Teaching as Decision Making

Successful Practices for the Elementary Teacher

THIRD EDITION

Alane J. Starko
Eastern Michigan University

Georgea M. Sparks-Langer
Eastern Michigan University

Marvin Pasch
Eastern Michigan University

Lisa Frankes
Eastern Michigan. University

Trevor G. Gardner
Northern Caribbean University

Christella D. Moody
Eastern Michigan University

Merrill
Prentice Hall

Upper Saddle River, New Jersey
Columbus, Ohio

To our families for their continuing support and encouragement. Special thanks to Bob, Peter, Judy, Patricia, and Charles

Library of Congress Cataloging in Publication Data
Teaching as decision making: successful practices for the elementary teacher / Alane J. Starko ... [et al.].— 3rd.
   p. cm.
  Marvin Pasch listed first on 2nd. ed.
  Includes bibliographical references and index.
  ISBN 0-13-028683-4 (pbk.)
   1. Elementary school teaching. 2. Lesson planning. 3. Classroom management. 4. Education, Elementary–Decision making. I. Starko, Alane J.

LB1555 .T38 2003
372.1102–dc21

2001056243

Vice President and Publisher: Jeffery W. Johnston
Executive Editor: Debra A. Stollenwerk
Editorial Assistant: Mary Morrill
Assistant Editor: Daniel J. Parker
Production Editor: Kimberly J. Lundy
Production Coordination: Carlisle Publishers Services
Design Coordinator: Diane C. Lorenzo

Photo Coordinator: Valerie Schultz
Cover Designer: Rod Harris
Cover Image: SuperStock
Production Manager: Pamela D. Bennett
Director of Marketing: Ann Castel Davis
Marketing Manager: Krista Groshong
Marketing Coordinator: Tyra Cooper

This book was set in Berkeley by Carlisle Communications, Ltd., and was printed and bound by R.R. Donnelley & Sons Company. The cover was printed by Phoenix Color Corp.

Photo Credits: Scott Cunningham/Merrill, pp. 20, 139, 150, 163, 237, 286, 334, 368, 395; Carmine Galasso/PH College, p. 404; Richard Hutchings/Silver Burdett Ginn, p. 261; KS Studios/Merrill, p. 412; Anthony Magnacca/Merrill, pp. 37, 100, 123, 209, 226; Pearson Learning, p. 55; Irene Springer/PH College, p. 1; Barbara Schwartz/Merrill, pp. 12, 181, 193; Anne Vega/Merrill, pp. 113, 311, 354; Todd Yarrington/Merrill, p. 75.

Pearson Education Ltd.
Pearson Education Australia Pty. Limited
Pearson Education Singapore Pte. Ltd.
Pearson Education North Asia Ltd.
Pearson Education Canada, Ltd.

Pearson Educación de Mexico, S.A. de C.V.
Pearson Education—Japan
Pearson Education Malaysia Pte. Ltd.
Pearson Education, *Upper Saddle River, New Jersey*

10 9 8 7 6 5 4 3 2 1
ISBN 0-13-028683-4

Preface

 ## THEORETICAL/CONCEPTUAL FRAMEWORK

Teaching as Decision Making: Successful Practices for the Elementary Teacher is the work of teacher-educators with deep roots in schools. In this book we have attempted to bridge the theoretical with the practical, recognizing the import of theory and skill development, carefully planned lessons and teachable moments, and the intangible but all important magic of the teacher-student relationship. At the heart of the book is the careful decision making necessary to plan lessons that address the needs of specific children while understanding the broader issues and context at hand. The text encourages its readers to reflect upon five key factors involved in making and implementing decisions about teaching and learning that are both ethical and effective:

> Students (culture, styles, needs, interests, development);
> Content (key concepts, outcomes and standards, required thinking);
> Pedagogy (methods, approaches, strategies, representations);
> Philosophy (moral aspects, beliefs, aims, values); and
> Context (physical environment, political conditions, social aspects).

A sample intermediate-level unit on the Revolutionary War is included in the Appendix and referenced throughout the text to develop future teachers' skills in unit and lesson planning within the context of local and state standards. Additional examples are drawn from a kindergarten-level interdisciplinary unit on patterns and a multitude of individual lessons. With every strategy learned, students are invited to critique

> its strengths and weaknesses;
> where, when, and with whom it might be most effective;
> how it might need to be modified for special student needs; and
> what values or social relationships it might be promoting.

Thus the reader learns not only technical reflection (How do I use this technique and improve upon it?), but also critical reflection (e.g., What long-range values are being promoted?). We believe that teachers need to ask themselves both kinds of questions. We also recognize that new teachers need information on the technical aspects of the job. Therefore, we have provided practical, concrete skill development and models for instruction. However, in the reflection journals, the "reflecting on the ideas" activities, and many of the practice activities, learners are prompted to consider the bigger picture of teaching and learning.

The teaching approaches and strategies presented in this text are grounded in contemporary learning theory and constructivist practice. Our view of constructivism centers on children actively engaged in building understanding, whatever the strategy or lesson design. We believe that engaged learners construct meaning across a range of strategies, as long as those strategies are used well: direct and inductive approaches, cooperative learning and independent learning, learning centers and role-play, storytelling and manipulatives.

Any approach that purports to be constructivist must start with children first. This edition of *Teaching as Decision Making* makes that process explicit by rearranging chapters so that information on individual student differences and cultural differences appears first, before the information on planning learning outcomes or lesson plans. Information on understanding, authentic learning activities, and differentiation is introduced early in the text, providing a framework for all subsequent learning.

Finally, the text uses a bridge metaphor to describe the process of building connections between students and content. One of the key aspects of this metaphor is that students must trust teachers enough to come across the bridge with them. The process of relationship building, both with individual students and across a learning community, is a thread through our discussion of instruction and the approaches to classroom management presented at the end of the book.

 ## ORGANIZATION OF TOPICS

Chapter 1 provides a model of teachers' reflective decision making and introduces the metaphor of bridge building for considering the many aspects of teacher reflection. It also considers the teacher-student relationships that lie at the heart of teaching.

Chapters 2 through 12 are organized into three themes: Planning for Instruction, Implementation, and Creating a Positive Learning Environment.

Topic 1. Planning for Instruction: Setting the Stage

- Understanding students and learning (Chapter 2)
- Teaching for understanding and authentic learning (Chapter 2)
- Choosing and analyzing classroom goals (Chapter 3)
- Teaching to content standards (Chapter 3)
- Planning for educational outcomes/objectives (Chapter 4)
- Assessing learning performances (Chapter 5)

Topic 2. Implementation: Getting Out There and Teaching

- Reflective lesson design and constructivism (Chapter 6)
- Designing and teaching the lessons and assessments (Chapters 5, 6, 7, 8, 9)
  - Direct approaches (Chapter 7)
  - Inductive approaches (Chapter 8)
  - Facilitating structures and strategies (Chapter 9)
- Differentiation and diversity (Chapter 10)

Topic 3. Creating a Positive Learning Environment

- Organizing the classroom for learning (Chapter 11)
- Dealing with misbehavior (Chapter 12)

The book concludes with Chapter 13, which leads the prospective teacher to envision his or her future as a continual learner and the importance of commitment and hope in shaping a career.

FEATURES OF THE TEXT

- *Teaching as Decision Making* emphasizes developing skills in classroom curriculum design—specifically, planning, teaching, and assessment skills. Students are prepared to create teaching units based on state or local curriculum standards.
- Emphasis is placed on both technical and critical reflective decision making. Readers learn not only technique, but also how to critique it for its long-range effects and ethical implications.
- The book recognizes both formal and informal modes of teaching and the role of teachable moments alongside carefully planned lessons.
- The analysis of content and outcomes stresses conceptual understanding based on facts rather than fact-centered planning.
- The curriculum design process uses backward design principles, beginning with substantial goals, planning assessment strategies, and then creating lessons to lead toward the goals.
- Authentic, real-life tasks for learning and assessment are emphasized (e.g., student-led research, problem-based learning, alternative assessment, and inductive models of teaching).
- Contemporary research on learning, memory, and brain functioning is summarized.
- Detailed explanations and concrete models develop the ability to design, teach, and reflect upon the results of a variety of approaches to learning:
  - Direct approaches (storytelling, minilectures)
  - Inductive approaches (inquiry, problem-based learning, student research, role-play, and simulation)
- Strategies and structures to support teaching approaches are presented:
  - Questioning
  - Group learning activities and cooperative learning
  - Academic service-learning
  - Integrating technology in instruction
  - Centers and contracts
- Short- and long-term planning strategies are described, across a day and across an academic year.
- The text focuses on the importance of differentiated instruction, including meeting the diverse needs of multicultural, gifted, special education, bilingual, and urban students.
- A practical and balanced approach to classroom management is presented in two chapters. Concrete strategies in behavioral, humanistic, and research-based traditions provide a base for developing a philosophy of classroom management and creating a learning community.

Pedagogical Features

- *Chapter Overview:* A short paragraph highlights the key ideas that follow.
- *Opening Activity:* These activities prompt the reader to reflect upon the topic to come, usually a case or situation.
- *Chapter and Section Objectives:* Each chapter (or each section within a chapter) has a list of learning outcomes that will be developed.
- *Check Your Understanding:* After a presentation of important ideas, readers are invited to check their understanding of the content.
- *Reflecting on the Ideas:* Throughout each chapter, readers are asked to consider their responses to the ideas or to take an alternate point of view.
- *Chapter Summary:* At the end of each chapter, key ideas are summarized.
- *Practice Activities:* At the end of sections and chapters, readers are asked to complete skill-building activities or reflection exercises.
- *Portfolio Activities:* Each chapter contains suggestions for items based on chapter content that may be included in a professional portfolio.
- *Search the Web*: Each chapter contains references from the World Wide Web and links to the Prentice Hall Companion Website that accompanies this text (www.prenhall.com/starko).
- *Glossary:* A glossary of key terms used in the text is included at the end of the book.

Special Features

- *Unit Preparation*: At the end of each chapter, students are asked to complete activities that will lead to the creation of a curriculum unit. Students who complete the activities at the end of each chapter will have a complete unit by the end of the book.
- *Model of Reflection:* The model is presented in Chapter 1 and is referred to throughout the book.
- *Appendix:* A sample unit on the Revolutionary War provides an example of each unit component, including various types of lessons.
- *Microteaching Activities:* At the end of the chapters on teaching approaches, readers are asked to design a lesson, teach it, and complete a reflection journal.
- *Reflection Journal:* The journal prompts readers not only to consider the technical aspects (e.g., What worked? Why? What would you do differently? Who learned what?), but also to reflect critically on the ethical and moral aspects of the lesson (e.g., What values were promoted today?).

 ## COMPANION WEBSITE

The Prentice Hall Companion Website: A Virtual Learning Environment

Technology is a constantly growing and changing aspect of our field that is creating a need for content and resources. To address this emerging need, Prentice Hall has developed an online learning environment for students and professors alike—Companion Websites—to support our textbooks.

In creating a Companion Website, our goal is to build on and enhance what the textbook already offers. For this reason, the content for each user-friendly website is organized by topic and provides the professor and student with a variety of meaningful resources. Each Prentice Hall Companion Website includes features for both professors and students.

For the Professor

Every Companion Website integrates **Syllabus Manager**™, an online syllabus creation and management utility.

- **Syllabus Manager**™ provides you, the instructor, with an easy, step-by step process to create and revise syllabi, with direct links into Companion Website and other online content without having to learn HTML.
- Students may log on to your syllabus during any study session. All they need to know is the web address for the Companion Website and the password you've assigned to your syllabus.
- After you have created a syllabus using **Syllabus Manager**™, students may enter the syllabus for their course section from any point in the Companion Website.
- Clicking on a date, the student is shown the list of activities for the assignment. The activities for each assignment are linked directly to actual content, saving time for students.
- Adding assignments consists of clicking on the desired due date, then filling in the details of the assignment—name of the assignment, instructions, and whether or not it is a one-time or repeating assignment.
- In addition, links to other activities can be created easily. If the activity is online, a URL can be entered in the space provided, and it will be linked automatically in the final syllabus.
- Your completed syllabus is hosted on our servers, allowing convenient updates from any computer on the Internet. Changes you make to your syllabus are immediately available to your students at their next logon.

For the Student

- **Topic Overviews** — outline key concepts in topic areas
- **Web Links** — a wide range of websites that provide useful and current information related to each topic area
- **Lesson Plans** — links to lesson plans for appropriate topic areas
- **Projects on the Web** — links to projects and activities on the web for appropriate topic areas
- **Education Resources** — links to schools, online journals, government sites, departments of education, professional organizations, regional information, and more

- **Electronic Bluebook** — send homework or essays directly to your instructor's email with this paperless form
- **Message Board** — serves as a virtual bulletin board to post—or respond to—questions or comments to/from a national audience
- **Chat** — real-time chat with anyone who is using the text anywhere in the country—ideal for discussion and study groups, class projects, etc.

To take advantage of these and other resources, please visit the Companion Website that accompanies *Teaching as Decision Making: Successful Practices for the Elementary Teacher,* Third Edition, at

www.prenhall.com/starko

ACKNOWLEDGMENTS

The authors wish to acknowledge the many instructors and hundreds of students at Eastern Michigan University who have helped us test and revise this textbook. They provided much valuable feedback and numerous insights. We appreciate their insights and are grateful for such individuals entering the field of teaching. Special thanks to Deborah Harmon, whose careful feedback on differentiation and diversity made this a much better book.

We would like to offer special thanks to our colleagues who served as reviewers: Sue R. Abegglan, Culver-Stockton College; Elinor V. Ellis, Florida A&M University; Michele Kamens, Rider University; Stephen Lafer, University of Nevada, Reno; Cynthia E. Ledbetter, University of Texas at Dallas; Anna Lowe, Loyola University Chicago; Connie H. Nobles, Southeastern Louisiana University; and Harry Teitelbaum, Kutztown University. Finally, thanks to Debbie Stollenwerk, Dan Parker, and all the folks at Prentice Hall and Carlisle Publishers Services for helping to make this often-long process more manageable. We particularly appreciate Valerie Schultz's fine collection of photographs. They remind us of the children at the heart of our efforts.

About the Authors

Alane J. Starko is department head and professor in the Department of Teacher Education at Eastern Michigan University. A former elementary classroom teacher and teacher of the gifted, she has been an active consultant in the areas of classroom differentiation, creativity, and education of the gifted and talented. Alane has been a board member and service publications editor for the National Association for Gifted Children. In addition to her work on *Teaching as Decision Making,* she is author of *Creativity in the Classroom: Schools of Curious Delight, It's About Time,* and a variety of articles, as well as coauthor (with Gina Schack) of two books on authentic research with young people.

Georgea M. Sparks-Langer has published extensively in the areas of staff development (as Georgea M. Sparks), teacher education, and teachers' reflective decision making in journals such as *Journal of Educational Psychology, Educational Leadership, Journal of Teacher Education,* and *Journal of Staff Development.* She has presented workshops nationally and internationally with the Association for Supervision and Curriculum Development (ASCD), Phi Delta Kappa, and in numerous states, countries, districts, and schools. She is currently a professor in the Department of Teacher Education at Eastern Michigan University and coordinator of a grant to improve teacher quality through a student-teaching performance assessment that documents K–12 student learning gains.

Marvin Pasch, recently retired from his role as a professor in the Department of Teacher Education at Eastern Michigan University, is the senior editor for social studies for the State of Michigan Merit Award Program's Sample Curriculum and Plans for Education (SCoPE) project. During his higher education career, he was a college administrator at EMU and Cleveland State University for 16 years and a faculty member for almost 30 years. Prior to making the transition to higher education, he taught junior and senior high school social studies for 11 years. For 5 years he taught in a team-teaching, flexibly scheduled high school where teams developed and implemented individualized learning packages. He has a 35-year interest in instructional planning and program evaluation and has published articles in the *Journal of Staff Development, Journal of Teacher Education, Social Education, Science Teacher,* and *Educational Leadership.*

Lisa Frankes is an assistant professor in the Department of Teacher Education at Eastern Michigan University. Her work for the past 4 years has involved developing university-school partnerships. She has collaborated with teachers to create and implement curriculum that promotes media literacy. Prior to this, she was the professional development school coordinator at the University of Maryland at College Park where her work involved the creation and facilitation of teacher-researcher inquiry groups. She began her career in education as a teacher in the Boston Public Schools.

Trevor G. Gardner is vice president for academic administration at Northern Caribbean University in Mandeville, Jamaica. A former professor in the Department of Teacher Education at Eastern Michigan University, he was also an elementary and secondary teacher, a high school principal, and a school board member. He is an international consultant in school discipline and positive parent participation, having created the Rational Approach to Practical School Discipline (RAPSD), which is featured in Chapter 12, as well as the Participating Parents for Progress (PPP). Over the past 19 years he has consulted with more than 100 schools and colleges on discipline, multicultural education, and desegregation.

Christella D. Moody was a public school teacher in the Chicago Public Schools for 11 years, and then spent 15 years in the Ann Arbor, Michigan, Public Schools as a teacher, school administrator, coordinator of multiethnic instruction, and coordinator of staff development. She has consulted in more than 10 states on effective teaching and multicultural education. She is the historian of the National Alliance of Black School Educators and the developer of the Young Educators Society for the State of Michigan. She is currently president of Current Directions Publishing Co. and executive director of the C. D. Moody Educational Foundation.

Brief Contents

Contents

NOTE: Every effort has been made to provide accurate and current Internet information in this book. However, the Internet and information posted on it are constantly changing, so it is inevitable that some of the Internet addresses listed in this textbook will change.

CHAPTER 1

Teaching as Decision Making

CHAPTER OVERVIEW

In this book, we explore how decision making contributes to the effectiveness and empowerment of teachers. Empowerment involves a feeling of self-efficacy—the knowledge that you make a difference in your work environment and that what you do as a teacher affects how students learn. An empowered teacher has assumed the responsibility to be a **reflective decision maker**—an active designer of instruction who reflects on teaching practices and student learning. We consider how reflective teaching is like bridge building and examine the power and importance of relationships in teaching.

Where Are We Heading?

Consider two alternative styles of teaching: the consumer versus the reflective decision maker. The **teacher consumer**, through preference or circumstance, permits the curriculum—the content and methods of what is taught—to be determined and organized by others. Typically, the teacher consumer has surrendered to the textbook the responsibility to define, analyze, and develop the curriculum. Consumers may follow the teacher's manual verbatim, without considering the worth of each topic or activity to the students in a particular school or classroom. They may not consult other teachers and experts to explore alternative methods and resources. Thus they do not participate in the creative process that brings curriculum to life.

Delegating all decisions about curriculum to a textbook poses significant risks. Textbooks present a wide variety of topics and often include an abundant assortment of important and unimportant, relevant and irrelevant information (Erickson, 1998). That information includes the concepts, skills, and phenomena that should be emphasized, with the addition of "details, embellishments, redundancies, illustrations, examples, facts, and names" (Dempster, 1993, p. 434). Too often, the student loses the point of the lesson in the midst of the profusion of information. Furthermore, the teacher is led by the extensive but shallow treatment of topics to cover everything superficially but little in enough depth for learning to take place. Similarly, teachers can become overwhelmed by the profusion of content standards that 21st-century students are required to master. Without careful attention to priorities and thoughtful planning, both teachers and students can be buried in ineffectively applied requirements (Carr & Harris, 2001).

Contrast the teacher consumer with the reflective decision maker, a **teacher designer** who uses content standards to develop district and/or grade-level goals, clarifies the outcomes to be learned and ways of assessing them, creates units of study, and only then decides what instructional materials, activities, and assessments are appropriate. Textbooks may be used, but the teacher (or team of teachers), not the textbook, is the major decision maker. Key topics are taught in sufficient depth to develop understanding; topics of little importance are eliminated.

Teacher decision makers have the fullest opportunity to flex and stretch their reflective thinking. They make *planning* decisions by choosing and analyzing content, clarifying outcomes, selecting learning activities, and assessing student performance. They make *implementation* decisions as they design and teach units and lessons, assess learning, make adjustments for individual student needs, and enhance their students' thinking skills. Finally, they make decisions about *classroom management,* applying their beliefs and principles about individual human beings and communities to create and maintain a positive learning environment.

After completing instruction, reflective teachers analyze student success and revise their teaching plans accordingly. But, these teachers are interested in more than just what goes on in their classrooms. They participate actively with others in **professional development**, activities, and constant learning (Beerens, 2000). They also take an active interest in the growth of their profession and the recurring need for educational change and improvement (National Board for Professional Teaching Standards, 1991; see also Darling-Hammond & Sykes, 1999).

The purpose of this text is to explore a wide range of issues, strategies, and topics that teachers must consider in the 21st century. But what are the characteristics of an effective decision maker? These questions have helped shape this textbook.

A number of teacher educators have used the term teacher reflection to describe a teacher's instructional decision making (Schon, 1987, 1991; Spring, 1985; Zeichner, 1996; Zeichner & Liston, 1996). There are many views of teacher reflection (Grimmett & Erickson, 1988; Valli, 1997), ranging from the **technical view** (e.g., How well are the techniques I'm using working?) to the **critical ethical/moral view** (e.g., What are the long-term effects on society of this content or this technique?) (Colton & Sparks-Langer, 1993). A common definition consistent with the approach taken in this book is "the teacher's ability to make rational educational choices and to assume responsibility for one's choices" (Ross, 1987, p. 2)—in other words, to make thoughtful instructional decisions. A key aspect of such decision making is to consider multiple points of view rather than acting on the first idea that comes to mind.

Our work has focused on the question, What do teachers need to think about when making a teaching decision? Good teaching decisions are based on much more complicated questions than, What shall I do on Monday? or What works? Decisions that appear to be straightforward considerations of teaching techniques or management strategies are embedded in multiple variables. Each must be weighed according to its impact on students both short and long term. Reflecting on these variables is a complex process and not every educator engages in it. In fact, we have observed that frequently a person who attempts to tell you there is one right way to teach hasn't taught very many children—or is trying to sell you something!

Reflective teachers ask themselves not only, Is this an effective technique for this type of lesson? but also, Is it suited to this group of students? Do I have the necessary skills? Does it model ethics I believe in? Is it fair? Is it important? Will I be able to look back on this day and feel I have done what students needed most? We cannot answer these questions for you—teaching would be much easier if we could. Rather than describing a single methodology, we have attempted to provide you with a broad range of options. We have our preferred strategies and you'll probably be able to discern them. But, in the end, what is most important is not whether you teach in a way consistent with our beliefs, but that you thoughtfully identify and follow your own. Of course, reflective teachers do not make choices in a vacuum. They carefully weigh knowledge of how children learn and develop with knowledge of best practice in pedagogy as well as a host of other variables. We hope this book will give you the tools you need to consider a wide variety of factors in making wise educational decisions.

CHAPTER OBJECTIVES

In each chapter of this book, you will find objectives to help you identify key skills and important ideas to be learned. In longer chapters, the objectives are sometimes divided by section. After this chapter, you will be able to:

1. describe reflective decision making and why it is important for teachers;
2. use a bridge analogy to describe five key factors in teacher reflection; and
3. describe the role of a caring learning community.

 ## SECTION 1. TEACHING AND BRIDGE BUILDING

This is a book about teaching. It is also a book about bridge building. That probably sounds a bit strange, but it is true. This book will help you learn a lot about the things teachers do and the ways they help students learn. It will help you begin to understand the way teachers think when they plan lessons, teach, and consider whether their lessons are successful. But it will also teach you about building bridges.

What Does Teaching Have to Do with Bridges?

Teachers build many kinds of bridges. We can imagine teachers building bridges to connect them to their students or bridges to connect students one to another. We can imagine building bridges between subjects or between one idea and another. Perhaps the most basic bridge a teacher must build is the bridge between a student and the content the teacher hopes the student will learn.

Metaphors, like this metaphor of a bridge, can be powerful tools in learning. They provide us with another view of important topics—in this case the process of reflective teaching. Stop for a minute and think, How is teaching like building a bridge between a student and the content? What would you need in order to build a good bridge? Jot down a few ideas before you continue reading.

There is no perfect answer to this question, but here are some of our ideas. First, in order to build a bridge between a student and the content, you need to know where the student is. There is no point building a bridge if the student can't get to it. This is also true in teaching. Before you can plan a lesson that will reach your students, you must know where your students are. You must know what each student already understands about the topic, what he or she might be interested in, and what skills the student has or needs. You also should know how the student learns best and how his or her background can help in the learning process. And that is just the beginning. You can tell that this end of the bridge will have to be deep, reflecting your deep understanding of your students. This will be a challenge, since you will have many students, each needing to cross a bridge.

The other end of the bridge is equally important. If you are going to build an effective bridge between students and content, you need to know the content well. This end of the structure must also be deep, reflecting your in-depth understanding of the subject to be learned. It is not enough to know *some information*. As a teacher, you need to know how to find the *most important information*, the ideas that will help students learn and grow for years to come. Time in school is too precious to waste on ideas that are trivial. You must anchor this end of the bridge to powerful ideas that will help students understand new content, solve problems, and ask important questions. This means your decisions about what to teach must be thoughtful.

Of course, once the two ends are firmly anchored, you must actually build the bridge. This is the part of the process we most commonly associate with the idea of "teaching." When we build the bridge we plan lessons and activities for students that will help them understand the content, moving them from what they know to what they do not know. We are sure that you will want to build a bridge that is not only strong enough to support students on their journeys, but beautiful as well—a bridge students may cross with joy and interest. To do that you will need lessons that are clear and well structured as well as interesting. They will need to be familiar enough to be comfortable, challenging enough to move students forward, and novel enough to be interesting. This is no small challenge!

It also will be important to understand the conditions under which the bridge is built. Just as bridge building needs to be appropriate for the weather, the climate, and the geography of the area, so will your teaching need to be suitable for the context in which you teach. Activities or goals that may be appropriate for one group may be unsuitable in another political, cultural, economic, or social environment. It would be interesting to consider what kinds of contexts might be analogous to sunny days, swampy ground, or sudden earthquakes! Think about the elements of this bridge-building metaphor as you consider the teacher decision-making model described in the next section.

SECTION 2. REFLECTIVE TEACHER DECISION MAKING

Teaching is a complex endeavor. There is no one learning activity that will work with all students, in all circumstances, or for all types of content and objectives. The teacher must make moment by moment decisions about what to do. Such decisions are based on a great deal of information and must often be made in a split second. At other times, you will be able to take more time to reflect on the complexities of teaching and learning—for example, when you are making lesson plans and redesigning lessons. The decision-making model attempts to clarify when teaching decisions are made and the factors to be considered when making them.

REFLECTING ON THE IDEAS

Reflective teachers make a full range of decisions about planning, implementation, and management. Imagine yourself sitting at your desk planning a lesson for a class you will teach. Make a list of all the factors, issues, and knowledge a teacher needs to consider when making such teaching decisions.

FIGURE 1.1   Five Factors Contributing to Teaching Decisions

In Figure 1.1 our bridge shows five factors that contribute to successful and re-sponsible teaching decisions: the students, the subject matter, pedagogy (knowledge about teaching), the context of instruction, and the teacher (Richardson, 1996; Shul-man, 1986). The base of the picture, **reflection**, indicates the importance of considering all five factors before, during, and after teaching.

Let's consider each factor in greater detail. The first factor influencing teaching decisions is **student needs and characteristics**. This is the first end of the bridge in Figure 1.1. The teacher needs to take into consideration students' home background and culture when trying to relate new ideas to students' prior experiences. For example, re-ferring to curling to illustrate a point in a science lesson may totally confuse a student who has never seen that sport. In contrast, a teacher who utilizes students' knowledge of seesaws when teaching the concept *fulcrum* makes a connection that facilitates learn-ing. If learners are tired or discouraged, the teacher may need to be especially enthusi-astic and creative. Students' developmental levels and learning styles may also influence the choice of activities. Teachers need to include multiple pathways for learning that in-clude all senses and appeal to all students' interests and talents.

Considering teaching situations from the perspective of students' needs can make the difference between technical and critical reflective thinking (Zeichner & Liston, 1996). For example, if a student is disruptive in class, a teacher who is thinking only about the technical aspects of, How will I complete this lesson? will approach the situation differently than one who considers, What might be causing the student to act this way? In the first instance, the teacher is likely to look for the quickest way to quiet the disruptive student—probably some type of disciplinary consequence. In the second case, the teacher might think of multiple possibilities ranging from lack of sufficient challenge in the lesson, to lesson content that conflicts with values taught in the student's home. Those needs would result in different strategies to address the problem.

The **subject matter**, or content (at the other end of the bridge), also influences teaching decisions. Each subject will have standards set by the state or district that specify key student-learning outcomes for the different grade levels. Teaching science may call for certain activities, whereas teaching literature may require different strategies. Understanding content is important, but it is not sufficient. A good teacher must be able to "translate" ideas so that students understand them. It may take several attempts before a teacher discovers how to represent a complex idea so it makes sense to students.

A significant influence on decision making is how much the teacher knows about **pedagogy**: *teaching, learning, assessment,* and *classroom management.* The teacher needs a professional knowledge base of concepts, theories, and techniques to draw upon. These ideas include knowledge of human development, learning theory, multicultural education, assessment strategies, and teaching methods, to name a few. They are important tools for bridge building.

Another very important aspect of a teacher's thinking is the **context**—the conditions that influence everyday classroom life. The social, cultural, and political forces in the school, district, and community help determine what is taught and, sometimes, how it is taught. For example, many state departments of education are currently focusing on major restructuring efforts that are forcing educators to become accountable for their students' learning of state standards.

Finally, **teacher characteristics and beliefs** have an important impact on decision making. Teacher traits such as self-confidence, enthusiasm, cultural background, intelligence, and commitment affect what a teacher will do on a particular day. Personal beliefs (philosophy) about students' ability to learn, the purposes of school, and social values will also influence a teacher's choice of actions. Teachers are shaped by their culture's assumptions about truth, learning, intelligence, and work. Often teachers' beliefs about teaching can be expressed in metaphors used to describe their work, like the metaphor of the bridge cited here. Think about the ways two teachers' practice might differ if one viewed teaching as planting seeds and waiting for harvest, while the other viewed it as parallel to athletic coaching. Reflective teachers are aware of the beliefs, values, and assumptions that undergird their teaching—and are able to reexamine those beliefs when appropriate.

Zeichner and Liston (1996) discuss a framework by Handal and Lauvas that describes three sources of teachers' personal and practical theories (beliefs) that shape their teaching practice. The first is their personal experiences. Liston describes three very different teachers who influenced his teaching practice: (a) a very formal social studies teacher who taught him the value of inquiry, (b) a more freewheeling teacher who taught him about thinking about experiences in unconstrained ways, and (c) a teacher who provided a more negative example. Liston's unhappy experience in the latter authoritarian classroom convinced him of the importance of problem solving and independent thinking in math class. All of us have beliefs about teaching that have been shaped by our experiences as students (and, as our careers continue, as teachers). A student who had a positive experience in the authoritarian math class might come away from that experience believing problem solving unnecessary or ineffective. If that student becomes a teacher, this belief will be a powerful influence.

The second source of teachers' practical theories about teaching is transmitted knowledge—the knowledge gained from teacher preparation programs, dicussions with other teachers, research on teaching, and books like this one. Those sources can be particularly helpful when research about teaching and learning brings new understandings that are not obvious, or even counterintuitive. In this case, increased knowledge of pedagogy results in a change in teacher beliefs.

The third source is teachers' values about what is good and bad, particularly in education. Those values shape the way we view everything that happens in our classrooms, what we choose as goals, what we view as successes, and what we view as failures. Teachers also exert a powerful influence on students' values—an influence that may become apparent only later on, as students imitate the models their teachers have provided for them. Considering the values—spoken and unspoken—that will shape your classroom community is an essential part of being a reflective teacher.

As you progress in your development as a reflective teacher, you will learn how to become sensitive to all these factors. For example, when making decisions *before teaching,* the teacher reflects on all five factors: students, subject matter, pedagogy, context, and teacher beliefs. For example, when designing activities and lessons, the teacher may consider the following questions: What do I know about the students' backgrounds and interests? What do students know or believe about this topic? What objective(s) do I want students to achieve? Which concepts are most important? What types of activities will I need for students to learn the necessary content? What problems may arise during the lesson? What strategies have I planned to confront problems if they arise?

During teaching, the teacher observes how well the lesson is being received by students and reflects on all five factors as possible explanations for why the lesson seems to be going well or not. For example, if students seem out of touch with the lesson, the teacher might reflect upon the following questions: Is this lesson out of sync with students' cultural experiences? Are the students distracted by something that happened at lunch? Am I continuing with the same activity too long? Do I need to get students actively involved? Using this information, the teacher makes adjustments as needed in the pace, depth, and complexity of the lesson. Such decisions may even require shifting to a different activity or, in unusual circumstances, changing to a different lesson and objective(s).

After teaching, the reflective teacher evaluates the success of the lesson by asking: What does the students' work/responses tell me about how well the students attained the objective(s)? Why was the lesson successful or unsuccessful? What could I have done differently? What have I learned about my students or about this topic? The five factors can help answer these questions. The teacher can then use this information to revise the lessons as necessary and to plan future ones more intelligently.

In your field experiences and early years of teaching, you will begin to see how these ideas can be woven together into the wonderful complexity of teaching.

Relationships and the Caring Community

But there is one important idea left—the way two of our factors come together: the students and the teacher. Consider once more our metaphorical bridge. Even if the bridge is built well, with strong ties to the students' world and strong links to the content, it is of little use unless the student crosses over with you. This is one of the great truths of teaching that is hard to learn from a book. *Teaching is about relationships.* You must know who you are and what you believe is important. You must know the student. You must know the content. You must know all the skills of lesson planning and assessment that will help you build a strong bridge between the two. But, in the end, the student must trust you enough to come across the bridge with you. Going to new places can be frightening. Only in a caring relationship can students find the courage to try new things, risk failure, and learn to grow. Developing these relationships is the heart of teaching. Caring relationships are not easy. Sometimes they mean being gentle; other times they mean being stern. But at all times they require us to view each student as one of our planet's most priceless treasures. Developing a safe community of learners is key to successful teaching.

The value of these relationships was described in one of a yearlong series of articles on Roslyn Ratliff, a first-year teacher in Detroit Public Schools (Seidel, 2000). Earlier articles had focused on teaching strategies, management challenges, and working with parents. In May the article was titled, "Miss Ratliff Connects." After describing the beginning-of-the-year trials of Brian, a third-grade student frequently taunted by bullies, the author describes the changes that have come in Miss Ratliff's room.

Do you hear it?

A gentle echo that bounces through the room, subtle as a breeze, lingering, nudging, reminding: "Positive people don't put others down."

Miss Ratliff has said the phrase so many times it rolls off her tongue without a thought. It is her class motto and, she believes her biggest success as a first-year teacher.

It is the side of teaching that can't be measured—certainly not by a state-mandated test—but you can feel it when it happens. You can see it. It is real and important and the reason she got into teaching in the first place: to make a difference in the lives of children at an age when they are most vulnerable.

Miss Ratliff has tried to teach her students to be kind to each other, to respect each other, to have patience with each other.

"Their patience, that's what I'm proud of," she says. "The patience they have with each other when it's time to read. If somebody is struggling, my kids don't blurt stuff out for the other kids. They give them an opportunity to sound it out. When one group of students or somebody at the table, doesn't get something, the students don't get frustrated. They really work with each other. They help each other, they are being patient, working with each other like a family." (p. K1)

Herb Kohl (Scherer, 1998) said:

> A teacher's task is not only to engage students' imagination but also to convince them that they are people of worth who can do something in a very difficult world. When children don't have access to resources, it's very easy to give up on hope. And if you give up on hope, what's the point of learning to read? What's the point of passing a Regent's exam if you believe the college won't accept you? What's the point of doing well in school if you know at the end of schooling all you will get is a McDonald's job? (p. 9)

In a caring community, we not only build students' skills, we build their hope. Each student who enters our door must understand that we know he or she can learn. All children must know we expect them to learn, we care whether or not they learn, and we intend to stick by them so that they do learn. The concept of caring as an essential element in effective teaching is an important lens through which we view the activities of teaching and learning (Noddings, 1992, 1995; Pang, 2001).

Authors have approached the goal of community building from varied directions. James Comer (1997; O'Neil, 1997) approaches teaching from the perspective of development. All children come into this world with many needs. With guidance from caring adults, they develop, learn, and grow. As a psychiatrist, Comer reflected on his own experiences growing up in a challenging environment. Despite many difficulties, he and his siblings were able to learn and succeed both educationally and professionally. Their development was facilitated as their social skills, their attitudes, their goals, and their accomplishments were nourished by a caring family and a close-knit neighborhood and church community. Other friends, equally bright but without similar family and community supports, floundered. These experiences led Comer to identify the need for relationships with caring adults as the center of educational planning.

We cannot count on all children arriving in our classroom with a full developmental support system. Comer believes we must be among the caring adults who provide that system. We cannot replace the systems of support in students' homes and neighborhoods, but we can contribute to them. Comer focuses on the need to help children develop—not just along a cognitive dimension but along six **developmental pathways**: physical, cognitive, psychological, language, social, and ethical. He believes that growth along all those pathways facilitates academic growth.

REFLECTING ON THE IDEAS

When observing a teacher interacting with students in a classroom, on the playground, or in any other location, think about the six developmental pathways. Observe the way the teacher's behavior facilitates—or does not facilitate—students' growth in each area. Do you think it is possible for schools to develop all those areas? Is it possible for schools to develop cognitive abilities in children *without* developing the other pathways?

Comer's (1997) model for school development focuses on building relationships throughout a school building. These include relationships between adults and children, but also relationships among adults. Clearly, from Comer's perspective, the ability to build strong relationships is one of the most important skills for a teacher.

Goleman (1995) makes the argument that **emotional intelligence** (EQ) is a set of patterns, behaviors, and kinds of thought that are essential for success both in learning and in the workplace. He believes that effective educators must both teach and model appropriate affective, as well as cognitive, development. These include such components as self-awareness, independence, optimism, accountability, empathy, and the ability to manage one's feelings. Goleman (2000) suggests that school curricula must include a more complete "emotional literacy curriculum" that addresses issues such as handling stress, conflict resolution, decision making, and group dynamics.

Given the many other demands on busy teachers' time and school schedules, some may question whether we can take on the responsibility for emotional development that has been traditionally centered in the home. Goleman and others would argue that we have no choice. In a culture in which school violence is a regular part of the headlines, taking time to teach emotional skills may be the most important thing we do. Still others suggest that the links between emotional intelligence and life success are more complex and that it is important to attend to the emerging body of research before making whole-scale changes in curriculum (see, for example, Cobb & Mayer, 2000; Mayer & Cobb, 2000). However the research emerges, it seems reasonable to assume that teaching to support healthy emotional development is most likely to occur in a climate of healthy relationships between students and teachers, with teachers modeling the kinds of affect—as well as the kinds of intellect—to which their students should aspire.

Still another way to focus on the types of relationships that are needed in classrooms is the increasing interest in the idea of linking spirituality and education—both as a means of fostering relationships and a vehicle for developing character. The thought that spirituality may have a place in public education is uncomfortable for many teachers. The important division between church and state makes any practice that could be interpreted as promoting specific religious beliefs inappropriate. And yet, writing in this area has increased to the point that a major publication, *Educational Leadership*, devoted an entire issue (December 1998/January 1999) to exploring "The Spirit of Education." Interest in the issue was such that it sold out more rapidly than any issue in the history of the publication.

Palmer (1998, 1998–1999) describes spirituality as "the ancient and abiding human quest for connectedness with something larger and more trustworthy than our egos—with our own soul, with one another, with the worlds of history and nature, with the invisible winds of the spirit, with the mystery of being alive" (1998–1999, p. 6). From Palmer's perspective, the courage to teach is the courage required to open our hearts and ourselves to the relationships required to teach. It requires asking the important questions that are embedded in all disciplines: Does life have meaning? What can I trust? How do we deal with suffering? How do we appreciate beauty? These are not questions we can answer for our students. They are questions that can be explored together while studying a myriad of academic subjects, both building and requiring relationships of trust in safe communities.

Communities are built in many ways. Sapon-Shevin, Dobbelaere, Corrigan, Goodman, and Mastin (1998) described the transformations that occurred in early elementary classrooms that adopted the rule "You can't say you can't play." No group of students was allowed to exclude a child who wanted to join an activity. Although the rule was focused

Caring Relationships Are at the Heart of Good Teaching

on social behavior, it is easy to imagine the way students' academic interactions could change when their patterns of interaction became more inclusive. Chapter 11 discusses other management strategies designed to develop a sense of classroom community.

Renard and Rogers (1999) have developed a more complex model of relationship-driven teaching. Their model centers on fulfilling students' fundamental emotional needs so that learning can take place. If students' emotional needs are being met in school, they are more likely to engage in learning (Rogers, Ludington, & Graham, 1998). When students believe teachers care about them, they are more motivated to learn—more likely to cross the metaphorical bridges we are building. Rogers and Renard describe two underlying principles and six standards that undergird relationship-driven teaching. They can be useful as we consider ways to build communities in a variety of classrooms.

The first principle is based on the work of Covey (1990), "seeking first to understand" (Rogers & Renard, 1999, p. 35). Our first goal in building relationships with students is to seek to understand them. We must understand the knowledge, beliefs, experiences, and interests of our students as they are—not as we would like them to be or think they should be. The second underlying principle involves managing the learning context, not the learners. It requires establishing school situations likely to foster **intrinsic motivation**, motivation that comes from within the students, rather than attempting to dominate or control students from the outside. Teachers who are able to manage conditions—rather than focusing on managing students—are more likely to help students want to do what needs to be done.

The six standards described by Rogers and Renard (1999) are designed to build a motivating teaching context. They are as follows.

1. *Safe*. Safety in school must include not just physical safety (although that certainly is important), but emotional safety as well. Students must know that they will be safe from threats, intimidation, or embarrassment. In a safe classroom, students are free to take risks and try new things.

2. *Valuable*. Students are more likely to engage and persist in learning if they perceive that what they are doing is valuable. Valuable content fills a need, solves a problem, or is interesting and enjoyable.
3. *Successful*. To maintain motivation students need evidence of their success. This means that students need activities that are challenging enough that they recognize their growth while still allowing for success.
4. *Involving*. Students are more motivated to learn when they feel they have a stake in what is going on. Students who have had a part in planning an activity or made meaningful decisions about the ways they learn are more motivated to continue.
5. *Caring*. Everyone wants to be liked. Students want to feel accepted by their teacher, valued, and cared about. The harder a child is to like, the more he or she probably needs to know you care. Caring is not always easy—often it is very hard work.
6. *Enabling*. Good teachers constantly seek out best practices that help their students learn. They continue to learn and grow in search of teaching methods that will be effective with all students rather than relying on "tried and true" methods that work with many students but leave some behind.

The **Responsive Classroom Model** (Charney, 1992; Horsch, Chen, & Nelson, 1999), briefly described in Chapter 11, is another example of a model of teaching and management focused specifically on the development of self-management and motivation in classroom communities.

REFLECTING ON THE IDEAS

Observe a teacher you consider to be effective. Be particularly attuned to the things the teacher does to develop positive relationships with students and foster intrinsic motivation. It may be helpful to divide a paper into the preceding six areas and make notes of behaviors that appear to fit each category. Share your observations with a colleague and look for similarities and differences.

As you study this text and learn about teacher reflection and planning, consider the ways the activities you are pursuing may facilitate strong relationships and student motivation. Fortunately, there are many times in education when an instructional choice can serve more than one goal. For example, in Chapter 2 you will learn that some scholars believe that an emotionally safe classroom atmosphere is more compatible with brain development than one that is highly competitive or negative. Other scholars would recommend the same type of atmosphere but for different reasons—in this case, to develop the relationships of trust necessary for student motivation. Be alert to other parallel recommendations. In many cases the strategies that are recommended for optimum cognitive growth will also serve important affective functions, and vice versa. In the end, whatever strategies you choose for teaching will form the structure of the bridge you cross with your students. It will be the heart of your teaching, the community of relationships you build in your classes, that will determine whether you cross successfully.

SUMMARY

We have provided a model for reflective teacher decision making, a metaphor for think-ing about teaching, and information on the importance of relationships in teaching. The rest of the book develops your ability to design instructional units and manage your class-room. As you explore the chapters that follow, examine the information in a careful and systematic way and respond to the exercises provided. In particular, be sure to follow the directions in each "Unit Preparation" section throughout the book. If you complete each section of the unit as you read the text, when you have completed the book you will have an original teaching unit prepared and ready for implementation. We have written this book because we believe the information can help you to be the best teacher possible. We hope that you will find the information both practical and thought provoking. It is our vision for you to become a reflective teacher "designer" capable of making thoughtful and appropriate instructional decisions. We wish you well on the journey.

UNIT PREPARATION

As you read this text we will describe a process for creating a teaching unit. If you com-plete each "Unit Preparation" section in turn, you will develop an original teaching unit by the time you complete this text. To begin, it is important that you determine the au-dience for your unit. Ideally you should prepare a unit for a real classroom, preferably one in which you are currently doing a variety of field experiences. Identify that class now. Begin talking to the teacher about content areas that would be appropriate for unit planning and special class needs you should consider. Find out whether content in that class is typically organized in single-subject or interdisciplinary units. You probably will find the unit-planning process easier to use in content that is organized around key con-cepts rather than skills. For example, a unit on Families Around the World or Habitats will fit this planning model more readily than a unit on how to read a map—although map reading could be embedded in many units. More detailed information on selected unit content will be found in Chapter 3. For now, it is most important to make a deci-sion about the class for whom you will be preparing materials and the general area(s) you might address. Begin reading in that area now. It is essential that you have a solid understanding of the content yourself before trying to teach it to others. Do not make the mistake of thinking that, because you are teaching young children, your content knowledge can be limited. Selecting the most important content for elementary school students requires teachers to know far more than they teach. Only by knowing the con-tent well can you make good decisions about content emphases and organization. Be sure to keep all relevant bibliographic information for your reference list. You should also keep track of any commercial materials or other materials that you use in the unit and reference them appropriately.

PORTFOLIO ACTIVITY

The "Portfolio Activities" in this text are designed to help you compile a collection of materials that can be helpful in demonstrating your knowledge and reflection about teaching and learning. In some cases the "Unit Preparation" activities can also serve as parts of your portfolio. In other cases we'll suggest additional activities.

For example, one of the most powerful means of describing our beliefs about teaching is through the metaphors we use to describe it. Choose a metaphor and write a brief reflection describing your view of the core role of a teacher. You may wish to develop this metaphor into a more formal description of your philosophy of teaching. It can be helpful to examine your metaphor—and your philosophy—periodically and see if they have changed as you have developed in experience and expertise.

SEARCH THE WEB

The World Wide Web can be a valuable resource for reflective teachers seeking information on content, research on teaching, or even lesson ideas. A strength of web publishing is that it is accessible to many individuals. Many teachers and organizations throughout the world post information for others to share. Of course, a related challenge is that information on the web must be carefully reviewed to determine the credibility of the source and accuracy of the information. Another challenge for those who want to share web information is that at this point in history many web addresses are unstable. That is, if you visit a website today (or we print one in this text), there is no guarantee it will exist next year when you try to find it. The teacher who created it may have taken another position with a different address, the organization may have lost its web-savvy organizer, or any number of other scenarios. To strengthen its web references against instability, Prentice Hall has created Companion Websites to support its education texts. The Companion Website for this text provides a gateway to Merrill Education's Links to General Method Resources Website. Links on the site are periodically updated in an effort to keep current information available. Specific topics within the Companion Website are referenced throughout the text, but take some time to explore the site and find out what is there. The home address is

http://www.prenhall.com/starko

Since it is an important resource, it would be wise to bookmark it. At the bottom of the screen you will find a space to select from a number of topics. Each topic will lead you to a number of web links and other resources. You'll even find a message board, chat room, and electronic bluebook that may be useful to your class.

We will also cite selected other web resources that are stable enough that we feel confident they will continue to be useful for many years. One of the most important of these resources is the Educational Resources Information Center (ERIC) system. There you will find links to virtually any type of document about education, as well as a variety of search services. To find the ERIC Clearinghouse on Elementary and Early Childhood Education go to

http://www.ericeece.org

To learn more about the Comer Model go to

http://info.med.yale.edu/comer

REFERENCES

Beerens, D. (2000). *Evaluating teachers for professional growth: Creating a culture of motivation and learning.* Thousand Oaks, CA: Corwin Press.

Carr, J. F., & Harris, D. E. (2001). *Succeeding with standards: Linking curriculum, assessment, and action planning.* Alexandria, VA: Association for Supervision and Curriculum Development.

Charney, R. S. (1992). *Teaching children to care: Management in the responsive classroom.* Greenfield, MA: Northeast Foundation for Children.

Cobb, C. D., & Mayer, J. D. (2000). Emotional intelligence: What the research says. *Educational Leadership, 58* (3), 14–18.

Comer, J. P. (1997). *Waiting for a miracle.* New York: Penguin Putnam.

Colton, A., & Sparks-Langer, G. (1993). A conceptual framework to guide the development of teacher reflection and decision making. *Journal of Teacher Education, 44* (1), 45–54.

Covey, S. (1990). *The seven habits of highly effective people.* New York: Simon & Schuster.

Darling-Hammond, L., & Sykes, G. (Eds.). (1999). *Teaching as the learning profession: Handbook of policy and practice.* San Francisco: Jossey-Bass.

Dempster, F. N. (1993). Exposing our students to less should help them learn more. *Phi Delta Kappan, 74* (6), 433–437.

Erickson, L. (1998). *Concept-based curriculum and instruction: Teaching beyond the facts.* Thousand Oaks, CA: Corwin Press.

Goleman, D. (1995). *Emotional intelligence.* New York: Bantam.

Goleman, D. (2000). *Toward a model emotional literacy curriculum.* [On-line]. Available: www.eq.org

Grimmett, P. P., & Erickson, G. L. (Eds.). (1988). *Reflection in teacher education.* New York: Teachers College Press.

Horsch, P., Chen, J., & Nelson, D. (1999). Rules and rituals: Tools for creating a respectful, caring, learning community. *Phi Delta Kappan, 81* (3), 223–227.

Mayer, J. D., & Cobb, D. R. (2000). Educational policy on emotional intelligence: Does it make sense? *Educational Psychology Review, 12* (2), 163–183.

National Board for Professional Teaching Standards. (1991). *Toward high and rigorous standards for the teaching profession.* Arlington, VA: Author. Available: www.NBPTS.org

Noddings, N. (1992). *The challenge to care in schools.* New York: Teachers College Press.

Noddings, N. (1995). *Philosophy of education.* Boulder, CO: Westview Press.

O' Neil, J. (1997). Building schools as communities: A conversation with James Comer. *Educational Leadership, 54* (8), 6–11.

Palmer, P. (1998). *The courage to teach: Exploring the inner landscape of a teacher's life.* New York: Jossey-Bass.

Palmer, P. (1998–1999). Evoking the spirit in public education. *Educational Leadership, 56* (4), 6–11.

Pang, V. O. (2001). *Multicultural education: A caring-centered, reflective approach.* New York: McGraw-Hill.

Richardson, V. (1996). Teacher thinking. In J. Sikula (Ed.), *Handbook of research on teacher education* (2nd ed.). New York: Macmillan.

Renard, L., & Rogers, S. (1999). Relationship-driven teaching. *Educational Leadership, 57* (1), 34–37.

Rogers, S., Ludington, J., & Graham, S. (1998). *Motivation & learning.* Evergreen, CO: Peak Learning Systems.

Ross, D. R. (1987, April). *Teaching teacher effectiveness research to students: First steps in developing a reflective approach to teaching.* Paper presented at the annual meeting of the American Educational Research Association, Washington, DC.

Sapon-Shevin, M., Dobbelaere, A., Corrigan, C., Goodman, K., & Mastin, M. (1998). Everyone here can play. *Educational Leadership, 56* (1), 42–45.

Scherer, M. (1998). The discipline of hope: A conversation with Herber Kohl. *Educational Leadership, 56* (1), 8–13.

Schon, D. A. (1987). *Educating the reflective practitioner.* San Francisco: Jossey-Bass.

Schon, D. A. (1991). *The reflective turn: Case studies in and on educational practice.* New York: Teachers College Press.

Seidel, J. (2000, May 21). Miss Ratliff connects. *Detroit Free Press,* pp. K1–K2.

Shulman, L. S. (1984). It's harder to teach in class than to be a physician. *Stanford School of Education News, 2,* 1–5.

Shulman, L. S. (1986). Those who understand: Knowledge growth in teachers. *Educational Researcher, 15* (7), 4–14.

Spring, H. T. (1985). Teacher decision-making: A meta-cognitive approach. *The Reading Teacher, 39,* 290–295.

Valli, L. (1997). Listening to other voices: A description of teacher reflection in the United States. *Peabody Journal of Education, 72* (1), 67–88.

Zeichner, K. M. (Ed.). (1996). *Currents of reform in preservice teacher education.* New York: Teachers College Press.

Zeichner, K. M., & Liston, D. P. (1987). Teaching student teachers to reflect. *Harvard Educational Review, 57* (1), 23–48.

Zeichner, K. M., & Liston, D. P. (1996). *Reflective teaching: An introduction.* Mahwah, NJ: Lawrence Erlbaum.

Planning for Instruction: Setting the Stage

Understanding Students and Learning

CHAPTER OVERVIEW

Our responsibilities as teachers begin and end with students. Only when we are successful in helping them learn are we really teaching. Understanding our students—what they know, what they care about, how they learn best, and how their knowledge relates to our content—is key to this process.

This chapter focuses on students, the ways they differ as individuals, and the factors that affect their learning. By considering the ways in which students' characteristics impact their responses to learning activities, teachers can plan lessons around the needs of the most important people in the classroom: the students.

■ *Opening Activity*

Throughout this text we will follow an imaginary fifth-grade teacher, Gloria Jackson, as she develops a unit on the Revolutionary War. Assume for a moment that Gloria has decided to use a textbook reading and a lecture to inform her students about major events in the Revolutionary War. As she is teaching, she is getting little response from her students. They seem to be bored. Suzie is staring out the window, and three students in the back are whispering. Gloria has planned her lecture carefully and provided much detail about the events. But the students seem uninterested.

What is going on here? Consider some of the factors that might be contributing to the students' lack of attention. Think about what influences your own learning. List as many factors as you can.

_____

_____

_____

_____

_____

_____

■ ■ ■

You may have thought of some of the following possibilities: The teacher never got the students' attention at the beginning of the lesson, she did not make the material relevant to their everyday lives, or the material was too abstract and complex for the students. Perhaps they were sleepy because it was right after lunch, the content was presented in a disorganized and confusing way, the lecture lasted too long, no visual aids were used, students were not directly involved through interaction with the teacher or with others, the presentation lacked variety, and so on.

There are many reasons that might explain why students are inattentive during a learning activity. If Gloria wants to redesign this activity so that it will be more effective the next time she uses it, she will need to know why it did not work very well. This chapter presents information about students and the ways they learn that can help you with such decisions.

CHAPTER OBJECTIVES

After you have completed this chapter, you will be able to

1. describe characteristics of students that may influence teaching decisions; and
2. explain how the mind constructs meaning, and the implications for teaching.

Teacher Reflection and Decision Making

Reconsider the theme of this book: teachers' decision making. In order to plan learning experiences, make modifications while teaching, and redesign activities so they are more effective in the future, teachers need to do some very complex thinking. Recall the discussion of the five factors involved in teaching decisions in Chapter 1. Figure 2.1 shows how teachers reflect on instructional decisions by taking into account student needs, content (ideas) to be learned, teachers' knowledge of learning theories and methods (pedagogy), the conditions (context) surrounding the learning, and teacher characteristics. These same factors are considered in selecting and implementing learning activities.

To decide which method to use with which content and with which students, you need to understand quite a bit about student characteristics and how students learn. The first section of this chapter examines the types of information you will want to consider about individual students. Section 2 explores various learning theories and their practical applications more generally, as they may affect any student in your classroom. Section 3 describes the concept of understanding and the way it relates to authentic learning activities.

FIGURE 2.1   Factors Influencing Teaching Decisions

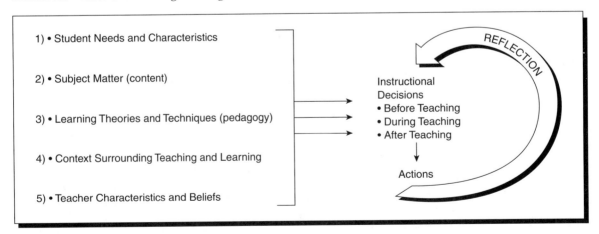

SECTION 1. THE LEARNER: STUDENTS' PERSONAL CHARACTERISTICS

All instructional decisions involve students. The most carefully conceived objectives or well-designed lessons have meaning only when they affect particular students. You will have to consider the ways the students' strengths, weaknesses, needs, desires, and interests will affect the teaching and learning process. The more you know about the individual differences among your students, the more effectively you can adapt instruction to your particular class and to each new group of students you encounter throughout your teaching career.

Gathering Information

Probably your most vital skill as a teacher is the ability to gather, understand, and use information about your students. Information will come in many forms. Some information about students' families, health, and past educational experiences will come with students' records. If, for example, you noticed that Peter was having trouble with math, it would be helpful to know that until last year his math grades were above average. With that knowledge you would need to consider what might have occurred last year and how that knowledge should affect your planning. Certainly you will need to make sure Peter learns the math skills and understandings he did not learn last year. But your approach may be different if you learned that Peter was absent for 2 months last spring due to a serious illness. You may find that by concentrating on the specific skills taught during that time you can bring Peter up-to-speed more quickly than with a general review of last year's material.

Some information about your students will come from **standardized tests**, particularly if the test is aligned with your curriculum and if test results are broken down into specific areas or subtests. Some information can be gathered as you observe your students' behavior and analyze their work. For example, you can learn about students' interests by observing their choice of library books or listening to their stories of weekend adventures. You can understand a great deal about their learning by analyzing the errors on their papers or considering areas of unusual insight. Still other kinds of information require you to go out into the community and interact with parents, families, and community members. This type of activity can be invaluable in understanding the community and cultures within which your students learn. All these types of information will be important as you preassess what students know before teaching and strive to understand their responses during learning activities.

In many ways, a good teacher's information gathering about students parallels the diagnostic skills we expect in physicians. A good physician is a careful observer, using a variety of skills to understand what is happening in a patient's body. But knowing the immediate symptoms is not enough. The physician must know a great deal about a patient's history, allergies, and lifestyle in order to determine the best course of action. Teachers have a similar challenge in understanding students' intellectual and emotional growth. Only as you understand what students know and how they are learning—both immediately and in a broader context—can you make good decisions about instruction.

Culture

One of the most fundamental ways in which students may differ from one another is in their culture (Banks, 1997, 1999). **Culture** has been defined as "the ideation, symbols, values, and beliefs that are shared by a human group" and include the ". . . institutions, or other components of human societies that are created . . . to meet their survival needs" (Banks, 1999, p. 115).

Each of us has been raised in a particular culture. We have spoken at least one common language; celebrated particular holidays; understood specific family structures; appreciated certain kinds of music, art, and literature; and shared values with those around us.

Students' cultures influence their way of perceiving, evaluating, behaving, and doing. Cultures affect the way students communicate, the structure of their family, the art and music they value, their social relationships, and many other important factors in their lives. Cultural influences have multiple layers, some more easily visible than others (Pang, 2001). Cultures vary in their means of communication (language, symbols, and artifacts), means of interaction (customs, practices, and interactional patterns), and values (values, norms, beliefs, and expectations). It is much easier to observe differences in dress and dialect than it is to understand the value orientations that impact your students' lives. Although most of us are aware that students from other countries have cultural differences that would make their school life different from ours, we should also recognize that there are many different cultures within our own country that affect students' lifestyles, values, attitudes, and school performance.

The dominant culture (*macroculture*) in the United States is Anglo–Western European. The formal institutions, official language, dominant social values, and other aspects of life in this society were shaped by the experiences of early settlers from Western Europe. For example, the individualism that has been a traditional American value has its roots in Judeo-Christian ethics, and our government was modeled on the English parliamentary system. Yet the United States is in actuality a multicultural society and consists of many microcultures. A *microculture* may be defined as the smaller cultures with their own unique cultural patterns that constitute the macroculture. As this nation has grown, many groups of immigrants have arrived, each bringing its own cultural traditions. Some of those who joined our society came voluntarily in search of a better life. Others, for example many African Americans, were involuntary immigrants who were brought against their will (Ogbu, 1983). All of these groups have made valuable contributions to the United States. One of the greatest riches of this country is the diversity of its people and the strengths and influences each culture has contributed to the whole.

At various times in our history, specific cultural groups have been deemed less desirable, less intelligent, or less valued because of their differences from the larger culture. For example, during the late 19th century, the Chinese and the Irish were considered undesirable and were subject to social and economic prejudice. Shops seeking employees sometimes posted signs reading, "No Irish need apply." Today exclusionary practices, although different in form, still persist. Schools can have an influence in reversing this trend. If educators increase their knowledge of the differences among and within cultures, the schools can better serve the diverse needs of students and affirm their many cultural heritages.

Culturally relevant teaching (Ladson-Billings, 1994, 1995; Pang, 2001; Wlodkowski & Ginsberg, 1995) requires that teachers be knowledgeable about, and responsive to, the cultural differences among their students. It recognizes that teaching for varied cultures is not as simple as using diverse pictures on the bulletin board or presenting units on different countries (although it would include both of those practices). Students' responses to learning tasks are affected by their understandings of importance, opportunity, novelty, and value. Culturally competent teachers (Ford, 1996; Ladson-Billings, 1994, 1995) learn from their students what they value, how they feel, and how they interact most comfortably. Only by knowing students well can teachers plan activities that will allow them to learn effectively.

Some students come not only from a culture whose traditions and values differ from those of the mainstream but from homes in which Standard English is not the primary language, or is not spoken at all. According to the 2000 census, one out of every five students speaks a language other than English at home (Census, 2000). Some of these students are truly bilingual, that is, they speak English and a second language; others speak little or no English. In fact, some "bilingual" students have had such limited or confusing language experiences that they are not proficient in either language. Although in many districts support is provided for large bilingual populations in the form of special classes or tutoring, many students for whom Standard English is not the preferred language may be in your classes for most or all of the school day. In order to serve the needs of this special population, it is important to consider both the characteristics of bilingual students and the strategies that help them succeed in English-language schools.

There is no single profile of a bilingual student. Their behaviors and achievement may vary enormously, depending on their previous educational experiences, familiarity with English, and cultural background. Some bilingual students display low academic achievement because of the difficulties in learning created by language barriers. Others have difficulties conveying, in an unfamiliar language, information they have learned in school, in their native country, or at home. Still other students feign lack of knowledge in order to avoid embarrassment or questions that they may not understand.

The insecurities that commonly develop from striving to communicate in a new language may be expressed in many ways. Imagine yourself in a foreign country, unable to speak the language in which others are communicating. Those around you think you are ignorant because you express your ideas so poorly, or do not express them at all. How might you react? Some students react to such situations by acting out, sometimes even creating their own cultural stereotypes: "We are tough in my country. We do not mix with weaker people." It is much easier to reject first than to feel rejected. Others respond by withdrawing, avoiding any circumstance that might demand communication.

Some students, especially as they gain experience in the mainstream culture, can become confused or uncertain about their identity. These students may be unwilling to speak their native language and reluctant to invite non-English-speaking relatives to school functions or to provide the necessary translation. The struggle to define a personal identity can be particularly acute for students who come from minorities within their native countries, or from countries in which the media are suppressed. Such students have difficulty defining their identity or role in either country.

Culturally diverse and bilingual students find themselves in the often uncomfortable position of straddling two or more cultures—the dominant culture and their own culture. Their cultural identity is directly influenced by their level of acculturation or acceptance of the dominant culture (Cross, 1995). Some students find strength in their home culture, wearing traditional clothing and bringing lunches unfamiliar to American students. Other students may exaggerate behaviors they associate with the United States—hiding their home culture by imitating the dominant culture. One student brought nothing but Twinkies for lunch, because they are "American food." Choice of hairstyle and preferences in music and dance are other means by which students from culturally diverse backgrounds indicate their feelings about the macroculture and their native culture.

All cultures have clearly defined gender roles that affect students' performance or behavior in schools (Cline, 1998). In some cultures a young girl's honor requires that she remain apart from young men, often beginning at an early age. In others, girls are expected to marry, or at least leave school and wait to marry, in their early teens. Such values create conflict for young women whose identities span two cultures and for the young men who feel obligated to protect them. Tensions can also occur when female school personnel interact with students or parents whose traditions preclude women from occupying positions of authority.

Other, less obvious differences in cultures can also cause misunderstandings. How might a student whose culture sees owls as symbols of bad luck view a Halloween decoration? How might a teacher for whom eye contact is a sign of integrity respond to a student whose culture requires lowered eyes in the presence of authority? Clearly, both language and cultural differences can affect students' interaction in school and, hence, their achievement. More information on teaching culturally diverse students is presented in Chapter 10.

REFLECTING ON THE IDEAS

Think about your own culture. Many ideas and values that are obvious to you seem that way because you have learned them from your culture. For example, if you value promptness, working before recreation, or striving to do your individual best, you learned those values as part of a culture. Or, you might have been taught that helping at home when needed is more important than the time one arrives at school, or that thinking about the feelings of those around you is more important than standing out as an individual. Think about the ways your cultural values will affect your teaching. When might they cause problems? Discuss your ideas with a friend, preferably someone whose background is different from yours.

Prior Knowledge and Experience

Students' prior experiences at home, at school, and in the community affect their responses and performance in many areas. Cognitive psychology has informed us that learning is not a passive event, like filling a cup, but an active process in which each individual builds knowledge, linking new bits of information or experience to internal circuits (or structures) called **schemata**. You might think of the knowledge and skills you plan to teach as links in a complex circuit or pieces of a Tinkertoy set. You may pass out the pieces, but students have to fit them into their own structures, and each structure is different.

In what ways might students' prior experiences affect their learning? If, for example, students have never seen the ocean or a movie of the ocean, they may have difficulty understanding lessons on the voyage of the *Mayflower*, sea life, or even the divisions of water and land masses on a globe. Students who have never traveled outside their hometown have fewer schemata available to provide the basis for a discussion of variation in climates. It is important to assess your students' familiarity with major concepts that underlie your instruction. For example, you might begin a lesson on sea life by having students brainstorm all the plants and animals they have seen living in water.

Some students' prior experiences, either at home or in school, have not provided them with the expected concepts or skills for their grade level. Effective instructional planning must include careful diagnosis of prior knowledge, experience, and skills related to your topic.

If some students lack important knowledge and skills, you must decide whether remediation or compensation would be more appropriate. A **remedial approach** entails teaching prerequisite knowledge and skills before proceeding with planned instruction. For example, before teaching a lesson on solving problems using area and perimeter, Gloria Jackson's colleague, Ms. Lee, identified several students who were unable to calculate perimeter and area or distinguish between them. Based on this finding, she divided the class into two groups for instruction. While most students worked independently on reviewing problem-solving skills, she took the students who needed review on area and perimeter aside for a brief small-group session. When this was completed, she was able to teach her planned lesson to the whole class. Since solving problems using perimeter and area is dependent on understanding the nature of those two concepts, she believed that review of the concepts was necessary before the second group could go on successfully to the more advanced material. If the necessary knowledge and skills can be attained in a reasonable length of time, remediation is the logical choice.

Sometimes, however, remediation is not possible or would represent an unreasonable use of class time. In such cases, a teacher may choose **compensatory instruction** instead. Compensation involves choosing an instructional approach that circumvents areas of weakness. For example, a teacher in an urban school might choose to alter a lesson on mammals to focus on cats, dogs, and squirrels, rather than the farm animals emphasized in the text. This would allow the teacher to proceed with the content (mammals) without spending time elaborately developing concepts about farms. (Of course, a good alternative would be to visit a farm to develop the necessary concepts.)

If a student is strong in math but has weak reading skills, the teacher might provide reading assistance to the student in interpreting a math story problem rather than delaying instruction in problem solving until the student's reading skills can be remediated. In each case, a compensatory approach would allow meaningful instruction to take place, despite weaknesses in prerequisite experiences or skills.

In addition to experiences, knowledge, and skills, students bring attitudes, values, and social patterns that have been shaped by prior experiences. Some students come from homes in which school success is highly valued. In other home environments, students may be encouraged to value street smarts, athletic success, or social status. Some families reward problem solving or independent thinking, whereas some emphasize conformity and the memorization of facts. Some homes are language-rich and encourage a variety of expression; other homes prefer children to observe quietly.

Students who come from homes that support the types of learning emphasized in school have intellectual and emotional advantages. It is the responsibility of all teachers to model both skills and attitudes that will support students in their learning. High expectations for all students, rewards for varied accomplishments, ties to personal experiences, and family involvement all set a classroom tone that balances recognition of the variety of values students bring to school with the encouragement of attitudes likely to promote achievement. Careful observation and attention to student and parent comments can help you identify students who need extra support in balancing values from home and school. Such observations can also make you aware of areas of student interests, allowing you to tap those interests through lesson planning or individualized activities.

Interests

Perhaps one of the least considered aspects of student characteristics is student interests. Certainly most teachers would agree that students are more likely to learn material if they are interested in it. Interests affect what we learn, how we pay attention, how much we persist in the face of difficulty, and how extensively we study particular subjects. Today, pressures (real or perceived) to adhere to prescribed curriculum can limit teachers' use of student interests. However, using students' interests in teaching does not necessarily mean we will plan units around baseball, dinosaurs, or the latest pop culture phenomenon—although such studies may sometimes be appropriate. It may mean using examples from students' interests to explain key ideas or practice essential skills. Understanding students' interests can help teachers tie curriculum to students' needs, identify fruitful areas for enrichment or independent study, and design powerful application projects.

Some of the interests and concerns of students at a given age are predictable. Primary-age children are interested in things they see in their immediate surroundings. They enjoy using their imagination and their growing sense of individual identity. Older elementary students are often interested in how things work, as they develop more sophisticated concrete thinking. Preadolescent students are interested in issues of personal identity and relationships. Strong, Silver, and Robinson (1995) referred to a "curiosity connection" when teachers tie curriculum to key adolescent issues. Similar curiosity can be encouraged when teachers tie instruction to key developmental issues at any age. However, other student interests may be idiosyncratic to a particular place, time, or individual(s). Identifying such interests can make the difference between students who are engaged in the lesson and those whose thoughts and concerns are anywhere but in the classroom.

Teachers have many informal ways of identifying students' interests. Certainly it would be difficult to miss the latest media/marketing craze attached to every fast-food meal, or the fact that every book Bruce takes out of the library is about medieval times. However, there may be times when you want to assess student interests in a more systematic manner.

In this type of formal data gathering, you may use *open-ended responses*, *closed-ended responses*, or a combination of the two. In an open-ended response inventory you might ask questions such as: I like to read about _____ , After school I like to play _____ , or, If I could invite anyone, living or dead, to visit our classroom, I would invite _____ . By examining the responses to several such questions, it is possible to identify themes and trends in students' concerns. Such analysis can provide a wealth of information and insight into the worlds of individual students. The parallel disadvantage is, of course, that **open-ended questions** are not easily tallied and may be time consuming to analyze for large groups. Another alternative is to present students with a closed-ended set of responses. One way to do this is to use a list of possible topics and ask students to circle the ones they would most like to study. (With younger children you may want to limit the number of things that may be circled to avoid students saying they are interested in absolutely everything!)

A helpful means for gathering information on students' interests in a topic for study is the KWL strategy. To use **KWL** you introduce a topic of an upcoming lesson or unit and create a three-column chart asking students what they know (K), what they want to know (W), and later what they have learned (L) about that subject. The KWL strategy provides reflective teachers with a rich source of useful information. Not only does it serve as an informal preassessment of students' prior knowledge, but it gives students a chance to share their interests—and hence the clearest ways to make the topic interesting to them. Of course it is important to make use of this information in planning later activities. Students will not continue to raise questions or share their interests if they never have a chance to investigate them.

Another possible source of information on students' interests is a more systematic recording of the informal data that is part of everyday life with a room full of children. You could keep records of topics mentioned in journal writing, sharing time, or informal conversation. You may want to consider anecdotal records of free play (especially dramatic play) or topics of library books in which students show interest. Whatever method you choose, the goal is to become as familiar as possible with students' interests and concerns.

Sometimes identified student interests may lead to independent investigations by individual students. For example, one primary-grade student, after a brief preclass exchange about his music lesson and the music he was practicing for a recital, said, " You know, Tchaikovsky wrote some happy music and some sad music. Do you think he wrote happy music when he was happy and sad music when he was sad?" A teacher suggested he make a dual time line that indicated the major events in Tchaikovsky's life and the works he composed. After labeling the happiness or sadness of events and compositions, the student could see what correlation, if any, existed between the two. In addition to learning about Tchaikovsky, this student learned that his interests were valued by his teacher (U.S. Department of Education, 1993, p. 29).

Other times student interests can form the basis for short- or long-term class activities. A teacher who knows that many students are interested in animals may plan an activity to teach measurement by measuring out the relative sizes of various animals on the classroom floor. A class interested in the circus may be challenged to plan activities for a metric circus. Students fascinated with motion pictures may hone their writing skills developing (and possibly videotaping) a screenplay. In each case, students' involvement in content would be facilitated by the ties to their interests.

Intellectual Abilities

Students differ in many other ways. In every class you will find a range of general and specific intellectual abilities. Traditionally, general intellectual ability has been measured by IQ scores derived from a test originally developed to predict success in school. Although IQ tests frequently provide information on the ease with which individuals approach school tasks, they have been called into question as measures of total intellectual potential. Since the early 20th century, psychologists have debated the importance of general intelligence versus sets of specific academic abilities. Are individuals generally either "smart" or "less smart" or do they differ in more complex ways? Might a person be intelligent in math and less intelligent in language? What kinds of important intellectual abilities might not be measured by paper-and-pencil tests, or a test given in 1 day?

Contemporary learning theorists continue to debate the nature of intelligence itself. Although a complete description of theories of intelligence is beyond the scope of this book, two examples will suffice. Sternberg (1985, 1997) has developed a **triarchic theory** of intelligence. He believes that intelligence includes three basic components: the componential system or workings of the mind in processing information, the response to novelty, and the ability of the individual to react to the environment—an ability we might call practical intelligence or street smarts. Individuals who have strengths in one of these three areas might show very different abilities. A person whose componential system is particularly strong might be a whiz at taking in and processing information. That student might have little trouble analyzing a complicated math formula or remembering factual information for a test. Individuals who deal well with novelty might come up with original ideas or be excellent problem solvers. They might write unique stories, invent interesting games at recess, or constantly suggest alternatives to class assignments. You have probably known someone with particular ability to interact with the social environment, someone who always knows the way to get things done— someone with practical intelligence. When students were taught in ways that emphasize all three types of intelligence, student achievement improved (Sternberg, Grigorenko, & Jarvin, 2000; Sternberg, Torff, & Grigorenko, 1998).

Gardner (1983, 1991, 1993) believes that we all have **multiple intelligences.** His original work identified seven independent intelligences: linguistic, musical, logical-mathematical, spatial, bodily-kinesthetic, interpersonal, and intrapersonal. According to this theory, each person has a unique profile of intelligences, strong in some, weaker in others. A fine dancer might have exceptional bodily-kinesthetic intelligence but not necessarily be outstanding in mathematics or music. A person with unusual interpersonal intelligence might make a particularly fine counselor, teacher, or friend. More than 10 years after the original model was developed, Gardner identified an eighth intelligence: naturalist intelligence (Checkley, 1997). Gardner believes that as he continues his work, other intelligences will be identified. Schools traditionally have focused their attention on only two of Gardner's seven intelligences: linguistic and logical-mathematical. Now, some educators are trying to identify the intelligences through which individual students learn best; they are also working to develop all types of intelligence in classroom settings (Armstrong, 1994; Gardner, 1993) (see Figure 2.2).

FIGURE 2.2 Gardner's Eight Intelligences

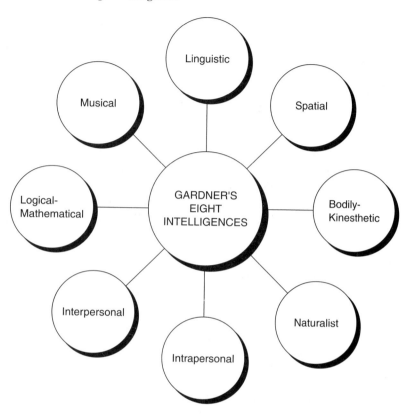

Cultural and language differences have a significant impact on traditional test performance. Students who have been exposed to key test vocabulary words clearly have an advantage over those who have not or those for whom the English language is unfamiliar. Students who have played with blocks before are likely to be more comfortable in a testing task involving blocks than those for whom manipulating blocks is a new experience. Are those students less "smart" than students whose previous experiences have enabled them to be more successful test takers?

While the roles of general and specific ability or the validity of test scores will continue to be debated, from a practical standpoint several things are clear. Students' intellectual abilities differ in complex ways. They can be thought of as having profiles of intelligence, with strengths in some types of thinking and relative weaknesses in others. Some students learn traditional school tasks quickly and easily. They can solve problems, think abstractly, and remember information more readily than others. It is important to provide appropriate instruction for such students, challenging their abilities with a depth and pace of instruction that would not be appropriate for all students. Others need more assistance in learning, extended opportunities for practice, and a careful linking of new and prior experiences. Most students demonstrate strengths in some areas and weaknesses in others. If a student shows advanced ability in language but difficulty in mathematics, it is important to investigate such patterns and vary instruction to meet them. Teachers may also wish to consider how to nurture less traditional forms of intelligence, and become more aware of students' strengths and weaknesses in spatial, kinesthetic, or interpersonal learning. It is much more important to match instruction to students' needs than to worry about whether a student's particular pattern of abilities means the student is or is not "intelligent."

Finally, teachers must be cautious about interpreting any test that attempts to assess intellectual ability. Any score represents performance on a particular day. Such a score may be influenced by factors as diverse as illness on the day of the test, familiarity with the language of the test, and prior experience with the vocabulary and materials of testing. In providing instruction that is appropriate to student needs and abilities, teachers must take into account not just IQ and standardized test information but also observations of performance under a wide range of circumstances.

REFLECTING ON THE IDEAS

List at least four ways in which students in a fifth-grade class might differ from one another. How might each of these differences affect Gloria Jackson's unit on the Revolutionary War?

1. _____

2. _____

3. _____

4. _____

Learning Styles

In addition to intellectual strengths and weaknesses, students vary in the ways they learn best. The way a student learns can be defined as **learning style**. Hunt (1979) said that learning style "describes a student in terms of those educational conditions under which he is most likely to learn. Learning style describes how a student learns, not what he has learned" (p. 27).

There are many theories of learning styles, but one principle underlies them all: Individuals do not all learn best in the same way. Circumstances or methods that may promote learning for one individual may not be helpful for others. Some learning styles are not better or stronger than others, merely different. Teachers must recognize that students learn in different ways. An approach may seem logical to a teacher and work well for some students—the students whose styles are similar to that of the teacher—but not be effective for other equally intelligent students whose styles are different.

Perhaps the simplest variation in learning styles may be found along sensory channels. Some individuals learn most effectively through visual information; they process information best if it comes to them through their eyes. Others learn best auditorily, processing information most efficiently if it comes to them through their ears. Still others benefit most from information presented kinesthetically, involving the sense of touch or whole body movement. These differences do not reflect the relative acuity of eyes, ears, or other senses. Although a student with poor eyesight would certainly have trouble with information presented only visually, it is possible to have 20/20 eyesight and still not process visual information well. The connection between the eyes and the brain may simply not function as well as that between the ears and the brain. For example, a student who is a strong auditory learner may best experience the story of the Constitutional Convention by listening to the teacher tell the story. A strong visual learner would absorb the lesson most successfully if the story were accompanied by pictures or text, and a kinesthetic learner would benefit from opportunities to role-play a dramatization of the event (Barbe & Swassing, 1979).

Numerous other theories of learning styles are based on various dimensions representing ways individuals take in and process information (Guild & Garger, 1998). For example, Gregorc (1982) developed a theory of learning styles that was not derived from the functioning of the individual senses but from the ways individuals organize and process information from all the senses. His model is representative of theories based on two opposing dimensions of learning processes. The model is based on two dimensions: perception and organization. *Perception* refers to the means by which an individual takes in information. While most people have the ability to perceive both concrete information (accessible to the senses) and abstract information (ideas, feelings), some people grasp information best when it is presented concretely. Others are most comfortable taking in and manipulating information in abstract form.

Individuals also vary in the ways they *organize* information. Some individuals organize information best in a sequential or linear way, with each bit of information leading to the next in a straight-line manner. Others are more comfortable with an organization Gregorc calls *random,* a nonlinear, holistic approach characterized by leaps of logic and the processing of several bits of information simultaneously. Each individual can be described as having preferences somewhere on the continuum between the two preferences.

Gregorc combines the perceptual and organizational abilities into four learning styles associated with particular behaviors and characteristics. Each style has a unique and organized view of the world and operates from a particular point of view. Although no individual operates in only one style, many people have strong preferences for one or more channels. Such preferences can be identified through a learning styles inventory, or more informal observations of behavior, language, and habits.

An individual with a dominant *concrete sequential (CS)* style prefers to work with concrete information processed in a sequential manner. Such an individual might be characterized as practical, structured, down-to-earth, and organized. A CS adult balances the checkbook carefully, organizes closets, and rarely forgets an appointment. A CS teacher is a natural at keeping complete records, arranging classroom materials, and developing logical units of study. A CS student learns best when information is presented in a systematic fashion, with practical applications and hands-on activity.

A person with a dominant *abstract sequential (AS)* channel prefers learning abstract information and organizing it sequentially. Such a person may be seen as studious and intellectual. AS adults are happiest when searching for new knowledge, analyzing problems, or evaluating issues through logic and reason. They may not be concerned with such concrete issues as whether two socks match or what the outdoor temperature is. AS teachers may present brilliant lectures or carefully structured research projects, and AS students may debate logically, analyze literature critically, and forget their lunch.

An individual with an *abstract random* (AR) style prefers abstract information, but processes it in a holistic, nonlinear fashion. This person may be seen as sensitive, emotional, and artistic. AR individuals may write poetry, counsel friends, and be expert at relationships, whether between individuals or academic disciplines. They may have moments of personal or professional insight without being able to explain them. An AR teacher loves interdisciplinary teaching, thematic units, and a classroom full of art (including on the ceilings). An AR student may be the life of the class, have an eye for beauty, and possess a wonderful imagination, but have little idea how to transfer ideas into concrete reality.

Finally, a *concrete random* (CR) individual processes concrete information in nonlinear ways. CR individuals are natural problem solvers, explorers, and inventors. CR individuals love to tinker with gadgets, appliances, or ideas. Their garages and cupboards may overflow with spare parts and unusual tools for future experimentation. As teachers, they have classrooms full of experiments and emphasize creative problem solving and independence. CR students flourish in such an atmosphere, often finding solutions to problems through intuitive leaps they cannot explain. Like AR learners, CR students have trouble when asked to show their work (Butler, 1986; Gregorc, 1982).

In this brief overview, you may have caught a glimpse of yourself or someone you know. In examining how these characteristics might affect teaching and learning, several questions are worth considering. What would happen to a student with a strong AR preference in a CS teacher's classroom, or vice versa? In either case, the mismatch between teaching style and learning style could create difficulties for both student and teacher. Neither style is "right," but the two styles are different. Regardless of the learning style model used to examine individual differences, the question of style differences among students and teachers remains.

Does this mean schools should try to match teachers' and students' styles in assigning classrooms? Probably not. Aside from the logistical difficulties of such a proposal, it would be a disservice to allow students to function in only their preferred mode. Students need to learn to adapt to different situations, taking on preferred or less preferred styles as needed. (For example, in filling out income tax forms, it is highly desirable to function in a CS manner or hire a CS accountant!) However, teachers can make sure that at least some of the activities for each topic or unit allow students to function in preferred ways. Teachers can also provide special support to students when assigning work outside their preferred styles.

Butler (1995, 1996) has developed materials to teach adolescents about their learning styles. She believes that helping students understand their personal style can help them study more effectively and interact more productively with teachers and peers. You may want to consider whether teaching your students about style difference may be an effective way to enhance their learning.

Dunn and Dunn (1975; Dunn, 1996, 1997) have described learning styles as "the manner in which 18 different elements of four basic stimuli affect a person's ability to absorb and to retain information, values, facts or concepts" (1975, p. 74). The four types of stimuli are environmental, emotional, sociological, and physical. For example, under environmental stimuli, students may prefer bright or dim places, warm or cool places, a specific noise level, or a particular physical arrangement. Emotional stimuli include variation in motivation, persistence, responsibility, and amount of structure preferred. Sociological variables include preferences for working individually, in pairs, in teams, or in groups. Physical variables include perceptual (sensory modalities) differences, and preferences for food and time of day. Each variable interacts with culture and prior experiences in complex ways. The fact that students vary in their responses to such a large number of variables helps to explain the number of individual differences found in each classroom. Dunn et al. (1995) found that despite these limitations, matching individual style preferences can have a positive impact on student learning.

One of the more interesting questions in learning styles research is whether styles vary along one or more dimensions across cultural groups (Dunn & Griggs, 1995; Shade, 1997; Smith, 1998). Gay (1994) notes that culture and ethnicity have a strong impact on shaping learning styles but that it is essential to use caution in interpreting research. There is an emerging research base suggesting patterns of learning styles differences across cultures. Boykin (1994, for example) examines learning styles in African American students, Swisher and Doyle (1992) review style patterns among Native Americans, and Shade (1997) provides a helpful summary across populations. As you learn about the cultural groups you teach, it may be helpful to consult literature on style differences. However, it is essential to remember that generalizations across an entire population are of limited value when applied to a specific individual. Each child in your classroom must be considered as an individual, not as a representative of a particular group.

REFLECTING ON THE IDEAS

Imagine you are teaching a unit on plants. List five activities that would appeal to varying learning styles. You may use any of the learning style frameworks presented earlier in this chapter. Label each with the learning style(s) to which it would appeal. For example, "Drawing the structure of a flower—visual."

1. _____
2. _____
3. _____
4. _____
5. _____

Which of the activities listed are most appealing to you? Think about how your own learning style may affect your teaching. In what ways might it be helpful? In what ways might it cause difficulties?

SECTION 2. LEARNING: HOW DOES LEARNING OCCUR?

As we prepare to think about teaching in ways that help students learn, it can be helpful to briefly review some of the things we know about how learning occurs. You probably learned these principles in more detail in your classwork in educational psychology. We cannot list all the important information here, but we can review a few key principles. You may want to consult a textbook in educational psychology (for example, Ormrod, 2000) for more details.

Students Learn Only What They Are Ready to Learn

One of the most commonly used phrases in early childhood education is **developmentally appropriate practice.** The phrase is equally appropriate for other stages of learning. It reflects the idea that individuals learn best when instruction is matched to their development and readiness. With some basic understanding of development and learning you can begin to identify the crucial ways in which you will need to vary your activities to match the unique needs of your students.

Your students will display varying levels of physical, cognitive, emotional, and moral development. Some of your students will struggle with the fine-motor skills related to handwriting; it takes a while to realize that some of what you may label as a "problem" (e.g., making a 5 backwards) is developmentally normal for a particular child and will resolve itself over time. In other cases you will need to be attentive to moral development; elementary children need to grow into the understanding that industry (trying hard) can pay off. If competition is common in the classroom they may become confused when others who work less are frequently "winners." In early years of teaching, theory and experienced teachers can be helpful in identifying what constitutes a problem that must be addressed immediately and what is normal for a child in this developmental range.

Students develop from concrete to abstract thinking over time. You may remember Jean Piaget (1970), the Swiss psychologist who studied his children and discovered distinct stages of cognitive growth. In the preschool years, the child may demonstrate little logical thought (at least from an adult perspective). But as children grow through the elementary years, their thought processes become more integrated and organized, with abstract thinking emerging largely in early adolescence. Thus, most elementary children will need concrete experiences on which to base their learning. They will need multiple hands-on experiences, including the exploration and manipulation of physical objects, in order to grasp abstract concepts. For example, students learning computation skills must have experiences putting together groups of objects before they are ready for the concept of addition. In these experiences, students should be asked to explain their reasoning and challenge explanations that seem illogical. Children with multiple experiences in any area will show greater development and more sophisticated thinking than those who have not had similar experiences. It will be important to identify students lacking developmental experiences shared by most of your students. For example, children who come from a home in which they have had few opportunities to converse with adults will need extra practice in presenting ideas and learning to listen. They may also need explicit teaching of vocabulary.

An appropriate level of challenge is an important part of readiness. You may have noticed that you are most successful—and most motivated—in learning a new skill if you move forward in ways that are challenging but allow for feelings of success. The same is true for children. Vygotsky (1997) used the term **zone of proximal development** to describe the "zone" in which the learning is beyond the child's current understanding but close enough to be reachable with careful scaffolding (support and direction) by the teacher. The best learning is neither so easy that it is obvious nor so difficult that it is overly frustrating. Young children, in particular, need frequent opportunities for success in order to develop a sense of efficacy as a learner. It can be a challenge for the teacher to find the level of instruction at which students have feelings of both challenge and success.

Students Construct Their Own Understanding

Piaget and Vygotsky contributed to our understanding of how knowledge is obtained. It is not transmitted intact from one individual to another. (Teaching would be much easier if that were the case!) Rather, knowledge is constructed by each individual as he or she interacts with the world and with other human beings. For example, imagine a child who sees a skunk for the first time. The child will try to fit this experience with other previous experiences and may well decide, since this animal is similar in color to the family's pet cat, it can be called "cat" too. If an adult is nearby, the adult is likely to challenge the child's understanding, probably emphatically, insisting that the animal is not a cat and the child may not pet it. Since this strange excited adult behavior is different than any the child has seen around a cat before, the child is likely to decide this experience does not fit with previous understandings of "cat" and begin to construct a new concept: skunk. In a calmer moment, the adult may be able to point out the fact that the cat and

*Students Construct Understanding
Through Their Experiences*

the skunk are the same colors but different in important ways. Should the child have the opportunity to smell the skunk, the concept will be more richly built. Powerful learning experiences also can come through modeling. In this case, the adult model of what to do when encountering a skunk is likely to be tied to the emerging concept. Still, the concept of *skunk* is built bit by bit through experiences—not through a 10-minute lecture on the nature and characteristics of skunks. Understanding that students' concepts have been constructed over time through interactions with those around them gives reflective teachers another reason to learn more about the cultures within which those ideas have been built.

A parallel principle is that students' existing concepts—built into their cognitive structure through experience—are not easily dislodged by simple explanations. Some of these are powerful cultural learnings. For example, a cultural norm of quiet respect for adults will not be reversed simply because a teacher says she hopes her students will ask many questions. Other existing concepts are misconceptions based on experience. For example, students who have had many experiences in which sweaters made them warm are likely to have developed a strong belief that sweaters generate heat. Explanations to the contrary will not be powerful enough to dislodge associations built through multiple experiences. Only through multiple new experiences that challenge the misconception can new learning occur. You'll read about such experiences in the next section. Teaching that is based on the assumption that students build their own understanding is called **constructivism** or **constructivist teaching**. There is a wide range of definitions for constructivism (Perkins, 1999; Philips, 1995) leading to considerable disagreement over what does and does not constitute constructivist teaching. Although constructivist teaching has been defined in varied ways, all definitions center around strategies that allow students to actively interact with ideas providing maximum opportunities for concept development. For some, constructivism means "objects and events have no absolute meaning, rather, the individual interprets each and constructs meaning based on individual experience. . . . Constructivists tend to eschew the breaking down of context into component parts in favor of environments wherein knowledge, skill, and complexity exist naturally" (Hannafin, Hannafin, Land, & Oliver, 1997, p. 109). Some individuals interpret this to mean that direct teaching must necessarily be ineffective or that shared knowledge is illusive, at best. Brandt and Perkins (2000) state:

> Perkins (1992) distinguishes between without-the-information-given (WIG) constructivism and beyond-the-information-given (BIG) constructivism. Ardent WIG constructivists argue that for real learning, students must virtually reconstruct knowledge for themselves, with appropriate support. BIG constructivists believe that giving learners information directly is fine and often preferable; but to learn it, they must then apply it actively and creatively. (pp. 167–168)

This book is designed to support a constructivist approach to teaching from a position more closely aligned with BIG constructivists. From our perspective, the key to constructivism is not whether learning takes place in a complex environment or whether objects do or do not have absolute meaning. The important concept for teaching is that although we can present information, we cannot give knowledge to students; they must construct it themselves. All of our teaching decisions must be designed to help them do so effectively. More information on constructivist teaching can be found in Chapter 6.

FIGURE 2.3 The Information-Processing Model

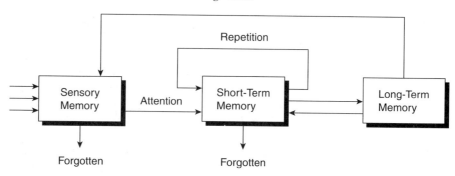

It can be helpful to understand the way information enters memory in order to build new concepts. The theory that describes this procedure is called information processing. Three elements of an information-processing model are illustrated in Figure 2.3: the sensory register, working (short-term) memory (STM), and long-term memory (LTM). Think of the child approaching the skunk. The sensory register receives information from the eyes that the skunk is present. If the child is distracted or does not care, the information is lost and no learning will take place. If the child attends to the skunk, information enters the short-term memory. The child searches long-term memory for previous experiences that will help in interpreting the information. It is from the cache of information filed in long-term memory that the (erroneous) association "cat" emerges. If a new association "skunk" is formed, it too will be stored in long-term memory—with strong ties to "cat," "black and white," and "excited adult."

Information-processing models can provide important understandings that assist us in teaching.

- Attention is a gatekeeper. If something is not noticed, it will not be learned. Human attention is limited—if your students are attending to something outside the window, something inside their desks, or even something inside their heads, they will not be able to attend to your lesson. It is important to keep students actively involved in lessons in order to keep their attention focused. Boredom and distractions are enemies of attention.
- Short-term memory is of short duration (5–20 seconds) and limited capacity. Once students are paying attention, they can only think about a few new ideas at a time. It is best to concentrate on a few key ideas at one time and use multiple experiences to reinforce them. The more different types of experiences, the better the opportunity to build the ideas. It is also helpful to tell students directly which ideas are the most important and to write them on the board.
- Long-term memory and short-term memory work together. The prior knowledge in the long-term memory provides the base to which new ideas are connected. Prior knowledge in the long-term memory also helps determine which information enters the short-term memory at all—with no prior experiences with skunks and no adult to intervene, a child may not even notice that the skunk is anything new

or interesting. It could pass out of sight without any learning taking place. It is important for teachers to provide the scaffolding that helps students find ties between the new concepts to be learned and their prior experiences in long-term memory.

- The types of experiences we provide for children have a direct impact on how effectively new concepts are processed. Meaning is enhanced by encountering concepts in multiple contexts—that is, the more diverse experiences students have with a concept, the more powerful it will become. For example, students learning about animals will build more powerful concepts if they read about animals, draw animals, measure the size of animals on the sidewalk, feed class pets, visit a zoo, watch videos of animals, visit animal sites on the web, observe insects on the playground, and so forth rather than simply reading about animals. Students who have—via electronic communication—compared the insects on their playground with those on another playground in a distant state, are actively involved in building the bases for concepts about geography and climate as well as those about insects. The more opportunities for active processing of information—activities that require students to do something with the information as opposed to just absorb it—the more ties are built in long-term memory and the more powerful the concepts.

- Well-organized information is easier to remember. When teaching, it is important to help students understand how ideas are related and which ideas are most important. This can entail the use of **graphic organizers,** lists of steps, and explicit ties to prior knowledge. When information does not have a logical structure, it can be helpful to create one. For example, many students have learned the names of the Great Lakes (a relatively random list) by remembering the mnemonic device HOMES. Repetition can be helpful in remembering less meaningful information that needs to be accessed quickly. Think about how much easier it is to remember phone numbers that you use frequently as opposed to those you rarely call. Similarly, drill and practice activities can be helpful in memorizing math facts or learning to spell nonphonetic words.

- Finally, because learning is built through experience, the ways information is processed will vary across cultures. Not only will the relevant prior knowledge be different, but cultures even vary in their models of effective teaching and learning. For example, many Native American tribes' traditional means of learning and teaching relies heavily on observation and modeling. Other contemporary American groups dive into new experiences and learn by doing. A thoughtful teacher will analyze his or her students' prior learning experiences when planning new learning activities.

Researchers in the area of *situated cognition* emphasize the importance of context in building understanding (Brown, Collins, & Duguid, 1989). New knowledge is not acquired in a vacuum. It develops through specific interactions with the environment. Only by understanding the situation in which learning occurs can we understand the learning. From this perspective, the more closely the circumstances of learning resemble the context in which the information is needed, the better. For example, solving "word problems" in math would be less powerful than solving actual problems for which mathematical information is necessary—figuring out the number of pizzas necessary for an upcoming activity or the amount of paint necessary to paint a stage set. Advocates of this model emphasize the importance of authentic learning activities as described in the next section. Designing instruction based on situated learning requires that teachers select a situation that will allow students to acquire the desired learning and provide "scaffolding" or supportive activities that allow students to succeed in a complex situation (Young, 1993).

Brain-Based Education

One of the more interesting trends in education today is the effort to link new information coming from neurology and neural psychology to classroom practice. If we understand more about how the brain functions, it seems logical that such knowledge would help us plan better for student learning. Writing from this perspective cites the need for "brain-based" or "brain-compatible" learning.

It is clear that information from brain research will bring important information to educators. However, as with any research, it is important to read (and listen) analytically. Any time you are told, "Research says you should. . . ." it is important to ask, "What research?" "Under what conditions?" "With what populations?" When we ask these questions about the recommendations being made for **brain-based education**, we find mixed results. In some cases, the conclusions and generalizations, particularly those drawn from animal research, seem a bit premature for the amount of data. For example, some writers have claimed that brain research "proves" that early development is so important that all the most critical learning occurs before students enter school. In fact, although early learning is important, the brain continues to develop in important ways throughout a healthy life (Bruer, 1999). However, despite this caution, research surrounding brain-based learning promises to bring more important information with each passing year. In the meantime, it is interesting to note that many recommendations made by writers in this area are consistent with the constructivist approaches rooted in cognitive psychology: students' active engagement in learning, clear organization of content, and students' involvement in complex activities (see, for example, Caine & Caine, 1997; Jensen, 2000; Scherer, 2000).

Both psychologists and brain researchers also study memory. Different types of information are stored differently in the brain (Sprenger, 1999). Most of what we teach in schools will be recorded as semantic memory, or information learned from words. The descriptions of long-term memory earlier in this chapter describe processes for semantic memory. Episodic or spatial memory is the memory associated with places. If you have ever walked back to the place you lost something in an effort to reconstruct your actions, you were hoping to trigger episodic memory. Procedural memory or "muscle memory" records the actions of your body. Because (unlike semantic memory) it operates outside the realm of conscious thought, it can allow human beings to do two things at once—for example, drive a car (using procedural memory) while having a conversation (using semantic memory). Automatic memory is described as "conditioned reflex memory" (p. 53). It stores information that has been memorized through repetition, perhaps the multiplication tables, but not the ability to comprehend the concept of multiplication. Finally, emotional memory is the most powerful type of memory. Experiences that trigger powerful emotions, for example a class celebration or special event, are much more likely to be remembered. The power of emotional memory also means that students who are thinking about emotionally powerful topics outside the lesson—a problem with a friend or family member, a party after school, a big game last night—are much more likely to attend to the emotionally laden memories than to the lesson at hand, unless the teacher takes special trouble to engage them. Educators are beginning to study the ways it may be possible to systematically provide experiences that will trigger different types of memory, providing multiple avenues for student learning.

The brain-based education movement has also brought an increased emphasis on the importance of emotion in learning. In addition to the importance of emotional memory, researchers also suggest that the emotional climate of the room, particularly the stress level, has an impact on student learning. High levels of stress, which may trigger a "fight or flight" response, are not conducive to optimum learning.

■ *Practice Activity: Classroom Observation*

Observe a classroom of your choice. Evaluate how well the teaching methods appeal to the brain's information processing, memory, and ways of constructing meaning. How brain-compatible is the classroom environment (curiosity, safety, rich materials without clutter, and so on)? Write a reflective paper that addresses each of these areas.

■ ■ ■

As you can tell, the ways you plan learning activities will greatly affect how readily students are able to learn and retain new ideas. When learning activities are at the appropriate level, tied to prior experiences, with multiple opportunities for active involvement with content, opportunities for learning are maximized.

CHECK YOUR UNDERSTANDING

With a friend, review the information on learning theory in this section. Examine a lesson in a teacher's edition of a textbook, or a sample lesson from one of the many Internet sites containing teaching materials. Analyze the extent to which the lesson optimizes the opportunity for student learning. List its strengths and weaknesses.

SECTION 3. UNDERSTANDING AND AUTHENTIC LEARNING

In planning for instruction, it is essential to plan so that students will understand the content. At one level such a statement seems so obvious as to be ridiculous—of course we want students to understand the content, that's why we are teaching. But, in fact, students are taught many things they do not really understand, even though they successfully answer test questions on that content. You probably have had this experience yourself. Think of a time you have taken a class in which some of the content never did make sense to you. This may have been a history class in which you learned a series of confusing events or a science class in which you learned a collection of rules or facts. In such circumstances, what did you do? If you are like many students, you memorized the things you needed for class (or tests) and forgot them as soon as the class ended. You did not apply the things you learned because you couldn't—you didn't understand what you had "learned." Although you could recall the information (possibly through some memory strategies), you were not able to make sufficient ties to your prior knowledge to connect to real-life applications. Gardner (1991) presents powerful evidence that teaching without generating understanding is common even in schools viewed as excellent.

Spending time in school in this type of learning is wasteful. If students cannot use what they've learned, what is the point of learning it? Contrast this to learning that produces **understanding**. When an individual understands a concept or skill, he or she can apply it appropriately in a new situation. For example, if I merely memorize the types and functions of simple machines, that information will not help me. However, if I understand that information I can apply it—perhaps the next time I need to move a heavy piece of furniture or when I encounter a large branch fallen across a rural road. Gardner (1999) describes what he calls an "acid test" for understanding, "posing to students a topic or theme or demonstration that they have never before encountered, and determining what sense they can make of those phenomena" (p. 119). In other words, if students can use what they have learned to make sense of a new situation, they understand it.

Unfortunately, teaching for understanding is not easy. If it were, the types of superficial learning described earlier would not be so common. Gardner (1999) describes the biggest obstacle to understanding as the theories children develop early in life. As you have learned, children are building schemata from the moment of their birth. An important part of that process is the identification of patterns that can be generalized across many experiences. The problem comes when patterns are misapplied in situations that seem very reasonable but are not, in fact, correct, as in our skunk example. Some of these patterns can be of long duration, building powerful misconceptions.

For example, Watson and Konicek (1990) describe several days of experiments in which fourth-grade students tested their belief that sweaters generate heat. Years of experience dressing for winter weather had taught the students that heat comes from fire, from the sun—and from sweaters, hats, and coats. When the initial experiment (placing thermometers inside sweaters and hats for 15 minutes) did not provide evidence of heat production, students designed new efforts using longer time periods and sealing the sweaters in enclosed spaces. Still, no heat was produced. Students were confused and probably frustrated as their predictions were not supported. Only then, when students seemed at an impasse, did the teacher offer an alternative hypothesis that might be tested. The article ends with students heading to recess, thermometers under their hats!

Gardner (1999) suggested four approaches that appear promising in teaching for understanding. The first recommends that we learn from "suggestive institutions" (p.126). By examining institutions outside schools in which understanding is fostered, we may gain clues that will enhance our repertoire of teaching strategies. For example, considering how learners function in apprenticeships or how children engage with content in museums may provide models for teaching. The experimentation facilitated in good science museums is very different from the science teaching experienced by many children.

The second avenue is illustrated by the sweater example: direct confrontations with erroneous conceptions. In this strategy, students are given experiences that force them to examine their current concepts. If students believe that metal sinks and wood floats, experimentation with a variety of toy boats can challenge that belief. If students believe all leaders are generals or team captains, that belief may be challenged when they learn how the Daughters of Liberty organized spinning bees that allowed the boycott of English textiles.

The third avenue is a framework for creating activities that demonstrate understanding as instructional goals, *performances of understanding*. Choosing understanding goals and planning for performances of understanding are discussed in Chapters 3 and 4. The fourth avenue suggests that understanding is enhanced as students are provided with learning through multiple intelligences. This is discussed in more detail in Chapter 6.

It can be helpful to think of a series of moments that can occur when we encounter new information in ways that promote understanding. The first moment comes when we say to ourselves, "Oh, wow!" An "oh wow" moment occurs when we approach new experiences or ideas with curiosity and openness. It allows us to look at things we do not understand and think, "How interesting" or "How curious" or "How puzzling." An experience that encourages students to be curious can serve not only to motivate them to learning but to help them recognize the need for additional understanding. The activity in which students put thermometers inside their sweaters encouraged that type of curiosity and led to further investigation.

Most healthy toddlers approach the world with a perpetual "oh wow" attitude, occasionally to the dismay of frazzled parents who try to ensure their children's safety without discouraging curiosity. Unfortunately, contemporary culture suggests that openness be displaced by cynicism at an increasingly early age. Even elementary school students can view themselves as too sophisticated to be interested, much less enthused, about learning. If we are to facilitate our students' understanding, we must provide them with experiences that intrigue.

The second type of moment is one in which new connections and insights occur. It is the moment of "aha!" An "aha" moment is one in which the child says (or thinks), "Of course" or "How logical" or "Now I see why that happened." You have probably experienced this type of moment, when information that had previously been confusing suddenly fell into place and made sense. You had enough connections to see a more fully formed logical pattern.

In order for aha moments to occur, students must have enough encounters with the information that purposes and patterns emerge. For example, students who never understood why the American Revolution occurred or who have attempted to apply an overly simplistic pattern from fairy tales or *Star Wars* (i.e., "There were good guys and bad guys. The bad guys won.") may have an aha moment when they learn about events from King George's point of view. Simply saying, "England needed money to finance the army" is not likely to generate understanding. Having experiences that help them envision the king as a human being, understand his personality and needs, and realize that different individuals can have different points of view can bring together connections that allow not just King George's actions but many of those in the war to make sense. Aha moments can occur when students make sense of how scientific principles are exemplified in the world around them, why historical figures acted the way they did, or why countries with particular geography or history develop as they do. They can make the difference between viewing another culture's traditions as strange and seeing them as logical—from another point of view. For example, one group of third graders thought it was strange that Japanese children ate so much rice, especially for lunch. Why didn't Japanese children eat sandwiches like they did? Once they studied how rice grows and how wheat grows, and compared that information to the geography of the two countries, it all made sense. Rather than viewing the use of this traditional food as peculiar, they saw it as a clever use of the available land.

The final type of moment may not occur often, but it is an important goal for many teaching situations. In this moment a student looks at a new understanding and thinks, "How wonderful" or "How beautiful!" Every discipline has patterns that are beautiful to those who are immersed in that world. Mathematicians find beauty in elegant equations, anthropologists in the traditions of diverse cultures, biologists in the complex interactions of living things. Helping students find appreciation when they learn things that are beautiful or true or good can be one of the finest moments of teaching.

Authentic Learning and Teaching

One of the concepts closely associated with teaching for understanding is the idea of **authentic learning**. It is exemplified in the following situations.

In one school, third-grade students studied their community. As part of the unit, the teacher had the students brainstorm community problems and identify the problem they saw as most critical. As true elementary students, they identified their community's most pressing problem as not having a McDonald's. Undaunted, the teacher asked how they might solve the problem. Data on new housing and roads were gathered, plans for new shopping areas were investigated, and the results were submitted to McDonald's. Students were convinced that the new fast-food restaurant ultimately built in their community was the result of their efforts.

In another school, fifth-grade students used systematic sampling to plan and conduct surveys regarding students' computer usage at home. Their results were used by the school board in making decisions about the types of technology, and technology instruction, necessary in the building. In a third school, students worked together to plan and carry out strategies to help students from a swelling immigrant population adjust to a new country.

In other schools, students studying animals have sponsored community celebrations of Be Kind to Animals Week, planted gardens to attract butterflies, and constructed birdhouses to lure birds back to a local park after construction drove them away. Those studying plants have planted gardens, marked nature trails around their schools, and created booklets warning of the dangers of poisonous plants. Young people studying languages have created skits to present to parents and translated informational signs in the school building; those studying local history have created school museums of local artifacts. In each case, students had the opportunity to use the information they gained in schools to solve a problem, investigate an issue, or create something of value to themselves or others. This process, in which teaching is organized around meaningful use of content, is sometimes called authentic learning or authentic achievement. Authentic settings for learning have been cited as part of situated learning theory in the previous section. Although situated learning research may not be sufficient to support all learning in authentic situations (Anderson, Reder, & Simon, 1996), there are other positions that result in similar recommendations.

Authentic learning mirrors the way much information has been learned throughout recorded history. Individuals have learned to weave in order to create tapestries, to play instruments in order to perform, and to calculate in order to run a business or a household efficiently. Only in schools (and quiz shows) are facts valued for their own sake. In the rest of the world, facts are useful because they help us understand the world around us, solve problems, or communicate ideas. Authentic learning allows studies to be grounded in appropriate context and used in purposeful ways, both powerful assets to learning.

Related constructs have been defined by others. Gardner (1991) distinguished between "rote, ritualistic or conventional performances . . . [that] occur when students simply respond . . . by spewing back the particular facts, concepts, or problem sets they have been taught" and "performances of disciplinary (or genuine) understanding" (p. 9). Many of the activities traditionally used in school to practice or assess information have not required students to understand the information, merely to repeat it. Perkins (1992) described "generative knowledge" as a combination of retention, understanding, and active use of knowledge "that does not just sit there but functions richly in people's lives to help them understand and deal with the world" (p. 5). In each case, theorists emphasize the importance of knowledge that is related to contexts the students understand and that is used in meaningful ways.

Newmann (1991, 1996) identified four characteristics of authentic achievement. First, authentic achievement requires the production rather than the reproduction of knowledge. In other words, traditional learning tasks ask students merely to reproduce information provided them by the teacher. The teacher gives students the facts; the students give them back. In authentic achievement, students must go further. They must do something with the facts: create something new, solve a problem, investigate a question, and so forth. In this mode of teaching, it is not enough to know something about your community—you must do something to investigate the community or make it a better place.

Second, authentic achievement requires disciplined inquiry. In disciplined inquiry, students investigate problems or questions within a particular discipline. Such investigation demands both in-depth knowledge of content and knowledge of how one conducts inquiry within a content area. Students studying the community need to know what kinds of questions professionals ask about communities and how they gather information. Clearly the sophistication with which students approach this inquiry will vary considerably from kindergarten to sixth grade, but all students can be taught to ask questions about content and investigate the answers. At each level, teachers should ask themselves, How do professionals in this discipline gather information, solve problems, and address issues? In many cases, the strategies that allow adults to address authentic tasks can be appropriately taught to students.

The third and fourth characteristics of authentic learning go hand in hand. Authentic learning includes assembling, interpreting, and synthesizing knowledge, and results in products that have aesthetic, utilitarian, or personal value. Many traditional school projects are summaries of information. Students read a convenient reference book or encyclopedia, restate the information in their own words, and create some kind of product. In most cases this is the ever-present school report. In other cases the information might be more creatively communicated through a poster, bulletin board, or display, but it is still basically a reproduction of someone else's ideas. An authentic product contains the student's own thoughts, questions, data, and interpretations, in addition to the ideas of others.

A vivid example of authentic learning is illustrated by the research of Hunter Scott from Pensacola, Florida (Leinwand, 1998). As an 11-year-old middle school student, Scott was impressed by the tale of the ill-fated cruiser *Indianapolis* spun by the sea captain in the movie *Jaws*. In 1997, Scott embarked on a personal crusade to learn all he could about the events leading up to the sinking of the *Indianapolis* on July 30, 1945, a few months before the end of World War II. When the ship was torpedoed by a Japanese submarine and sunk, 1,196 sailors were cast into the sea. Only 316 survived 5 days in the water as thirst, exposure, and shark attacks took their toll. As Scott continued his study, he contacted the surviving members of the crew using the postal service, telephone, and e-mail. He became convinced that the ship's captain had been unjustly blamed for its demise. After presenting his findings in local and county history fairs, his study received national publicity and led to a congressional inquiry to determine if the history book of the *Indianapolis* tragedy should be reopened.

Interestingly, the characteristics of authentic learning identified by researchers as key to learning parallel those identified in a study that asked young adolescents to identify their most memorable and engaging work (Wasserstein, 1995). Although some teachers might guess that students prefer easy assignments, "Again and again, students equated hard work with success and satisfaction. Moreover, they suggested that challenge is the essence of engagement; when students feel they are doing important work, they are more likely to buy in than not" (p. 41). When students were exploring ideas in ways that seemed meaningful and important, they worked hard and felt proud of their efforts. When assignments were perceived as "busywork," or unrelated to the real world, students were resentful and uninterested.

What Makes a Problem Real?

What characteristics define "real" or "authentic" problems or tasks and how are they distinct from the kinds of problems typically addressed in schools? While Newmann's guidelines provide a beginning, helpful insights can be found in the work of Renzulli (1977), whose Enrichment Triad Model centers on individual and small-group investigations of real problems. Although the triad model was originally developed for education of the gifted and talented (see Chapter 9), many of its components are appropriate for all students, and the strategies for pursuit of real problems can hold the key to authentic learning in many arenas.

First, a real problem has personal interest and value to the student or students who pursue it. Clearly, individual students can be engaged in authentic problems or tasks based on personal interests. Group projects can involve shared interests or contain diverse opportunities for involvement that necessitate differing interests and abilities. The class involved in gathering data for the McDonald's project utilized the group's shared interest in fast food as well as diverse individual interests and skills in many areas. Budding statisticians had the opportunity to become more deeply involved in the mathematical data supporting the presentation. Others were more involved in other phases of data gathering, composition, illustration, and so on. At least some part of the project could be interesting to virtually every student.

Second, a real problem does not have a predetermined correct response. It involves processes for which there cannot be an answer key. The real problems with which our students become involved seem to fall into three general categories.

1. Some real problems are *research questions*. They involve gathering and analyzing data and drawing conclusions. True research questions entail collecting information from primary sources through observation, surveys, interviews, or document analysis. The students who survey food preferences in the school cafeteria, those who interview local citizens on life in the community during World War II, and the first graders who observe the effects of milk on plant growth are all investigating research questions. Students involved in Gloria's unit on the Revolution might become curious about whether anyone from the Revolutionary period was buried in a local cemetery or what kind of clothes people wore in everyday life. These could lead to gathering data on the dates of death, life span, and cause of death recorded on cemetery markers or studying reproductions of engravings of the period with an eye to workers' clothing. Either project would parallel strategies used by historians in investigating similar questions.

2. Other real problems might be categorized as *activism* or service-learning. In these activities, students work in the community or attempt to improve some aspect of the world around them. Students who organize clothing drives for the homeless, teach peers what to do if they suspect a friend is being abused, set up school recycling programs, or lobby for bike paths are pursuing this type of real problem. Increasingly, electronic communication makes it possible for students to join with others in global activism. The Rope Pump Project is a good example of this type of activism. Students raise funds to purchase rope-operated pumps for villages in Nicaragua, then have the opportunity to communicate with students from the village. If Gloria's students became interested in local grave markers, they might become involved in efforts to preserve them.

3. Real problems in the arts entail the *expression* of some theme, aesthetic, or idea. Adult creators use words, movement, paint, or clay as tools for expression. Students whose art explores the changing light, whose stories reflect their ideas about friendship, or whose dance reflects their frustration over injustice are addressing real problems in meaningful ways. Students who create historical fiction set in the Revolutionary War period would be addressing this type of problem.

In pursuing real problems, students should use authentic methodology—that is, they should address the problem as much as possible in the way a professional adult would address it. Newmann's criterion of "disciplined inquiry" reflects this idea. The students who want to survey cafeteria preferences must learn something about survey design. The first graders experimenting with bean plants should make a hypothesis and have a control group. Although some types of authentic methodology are easier to implement than others, each aspect of a project provides opportunities to stretch students toward professionalism. It will be much easier for students to use authentic historical research techniques in a local history project as opposed to one on a distant locale (although electronic networks are making this process more feasible). However, even the student for whom primary sources are limited can use professional techniques for sharing information in a manner that is appropriate to the discipline.

When pursuing real problems, students eventually share information with a real audience. What constitutes a real audience will vary enormously with the age of the students and the sophistication of their problems. The key is that the audience should have a genuine interest in the product, rather than viewing it as a source for a grade or other evaluation. Some real audiences are part of the natural school environment. For example, a group of primary students may write an original play and produce it for the class next door. Other audiences may be created within schools to provide a vehicle for student efforts: art exhibits, literary magazines, invention conventions, science fairs, and so on (Schack & Starko, 1998; Starko & Schack, 1992). Still other audiences may be part of the local community. In one community, the local chamber of commerce was pleased to display a student-produced brochure on the history of local buildings. Results of a water pollution study were shared with interested faculty at a local university. The radio station often aired student-generated public service announcements. Local access cable TV, historical societies, and other community organizations can provide enthusiastic audiences for appropriate student products.

Certainly, the types of problems pursued, the methodology employed, and the audiences approached will vary enormously from the first kindergarten puppet show or garden experiment to the sixth-grade investigation of pollution in a local stream. However, at each stage, students may be nudged just one notch closer to professionalism: the kindergartner to plan the puppet before building it, the fifth graders to prepare a brochure for the town's birthday festival. Each represents a legitimate step toward pursuing real problems.

During your instructional planning it would be wise to consider authentic learning activities and projects as you design your outcomes. Whatever the subject, the ultimate goal should be to have students use the content in meaningful ways. The more aspects of real-world problem solving that can be incorporated into the process, the better. Of course, the types of authentic learning activities that can be planned will vary. For example, second-grade students engaged in a study of the neighborhood surrounding the school could gather survey and observational data about the types of buildings in the neighborhood, available recreational activities, and community services. They might even start a petition to have a vacant lot turned into a park, or lobby the local government to fix the broken swings in the park.

A unit on Greek mythology would not offer parallel opportunities for activism. If their teacher wished to teach techniques of historical research, students might learn to analyze photographs of Greek artworks for evidence of the influence of myth. Their results might be compiled in an "archaeologist's report." Alternatively, the teacher might plan to engage students in personally meaningful problem solving by helping students make ties between mythological heroes and heroes today. Students could examine the mythology surrounding contemporary heroes in sports or entertainment and analyze how those heroes influence our lives. Such analyses could result in a variety of literary or artistic products.

There are several opportunities for different types of authentic learning in Gloria's Revolutionary War unit. Certainly the opportunity to write a play about an event of the period could result in a production for another class—or even for a local veterans' association. Students could also be involved in a variety of questions involving historical research (see Chapter 7): examining accounts of events as portrayed by colonial and British publications or studying paintings to see if fashionable dress differed across the ocean. Or students might study period recipes and attempt to create a Revolutionary meal!

REFLECTING ON THE IDEAS

Think about your own learning experiences in and out of school. When have you been involved in authentic learning? Were most of your experiences in class, in extracurricular activities, or outside school? In what ways were your experiences powerful for you? What implications does that have for your teaching?

SUMMARY

This chapter considered the characteristics that influence how students learn and what is known about the process of learning itself. We also examined what it means to understand something one has learned. In making decisions about learning activities, teachers must consider students' intellectual abilities, prior knowledge and life experiences, cultural background, interests, and learning styles. Teachers must also understand that students do not learn by passively receiving information. They construct their own meaning out of what they experience, and this meaning is profoundly influenced by what they already know and have experienced. If students are to understand content, teachers must provide a variety of complex experiences that allow students to encounter information in many ways and have the opportunity to use it meaningfully.

■ *Practice Activity: Student Interviews*

Select an elementary school student to interview three times during the term. Conduct your first interview while studying this chapter. Each interview should take no more than 10 to 15 minutes. For each interview, choose something the student has been learning about in school. Then try to determine the student's understanding of the topic and how he or she acquired it. Write a case study, but do not use the student's real name. Maintaining confidentiality regarding student characteristics and behaviors is an important professional standard you should begin now. Include the following information in your study:

Age, grade, gender of student
Topic(s) discussed
Understandings, misconceptions, and interesting ideas you identified
Ways the student used prior knowledge to construct understanding
Teaching strategies that were or were not helpful

■ ■ ■

UNIT PREPARATION

In order to plan effectively for the class you are observing, it will be important to learn as much as you can about the students. Begin by learning as much as you can about the general developmental characteristics of the age and grade you are preparing to teach. By reading and observation, consider how those developmental characteristics will affect the types of lessons that are most effective. Compare your findings with a classmate studying the same grade. Next, consider the characteristics of the specific class for which you are planning. Learn about the major cultural groups represented there. Discuss with the teacher any students who have special needs or interests related to your unit topic. If you have the opportunity to correct student work, use it as a chance to analyze student thinking and try to anticipate ways to make your teaching as clear as possible. Although it certainly will be impossible to learn everything there is to know about the class, this study will help you remember that unit planning must always focus on students' needs, interests, and characteristics in order to be successful.

PORTFOLIO ACTIVITY

In your field placement or other school setting, conduct an assessment of student interests. Prepare a summary for your portfolio. Be prepared to discuss how you will use this information in instruction.

SEARCH THE WEB

You can find a variety of resources to help you learn more about chapter topics on the Companion Website, at www.prenhall.com/starko. Go to the topic area called "Child/Adolescent Development." There you will find links pertaining to development, brain research, learning styles, multiple intelligences, and more. Under the topic area "Diversity in the Classroom" you will find information on language and cultural differences.

REFERENCES

Anderson, J. R., Reder, L. M., & Simon, H. A. (1996, May). Situated learning and education. *Educational Researcher, 25* (4), 5–11.

Armstrong, T. (1994). *Multiple intelligences in the classroom.* Alexandria, VA: Association for Supervision and Curriculum Development.

Banks, J. (1999). *An introduction to multicultural education.* Boston: Allyn & Bacon.

Banks, J. (1997). *Teaching strategies for ethnic studies* (6th ed.). Boston: Allyn & Bacon.

Barbe, W. B., & Swassing, R. H. (1979). *Teaching through modality strengths: Concepts and practice.* Columbus, OH: Zaner-Bloser.

Boykin, A. W. (1994). Afrocultural expression and its implication for schooling. In E. R. Hollins, J. E. King, & W. C. Haymen (Eds.), *Teaching diverse populations: Formulating a knowledge base* (pp. 105–127). Albany, NY: State University of New York Press.

Brandt, R. S., & Perkins, D. N. (2000). The evolving science of learning. In R. S. Brandt (Ed.), *Education in a new era: ASCD yearbook 2000.* Alexandria, VA: Association for Supervision and Curriculum Development.

Brown, J. S., Collins, A., & Duguid, P. (1989). Situated cognition and the culture of learning. *Educational Researcher, 18* (1), 32–42.

Bruer, J. T. (1999). Neural connections: Some you use, some you lose. *Phi Delta Kappan, 81* (4), 264–277.

Butler, K. (1986). *Learning and teaching style in theory and practice.* Columbia, CT: Learner's Dimension.

Butler, K. (1995). *Learning styles: Personal exploration and practical applications.* Columbia, CT: Learner's Dimension.

Butler, K. (1996). *Viewpoints.* Columbia, CT: Learner's Dimension.

Caine, R. N., & Caine, G. (1991). *Making connections: Teaching and the human brain.* Alexandria, VA: Association for Supervision and Curriculum Development.

Caine, R. N., & Caine, G. (1997). *Educating on the edge of possibility.* Alexandria, VA: Association for Supervision and Curriculum Development.

Checkley, K. (1997). The first seven . . . and the eighth. A conversation with Howard Gardner. *Educational Leadership, 55* (1), 8–13.

Cline, Z. (1998). Buscando su voz en dos culturas—Finding your voice in two cultures. *Phi Delta Kappan, 79,* 699–702.

Cross, W. (1995). The psychology of Nigrescence: Revising the Cross model. In J. G. Ponterotto, J. M. Casas, L.A. Suzuki, & C. M. Alexander (Eds.), *Handbook of multicultural counseling* (pp. 93–122). Thousand Oaks, CA: Sage.

Delpit, L. (1995). *Other people's children: Cultural conflict in the classroom.* New York: New Press.

Dunn, R. (1997). The goals and track record of multicultural education. *Educational Leadership, 54* (7), 74–77.

Dunn, R. (1996). *How to implement and supervise a learning styles program.* Alexandria, VA: Association for Supervision and Curriculum Development.

Dunn, R., & Dunn, K. (1975). *Educator's self-teaching guide to individualizing instructional programs.* New York: Parker.

Dunn, R., & Griggs, S. A. (1995). *Multicultural curriculum and learning styles.* Westport, CT: Praeger Publications.

Dunn, R., Griggs, S. A., Olson, J., Beasley, M., & Gorman, B. S. (1995). A meta-analytic validation of the Dunn and Dunn model of learning styles preferences. *Journal of Educational Research, 88* (6), 353–362.

Ford, D. Y. (1996). *Reversing underachievement among gifted black students: Promising practices.* New York: Teachers College Press.

Gage, N. L., & Berliner, D. (1990). *Educational psychology* (4th ed.). Boston: Houghton Mifflin.

Gardner, H. (1983). *Frames of mind: The theory of multiple intelligences.* New York: Basic Books.

Gardner, H. (1991). *The unschooled mind.* New York: Basic Books.

Gardner, H. (1993). *Multiple intelligences: Theory into practice.* New York: Basic Books.

Gardner, H. (1999). *The disciplined mind.* New York: Simon and Schuster.

Gay, G. (1994). *At the essence of learning: Multicultural education.* West Lafayette, IN: Kappa Delta Pi.

Gregorc, A. (1982). *An adult's guide to style.* Maynard, MA: Gabriel.

Guild, P. B., & Garger, S. (1998). *Marching to different drummers* (2nd ed.). Alexandria, VA: Association for Supervision and Curriculum Development.

Hannafin, M. J., Hannafin, K. M., Land, S. M., & Oliver, K. (1997). Grounded practice and the design of learning environments. *Educational Technology, Research and Design, 45* (3), 101–117.

Hunt, D. E. (1979). Learning and student needs: An introduction to conceptual level. In J. W. Keefe, *Student learning styles: Diagnosing and prescribing programs* (pp. 27–28). Reston, VA: National Association of Secondary School Principals.

Jensen, E. (2000). Brain-based learning: A reality check. *Educational Leadership, 57* (7), 7–80.

Kovalik, S. (1994). Brain compatible learning. *Video Journal of Education, 3* (6).

Ladson-Billings, G. (1994). *The dreamkeepers: Successful teachers of African American children.* San Francisco: Jossey-Bass.

Ladson-Billings, G. (1995). But that's just good teaching! The case for culturally relevant pedagogy. *Theory Into Practice, 34,* 159–165.

Leinwand, S. J. (1998). Classroom realities we do not often talk about. *Mathematics Teaching in Middle School, 3* (5), 330–331.

Newmann, F. K. (1996). Authentic pedagogy and student performance. *American Journal of Education, 104* (4), 280–312.

Newmann, F. K. (1991). Linking restructuring to authentic student achievement. *Phi Delta Kappan, 41,* 463.

Ogbu, J. U. (1983). Minority students and schooling in pluralistic societies. *Comparative Education Review, 27* (2), 168–190.

Ormrod, J. E. (2000). *Educational psychology: Developing learners* (3rd ed.). Columbus, OH: Prentice Hall/Merrill.

Pang, V. O. (2001). *Multicultural education: A caring-centered, reflective approach.* New York: McGraw-Hill.

Perkins, D. (1992). *Smart schools.* New York: The Free Press.

Perkins, D. (1999, November). The many faces of constructivism. *Educational Leadership, 57* (3), 6–11.

Philips, D. (1995). The good, the bad, and the ugly: The many faces of constructivism. *Educational Researcher, 24* (7), 5–12.

Piaget, J. (1970). Piaget's theory. In P. H. Mussen (Ed.), *Carmichael's manual of psychology.* New York: Wiley.

Renzulli, J. S. (1977). The enrichment triad. Mansfield Center, CT: Creative Learning Press.

Schack, G. D., & Starko, A. J. (1998). *Research comes alive.* Mansfield Center, CT: Creative Learning Press.

Scherer, M. (Ed.). (2000, November). *Educational Leadership, 58* (3). [The Science of Learning].

Shade, B. J. (1997). *Culture, style, and the educational process: Making schools work for racially diverse students.* Springfield, IL: Charles Thomas, Publishers.

Smith, G. P. (1998). *Common sense about uncommon knowledge: The knowledge bases for diversity.* New York: American Association of Colleges for Teacher Education.

Sprenger, M. (1999). *Learning and memory: The brain in action.* Alexandria, VA: Association for Supervision and Curriculum Development.

Starko, A. J., & Schack, G. D. (1992). *Looking for data in all the right places.* Mansfield Center, CT: Creative Learning Press.

Sternberg, R. (1985). *Beyond IQ: A triarchic theory of human intelligence.* New York: Cambridge University Press.

Sternberg, R. (1997). What does it mean to be smart? *Educational Leadership, 54* (6), 20–24.

Sternberg, R. J., Grigorenko, E., & Jarvin, L. (2000). Improving reading instruction: The triarchic model. *Educational Leadership, 58* (6), 48–54.

Sternberg, R. J., Torff, B., & Grigorenko, E. (1998). Teaching for successful intelligence raises school achievement. *Phi Delta Kappan, 79,* 667–669.

Stiggins, R. J. (1994). *Student-centered classroom assessment.* New York: Merrill.

Strong, R., Silver, H. F., & Robinson, A. (1995). What do students want. *Educational Leadership, 53* (1), 8–12.

Swisher, F., & Doyle, D. (1992). Adapting instruction to culture. In J. Reyner (Ed.), *Teaching American Indian students* (pp. 81–95). Norman, OK: University of Oklahoma Press.

U.S. Census Bureau. (2001). *Census 2000 Supplementary Survey*. [On-line]. Available: http://ourworld.compuserve.com/homepages/jwcrawford/census03.htm.

U.S. Department of Education. (1993). *National excellence: A case for developing America's talent*. Washington, DC: Author.

Wasserstein, P. (1995). What middle schoolers say about their school work. *Educational Leadership, 53* (1), 41–43.

Watson, B., & Konicek, R. (1990). Teaching for conceptual change: Confronting children's experience. *Phi Delta Kappan, 71,* 680–685.

Wlodkowski, R. J., & Ginsberg, M. B. (1995). Framework for culturally responsive teaching. *Educational Leadership,* 53 (1), 17–21.

Vygotsky, L. S. (1997). *Educational psychology*. Boca Raton, FL: St. Lucie Press.

Young, F. (1993). Instructional design for situated learning. *Educational Technology, Research and Design, 41* (1), 43–58.

CHAPTER 3

Choosing and Analyzing Classroom Goals

CHAPTER OVERVIEW

One of the most important decisions a teacher makes is what to teach. Of all the knowledge, skills, and attitudes that are possible, of all the content suggested as appropriate for a particular grade level, some portion must be selected for a given class in a given day, month, or year. How teachers make decisions about what to teach is the focus of this chapter. The chapter addresses several key questions about selecting classroom goals: Why is there so much debate and disagreement about the goals and achievements of American education? From what sources does a successful teacher derive educational goals? How does the reflective teacher choose goals that are best for the students?

The chapter consists of three sections. In Section 1, the focus is on three major educational philosophies and their impact on curriculum goals. In it we will examine the ways varying educational philosophies can shape the ways individuals think about the purposes of schools and the content that is most valuable. In Section 2 we will discuss the processes of selecting educational goals or outcomes—deciding what it is we hope students will know or be able to do as a result of our instruction. We will examine the way key concepts and generalizations can help shape the content in ways that will facilitate student understanding. Finally, Section 3 provides an overview of unit design, illustrating how curriculum goals and content analysis fit into the overall planning process.

 ## CHAPTER OBJECTIVES

After completing this chapter you will be able to:

1. Classify examples of educational statement that reflect progressive, essentialist, and reconstructionist or critical pedagogy philosophies;
2. Create curriculum outcomes using content standards;
3. Classify examples of affective, psychomotor, and cognitive goals; Relate concepts, generalizations, and facts in a content area of your choice;
4. Sort examples of concrete and abstract concepts;
5. Construct a concept map for a single subject or interdisciplinary unit; and
6. Break down a content area into a generalization, concept and facts network.

 ## SECTION 1. CHOOSING WORTHWHILE EDUCATIONAL GOALS

The process of choosing educational goals can be thought of as the answers to a series of questions:

1. What is my philosophy? What kinds of learning do I believe are most important in schools?
2. What do I want my students to understand and be able to do as a result of my instruction?
3. What content will I teach?
4. What concepts and generalizations will focus and structure the content for understanding?

These questions are not always answered in this order, or even in any order that is clear and sequential. A teacher's educational philosophy is shaped over time and tends to be slow to change. In most cases teachers do not stop to consider their philosophy each time they begin to plan a lesson or unit. However, that philosophy shapes all the decisions the teacher makes in important ways, determining what a teacher believes is valuable in school, what is essential, and what is trivial.

The answers to the next three questions often are intertwined. A teacher may identify a series of goals shaped by district guidelines, state standards, and personal beliefs. Once the teacher identifies the specific content to be taught, that may bring to mind additional goals—or lead the teacher to decide a particular goal is not suitable for this content. Identifying the key concepts and generalizations that can be used to help students understand the content will shape the content to be selected and the areas to be emphasized. In this weaving of goals, content, and core concepts, important teaching decisions are made.

Section 1 Objectives

After you have completed this section, you will be able to classify examples of educational statements that reflect progressive perspectives, essentialist perspectives, and critical pedagogy and describe how they relate to your personal philosophy.

■ Opening Activity

Read the following scenario. Try to determine the different curriculum philosophies expressed by the various speakers:

It was a warm evening in early May as the sun filtered into the school board room of the Taunton, Michigan, schools. Taunton is a suburban community of 110,000 persons. The Taunton families are primarily White and of European background, although in recent years there has been a growing presence of African American and Asian students in the schools. A large majority of the public school students come from middle and upper income families, although a significant number of families would be classified as lower income. About 80% of the youngsters who graduate from one of the two high schools go on to higher education. Many Taunton residents pressure the schools to concentrate their attention on intellectual development—in part, so high school graduates are prepared to make the transition into higher education. There are an equal number who urge the schools to play a much larger role in enhancing students' personal and social development. Taunton Public Schools participate in a far-reaching inclusion program, in which children with disabilities are included in the regular classroom for most educational activities, seeking to maximize both intellectual and social development for that population.

Lastly, there is a small but vocal group of parents and other members of the community who push the schools to be more involved in community action and improvement projects. Marvin Pancett, the school board president, tried to remain calm in the midst of a spirited exchange between two members of the community task force, which was charged with an examination of "The School Curriculum in the 21st Century." The task force chair, Maude Jones, was completing her majority group report on the place of multicultural education in the school curriculum:

"In Orwell's novel of tyranny, *1984,* the Party in power's banner reads, 'who controls the past controls the future; who controls the present controls the past.' Clearly, White males, primarily from western European backgrounds, have controlled the past in the United States. That control is clear in the education we give our children in Taunton. The cultural contributions of women; people of color; White males from southern and eastern Europe; Jews, Muslims, and individuals of many other faiths have been largely overlooked or marginalized. The task force majority is unhappy with the lack of meaningful multicultural content in the curriculum. We note the increasing numbers of children of color entering the Taunton schools. However, all students, not just students of color, benefit from a multicultural education. Consequently, the task force majority recommends the inclusion of cultural and historical content about Asia, Latin America, and Africa, in addition to content about diverse people in America. In fact, many would like to see Taunton become a leader in the development of a multicultural/global curriculum" (Banks, 1994, 1995; Davidman, 1994; Davidman & Davidman, 1994).

A representative from the task force minority, Paul Smith, was visibly angry as he rose to speak:

"The task force minority cannot defend the past. We agree with Ms. Jones's conclusion that the school curriculum misrepresented the history, cultures, and contributions of the groups she mentioned. We agree that a more balanced curriculum is needed. However, we disagree that a multicultural curriculum is the answer. The saga of human history has both its heroes and villains; its uplifting events, ideas, and individuals and those whose direction is otherwise. If western civilization has much for which to apologize, it also gave birth to democratic thought and practice, the flowering of human reason, artistic creation, and advancements in science, mathematics, and technology that have bettered the lives of all. To replace the study of western civilization because some groups feel slighted would be a serious mistake and I will never endorse it."

Carla Martinez, a member of the task force majority, responded:

"Mr. Smith and his followers refuse to recognize that American society is diverse. In many communities and schools people of color are a majority of the residents. Soon after the next century begins we shall see African American and Latino/Latina children become the majority group in the public schools. A multicultural perspective to the study of history, the humanities, and the arts will do honor to the heritage and backgrounds of all children. Multicultural education can lead to greater understanding of people from diverse ethnic and racial groups and thus lead to a decline in prejudice and stereotyping. The use of learning activities that have proven to be successful enhances learning opportunities and increases academic achievement for all students. Multicultural education also can be a productive element in a process for school restructuring and empowerment for students of color" (Banks, 1993).

The board members listened as advocates with different viewpoints rose to speak. Finally, school board president Pancett, distressed because the hour had reached midnight, adjourned the meeting for one week acknowledging the need for further discussion. The next morning Mr. Pancett showed up at the door of the school superintendent, Dr. Ruth Borkman, to discuss the confusing series of events at the school board meeting the previous evening:

"Dr. Borkman, what in the world happened last night? I have to admit that the arguments between the two segments of the task force overwhelmed me. Why is the committee so split?"

"Marv, what happened last night brings the wide differences of opinion about what should be taught in the schools to the surface. These differences obviously are present in the task force. When individuals differ in their fundamental beliefs about the purposes of school, their opinions on many educational matters are likely to vary."

Dr. Borkman then proceeded to explain the educational philosophies that one might expect to find in a public school in the United States and how the philosophies affect the school curriculum and the teachers' instructional approaches.

■ ■ ■

REFLECTING ON THE IDEAS

The positions taken by members of the curriculum task force reflect the two most common educational philosophies found in American schools today. Consider what appear to be the key beliefs or values held by each side. Have you seen similar differences played out in schools in your area?

Three Views of Educational Philosophy
Progressivism: Social and Personal

As Dr. Borkman explained to school board president Pancett, the majority group members of the curriculum task force were defending a progressive educational philosophy about society in general and education in particular. **Progressivism** developed as the United States was transformed from a rural to an industrialized society. Although the transformation of American society occurred over generations, social scientists and historians label the period 1880–1914 as the major era of change.

As the pace of industrialization quickened, millions of immigrants thronged into the United States. The surge in population with many new Americans living in crowded homes in big-city neighborhoods changed forever the simplicity of the one-room schoolhouse focusing on the three Rs. Such schools were replaced by multiroom and multigrade comprehensive schools that housed hundreds, even thousands, of students. With rapid and massive changes in the size and composition of the schools, together with similar changes in the society at large, advocates of progressivism believed that education beyond the basics was also required. "Progressivism was based on the assumption that the quality of human existence could be improved by the application of scientific reasoning to social problems. Consequently, education as a major social institution, could play a key role in developing competent citizens, who would be better prepared to deal with the new challenges facing our modern industrial society" (Stanley & Nelson, 1994, pp. 271–272).

Although it is difficult to identify what beliefs and values were shared by all educational progressives, most favored curriculum experimentation and flexibility rather than a prescribed program for the transmission of subject matter (e.g., John Dewey). Thus a major focus of the progressive curriculum was on learning to think rather than on learning particular subject matter. In addition, progressives were committed to a child-centered educational program in schools that exemplified democratic values and processes. Ironically, progressive teachers found themselves having to choose between supporting the educational and social choices made by an individual child and a desire to support democratic values in the classroom. For example, a large majority of students might decide to pursue a particular unit of study, with a small group refusing to abide by the decision. Ultimately, it was this recurring dilemma that led to a split in the progressive movement.

One group of progressives—let's call them **social progressives**—retained the belief that social development is the primary function of modern education. Social progressives see schooling as a process of preparing young people to be successful adults in a democratic society. They view curriculum in terms of the knowledge, skills, and attitudes that assist young people to confront and master the tasks they will face as adults. In the contemporary educational area, social progressives can be seen leading the fight for an increased emphasis on citizenship education: nutrition, health, and family issues; career education; dropout prevention; and emotional, moral, and character development.

Often, social progressives are spokespersons for an educational community that values and respects diversity. Inherent in that respect is emphasis on the nature and contributions of many cultural groups. Social progressives maintain that the result will be a classroom marked by mutual support and harmony. A curriculum that accomplishes this objective must extend its scope to include instruction about the nature and contributions of multiple groups, including Native Americans, African Americans, Latinos, Asians, and Europeans (Association for Supervision and Curriculum Development, 1993).

Although many members of the "School Curriculum in the 21st Century" task force support a social progressive view of the curriculum, a second group of progressives is also represented on the task force—the **personal progressives**. Personal progressives argue that instruction must be tailored to meet the needs and interests of the many kinds of children who enter the public schools. They are opposed to a predetermined curriculum that rigidly organizes and structures what all children are expected to learn. Many progressive teachers in the period 1930–1960 were influenced by the ideas of William Heard Kilpatrick, who espoused the project method. According to this view, the child's experiences should provide the basis for curriculum decisions; these decisions should not be dictated by subject matter fixed in advance. Understandably, Kilpatrick argued that "subject matter was useful only when it could be combined with the child's interests" (Ravitch, 1983, p. 52).

One of the best known contemporary personal progressives, John Holt, was influential in the 1960s through his books *How Children Fail* (1964) and *How Children Learn* (1970). Holt derided the authoritarian climate he perceived in many schools where control and docility were prized and freedom and spontaneity extinguished (1964). He was a leading proponent of the movement that became known as "open education" or "informal education." In such an approach, learning is individualized, teaching is informal, content is based on student expressions of needs or interests, play is valued, children are active, and learning takes place in a noisy and joyful setting. Personal progressives view multicultural education as a process of enhancement of individual children, making each a stronger, more capable, and more independent person. Such persons become "self-directed learners" who gradually take more responsibility for their own educational plans and goals (Davidman, 1994).

Essentialism

A second educational philosophy, espoused by the members of the task force minority group, is essentialism. **Essentialism** is a belief that the purpose of schooling is to impart necessary knowledge, skills, and attitudes to enable young people to function as fully developed human beings. Essentialists believe that to achieve maturity, the learner must understand the external world of observable reality and abstract ideas. Some essentialists focus their attention on what has been called the "basic skills"—reading, writing, and arithmetic. Others have a more extensive list of essentials. Still others argue that the essentials are contained in the school subjects that have been grouped by disciplines— literature, English and other languages, history, the social sciences, chemistry, physics, biology, mathematics, and the fine arts. These essentialists argue that disciplinary knowledge has stood the test of time. Because it has been examined, refined, and revised over the centuries, the knowledge gained from disciplinary study is more valuable than knowledge gained from any other source of educational content.

An example of the essentialist position can be found in the book *Cultural Literacy: What Every American Needs to Know* by E. D. Hirsch, Jr. (1987). Hirsch maintained that "no modern society can think of becoming a classless society except on the basis of universal literacy. To be truly literate, a high school graduate must be able to grasp the meaning of written materials in any field or subject provided that those materials are addressed to a general audience" (p. 129). Hirsch continued his analysis of productive schooling to argue that the curriculum should impart intensive knowledge, consisting of "mental models"—commonly labeled as concepts or ideas. However, Hirsch believed that extensive knowledge is also necessary. Extensive knowledge is background information in the form of essential facts, names, places, terms, dates, and events.

According to Hirsch, the dominant concern for relevance and pluralism so prevalent in most schools results in a fragmented curriculum and youngsters who learn few topics, such as literary and historical works, in common. Thus he concluded that U.S. youngsters share little knowledge of the culture that has shaped and enriched the Western world.

Support for Hirsch's position came from the study *American Memory: A Report on the Humanities in the Nation's Public Schools* by Lynne Cheney, chair of the National Endowment for the Humanities (1987). Cheney drew on the data from an NEH study to reveal that two thirds of U.S. 17-year-olds who were tested did not know when the Civil War was fought (even granting them a 50-year margin of error), could not correctly identify the Reformation and the Magna Carta, and were unable to identify such literary giants as Nathaniel Hawthorne, Jane Austen, Geoffrey Chaucer, and Walt Whitman (Ravitch & Finn, 1987). Essentialists would argue that these results indicate a need for increased emphasis on traditional disciplinary content.

Reconstructionism and Critical Pedagogy

The two educational philosophies known as progressivism and essentialism were in conflict within the Taunton schools curriculum task force and are at war in the general society, as reflected by the various reactions to the cultural literacy controversy. However, there is a third philosophy that should not be overlooked. This philosophy, originally identified as **reconstructionism** or, more recently, **critical pedagogy**, is characterized by a belief that schools should prepare the future adults of society to work for social justice and to demand societal change. Proponents maintain that the present society is seriously flawed by inequities based on class, race, and gender, and that schools have a responsibility to respond to those inequities. "It is a view concerned with promoting more democratic, equitable social relations even if that means challenging the existing order of things" (Reynolds & Martusewicz, 1994, p. 226).

Reconstructionism had its roots in the 1930s when social reconstructionists introduced critiques of traditional educational ideas and institutions in relation to surrounding social, political, and economic structures. George Counts, a noted reconstructionist in the 1930s, wrote:

> There can be no good individual apart from some conception of the character of a good society; and the good society is not something that is given by nature: it must be fashioned by the hand and brain of man. This process of building a good society is to a very large degree an educational process. (1932, p. 26)

Counts' book title, *Dare the Schools Build a New Social Order?* reflects the reconstructionists' hope.

Contemporary philosophers with a similar perspective espouse critical pedagogy, an approach to teaching that entails a commitment to classroom practices that encourage critical analysis of issues such as race, class, and gender, and reflect democratic social relationships. Many of those involved in critical pedagogy are political and social activists who believe that schools often unwittingly serve to reproduce these inequalities. They may seek to encourage young people in political activity and in social action projects in the community.

If an individual committed to critical pedagogy had been active on the "School Curriculum in the 21st Century" task force, what might that advocate have written as a minority report? Think about what that report might sound like before continuing.

The remarks would probably be similar to the following:

> There must be more to multicultural/global education than learning some things about persons and groups who have different ways of speaking and dressing, different religions or customs, or different previous histories. Multicultural education must also be an agent for societal change and improvement. It must contain a parental and community component that encourages participation in the education of children and extends that participation beyond the classroom to influence the actions and decisions of school committees, boards, and other community agencies. It must be at the center of an activist education that improves the quality of life in communities that have been oppressed by racism and/or the lack of economic opportunity.

REFLECTING ON THE IDEAS

Which of the three educational philosophies do you support? If you were a member of the community task force examining the topic "The School Curriculum in the 21st Century," what would you include in your report on multicultural education? Would your report have a progressive, essentialist, or critical emphasis?

Planning Educational Outcomes

Given the complexity and diversity of potential educational content, and with a philosophical perspective as a backdrop, how does a reflective teacher go about the task of deciding what to teach? The beginning of this process is deciding what it is we are trying to accomplish—what it is we hope students will learn and understand, sometimes described as the **outcomes** we hope will result from our teaching. Outcomes for teaching and learning may be called goals, standards (usually broad, long-range outcomes), benchmarks (usually more specific outcomes), or objectives (usually short-term and specific outcomes, see Figure 3.1). This chapter will guide you in clarifying educational goals—the broad learning outcomes for your students.

Educational goals (often referred to as outcomes) are statements of educational intent that provide general direction to the teacher in developing instruction. Educational goals or outcomes are often written to describe student learning within large blocks of content such as a course of study or a unit of study. Although a goal may be written in specific and precise language, most goals are general in form. Thus they must undergo further analysis before they can be useful as guideposts in the design of teaching lessons.

There are dozens of models to assist teachers to select educational goals. In the 1930s, Ralph Tyler, one of the major figures in curriculum development in the 20th century, developed a systematic framework that has since been popularly referred to as Tyler's Curriculum Rationale (1969). The rationale appears in Figure 3.2. In Tyler's conception of the process of curriculum design, the teacher begins by examining a range of available materials on the subject matter to be taught. Such materials include textbooks, books written on the topic, curriculum guides, magazines and newspapers, and information gained through interviews with knowledgeable educators, students, parents, and other resource people in the community. When the examination has been completed, the teacher lists all the possible goals that emerged.

FIGURE 3.1   Common Terms for Student Learning Outcomes

Common Terms for Student Learning Outcomes (Results)		
Term	**Broad, Long-Term**	**Specific, Short-Term**
Goal	X	
Standard	X	
Benchmark		X
Objective		X

FIGURE 3.2 Tyler's Curriculum Rationale

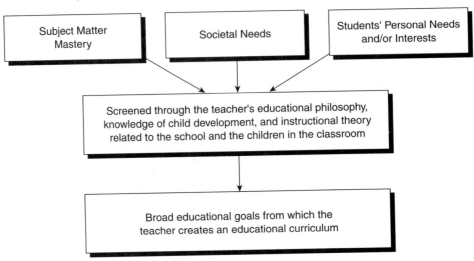

To utilize the rationale, the teacher might divide the goals into three groups based on their philosophic source: (a) goals that assist the student to master important subject matter, (b) goals that relate to contemporary societal needs, and (c) goals that relate to the students' personal needs and/or interests. Do you recognize in Tyler's three sources of goals the educational philosophies discussed previously in the chapter? Subject matter mastery is consistent with an essentialist philosophy. Goals in that area would include competence in communication skills, mathematics, history, and the arts. Societal needs can be confronted from either a progressive or a critical pedagogy perspective. Goals emerging from societal needs could include learning about the environment, health education classes, or gaining skills in decision making that can be used to address a variety of social crises. Attention to student needs or interests is progressive in nature.

REFLECTING ON THE IDEAS

Review the process recommended by Tyler for selecting content goals. Examine the list of goals found in a curriculum guide or teacher's edition of a textbook. Count the number of goals that appear to reflect each of Tyler's sources: subject matter mastery, societal needs and students' personal needs and interests. Where does the emphasis lie in your document?

SECTION 2. ANALYZING CONTENT GOALS

Section 2 Objectives

After you have completed this section, you will be able to

1. classify examples of affective, psychomotor, and cognitive goals;
2. describe the use of standards in planning;

3. relate concepts, generalizations, and facts in a content area of your choice;
4. sort examples of concrete and abstract concepts;
5. construct a concept map in a content area of your own choice; and
6. structure a content area into a network of generalizations, concepts, and facts.

Teaching with Content Standards

The "Curriculum in the 21st Century" task force recommended that the Taunton Schools revise its curriculum to make it more inclusive of persons whose voices in the past were left out of history, literature, and fine arts school lessons. The task force also made it clear that the school board wanted the positive contributions of the United States to be emphasized as the scope of the curriculum is broadened to include more content about women and people of color. Fairhill Elementary School was given the responsibility to demonstrate this new approach to curriculum by developing a new version of the fifth-grade American History unit.

Gloria Jackson, a fifth-grade teacher at Fairhill, stared out the window of her classroom on a warm June morning and recalled the meeting with her principal, Janet Martin. Ms. Martin had asked Gloria to lead the curriculum team of fifth-grade teachers to develop a new American Revolution unit. On the positive side, Gloria had been a social studies major in college and had enjoyed her courses in history. On the negative side, Gloria recognized that she lacked sufficient knowledge of curriculum design and analysis to give her confidence that she could lead a team of teachers to develop the unit. She pondered the challenges she would face. She would have to focus on important ideas. She was particularly interested in highlighting the contributions of women and people of color. She thought back to an article she had read recently on the benefits of interdisciplinary planning. With so much to teach and never enough hours in a day, it made sense to find ways to integrate two or more subjects, in this case social studies and language arts.

Gloria decided to speak with Stan Winder, the fifth-grade teacher across the hall. Stan was on the district social studies committee and could be depended on to have something creative to offer.

Gloria: Hi Stan! Are you ready for the new year?

Stan: You bet. You know me, always ready for a new adventure!

Gloria: Well, the American Revolution unit will be a new adventure for all of us. I thought you might have some ideas to help me make this a strong interdisciplinary unit.

Stan: Interdisciplinary unit planning has certainly helped me. I've found that linking subjects together helps my students—and me—to focus on important ideas. It also has helped me to find the time for some interesting projects for students to do.

Gloria: In the American Revolution unit, social studies and language arts seem to be natural companions.

Stan: I agree. Have you thought about which areas of language arts you would integrate with social studies?

Gloria: Historical fiction would be included and essay writing, certainly. The Declaration of Independence is a wonderful example of persuasive writing, although it is going to be a challenge for many fifth-grade students.

Stan: I would love to help with the planning. By the way, you know I was on the state committee that created the new framework for social studies. The framework contains content standards in social studies together with benchmarks that students would be expected to know and be able to do at the conclusion of their early elementary, later elementary, middle school, and high school years. We will have to align the goals for the new American Revolution unit with the standards and the appropriate later elementary benchmarks.

Gloria: I'm not sure I understand the big push to incorporate standards.

Stan: I have some concerns about the top-down nature of the reform; however, I value the framework as one tool for my curriculum development. The primary purpose for the creation of the standards is to assist us in identifying student performance expectations in both content knowledge and thinking processes.

Later Gloria thought back to her teacher education preparation program and wished that more class time had been spent on the process of designing curriculum using standards. Her state's curriculum framework appeared a bit confusing. She struggled to define the terminology—for example, how to distinguish differences among outcomes, goals, standards, and benchmarks. Upon locating her copy of the *Michigan Curriculum Framework* (1996), she first examined the various strands, or broad categories of subjects, that define social studies education. From within each strand, she would have to select standards, or broad goals, and then more narrowly defined learning objectives or benchmarks (see Figure 3.3).

She noted that among the strands, the development of discourse and decision-making skills, inquiry or research skills, and civic involvement in the community all emphasize the development of thinking processes and communication skills. The other four emphasize content knowledge in specific disciplines. Next she turned her attention to the standards and benchmarks found within each strand. She observed that standards

FIGURE 3.3   Strands in Social
Studies Education
Source: *Michigan Curriculum Framework*, Michigan Department of Education, 1996.

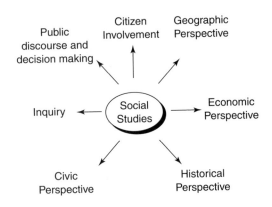

are global, long-range outcomes or goals for all students. For example, in the social studies a sample content standard in the area of history is stated as follows:

> Students will reconstruct past events in United States history by comparing interpretations written by others from a variety of perspectives and creating narratives from evidence.

She contrasted this content standard with one found within the inquiry strand that emphasizes thinking processes and communication skills:

> Students will engage their peers in constructive conversation about matters of public concern by clarifying issues, considering opposing views, applying democratic values, anticipating consequences, and working toward making decisions.

After examining the seven strands, Gloria scanned the numerous benchmarks numbered under each strand. She thought they seemed more akin to lesson objectives because they were quite narrow in scope. She also observed the developmental progression of the benchmarks. For example, under the sample history content standard, there are different benchmarks for various age groups:

Early Elementary: Explain why accounts of the same event differ.
Late Elementary: Interpret conflicting accounts of events in United States history and analyze the viewpoints of authors.
Middle School: Show that historical knowledge is tentative and subject to change by describing interpretations of the past that have been revised when new information was uncovered.

Gloria noted the spiral nature of the benchmarks. As students mature they are able to grapple with more complex ideas and apply increasingly sophisticated thinking skills. The curriculum directors in her district were working with teachers on the use of the curriculum framework as one means of ensuring that content and skills would be taught in a logical developmental sequence from elementary through secondary school.

Gloria then looked at the initial planning for the American Revolution unit. She thought that the unit would take 3 to 4 weeks of class time, assuming that the students would be engaged in unit activities about an hour each day. She made an initial decision that the unit would be divided into three sections.

Phase 1 would cover the background necessary to understand why the American Revolution occurred: the political relationships between king and parliament and between England and the American colonies, the economic ties of mercantilism, and the territorial issues that evolved from the movement of settlers west as a result of the French and Indian War.

Phase 2 would cover the actions of king and parliament between 1765 and 1783 and the reactions of the American colonists that led ultimately to the creation of the United States as an independent country.

Phase 3 would cover the aftermath of independence as the new nation struggled to find a system of government that would be small enough not to be a threat to liberty and yet have sufficient revenue to pay for the necessary expenses of government.

Based upon this outline, Gloria would seek to identify a number of standards and benchmarks she wanted students to achieve. For example, one later elementary benchmark for Michigan is "place major events in the early history of the United States in chronological order." This unit could be a good place to work toward part of that benchmark. Another benchmark that could be appropriate is "interpret conflicting accounts of events in both Michigan and the United States and analyze the viewpoints of the authors." Since the Revolutionary War represents a conflict between two points of view, this is another logical benchmark for that unit.

Gloria Jackson's Puzzle

After studying the curriculum standards, Gloria Jackson was ready to begin planning the interdisciplinary unit on the American Revolution for her fifth-grade class. In preparation she gathered a variety of materials for instruction, influenced by the kinds of resources available:

1. State and district standards for language arts and social studies
2. The district's newly adopted textbook
3. A collection of children's historical fiction from the local library
4. *Cobblestone* magazines (a children's periodical about history) pertaining to the American Revolution
5. Assorted videos on the colonial period
6. Websites that provide primary source documents, paintings, time lines, and so on
7. Nonfiction books on the American Revolution at diverse grade levels
8. Materials on the local historical society and history museum
9. A variety of texts on methods for teaching social studies and language arts

Along with the collection of resources, she came to this planning session having read some books on the American Revolution and constructed a content outline that will guide lesson development. Gloria sat at her desk staring at the materials and content outline. Where to begin? First, she reflected, "I have to know what outcomes are important—what do I want the students to know (content goals) and be able to do (process goals)?" Reflecting upon her recent conversation with Stan, she recognized the importance of beginning with the standards. Standards-based reform is an important educational trend both in Gloria's district and across the nation (Carr & Harris, 2001; Feuer, 1995; Ravitch, 1993). However, there is a difference between genuine standards-driven reform, in which standards are used to focus and improve instruction, and what one author has called its "evil twin," teaching focused on high-stakes testing (Thompson, 2001). Emphasis on a single test is not the only danger in standards-based planning. Agreeing with some of the concerns voiced by educational reformers such as Deborah Meier and William Ayers (Meier, 2000), Gloria recognized that there is a danger in placing too much authority in others while denying one's own abilities as a reflective decision maker. The state curriculum framework, while a valuable tool for curriculum development, must not become a rigid and prescriptive set of directives. Gloria will examine the standards and select those that appear most relevant and important to the unit. However, she will do this in conjunction with defining for herself those goals she believes should guide unit development. In particular, Gloria will be attuned to goals that are essential for this particular class of students in this particular community—a decision-making process that is impossible to manage at a state or national level.

Gloria sought to identify some priorities for herself regarding goals for the unit. First, she reflected on the importance of introducing multiple perspectives in any social studies unit. History is so often taught as a set of facts and truths when, in reality, events of life are marked by controversial interpretations depending upon who is viewing the events. She thought of the many voices that might frame the unit on the Revolution. There were loyalists and patriots, free and enslaved, wealthy and poor, men and women, and each group had its own perspectives on the Revolution (Hakim, 1999). An examination of multiple perspectives goes hand in hand with the inclusion of ethical questions regarding the morality of certain decisions and events in history. Threaded throughout Gloria's instruction is her belief that social studies education must further the development of empathic people who consider the moral and ethical sides of any issue (Brophy & VanSledright, 1997). If some members of Gloria's class were having trouble getting along and understanding the differences in their perspectives, instruction in understanding varying points of view could be particularly crucial.

In addition, she recognized that almost any body of knowledge can be a vehicle for teaching important higher level thinking processes such as analysis, evaluation, and synthesis. Instruction in important skills such as those related to inquiry—locating materials, taking notes, organizing the content, and presenting it—can also be inserted into any subject matter being taught (Costa & Liebmann, 1997). For Gloria, the larger goal of teaching students to independently inquire and solve problems influences the study of any subject.

Another challenge for Gloria is to construct a unit from an interdisciplinary perspective. She reflected upon an article she'd read recently about the benefits of interdisciplinary planning. With so much to teach and never enough hours in the day, it made sense to think about planning ways that two or more subjects could be integrated. Incorporating content standards from language arts seemed like a natural fit (Zarnowski & Gallagher, 1993). For example, reading historical fiction can help students imagine an historical period and become empathically involved in the lives of historical figures. Diverse writing activities such as constructing a Revolutionary newspaper, creating plays of key events, and constructing diaries from the perspective of different historical figures promote deeper understanding (Lindquist & Selwyn, 2000). Because social studies is by nature an interdisciplinary subject, Gloria will also include goals pertaining to civics, geography, and economics in addition to history. Drawing upon her knowledge and belief in the value of the theory of multiple intelligences and the importance of seeking multiple entry points to any given concept or idea, she will seek ways to develop goals that incorporate analysis of the artwork and music of the period as well (Gardner, 1999).

Finally, Gloria will develop goals that link the past to the present. One of the greatest challenges social studies teachers must tackle is the seeming lack of relevance between events of the past and students' daily lives. She knows that without ties to prior knowledge, it will be impossible for students to interpret, understand, and remember the information. In the Revolutionary War unit, Gloria will purposefully connect concepts such as monarchy and democracy to her classroom community so that students can easily relate the content to their lives (Wiske, 1998). She is excited about implementing a simulation she read about in which the teacher acts as king for a day in an attempt to help children understand the oppression the colonists experienced.

Later Stan and Gloria worked together to create a comprehensive list of goals for the unit. They shared their individual lists and struggled to come to consensus regarding the most important ones. Their final list incorporated goals from both the language arts and social studies standards.

Social Studies Outcomes

Students will

1. analyze and explain the political, economic, and territorial causes of the American Revolution
2. develop a deep understanding of basic concepts such as revolution, liberty, democracy, equality, and so on
3. place the major events in the Revolutionary War period (1763–1787) in accurate chronological order using a time line
4. explain how the French and Indian War led to the imposition of taxes in the colonies
5. give examples of different forms of governmental authority as they are enacted through a monarchy and a democracy and the use of power without authority
6. create analogies between the different forms of government and rules and structures in their own classroom community
7. describe the different forms of resistance the colonists employed and compare them with forms of social protest used today
8. value the importance of political participation as an instrument of societal improvement
9. define the term *revolution* and explain why the concepts of independence, equality, and democracy as used in 1776 were revolutionary for the period
10. interpret the development and summarize the main points of the Declaration of Independence
11. pose a research question pertaining to a major event, cultural group, or person of the American Revolutionary period, gather information, construct an answer to the question posed, and report the results of their investigation
12. explain how the American Revolution affected various persons including patriots, loyalists, rich, poor, women, Native Americans, African Americans
13. evaluate one or more major events of the Revolutionary War from two contrasting points of view and use these multiple perspectives to create a story, play, newspaper, or three-dimensional model
14. strive to value and appreciate the perspectives of others
15. compare and contrast multiple perspectives among students regarding everyday classroom issues and life events
16. develop a class definition of a leader and evaluate why an individual from the Revolutionary War should or should not have been considered a leader
17. evaluate the major dilemmas facing the Continental Congress and determine if the compromise regarding slavery was justified. Predict what might have occurred had the congress reached a different decision

18. value the importance of ethics when making decisions
19. pose a question regarding the music or art of the Revolutionary period, gather information, construct an answer to the question posed, and present the results in a musical performance

Language Arts Outcomes

Students will

1. express their responses to oral, visual, and electronic texts, and compare their responses to those of others
2. describe and discuss the shared human experience depicted in a work of historical fiction
3. identify the persuasive forms of communication used by the individual authors and speakers of the American Revolutionary period and analyze how their words influenced audience expectations
4. analyze the Declaration of Independence in terms of content, structure, and style
5. use the writing process to construct a simple narrative depicting specific events of the Revolutionary War
6. participate in a literature discussion circle regarding a biography of one important leader or common person of the Revolutionary period

As Gloria works to prepare her unit, she will use these general goals to help her shape the specific teaching objectives for her lesson plans.

Three Domains of Educational Content

Reflective teacher decision makers are aware of and purposeful about the kinds of learning they are trying to promote. Educational goals can be classified in a number of ways. In the previous section we learned that goals can be classified according to philosophical positions—progressivism, essentialism, and critical pedagogy. Another way to classify goals is to subdivide them into knowledge (to know), skills (to be able to do), and attitudes (to feel, or to be like). Another classification scheme organizes goals into affective, psychomotor, and cognitive groupings or domains. Some goals are clearly classified in one of the three domains. Other goals have characteristics that suggest they reside in more than one domain.

The **affective domain** involves emotional behavior—that is, feelings, attitudes, preferences, and values. The range of possible behaviors around which affective goals can be written is quite large. For example, an affective goal might be expressed as an appreciation of the differences that exist in the behavior of people in various ethnic and racial groups. A more specific and significant goal would be to expect students to respond to classmates from a different ethnic, racial, or cultural group in ways that are appropriate and supportive. In Gloria's list of social studies outcomes, goals 8, 14, and 18 are affective. The concern is for students' appreciation and valuing of the importance of political participation, multiple perspectives, and the place of ethics in decision making.

The **psychomotor domain** consists of learning that is sensory in nature, ranging from involuntary, reflexive movements to complex chains of skillful and purposeful

FIGURE 3.4   Key Concepts to Be Taught

Key Concepts to be Taught/Retaught

Democracy, Monarchy, Colonies, Taxation, Equality, Freedom, Inalienable rights,

Independence, Leader, Liberty, Oppression, Multiple Perspectives, Representation,

Democracy, Republic, Protest/Resistance, Revolution

---

behavior, such as dancing and playing quarterback. Any physical skill that requires repeated practice to perfect has psychomotor elements—for example, playing the piano or pronouncing words in an unfamiliar language. In school, sports and the practical and fine arts play a special role in the physical development of learners. Early instruction in the primary grades emphasizes play and motor development. Some goals for students with mental impairments are largely psychomotor—for example, dressing or eating independently. In Gloria's list of goals, numbers 13 and 19 have psychomotor elements although neither is primarily psychomotor in focus. Goal 13 may involve acting in a play or constructing a model; goal 19 involves performing a musical composition.

Cognitive (intellectual) goals require students to learn and recall information or to use their intellectual skills to determine meaning and to relate new information to previous learning. Higher level cognitive goals require the learner to disassemble information or to assemble it in new forms, to judge its worth and merit, and to apply it in complex ways to solve everyday problems and those in the workplace. The other goals in Gloria 's list are clearly in the cognitive domain. They range from the memorization of information to the interpretation and evaluation of events and ideas.

Structure of Subject Matter

Teacher decision makers need to identify the depth and breadth of the particular subject that will be taught. In cases in which the teacher has limited content knowledge, it is often necessary to clarify key ideas within content before identifying goals. The following outline shows how the three phases of Gloria's Revolutionary War unit could be outlined. The content outline for Phase II, "Actions and Reactions: The Revolutionary War," is shown in detail. Key concepts to be taught are listed in Figure 3.4.

Content Outline: Revolutionary War Unit

    I. Taxation Without Representation British Rule: Roots of the Revolution
        A. The Monarchy and Parliament
        B. John Locke and the Rights of Englishmen
        C. Restricting representation in the American colonies

      D. Restricting trade in the American colonies (mercantilism)

      E. The French and Indian War (1756–1763)

         1. Colonial powers fight for territory in the New World

         2. The Native American perspective

         3. Quebec, Treaty of Paris, and the end of French control

II. Actions and Reactions: The Revolutionary War

      A. War debt and the cost of British protection: Taxation in the colonies

      B. Parliamentary actions and colonists' reactions

Crown and Parliament Actions	American Colonists' Reactions
Stamp Act (1765)	Stamp Act Congress (1765)
Boston Massacre (1770)	Founding of Sons of Liberty (1772)
Tea Act (1773)	Boston Tea Party (1773)
Intolerable Acts (1774)	Continental Congress (1774)
(Boston Port Act, Quartering Act)	Paul Revere's Ride (1775)
Battles of Lexington and	Minutemen Gather at Lexington and
Concord (1775)	Concord (1775)

      C. Multiple Perspectives

         1. Patriots and Loyalists

         2. Free and slave

         3. Rich and poor

         4. Merchants and farmers

         5. Men and women

         6. Northerners and southerners

      D. Patriot Leaders

         1. John Adams

         2. Samuel Adams

         3. Benjamin Franklin

         4. John Hancock

         5. Patrick Henry

         6. Thomas Jefferson

         7. Thomas Paine

         8. George Washington

      E. Leaders (English)

         1. Monarchy (Crown)

         2. Parliament (House of Commons, House of Lords)

            a. Edmund Burke

            b. George Grenville

            c. Lord North

            d. William Pitt

      F. The Declaration of Independence (1776)

         1. Committee of the Continental Congress

         2. Thomas Jefferson the primary author

         3. Model document for others to emulate

         4. Issues of freedom, independence, equality, rights, slavery, revolution

        G. The Revolutionary War (1776–1783)
          1. American military leaders
          2. British military leaders
          3. Battles and events
          4. Problems of finance and supply
          5. America gains European allies
          6. The home front
          7. Surrender at Yorktown and Treaty of Peace

III. The Aftermath: Struggles for a New Nation
        A. The Articles of Confederation
          1. Nature
          2. Weaknesses
        B. Calls for a new pattern of government
          1. Federalist papers
          2. Constitutional Convention (1787)

Although the creation of a content outline is a necessary task in the development of a curriculum unit, it is only one task in a long process of decision making. The curriculum developer must also have an understanding of the nature of cognitive knowledge so that the content does not become merely a list of unconnected information. When a content outline is tempered by an understanding of the nature of subject matter, the logical chunks —the groupings and relationships that organize the content— will become apparent.

To understand more deeply the nature of subject matter, consider the work of Jerome Bruner, an internationally acclaimed psychologist. In 1960, Bruner's influential book *The Process of Education* was published. One of these ideas focused educators' attention on the nature of subject matter and the way that subject matter ought to be organized for teaching purposes. Bruner supported the notion that every subject taught in schools has a structure, and that structure has a particular form composed of three elements— concepts, generalizations, and facts. He considered all three elements as appropriate for student learning. However, Bruner's central position was that the school "curriculum of a subject should be determined by the most fundamental understanding that can be achieved of the underlying generalizations that give structure to that subject" (p. 31). He argued that instruction should center on the "fundamentals"—the generalizations and concepts of the subject rather than the individual facts. To illustrate his belief he used the analogy of the fully blooming shade tree: its trunk and branches represent the subject's organizing generalizations and major concepts, and the leaves represent the multitude of specific facts that describe the nature, history, and scope of the subject and provide examples of its application.

Bruner argued that understanding the structure of subject matter assists learners to make the subject more understandable. It increases retention and transfer of learning, enhances the capability of the learner to relate newly introduced content to previously learned content, and provides a path for learning additional content within the same subject. Philip Phenix, a philosopher and educator, summarized the advantages of teaching through a structured approach by noting that:

Understanding the Structure of the Content Makes Learning Easier

One of the secrets of good teaching is the practice of clearly charting a way through the subject of instruction so that the students know how each topic as it comes along fits into the whole scheme of the course and of the discipline to which it belongs. They understand where they are in relation to what has gone before and to what is to be studied subsequently. The effect of such teaching is a growing appreciation of the inner logic of the subject, resulting at length in a grasp of its spirit and method which will be proof against the erosions of detailed forgetting. (1960, p. 307)

Gloria Jackson showed an understanding of the underlying structure of subject matter by the way she confronted the task of forming goals for the American Revolution unit. Gloria recalled her first course in history from a respected professor who emphasized the conceptual structure of a given topic. In her introductory lecture, the professor emphasized that the following fundamental generalizations help to make sense of historical events, issues, and trends:

1. The binding of people through language, religion, tradition, common history, and political boundaries into nationalistic movements has often altered the course of history.
2. Historical events have multiple causes.
3. When two cultures clash, both change. The more powerful culture can be expected to dominate and transform the weaker, while often denying any positive contributions from the weaker culture.
4. Historical events can be interpreted from multiple perspectives.
5. Historical method involves both an examination of evidence from the past and those who produced that evidence.

Similar generalizations could help Gloria's students make sense of the information they learned about the American Revolution.

Another fundamental generalization is derived from the study of history. Regardless of when or where they lived, regardless of their race, nationality, or religion, all people possess many characteristics in common. The student who examines unfamiliar cultures with this understanding will be a more accurate, reliable, and productive investigator than will one who has not understood this concept. In the hands of a creative and knowledgeable teacher, this idea can be a connecting thread that is applied as students learn about new peoples and cultures.

It is clear from even this brief discussion that making good decisions about content will take considerable study and content expertise. It is one of the great dilemmas of elementary education that many elementary school teachers need to be experts in multiple subjects—a challenging expectation, indeed. There are many strategies and resources to use as you become more expert in various subjects. Good teachers are avid readers, and you will find many kinds of print resources helpful to you, much like the list of resources Gloria collected earlier in this chapter. Other teachers can be helpful, as can content experts in your area. Local museum or historical society personnel might have suggestions regarding the Revolutionary War unit. Also, do not forget the vast network of resources available through the World Wide Web and other technological resources.

Concept Learning

After studying her resources, Gloria knows she cannot teach everything of importance related to the American Revolution. Therefore she has some very important decisions to make regarding what ideas are most important for her class. The outline is a first step in developing a structured analysis of cognitive content. However, before proceeding further, it is necessary to look more deeply into the nature of the three elements of that content—concepts, generalizations, and facts. Let's first examine the concept.

Concepts are categories or classes of things that share a set of critical characteristics. Concepts are like lenses or road maps that human beings use to examine the world as identified by the five senses. They permit us to use previous experience and knowledge to place new information in a context, to associate the present with the past, and to recognize new information as a variation of what we have learned previously. We learn many concepts through direct experience, outside of school. In fact, preschoolers and primary-age youngsters often learn to use concepts to classify new experiences prior to learning the verbal labels, or names, they will later use to identify the concepts to others. (This may have been the case with the skunk example in Chapter 2.) However, the learning of concepts, together with the words used to label and describe them, is an essential element in successful school instruction. Many learning psychologists and instructional planners believe that concepts are the essential building blocks in a quality curriculum.

To illustrate how concept learning aids us in understanding what may at first seem like a novel experience, imagine disembarking from a train in a place you have never been before, in a country where you do not speak or understand the language—on the surface a frightening prospect! However, the more you analyze the problem, the lower is your level of fear. Safely stored in your long-term memory are the concepts of *hotel*, *restaurant*, and *bank*. Train stations typically have tourist information centers where it is likely that someone will speak English and provide you with a simplified dictionary that can help you to interpret the unfamiliar language. You know that the bank can exchange your U.S. dollars for the local currency. You can expect to find taxicabs or public transportation. All in all, the concepts you have learned make it possible for you to function in what appears at first to be a totally alien environment.

Concepts have characteristics, often called *attributes*. Attributes allow us to distinguish between examples of the concept and nonexamples. Nonexamples are not members of the concept class but are similar enough to confuse the unwary observer. For example, a particular table may look something like a chair but it is not a chair. A skunk looks like a cat but it is not a cat. In making the distinction, it is important to distinguish between critical and noncritical concept attributes. Only critical attributes can be used to determine whether a given example fits within the concept class. From the American Revolution unit, consider the concept of equality. Two persons, things, or ideas may be considered equal when they are treated in a uniform fashion. Two entities that are the same in size, value, rank, degree, and so on are considered equal. Thus two critical attributes are equivalency and uniformity.

Concepts can be classified as concrete or abstract. A *concrete concept* is one that exists in the physical world and can be described in terms of its observable attributes. For example, *chair* is a concrete concept, as are *yellow*, *dog*, and *girl*. The critical attributes that determine whether something is a chair are that (a) it is used to sit on, (b) it stands on, usually, four legs, (c) it has a back rest, and (d) it is built to seat only one person (*Webster's New Collegiate Dictionary*, 1981). Using these attributes to guide us, we can distinguish among chairs, tables, couches, stools, and so on. We can distinguish between examples and nonexamples.

An *abstract concept* is one that cannot be observed, either because it does not possess physical dimensions or because its physical dimensions are not critical in distinguishing between examples and nonexamples. Consider the concept *citizen*. Although citizens have physical attributes, in that all citizens are human beings and can be observed, you can't tell a citizen from a noncitizen by physical appearance. The physical attributes are not critical in identifying examples. Thus it is an abstract concept. As a rule, the preparation for teaching an abstract concept is more extensive and detailed than the preparation needed to teach a concrete concept.

As complicated as it is, *citizen* is an example of an abstract concept that has a clear definition and attributes that together can be used to distinguish examples from nonexamples. Thus a citizen of the United States is either natural born (a child of a U.S. citizen or born on U.S. territory) or completes a process of naturalization. In the American Revolution unit, some of the abstract concepts have clear definitions and attributes. Among them are *parliament*, *representative*, *republic*, and *taxation*.

Concepts whose attributes and/or definitions cannot be used to distinguish all examples from all nonexamples are more difficult to teach and learn. Examples of such concepts in the American Revolution unit are *equality*, *freedom*, *democracy*, and *liberty*. Although these concepts have definitions and attributes, neither can be used to distinguish all examples from all nonexamples. For example, the dictionary definition of *political freedom* is the "absence of necessity, coercion, or constraint in choice or action"

(*Webster's New Collegiate Dictionary,* 1981). Are we free in the United States? Reasonable people would agree that we are. Yet there are restrictions on our freedom. Traffic regulations control how fast we drive. In some communities, smoking is forbidden in public buildings or restricted to designated locations. Individuals must obtain a license to get married, own a dog, or drive a car. In all these cases, our freedom of choice and action is limited. Thus attempting to define the limits of a complex concept such as freedom yields a continuum of examples ranging from the clearly defined to the ambiguous and debatable. Still, concept learning is critical. We want students not just to memorize definitions of concepts but to understand them—to be able to use them in new situations and tie them to other ideas.

REFLECTING ON THE IDEAS

To assess your understanding of different concepts, create two groups of five concepts in a subject area of your choice. You may find it helpful to do this exercise in the area for which you are planning your unit. The first group of concepts should contain concrete concepts; the second group should contain abstract concepts. In your group of abstract concepts, include concepts with clear definitions and/or attributes, and concepts with unclear definitions and/or attributes. Check your groupings with a colleague.

Concept Mapping

Gloria Jackson and the fifth-grade curriculum team were fortunate to have attended a timely in-service workshop on content structures. The in-service leader defined the meaning of a content structure as "the web of facts (words, concepts) and their interrelations in a body of instructional materials" (Shavelson, 1974). She then reviewed the advantages of learning the structure of content as observed by Bruner: (a) it makes the subject more understandable by relating general and specific knowledge, (b) it improves the retention of knowledge by learning concepts and facts as a network of information, and (c) it enhances the capability to relate new knowledge to previously learned content. Finally, she identified *concept mapping* as a helpful curriculum development tool for teaching content structures. **Concept mapping** is a thought process that culminates in a visual display of relevant knowledge and relationships. Each concept, concept attribute, or example is contained in an individual circle. Relationships among concepts, attributes, and examples are shown through connecting lines and arrows and by "linking words" that describe the nature of each relationship.

The resulting diagram represents a personalized map of the important elements and relationships in a curriculum topic. Typically, a concept map begins with the selection of a focal topic "that is of special interest to the mapper and is the focus of the particular map" (Naidu, 1990). The mapper may choose to begin the map by placing the focal topic at the top, the middle, or the bottom of the map. In any case the direction of the arrows reveals which concept is to be the focus of the map.

Concept mapping has been shown to assist teachers and learners to broaden, deepen, and sharpen their understanding of curriculum topics. It broadens understanding by forcing the consideration of meaningful relationships among concepts. It deepens understanding by requiring the learner to identify concept attributes and examples. It sharpens understanding by providing a visual display of the total set of relationships and elements. The end result may be greater initial learning and retention over time (Heinze-Fry & Novak, 1990). It can also assist teachers to plan by helping them identify important relationships among concepts.

Gloria began her concept map by identifying the focal concepts about the American Revolution that she wanted to emphasize: *democracy, monarchy, colonies, taxation, equality, freedom, inalienable rights, independence, leader, liberty, oppression, multiple perspectives, representation, democracy, republic, protest/resistance,* and *revolution.* Next, she sought to connect these major concepts using linking verbs that demonstrate meaningful connections among the concepts. A concept map demonstrating important conceptual relationships on the topic of the American Revolution is presented in Figure 3.5. A second map (see Figure 3.6) displays connections among a single language arts concept, *persuasive communication*—a concept that would be integrated into the Revolutionary War unit.

Generalization Learning

If concepts are the road maps for teaching and learning, then generalizations are the destinations teacher decision makers attempt to reach. A generalization is a statement that expresses a generally true relationship between two or more concepts. Understanding a generalization is most likely to lead to the "aha" experiences described in Chapter 2. Whereas a concept is usually expressed in a word or two, a generalization is always expressed as a statement, often as a complete sentence. As opposed to concepts or facts, generalizations allow students to make sense of events in a variety of settings.

FIGURE 3.5 American Revolution Concept Map

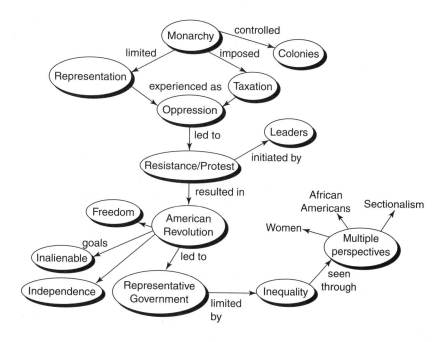

FIGURE 3.6   Connections Among the Concept of Persuasive Communication

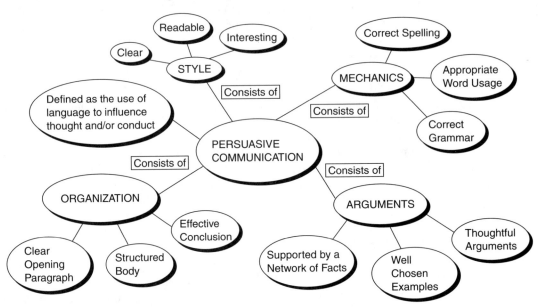

The following are examples of generalizations:

- Metals expand when they are heated.
- The pace of life is slower in small towns than it is in large cities.
- Retired people tend to vote in greater numbers than do voters between the ages of 18 and 21.
- Division is the reverse of multiplication.

A second way to distinguish a generalization from the other elements of subject matter is to contrast it with a fact. Both generalizations and facts have the attribute of being statements. However, facts include specific information about particulars—people, things, places, time, and events. In addition, a fact is typically verified by making a single observation, by conducting a simple experiment, or by consulting a credible reference. The following examples are facts:

- Henry Ford was the father of the modern assembly line.
- Count Basie played the piano in his orchestra.
- Whales are the largest mammals.
- The U.S. Constitution can be changed through the passage of amendments.
- Gold is more malleable than iron.

A generalization cannot be checked through a single observation; experimentation through repeated trials over time is required. In some cases, many references must be consulted and compared before we can feel confident that a particular generalization is an accurate description of reality. Even then, we would not be surprised to find that some

TABLE 3.1   *Generalizations and Facts*

Generalization	Fact
Is not absolute (contains some "wiggle")	Is concrete, definite, with no reasonable doubt
Verification requires a good deal of observation/experimentation	Is usually verified by a single observation or reference
Expresses relationship between two or more concepts	Usually refers to one person, event, thing, or place
Applies to many examples	Applies to a single example
A hypothesis, explanation, or theory	Evidence that may support a hypothesis, explanation, or theory.

knowledgeable people would disagree about the accuracy of that generalization. We know, after all, that generalizations are constructed from concepts. Abstract concepts with unclear definitions and/or attributes, as we have learned, are difficult to apply to all cases we may encounter. Table 3.1 shows the difference between facts and generalizations.

After a period of reflection on the goals of the American Revolution unit and the outline of the content, Gloria created three generalizations for the unit, one for each of the three unit phases, that she believed would provide a meaningful structure for the unit. A focus question and student goals are presented with each generalization. For each goal, she created a focus question to help students identify key ideas in that section of the unit.

Phase I. Mercantilism (restricting trade) was used by England to exercise political and economic control of colonies.

Focus Question: What is the proper role of government?

    a. understand the mother country/colonial relationship
    b. examine a monarchy in the context of a classroom community and our national government

Phase II. The colonists used various kinds of resistance to end what they perceived as oppression by crown and parliament.

Focus Question: How should people respond to limits placed on their freedom?

    a. understand various kinds of resistance and their relation to justice and injustice
    b. examine parent-child and teacher-student relationships in comparison to crown/parliamentary-colonial relationship

Phase III. Although the American Revolution created a new nation based on inalienable rights, for many years after, these rights were available only to certain White men who owned property.

Focus Question: What were the key issues to be addressed in creating a government for the new nation?

    a. understand multiple perspectives: race, class, gender, religion
    b. explore ways to organize our classroom community

CHECK FOR UNDERSTANDING

Examine the following examples. Identify those that are *generalizations* by writing G and those that are *facts* by writing F in the space to the left of each example.

_____ 1. In a democracy, the decision-making power is placed in the hands of the majority while at the same time the rights of the minority are protected.
_____ 2. Teaching is both a science and an art.
_____ 3. The color green can be made by combining yellow and blue.
_____ 4. The number of seconds in 1 month (30 days) is 2,592,000.
_____ 5. As the supply of a substance increases, price generally decreases.
_____ 6. If there are x ways of doing one thing and y ways of doing another thing, then there are x plus y ways of doing both.
_____ 7. The term *Karma* is associated with Hinduism.
_____ 8. The earliest alphabet originated in the Middle East.
_____ 9. Paul Bunyan was the subject of tall tales.
_____ 10. Residents of Washington, D.C., began voting for president in 1964.

Examples 3, 4, 7, 8, 9, and 10 are facts; examples 1, 2, 5, and 6 are generalizations.

Although generalizations are powerful tools in understanding the past, present, and future, they must not be interpreted mindlessly. In the spirit of scientific investigation, the generalization is valid only if there is no external intervention that changes the relationship between the concepts. For instance, consider the following generalization about past and future educational performance:

> The best single predictor of a young child's educational performance in high school and college is the number of years of schooling (8, 12,16, 16+) of the child's parents.

That prediction is accurate if nothing intervenes to alter the relationship between the level of education of the child's parents and his or her predicted school performance. However, that is precisely what we expect a good teacher to do—to make it possible for the child to prosper intellectually and emotionally as a consequence of schooling. Good teachers do intervene and alter, for the better, the expected result. Thus a generalization has to be interpreted as a general truth that will prove to be an accurate prediction in a majority of cases. It doesn't guarantee that a particular child will fit the pattern or that intervention from the home or the school or from another significant person in the child's life will not alter the balance in some dramatic way.

Factual Learning

The analysis of the three elements of content concludes with the third element—facts. As indicated in the discussion of generalizations, a fact, for purposes of instruction, is a statement about particulars (people, things, places, times, or events) and is typically verified by making a single observation, by conducting a simple experiment, or by consulting a credible authority.

Don't underestimate the importance of facts in learning and living. To illustrate their importance, imagine that you begin reading an article in a newsmagazine about the stock market. You read the following sentence:

Wall Street remembers the shantytowns and bread lines of the 1930s caused by the "Great Crash of 1929."

Assume you do not know that the major financial institutions in the United States, as well as the New York Stock Exchange, are located in and around Wall Street in New York City or that a stock market crash in 1929 brought many to financial ruin. You do not remember that in the Great Depression of the 1930s many unemployed people lost their homes or could not afford to pay rent and buy. Thus they were forced to live in temporary shacks made of scrap, wood, tin, or cardboard known as "shanties." They also stood for hours in long "bread lines" to receive food donated by the government or by private charities. You do not know that "crash" refers to the stock market collapse that led to the widespread failure of banks, businesses, and farms and then to a worldwide depression. If you had not known one of these facts, what sense can you make of the sentence?

Collectively, the facts that we possess add to our reputation as educated persons— and potentially to our success on quiz shows. However, if facts are to be useful in increasing our understanding and ability to interpret the environment, they must be related to generalizations and concepts. For example, being able to list the names of the U.S. presidents has little meaning unless the list is organized under concepts such as effectiveness, political party affiliation, and philosophy. A student's ability to recall the scientific names of all mammals would be of little value unless he or she could identify animals that were mammals and could recognize the critical attributes of a mammal. In the stock market example, you would read with optimum understanding if you were able, mentally, to place the facts into an existing structural network in your long-term memory. That structure includes knowledge of how the stock market functions, together with generalizations that relate the stock market to the U.S. economy and the banking and monetary system. Finally, it includes the capability to evaluate the likelihood that a stock market collapse today would initiate a catastrophic depression similar to the one that occurred in the 1930s.

Content Analysis

Having analyzed educational content and identified the three elements of that content— concepts, generalizations, and facts—we can return to Bruner's suggestion to teach content in the form of a fully blooming tree with the trunk and the major branches representing the generalizations and concepts and the leaves representing the specific facts. Gloria Jackson and her fifth-grade teacher planning group would do well to organize their content analysis of the American Revolution unit using the fully blooming tree scheme (see Figure 3.7).

Content Analysis in Interdisciplinary Units

Curriculum has been organized by traditional subject areas (i.e., language arts, math, science, social studies, art, music) through much of this century, and the subject-based

FIGURE 3.7 The Fully Blooming Tree Example Applied to the American Revolution

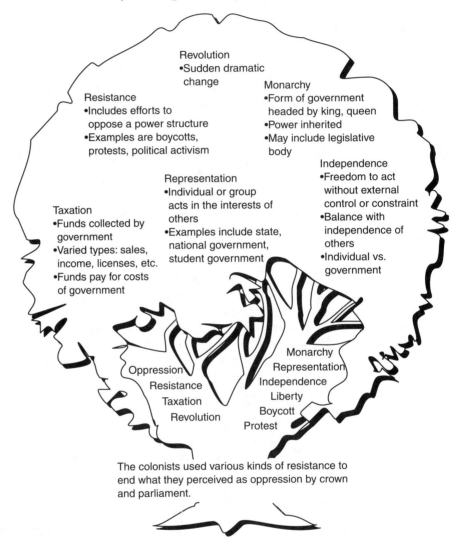

Revolution
•Sudden dramatic change

Monarchy
•Form of government headed by king, queen
•Power inherited
•May include legislative body

Resistance
•Includes efforts to oppose a power structure
•Examples are boycotts, protests, political activism

Representation
•Individual or group acts in the interests of others
•Examples include state, national government, student government

Independence
•Freedom to act without external control or constraint
•Balance with independence of others
•Individual vs. government

Taxation
•Funds collected by government
•Varied types: sales, income, licenses, etc.
•Funds pay for costs of government

Oppression
Resistance
Taxation
Revolution

Monarchy
Representation
Independence
Liberty
Boycott
Protest

The colonists used various kinds of resistance to end what they perceived as oppression by crown and parliament.

patterns can be hard to break. However, this pattern is changing rapidly. Educational reform proposals have identified a number of advantages to organizing curriculum around interdisciplinary content (Beane, 1997; Jacobs, 1989, 1991; Roberts & Kellough, 1996). First, an interdisciplinary approach models the real world. Nowhere except in schools do we divide our days and tasks into a time for math, a time for language, and a time for science. In everyday life, disciplines intermingle and relate to one another as individuals use them to solve problems. Scientists use language; reporters use math.

Second, interdisciplinary content can help students create multiple ties to important ideas. A student who learns about the concept of balance only in mathematics has fewer opportunities for understanding this concept than a student who examines the same concept in art, biology, and political science. Third, interdisciplinary approaches can provide novelty and allow students to look at familiar content with new eyes. Students who think they know all there is to know about pioneers, having studied westward migration in previous years, may come to new understandings if they begin to question what would constitute a pioneer in art, technology, music, or science. Such questions provide opportunities for analysis and critical thinking that would be absent if questions were limited to a single discipline.

There are many ways to structure interdisciplinary content. We will describe three:

- Using multiple disciplines to investigate a topic
- Examining interdisciplinary themes
- Addressing complex problems

The simplest approach to interdisciplinary content is using *multiple disciplines to investigate a single topic or time period.* Such investigations may be largely teacher directed or based on student questions. This approach could be used to study the Revolutionary War period; that is the approach used by Gloria and her colleagues in incorporating both history and language arts. Students may learn about lifestyles and politics in social studies, about literature or propaganda in language, about flags and symbols in art, about the distances traveled by the armies in math, and about period dance or games in physical education.

A unit based on a time period usually starts as a "topic web," with the topic in the center and the content areas at the end of each spoke as shown in Figure 3.8. These topics can be used to identify key content, goals, and class activities. Although this web appears similar to a concept map, note that key concepts in each topic remain to be identified. An alternative to teachers designing the web is to ask students what they know about the topic, and allow those questions to give direction to the unit. In most cases, student questions range over a wide variety of disciplines. If not, teachers may prompt additional inquiries with a few well-chosen questions of their own. Still, the process will not end there. It will be important for the teacher to do the same in-depth planning for teaching generalizations, concepts, and facts—and make the same key ties to curriculum standards—regardless of whether a unit is centered on a single discipline or multiple disciplines, entirely teacher planned or directed by student questions. The ability to tie student interests and questions to key concepts is an important teaching skill.

Similar processes could be followed for a more concrete topic such as kites. Students could design kites in art, learn about aerodynamics of kites in science, and investigate the use of kites in different cultures in social studies. In most cases, interdisciplinary planning starts with a wide-ranging web that is pruned to fit the demands of scheduling, interest, and required curricula. It is, however, better to start with a complex web and select the most important ideas rather than use a sparse web and risk missing important connections.

Selection of the organizing topic is key to a successful interdisciplinary unit. The topic must be interesting to students while also allowing reasonable ties to key areas of curriculum. For example, the topic *kites* could be well suited for a primary grade in which a key social studies emphasis is family activities in different cultures and an emphasis in

FIGURE 3.8   A Web for a Topical Unit on Medieval Life

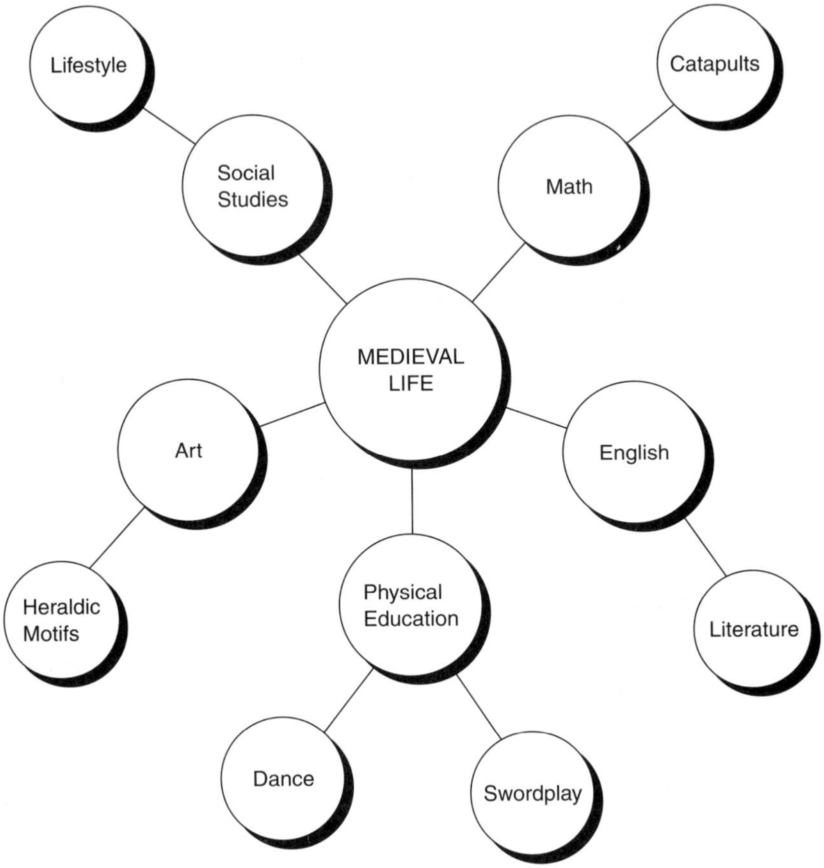

science is learning through inquiry. Students could gain insight into the ways families play together and the importance of celebrations across cultures by examining the use of kites in the United States and China. They could learn inquiry processes by hypothesizing how modifications in a basic kite design could enhance its flying and by experimenting with their designs. Ties to basic language arts skills could easily be made by writing about kite activities. However, kites would be a less appropriate topic for a grade level in which the primary social studies focus is American history.

Many teachers in primary grades plan a large part of their curriculum in interdisciplinary units organized around topics or works of literature. This type of planning is facilitated because so much of the curriculum in the early grades is focused around skills that can be taught within a number of topics. For example, imagine a first-grade teacher whose students are entranced with *Clifford the Big Red Dog*. The teacher might decide to capitalize on that interest by planning a short unit focused on Clifford. Naturally, the unit would not be focused on concepts and generalizations about Clifford but would use

Clifford as a vehicle to teach important parts of the curriculum. For example, early elementary benchmarks in mathematics in Michigan include:

Locate and describe objects in terms of their position including front, back, inside, outside, right, left, over, under, next to, between.

Explore what happens to the size, shape, and position of an object after sliding, flipping, turning, enlarging, or reducing it.

Use concepts of position, direction, and orientation to describe the physical world and to solve problems.

Explain the meaning of measurements and recognize that the number of units it takes to measure an object is related to the size of the unit.

Collect and explore data through counting, measuring, and conducting surveys and experiments.

Early elementary benchmarks in language arts, social studies, and science include:

Write with developing frequency for multiple purposes to produce a variety of texts, such as stories, journals, learning logs, directions, and letters.

Explain how conflicts at school or in the local community might be resolved in ways that are consistent with core democratic values.

Use simple measurement devices.

Construct charts and graphs and prepare summaries of observations.

Focusing on these benchmarks as general goals, the teacher could plan a unit that included activities such as reading and writing about Clifford; locating Clifford above, behind, and next to a house; predicting what would happen if other animals or items were magnified to fit Clifford; using a variety of devices to measure Clifford (perhaps drawn in chalk on the playground); surveying peers regarding their preference for a giant red dog or a standard-sized dog; anticipating problems that might arise with a giant dog in the house; and solving a hypothetical problem with a neighbor who is inconvenienced by a large dog and writing a letter describing the solution. After identifying the benchmarks to be addressed, it would be important for the teacher to identify the key ideas about measurement, problem solving, and so on, that will be taught in the unit.

A slightly more complicated version of interdisciplinary content involves the use of **interdisciplinary themes**. An interdisciplinary theme is one that is an important idea in a variety of disciplines. Although we could use mathematics to learn about kites, they are not particularly important in the study of mathematics. A true interdisciplinary theme is *genuinely meaningful across disciplines*. The concept of balance is a good example of an abstract interdisciplinary theme. One could easily study the idea of balance in a variety of disciplines. Other examples of interdisciplinary themes are power, revolution, symbols, interdependence, and cycles. In each case, studying the same theme in a variety of disciplines can add to students' understanding. Units planned around interdisciplinary themes often are particularly appropriate for upper elementary and middle school classes, where students are beginning to develop more abstract thinking.

Planning a unit around an interdisciplinary theme begins in much the same way as one centered on a topic. Disciplines for webbing are selected by their relevance to the concept addressed. If Gloria Jackson's fifth-grade planning group wanted to create a thematic unit, they could explore the concept of power: how various groups gained and lost power during the Revolutionary period, force (power) in science, exponents in math, literature on personal empowerment, and so on. Imagine that Gloria's colleague, kindergarten teacher Diane Jordan, decided to focus a thematic unit around the concept *patterns*. Even though patterns is an abstract concept, it is a good choice for Diane, since her kindergarten curriculum emphasizes pattern books and rhyming patterns in literacy activities and geometric patterns in math. These will provide the concrete experiences necessary to develop the concept. She knows that the music teacher emphasizes rhythmic patterns in her kindergarten music activities. She feels confident that the music teacher will be pleased to help her students make ties between those patterns and the others they study in class. Diane might start her interdisciplinary planning with a web like that in Figure 3.9.

The third type of interdisciplinary curriculum is structured around *real-world problem solving*. Virtually all real-world problems, by their nature, are interdisciplinary. An investigation of life in the pond behind the school may initially appear to be a science problem. However, even the most superficial investigation is likely to require graphing and mathematical problem solving, as well as report writing. If the investigation is extended or the analysis complex, additional disciplines such as computer science, graphic design, or public speaking may be necessary. As in other types of interdisciplinary plan-

FIGURE 3.9   A Web for a Thematic Unit on Patterns

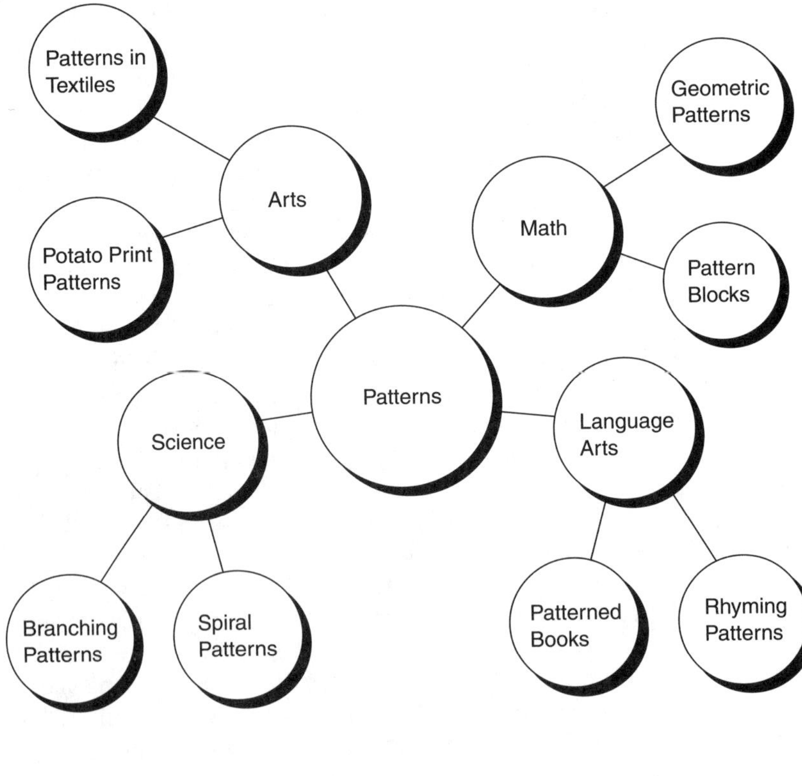

ning, it is important to keep track of the content and skills emphasized in real-world activities, particularly if the class engages in several such activities over the course of the year. With careful planning and record keeping, a reflective teacher will be able to identify areas that have been well taught within interdisciplinary activities and others that will need additional emphasis. For example, if students have created multiple graphs in conjunction with their fall pond life study, the chapter on graphing in the math book may need little or no attention—that content may already have been taught, along with important information on living things and ecosystems. However, other key areas of science (for example, electricity or simple machines) that did not tie to the pond life study would not have been addressed and may need additional emphasis second semester.

Final Thoughts on Structure of Content and Analysis of Learning Process

This section presents two of the most common concerns expressed by future teachers, followed by advice that should reduce any anxiety you may have about your ability to analyze content and learning processes.

Question 1

"I can't identify generalizations or key concepts in the subject matter I am expected to teach. The textbooks don't identify them. I feel the way Gloria Jackson did before she began her curriculum development task. Can you help me?"

Unfortunately, too few subject matter textbooks are organized in a structural way so that the fundamental generalizations and concepts are identified and highlighted and then related to factual information. Many textbooks, especially in social studies, provide information without any mention of the concepts and generalizations that help to classify and explain the information. If the teacher does not organize the text material into a structural outline, much of what will be read and discussed will probably be forgotten.

As bleak as the situation appears, there are some strategies you can use to increase your ability to identify key generalizations and concepts in the subjects you teach. First, the professional journals and national standards of such associations as the International Reading Association (IRA), National Council for the Social Studies (NCSS), National Council of Teachers of English (NCTE), National Council of Teachers of Mathematics (NCTM), National Science Teachers Association (NSTA), and their state affiliates provide articles, papers, and presentations focused on the organization of content for teaching purposes. Some of these associations publish monographs containing lesson and unit plans grounded in fundamental generalizations and concepts.

In addition, there are specialized curriculum resource and development centers in some subject areas, such as the Joint Council on Economic Education, and instructional journals for elementary and secondary teachers that publish lesson and unit plans and produce special issues on curriculum. To use magazines and journals productively, you can consult specialized reference guides to published material organized by topics, titles, and author names.

School district curriculum guides are a second useful source for structural lesson plans. Most include sample lesson plans and are oriented toward the teaching of generalizations and concepts. Often the unit or lesson you want to develop has been prepared by someone in some other school district and you can adapt it for your use.

A third source is textbooks and other works on the topic written for adults or for students at a higher or lower grade level than your class. Someone may have organized the topic in a structural way, and you can use the organizing framework while increasing or reducing the level of complexity of the reading material and other activities. A final source consists of other educators with whom you come into contact. Teachers who are active members of the profession, attend meetings and conferences, and take in-service and graduate course work can be expected to gain more insights into the structure of subject matter than will those who do not.

Question 2

"This whole idea of taking so much time to (a) plan outcomes, (b) analyze facts, concepts, and generalizations, and (c) create content outlines seems like overkill. Do I really need to know all this just to be a teacher?"

Yes! Recall the discussion in Chapter 1 about consumer teachers (who follow others' materials blindly) and reflective decision makers who design their own curriculum. If you cannot perform content analysis and learning process analysis, you will be at the mercy of commercially available teaching materials. With the ability to identify key ideas and structure students' cognitive learning in a logical order, you will have the option of designing your own curriculum when other materials fail you. Further, quite often when a textbook-based order of presentation fails to develop the learning you desire, you can analyze the lessons by examining the appropriateness of the order of the objectives and tasks.

SECTION 3. PLANNING A UNIT OF INSTRUCTION

This section will help you form a vision of what Gloria's unit will look like by the time it is completed—and what you will be able to do by the time you finish this course. It provides a review of information in this chapter and a preview of the next stages in the planning process. If you read the text for understanding, complete each "Unit Preparation" exercise, and receive feedback on your unit elements from an expert, you should be able to enter your student teaching semester with confidence that you can plan and carry out units and lessons. The components of the unit on the Revolutionary War in this section are taken from an example of an interdisciplinary unit of instruction that combines social studies with language arts. More details on the unit are presented in the sample unit at the end of this text.

General Unit Planning

Wiggins and McTighe (1998) describe effective curriculum planning as "backward design" (p. 8). Backward design begins at the end, by identifying the desired results (goals, standards, and performances) first and then selecting the learning experiences necessary to get there. They identify three stages in backward design: (a) identify desired results, (b) determine acceptable evidence (assessment) that will help you determine whether you have achieved the desired results, and (c) plan learning experiences and instruction. Good unit planning is an example of backward design. A **unit** is a series of lessons that lead to the accomplishment of a broad goal. You will notice that the chapters in this text follow the stages of backward design as we progress through the unit-planning process: identifying outcomes and objectives, planning assessment strategies, and then considering various types of lessons. Of course there are times when an interesting lesson idea will impact your unit design, but in all cases unit planning should lead toward the achievement of an important goal, not simply provide an opportunity for a favorite activity. The final product usually includes the following components:

- Rationale and key questions
- Concept map with generalizations and facts
- Outcomes (goals), objectives, and preassessment activities
- Lesson plans with modifications for special needs
- Evaluation/assessment procedures (including an authentic culminating activity)
- Materials and resources

Rationale and Key Questions

The unit **rationale** is a brief statement that explains the content and purposes of the unit. The rationale is written for the students and for those who will be using the unit. It can focus attention on key unit issues, provide motivation, and justify the importance of the content in terms of subject matter, societal needs, and needs or interests of learners (see the discussion of Tyler's Curriculum Rationale earlier in this chapter). The rationale should be no more than a paragraph or two in length. An example of a rationale for the Revolution unit is found at the end of this text.

The **key questions** focus learners' curiosity on the unit because they have no easy answers and therefore invite exploration. Possible key questions for the Revolutionary War unit are: What made the Revolutionary War revolutionary? What kinds of leaders were important in the Revolution? What is the proper role of government?

Concept Map with Generalizations

As you have learned, the concept map creates a structure showing the main ideas, concepts, generalizations, and facts the students are to learn. Your district and state curriculum frameworks, along with your professional organization's content standards, will prove valuable in making these decisions. A teacher can present information in an orderly way only after a thorough and searching analysis of the content. Since it is not possible to teach everything about a subject, teachers must make decisions about essential ideas—concepts, generalizations, and facts—and then organize those ideas logically. Examples of content outlines and concept maps are provided earlier in this chapter as well as in the sample unit.

Of course, content can be organized through a single discipline, by multiple disciplines around a single topic, or around an interdisciplinary theme. If your unit is interdisciplinary, or thematically linked to other subjects your students are studying, your concept map would include multiple disciplines. A thematic unit would have the theme as a main concept, and the key question would be interdisciplinary in nature. For example, a unit focusing on the theme "Revolution" might center on the key question, What makes something a revolution? Content in that unit could include revolutions in science, music, or art in addition to political revolutions.

Outcomes and Preassessment

After deciding on the most important ideas in the unit, the teacher must decide what students should be able to do in order to demonstrate they understand the key ideas. These student performances are often called outcomes. They should include all cognitive, affective, and psychomotor outcomes relevant to the unit. Each outcome will need to be broken down into smaller, more specific objectives that lead to the outcome. These smaller objectives are sometimes known as **benchmarks**. (At other times the term *benchmark* is used to refer to a larger grade-level outcome that is used to meet a broad state or district curriculum standard. In either case a benchmark is a marker of progress on the way to a larger goal.)

Planning specific objectives will be presented in Chapter 4. How might this breakdown look in the unit on the Revolution? Refer to the social studies outcomes for the sample unit (listed earlier in this chapter). Look at outcome 13, "Evaluate one or more major events of the Revolutionary War from two contrasting points of view and use these multiple perspectives to create a story, play, newspaper, or three-dimensional model." This outcome may need to be broken down into several benchmarks or **enabling objectives** (smaller objectives that, combined, enable the student to accomplish the higher order task):

Long-Range Outcome

Students will be able to evaluate one or more major events of the Revolutionary War from two contrasting points of view and use these multiple perspectives to create a story, play, newspaper, or three-dimensional model.

Enabling Objectives

Students will be able to

1. describe events surrounding the Boston Tea Party, the Boston Massacre, the meeting of the Continental Congress, the winter at Valley Forge, and the signing of the Declaration of Independence
2. identify point of view in narrative and expository text
3. identify the major goals of the colonial and loyalist factions in the colonies
4. create a product of the student's choice (story, newspaper, play, etc.)

With this knowledge, students will be well equipped to create a product expressing multiple points of view. Without such clear breakdowns of necessary learning, the teacher may fail to provide the proper knowledge base for higher level tasks. For example, if students are never provided with guidance as to how to create and format the dialogue for a play, it is unlikely they will do so successfully. If the teacher presents content in a random order, it is impossible for students to incorporate key facts and understandings into the higher level projects that culminate the unit.

Instructional outcomes and objectives are valuable for two reasons. First, they help teachers assess the learners' readiness for the content and thinking required by the unit. You have read about the importance of diagnosing learners' prior knowledge, interests, and needs. A list of outcomes can help the teacher design a preassessment activity to discover what skills and understandings students bring to the unit. For example, before setting up a school store, the teacher would need to know if students are able to perform the required math and bookkeeping. Having such information before teaching allows the teacher to fill any gaps or provide extra support for the few students lacking the essential skills required for the unit.

Early diagnosis (preassessment) also helps to determine which students have already learned some of the unit's key concepts or skills. For example, imagine you are teaching a fourth-grade unit on the ecosystems. If some students had a third-grade teacher who devoted a good deal of time to the subject of the environment, you would want to find out what those students already know and believe about this topic. These students may need more advanced activities—for example, presenting their knowledge to others through a skit or a small play. Or they could be encouraged to pursue their learning in another area.

A second reason for creating enabling or benchmark objectives is that they indicate the logical progression of activities. As we saw in the example, without knowledge of major events, point of view, and the construction of various product options, students will have difficulty accomplishing the higher level task of creating a product that presents multiple points of view regarding a specific event.

After this process of choosing outcomes, preassessing students, and arranging smaller objectives in a logical order, you'll be ready to select an objective for your first lesson that is at the correct level of difficulty for most students. You will also know what knowledge, skills, and preconceptions students bring to the learning experiences you will provide in the unit. Finally, you will have considered your assessment methods, perhaps a combination of tests and projects (exhibits, portfolios, or performances). When you have completed these tasks, your instruction (and your students' learning) is likely to be more successful.

Assessment Procedures

In the assessment component, you plan how you will determine students' achievement of your objectives. Obviously, you should not wait until the end of your teaching to find out if students have learned anything. Chapter 5 stresses the importance of continuous assessment of students' learning. **Continuous assessment** means that you will want to find out how well students are learning throughout your teaching—before, during, and after learning activities (Wiggins, 1998).

As a teacher, you must think about what meanings, understandings, and beliefs your students are constructing out of the activities you design for them. But how do you find out what is actually going on in your students' heads—the meanings they are developing?

This is where continuous assessment comes in. The term **assessment** is used here instead of *evaluation* or *testing* in order to convey a less formal, but more continuous process.

One of the best ways to assess student progress is to talk to individual students (or listen in as they work in groups) and hear them explain their thinking. If you begin to use portfolios to document student learning, you will probably include a conference with students that will allow you to gather such information. Much can be learned by having students write about a product they have created, telling you why they like it and what makes it a "good" product. It is fascinating to read students' analyses of their own reasoning as they approach a problem or a project.

What can be gained by such ongoing inquiry into students' emerging constructions of meaning? The first insight most teachers report is how surprised they are at what they find. Quiet students often evidence profound insights when given time and an attentive ear. Troubled students begin to open up and share their thoughts. Students who take more time to learn are often constructing meanings in a mode (e.g., interpersonal, kinesthetic, spatial, musical) that is not being accessed by typical classroom activities. Paper-and-pencil tests given at the end of a unit cannot yield these insights. Nor are they very useful in pointing the way toward helping students learn more successfully. Continuous assessment of students' thinking through both written and spoken evidence can be a powerful force in redesigning instruction on the spot.

At the end of your unit, you will conduct a more comprehensive assessment that lets you know which students met which objectives. The final unit evaluation may be a combination of a test or other individual assessment and an authentic culminating project that combines many of the objectives. In the Revolutionary War unit, students might create a play that illustrates how individuals reacted to events of the time period. They would create the characters, give their backgrounds, and act out a situation that might exist in response to a particular event. The small plays would be presented to the class or to another grade level. They would be graded using a rubric to assess accuracy of life events and other quality standards.

Regardless of the method of assessment, the unit evaluation procedures should provide adequate information about each student's mastery of the most important unit objectives. As a result of this information, the teacher may choose to reteach certain crucial content, especially if later learning is dependent on that content. Continuous assessment of each objective provides information on how to modify the activities for students' individual needs. Many teachers refer to this decision-making process as *monitoring* (assessing) *and adjusting* (making needed changes).

Lesson Plans with Modifications for Special Needs

A *lesson* is a sequence of activities designed to help all students achieve one or more objectives. Once you have an objective for your first lesson, you are ready to design activities that will help students learn. What will these lessons look like? How will you modify some activities so that all students can succeed and be sufficiently challenged? That's what Chapters 4 through 9 are about: how to plan activities that systematically lead students to meet the learning objectives. Of course, all learners are not the same, so the lessons will need to be adjusted for individual learning needs.

Materials and Resources

What materials and resources do you need in order to teach the unit? Any books, visual aids, videos, or other media or materials should be listed at the end of the unit. You should also include a copy of any worksheets, overhead transparencies, computer resources, and other materials you plan to use. Organizing your material helps you stay on top of the logistical planning for each lesson. Often a video or special materials must be ordered well ahead of time. This long-range planning is crucial to smooth-running lessons. It also makes it easier to share your unit with others.

A bibliography will be of use for those who wish to use your unit. It provides the references for further reading, electronic information (e.g., websites), and other helpful resources on the unit topic.

SUMMARY

The chapter opened at a school meeting in the Taunton, Michigan, school system during which the approval of a multicultural/global education program became entangled in the continuing debate over the nature and mission of public schools in the United States. A review of the three major educational philosophies—progressivism, essentialism, and critical pedagogy—and the recommended process for generating educational goals using Tyler's Curriculum Rationale were presented. The central problem of Chapter 3 was introduced when Gloria Jackson agreed to lead the fifth-grade team of teachers to develop and design a new American Revolution unit by creating a set of goals for the unit and analyzing the content to be included in the unit. She chose to use concept mapping to display the relationships among key concepts. The final section of the chapter previewed how these goals could be used to shape a curriculum unit.

When you face the challenge of analyzing educational content, you will be aided by your understanding of the distinctions among cognitive, affective, and psychomotor content, especially the breakdown of cognitive content into generalizations, concepts, and facts. You should be able to analyze cognitive content and connect it to the analysis of learning process.

Practice Activity: Creating a Map for an Interdisciplinary Unit

Imagine you are on an interdisciplinary team planning a unit to be shared with two colleagues. Think of a topic or theme that would apply to at least three content areas. Place the central topic or theme in the middle of a sheet of paper and create a concept map that shows how concepts and topics from the various subject areas might be connected.

■ ■ ■

UNIT PREPARATION

One of the most important parts of your unit preparation is the selection and analysis of content. By now you should have chosen your unit topic, gathered information about it, and talked with the teacher about your students' particular needs. The next step in preparing your unit is choosing the specific content to teach. This will involve several steps. The order in which you take the steps may vary depending on your learning style.

Once you have identified the topic, you should review relevant state and national standards. The links listed under "Search the Web" will help you locate them. Plan an initial set of outcomes and match them to the relevant standards. Depending on your unit topic or theme, this may entail standards from one or more than one discipline. Probably most of your outcomes will be cognitive, but you should consider affective goals as well. Occasionally a psychomotor goal will also be appropriate.

Next you will need to organize the key content using an outline, a concept map, or both. Those with more linear (sequential) learning styles are likely to prefer to outline first, whereas those who prefer more holistic approaches may find it easier to start with a branching map. The more clearly the map delineates the relationships among concepts, the more helpful it will be.

Finally, you should list the key generalization(s) and/or focus question(s) and concepts that will form the core of your unit. You could even display these on a tree like that in Figure 3.7. You will want to select facts that will help students understand the concepts and generalizations that frame your unit. In order to keep your unit focused you probably will want to limit yourself to one to three generalizations and/or questions around which all other content is organized.

At the end of this process you should have the first draft of your content analysis including (a) a list of outcomes linked to relevant standards, (b) a concept map and/or content outline, and (c) a list of key generalizations and/or focus questions, concepts, and facts to be taught. Do not underestimate the importance of this section of unit planning. For many students, this is the most difficult—and most crucial—part of the planning process. In our experience, often students who have trouble planning teaching activities find that the core of their difficulties lies in confusion over the key content to be addressed. Take time, share your ideas with colleagues, and get feedback from your instructor. Since this is your first attempt, it is likely that you will need to revise your content analysis at least once before it is ready to use.

PORTFOLIO ACTIVITIES

A common interview question for beginning teachers is, "Describe your philosophy of education." You may find that your philosophy flows naturally from the metaphor you developed in Chapter 1. Begin now to write your educational philosophy. Consider what you believe to be the most important purpose(s) of schools and how that will affect your teaching decisions.

Several of the unit development activities discussed in this chapter can be adapted as part of a portfolio. A clear concept map can make the structure of your unit (and its emphasis on core concepts) evident to a reader who may not take the time to read every lesson. A "tree" illustration can serve a similar purpose.

It will be important to delineate the outcomes for your unit and how they relate to state standards, national standards, or both. This could be done either through a list of standards and benchmarks addressed or a grid relating unit outcomes to standards. If you plan to apply for teaching positions in more than one state, it would be wise to provide information on state standards for each locale.

 ## SEARCH THE WEB

State and national standards can be found through a variety of websites. Check the Companion Website under "Standards" for information on standards and standards sites. At this writing there are two exceptionally well-organized sites that may be helpful to you.

To find the state education agencies across the nation, go to

www.ccsso.org/seamenu.html

To find national professional organizations in various disciplines, go to

www.edweek.org/context/orgs/orgs.html

Also check the Companion Website for examples of discipline-based and interdisciplinary planning. You will find them under both "Curriculum" and "Instructional Strategies."

REFERENCES

Association for Supervision and Curriculum Development. (1993, September). *ASCD curriculum update* (p. 2). Alexandria, VA: Author.

Banks, J. A. (1993). Multicultural education: Progress and prospects. *Phi Delta Kappan, 75* (1), 25–27.

Banks, J. A. (1994). Transforming the mainstream curriculum. *Educational Leadership, 51* (8), 4–8.

Banks, J. A. (1995). *Multicultural education: Historical development: Dimensions, and practice.* Washington, DC: Educational Resources Information Center. (ERIC Document Reproduction Service No. ED 382 696)

Beane, J. (1997). *Curriculum integration: Designing the core of democratic education.* New York: Teachers College Press.

Bolte, L. (1997, March 24). *Assessing mathematical knowledge with concept maps and interpretive essays.* Paper presented at the Annual Conference of the American Educational Research Association, Chicago. (ERIC Document Reproduction Service No. ED 408 160)

Bridwell, N. (1997) *Clifford the big red dog.* New York: Scholastic Books.

Brophy, J., & VanSledright, B. (1997). *Teaching and learning history in elementary schools.* New York: Teachers College Press.

Bruner, J. E. (1960). *The process of education.* Cambridge, MA: Harvard University Press.

Carr, J. F., & Harris, D. E. (2001). *Succeeding with standards: Linking curriculum, assessment, and action planning.* Alexandria, VA: Association for Supervision and Curriculum Development.

Cheney, L. V. (1987). *American memory: A report on the humanities in the nation's public schools.* Washington, DC: National Endowment for the Humanities.

Costa, A.L., & Liebmann, R. M. (Eds.). (1997). *Envisioning process as content: Towards a renaissance curriculum.* Thousand Oaks, CA: Corwin Press Incorporated.

Counts, G. S. (1932). *Dare the schools build a new social order?* (pp. 7, 9–10). New York: John Day.

Davidman, L. (1994). *Teaching with a multicultural perspective.* New York: Longman Publishing Group.

Davidman, L. (1995). Multicultural education: A movement in search of meaning and positive connections. *Multicultural Education, 2* (3), 8–12.

Davidman, L., & Davidman, P. (1994). *Teaching with a multicultural perspective.* Washington, DC: Educational Resources Information Center. (ERIC Document Reproduction Service No. ED 382 696)

Feuer, M. J.(1995). *Anticipating goals 2000. Standards, assessment and public policy.* Summary of a workshop. Washington, DC: Educational Resources Information Center. (ERIC Document Reproduction Service No. ED 389 744)

Gardner, H. (1999). *The disciplined mind.* New York: Simon & Schuster.

Hakim, J. (1999). *From colonies to country.* New York: Oxford University Press.

Heinze-Fry, J. A., & Novak, J. D. (1990). Concept mapping brings long-term movement toward meaningful learning. *Science Education, 74* (4), 461–472.

Hirsch, E. D., Jr. (1987). *Cultural literacy: What every American needs to know.* Boston: Houghton Mifflin.

Holt, J. (1964). *How children fail.* New York: Pitman.

Holt, J. (1970). *How children learn.* New York: Pitman.

Jacobs, H. (1989). *Interdisciplinary curriculum: Design and implementation.* Alexandria, VA: Association for Supervision and Curriculum Development.

Jacobs, H. (1991, October). Planning for curriculum integration. *Educational Leadership, 49* (2), 27–28.

Lindquist, T., & Selwyn, D. (2000). *Social studies at the center.* Portsmouth, NH: Heinemann.

Meier, D. (Ed.). (2000). *Will standards save public education?* Boston: Beacon Press.

Michigan Department of Education. (1996). *Michigan Curriculum Framework.* Lansing, MI: Author.

Naidu, S. (1990). *Concept mapping.* Washington, DC: Educational Resources Information Center. (ERIC Document Reproduction Service No. ED 329 247)

Phenix, P. H. (1960, April). The topography of higher liberal learning. *Phi Delta Kappan, 41,* 307.

Plotnick, E. (1997). *Concept mapping: A graphical system for understanding the relationship between concepts.* (ERIC Document Reproduction Service No. ED 407 938)

Pruisner, P. (1996, October). Using graphics for integrated planning. In *VisionQuest: Journeys toward visual literacy.* Selected readings from the annual conference of the International Visual Literacy Association, Cheyenne, WY. (ERIC Document Reproduction Service No. ED 408 979)

Ravitch, D. (1983). *The troubled crusade: American education 1945–1980.* New York: Basic Books.

Ravitch, D. (1993). Launching a revolution in standards and assessment. *Phi Delta Kappan, 74* (10), 767–772.

Ravitch, D. E., & Finn, C. E., Jr. (1987). *What do our 17-year-olds know?* Washington, DC: National Endowment for the Humanities.

Reynolds, W. M., & Martusewicz, R. A. (1994). The practice of freedom: A historical analysis of critical perspective in the social foundations. In R. A. Martusewicz & W. M. Reynolds (Eds.), *Inside out: Contemporary critical perspectives in education* (pp. 223–238). New York: St. Martin's Press.

Roberts, P.L., & Kellough, R.D. (1996). *A guide for developing an interdisciplinary thematic unit.* Upper Saddle River, NJ: Merrill/Prentice Hall.

Shavelson, A. J. (1974). Methods for examining representations of subject-matter structure in a student's memory. *Journal of Research in Science Teaching, 11* (3), 231–249.

Shulman, L. S. (1986, February). Those who understand: Knowledge growth in teaching. *Educational Researcher, 15* (2), 4–14.

Stanley, W. B., & Nelson, J. L. (1994). The foundations of social education in historical context. In R. A. Martusewicz & W. M. Reynolds (Eds.), *Inside out: Contemporary critical perspectives in education* (pp. 265–284) New York: St. Martin's Press.

Thompson, S. (2001). The authentic standards movement and its evil twin. *Phi Delta Kappan, 82* (5), 358–362.

Tyler, R. (1969). *Basic principles of curriculum and instruction.* Chicago: University of Chicago Press.

Webster's new collegiate dictionary. (1981). Springfield, MA: G. & C. Merriam.

Wiggins, G. (1998). *Educative assessment: Designing assessment to inform and improve practice.* San Francisco: Jossey-Bass.

Wiggins, G., & McTighe, J. (1998). *Understanding by design.* Alexandria, VA: Association for Supervision and Curriculum Development.

Wiske, M. S. (Ed.). (1998). *Teaching for understanding.* San Francisco: Jossey-Bass.

Zarnowski, M., & Gallagher, A.F. (1993). *Children's literature and social studies.* Washington, DC: National Council for the Social Studies.

CHAPTER 4

Planning Educational Outcomes

CHAPTER OVERVIEW

Once upon a time a Sea Horse gathered up his seven pieces of eight and cantered out to find his fortune. Before he had traveled very far he met an Eel who said, "Psst. Hey bud. Where 'ya goin'?"

"I'm going out to find my fortune," replied the Sea Horse, proudly.

"You're in luck," said the Eel. "For four pieces of eight you can have this speedy flipper, and then you'll be able to get there a lot faster."

"Gee, that's swell" said the Sea Horse, and paid the money and put on the flipper and slithered off at twice the speed.

Soon he came upon a Sponge, who said, "Psst. Hey bud. Where 'ya goin'?"

"I'm going out to find my fortune," replied the Sea Horse, proudly.

"You're in luck," said the Sponge. "For a small fee I will let you have this jet-propelled scooter so that you will be able to travel a lot faster." So the Sea Horse bought the scooter with his remaining money and went zooming thru the sea five times as fast.

Soon he came upon a Shark who said, "Psst. Hey bud. Where 'ya goin'?"

"I'm going out to find my fortune," replied the Sea Horse.

"You're in luck. If you take this short cut," said the Shark, pointing to his open mouth, "you'll save yourself a lot of time."

"Gee, thanks," said the Sea Horse, and zoomed off into the interior of the Shark, and was never heard from again.

The moral of this fable is that if you're not sure where you're going, you're liable to wind up someplace else. And if you have not clarified what it will look like when you get there, you might never know it when you do arrive!

"The Sea Horse Fable*" (Mager, 1997) provides whimsical support to those who value clearly written instructional objectives. Furthermore, it introduces you to the content of Section 1 of this chapter, the transformation of curriculum goals into clearly stated instructional objectives. Whether you plan to develop your own educational goals or use the standards and benchmarks developed in state or national curriculum frameworks and assessment programs, the process of transforming goals into teachable objectives will enhance your effectiveness. It is probably obvious that you will be most effective in helping children learn something if you know exactly what it will look like if they have learned it. But, clearly stated learning objectives provide another bonus: they help you develop assessments that will provide concrete evidence of what children know, can do, and are like. You can then use this information before, during, and after lessons to tailor your activities for specific student needs. Without a clear vision of the desired learning, it will be almost impossible to design assessments to determine if that learning is present.

In Chapter 3 you learned how to select and analyze educational goals. In the first section of this chapter you will learn how to write, classify, and evaluate clearly stated objectives for your students' learning. In Section 2 you will learn how to write clearly stated objectives at differing levels of cognitive development. Chapter 5 will help you learn how to assess student learning; but it all begins with clearly stated learning outcomes/objectives.

SECTION 1. WRITING CLEARLY STATED OBJECTIVES

■ *Opening Activity*

It's early October and time for family night at the Fairhill Elementary School in the Taunton, Michigan, school district. The evening begins with remarks by school officials, who request parent participation on district committees and task forces. The principal closes the general session by reporting on school progress as well as the opportunities and challenges of the coming year. Finally, the parents disperse to follow their children's class schedule and meet with the teachers. This will give them an opportunity to form a personal impression of the teachers. As a result of their children's enthusiasm, many of the parents come expecting to be impressed. Only a few anticipate being bored or irritated. Most parents have a "give the teacher credit, it's a difficult job" attitude. They arrive hoping to be informed about the work their children are doing in school. A substantial number of parents seek guidance from the teacher concerning the parents' role in reinforcing school goals and tasks.

Imagine yourself as an invisible observer able to flit from room to room, listening to the teachers introducing their educational plans and programs for the coming year to groups of parents. Specifically, you attend the sessions in two fifth-grade classrooms where the focus of attention is on a new unit titled "American Revolution." What follows is a partial transcript of the sessions in these classrooms, in the form of two case studies. After reading the two case studies, answer the questions that follow.

Room 214: Mr. Abrams

Mr. Abrams: A school district curriculum group led by Ms. Jackson developed this unit last year and we are expected to teach it at Fairhill and at the other elementary schools in the district. So that's what we will be doing as an interdisciplinary study combining social studies and language arts this marking period.

Mr. Vasquez (parent): Mr. Abrams, what are the goals you hope to achieve as you teach the unit to our children?

Mr. Abrams: I would have to reexamine the teacher's guide that came with the unit to describe the specific goals, but in general, I expect to teach my students about the key events from 1763–1783 and the people who lived through them.

Mrs. Washington (parent): That sounds OK to me, but can you tell me a little more about what my daughter will know when she completes this unit?

Mr. Abrams: I really am not prepared to do that at this time. Remember, some of the responsibility for learning rests with the student and also with the parents. My responsibility is to provide general direction for the students and give them the materials from which they will learn.

Mr. Lassiver (parent): I believe in assisting the teachers by knowing what's expected of my child and encouraging and helping my child to study at home. Under your approach it will be difficult for me to do that.

Mr. Abrams: Possibly we should discuss that at the parent-teacher conference scheduled between us. Thank you all for coming tonight, and I look forward to meeting individually with you on conference day in November to discuss your child's progress.

Room 212: Mrs. Calzone

Mrs. Calzone: One of the highlights of this year's social studies course of study is the interdisciplinary, social studies and language arts unit, "The Revolutionary War" developed last year by a school district curriculum group led by Gloria Jackson, one of our fifth-grade teachers here at Fairhill. I have examined the unit and am prepared to teach it. I have added some features to the unit that make it especially useful for my students.

Mr. Sarason (parent): Mrs. Calzone, what are the goals you hope to achieve as you teach the unit to our children?

Mrs. Calzone: That's a good question. In fact, I have prepared a handout to give to each of you. The handout includes the goals as well as some recommended activities you can do at home to assist your youngster to achieve the goals.

Mrs. Rodriguez (parent): I'm glad these are written clearly! I also appreciate the fact that the goals are written directly to students. The goal to "explain how the American Revolution affected various persons—patriots, loyalists, rich, poor, women, Native Americans, and African Americans" is especially interesting to me as a Native American. I hope you succeed in getting my son, Tony, to see the differences.

Mrs. Calzone: Thanks for the expression of support, Mrs. Rodriguez! I am hoping that the adults and the older brothers and sisters will be involved in some of the goals and activities in the unit. There are two instructional objectives that you might ask your son or daughter about. They involve class projects that we will all do together. One of these objectives is for students to select a work of historical fiction written about the Revolutionary War period and "describe and discuss the shared human experience depicted in that work of fiction." A second is to "evaluate one or more major events of the Revolutionary War from two contrasting points of view and to create a story, play, newspaper, or three-dimensional model." I hope you will all show interest in those projects. In fact we will be beginning the second project in two weeks. May I have your participation?

All Parents in Unison: Yes. (enthusiastic applause)

Mrs. Calzone: Thank you all for coming tonight, and I look forward to meeting individually with you on conference day in November to discuss each student's progress.

Consider the interactions that occurred in this scenario. Which teacher do you think was more effective in developing a positive relationship with parents? Why? Think about the relationship between "The Sea Horse Fable" and the two case studies. This chapter will consider what it means to "know where you are going" in planning for instruction and how that will be reflected in your activities as a teacher.

■ ■ ■

CHAPTER OBJECTIVES

After you have completed this section, you will be able to

1. defend or reject the position that teachers who use instructional objectives are more successful in generating student learning than are those who do not;
2. explain the advantages and disadvantages of using instructional objectives and make decisions accordingly;
3. analyze the argument for the use of understanding performances;
4. define the A, B, C, D characteristics of a clearly stated objective; and
5. classify examples of educational statements as clearly stated objectives.

Objectives and Understanding Performances

Few will argue that one of the most important decisions a teacher makes involves the intended learning of students—the outcomes or results of teaching. Although there has long been a controversy about the value of instructional objectives, those who support them argue that if teachers expect to achieve success, they must be able to define success, and then assess students' progress in reaching it. To advocates, the success of teaching is measured by the congruence between their objectives and student learning. That is, objectives enable the teacher to be sure the learning experiences provided for the children match or support the development of the learning described in the objective.

Some supporters of the use of instructional objectives believe that all learning outcomes can be measured in some useful way. Other, more pragmatic proponents are willing to concede that some outcomes are beyond easy measurement by the teacher. However, all advocates agree that teachers who use clearly stated instructional objectives are likely to be more successful in enhancing the learning of their students than are teachers who do not use them. Opponents of instructional objectives voice concern that focus on measurable outcomes may cause educators to focus on objectives that are easy to measure rather than those that are important, leading to fragmented or shallow instruction.

The authors of this text believe that the argument for and against the use of instructional objectives is a false one. Consider the benefits of planning instruction using meaningful criteria that includes *both* the use of higher level cognitive objectives *and* the use of meaningful, open-ended, creative activities. When teachers teach for understanding they structure learning to engage students in **understanding performances**, authentic tasks that enable students to achieve powerful learning outcomes (Gardner, 1999). Teaching for understanding through the creation of understanding performances differs from the traditional view of successful learning as demonstrated by students answering worksheets correctly or receiving 100% on an exam. The view of *understanding as performance* requires that each student continuously apply specific knowledge and skills within a meaningful context—an authentic task, project, performance, or exhibit. That is, students do something that demonstrates their understanding. It is important to clarify that an understanding performance is only meaningful *if it has been carefully designed to meet important higher level learning objectives*. Simply because an activity is "hands-on" does not mean it addresses central concepts and generalizations or builds important skills. Wiske (1998) makes this point clear when summarizing the characteristics of an understanding performance.

An understanding performance

- relates directly to important learning goals
- allows students to develop and apply understanding through practice
- engages students' multiple learning styles and encourages diverse forms of expression
- promotes reflective engagement in challenging, approachable tasks
- requires students to perform in ways that others—peers, parents, or community members—can view and respond

What do these criteria look like when enacted within the classroom setting? Enter a classroom where cooperative learning groups are engaged in understanding performances. In one area, huddled around a computer, four children use a search engine to find information on a research topic. In the class library another group has pulled some books from the shelves. Children are sitting on the rug reading in pairs with their learning logs open. In other areas of the room children sit in clusters designing maps from clay and cardboard, using an atlas as a reference. The teacher is meeting with another group to assist them with the organization of their report. Posing questions, asking for clarification, and offering suggestions, the teacher guides from the sidelines. Charts, graphs, a word wall, learning centers, and reference materials all signal a room where children have opportunities to learn according to their needs and interests. In such a learning environment mistakes are expected as opportunities for understanding as a student gradually approximates more refined ways of thinking and performing. The environment may be more analogous to a laboratory where children explore, analyze, draw conclusions, and present their ideas in creative and meaningful ways.

In this scenario, the teacher recognizes the rich possibilities for learning inherent in research activities. Her main instructional objectives include teaching students to access multiple resources; to efficiently and effectively gather, organize, and present information; and to analyze and evaluate a body of content in order to draw important conclusions. These instructional objectives will be reached by *all* students, even while individual students will achieve other outcomes depending upon their ability, interest, and learning styles. In this classroom the conflict over the use of instructional objectives has been resolved. Clear purposes and instructional objectives are coupled with the use of open-ended and generative activities that lead to diverse and complex learning outcomes. The focus on understanding performances represents a synthesis, the creation of a new idea that incorporates the best elements of instructional objectives with the important elements of creativity and higher level thinking. Proponents of understanding performances set goals for student behavior and organize instruction to meet those goals. They are concerned with complex learning, problem solving, and individual variation.

An important decision teachers must make in unit planning is which aspects of the unit are important enough to merit demonstration in an understanding performance. Given a finite amount of time, choices must be made about which content will be taught for understanding and which will be taught in less depth—or not taught at all. Wiggins and McTighe (1998) offer four guidelines for selecting knowledge to be taught for understanding. They believe such material should:

- Represent a big idea having enduring value beyond the classroom.
- Reside at the heart of the discipline (involve "doing" the subject").
- Require uncoverage (of abstract or often misunderstood ideas).
- Offer potential for engaging students. (p. 23)

Notice how your analysis of key generalizations and concepts, as well as your understanding of authentic learning, provides you with the keys for choosing content to be demonstrated in understanding performances.

As discussed in Chapter 3, an educational goal or outcome provides general direction to the teacher in making crucial decisions about instruction. Although both goals and objectives describe student rather than teacher behavior, a goal generally covers more content than an objective does and thus is phrased more broadly. In that respect, a goal is similar in nature to a standard as it is used in curriculum frameworks and assessment programs. For example, a goal might encompass the content that will be taught in a semester or yearlong course or even a long unit, whereas an instructional objective might cover the content for a weeklong unit or for a single day's lesson plan. An **instructional objective** is defined as a specific statement of what the student will know or be able to do after the unit or lesson ends. Whereas goals are related to standards, instructional objectives are related more closely to benchmarks. Instructional objectives can be developed for all types of content (affective, psychomotor, or cognitive), in all subject areas, and across all grade levels. They can be conceived and written at all levels of subject matter, from facts to concepts to generalizations, and at all levels of learning process, from knowledge to evaluation. When prepared properly, instructional objectives can be used to plan learning activities that will teach the content as well as provide evaluation procedures to assess student learning of that content.

Recognizing Clearly Stated Instructional Objectives

To help you assess what you know already about clearly stated instructional objectives, read the following examples and be ready to explain which ones are complete instructional objectives.

Students will

1. analyze and explain the political, economic, and territorial causes of the American Revolution
2. show a deep understanding of basic concepts such as *revolution, liberty, democracy, equality*, and so on
3. value the importance of ethics when making decisions
4. describe the conflict between the views of loyalists and patriots by writing an original short story that accurately reflects the views held during the Revolutionary War period
5. participate in a literature discussion circle regarding a biography of one important leader or common person of the Revolutionary period

6. create an original five-line poem or song lyric related to the Revolutionary War period that is similar in style to those presented in class
7. strive to value and appreciate the perspectives of others
8. summarize the main points of the Declaration of Independence
9. identify the persuasive forms of communication used by the individual authors and speakers of the American revolutionary period and analyze how their words influenced audience expectations
10. develop an argument by writing a one-page essay explaining why the concept of equality was considered revolutionary in 1776

Items 4, 6, and 10 are the most complete instructional objectives. Why are they classified as complete instructional objectives while the other items are not? Using the language of instructional designers, they pass the "behavior test" that distinguishes an educational goal from an instructional objective; that is, both the content to be learned and the expected learning process and level are described. Let's examine item 4 and determine what elements contained within it make it an acceptable instructional objective:

> Students will describe the conflict between the views of loyalists and patriots by writing an original short story that accurately reflects the views held during the Revolutionary War period.

Element 1. *What is to be learned?*

What is to be learned is the knowledge of the views held by loyalists and patriots during the Revolutionary War period (clear content description).

Element 2. *Learning process and level.*

The learning process is to write (clearly understood process). The learning level is synthesis, since the verb *write* refers to tasks at that level. (See Table 4.1 later in this chapter.)

An instructional objective must describe how the student is to demonstrate achievement of the objective. In item 4 it is by writing an original short story. In item 6 it is by creating a poem or song lyric. In item 10 it is by writing an essay. These examples illustrate the "by clause" of an instructional objective. Sometimes the by clause adds clarity to the verb that identifies the learning process as in item 4, in which the learning process is to "develop," and the by clause is "by writing an original short story." Another approach is illustrated in item 6, in which the by clause "create an original five-line poem or song lyric" contains the action verb *create*.

When used in conjunction with curriculum frameworks and assessment programs, instructional objectives add clarity to benchmarks. Benchmarks typically describe "what is to be learned." Often the **learning process** is included, but they seldom include the way students are expected to demonstrate achievement of the benchmark. This is especially true for "understanding performances" as we have defined them. For example, consider the "Historical Perspective" standard in the Michigan Framework for Social Studies Education Content Standards (1996). One of the benchmarks to be achieved within that standard is to "differentiate between historical facts and historical interpretations." When a by clause is added the instructional objective becomes:

> Students will differentiate between historical facts and interpretations by identifying them in an account of an event such as the Boston Massacre of 1770.

A second example is from the "Time and Chronology" standard. A benchmark to be achieved is to "distinguish among the past, present and the future." When the by clause is added the instructional objective becomes:

> Students will distinguish among the past, present and the future by identifying examples of each from a diary entry written by a Revolutionary War character.

Let's turn our attention to some items in the list that are *not* complete instructional objectives.

Item 2. Students will show a deep understanding of basic concepts such as *revolution, liberty, democracy, equality,* and so on.

Item 5. Students will participate in a literature discussion circle regarding a biography of one important leader or common person of the Revolutionary period.

CHECK YOUR UNDERSTANDING

Why are items 2 and 5 not complete instructional objectives? Stop and consider your answer before continuing.

First, consider item 2: Students will show a deep understanding of basic concepts such as *revolution, liberty, democracy, equality,* and so on.

Element 1. *What is to be learned?*

> What is to be learned is a "deep understanding" of a set of named concepts. (Although the list of concepts is clear, what does a "deep understanding" mean? Unclear content description.)

Element 2. *Learning process and level.*

> The learning process is *to show.* How will the student show a deep understanding—through a written exam, in a paper, in an oral exam? (Unclear process.)

An example of a rewritten item 2 that conforms to the behavior requirement of an instructional objective follows:

> When given a paragraph that describes one of the following concepts— *revolution, liberty, democracy,* or *equality*—without naming it, the student will identify which concept is being described and explain in a written paragraph why it is the correct one.

The second unacceptable example of an instructional objective is item 5. This item is actually a classroom activity, not an instructional objective, the expected outcome from an activity. Be careful of this trap when writing objectives. Many teachers are more comfortable writing the activity the student will engage in rather than the learning that will result from the activity and how it will be demonstrated in an assessment.

Take a closer look at item 5: Students will participate in a literature discussion circle regarding a biography of one important leader or common person of the Revolutionary period.

Element 1. *What is to be learned?*

What is to be learned is the important facts and other information about a person who lived during the Revolutionary War period. The topic is somewhat broad.

Element 2. *Learning process and level.*

The learning process is to participate in a discussion, which is a learning activity, not the result or outcome of the activity. Thus an appropriate by clause is needed to accompany the verb. (Unclear learning process.)

An example of a rewritten item 5 that conforms to the behavior requirement of an instructional objective follows:

After participating in a literature discussion circle regarding a biography of one important leader or common person of the Revolutionary period, the student will list five facts from that person's life that affected his or her views about the Revolutionary War.

Writing Clearly Stated Instructional Objectives

A clearly stated instructional objective must contain a behavior statement and may include several other characteristics. A helpful way to remember four characteristics of a traditional behavior objective is to use the A, B, C, D mnemonic aid, or memory device. Although not all instructional objectives will contain all four components, some beginning teachers find it helpful to consider each characteristic in turn. (You might want to stop for a moment and consider which teacher learning style might be reflected in this preference.)

Clearly stated instructional objectives are developed from educational goals to be achieved by a particular student or students, identified in the *audience (A)* statement. The following examples are audience statements:

Fifth-grade students will demonstrate the ability to:
Art students will be able to:
Students who complete their other assignments will show they can:
Students in language arts will:

Often the audience statement becomes the stem for a set of instructional objectives, as in the following example for a unit:

After completing this unit, fifth-grade students will be able to:

The *behavior (B)* requirement must be a concrete, observable action that illustrates the nature of the learning. Therefore, statements such as "Students will learn their action verbs" and "Students will know how to design an experiment" are not observable specific behaviors. Similarly, statements that describe activities designed to produce learning (e.g., "Students will watch a movie") are not clearly stated instructional objectives.

A *conditions (C)* statement is included when special circumstances are present that may affect student performance. Conditions may be equipment or material to be used by the student, a time requirement, or some other limitations within which the student is expected to perform. If there are no special circumstances, a conditions statement may be omitted from the objective. The following are four examples of conditions statements:

Using the outline map provided
Given a set of data never seen before and class notes
Given a calculator
As a volunteer

Conditions often describe the materials that may be used by the student when producing the product or performance to be used as evidence of learning. Referring to the preceding examples, there is an assumption that if the student in the second example can perform the problem-solving activity with the materials available, the learning is considered acceptable. The fourth example is used with an affective objective that aims to increase student participation in voluntary social improvement projects.

A *degree (D)* statement describes the criteria or standards that will be used by the instructor to determine whether the student has achieved the instructional objective being tested. The degree statement explains how the student product (i.e., written exam, model, painting, short story, research paper) or performance (i.e., speech, song, sprint, discussion) will be graded. There are two ways that a degree statement may be expressed. The first is in quantitative terms. *Quantitative degree statements* are typically associated with teaching lessons in which the subject matter yields "right" answers rather than "best" answers. Quantitative degree statements also are associated with the lower level learning processes of knowledge and application rather than the higher level processes of synthesis and evaluation. The following five examples are quantitative degree statements:

Achieving 7 out of 10 correct
With 75% accuracy
Listing at least 3 reasons
Using 10 of the unit's vocabulary words
Making 5 of 10 free throws

Qualitative degree statements refer to the teacher's assessment of a complex student behavior. Often, qualitative degree statements are difficult to construct. They require teachers to determine the form and substance of the minimally acceptable student product or performance, and guide students in the preparation of their assignments. These criteria, when used to assess a complex task, are often configured as *scoring rubrics*. Four examples of qualitative degree statements follow:

Essays will be judged on the accuracy of factual statements, relevance to the topic, persuasive appeal, and mechanics (sentence structure, spelling, word usage, organization, and coherence).
Radio commercials will be judged on how appealing they make the product to potential customers, on clarity, and on proper use of language.

Art projects will be graded on whether they show three or more colors, and use perspective to present a street scene as described in the assignment.

Travel brochures will be graded according to the following criteria (rubric): (a) accurate information on costs, mileage, and other details, (b) attractive pictures and drawings, (c) interest and appeal for the potential customer, and (d) correct use of the language.

For additional examples of clearly stated objectives, let's return to the Revolutionary War unit developed by Gloria Jackson and her interdisciplinary team of fifth-grade teachers. Following are (a) a unit rationale that describes the content to the student and justifies its importance, and (b) some clearly stated objectives that the team created to guide student learning.

Unit Rationale: Revolutionary War Actions and Reactions (1763–1783)

Have you ever wondered what it would be like to live in Philadelphia in 1776 at the time when the United States was born? Why did some people wave the flag of the new country while others still were loyal to England? How did the Revolutionary War affect different kinds of people such as farmers, merchants, Native Americans, African Americans, the rich, and the poor? What ideas that were discussed at the time of the Revolutionary War have become identified with our country? How well do we as a country live up to our beliefs in democracy, freedom, and equality? When do people have the right to rebel against their government? What people and events should we remember about the Revolutionary War period? These questions among others will be answered in our Revolutionary War unit.

Unit Objectives

When this unit is completed, fifth-grade students will

1. when given a list of facts about the people, events, things, and ideas from the Revolutionary War period , identify them on an exam and match each fact with a statement that identifies it
2. when given the facts about the Revolutionary War described in objective 1, create a poster or handbill or newspaper editorial that attempts to persuade the reader to support a position about some event or idea
3. after participating in a literature discussion circle regarding a biography of one important leader or common person of the Revolutionary period, list five facts from that person's life that affected his or her views about the Revolutionary War
4. after listening to the lyrics of a song written during the Revolutionary War period, express an emotional reaction to it from different points of view such as a patriot or loyalist
5. when given a paragraph that describes one of the following concepts—*revolution, liberty, democracy*, or *equality*—identify which concept is being described and explain in a written paragraph why it is the correct one

6. create a description of life in colonial America in 1775 by writing an original diary entry between 250 and 500 words that accurately reflects the lifestyle of a person who lived there
7. rewrite the first paragraph of the Declaration of Independence in his or her own words and justify in a classroom presentation that the meaning has not been changed
8. develop an argument, by writing a brief, one-page essay that contains at least three reasons why the concept of equality was considered revolutionary in 1776
9. create an original five-line poem or song lyric related to the Revolutionary War period that is similar in style to those presented in class
10. place at least 10 events from the Revolutionary War period (1763–1783) on a time line that can be displayed in the classroom (the display should be on butcher paper that is at least 5 feet long)

Diane Jordan's unit on patterns might include objectives like the following.
     Kindergarten students will

1. describe the characteristics of a fabric that define it as a pattern
2. when shown the first three to five cubes in a block sequence on an overhead, arrange colored cubes in a pattern that repeats at least twice
3. when given a page patterned after the book *Brown Bear Brown Bear What Do You See?*, draw a picture and dictate a sentence continuing the pattern
4. when given a collection of leaves, sort them into those that have a branching pattern and those that do not

     ■ *Practice Activity: Writing Clearly Stated Instructional Objectives*

Write three clearly stated instructional objectives for a teaching lesson or unit of your choice: one psychomotor, one cognitive, and one affective (see Section 2 of Chapter 3 to review these categories). Each objective should include the behavior requirement and either or both the conditions and degree requirements. Label the behavior, conditions, and degree elements of the objectives.

■ ■ ■

REFLECTING ON THE IDEAS

Objectives can give important focus to your teaching, but there may be times when the wisest course is to alter your planned objective or abandon it entirely. When might this occur?

SECTION 2. WRITING OBJECTIVES AT DIFFERENT LEVELS OF COGNITIVE LEARNING

Section 2 Objectives

As a result of working with this section, you will demonstrate the ability to

1. identify the six levels of Bloom's taxonomy and how they relate to teaching for understanding;

2. correctly label an unfamiliar objective using the taxonomy;
3. create clearly stated objectives at the knowledge, comprehension, application, analysis, synthesis, and evaluation levels of the cognitive domain; and
4. use the taxonomy to put objectives into a logical teaching order.

Teaching for Understanding

What does understanding look like? As you consider ways to help students understand key content, one of the most important decisions you will make is what you will ask students to *do* with the content to demonstrate their understanding. What understanding performance will you require? You know that demonstrating understanding requires that students do more than just recall information. Wiggins and McTighe (1998) list six facets of mature understanding. Consider what these facets might look like when demonstrated by young people.

When we truly understand, we

- Can *explain:* provide thorough, supported, and justifiable accounts of phenomena, facts, and data.
- Can *interpret:* tell meaningful stories; offer personal dimension to ideas and events; make it personal or accessible through images, anecdotes, analogies, and models.
- Can *apply:* effectively use and adapt what we know in diverse contexts.
- Have *perspective:* see and hear points of view through critical eyes and ears; see the big picture.
- Can *empathize:* find value in what others might find odd, alien, or implausible; perceive sensitively on the basis of prior direct experience.
- Have *self-knowledge:* perceive the personal style, prejudices, projections, and habits of mind that both shape and impede our own understanding; we are aware of what we do not understand why understanding is so hard. (p. 44)

As you plan for understanding performances, you will want to plan activities that require students to explain, interpret, and apply information; to view ideas from differing perspectives; and to consider their own thought processes. Considering students'

How Will You Ask Students to Demonstrate Understanding?

own thought processes is discussed in the section on metacognition in Chapter 8. However, one of the most common frameworks for considering the remaining activities is Bloom's taxonomy of cognitive objectives. As you consider possible instructional objectives, the taxonomy can be a powerful tool in analyzing whether the objectives are demonstrating understanding or simple recall.

Bloom's Taxonomy

The most widely used process for ordering cognitive learning tasks is the taxonomy of educational objectives, first conceived by educational psychologist Benjamin Bloom and his colleagues in the 1950s. There are separate taxonomies for each of the three domains of learning objectives: one for cognitive tasks, a second for affective tasks, and a third for psychomotor tasks. This section concentrates on the cognitive domain, first presented in *Taxonomy of Educational Objectives: Handbook I. Cognitive Domain* (1956).

Through Bloom's taxonomy you can accomplish all of the following:

1. Place instructional objectives into a logical teaching sequence
2. Be more precise in planning objectives and learning activities
3. Plan and implement lessons at higher thinking levels
4. Create assessment procedures and items that are consistent with instructional objectives and activities
5. Decide when to pursue an alternative objective that is suggested by students

There are six categories of intellectual objectives included in the cognitive domain taxonomy: knowledge, comprehension, application, analysis, synthesis, and evaluation. These categories are also considered to be hierarchical. Thus they are designated as levels. The levels range from the lowest cognitive learning tasks (knowledge) to the most complex tasks (evaluation). It is assumed that higher level tasks subsume tasks at a lower level. Thus an application level task also obligates students to demonstrate knowledge; an evaluation level task requires the student to perform successfully at all the other levels of the taxonomy.

The taxonomy was developed to assist teachers as they create instructional goals and objectives, plan instructional tasks and activities, and design testing procedures. Over the years, thousands of teachers have derived benefit by using Bloom's taxonomy. For example, as teachers define tasks for each of the six taxonomic levels, they develop lessons that provide variety and more complex thought for students. Furthermore, the higher level tasks (synthesis and evaluation) can only be found within complex activities with generous amounts of student participation. As teachers attempt to include these tasks, they implement activities that otherwise might be overlooked. The activities of applying, interpreting, and evaluating knowledge from multiple perspectives are all found in the higher levels of Bloom's taxonomy.

As useful as the taxonomy is, two caveats must be issued. First, the boundaries between some category levels are not sharply defined (e.g., between application and analysis). Second, many complex tasks include a bundle of behaviors. Thus it may be difficult to classify the task into only one of the six levels. Reasonable people can argue over the decision to classify an objective into a particular level. Although these arguments may be interesting, the precise placement of an objective into a particular level is usually not of fundamental importance. What is fundamental is that the instructional tasks planned, implemented, and evaluated by the teacher include the higher levels of the taxonomy. Students will then have the opportunity to manipulate information (apply, analyze, synthesize, and evaluate) rather than simply repeat it back to the teacher. When students manipulate information in meaningful ways, learning is more likely to be enhanced. Each level of the taxonomy is described in the paragraphs that follow.

Knowledge (Memory)

The first level of the taxonomy is knowledge. Tasks at the knowledge level oblige the student to recall, recognize, or reproduce what has been previously learned. Usually, the teacher prompts the recall in the same or similar manner as it was originally learned. Answers are predictable and tend to be either right or wrong. For example, a teacher writes the words *patriots* and *loyalists* on the chalkboard and the next day asks the class to recall them from memory and to write them on a sheet of paper. If the teacher had asked for an oral recitation of the names, the task would remain at the knowledge level. Regardless of the nature of the content that must be recalled, whether generalizations, concepts, or specific facts, if the task is only to recall what was learned from the teacher or from some other source of information, the task remains at the knowledge level.

Examples of knowledge tasks are:

1. Recall the definition of *democracy*.
2. State the name of the king of England during the Revolutionary War.
3. List three events that occurred during the Revolutionary War.
4. Identify the 13 colonies on a map.
5. Recognize the names of English and American military leaders during the Revolutionary War.
6. Identify circles, squares, and triangles in a pattern.
7. Recognize words with an "at" ending.

Comprehension (Understanding)

The second level of the taxonomy is comprehension. At the comprehension level, students understand material and can express it in their own words or in a similar form. They may recall previously learned material and either express it in a different way or the teacher may prompt the understanding in a new form. If the teacher asks students to describe in their own words the meaning of *colonialism*, the task is at the comprehension level. Or, if the teacher asks students to pick out the definition when written by different persons using different words to communicate the same meaning, the task is also one of comprehension.

Other examples of comprehension tasks are:

1. Summarize the major events during the Revolutionary War period.
2. Discuss the differences between loyalists and patriots.
3. Describe the meaning of the first paragraph of the Declaration of Independence.
4. Draw a map showing the encirclement of the British at Yorktown.

5. Define *democracy* using your own words.
6. Describe the pattern in a drawing or piece of fabric.
7. Define a patterned book.

Because both knowledge and comprehension involve only the retrieval of information, they are sometimes referred to as the lower levels of Bloom's taxonomy. That does not mean that lower level tasks are easy or unimportant. Describing the mathematical processes involved in stepwise multiple regression is, after all, a comprehension level task! The information gained at the lower levels often forms the background knowledge needed to successfully complete tasks at the higher levels.

Application

It is at this level (and those that follow) that students are required to exhibit complex thought as well as the retrieval of information. There is a guiding rule that distinguishes application and the other higher levels of thought. Students must not only recall and understand content, they must do something with it. If students are to demonstrate that they can manipulate information, the teacher must include some novel element in the task the student is expected to complete. A typical task at the application level is to provide unfamiliar math or science data, a historical incident, a quotation, a painting, or a musical selection and ask the student if it is an example of a concept that has been previously learned. Students might also be asked to make a relatively simple computation to illustrate that they can apply the concept appropriately.

Some examples of application tasks include the following:

1. Given a mixed set of items that are either revolutionary or evolutionary, correctly classify them.
2. Generate new examples of the revolutionary developments in the world today.
3. Identify an example of democracy in a piece of literature not previously studied.
4. When given a description of colonial life in America in 1775, identify the entries that do not fit with what we know about the period.
5. Classify arguments that support the patriot and loyalist positions in 1776.
6. Cut out a section of a magazine that could be considered a pattern.
7. Sort series of shapes into those that are patterns and those that are not.

Analysis

At the analysis level, the task given to the student consists of unfamiliar data and/or examples but requires a more complex thought process than is elicited from an application task. Analysis requires the taking apart of a complex stimulus. Students examine the information or data provided as evidence and make inferences or hypotheses. Analysis demands that students go beyond the information to draw conclusions. For example, students could be given a story of a family's activities including purchases of goods and services. They are told to find the three purchases that are "poor" buys and three that are "sensible" buys and write a sentence explaining why their choices are either poor or sensible, given the family's income and wants. A second example of an analysis task would be for students to explain why a given household's budget is appropriate or not, given the family's income.

Other examples of analysis tasks are:

1. Given period maps, determine the dimensions of a typical tidewater plantation at the time of the American Revolution.
2. Explain why the Revolutionary War was either inevitable or not.
3. Compare and contrast the life of the slave and master in tidewater Virginia at the time of the American Revolution.
4. Research and trace the origins of the musical tradition of Appalachia.
5. When given an account of democracy, explain why it could not have been written at the time of the American Revolution.
6. Compare two books by Bill Martin, describing the use of patterns.
7. Listen to a piece of music and describe the patterns in rhythm and melody.

Synthesis

At the synthesis level, students create an original product, exhibit, or performance that involves the selection, organization, and implementation of a number of concepts and generalizations and requires substantial thought. The key distinction between a synthesis level task and those at a lower level is the necessity that the student produce something that did not previously exist, at least for that student. For example, if students are asked to create a new flag symbolizing the United States in 1776 (or in 2006), they would be engaged in a synthesis task. Original stories, artistic creations, musical compositions, and most projects are also at the synthesis level.

Other examples of synthesis tasks are:

1. Develop an argument why the American Revolution succeeded.
2. Develop original stories of life in Boston during the second half of the 18th century.
3. Write an original song lyric expressing some aspect of life in the Revolutionary War period.
4. Write an original story about slavery at the time of the American Revolution.
5. Create a visual or verbal image of your impressions as if you were a visitor to the American colonies about the time of the Revolutionary War.
6. Dictate an original patterned book of at least four pages.
7. Create an original rhythm pattern using hands and feet.

Evaluation

The highest level of Bloom's taxonomy of the cognitive domain is evaluation. When engaged in an evaluation task, individuals make a judgment about the worth or merit of two or more plausible alternatives, select the preferred alternative, and defend that choice using specified criteria. For example, assume you attend an auction of Renaissance style paintings created by contemporary artists. If you elect to purchase one, the decision combines an affective preference ("This painting appeals to me more") with a cognitive judgment at the evaluation level ("It uses the materials used during the artistic period, accurately uses perspective, and is faithful to the dress and man-made structures of the period").

In an evaluation task, students must defend their decision using a combination of logical argument supported by evidence in fact and the application of predetermined criteria. For example, an essay can be judged on one or all of the following standards: organization, coherence, use of language appropriate to the audience, succinctness, and evocative impact.

Other examples of evaluation tasks are:

1. Critique song lyrics or poems written by classmates using the criterion that they accurately reflect the style and time of the Revolutionary War .
2. Defend or reject the position that Thomas Jefferson was an advocate of slavery.
3. Argue the loyalist or patriot position in a letter to the editor written to a newspaper in the year 1776.
4. In a debate, be prepared to argue for or against the view that the framers of the Declaration of Independence were advocates of democracy.
5. Support or defend this statement: "George Washington was a great military leader."
6. Determine which of three books has the most interesting pattern and explain why.
7. Explain which arrangement of the class (one line, two lines, partners, whole group, other) is the best for walking down the hall. Give at least one reason for your choice.

The levels of the cognitive domain, a description of each level, and appropriate learning process action verbs often associated with each level are displayed in Table 4.1.

Using Bloom's Taxonomy to Break Down Complex Tasks

Knowing whether an objective is at the higher or lower levels of cognitive complexity can help you decide the order for your lessons. Look back at the four objectives at the beginning of this section. Note how the first objective in the list is lower level and the others build until the highest level task is last. Bloom's taxonomy is especially helpful for doing this kind of content analysis.

Common Questions About Bloom's Taxonomy

Question 1

"Just as soon as I think I can classify tasks and objectives at some level of Bloom's taxonomy, I come across one that I can't classify. Or a group of us get together and we have three different answers. Even the instructor is unable to persuasively justify why an objective is at the application level or the analysis level. Why does this happen?"

Bear in mind that you are attempting to accomplish one of the most complex intellectual tasks in teaching. In terms of learning process, the creation of a higher level task—analysis, synthesis, or evaluation—requires you to select and organize a set of related concepts, generalizations, and facts into a meaningful network of content. Perhaps you are not knowledgeable enough about the topic you must teach to be able to analyze its structure quickly. Furthermore, the content and learning process frameworks are composed of

TABLE 4.1 *Bloom's Taxonomy of the Cognitive Domain*

Level	Description	Suggested Action Verbs
6. EVALUATION	Students can use previously learned standard/criteria to determine the worth or merit of a complex product.	defend or reject, develop and critique, judge, state or support a position, justify, argue, decide, appraise
5. SYNTHESIS	Students can create an original and complex product out of a set of simpler components.	create, build, develop an original, compose, write, solve, perform, establish, predict, produce, modify, plan, formulate
4. ANALYSIS	Students can take a complex set of material and break it down into its component parts and/or explain why a complex set of relationships is organized as it is or what caused it to be or predict from the present to the future.	compare and contrast, analyze, break down, explain why, show how, draw a diagram, deduce
3. APPLICATION	Students can apply previously learned material such as concepts, rules, or generalizations to newly taught material.	classify, apply, find, choose, compute, sort, generalize, organize
2. COMPREHENSION	Students can express previously learned material in their own way.	define, put in your own words, describe, summarize, translate, illustrate, restate, demonstrate
1. KNOWLEDGE	Students can recall, reproduce, or recognize previously learned information as it was taught to them.	reproduce, recognize, recall, list, identify, name, label, underline, place in order

abstract concepts, and it may be difficult to define them, to identify critical attributes, and to classify examples and nonexamples. Finally, because you are likely to be teaching abstract concepts, it is understandable that you find it difficult to determine whether some element of the content is a generalization or a fact or whether a given instructional objective is at the synthesis or evaluation level. Eventually, however, after teaching a topic and thinking about the ideas within the topic, the conceptual structure begins to emerge and higher level tasks become easier to design and distinguish.

Question 2

"If it is so difficult to distinguish among the levels wouldn't it make sense to create new categories? Can't you simplify it further?"

Good question! Here is a simplified version of the taxonomy for you to consider. These become the three levels of the taxonomy.

Level A. knowledge/comprehension
Level B. application/analysis/synthesis (higher level)
Level C. evaluation

Level A consists of familiar tasks at the knowledge or comprehension level. At level A, students are asked to remember or recall information such as names, dates, definitions, items, numbers, labels, statements—either exactly as it was taught or to summarize it, express it in their own words, or do a simple computation as in making change. For example, the question, What happened in the Year 2000 to the price of gasoline when the supply was drastically reduced? is at level A.

Level B includes application, analysis, or synthesis tasks. Tasks at level B are triggered by an unfamiliar example, a novel situation, or a set of data that the student must manipulate in some way—classify, reorganize, explain, break down, identify cause and effect, and so on. In contrast to the knowledge level, the testing situation must contain an unfamiliar element. For instance, "If you were a wheat farmer in the United States and you knew that there would be a severe drought in wheat-growing regions of Canada and Russia in the coming year, would you plan to plant more or less wheat next year? Why or why not?" In synthesis tasks, the students must also create something unique that is prompted by the testing situation: a story, essay, painting, performance, model, or exhibit.

Level C includes evaluation tasks. For instance, "Write a 500-word essay in support of or opposition to the rationing of health care in the United States as a way to control health costs" or "Present your arguments in support of or opposition to the rationing of health care in the form of a 5-minute speech to classmates." If you are careful to include these three levels of thinking in your unit planning, you are likely to plan activities that genuinely demonstrate understanding.

For appropriate verbs to use in creating instructional objectives at all levels of the taxonomy, consult Table 4.1.

■ *Practice Activity: Classifying Tasks into Bloom's Taxonomy*

Classify the following objectives: KC for knowledge/comprehension, HL (higher level) for application/analysis/synthesis, or E for evaluation.

_____ 1. Put in your own words the definition of a leader.

_____ 2. Recall the definition of *democracy*.

_____ 3. Explain why an unfamiliar example of the struggle for independence in the 19th or 20th century is similar to the American Revolution.

_____ 4. Provide a definition of *liberty* as it is used in a newspaper story.

_____ 5. Identify the key events of the Revolutionary War that were presented in class.

_____ 6. Defend or reject the thesis that the American Revolution was not a revolution but simply a change in government.

_____ 7. Recall a source of information about the English parliament taught in class.

_____ 8. When given a brief description of a person who lived during the Revolutionary War period, explain whether this person was or was not a leader.

    9. Sort a group of unfamiliar statements into a group consisting of historical generalizations.

   10. Create an original short story that accurately reflects the Revolutionary War period.

ANSWERS: 1. KC (comprehension), 2. KC (knowledge), 3. HL (analysis), 4. KC (comprehension), 5. KC (knowledge), 6. E (evaluation), 7. KC (knowledge), 8. HL (analysis), 9. HL (application), 10. HL (synthesis).

■ ■ ■

■ *Practice Activity: Bloom's Taxonomy*

Using the three clearly stated instructional objectives you wrote in the practice activity at the end of Section 1, revise, if necessary, so that one is at the knowledge level, a second at the application level, and a third at the analysis, synthesis, or evaluation level.

■ ■ ■

SUMMARY

The first section of Chapter 4 began with the parable "The Sea Horse Fable." Its theme supports the use of instructional objectives as a valuable decision-making tool for teachers. The text provided two arguments in favor of the use of instructional objectives: (a) they assist the teacher in focusing student attention on what is expected in the lesson and unit, and (b) they increase the likelihood that assignments and assessments will be related to what was actually taught. The section then listed two arguments against the use of instructional objectives: (a) since lower level (memory-type) instructional objectives are easier to construct, important higher level thinking and affective outcomes may be lost, and (b) some spontaneity may be lost when the classroom is focused on predetermined outcomes.

The remainder of the section was devoted to preparing you to write clearly stated objectives. A unit rationale and objectives for the "Revolutionary War Actions and Reactions (1763–1783)" unit were presented as an example of how clearly stated objectives can describe the intended learning in a unit.

In Section 2 the focus changed from writing clearly stated objectives, to using Bloom's taxonomy to analyze cognitive learning tasks and to write cognitive learning objectives at different levels: knowledge, comprehension, application, analysis, synthesis, and evaluation.

UNIT PREPARATION

Look at the list of outcomes you prepared in Chapter 3. Analyze whether the outcomes you planned will lead you to engage students to demonstrate understanding. One way to assess that is to consider whether your outcomes use the upper levels of Bloom's taxonomy. If not, you'll want to reconsider your list. If you are satisfied with your list of outcomes, your next step is to create a set of lesson objectives that will lead students to attain the desired goals. Your lesson objectives will include both higher level behaviors and the lower level behaviors necessary to prepare students for understanding performances. You should include a culminating objective that will require students to combine and synthesize unit information. Again, consider these objectives as a first draft. As you learn more about different types of lesson planning, you are likely to envision alternative ways students may demonstrate understanding. At this stage you want to make sure that your draft objectives focus on key content and require students to use information in complex ways.

PORTFOLIO ACTIVITY

Choose one or two of your outcomes and prepare a chart showing how they could be broken into lesson objectives, labeling with the appropriate level of Bloom's taxonomy. Your goal is to demonstrate your mastery of a congruent planning process leading to higher level thinking. Be prepared to talk about how your activities will lead students to higher level thinking and demonstrations of understanding. You may want to practice this conversation in a mock interview.

SEARCH THE WEB

Check the Companion Website under "Planning Instructional Objectives and Goals" for examples of planning guides and templates for creating learning outcomes. Be sure to analyze the materials carefully. Do they lead readers to create outcomes most likely to lead to understanding performances or outcomes that are easiest to assess? Compare notes with colleagues to see which site(s) they find most helpful.

REFERENCES

Bloom, B. (Ed.). (1956). *Taxonomy of educational objectives: Handbook I. Cognitive domain.* White Plains, NY: Longman.

Gardner, H. (1999). *The disciplined mind: What all students should understand.* New York: Simon & Schuster.

Mager, R. F. (1997). *Preparing instructional objectives.* (3rd ed.). Atlanta, GA: CEP Press, Inc.

Michigan Department of Education. (1996). *Michigan Curriculum Framework.* Lansing, MI: Author.

Wiggins, G., & McTighe, J. (1998). *Understanding by design.* Alexandria, VA: Association for Supervision and Curriculum Development.

Wiske, M. S. (Ed.). (1998). *Teaching for understanding.* San Francisco: Jossey-Bass, Inc.

CHAPTER 5

Assessing Learning Performances

CHAPTER OVERVIEW

Selecting instructional objectives, planning and implementing instruction, and selecting and assessing learning performances are all part of a cyclical process. Objectives must be carefully aligned with assessment methods to accurately measure student performance. A well-constructed assessment provides critical information to students regarding their strengths and needs, and provides feedback to teachers regarding the strengths and weaknesses of their instruction. Assessment involves (a) determining what students already know and need to learn (preassessment), (b) using the information to make instructional planning decisions, (c) selecting assessment methods that align with content standard benchmarks and instructional objectives, (d) measuring how well students attain these standards and objectives, (e) providing informative and useful feedback to students and parents, and (f) modifying instruction to better address student learning needs.

CHAPTER OBJECTIVES

After you have completed this section, you will be able to

1. Explain the roles of assessment throughout the instructional cycle;
2. compare and contrast common assessment terms such as diagnosis, norm- and criterion-referenced assessment, formative and summative assessment, and grading;
3. list common assessment procedures on a continuum from most controlled to most natural;
4. explain the importance of validity and reliability when evaluating student learning;
5. describe strategies for increasing validity and reliability of classroom assessment;
6. explain alternative assessment approaches such as authentic assessment including portfolios and exhibitions, and criterion-referenced assessment including peer and self-assessment, contract and mastery learning; and
7. use recommended strategies to assess student learning.

PRINCIPLES OF ASSESSMENT

This section begins with an examination of a particular student's performance. When you have completed your work on the section, you should be able to define key terms of importance in educational assessment and make decisions about the kinds of assessments and grading systems you will use in your teaching.

■ *Opening Activity*

Read the following classroom dialogue between a teacher and a parent at Gloria Jackson's school. Then answer the questions that follow.

> *Mrs. Campison (parent of a fifth grader):* Mrs. Samson, my daughter, Loretta, is in your fifth-grade class this year. I'm afraid that she is very upset about the

grade she received from you in social studies this marking period. She has complained often since she received her report card the day before yesterday.

Mrs. Samson (fifth-grade teacher): Mrs. Campison, I'm sorry about Loretta's reaction to the grade she received. My purpose in teaching is to assist students to be more confident and knowledgeable persons rather than to make them unhappy.

Mrs. Campison: Mrs. Samson, is it true that you are a harder grader than Mr. Carson? Loretta told me that students in your class do more work than their friends in Mr. Carson's classroom.

Mrs. Samson: I won't compare my requirements to another teacher's requirements. However, it is true that I expect students to do their best work. I have found that if I have high expectations for my students, they will make more learning progress than if I were less demanding.

Mrs. Campison: But what about the students who are frightened by your approach to teaching, as Loretta is? What do you do to accommodate these students?

Mrs. Samson: First, there are very few students who do not benefit from my approach. Consider that we are at the end of the first marking period. Some students need more time to understand that I am serious. Second, I believe that it is the teacher's responsibility to motivate students and to provide the best instruction possible. However, it is also the teacher's responsibility to judge how well the students have learned what has been taught and to assign a grade to that judgment.

I appreciate the concerns you express about Loretta's schoolwork and hope you will encourage her to respond positively to the challenge to do better in school.

Mrs. Campison: Where is the place for effort in your scheme of things? Loretta tells me that she tries as hard as she can but she still fails to satisfy you.

Mrs. Samson: Effort, if it is strong and persistent, results in improvement. I am absolutely convinced of that.

Mrs. Campison: I see that we are not getting anywhere with this discussion. I do intend to speak with Loretta and to offer her additional assistance and to encourage her to pay more attention in class and to ask for help from you when she needs it. However, I must say that I find your approach to teaching children unduly threatening and unbending. After all, these children are only 10 and 11 years old. I believe they ought to enjoy their youth and be encouraged to cooperate with each other rather than to compete for your approval and for grades.

Mrs. Samson: Mrs. Campison, if you and I support each other and motivate Loretta to do her best work in my classroom, I am confident that we can make a significant contribution to her educational development.

What is your reaction to the two persons featured in the dialogue? Do you find yourself more in agreement with the ideas expressed by Mrs. Campison or Mrs. Samson? Why?

■ ■ ■

Educational Assessment and Grading

Educational assessment is a systematic process that leads to a judgment about the ability or achievement exhibited by a person or persons, or by an instructional program. Educational assessment is considered systematic because it is planned, organized, and completed periodically, and its judgments are subject to revision or redress through established review procedures. Compare this systematic process to the assessments we make in everyday life. How often do we decide whether something is attractive or unattractive, fair or unfair, good or bad? Normally, we are not called upon to defend these evaluative decisions. However, the assessments that teachers make are subject to public scrutiny.

Often an educational assessment entails judgments about both the learner and the instructional program that produced the learning. The conversation between Mrs. Campison and Mrs. Samson involved the assessment of a student's performance. However, the parent implied that the teacher's instructional approach was a factor affecting the student's performance. Parents have the right to demand that when teachers make educational assessments, they can defend them with appropriate reasoning and evidence using language that a noneducator will understand.

Educational assessments can be made at any time and for a variety of purposes. Two of these purposes are labeled formative and summative. **Formative assessment** provides information for improvement while the person or program has the opportunity to improve. Thus formative assessment helps a teacher make better decisions about student performance and instructional success. Examples of formative assessment methods are checks for understanding and discussion questions, pretests and self-tests, quizzes, drafts of assignments that are reviewed and returned for revision, practice exercises, and so forth.

Summative assessment is used to make educational decisions about persons or programs after instruction. Examples of summative assessment of learners include student-created exhibits, large research projects that require students to demonstrate understanding of major generalizations and concepts, unit tests, final exams, term papers, student-led conferences, report cards, decisions to retain or promote a student, and the like. The purpose of the assessment determines whether it is formative or summative. In reality, a given assessment procedure may serve both purposes. Think for a moment about a unit test that is designed as a summative assessment of students' performance after the completion of one unit and that also serves a formative purpose to guide students toward improved performance in the next unit.

Assessments can be placed on a continuum between controlled and natural. A highly controlled assessment suggests the use of a special testing environment—chairs arranged to discourage copying from neighbors, no books or papers on desks, the requirement that the test be completed within a given time period, and so on. In a controlled assessment, the learners are always aware they are being assessed. The most common form of controlled assessment is a standardized or teacher-made paper-and-pencil test, typically administered in the classroom.

Nevertheless, there are other kinds of controlled assessments that a wise teacher should use when appropriate. For example, the observation of a student product or presentation offers a different view of student skill or achievement than does a paper-and-pencil test. Written homework assignments, interviews, questionnaires and check-

FIGURE 5.1   Assessment Continuum: Most Controlled to Most Natural

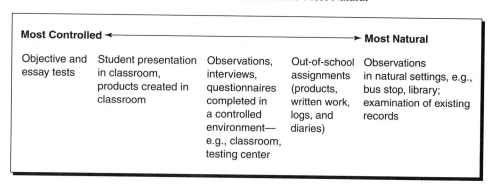

lists, observations, and examination of existing records are types of less controlled assessments. At the far end of the spectrum are natural assessment procedures. Natural assessment requires no artificially constructed testing environment, and the learners are not aware that they are being assessed. For instance, the teacher might observe play during recess, check the kind and number of library books students choose, and so on. A continuum of assessment procedures from most controlled to most natural is shown in Figure 5.1.

The Relationship Between Instruction and Assessment

Consider the following scenario:

A first-year teacher working with Gloria Jackson on the Revolutionary War unit has begun assessing her fifth-grade students' first drafts of a formal research report. Using a minimum of three resources, students created two-page reports on the differing perspectives of loyalists and patriots during the Revolutionary War. The teacher is shocked and dismayed by the poor quality of student work. Only 4 of the 25 students have followed the written instructions accurately. Perplexed by the number of students who have submitted papers without important headings, specific comparisons between loyalist and patriot points of view, and properly labeled time lines, the teacher reflects upon possible reasons for such results. Although some teachers might be inclined to find fault with the students by concluding that they lack research experience or ability, this teacher recognizes that the sheer number of students who failed to meet expectations indicates other causes. An honest assessment of her instruction yields some important insights: the need for clearer expectations and new forms of scaffolded instruction to promote success. Perhaps a minidemonstration lesson on comparing and contrasting ideas using a Venn diagram will assist students in their effort to compare and contrast loyalist and patriot perspectives. The teacher considers creating a self-check list of report components that students will complete before turning in their final report. Finally, she weighs the potential benefits and drawbacks of presenting students with a model report she could create herself.

FIGURE 5.2   The Instructional Cycle

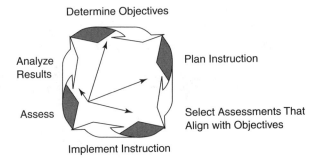

This first-year teacher has made an important connection between assessment and instruction. Her students' work provides critical information for the improvement of her own instruction and for her future planning decisions. Selecting instructional objectives, planning instruction, assessing learning performances, and analyzing results are all part of a continuous cyclical process (see Figure 5.2). When viewed as an integral part of the instructional cycle, assessment data can be used to generate a wealth of information regarding the quality of our goals and objectives, the effectiveness of our instruction, and of course, the strengths and needs of our students.

Traditionally, assessment has occurred at the end of an instructional cycle; however, teachers currently use assessment methods at each phase in the cycle (represented by the inner arrows in Figure 5.2). We call this *continuous assessment*. For example, during the implementation phase, teachers informally assess students through the use of observation, anecdotal records, discussion questions, and one-to-one conferences. Why have teachers begun to embed formative assessment practices throughout the instructional cycle? If the primary purpose of assessment is to improve student learning, then students must have opportunities to benefit from assessment data—to change, refine, and extend their thinking. When formative assessment is embedded throughout the instructional process, students receive continuous feedback, teachers regularly clarify and revise their expectations and objectives, and instruction is continuously modified to better address student needs. Teachers have more information on which to base their decisions and their planning. As a consequence, greater numbers of learners will succeed in achieving instructional goals and objectives.

There are systematic methods for embedding assessment practices within the instructional cycle. For example, one teacher we know selects five students each week whose work will be analyzed in detail. This teacher becomes genuinely curious about why these five students perform as they do and she attempts to discover the best way to help each child progress. As she analyzes a child's work, she consults other resources—teachers, books, experts, or other professionals—to help her understand the learners' needs more deeply. Working together with other professionals to interpret and understand student work can be a particularly powerful strategy.

Here is how the process looked with Norma Madsen's second-grade student, Ted. To find out more about the children's interests and to assess their writing skills, the teacher

FIGURE 5.3   Second Grader's Work Sample

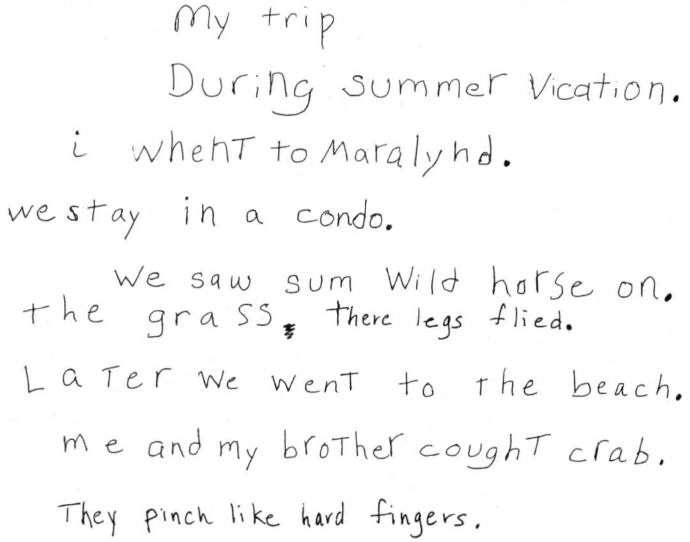

> My trip
>   During summer Vication.
>   i whehT toMaralyhd.
>   westay in a condo.
>   We saw sum Wild horse on.
>   the grass, there legs flied.
>   LaTer we wenT to the beach.
>   me and my broTher coughT crab.
>   They pinch like hard fingers.

asked the children to write about one experience they had during the summer. The content of Ted's paper (see Figure 5.3) was creative and he used quite a few expressive words (spelled phonetically) in his eight-line response. However, Ted wrote outside of the lines, put a period at the end of each line, used "I" and "i" to refer to himself, and sometimes used a capital letter at the beginning of the sentence. Norma was not sure what to focus on, but since mechanics was one goal for second grade, she had some concerns. She took the paper to another teacher and asked for some insights. Together, they decided that the errors might be due to (a) Ted's misconceptions regarding the rules, or (b) his being in a hurry to write the exciting things he reported. Wishing to nurture each child's strengths, Norma shared her enthusiasm with Ted regarding his creative and engaging description. She then asked Ted to revise the paper and found that some areas improved, but capitalization was still a problem. So, she asked him to describe what he knew about the rules for the beginning and ending of a sentence. He thought they always ended at the end of the line. Upon identifying this misconception, she had a clear understanding of how to proceed with instruction.

This "Collaborative Analysis of Student Learning" (Goff, Langer, & Colton, 2000) process helps teachers analyze and interpret classroom data to inform their instructional decisions. As one teacher using this process stated, "I never had training in analyzing student work. I was upset naturally because they [students] weren't doing well but I didn't have a vehicle for understanding . . . from their paper what was going on." Teachers in a study of the collaborative process changed from using student work to merely enter a grade or check in the grade book to analyzing the exact nature of a student's learning and using that information to make instructional decisions.

Diagnosing Learners: Preassessment

Many teachers assume that students know little or nothing about the subject or skills they are about to teach. Or, they assume the children have all the necessary skills to succeed in the planned activities. But, what if some children already have mastered what you are about to teach? What if others are lacking the prior skills or knowledge to succeed in the lesson—for example, they cannot read the directions for a task? Information gained from a preassessment of student knowledge, skills, interests, and attitudes enables the teacher to tailor instruction to the needs of diverse learners.

The issue of preassessment is particularly crucial at the beginning of the school year, when you have little knowledge of your new students. You may have read their cumulative folders; or, as some teachers do, you may have decided to gather information on your own. In any case, you certainly will want to see what skills, knowledge, interests, and attitudes the children bring to your classroom as you begin to plan the curriculum. Indeed, many teachers devote the first weeks of the school year to two very important tasks: (a) teaching children about the routines, procedures, and codes of conduct of the classroom, and (b) assessing where students are in relation to the outcomes (standards and benchmarks) for their grade level.

But, what will you do with this information? You can think of the results of your preassessment as being a guide for how to best design the lessons and activities to successfully lead your students from their experiences to the new content. If you find students have vast experience and background with certain subjects, you can provide more challenge for them. If you find some children struggle with simple reading tasks, you will have to provide additional support, practice, reinforcement, and alternatives (e.g., by reading directions aloud to the student). If you find a child has had a bad experience in science and is not interested in the subject, then you will need to find a way to provide high success early in the school year. In short, without accurate information about where each child is in relation to curriculum, our lessons and activities are likely to miss the mark, and increased student failure may result. If we want to plan instruction that is appropriate for a specific group of students, we need to know their attitudes, interests, general skills, prior life experiences, and specific knowledge of the content to be taught. There are many ways to determine this information. Figure 5.4 illustrates four categories of preassessment.

In addition to preassessing student entry abilities at the beginning of the school year, teachers use preassessment at the beginning of a unit of instruction. For example, if Gloria is about to teach her unit on the Revolutionary War she should think about preassessing the students' entry level knowledge and skills so that she can identify and address any student misconceptions, as well as determine how to build instruction upon students' prior knowledge, interests, and skill levels. At the beginning of the unit she might ask students to select from the following options and respond individually: (a) respond to some general questions, (b) write a story telling about the American Revolution, or (c) draw pictures and captions to describe their understanding. She might also ask them to complete an attitudinal survey regarding interests and attitudes toward the unit topic. Then she would collect the responses and read them carefully that evening. She might sort the responses according to the levels of knowledge and/or types of atti-

FIGURE 5.4 Four Categories of Preassessment

Preassessment Purposes and Strategies	
Area Assessed	**Examples of Preassessment Strategies**
Interests/feelings	Survey, questionnaire, free-write, rating scales, KWL
General learning skills	Perform (e.g., read aloud, write, do math)
Prior experiences	Free-write, log, daily journal, discussion
Knowledge of content	Pretest, anticipation, guide game, perform task(s), self-assessment (KWL), concept maps

tudes and interests. This preassessment information can enable the teacher to "differentiate" the lesson activities and assignments—that is, tailor them to the needs and interests of the students.

Formal and Informal Types of Preassessment

There are two related issues involved in the diagnosis of students' entry level competence through preassessment—what methods to use to gather the information and what content and skills to assess. Preassessment can be accomplished through both *formal* and *informal methods*. An example of a formal method would be a written test, similar in style, length, and degree of difficulty to the posttest that you will administer when the unit instruction has ended. Formal methods take more time to develop and administer but can yield more precise information about student entry level competence. Formal methods are more frequently used prior to beginning a unit of instruction; however, as a general rule, you will want to use an informal method for preassessment of individual lesson content. For example, you could use a class discussion as an informal preassessment for a lesson.

In regard to creating the content of a preassessment, consider some general knowledge and skill issues. What prerequisite knowledge and skills do students need to be successful in achieving the standards and objectives in this unit? Do students have the necessary background knowledge to read successfully the written material about life in the Revolutionary War period that you have gathered? Can they take notes on lectures, reading, and research? Do they know how to cooperate with others during group work?

If you wish to assess students' knowledge of content, first determine the important concepts to be taught. A concept map, discussed in Chapter 3, is very helpful for clarifying important ideas. Concept maps can be developed for individual lessons as well as for larger bodies of content. If you were preparing a lesson on the different perspectives of merchants and frontiersman toward the monarchy, your map would incorporate common perspectives for both groups. For example, you would know that a New York merchant may have an interest in promoting or restricting trade with England depending on what the merchant buys or sells. It is likely that he or she, living in a busy, politically active area, would be very interested and probably involved in politics. Those living on the frontier would be more likely to feel isolated from the more populated and urban areas and thus, less concerned with the economic issues. Instead, he or she might be angry that the English government in far-off London has tried to restrict movement of settlers into the western Indian land. When you preassess students by asking them to list ideas they have about the lives of merchants and those on the frontier, you would look for evidence of these understandings.

In contrast to the lesson assessment described here, a unit-specific preassessment will determine if the students' prior knowledge is sufficient to begin the unit at the entry level you had expected. With a typical group of fifth graders, you can expect that many students will need some review material to study before beginning the unit. You may also discover through the preassessment that a few students have already learned what you planned to teach. If you have anticipated this, you will have planned independent study or special projects for these students. In any event, the responses you receive from students on a preassessment can be used to determine the complexity of the content to be taught in the unit, the nature of the activities you will use to initiate study of the unit, as well as other planned activities.

REFLECTING ON THE IDEAS

If you were Gloria Jackson, what would you wish to know about the fifth-grade students' entry level competence before you begin teaching the Revolutionary War unit? Think for a moment before reading further.

You might have considered: Are the students able to read a chapter and gain meaning? Can they take notes from a lecture or movie or field trip? How much do they know about the major causes or outcomes of the war? Can they define important concepts such as *colony* or *monarchy?*

Accuracy in Assessment

Gloria used a preassessment to assess how well students were prepared to study the proposed Revolutionary War unit. Using the preassessment helped her to customize the unit to meet the particular learning needs of the students in the class. At the end of the unit, she will assess the students on what they have learned and will assign a grade to communicate her judgment about their success to the student, to parents, to other educators, and to interested and appropriate others. Bear in mind that a grade is a label that has traditionally been used to represent learning. It is a kind of certificate that communicates achievement to educators, employers, and the general public. If they are to be useful, grades have to be sufficiently accurate so that they can predict future performance in a particular subject area. Thus a student who receives nothing but A's in math in elementary school should expect to be successful in math in middle school.

No doubt you are aware of the intense debate about the relative worth of the grading process. The decision whether to assign grades, the process used to determine the value represented by the grades, and the particular symbols used as grades are political decisions as much as educational decisions. Some educators argue that the symbols traditionally used for grading do not clearly represent the complexities of student achievement and that more specific information is more helpful (Marzano, 2000). Tomlinson (2001) suggests that grading needs to accommodate individual differences and differences in instruction. For example, how would a teacher grade a student who is making excellent progress but is working at an instructional level below grade level? Similar puzzles arise for a student who is struggling but working on exceptionally advanced material. In most school settings, these decisions are only partially under the control of the teacher. Remember that the value of a grade as an indicator is only as good as the assessment decisions upon which the grade is based. If grades are not given, the teacher must evaluate student performance and communicate the judgments about that performance in some other form.

Validity

The grading controversy illustrates the most important criterion on which the field of educational assessment rests—**validity**. *Educational validity* can be defined as the property of an assessment that makes it an accurate measure of what it purports to measure. Although there are several kinds of validity, only content validity is directly under the teacher's control and responsibility. *Content validity* has often been described through the following teaching prescription: Tell them what they will learn, teach them what you told them, and test them on what you taught.

However, achieving a high level of content validity is more complex than the simple prescription suggests. Fortunately, your analysis of the content you will teach and the use of clear instructional objectives are the foundations on which valid tests are developed. There are two dimensions of content validity. First, a valid assessment is one that provides an adequate coverage of the content taught in the unit. In the case of the Revolutionary War unit, adequate assessment of the content includes evaluation of the specific information and the concepts and generalizations that organize the unit.

If some aspect of the content is missing from the assessment, students can rightfully argue that too much emphasis was placed on some portion of the unit and too little on other portions. Another common violation of validity occurs when students are assessed on skills or knowledge not taught in class but instead acquired previously—material learned in earlier courses or through students' personal experiences. For example, consider the injustice that is created when the teacher permits a student to submit a unit project on colonial America that was the result of last summer's family excursion through the original 13 colonies rather than the library research that was expected of other students. Obviously, one family provided a student with opportunities for cultural enrichment that were far beyond the capacity of other families. To give substantial credit to the student for a project based on an outside experience compounds the effects of economic and class inequity.

The second dimension extends the issue of educational validity into the learning process. It is necessary not only to "test on what you taught" but to assess at the appropriate level of learning. Thus the match between objectives, activities, and assessment procedures includes the requirement that objectives written at any given learning level be matched with activities and assessment procedures at the same level. Perhaps you know of instructors who promise lofty aims such as "enhancing thinking skills," "learning to make informed judgments," and "exploring ways to solve problems" and then test for the recall of bits and pieces of information. To avoid this error in assessing the Revolutionary War unit, any tests given must include (a) questions on the applications of concepts such as democracy, liberty, and equality, and (b) questions that require students to analyze data and to create original responses. Of course, these formal tests would be only part of the total assessment of the unit.

Reliability

A second assessment concept of importance to the classroom teacher is reliability. Whereas validity is concerned with accuracy of assessment, **reliability** is concerned with consistency or stability from one performance to the next. Educational assessments that have high levels of reliability ensure that a student who is assessed again on the same instrument will achieve an identical or nearly identical score. Thus if an assessment is both valid and reliable, the teacher can rely on the information as being a reasonable indication of what the student has learned. A common way of expressing the relationship between validity and reliability is that validity is the foundation of assessment. Without validity it makes no difference whether the assessment provides a consistent score from one test administration to the next. Assuming an assessment is valid, there are some strategies and techniques that will increase its reliability. For purposes of illustration, we will assume the assessment is a written test developed by the teacher.

Enhancing Reliability of Teacher-Developed Assessments

There are a wide variety of teacher-developed written tests. They can be classified into two types. In an *objective test* the student is expected to identify or provide the right or best answer. A multiple-choice test is the most common example of an objective test. Other examples include matching, true-false, and fill-in-the-blank. In a *constructed test* the student is expected to build a response requiring the planning, organization, and display of multiple elements. An essay test is the most common example of a constructed test. Of course, the use and complexity of written tests vary considerably K–6. The following suggestions may assist you to plan objective and essay tests most commonly used in older grades.

1. Are all students expected to complete all items on the test? If so, make sure it is not too long. This is especially important if essay items are included, since they require additional time for reading, organizing, and editing.
2. Will all students understand the directions for all segments of the test? Are the directions brief and understandable? Is there a potential for the student to misinterpret what is expected? If so, take time to go over the directions for each segment of the test before administering it.
3. Are there a sufficient number of items to adequately sample the content covered by the test? Remember, longer tests are more reliable than are shorter tests. However, a series of quizzes that divide up the content among a number of periodic assessments can enhance reliability. In addition, frequent assessments even out the variation that affects the reliability (a student's health on a given day, the amount of study time, etc.).

4. Are there any other assessments that will be used to sample student performance over the same content? Some students perform better on tests where they select the right answer (multiple-choice, matching, true-false). Others perform better on essay tests or when asked to create a product such as a model. A variety of testing procedures provides a more reliable assessment of a student's learning than does a single assessment.

5. The construction and scoring of paper-and-pencil tests will affect their reliability. An objective test takes more time to design and construct than does an essay test. However, because of the ease of scoring, objective tests tend to be more reliable, take less time to score, and provide for a wider sampling of content than does the essay test.

The concept of reliability is not only important in formal paper-and-pencil testing. Thinking about reliability can provide a rationale for systematizing the less formal observations that are an essential part of assessment in elementary grades. For example, a teacher who has given several assignments that require students to identify beginning consonant sounds may have a general impression that Suzie knows most of the sounds and Jane is having trouble. This can provide some general guidance for instruction, but it is much less helpful than a more systematic analysis. If the teacher creates a checklist of specific sounds and records each child's success at identifying each one, she will have more useful information. This might be done through individual meetings with each child (perhaps with the assistance of a parent volunteer) or by looking at a series of assignments and collecting the data.

Similarly, running records of a child's oral reading in which each miscue is noted and analyzed are a much more reliable and helpful source of information than depending on a general impression of a student's accuracy. A student who is consistently having trouble with common but nonphonetic words like *the* or *of* needs different kinds of assistance than one who is unable to decipher *cat* or *pig*. It is important to understand that elementary classrooms provide many opportunities for assessment, both formative and summative. The more valid and reliable—generally the more systematic—those assessments, the more useful. For example, in the kindergarten unit on patterns, Ms. Jordan may use an activity in which students create patterns from wooden blocks to assess her students' ability to identify shapes and create patterns. She may pose a challenge such as, "On your desk, create a pattern using only squares and triangles." By walking around the room with a clipboard listing students' names, she can observe and record their success.

Many elementary teachers find that checklists that can be used to record a variety of skills are helpful in increasing the reliability of their observations. Another strategy for increasing the reliability of informal assessments or gaining useful information from informal observations is to create a system for gathering and recording information observed throughout the school day. While there are some times, as in the clipboard example above, when a teacher plans to observe a specific skill, behavior, or evidence of understanding, there are other times when careful observation of students can result in unplanned but important insights. Gathering and recording these bits of information can increase the reliability of your information—just as multiple quizzes increase the reliability of those assessments, so multiple observations are more reliable than a single instance. In addition to a clipboard, one useful tool for observation is a pad of stick-on notes and a pen handy in a pocket at all times. When the teacher notices something that may be of note—John has mixed up *b* and *p* again, Simone has taken leadership in a co-operative group for the first time, Lastisha expressed interest in learning more about a conflict that came up in a discussion of current events—a quick note can be made and saved for the end of the day. Some teachers keep a notebook with pages for each student. By sticking dated observation notes on the pages—and eventually transcribing them—it is easier to spot important trends in learning or behavior. Such notes can be particularly useful in documenting the progress and difficulties of students with special needs.

Norm-Referenced and Criterion-Referenced Assessment

A classroom is sometimes viewed as containing a group of 20 to 35 students who compete against classmates for grades, awards, scholarships, and admission to college. College students may be accustomed to seeing an instructor put a grade distribution on the chalkboard showing how many students received an A, B, C, D, and F. The instructor may explain how the grade distribution was developed—how many correct answers were required in order to receive which grades, and what curve the instructor developed to ground and defend the assessment. Although the concept of *normal distribution* may remain mysterious, students know that the instructor arranged all the grades in a row and then established cutoff scores between grades—for instance, 92–100 = A, 85–91 = B, and so on.

This view of assessment is referred to as **norm-referenced**. That is, the evaluator examines all the scores and determines where each individual's score fits within the distribution. The average score and other scores that deviate from the average as computed through a statistical procedure become critical determinants of an individual's grade. Scores that fall well above the average get A's and B's; scores that fall well below the average get D's and F's. Scores that cluster around the average get C's. One major disadvantage of norm-referenced assessment is that, as student performance improves, the teacher is likely to raise the curve to retain a similar proportion of A's, B's, and C's. Thus students experience the phenomenon of working harder or doing better without seeing any grade change. A second major disadvantage is that the value of the grade is difficult to interpret from one group to the next. Since the grade is determined by the performance of students in a particular group, a grade in social studies in one fifth-grade classroom taught by teacher A, may represent much more or much less educational value than an identical grade in a fifth-grade classroom taught by teacher B. To avoid this problem, well-known testing programs such as the National Assessment of Educational Progress (NAEP), Scholastic Aptitude Test (SAT), and American College Testing (ACT) compare an individual's score against standards determined through the analysis of scores from a national sample group.

In contrast, criterion-referenced assessment considers each student as an individual, and the individual's performance is assessed against predetermined performance standards or criteria, known in the assessment literature as **criterion-referenced**. An assessment that is criterion-referenced enables the teacher to determine with confidence whether a student's response reaches a predetermined standard. Using standards as the definition of success rather than student-to-student comparison makes it theoretically possible for all students to be successful and receive A's. The list of standards or criteria for success is referred to as a **rubric** (Wiggins, 1996).

One example of a teaching/learning model based on criterion-referenced assessment is called **contract learning**. In such a model, the standards for receiving a given grade are described to all students. Each student contracts with the teacher to perform certain tasks at a given quality level in order to receive the agreed-on grade. Objectives and activities are identified, requirements determined, and deadlines established. Contract learning has the advantage of permitting a student to concentrate on certain subject areas or units within a subject and not on others. It also helps prevent the teacher from labeling students, for instance as A or C students, since students can choose the grade they will seek to achieve.

An example of contract learning is the Brain-Flex program implemented in a secondary school in New South Wales, Australia (Bounds & Harrison, 1997). Each student in the program completes two or three independent projects during a school year. These projects enable them to flex their minds in pursuit of intellectual topics and outcomes of interest to them rather than those selected by the state. The topic must have sufficient breadth and depth to justify the effort that will be devoted to it. That decision is made after the student has written an explanation of the topic and justified its worthiness. Once a suitable topic has been determined, a learning contract is developed with that student's tutor (teacher). The contract includes a rationale of what the student expects to learn, clearly written goals to be achieved, and standards for assessment of the expected outcomes. During the self-paced, instructional period, students attend sessions on thinking and learning skills. Other than these required sessions, each student on a learning contract is free to use whatever facilities, equipment, and materials are needed to study the topic. Faculty and staff are available to provide counsel and assistance as needed. At the end of the contract, students submit the outcomes of their study which must include a written summary of what they have learned. Of course, contracts for elementary-age students would necessarily be simpler and of shorter duration, but the principle of using criteria to establish a grade would remain the same.

A second example of a criterion-referenced assessment is known as **mastery learning** (Bloom, 1984; Carroll, 1963). Mastery learning is an individualized approach for use in a structured instructional program. It is based on the belief that all students can be successful in achieving all objectives if additional learning time is allowed for those who may need it. Mastery learning, if it is to be successful, requires that teachers use clearly stated objectives, employ preassessment and other kinds of formative assessment procedures, and use alternative strategies and learning activities. Finally, they must be prepared to reteach lessons when necessary, using alternative methods and materials. Advocates claim that if these assumptions are met and if a sufficient time for learning is provided, all students can master all objectives. The only distinction among students is in the time required to achieve mastery.

Selecting an Assessment Method

The two most important questions regarding assessment are (a) What do you want students to know and be able to do? and (b) How will you know students have achieved the goals and objectives you have established? This second question requires thoughtful reflection on one's choice of an assessment method. While some methods of assessment can effectively measure students' ability to apply skills and knowledge in real situations, others are more effective choices for analyzing students' thought processes, and still others are designed to measure a broad array of content knowledge.

Currently, performance assessment tasks are recognized as a powerful form of assessment (Feuer & Fulton, 1993; Worthen, 1993), sometimes to the exclusion of other strategies. Dismissing arguments that advance one form of assessment over another, Stiggins (1997) advocates the use of diverse forms of assessment. He claims there is a place for both teacher-made tests and performance assessment in the elementary classroom. Stiggens identifies four primary forms of assessment that offer different assessment capabilities:

- selected response
- essay
- performance assessment
- personal communication

Selected response assessments include short answer, multiple-choice, true-false, and matching exercises. These are particularly useful if the teacher seeks to assess broad areas of knowledge mastery; however, selected response assessments cannot directly assess skill application and mastery in an authentic context.

Essays are defined as exercises that call for extended written answers. They provide an excellent opportunity for the examination of student reasoning processes. Similar to selected response tests, essays often do not directly assess skill development and application in context.

Performance assessments are used to accurately assess problem-solving ability, skill development and mastery as observed in a performance, and student proficiency in applying knowledge through project or product development. However, performance assessments are not effective tools for assessing student mastery of a broad area of content.

Finally, personal communication forms of assessment include strategies such as conferencing, oral examinations, interviews, debates, questions posed during instruction, and group discussion. These strategies allow the teacher to assess student thinking processes and depth of knowledge mastery. They are less effective as tools for assessing knowledge of a large body of content. Each of these four assessment methods can be effective tools when matched thoughtfully with a specific set of objectives. Consequently, a primary challenge for the teacher concerns the alignment of objectives with assessment methods.

REFLECTING ON THE IDEAS

Examine the following instructional objectives and match them with an appropriate assessment method or methods:

1. Students will be able to evaluate the pros and cons of separation from England and defend a position.
2. Students will be able to select and evaluate resources for perspective and bias.
3. Students will be able to locate, organize, and present information regarding the characteristics and contributions of a key leader of the Revolution.
4. In chronological order, students will be able to list the major events of the American Revolution.

Assessing Student Performance

UNDERSTANDING PERFORMANCES AND ASSESSMENT

While selected response, essay tests, and personal communication forms of assessment have important and necessary uses in the classroom, performance assessments offer some unique strengths that require elaboration. The terms *authentic, alternative,* and *understanding performances* can be used to describe forms of assessment that engage students in the application of learning in meaningful contexts. These trends will be discussed here under the general label of performance assessment. When understanding is demonstrated through performance in a real context, students clearly perceive the value and relevance of learning. They are engaged in experiences that are valued and useful in the adult world. For example, consider the following performance assessment task:

> The men who wrote the Declaration of Independence feared that true equality for enslaved Africans would tear the nation apart. Patriots such as Benjamin Franklin and Thomas Paine disagreed. After reading about the views of both sides, write and present a speech in which one of these figures defends equality for all. Use at least three pieces of evidence found in the Declaration to support your ideas.

In this example, students learn the discipline of history through examining primary source documents as real historians do. They analyze and evaluate evidence, and draw conclusions in order to present an argument. The ability to articulate and support an argument with evidence is a skill students will utilize throughout their lives. Performances such as this speech assignment (other examples include playlets, news broadcasts, musical performances, debates) and products (exhibits, research reports, models, charts, diaries and logs, other writing assignments, experiments, art projects), created for real purposes and audiences also enhance student motivation. Finally, an emphasis on depth versus breadth of content coverage increases students' knowledge retention and understanding (see, for example, Associated Press, 1998).

FIGURE 5.5   Steps in Designing Performance Assessments

Designing Performance Assessments

The creation of performance assessments is challenging and time consuming; however, the rewards in student learning are well worth the effort. Performance assessments can be used as a form of formative assessment in which students develop new understandings, and as a form of summative assessment at the conclusion of a unit to assess students' cumulative knowledge. In order to construct a performance assessment teachers will need to (a) select goals and objectives, (b) design a performance task, and (c) determine assessment criteria (see Figure 5.5).

The following narrative will allow you to follow the decision-making processes of one teacher as she follows this three-step process in the construction of a performance assessment for her fifth-grade students.

Step 1: Selecting Goals and Objectives

Gloria Jackson is attempting to design an assessment task that will include the following instructional objectives based upon her state's curriculum framework:
Students will be able to

1. gather and analyze information in order to answer the question posed
2. locate information using a variety of traditional sources and electronic technologies, and report the results of their investigation
3. use primary sources to reconstruct past events in U.S. history
4. recount the lives of characters of a variety of individuals from the past representing their local community, the state, and other parts of the United States
5. identify and explain how individuals in history demonstrated good character and personal virtue
6. compare and contrast the struggles and achievements of historical figures with those of people in contemporary society

The list complete, she turns her attention to the next stage in the development process.

Step 2: Developing the Performance Task

After defining her objectives, she attempts to brainstorm the elements of a task that will incorporate all of these objectives in a project or a performance. She wants to motivate students in a meaningful way through having them empathically enter into the lives of the patriot leaders through exploring their aspirations and ideals. She also wants students to link the present with the past. What if students could research a figure from the

Revolution and present that person's life in some form of dramatic performance? In this performance they could speak to people of today about their participation in the Revolution. They could describe their goals, and struggles to achieve these goals. Perhaps they could pose questions to the modern audience that cause them to reflect upon their own lives. The process of brainstorming complete, Gloria Jackson seeks to refine the task and create directions for the students. Here is her formulated task:

> Next month we will invite parents and community members to learn about famous patriots of the past. Our challenge will not only be to help them understand the lives of these people, we will also challenge our audience to compare people's lives today with those heroic patriots who lived long ago. Do you think life is easier or more challenging for us today? What kinds of goals do adults have today and how do they differ from the goals of the patriots during the Revolutionary period? After conducting research with a partner, you will create an interview. One of you will be a patriot leader, the other a modern newscaster conducting a live interview. In this interview you will discuss specific information including your patriot's beliefs, important life events, and major contributions to the Revolution. Throughout the interview you will be asked to turn to your audience and pose questions that will require them to compare and contrast their lives to that of your patriot.

With this second step sufficiently outlined, Gloria tackles the most challenging part of the project, creating standards for effective assessment (Luft, 1997; Pate, 1993).

Step 3: Creating Assessment Criteria and Scoring Guides

Gloria returns to her instructional goals and objectives to determine important content and processes that must be assessed. She wonders whether there should be a written component to the project? What kinds of performance criteria will help students develop an exemplary dramatic performance? It may be important for her to create a model performance so students can identify the characteristics of an exemplary performance. This year she will videotape the performances so that next year's class can view an exemplary performance and co-construct a scoring guide, or rubric, with her. She first outlines the major elements that encompass the task: they will have to research and take notes on different topics, they will have to create questions that encourage comparison and contrasts, and they will have to construct the interview performance. Next she begins to elaborate upon the subelements in each area. Under content she determines that students will have to examine a minimum of three sources and submit a series of index cards that contain their notes on specific topics: important life events, beliefs, and major contributions to the Revolution. All of these elements will have to be addressed through the interviewer's questions. Perhaps along with each note card they can submit an interviewer prompt. Next, she lists characteristics of a good dramatic performance such as eye contact, dynamics, fluency, and knowledge of content. Finally she constructs a rubric that attempts to define these categories more elaborately through distinguishing the difference between an exemplary, satisfactory, and poor performance (see Figure 5.6).

Similar rubrics can be used to evaluate complex activities for younger students. Although early primary grade students are not able to complete highly complex projects, they are able to engage in many tasks that demand higher level thinking, and hence,

FIGURE 5.6   Performance Assessment Rubric for Revolutionary Leader Project

Elements: Note Cards	Levels of Proficiency		
	3 Points	2 Points	1 Point
Sources and Note Taking	Uses three or more resources to locate information	Uses three resources to locate information	Uses less than three resources to locate information
Important Dates	Includes all important dates: Birth, important events, death	Includes most important dates	Includes few important dates
Beliefs	Describes important beliefs, creates clear links between beliefs and actions	Describes important beliefs, creates some links between beliefs and actions	Describes few beliefs, links between beliefs and actions are undeveloped
Important Life Events	Provides detailed descriptions of all major life events	Provides some description of most major life events	Provides little description of major life events, important events not included
Major Contributions	Provides detailed description of major contributions and explains clearly why these contributions are important	Provides description of major contributions and some explanation of why these contributions are important	Provides little description of major contributions with little or no explanation of why these events are important
Interviewer-Interviewee Questions	Questions pertain to all four project topics and call for detailed responses	Questions pertain to some project topics and call for some detailed responses	Questions pertain to few project topics and call for minimal responses
Interviewer-Audience Questions	Questions for the audience require three to four comparisons between modern and historical beliefs, goals, struggles, and contributions	Questions for the audience require one or two comparisons between modern and historical beliefs, goals, struggles, and contributions	Questions for the audience require no comparisons between modern and historical beliefs, goals, struggles, and contributions
Performance			
Eye Contact	Both interviewer and patriot maintain eye contact with the audience	Both interviewer and patriot maintain some eye contact with the audience	Both interviewer and patriot maintain little eye contact with the audience

FIGURE 5.6 *Continued*

Elements: Note Cards	Levels of Proficiency		
	3 Points	2 Points	1 Point
Vocal Dynamics and Gestures	Both interviewer and patriot creatively and appropriately are dynamics and gestures for emphasis and dramatic effect	Both interviewer and patriot creatively and appropriately use some dynamics and gestures for emphasis and dramatic effect	Both interviewer and patriot incorporate little or no use of dynamics and gestures for emphasis and dramatic effect
Fluency	Both interviewer and patriot speak freely and with confidence throughout the interview	Both interviewer and patriot speak somewhat freely and with confidence throughout the interview	Both interviewer and patriot appear uncertain and lack confidence throughout the interview
Understanding of Content	Elaborate understanding of all four topic areas (dates, beliefs, life events, contributions) is clearly demonstrated	Sufficient understanding of most topic areas (dates, beliefs, life events, contributions) is clearly demonstrated	Little or no understanding of most topic areas (dates, beliefs, life events, contributions) is demonstrated

qualitative assessment. For example, one of the objectives in Ms. Jordan's pattern unit was for students to create and explain an original woven pattern using yarn and paper strips. The objective included a statement that the pattern must repeat at least once and students must include the idea of repetition in their explanation of why the design is a pattern. This project can appropriately be assessed using a rubric. Before going on, you may want to sketch out how such a rubric might look.

If you created a rubric for the weavings, the left side of the rubric probably included criteria such as whether the strips were woven correctly (this might reflect a psychomotor objective), whether there was a repeated pattern in the weaving, and whether the student could accurately describe why the weaving was a pattern. You may have chosen to describe several possible levels of performance or only to describe satisfactory achievement of each criterion. In either case, the rubric would be helpful in assessing student success.

Similarly, rubrics (or associated checklists) can be helpful in assessing ongoing complex activities such as journal writing or other writing assignments. A rubric describing the desired skills for a particular grade level can be used to evaluate students' writing and make decisions about skills instruction, both for individuals and for groups of students. For example, imagine that for one grade level, one of the areas of focus for writing instruction was figurative language. The section of the writing rubric for that area might look like that in Figure 5.7. The teacher could use this rubric to determine which

FIGURE 5.7 Rubric Section for Figurative Language

Focus Area	Emerging	Satisfactory	Target
Figurative Language	Identifies examples of figurative language in text. Successfully generates some examples of similes and metaphors, with cuing.	Successfully generates examples of similes and metaphors. Can use them in independent writing when assigned.	Appropriately uses similes and metaphors in independent writing without prompting.

students needed additional instruction on the similes and metaphors and which might better use the time in independent writing or some other activity.

If desired, the rubric could be expanded to five categories to include a description of unsatisfactory performance and an exemplary performance, not expected for all students—for example, the creation of multiple unique or exceptionally complex metaphors. Providing exemplary levels for some rubrics, and sharing them with students, can be particularly helpful in promoting self-assessment and goal setting for students with exceptional ability in a particular area.

Self-Assessment, Goal Setting, and Student Ownership of the Learning Process

Involving students in the creation of scoring guides and rubrics is one fundamental way to help students understand teacher expectations and criteria for successful achievement. Including students in performance assessment through peer evaluation, self-evaluation, and personal goal-setting practices promotes greater individual autonomy and responsibility for learning. Self-assessment enables students to internalize criteria for exemplary performance that they can then apply to new situations. Simple reflection forms such as the one in Figure 5.8 enable students to analyze their performance and establish goals for future performance.

Self-assessment prompts can also be used to facilitate student discussion about their work during peer, teacher-student, and student-led parent conferences. These self-assessment activities foster the development of an assessment vocabulary and communication skills that enable students to assume greater ownership for their learning. Once they have experience with performance assessment, students also can be appropriately involved in the creation of the rubrics themselves. Sample exemplary products from previous years can be helpful in allowing students to identify characteristics of successful examples.

Portfolios

One approach to performance assessment emphasizes the collection and display of student work in a **portfolio**. The elements recommended for placement in a portfolio include various kinds of products and exhibits. In some cases, students are encouraged to

FIGURE 5.8 Reflection Form

Reflection and Goal-Setting Form

Name: _____ Date: _____

Project: _____

1. I think the strengths of my project are . . .

_____

_____

2. My favorite part of the project was . . .

_____

_____

3. Some things I understand now that I did not before . . .

_____

_____

4. One thing I would do differently next time . . .

_____

_____

5. A learning goal I have as a result of this project is . . .

_____

_____

---

maintain a portfolio of increasingly polished versions of a significant assignment such as a research report, story, or art project. Students often attach their own assessment of the development of their competence to these exhibits. Thus, the students demonstrate a continuing commitment to the task.

For example, in the Revolutionary War unit, an assessment portfolio could include some of the following assignments:

A brief account of a fictional person living in colonial times written by the student
An original poem or song lyric appropriate to the Revolutionary War time written by the student
A drawing or scale model of a tidewater plantation at the time of George Washington
An excerpt of a Revolutionary War document rewritten by the student

A set of definitions of key terms from the Revolutionary War period

A letter to the editor of a colonial newspaper written by the student espousing a patriot or loyalist position on the coming struggle

A letter home from a soldier in either the English or American armies

The assignments contained in the portfolio could be evaluated (by the teacher, peers, or the student) and become important elements in determining the summative grade for the unit.

Another form of performance assessment is known as an exhibition. An **exhibition** is designed to be a broad, preferably interdisciplinary, culminating experience that requires the application of knowledge within a stated set of conditions. Typically an exhibition entails some type of presentation to an audience outside the class. For example, students completing a unit on the rain forest might transform their classroom into a simulated rain forest, with students stationed at various locations in the room to explain the ecology of the rain forest, products made from rain forest materials, threats to the rain forest, and so on. Other exhibitions might entail students creating portions of a class museum or giving presentations on mythological characters by taking on the persona of a god or goddess.

In an elementary school, imagine a simulation in which students were challenged to create and run a market economy complete with producers and consumers. The centerpiece of the economy is the creation and operation of a bank. Businesses producing and selling a variety of goods and services within the school and the community are planned and created. Students assume the duties and responsibilities of entrepreneurs, salespeople, advertisers, illustrators, bankers, and so on. Banks lend money to entrepreneurs; consumers invest in new and existing businesses, save, and borrow money from the bank. Parents and community people add their expertise as guest speakers and consultants. An end-of-year school fair is the exhibition—an occasion for all participants and sectors of the economy to exhibit their products and services and explain their roles and contributions to the economy.

Returning once more to the Revolutionary War unit, the portfolio requirement could be organized as an exhibition. Students from other classes, faculty, school board members, parents, and community guests would be invited to view exhibitions of student work from the unit. Models, letters, and scenes from short stories created by groups of students could be featured in displays and performances in the auditorium. Another Revolutionary War exhibit could be a staged debate in the House of Burgesses or at the meetings of the second Continental Congress in Philadelphia between advocates of independence and those advocating moderation.

You might argue that the creation of a working market economy, a model town, or a Revolutionary War exhibition would stretch the capability of school personnel and students. It would take a number of weeks of planning and implementation to complete. Teachers, administrators, and students would have to work together to accomplish the many tasks involved. It is no wonder that advocates of performance exhibitions see changes in the curriculum, organization, and management of the schools as necessary elements in their approaches to alternative curriculum and assessment. A variety of educators view high-quality assessment as a potential driving force for school improvement (Rothman, 1997; Simmons & Resnick, 1993; Smith, 1997).

SUMMARY

The chapter began with a confrontation between a teacher and a parent over a student's academic performance. The confrontation brought to the surface the complex and difficult issues involved in assessing and judging academic learning. Often, assessment problems occur because the evaluator has made a validity error, either (a) assessing what was not taught or failing to assess adequately what was taught; or (b) assessing at a different level of learning from what the student had practiced. Diverse assessment methods including selected response, essays, performance assessments, and personal communication must be carefully chosen to align with instructional objectives. Of the four types, performance assessment has unique qualities that facilitate student application of knowledge and skills within a realistic context. When students participate in the development of assessment criteria and reflect on their own progress through self-assessment and goal-setting activities, they develop assessment skills and increased responsibility for their own learning. Whatever the evaluative method used, thoughtful educational assessment will enable the teacher to make wise judgments about the performance of students and the quality of the educational program.

■ *Practice Activity: Designing a Performance Assessment*

Imagine you are teaching a unit. You have analyzed the content and identified the key generalizations, concepts, and facts. Write out your instructional objectives for your unit. Order the cognitive ones in a logical sequence. Be sure to include affective and psychomotor objectives as appropriate. Design a culminating exhibition in the form of a project or performance task that would assess the students' learning in your unit. Finally, create a scoring guide that includes key categories for assessment and the criteria that apply to each category.

■ ■ ■

■ *Practice Activity: Analyzing Student Work*

One of the most important assessment skills you will need is the ability to analyze student work, both individually and in groups. Gather two sets of student papers from a teacher or your own field experiences. You will need a preassessment and an assessment completed after teaching specific content. Examine the papers. Don't just score them but analyze which concepts were learned and how common errors may have been made. Look for evidence of student thinking. You may want to compare the learning of boys and girls or some other sub-groups. Think about how the results would impact your next teaching decisions.

■ ■ ■

UNIT PREPARATION

Prepare an assessment plan for your unit. Start with a grid listing your outcomes and how each one will be assessed. Outline your assessment materials, including at least one sample of a traditional test, an authentic assessment with rubric, and a structured observation. In most cases your authentic assessment will parallel the culminating objective you created in the last chapter. You should continue to develop and refine assessment materials as you develop your lessons.

PORTFOLIO ACTIVITIES

The assessment plan and materials created for your unit are good items to include in any portfolio. Be prepared to discuss why you made the assessment decisions you did and how your choices reflect valid and reliable assessments.

Complete an individual student work analysis. Select a sample of a student's work and remove any identifying information. Analyze the work sample and write a brief description of what you learned from the work and how it affected (or would affect) your teaching decisions. Be prepared to talk about using student work to plan instruction.

SEARCH THE WEB

Examine the materials on "Tests and Testing" found on the Companion Website. You will find information on developing rubrics and compiling portfolios as well as information on a variety of standardized tests. You may find it interesting to compare testing information across sites. How does information on sites critiquing tests (for example, Fairtest) compare to that prepared by testing companies?

REFERENCES

Associated Press. (1998, April 23). Top teacher has students act out history. *Detroit Free Press.*

Bloom, B. S. (1984). The search for methods for group instruction as effective as one-to-one tutoring. *Educational Leadership, 41* (8), 4–18.

Bounds, C., & Harrison, L. (1997). In New South Wales: The Brain-Flex project. *Educational Leadership, 55* (1), 69–70.

Carroll, J. (1963). A model of school learning. *Teachers College Record, 64,* 723–733.

Feuer, M. J., & Fulton, K. (1993). The many faces of performance assessment. *Phi Delta Kappan, 74* (6), 478.

Goff, L., Langer, G., & Colton, A. (2000). The collaborative analysis of student learning. *Journal of Staff Development,* Fall.

Luft, J. (1997, February). Design your own rubric. *Science Scope, 20* (5), 25–27.

Marzano, R. (2000). *Transforming classroom grading.* Alexandria, VA: Association for Supervision and Curriculum Development.

Pate, E. P. (1993, November). Rubrics for authentic assessment. *Middle School Journal, 25* (2), 25–27.

Rothman, R. (1997). *Measuring up: Standards, assessment, and school reform.* San Francisco: Jossey-Bass.

Simmons, W., & Resnick, L. (1993). Assessment as the catalyst of school reform. *Educational Leadership, 50* (5), 14.

Smith, J. (1997, December). Alternative assessment and successful school reform. *Equity and Excellence in Education, 30* (2), 61–70.

Stiggins, R. J. (1997). *Student-centered classroom assessment.* Upper Saddle River, NJ: Prentice Hall.

Tomlinson, C. A. (2001). Grading for success. *Educational Leadership, 58* (6), 12–15.

Wiggins, G. (1996, January). Designing authentic assessments. *Educational Leadership, 153* (5), 18–25.

Worthen, B. (1993). Critical issues that will determine the future of alternative assessment. *Phi Delta Kappan, 74* (6), 444–454.

TOPIC 2

Implementation: Getting Out There and Teaching

CHAPTER 6

Reflective Lesson Design

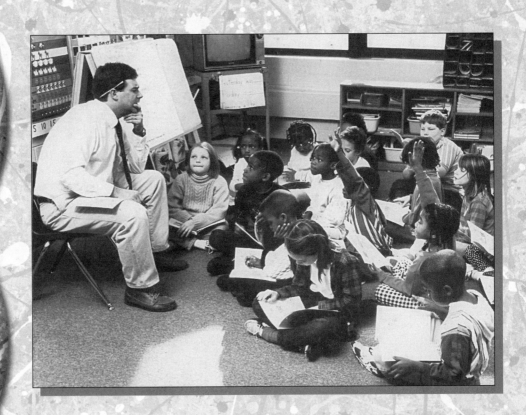

CHAPTER OVERVIEW

Teachers frequently ask themselves, What experiences can I design that will allow students to construct the intended understandings and attitudes specified in my district's curriculum guide? This chapter provides frameworks for planning lessons and activities. *Activities* are the elements of well-designed, well-organized *lessons* that help students attain specific learning objectives (outcomes). These lessons should not be isolated events. When organized into *units,* they lead systematically to the accomplishment of long-range goals (standards/benchmarks) that reflect useful skills and ideas for daily living.

This chapter and the next two introduce principles for planning that can help you think reflectively about a variety of teaching approaches, particularly as they relate to a constructivist approach to teaching. They will provide a structure for lesson planning and two basic approaches to teaching: direct and inductive. The chapter will discuss formal and informal modes of instruction in elementary classrooms and the need to think about differentiated instruction—instruction that flexes to meet many students' needs simultaneously, even in the beginning stages of planning.

The choice of lesson types and activities is based on the students' needs, the content and outcomes, the teacher's philosophy and style, and the context. A reflective teacher decision maker attempts to weave together a variety of types of activities when designing lessons and units.

■ *Opening Activity*

Look over the headings of the previous chapters in this book. If you were asked to design a unit on living things or the history of your local community, what steps would you take to help yourself plan? What would you need to do before teaching your first lesson? List the steps on a scrap of paper.

You should have listed the following steps: selecting goals (aligned with standards/benchmarks), analyzing content and creating a concept map, preassessing students, writing lesson objectives, planning lessons and learning activities, and designing assessment/evaluation procedures. (An explanation of these unit components is provided in Chapter 3.) Each of these steps will require careful thinking about many factors. One daily challenge for teachers is selecting learning activities.

Many times teachers implement activities because they are in the teacher's guide, because they have used the same activity for many years, or because, as inexperienced teachers, they could not think of any other way to present the material to students. Yet the design of learning activities is one of the most important decisions a teacher makes. This section explores principles and guidelines to help you create the most appropriate and effective learning activities for your students.

■ ■ ■

SECTION 1. PRINCIPLES FOR DESIGNING LEARNING EXPERIENCES

Section 1 Objectives

At the end of this section, you will be able to

1. describe elements of constructivist teaching; and
2. explain six principles for designing learning experiences and use them to analyze lessons.

Constructivist Learning Theory: Schooling for Democracy

One of the theories that undergirds the strategies for teaching and learning in this book is constructivism. Recall from Chapter 2 that constructivism is the result of a synthesis of the work of Piaget, Vygotsky, Bruner, and others. The term *constructivism* implies that learning is an active process—that individuals construct the schemata that constitute their understanding, as opposed to passively absorbing information. The theory suggests that in-depth learning of concepts and ideas occurs only when a person has the opportunity to actively construct knowledge through inquiry and exploration. Most constructivist theorists also emphasize the important role that dialogue and cooperative learning play in the development of understanding. The following are general principles of instruction and learning derived from constructivist theory. Consider how they mesh with what you know about the ways human beings learn.

1. Learning is not the result of development; learning *is* development. It requires invention and self-organization on the part of the learner. Thus teachers need to allow learners to raise their own questions, generate their own hypotheses and models of possibilities, and test them for viability.

2. Disequilibrium facilitates learning. Disequilibrium occurs when an individual perceives something that does not fit easily into his or her existing cognitive structure. Remember the child encountering the skunk cited in Chapter 2. Initially the child labeled the skunk "cat." When the child recognized that events surrounding this animal were inconsistent with previous experiences with cats (producing disequilibrium), new learning was possible. Errors, such as the mislabeling of this animal, need to be perceived as a result of the learners' conceptions and therefore not minimized or avoided. Challenging, open-ended investigations allow learners to explore and generate possibilities, both affirming and contradictory. Contradictions, in particular, need to be illuminated, explored, and discussed as opportunities for learning.

3. Reflective abstraction is the driving force of learning. Human beings seek to make meaning, to organize and generalize across experiences in a representational form. That is, we put labels to the patterns in our experiences, usually through language. Allowing reflection time through journal writing, discussion, or representation in other symbolic forms may facilitate reflective abstraction.

4. Dialogue within a community engenders further thinking. Human beings learn through interactions with others. For this type of learning to take place, the classroom needs to be seen as a community of discourse engaged in activity, reflection, and conversation. The learners are responsible for defending, proving, justifying, and communicating their ideas to the classroom community.

5. Learning proceeds toward the development of structures. As learners struggle to make meaning, progressive structural shifts in perspective are constructed—in a sense, "big ideas." These big ideas are learner-constructed, central organizing principles that can be generalized across experiences and that often require the undoing of earlier conceptions. Children who have learned about cats, skunks, and horses can begin to develop generalizations about animals. When they learn about coral, the generalizations need to change and become more sophisticated. This process continues throughout development (Fosnot, 1996). Organizing teaching units to emphasize the structure of generalizations can facilitate the development of big ideas.

From an examination of these principles, the role of the constructivist teacher emerges. The teacher must first seek to understand students' conceptions and then extend, refocus, or direct their thinking while preserving students' ownership of the learning process. Perhaps the greatest challenge for the teacher involves the preparation of learning experiences that include appropriate forms of **scaffolded instruction**. Just as scaffolding can be used to support and facilitate the construction of a building, scaffolded instruction is designed to help students build understanding, bridging the gap between current understanding and new meanings. It refers to the use of graphic organizers, graduated instruction, verbal hints and guiding questions, and some forms of direct instruction that act to guide the students while enabling them to maintain independence and move forward. M. G. Brooks and J. G. Brooks (1999) describe the challenge that is implicit in constructivist teaching.

> As educators, we develop classroom practices and negotiate the curriculum to enhance the likelihood of student learning. But controlling what students learn is virtually impossible. The search for meaning takes a different route for each student. Even when educators structure classroom lessons and curriculums to ensure that all students learn the same concepts at the same time, each student still constructs his or her own unique meaning through his or her own cognitive processes. In other words, as educators we have great control over what we teach, but far less control over what students learn. (p. 21)

Still, there are principles that emerge to define effective constructivist teaching. J. G. Brooks and M. G. Brooks (1999) outline five overarching principles evident in constructivist classrooms. Consider how each principle ties to what you know about student learning and development.

- Teachers seek and value their students' points of view.
- Classroom activities challenge students' suppositions.
- Teachers pose problems of emerging relevance.
- Teachers build lessons around primary concepts and "big" ideas.
- Teachers assess student learning in the context of daily teaching.

These principles can be used to shape instruction in a variety of lesson types, enhancing their effectiveness in facilitating student learning.

But effective student learning is not the only rationale for constructivist teaching approaches. In the title of their engaging book about exemplary instructional practices, Daniels and Bizar (1998) declare, "Methods Matter." When we plan a lesson, we are choosing both a method of instruction and a process that sends implied messages about who holds information and how learning takes place. We cannot separate our means and ends for they are related—each lesson teaches content, but it also teaches about learning. For example, imagine a classroom where teacher-directed learning predominates. If students spend the large majority of their time listening, they may learn that the only way one gains information is to listen to others. In such a classroom, students are likely to associate learning with passivity and obedience. They may have little opportunity for realizing the power that comes through personal discovery or to envision themselves as individuals who can take initiative toward learning. Of course, it would be foolish to suggest that students should not listen to teachers or that teacher-directed learning is unacceptable. But that type of teaching is only one of many available approaches. Used as an exclusive option it can teach unintended lessons. It is important to consider the lessons you teach through your instructional choices—both the effectiveness of your explicit instruction and the implicit learning that the lessons provide. Fortunately, you will have the opportunity to select from a variety of methods to help your students attain important outcomes.

In order to wisely select instructional practices it is helpful to look beyond the immediate classroom context to the skills and abilities students will need for participation in our society. Passivity and obedience, for example, are more appropriate citizen behaviors in an authoritarian society. In a democracy, skills such as locating, analyzing, and evaluating information; community problem solving; and reasoned public decision making are of critical importance (Beyer, 1996). Advocates of democratic classroom practices speak of the value of providing students with the opportunity for choices and increased ownership over the learning process. Substantive conversation among students in which they challenge each other's thinking through debate and articulate multiple perspectives also fosters democratic sensibilities. As you consider the principles and teaching methods in the next two chapters, think about how the teaching practices you select will affect both your students' understanding of content and their preparation to be citizens in a democracy.

Six Principles for Instruction

This section synthesizes much of what you have learned about students and authentic learning into a small number of learning principles to be used in designing student-learning experiences. These guidelines can serve as a mental checklist not only for planning, but also for problem solving and redesigning lessons.

Let's return to Gloria Jackson's situation at the beginning of Chapter 2. Remember, she was conducting a textbook-based lesson and her students were inattentive. She was frantically trying to figure out how to change the lesson so that students are more engaged and interested. In addition to reviewing what she knows about her students' (a) characteristics and (b) best ways of learning and creating meaning, she may want to refer to the following principles: *cultural context, conceptual focus, prior knowledge, higher level thinking, active processing,* and *variety.* You, too, may use these principles, not just to plan lessons but to understand how and why lessons were successful—or less successful—whether you were the teacher or the student. Using these principles to guide your analysis, you will find it easier to figure out why lessons worked or didn't work, or perhaps why your own study strategies are more or less effective.

1. Cultural Context Principle: Make sure classroom events and activities draw on the strengths of a variety of cultures and both males and females.

The discussion of this principle is divided into two sections: race, class, and gender issues; and political and social contexts. Treating people of various races, classes, and genders with equity differs somewhat from having an awareness of the political and social realities of the society in which our schools exist. Both are important for reflective teacher decision making.

Race, Class, and Gender Equity

Recall the discussion of students' cultural backgrounds in Chapter 2. Every activity you undertake, every example you use, and all the written or visual materials you provide can influence students' appreciation for diversity. These activities can also impact students' self-esteem. If students see examples of people like themselves in the stories they hear, the history they learn, and the images they see around them, they are more likely to make ties to their own experiences. If the stories, history, and images are affirming, students develop more positive images of themselves. If, in addition, they hear positive anecdotes, learn important history, and see beautiful images of people very different from themselves, they learn to value diversity.

Planning lessons to enhance these understandings entails more than teaching about Crispus Atticus while studying the American Revolution or discussing women's history during March. It involves awareness of the examples and images used in every aspect of the curriculum. For example, when developing activities in which students role-play story problems, be aware of stereotypes that may be inadvertently reinforced. Are boys and girls portrayed in equal numbers? Do the examples using girls all entail cooking? Are cooperative groups organized so that roles rotate among boys and girls, majority and minority students? How do the stories we read or the accomplishments we praise reflect the ethnic diversity of the world around us?

Activities designed to teach about important contributors to our society should include males and females representing various cultural groups. If, however, the important Native Americans are all warriors and the important African Americans are all entertainment or sports figures, stereotypes are still reinforced. These are subtle, but very important aspects of teaching, because you as a teacher exert a powerful influence over your students' attitudes toward themselves and others. Think about the scientists with whom your students may become familiar in the traditional curriculum. In most cases, it is not a very diverse group. Bringing in additional information about the contributions of women scientists and people of color will help all students envision their potential in those roles (see, for example, information on "Women of NASA" at NASA's website).

You may need to stretch yourself into greater cultural awareness so you can communicate an appreciation of all cultures. In every classroom, the examples, materials, and treatment of students need to reflect a bottom-line respect for all classes, races, genders, and religious beliefs. To do this takes commitment and time to become culturally competent. First, teachers need to search their own hearts and acknowledge that they too have been conditioned by society to hold certain prejudices. This is a hard pill to swallow, but it is better than denying the fact and inadvertently sending demeaning messages to students.

Second, they need to learn about the cultures represented in the community. This may require "hanging out" in gathering places, attending community functions, and becoming active in other ways. Join an organization or group that has many people from different cultural and economic backgrounds than your own. Get to know well someone who has had very different experiences in this society. As you get to know this person, begin to see how each social group comes with its own strengths and challenges. Finally, equipped with a better understanding of themselves and cultural diversity, teachers need to examine the available teaching materials for obvious or hidden biases.

Cultural competence is the essence of caring for students—respecting them and their backgrounds. Such caring and respect may provide a powerful model of democracy and fairness for students. In Lisa Delpit's (1995) view, this respect should not extend so far that the teacher fails to teach the student Standard English and other keys to success in the dominant culture. A teacher can celebrate and highlight the expressiveness of Ebonics while at the same time teaching children the conventions of English as used in the workplace. Helping students learn to understand and appreciate the cultural conventions appropriate to a given time and place is a valuable lesson that demands flexible and complex thinking.

Social and Political Context

This aspect of cultural context refers to the power relationships among groups and their influence on your decisions as a teacher. Figure 6.1 shows concentric circles expanding out from your classroom—school, community, district, state, nation, and planet. Each of these social and political entities is important to consider in your decision making. Sometimes you will find yourself selecting activities based on school factors. One such factor might be your school's collaboratively developed "school improvement" goals. For example, a school-planning team might set a goal to improve students' informational reading scores. You would then emphasize reading for information, especially in your social studies, math, and science activities. Or the school improvement team might plan to work on students' self-esteem. Your response might be to give more specific positive feedback to students as they show progress in their work, or you might set up a weekly game that many of the lower achieving students could play successfully, raising their status among other children (Cohen, 1994).

Other school factors that may influence the choice of activities include the size of the school, the grade levels served, and the physical facility. Some schools are designed for open-space learning, reflecting a progressive orientation. In such schools, classes can be easily combined for joint activities, offering greater flexibility for team teaching and sharing of resources.

School district policies and politics also influence greatly what goes on in your classroom. Most teachers work for a school system that is governed by a school board—a group of elected citizens or appointed officials. Members of the board reflect the attitudes, values, and philosophy of the community served by the schools. Thus board members exercise an important influence on school programs, policies, regulations, and curriculum. Although the school board members rarely spend large amounts of time ex-

FIGURE 6.1 Influences on Teacher Decision Making

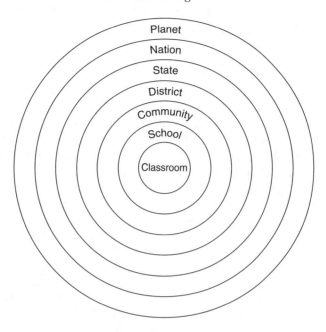

amining the actual teaching activities used, they do have a vested interest in what happens in classrooms. As representatives of the community, they want to be sure that students are learning appropriate skills and attitudes.

Imagine yourself teaching in an ethnically diverse community that has experienced conflict between the Latino and Anglo cultures. The school board has expressed concern over this conflict and has made conflict resolution a goal for the year. You would then strive to select classroom activities that would enable students to deal with conflict and learn how to resolve it. When deciding how to teach about representative government, for instance, you might select a learning activity in which teams of students work together to solve a problem. You would teach, model, and give feedback on the social skills needed for students to work constructively together. This type of activity would more likely meet the district goal than would a straight lecture that offers little opportunity for interaction or conflict resolution. Think, too, about how attention to differing cultures would apply to this goal.

State and national policies also influence what happens in the classroom. State curriculum frameworks, testing programs, statewide school improvement initiatives, and funding formulas are only a few of these larger factors that need to be considered by teachers on a daily basis.

The point of the cultural context principle is that classrooms do not exist in a vacuum. Teachers form an important socializing function in this society. The attitudes they develop and model will influence future generations' actions toward the opposite sex, people of color, and other cultural and economic groups. Chapter 10 contains more information about working with diverse students.

2. Congruent Continuous Assessment: (a) Match your objectives, activities, and assessment; and (b) find out what your students understand about a topic, plan activities to build on or reconstruct that knowledge, and assess continuously.

Congruence

Congruence refers to the crucial match between the lesson objectives, the activities, and the assessment procedures as shown in Figure 6.2. An example may help clarify this concept.

One high school chemistry teacher started every class with a story about football. As the students continued to ask questions, he would go on and on about his experiences as a football star, until the bell rang. There was no congruence between his chemistry objectives and his football-story activities. Even worse, he used tests from the teachers' manual, even though he had spent only a fraction of class time on the content covered by the test. His teaching method was clearly an infraction of the congruence principle.

Simply put, when you select activities, you should make sure they lead to your objectives. You will also want to be certain that your tests and projects assess the skills and ideas you have developed through your learning activities (Stiggins, 1994; Wiggins, 1996). For instance, if you want students to be able to solve word problems of a certain type, they will need adequate demonstration and practice activities on solving those word problems. When you evaluate your students' learning, your test should include new word problems of the same type. You may be reminded of the idea of validity (see Chapter 5) as you read about congruence.

One important aspect of congruence is to match the activities with the level and type of learning stated in the objective(s). If you want students to be able to recall the names of letters or identify states on a map, then one set of activities may be appropriate—for example, drill with flash cards, creating clay letters, drawing maps, group oral games, and so on. However, if your objective is that students be able to write stories or make predictions about an area's economy based on geography, then your activities might include small-group problem solving, peer editing, demonstration of creative thinking strategies, or a simulation that focuses on the use of natural resources. Thus lower level and higher level objectives may require different types of activities.

Whether the objective is affective, psychomotor, or cognitive will also influence your choice of activities. Affective outcomes usually take a longer time to develop and are often best taught through direct experience—for example, role-playing. Imagine that you want students to be able to disagree in a courteous way (your objective). For your activities, you might discuss and demonstrate the specific words and actions you desire and the put-down words and actions you want to discourage. You could bring two students to the front to act

FIGURE 6.2 Congruence in Planning

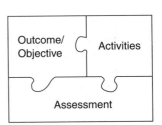

out both types of behavior and discuss the reactions. Then you could observe students during classroom group work and give feedback on their treatment of their classmates. This objective is one that you might address continually throughout several weeks or months.

A second important aspect of congruence is to match the assessment or evaluation with the objective(s). Congruence can be a bit tricky with higher level objectives. For example, if you want students to be able to compare and contrast the characteristics of a mammal and a reptile, you may discuss in class the similarities and differences between a cat and a snake. In evaluation however, if you included a question about a cat and a snake, you would only be testing memory of a prior lesson. To see whether students can engage in higher level thinking, you need to evaluate them with new situations. In this case, students would be asked to compare a mammal and a reptile not previously discussed in class, perhaps a dog and a lizard, or have them create an imaginary mammal or reptile with the correct characteristics. This task would require students to apply their ability to a situation not previously encountered.

In addition, you must make sure that, if you are teaching to a higher level objective, your class activities provide opportunities to practice functioning at those higher levels of learning. Too often, teachers teach to memory level and understanding level objectives and then expect students to be able to apply the knowledge at higher levels on an assessment, without ever having been asked to do so before.

One way to help yourself provide congruent activities is to tell students repeatedly the instructional objective(s) and remind them periodically of how they'll be assessed. In this way, you remind yourself and the students of where the lesson is heading and how the classroom activities relate to the objective. One excellent teacher kept showing his students the final project on water quality that his previous year's class had done. Seeing the project kept students motivated and focused on the outcome while they were learning the content and skills required for the project.

CHECK YOUR UNDERSTANDING

Mrs. Zarett is teaching limericks, and her objective is for students to be able to write a limerick. She shows them examples and describes the characteristics of a limerick. She provides practice by having students describe the characteristics and point them out in examples. Then, for her evaluation of their learning, Mrs. Zarett asks students to write a limerick. Determine whether the principle of congruence has been followed by comparing the objective with the activities and evaluation.

Answer: The assessment was at the higher level (synthesis), while the activities took the students only to the lower levels of comprehension (understanding). There is a mismatch here, a lack of congruence. Mrs. Zarett should have provided modeling and practice on the actual writing of limericks before asking the students to do so.

Continuous Assessment

Often teachers begin a lesson with a preassessment activity that will show what prior knowledge, experiences, or feelings students have about the topic in the lessons to come.

One teacher we know wanted children to conduct inquiries into local water quality. To find out about their prior experience with the topic, she had them write down everything that came to mind about how water is made safe for cooking or swimming. Reading her students' responses helped her find a few students with a deep interest in the subject, and others who had never played in a stream or considered the cleanliness of water. She could then ask the students with more background knowledge to share their experiences and build a knowledge base for the others.

Many teachers assume children have no knowledge of something because it has not been formally taught to them. Take, for example, the topic of historical accuracy. Although students may not have had any lessons in school on how history is written, they have been around history, stories, and the news media their entire lives. And the concept of history also has been around them in their families' discussions and activities. Wouldn't it make sense for the teacher to preassess students to find out what conceptions about history, stories, and the news they bring to the classroom? Helpful ideas can be built upon (e.g., "History is a record of events") while misconceptions ("There is only one interpretation of an event—the true one") can be corrected through hands-on, mindful experiences with various accounts of the same event, told from different perspectives.

This idea of *misconceptions* is an important aspect of constructivist teaching. Recall our discussion on misconceptions in Chapter 2. For example, most students (and many adults!) believe that plants gain their nutrition solely from plant food, just like humans do. The mind's early search for meaning has constructed an explanation that seemed very reasonable. This entrenched belief interferes with student learning about photosynthesis. Such early constructions of meaning (misconceptions) are very powerful and must be identified and challenged in order to change them. Teachers need to learn about such prior conceptions and then design experiences that clear up the student's misconceptions.

In the photosynthesis example, students could be asked to find out what would happen if plants received plenty of plant food, but no light. They would be pressed to explain the results, given their old ideas. Such discrepant events are very powerful in helping students reconstruct misconceptions. Just lecturing on new information with no acknowledgment of how students have created meaning is not likely to produce the kind of learning that stays with students.

Why do we have "and assess continuously" in this principle? Because whether it is before you begin to teach, during your teaching, or after, you will need to know how well the students are doing in achieving the desired learning objectives. Examining students' work, asking them to "think aloud," and observing their work in groups are all valuable sources of informal "assessment" information. Without such assessments, students' developing understandings (or misunderstandings) will be a mystery to you, and a crucial source of information for teacher decision making will be lost.

3. Conceptual Focus Principle: Make sure the activities are focused on developing a few key concepts and generalizations—the structure of the information—rather than memorizing a series of facts.

This principle relates to the discussion of concepts in Chapter 3. Concepts allow us to classify ideas and objects we've never seen before. They also allow us to transfer our learning. Consider a unit introducing your state—many students near our university study Michigan in the fourth grade. If a large percentage of the introductory unit is devoted to memorizing the state bird, the state flower, the state tree, and so on, little transferable learning occurs.

But what if, instead of being organized around isolated facts, the unit was organized around the concept of symbols? Students could discuss what symbols are and how they are chosen. They might discover that many symbols of the state were selected because they represent an important aspect of the state or played an important part in its history. Students may come to wonder if other symbols are chosen in similar ways. They might also learn that every group—nation, state, ethnic group—has specific symbols of its own culture. This is a powerful idea that will transfer to many settings and will aid students in understanding the world around them.

You can see how important it is to clarify for yourself the main ideas before beginning to teach a topic. There simply is not enough time to teach thoroughly everything in a given textbook or unit. How can you sift out what is crucial? One suggestion is to talk to the curriculum coordinator in your district about the district outcomes (standards or benchmarks). Then you can select the ideas and skills that relate most directly to the district grade-level and long-term goals. Other teachers are also a valuable source of information on curriculum. Try to become as knowledgeable as possible about the topics of importance at your grade level and subject areas. As you develop your own deeper understanding of the content, it is easier to pick out the most powerful ideas.

Once you have identified the key concepts and generalizations (remember the concept map from Chapter 3?), you will want to design instruction so the conceptual structure of the content is clear to students. Since the brain naturally wants to organize information into meaningful networks, or schemata, the teacher can capitalize on this inclination by helping students see the patterns and structure in new information.

How can this be done? Many teachers use an overhead projector, computer display, chalkboard, or poster to display information as they explain it. When deciding how to show the organization of the material, remember that your learning style may not match your learners' styles. You may prefer lists and outlines, whereas some of your students may need to see the information displayed spatially or in pictures. A variety of visual tools, from brainstorming maps to task-specific tools like sorting trees, can help students visualize the structure of the information (see Hyerle, 1996 for a good assortment of examples). Nonlinguistic representations, both as used by the teacher and as created by students, are powerful tools for enhancing memory (Marzano, Pickering, & Pollock, 2001). The outline and figure on the Revolutionary War unit found in Chapter 3 show how the information is organized. The list is a sequential one; the figure is more abstract and spatial. Concept maps, graphic organizers, and webbing are among the ways to show the "big picture" and the interconnections among ideas.

Many people have trouble making sense of information when it is unclear how one piece relates to another. Such people like to see the big picture first and then fit the details in later. Others can't find the big picture until they have understood all the details. You will have both types of learners in your classes. Therefore you can show the structure before, during, and after providing information so that all learning preferences are taken into account. In any case, be sure to focus students' attention on the structure and organization often during presentation of information. Statements such as these help students focus on the relevant information: "This next point relates to the one we just discussed in this way . . ." or "We've been talking about mammals. Now look up here and see how our next topic, reptiles, relates to. . . ."

Not all information lends itself to easy organization. For example, when there are many disparate facts to be memorized (e.g., the times tables), it may be hard to find any meaningful way of categorizing them. In such cases, you may wish to use a mnemonic device—a memory aid. You have probably used such devices at one time or another, especially when cramming for a test. A mnemonic device used to remember the names of the Great Lakes is HOMES: Huron, Ontario, Michigan, Erie, and Superior. Other mnemonic devices include making up a story or sentence using the first word or letter of items in a list (e.g., "Every Good Boy Does Fine" for the lines on the treble clef) and creating an image for each item on the list.

REFLECTING ON THE IDEAS

Imagine you are creating a checklist to help remind yourself of important ideas in the first three principles for designing learning experiences. You plan to tape the checklist inside your plan book as a reminder to use as you create lesson plans. What questions would you list?

4. Higher Level Thinking Principle: Aim learning activities toward an authentic project or display that requires higher level thinking.

When designing learning activities, it is important to look down the road toward a culminating experience that will allow students to create something original with their knowledge. This is the essence of authentic learning—an activity that requires students to develop a product for a real audience that illustrates their learning.

Note how such activities allow students to develop the kind of higher level thinking that will be required of citizens in the 21st century. In short, higher level thinking requires students to use information rather than merely recall it. They may be asked to compare one concept or generalization with another; to use a skill in a new situation; to analyze the causes, effects, motivations, or other aspects of an event; to make judgments; to apply logic; or to combine information and prior experience in new and creative ways. Higher level thinking also includes the use of processes such as problem solving and decision making in real or simulated situations.

This type of learning is in marked contrast to rote learning or memorization of facts that are not used in a meaningful way. This is not to suggest that lower level learning—recalling and understanding basic facts, concepts, or generalizations—is unimportant. However, it is only one step in a larger process. Good higher level thinking is built on a solid foundation of understanding. You will need to find out where students are in their understanding of an area, and then provide the guidance and encouragement they need to build toward higher level tasks.

In selecting learning activities, note that some have greater potential for enhancing higher level thinking than others. Role-playing, simulations, and writing assignments that require students to relate a number of generalizations to one another in a debate or to solve a complex problem are especially good for this purpose. Authentic student projects that extend beyond description to include performances and problem solving are also excellent vehicles for developing thinking skills.

Students Actively Involved in Learning

5. Active Processing Principle: Help students make new ideas more meaningful through direct experience and active involvement with the ideas in meaningful contexts.

Information is more easily stored and recalled when it is embedded in a rich network of experiences, facts, ideas, concepts, and so on. Such a meaningful network is created through direct experience with the ideas, concepts, and generalizations to be learned. The idea of active processing is fairly obvious: If teachers can engage students' minds in thinking about, using, applying, and reflecting upon new ideas or skills, the learning will be deeper and more permanent. When giving an explanation, a teacher can pause after each one or two main ideas and ask students to think about and answer a question, write down a brief summary, or discuss one of the ideas with their partner. These activities require students to work with the ideas in their short-term memories so the new ideas can become integrated into the structures of meaning in the long-term memory.

Take the Revolutionary War unit as an example. One of the objectives was for students to be able to contrast points of view. Rather than just lecture or assign a worksheet on the topic, the teacher could have students form literary criticism groups. In the groups, roles would be assigned requiring each student to analyze the point of view of a particular character in a story or novel. These could be summarized in a group presentation using a dialogue or a visual representation. Such direct experience and active involvement promote a significantly deeper understanding of the topic than would a teacher-centered lecture with follow-up worksheets.

FIGURE 6.3　Cone of Experience Illustration from *Audio-Visual Methods in Teaching, third edition,* by E. Dale © 1969. Reprinted with permission of Wadsworth, an imprint of the Wadsworth Group, a division of Thomson Learning. Fax 800 730-2215.

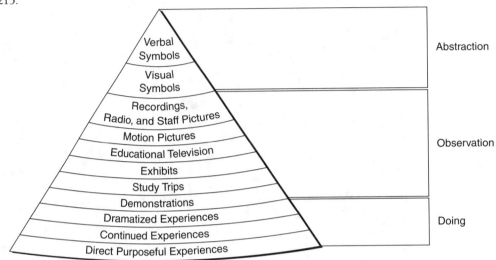

The "active processing" part of this principle has been discussed, but what is meant by "direct experience in meaningful contexts"? Imagine Gloria thinking about different ways to teach her students about the lifestyles in colonial America. She considers the following ideas: using a worksheet, demonstrating some of the customs, showing a movie or video, taking a virtual tour of a restored village, creating a classroom simulation of a colonist's activities in rural and urban locations, and having students analyze period drawings of everyday life. Which activities seem most meaningful to you in terms of actual real-life applicability? The last two occur in a meaningful context where students can have direct experience with the ideas being learned. Students can learn important information from the other activities, but to exclude the more authentic ones would greatly curtail meaningful learning.

The "cone of experience" (Dale, 1969) in Figure 6.3 is a useful way to portray this continuum from concrete, more meaningful contexts for learning to abstract, less meaningful contexts. An explanation of each layer from the base to the top follows. As you consider each level, recall what you know about Piaget's theory of cognitive development—your students are moving slowly from concrete to more abstract thinking (formal operations). Also recall what you learned about multiple intelligences theory and learning styles.

Doing

Direct purposeful experiences involve students in activities in the world outside the classroom and outside school. Examples include participating in community cleanup projects, establishing a working banking system in the school, managing and staffing a school store, and assuming the duties of tutor in a kindergarten. Kavolik (1994) referred to this level as "being there."

Contrived experiences approximate real-life situations. They are an edited version of reality. For example, children simulate three branches of government in the classroom or may use a computer simulation to experiment with physical and chemical changes. In this case the simulated situation is preferred over the real-life one because of safety concerns.

Dramatized experiences include role-playing and dramatic re-creations of actual or fictional events—for example, of scenes from history or literature. Kavolik (1994) referred to these activities as "immersion or simulation."

Observation

Demonstrations, study trips, virtual trips via the web, exhibits, educational television, motion pictures, recordings, radio, and *still pictures* all represent gradations from more concrete to more abstract learning activities. The more hands-on, the better (Kavolik, 1994).

Abstraction

The layer *visual symbols* includes activities where students work with maps, games, and other kinds of diagrams. *Verbal symbols,* the top layer, refers to activities such as writing, speaking, and reading, in which students work with symbols (e.g., words and numbers) that do not look like the objects they represent. That is, the symbols, in and of themselves, do not provide any visual clue to assist in meaning. In these cases, students are working with abstract concepts.

One implication of the cone of experience is that teachers should think about whether they are providing enough "learning by doing" activities. In most classrooms, there are too many abstract reading, writing, and listening activities and too few direct experience activities. Too often students are rushed through the concrete activities so they can function at the abstract level. Unfortunately, most elementary students are not developmentally ready to learn from many abstract activities. They need more time with concrete experiences.

However, one goal of schooling is to allow students to function at the higher, more abstract levels. Thus as students reach the higher grades in middle and high school, they need to be weaned away from a predominance of concrete experiences. Even among older students, however, many concepts are often best introduced through concrete, real-life activities.

CHECK YOUR UNDERSTANDING

Assume you are teaching students about bird migration. Label the following activities according to the type of learning: D for doing, O for observation, or A for abstraction.

_____ 1. Teacher lecturing from a textbook on migration

_____ 2. Field trip to a bird sanctuary, including an interview with a sanctuary guide

_____ 3. Reading and then completing a workbook exercise on the topic

_____ 4. Seeing a filmstrip about bird migrations

_____ 5. Groups of students role-playing movements of birds on a map

Did you label items 2 and 5 as doing, 4 as observation, and 1 and 3 as abstraction?

6. Variety Principle: Appeal to the different styles, needs, and preferences of students.

Having read the discussion in Chapter 2 of students' learning needs and styles, you are probably not surprised by the need for variety. We do not all learn in the same way, and teachers need to acknowledge this in planning and teaching. Students must attend to information in order to learn it. Most children have trouble attending to one topic for any length of time. In light of these facts, teachers can plan a variety of activities that will appeal to learners' multiple learning styles, preferences, and intelligences. In addition to enhancing learning, such variety also holds students' attention throughout the lesson.

Consider a language arts lesson that might be part of the unit on patterns described in Chapter 3. The teacher started out by showing the cover of the big book *Brown Bear, Brown Bear, What Do You See?* (Martin, 1983) and asking students to predict what the book might be about. She then read the book, encouraging students to join in as they perceived the pattern. Next the class was divided in half to read the book again, with each group assigned to read along with one part and clap with the other. In the following days students read along in their own copies of the book, took turns acting out the animals on cue, created charts of the animals, made lists of words that rhyme with *me,* and created their own original pages for the book.

In this lesson, the teacher used visual, auditory, and kinesthetic learning modes. She also appealed to musical intelligence as students worked with rhythmic patterns. The listing may have appealed to sequential learners, whereas those who prefer a more random style would probably feel comfortable acting out the animals or creating original additions to the story. Having students work in groups and alone also allowed for different learning preferences.

Because their teacher included a variety of activities that appealed to different learning styles and needs, more students are likely to achieve success. Their brains will accept and process the information more easily when they are tuned in and when their particular strengths are appealed to. The guideline to follow is to have a good deal of variety in your lessons, not only to maintain students' attention but also to hook into your learners' particular styles.

There is one aspect of this principle that deserves greater attention—**modeling,** which is a variation on appealing to the visual learner. To model is to show, demonstrate, or illustrate something as you explain it. Most educators suggest that explanations, stories, or other verbal lessons be illustrated visually. Another important aspect of modeling is to provide an example of an assignment or project so students can see the specifics of the qualities being sought in the product. Some experts (e.g., Stiggins, 1994) call this a "target paper." Modeling is not always easy to do, but it is worth making an effort to reach the variety of learners in your class.

What techniques might you use? One teacher we know put on a costume each Friday to illustrate a different idea the class had been studying. In a unit on westward expansion, for instance, she dressed up as a pioneer one Friday and as an explorer on another day. It is not necessary to go to such extremes, of course. You can draw pictures on the board to illustrate how sod huts were built, or fill a tank with water to show how different weights and densities of materials float and sink. You can have students role-play the numbers in a problem to illustrate the process of double-digit addition in math. Colored chalk may also be used; for example, if students are working on recognizing nouns, a story on the board might have all nouns highlighted in red.

There are many ways to add variety to your lessons. Talk to other teachers, read teachers' magazines, and be creative. It's fun to try new approaches, and it's rewarding when you finally see a hard-to-reach student tune in. Finally, don't forget that *humor, novelty,* and *emotion* are excellent ways of providing variety. Dare to be a little outrageous occasionally. You'll be pleasantly surprised with the results.

REFLECTING ON THE IDEAS

Complete the list of questions you began in the last activity by writing prompts or thought questions for the remaining three principles. As you prepare lesson and unit plans, look back at your list of questions to see if you are using the planning principles to guide you.

_____

_____

_____

▦ *Practice Activity: Remembering the Learning Principles*

First review the six principles of learning and make notes for yourself. Then create a mnemonic device, or memory aid, that will help you remember the six principles. Practice saying them from memory until you know they are in your long-term memory. Write or draw your mnemonic device in the space provided.

_____

_____

▦ ▦ ▦

▦ *Practice Activity: Applying the Learning Principles*

Use the six principles of learning to analyze the actions taken in the scenario that follows. In the margin, write the name of the principle that is illustrated by the activity described in the scenario. Be ready to explain why this principle aids learning. You also can use the principles to analyze real-life classroom observations and your own teaching.

Mr. Jones is working with a group of third graders on a unit about the local community. One objective of his lessons is for students to be able to create a bulletin board based on information from workers from the community who provide goods and services.

First, Mr. Jones focuses students on the lesson by asking them to name some of the kinds of jobs people hold in the community. Next he asks what they know about the impact those people have on their everyday lives. After a short discussion, he describes the objectives and presents the project to the students. The class is divided in half, with one half assigned to write to workers who produce or sell goods, and the other to write to those who sell services. Together the class divides the list of workers into the two categories, creating a chart. When students are not sure, those workers are put in a "research" category. The teacher adds workers to the list, making sure the major categories he wants to include (for example, health care workers) are not missed.

Students are divided into pairs and assigned a worker. They must research the responsibilities of their worker and prepare a list of three questions they might ask. Questions are to be prepared in a brief survey with a cover letter and mailed to the workers. As the letters return, each pair of students is responsible for sharing their information on the class bulletin board, divided into two sections: "Workers Provide Goods" and "Workers Provide Services."

Your responses may have included some of the following observations:

- Mr. Jones has selected an authentic activity as his outcome, which represents the meaningful context aspect of the active processing principle. Students will be active as they research their jobs and prepare their portion of the bulletin board. The survey prepared for a real community member is also meaningful and rich.
- The lesson represents an awareness of the surrounding social and political realities, illustrating the cultural context principle.
- The conceptual focus principle is evident in the focus on the key concepts of goods and services.
- The prior knowledge principle is used when the teacher asks students to list the workers in their community and to divide them into those providing goods and services.
- Higher level thinking is involved in designing the questions, analyzing the responses, and preparing the bulletin board.
- Finally, the lesson is rich in variety. Students write, read, listen, create, work in large and small groups, and work at more concrete and abstract tasks.

■ ■ ■

SECTION 2. TEACHING APPROACHES AND LESSON PLANNING

Section 2 Objectives

After you have completed this section, you will be able to

1. describe two categories of instructional approaches;
2. describe a format for lesson planning;
3. explain the difference between formal and informal instruction; and
4. describe differentiated instruction and why it is important.

Assume that you are about to plan a lesson to fit into Gloria Jackson's Revolutionary War unit. You must decide what learning activities you will select to lead students from where they are to where you expect them to be (as stated in your outcomes). There is no one activity or single lesson type that will work with all objectives, classroom environments, and students. Teaching involves not only planning but also day-by-day experimentation and responsive adjustments as you discover what works best for you and your students. Consequently, an effective teacher must possess a wide repertoire of skills, methods, and learning activities and be willing to employ them in the classroom. Our goal in this section is to provide a simple yet powerful format with the flexibility and creativity you need to provide rich learning experiences for your students.

Plan your lessons carefully, keeping your students, goals, and objectives clearly in mind. Use what you can glean from research, teaching principles, your experience, and your intuition, while also considering your classroom conditions and surrounding context. After you teach the lesson, take a few minutes to reflect on it. Note what went well and what did not. Use the learning principles in this chapter and other resources to try to figure out why things turned out as they did. Think of changes you could make that might improve the lesson; share your thoughts with colleagues and ask for their suggestions. Using your notes, redesign the lesson and try it again with a different class, then revise again, and so on. With this approach you will find that teaching will be ever fresh, and always a learning experience (Garrison, 1997).

Two Approaches to Teaching

This chapter and the next two will provide you with several approaches to teaching. The purpose here is to preview these different types of lessons before taking them up in detail. This will be most helpful for those of you who like to see the big picture first. If you are a more concrete learner, you may wish to come back to this section after reading about the various approaches.

REFLECTING ON THE IDEAS

To further understand the first two types of lessons, examine the following two teaching episodes involving a sixth-grade classroom.

Lesson 1

> *Teacher:* Class, I have written the definition of *honesty* on the board. It is freedom from fraud and deception. Raise your hand if you know what *fraud* is. (Wait) Janet?
>
> *Janet:* Miss Morrison, I think it means cheating to get something you want from someone else.
>
> *Teacher:* Good! Now, everyone think; what does *deception* mean? (Wait) Larry?
>
> *Larry:* It means using tricks or not telling the truth.
>
> *Teacher:* That's right. Now that we have looked at the definition and agreed that honesty requires that you tell the truth and don't use trickery or cheat to get what you want, I would like you to examine these three newspaper stories that I have gathered. Be ready to tell me if the person identified in each story is being honest. Later, we'll apply this idea in your courtroom plays.

Lesson 2

> *Teacher:* Class, we are going to examine a very important aspect of people. Instead of telling you what it is, I would like you to examine three newspaper stories that I have gathered. I want to know what the stories have in common. Also, be ready to tell me what the person identified in each story is like.

(Students look at the stories provided)

Teacher: Raise your hand if you have an idea of what the three stories have in common. (Wait) Larry?

Larry: The people in each story tell the truth even though they could make more money or be thought of as more important if they lied. In one story, a greeting card company wanted to pay a thousand dollars for a poem written by this man's great-grandfather to use on a greeting card. They thought it had been written by the man. He told the company the truth even though the company could then use the poem without paying anything for it. In the second story, this woman returned a purse with over five thousand dollars in it. In the third story, a woman told her daughter that the daughter had been adopted, although the mother could have kept it a secret. They were all honest!

Teacher: Excellent, Larry! Now, everyone jot on your paper your ideas about what it means to be honest. (Wait) Lauri?

Lauri: It means to tell the truth, even when the truth hurts!

Teacher: That's an excellent answer, Lauri. That is one of the lessons to be learned from the story you have been reading this week. Now let's look at three different news articles and see if the people involved in them are being honest.

What are the key differences you notice between the lessons? Which lesson do you think is better? Why? How might you label each?

The first type of lesson is the **direct lesson.** When the lesson begins, the teacher tells the students the concept or generalization to be learned and leads them through most of the activities. A direct lesson is also referred to as *deductive.*

Direct lessons are deductive because the teacher typically states the instructional objective(s), presents the material to be learned with examples and nonexamples, provides practice, and assesses students' learning. For instance, assume that Gloria Jackson's team wants to teach students about the concept *analogy* before having them write analogies between forms of "government" in the United States and in their classroom. If she decided to use a direct approach to teach students to identify examples of analogies, she would tell them the objective, present the definition and characteristics of analogies, show students examples and nonexamples, engage them in practice exercises, give them feedback and more practice, and then test them. Figure 6.4 illustrates the structure of the direct (deductive) lesson.

In contrast to a direct lesson, an **inductive lesson** begins with exploratory activities and leads students to discover a concept or generalization. For the preceding topic, Gloria might begin by giving students several passages containing analogies and some that

FIGURE 6.4 A Direct (Deductive) Lesson

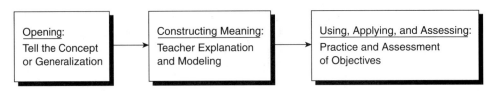

FIGURE 6.5   An Inductive Lesson

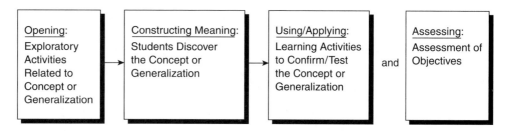

do not. She would ask them to select the passages that give them the most vivid image of the idea being presented. Next she would ask them to identify the phrases that made the passages so interesting. Only then would she label these phrases as examples of analogies, define the term, and describe its essential characteristics. As with the deductive lesson, the final step would be to provide practice exercises and then to assess students' accomplishment of the objective. You may have noted that inductive lessons require the student to do more of the thinking, at least in the beginning of the lesson. That is an added bonus of inductive lessons. Figure 6.5 illustrates the structure of an inductive lesson.

You can think of these approaches as a starter kit for your first year of teaching. Please note, however, that these are not the only approaches to teaching. An excellent presentation of several different strategies is available in Joyce, Showers, and Weil (1996). There are many approaches to be explored, especially in the area of student-directed learning (Darling, 1994).

The two lesson categories are not necessarily kept separate in daily teaching. It is not uncommon to see them combined in a particular lesson or unit. For example, a lesson might have an inductive introduction and a direct section that builds understanding—or vice versa. As you observe and practice teaching, you will be able to make decisions about the various types of lesson categories and to mix and match them yourself.

CHECK YOUR UNDERSTANDING

Without reviewing the text on the two lesson categories, explain their definitions to a colleague and describe how they differ from one another. See if you agree on the critical attributes of each lesson type.

A Lesson-Planning Framework

This section will describe a basic framework that can be used to structure many types of lessons. When beginning lesson planning, it is helpful to note the distinction between a lesson plan and a lesson design. A **lesson plan** describes your activities for 1 day of instruction. A complete **lesson design** includes all the activities you will need to help students achieve mastery of one or more objectives. It will include your plans for differentiation, and some assessments of how students are progressing. Such a lesson design may span 1 or more days. When planning for a week of teaching, it is most helpful to think of a lesson design rather than a lesson plan. A lesson is rarely a 1-day event to be performed

FIGURE 6.6 Activities, Lessons, and Units

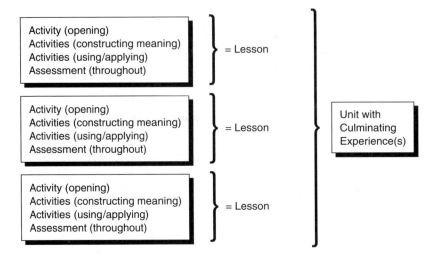

and then to be left, with no further work on that topic. Even if you think you have taught something well on a particular day, you should definitely plan to revisit the same topic or skill on another day. One-shot lessons have little lasting power.

A series of lessons may not necessarily be all in the same content area; they may form the puzzle pieces of an interdisciplinary unit, like the Revolutionary War unit Gloria Jackson's fifth-grade team has planned. In any case, the lessons will build upon one another and culminate in an authentic activity that illustrates much of what students have learned. Figure 6.6 shows how activities are combined to form lessons and units. The lessons are all congruent with the central themes and objectives of the unit. The learning is then demonstrated through the authentic culminating project(s) and other assessments.

How is a beginner to think about lesson planning? A simple but powerful frame for lesson design, which can accommodate most approaches to teaching, organizes lessons into four phases: *opening, constructing meaning, using and applying,* and *assessment.* Each of these is summarized in Figure 6.7 and described in more detail in the paragraphs that follow.

Opening

The beginning of any lesson should serve to *focus students' interests and attention* on the topic at hand. Showing a puzzling event, having students discuss their personal experiences, asking a provocative question, or sharing a story, popular song, or poem may all serve to focus students.

The opening is also a time to access students' **prior knowledge**, ideas, or skills that may be relevant to the lesson. For example, if students will need to use the concept of equality for the poem they will write, the opening should require them to recall what they know about equality. If students are to learn about telling time to the half hour, it will be helpful to have them demonstrate their knowledge of time on the even hours—

FIGURE 6.7   Lesson-Planning Framework: Four General Phases

OPENING: Readiness, preassessment, activate prior knowledge and experience, focus attention, invite inquiry/puzzlement, clarify culminating authentic projects/assessments, state objectives and purpose.

CONSTRUCTING MEANING: Students receive, gather, interpret, share, and digest: information, data, problems, ideas, events.

USING/APPLYING: Students apply new learning in problems, experiments, group or individual projects, productions, or exhibitions.

ASSESSING LEARNING: Teacher continuously gathers information from student responses and products to provide feedback and design next steps.

perhaps with the use of simulated clocks. Note that having students review prior concepts (rather than you reviewing them) also gives you valuable preassessment information about who may need reteaching in that area. Another reason to have students access prior experiences, feelings, or knowledge relates to how students construct meaning through experience (Chapter 2). Recall how new information is not retained when it is seen as unconnected to information in one's own mind. Having students activate their prior knowledge creates this readiness for learning new concepts.

Finally, often the opening helps students understand the *objective* of the lesson and how they will be *assessed* on this knowledge or skill. This is also the time to let students know the *purpose* of the lesson—why it is important, how it will be used in their personal or work lives, and how they will apply the knowledge in their authentic culminating projects.

Constructing Meaning

The next section of the lesson is where the learner's mind constructs new meanings and understandings through interacting with stories, ideas, objects, materials, and other learners. The authentic learning activities described in Chapter 2 would fit into this category, as would many less complex activities that help prepare students for higher level thinking. Teachers can provide inductive or cooperative group activities to help students construct meaning. Finally, more direct approaches, including teacher lecture and demonstration or storytelling, can be helpful to children's learning. This phase may require more than 1 day.

Using and Applying Understandings

This section of a lesson allows the students to actively use the new understandings in a variety of settings. Problem solving, application activities, writing a story or poem, and classroom practice all fit into this category. The idea is that even though a new understanding has been gained, it may not be permanent. New ideas and skills become more solid and meaningful through using them multiple times in meaningful settings. During the using/applying phase the teacher also gathers assessment information in both formal and informal ways to determine how well each child is achieving the desired outcomes of the lesson. At any time, reteaching or enrichment may be provided for those students with specific needs. This phase, too, may require more than 1 day.

Assessing Learning

In addition to continuous assessment during the lesson, the teacher will later provide more formal assessments of the learning resulting from one or more lessons. These may take the form of projects or tests that assess the learning developed over a series of lessons. Figure 6.7 shows the four lesson phases and key characteristics. The teaching approaches presented in the next chapters may be used in any combination and at any phase of a lesson.

Formal and Informal Instruction

In considering how teachers plan for student learning, it is helpful to consider the different types of learning activities that are important in the ebb and flow of elementary teaching. Unlike secondary teachers, elementary teachers usually are with the same group of students for most of the day. That kind of intimacy is challenging but does allow many opportunities for developing community as well as opportunities for learning. It also means that many interactions throughout the school day form the totality of student learning, not just the parts of the day that are outlined in formal lesson plans.

You will find that the formal designs for different types of lessons are helpful in planning, particularly for beginning teachers. In fact, such designs are often like the training wheels on a bicycle, good for getting a sense of how things work best until you are ready to ride more flexibly on your own. You will learn a number of formal lesson designs in Chapter 7. You will use them to plan the instruction throughout the school day. However, it is important to understand that many teaching opportunities are less formal.

For example, many concepts can be built simply by the way you arrange your room and the things you place there. Remember from Chapter 2 that we develop concepts through interactions with our environment. As individuals notice patterns in those interactions, concepts emerge. Many elementary classrooms are planned so that the learning environment provides experiences necessary to develop concepts. For example, classrooms that are equipped with plants, fish, and gerbils provide important experiences for developing concepts about living things. Classrooms with shelves that are numbered can allow young children to develop concepts regarding sequencing and ordinal numbers. Classrooms where the calendar includes birthdays of notable men and women from multiple cultures provide important data for developing the concepts of *famous* or *important*. Sometimes these ideas are also taught directly, but many times students learn them inductively through many experiences over time.

Of course, the classroom environment also can teach important lessons about how work is conducted, how materials are cared for, and what kinds of work are valued. The arrangement of the furniture, decorations on the walls, and routine interactions of the day all combine to teach students concepts like *work, leader, team,* and *adult.* It is important to think about the unspoken lessons our classrooms will teach and make sure they are the ones we want.

It is also important to note that the daily interactions with children bring countless opportunities for teachable moments—both big and small. The morning when a child arrives with a jar of tadpoles is a teachable moment. It might result in an impromptu explanation of the stages of a frog's life cycle or the opportunity to investigate that cycle by observation. A brief conversation on the nature of friendship with a student whose best friend is moving away, a class discussion on drugs spurred by a flippant remark, or a morning spent in preparing cards in response to a tragedy in a student's family all develop concepts that are essential for students' development. Balancing the immediacy of those moments with carefully planned lessons is one of the skills of an accomplished teacher.

Differentiation

Finally, before we begin our discussion of models for lesson planning, it is important to recall the complex dynamics of individuals and learning discussed in Chapter 2. Any class—or even small group—of students is made of multiple diverse individuals. Those individuals vary in many ways—their prior experiences, their culture, their patterns of intelligences, their learning styles, and so forth. Each different individual must find a way to link new information into his or her existing cognitive structure. And, of course, each structure is different.

When we think about it that way, the idea that we can plan one lesson for a class and expect all students to learn similar things doesn't sound very realistic. In fact, whatever your subject, you will have some students for whom particular activities are a good match and some students for whom they are not. A teacher who is committed to all students learning must recognize that it often will require not one lesson, but multiple differentiated lessons, in order to accomplish that goal.

Differentiated instruction is instruction that "flexes" to meet the needs of multiple learners simultaneously. It recognizes that in any given classroom there will be some times when everyone works together, some times when students work in small groups, and other times when students work individually. Sometimes individuals or small groups will be working on the same or very similar tasks. Other times their tasks will be completely different.

It is possible to consider differentiation both across lessons and within lessons. Differentiation across lessons requires that key concepts and skills be taught in multiple ways, targeted at different needs. In many ways it parallels the variety principle, and its implementation may look very similar. But when teachers differentiate across lessons, they use varied methods and materials not just as a global strategy, but in an effort to match specific student needs and characteristics. For example, a teacher who has observed several students who learn best through kinesthetic (using the whole body) experiences might make sure to include activities in which students shape their bodies like the letters of the alphabet in the teaching of letter sounds or patterns. This would be a good general strategy for all students. With similar knowledge, a teacher who is having a small number of students demonstrate the relative movement of the sun, earth, and moon would select students who learn best kinesthetically to portray the earth or moon, knowing that experience would particularly help those students internalize the concept. A teacher who is teaching about families or communities could differentiate across lessons by including a variety of children's literature that portrays families and communities similar to those that specific students have experienced. In this way more students have the opportunity to tie to prior knowledge.

The variety in students' needs also requires that teachers be able to differentiate within lessons. There are at least three overarching organizational patterns that comprise this type of differentiated instruction. First, there are some times when particular lessons or activities are not appropriate for some students. This is most likely to be true when students have very strong skills or interests or a great deal of prior knowledge. If, after preassessment, a teacher determines that one or more students are highly skilled in basic computation, it would not be a good use of those students' time to spend a great deal of time reviewing and practicing computation exercises. If students already know how to punctuate the ends of sentences, read a map key, or distinguish a noun from a verb, they may be assigned alternate activities rather than spend large amounts of time on already-mastered skills. There also may be occasions when a skill that is being taught is so far beyond the prior knowledge of a student or group of students that it would present an unreasonable level of frustration. In this case, too, that student or students may be assigned alternative activities. This strategy, of course, requires that both teacher and students be able to manage multiple activities occurring simultaneously in the same room.

Another general strategy that can be used for differentiation is multiple levels of activities or assignments within the same lesson or series of lessons. For example, if Gloria Jackson wants to teach the genre of historical fiction, all students could read historical fiction but they would not necessarily all read the same book. Students could choose from among a collection of historical fiction or students could be divided into groups and assigned texts of varying levels of difficulty. Class discussions could compare the accuracy, plot development, and use of language across texts. This approach not only allows for a variety of reading levels to be accommodated, but provides multiple examples for a richer development of the concept.

Finally, curriculum can be differentiated through the levels of supports or extensions offered individual students. Struggling students may be quietly offered a guide for note taking or allowed to do alternate problems on a math assignment to accommodate a slower pace of work. Students who complete assignments quickly and easily may be offered the opportunity to study topics of interest or work with a mentor from an older class on a challenging project. Whatever the strategy chosen, differentiated instruction requires that planning be done not for a "class" but for the individuals who comprise it.

Planning for multiple levels or types of instruction simultaneously is a daunting task, particularly for beginning teachers. It will not be possible to plan differentiated instruction for every moment of the day. Nevertheless, it is important to understand from the beginning of your career that effective teaching requires that we acknowledge and accommodate differences among individuals. Even if your beginning adjustments are somewhat limited, they will provide important connections to your students, and important inroads into expert teaching.

■ *Practice Activity: Why Plan Lessons in So Much Detail?*

You may have asked yourself, Why should I spend a lot of time writing lesson plans when the teachers I observe seem to do so little planning? Their lesson plans fit into a 2-inch by 2-inch box! Attempt to answer that question.

_____

_____

_____

Answer: You are a new teacher; teachers with years of experience rely on memory of prior years to guide them, and they have last year's lesson plans. A novice needs to do much more detailed planning (e.g., logistics, questions, group size, directions) than does an expert. You will not always need to plan at this level of detail, but it is a good idea to plan extra carefully when you teach something new, use a new strategy, or have an evaluation visit by a supervisor.

■ ■ ■

■ *Practice Activity: Differentiated Instruction*

Examine a lesson plan, either from a teacher's edition of a textbook or from your own collection of materials. What information is provided there that could help you plan for differentiated instruction? Is the lesson designed to be one-size-fits-all? Is that appropriate? Compare notes with a colleague. Think about how you might adapt the lessons as needed.

■ ■ ■

SUMMARY

This chapter has provided information on principles for planning, approaches to teaching, and lesson planning. It has discussed formal and informal teaching opportunities and the importance of differentiation.

A key concept of this book is that teaching is a sophisticated process of decision making in which many factors are considered. However, not all decisions are purely intellectual. Your own personal philosophy of teaching and learning will certainly come into play. Your emotions and health will influence your decisions; your personality and style will affect your teaching. Although these factors cannot be ignored, teaching can be an intelligent and purposeful activity, guided by cognitive reasoning.

Therefore it is important to avoid a haphazard method of planning. Many teachers select activities only on the basis of convenience or student interest, without regard to whether they match the instructional objectives, relate to students' learning needs, and so on. A purposeful, analytical approach to teaching will help you make the best decisions possible for the students, content, and conditions at the time.

Your growth as a decision maker is a gradual process. First, you will plan your activities to meet your objectives while taking into consideration the context, content, students, learning theories and principles, and teaching techniques. Then you will design a lesson or action plan for the teaching period. Finally, you will try it out, modifying it as necessary as you go.

The next step—reflection and redesign—is crucial to your development as a teacher, and it will be hard to find time for it. The payoff, however, is worth it. When you finish a lesson, spend a few moments reflecting on what went well and what did not go well. It is easiest to pick one successful and one less successful event for analysis. For each event, go back through your decisions, considering the context, students, content/objectives, learning theories, and techniques. Also consider the six learning principles. Ask yourself if any of these ideas can help explain why things went as they did. Then you can decide how to pursue or develop the successful parts of the lesson, emphasizing the factors or principles that made them work. You can also plan an alternative approach that might make the less successful parts of the lesson work better. The practice activity at the end of this chapter contains a reflection journal to be used for this purpose.

Your choice of an alternative is informed by your prior analysis, so it is likely to represent a real improvement. You try out your modification, rethink it, redesign it, and try again until you have a sequence of activities that work reasonably well. But be prepared, because you may need to modify further when students, goals, or content change. Teaching is an ever-renewing process.

■ *Practice Activity: Reflection Journal*

Observe a teacher or teach a short lesson yourself. Then fill in the following journal using the ideas from Chapters 4 and 5 to help explain what you saw. (Use extra paper if you need more space.)

Reflection Journal

What was done:

How it worked:

One successful aspect of the lesson:

Why did this part go well? What do I know about teaching and learning that might explain why? What conditions were operating that might explain why?

One less successful aspect of the lesson:

Why did this part not go well? What do I know about teaching and learning that might explain why? What conditions were operating that might explain why?

Ideas for next time. What I learned from this experience:

■ ■ ■

UNIT PREPARATION

This chapter provides general background information that will help you prepare the lessons for your unit. At this point you should have studied needs of the class you are to teach, prepared your content hierarchy and concept map, written lesson goals and objectives, and outlined your assessment plan. It is important to understand that none of these unit components are carved in stone yet. As you continue in unit planning you may find that the goals you have set are too lofty—or not lofty enough. You may identify a better culminating activity than the one you first planned. Unit planning is an iterative process, that is, each new stage may affect those that came before and it often is necessary to review and revise each piece many times. At this stage in the planning process you should create a time line for your unit, outlining which objectives you plan to emphasize each day. Think about the order that will best help students understand the structure of your content and build toward your culminating activity. Planning the time line before doing specific lesson planning can help you focus on the content to be addressed each day and may give you information on whether the goals you have set are realistic for the time available. Of course, as you actually teach the unit your time line will almost certainly have to flex to account for student learning—which is frequently at a different speed than we anticipate!

 ## PORTFOLIO ACTIVITY

The reflection journal in the preceding practice activity can make a good portfolio activity. Choose a lesson in which you are able to discuss students' learning and what you learned from the experience. Many beginning teachers make the mistake of focusing their attention solely on whether students are behaving and enjoying themselves. Of course it is important that your classroom atmosphere be conducive to learning. We also hope it will be a happy place. But the most important question for your reflection is, What were students learning and why? If you focus your reflections in that direction, they can be very powerful. Another possible portfolio activity is a plan for parent involvement. Carefully considering ways to involve parents and other community members in your class is an important part of the cultural context principle. The web links cited in the next section may help you compile a set of strategies that will enhance both your teaching and your communication with students' families.

 ## SEARCH THE WEB

If you have not yet looked at the "Diversity in the Classroom" section of the Companion Website, this would be a good time to explore. As you explore the sites, consider how they may help you utilize the cultural context principle. Similarly, think about how the links under "Parent and Community" can help you reach the same goal. You also may want to visit the "Critical Thinking Skills" section, found under "Instructional Strategies." Think about how the activities there relate to our principle of higher level thinking.

REFERENCES

Beyer, L. E. (1996). *Creating democratic classrooms: The struggle to integrate theory and practice.* New York: Teachers College Press.

Brooks, J. G., & Brooks, M. G. (1999). *In search of understanding: The case for constructivist classrooms.* Alexandria, VA: Association for Supervision and Curriculum Development.

Brooks, M. G., & Brooks, J. G. (1999). The courage to be constructivist. *Educational Leadership, 57* (3), 18–24.

Cohen, E. G. (1994). Complex instruction: Higher-order thinking in heterogeneous classroom. In S. Sharon, *Handbook of cooperative learning methods.* Westport, CT: Greenwood Press.

Dale, E. (1969). *Audiovisual methods in teaching.* New York: Holt, Rinehart and Winston.

Daniels, H., & Bizar, M. (1998). *Methods matter.* Portland, ME: Stenhouse Publishers.

Darling, J. (1994, Fall). Summerhill from Neill to the nineties. *Educational Forum, 58* (3), 244–251.

Delpit, L. (1995). *Other people's children: Cultural conflict in the classroom.* New York: New Press, Norton & Co.

Fosnot, C. T. (Ed.). (1996). *Constructivism: Theory, perspectives, and practice.* New York: Teachers College Press.

Garrison, J. S. (1997). *Dewey and Eros: Wisdom and desire in the art of teaching.* Monograph Accession No. BEDI970031555, *Education Abstracts* (Internet).

Hyerle, D. (1996). *Visual tools for constructing knowledge.* Alexandria, VA: Association for Supervision and Curriculum Development.

Joyce, B., Showers, B., & Weil, M. (1996). *Models of teaching.* Boston: Allyn & Bacon.

Kavolik, S. (1994). Brain compatible learning. *Video Journal of Education, 3* (6).

Martin, B. (1983). *Brown bear, brown bear, what do you see?* New York: Henry Holt & Company.

Marzano, R. J., Pickering, D. J., & Pollock, J. E. (2001). *Classroom instruction that works: Research-based strategies for increasing student achievement.* Alexandria, VA: Association for Supervision and Curriculum Development.

Perkins, D. (1999, November). The many faces of constructivism. *Educational Leadership, 57* (3), 6–11.

Powell, R. R. (1992). The influence of prior experiences on pedagogical constructs of traditional and nontraditional preservice teachers. *Teaching and Teacher Education, 8* (3), 225–238.

Stiggins, R. J. (1994). *Student-centered classroom assessment.* New York: Merrill.

Wiggins, G. (1996, Spring). Anchoring assessment with exemplars: Why students and teachers need models. *Gifted Child Quarterly, 40* (2), 66–69.

CHAPTER 7

Models for Teaching: Direct

CHAPTER OVERVIEW

Elementary teachers plan a lot of lessons. Every day there are many opportunities to teach—some planned, some unplanned. In order to address the variety of intelligences, learning styles, interests, and backgrounds of your students—and to keep teaching fresh and interesting—it will be important to have a wide repertoire of teaching strategies. The next three chapters will help you build this repertoire. This chapter examines approaches to teaching that can be categorized as direct instruction. The next chapter features approaches that can be described as inductive. Both chapters describe how direct and inductive teaching are exemplified in both formal lesson plans and informal teaching moments. Chapter 9 will describe structures and strategies that can be used with both types of teaching.

■ *Opening Activity*

Think about two things you have learned recently: one in school and one outside a formal educational institution. Now, imagine how you might have responded to that question when you were in elementary school. You may have listed a wide variety of things. As an adult you might have remembered learning about Bloom's taxonomy, laws of planetary motion, or how to read an e-mail attachment, bake bread, install a muffler, or develop photographs. Perhaps you learned what plants grow best on the west side of the house or how to calm an anxious child. At elementary age you may have learned to multiply, to play the piano, how to set up a tent, or what makes a good friend.

■ ■ ■

How did you learn these things? Probably in many different ways. Some things you may have learned when someone explained them to you—either in person or through the written word. Perhaps a professor explained the planets or a friend taught you the finer points of working with yeast. You may have learned to install a muffler from a clear how-to book, complete with photographs. Other things you are likely to have learned through multiple experiences that led you to draw conclusions. After several years of gardening, you may have drawn conclusions about what kinds of plants thrive in your soil. Probably experiences in elementary school taught you about friendship. Your learning has been a combination of direct and inductive learning throughout your lifetime. This chapter will help you build on those experiences to structure effective direct learning experiences for your students. Chapter 8 will present similar information regarding inductive teaching.

 ## CHAPTER OBJECTIVES

After you have completed this section, you will be able to

1. describe formal and informal instances of direct teaching;
2. debate the advantages and disadvantages of direct lessons;
3. evaluate appropriate and inappropriate uses of direct teaching; and
4. design a direct (deductive) lesson consistent with the principles of such lessons, teach it, and reflect upon it.

DIRECT TEACHING: FORMAL AND INFORMAL

Direct, or deductive, teaching is exemplified by the word *direct*. Direct teaching is to the point, straightforward, and clear. In it, someone gives someone else the information they need to learn. Direct teaching may be in person or in some mediated form—for example, through an instructional video or videoconference. Many lessons in many venues are taught directly. In families, children may be taught to tie their shoes, operate appliances, distinguish weeds from carrots, or cross a street safely. They learn the stories of ancestors' lives, the location of the Big Dipper, the way to hold a guitar, or the best way to locate a good fishing hole through the direct information sharing of family and friends. Successful examples of informal direct teaching usually include giving information, modeling skills, and providing the opportunity for practice. The clearer and more interesting the information, the more effective the modeling, and the more opportunities for real-world practice, the more successful the teaching is likely to be. Think of a child learning to hit a baseball, light a campfire, or use a sewing machine. In each case the adult is likely to explain what is needed, demonstrate a model performance, and allow the child to practice. Practice is understood as important and worthwhile because it will lead to success in playing a game, cooking a meal, or creating something new.

Such lessons have much to teach us about direct teaching. Children are given information in clear and purposeful ways, with plenty of opportunities to see how it is useful and how to use it successfully. They have the opportunity to practice and have additional modeling as they become more skilled. Good direct teaching in school will have similar characteristics. Some beginning teachers have the impression that direct teaching is equivalent to long boring lectures and that it is to be avoided. This is not true. Many types of information and skills are well suited to direct teaching. Human beings have been using direct teaching strategies since the beginning of communication. The key is to use it well. Like all good teaching, good direct instruction engages students in constructing their own knowledge by, in part, sharing information with which students are then engaged through questioning, deductive reasoning, or practice activities.

Other types of informal direct teaching come in the form of stories. Family history, like the history taught in school, is learned through teaching. It is interesting to compare typical textbook learning of history with the learning that occurs when families share the stories of ancestors crossing the ocean or the plains, starting a family business, or surviving hardship or adventures. Good direct teaching can also be storytelling.

You will use direct teaching in school in formal and informal ways. Informal direct teaching is likely to be used in brief teachable moments when you find a student needs instruction in a skill you hadn't planned to teach or when a child asks a question about content outside your plans. You may notice a child who needs instruction on holding a gerbil, setting up equations, or even asking others to join a game. A student might come in after a storm asking how hail is formed. In those moments it is helpful to remember basic components of effective direct skill instruction: sharing useful and interesting information, modeling, and giving students the opportunity to practice.

For example, if a student is not holding the gerbil correctly, a direct teaching moment would have the teacher take the gerbil and say, "Holding George that way isn't comfortable for him and may hurt him[*explaining why information is useful*]. Let me show you a better way [*giving information and modeling*]. Now, you try it [*providing opportunity for practice*]. Good, I can see George is comfortable now." This teaching moment is not only kinder than a brief, "Hold that gerbil correctly or put him away," but is more likely to lead to learning.

Other times informal teaching moments may result in direct teaching in storytelling mode. One of us used the story of learning to ride a bicycle to illustrate the need to listen to directions all the way through. As a child, this individual had been so anxious to ride a two-wheel bicycle that she took off on her own before learning how to use the brakes. This resulted in several frantic trips around the block before figuring out how to stop the bicycle. In virtually every primary class, there arose an occasion to discuss the need to listen to directions. In those moments this teacher was able to say, "Let me tell you what happened to me when I did not listen to directions" followed by a dramatic rendition of the bicycle adventure. The direct telling of this vivid bit of history was invariably remembered, and helped students think about listening more than a simple, "You need to listen" ever could. Good storytelling is an important skill for any teacher, and can be used in formal lesson plans as well as less formal opportunities.

 ## STORYTELLING AND CURRICULUM

Storytelling should be part of the language arts curriculum throughout elementary school. It provides opportunities to learn story structure, hear (and later practice) oral expression, and share a variety of cultures. However, storytelling can also be a vehicle for direct teaching in a variety of curriculum areas.

Stories, told well, almost always hold students' attention. They include vivid descriptions, interesting characters, and conflicts to be resolved. Much of the information we want to share with students in the social studies curriculum can be viewed as story rather than lecture, epic tale rather than textbook requirements. The unit on the Revolutionary War offers multiple opportunities for interesting storytelling. For example, the lesson on point of view based on the book *Can't You Make Them Behave, King George* (Fritz, 1977) offers the opportunity to tell the story of a king with a problem—a real king, a real person, with a family, a set of traditions, and a personality that makes some of his actions make sense. Although the information is simplified, it provides a clear example of differing points of view on the same event. It also gives students a chance to "know" King George so that later in the unit they can be asked, "And what do you think King George thought then?" and be able to envision likely responses.

History told as story can be as interesting as any television drama. To be a successful teller of history, you must have a sense of the big and the small, an overall sense of the structure of the story you are telling, and an alertness to the details that make it interesting. In much of western culture, stories have a beginning, a middle, and an end. Some conflict or challenge forms the "backbone" of the story, and the resolution (even temporarily) of the challenge provides a natural ending. Portions of the curriculum that can fit into that story structure are naturals for storytelling. For example, Washington's crossing the Delaware to attack the Hessians at Trenton is a dramatic story. In textbooks, however, it is often reduced to colorless recounting of facts. Once you have established the story outline, you must find the details of sight and sound that can bring the story to life for your students. In this case, you would want to help them picture the comfortable well-trained Hessian forces and the untrained, cold, and discouraged colonial soldiers. Sometimes you might have access to the actual words of those present at key moments. Imagine, for example, the soldier who wrote these words.

> Christmas, 6 P.M. it is fearfully cold and raw and a snow-storm [is] setting in. The wind is northeast and beats in the faces of the men. It will be a terrible night for the soldiers who have no shoes. Some of them have tied old rags around their feet, others are barefoot, but I have not heard a man complain. They are ready to suffer any hardship and die rather than give up their liberty. I have just copied the order for marching. . . .
>
> December 26, 3 A.M. I never have seen Washington so determined as he is now. He stands on the bank of the river, wrapped in his cloak, superintending the landing of his troops. He is calm and collected , but very determined. The storm is changing to sleet, and cuts like a knife. . . . We are ready to mount our horses. (Peacock, 1998, pp. 25, 28)

Notice how the details of the wind beating, the snow turning to sleet, and the image of Washington wrapped in his cloak against the wind as the barefoot soldiers land their boats bring this story to life. If you share details of history that make its humanity real, students will learn and remember. They will be able to make ties, not just to their textbook but to all their memories of cold, rain, determination, and courage. Good stories can also come from less dramatic moments, brought to life through the sights, sounds, and smells that made them come alive.

Becoming a good storyteller will take practice, but it is worth the effort. Take the opportunity to hear professional storytellers, either in person or through good children's television. Sometimes reading historical fiction can help you envision a time and place well enough to make it real for your students. Visiting museums and restored historical sights can help bring a time and place to life for you as well as for your students. McGuire (1997) suggested that organizing the social studies curriculum into a "Storypath" (p. 70) makes learning experiences more memorable. Her students created characters who could have lived at a particular time and place. By envisioning those characters' involvement in critical incidents in history, students became involved in complex and meaningful learning activities. But storytelling does not have to be limited to social studies.

Egan (1986) has suggested that the components of storytelling can be used to organize any area of curriculum. Planning curriculum in his story form model includes five steps:

1. Identifying importance
2. Finding binary opposites
3. Organizing content into story form
4. Conclusion
5. Evaluation

The first step, identifying importance, parallels our description of the need to identify core concepts. These concepts will direct the creation of the story. Whatever path the story takes, it should lead to the main ideas.

The second step, finding binary opposites, is a bit like concept mapping, except that the form of the map is determined in advance. Since every good story must have a conflict, this form of lesson (and curriculum) planning demands that some kind of opposites be addressed. These are selected to best suit the storytelling format. In history, opposites might be change and stability, monarchy and democracy, dependence and independence, or even survival and destruction. In science, opposites might be hot and cold, adaptation and failure to adapt, living and nonliving.

The next step in this curriculum model is to organize your content into story form. In the historical examples earlier, the history was the story. In other subject areas you will need to find or invent a story that brings your key concepts to life. For example, in science, the concepts of independence and interdependence might be introduced by a story about an animal who decided he didn't need any of the creatures in his habitat—perhaps a frog who takes off for the city. Egan uses a story about the King of Madagascar's difficulty in trying to count his army by matching them to pebbles in bowls to begin teaching about place value.

The final two stages reflect the need for each story to have a resolution (step 4: conclusion) and the need for the teacher to evaluate students' learning. Although the five steps of this model seem occasionally stretched by Egan's illustrations (for example, the binary opposites in the place-value story are "clever" and "clueless" for the king's successful and unsuccessful counselors), the idea that many important concepts can be illustrated through story is an important one. The key is to find a story that helps students envision the key ideas through some kind of situation in which a problem or challenge can be addressed and resolved. Think about how you could help students envision the circulatory system through a story of a trip in a blood cell, understand communities through a story of a village coming together to face a challenge—be it a dragon or a flood or a factory closing—or picture the "life" of a water droplet or a bit of molten lava. In each case, the structure of a story and the sensory details that make it real will enhance students' learning.

In informal learning, stories are often told over and over again throughout a family's history. Similarly, when you use storytelling in teaching you will want to give students the chance to "retell" the story but using it in some way. In some cases students might be asked to literally retell the story in their own words. In others they might be asked to transform it into another form—to illustrate it, write a song about it, dance it, or create a model. In any case, your storytelling lessons should fit the phases of a lesson described in Chapter 6. Any good story needs an interesting *opening* to catch the listeners' attention. This could be a puzzling question, a dramatic description, or any other story technique that signals to the listener that something interesting is coming. A good story *builds meaning* by tying to concrete images that students can imagine—sights, sounds, smells, and experiences that are vivid enough to become real. Students *apply understanding* through activities that follow the story, transforming it into some new form or using information in a new way. And, of course, both through application activities and other types of assessment, you must be constantly *assessing students' learning*.

CHECK YOUR UNDERSTANDING

Think about a unit you plan to teach. Consider how storytelling might be used in the unit. You may identify material that may be shared in story form or devise a story that contains principles you want to teach. Try telling the story to a friend or colleague. Ask for feedback on the parts that were the most vivid or interesting.

DIRECT LESSON DESIGN

Another, perhaps more traditional, form of direct teaching provides information in a straightforward manner rather than in story form. Formal direct teaching of skills is often organized in a format called (naturally enough) a direct lesson. The direct lesson design presented here is based on research on teaching effectiveness conducted in traditionally structured classrooms during the 1970s and 1980s (Hunter, 1976; Rosenshine, 1987; Wang, Haertel, & Walberg, 1993). Researchers prepared teachers to use the methods of more successful teachers, and determined that direct teaching tended to produce higher student learning scores on standardized tests in reading and math. This method, however, did not produce more creative thinking or better attitudes toward learning. Direct teaching, then, is not necessarily the best way to teach everything that is important, but it does have its advantages and is the best decision under certain circumstances. In elementary grades, this model is most commonly employed in brief "minilectures" in which teachers share information on important topics, procedures, or skills. They may include lessons on traditional school content and lessons on procedures within the classroom.

For example, the method for participating in a literature discussion circle (a strategy used in the Revolutionary War unit)will need to be taught directly. The technique for organizing the group, taking turns, and providing reactions will need to be shown and explained directly by the teacher. It would be very difficult and time consuming for students to "discover" this process on their own. Of course, the opening of the lesson might invite students to figure out ways to participate productively in a group discussion, but the teacher would not spend more than a few minutes on this part before going on to direct teaching. You might also use direct teaching to explain procedures for putting away materials, the correct way to set up an equation with "+" and "=", or any other body of content best explained through a series of steps or rules. Selecting those portions of content best suited to direct instruction, as opposed to guided discovery or inductive teaching, is an essential skill for teaching that is both effective and efficient (Wiggins & McTighe, 1998). Throughout this discussion, notice how good direct instruction is not a passive transmission of information from teacher to student. Rather, it is carefully planned to involve students in constructing new knowledge through activities that include some presentation of information.

Direct teaching provides valuable guidelines for strengthening the effectiveness of your minilectures (Cruickshank, 1990). The following seven elements in a direct lesson design are labeled to indicate how each fits into the general phases of most lessons.

Please remember that for many objectives, not every element can be included in a single period of instruction.

1. Set (opening)
2. Objective(s) and purpose (opening)
3. Information and modeling (constructing meaning)
4. Checking for understanding (constructing meaning)
5. Guided practice (using/applying)
6. Assessment (assessing learning)
7. Independent practice and reteaching (follow-up)

When you plan and teach your first direct lessons, you may wish to use all the elements in the order presented—or at least ask yourself if each one is necessary and make a conscious decision whether to include it or not. However, as you gain experience, you will become more comfortable using the sequence flexibly. You can develop your own order, bring in other steps, and blend the direct design with elements of other types of lessons. Please remember that any one approach to teaching is not a recipe to be followed exactly (Hunter, 1976). It is best thought of as a road map that suggests alternative pathways—some direct and quick, others less direct but possibly more picturesque.

1. Set

* Provides focus (active involvement of learner)
* Transfers relevant prior knowledge
* Provides an advanced organizer for key ideas
* Preassesses appropriate skills as necessary (diagnosis)

The *set* activity begins or introduces a lesson. You may also use a set after any break in a lesson (or when continuing a lesson from a previous day) to focus students' attention. A set activity is not merely saying to students, "OK, now we're going to work on math" or "Please turn to page 26." Remember that the sensory memory is the gatekeeper for what we remember. If you don't stimulate students to attend actively to the information you present, they will probably forget it immediately. If the set activity doesn't tie to students' prior knowledge, they are unlikely to understand the new information.

Set activities are usually short, lasting no more than 3 to 5 minutes for older students—much less time for younger ones. A film or a field trip would not typically be considered a set activity because such an activity might take several hours and would support a variety of topics. (You may select such an activity, however, to build prior experience and knowledge which you will later draw on in your lessons and activities.) You will also want to pick a set that is interesting, but not so engrossing that it distracts students from the activities that follow. As Madeline Hunter used to say in her workshops, "Don't bring in an elephant to teach the color gray." A friend humorously referred to this—and other instances of emphasizing "flash" over substance—as bungee jumping off our metaphorical bridge. You may have fun but you don't get to the other side! The main purpose is to focus the students on the content actively, to transfer existing knowledge to the new topic, and, when necessary, to assess students' prior relevant skills and understandings.

There are three key aspects of the set. First, a set activity provides a focus for the learners' minds by requiring *active involvement* with the content. Active involvement means more than passive listening. The active student imagines, writes, pictures, says, or reads, always with some question in mind. For example, one teacher introduced a lesson on creative writing by asking students to discuss in pairs a new ending to a story they had just finished reading. Then, after a short period of time, the teacher called on students to share what they were thinking.

A second aspect of the set is *prior knowledge*. The set activity should enable students to relate the new information to something they have learned before. In the previous example, the active involvement activity motivated students to relate the new topic (creative writing) to a familiar story. Think about how this example relates to what you learned in Chapters 2 and 5. Students construct information in long-term memory in networks of meaning (schemata). New information is more meaningful and more memorable when it is hooked in with relevant information in the brain. The beginning of the lesson is an excellent time to provide what is called an **advanced organizer**, or a structure to help students organize the information in their minds (Ausubel, 1968; Cawelti, 1995). For example, when introducing a direct lesson on the history of colonial America, it is helpful to let students get the big picture first. This might be done by reading a passage from a journal of a child who lived in the mid-1700s, or by a short written passage or discussion. These ideas then provide "ideational anchors" for the information to follow (Joyce, Showers, & Weil, 1996).

A third aspect of the set activity is *preassessment* or diagnosis. This step is optional, because you may have recently finished a prior lesson or activity that gave you good information about students' levels of performance. For example, consider a math class that just completed a lesson on telling time to the hour. The next lesson, on telling time to the half hour, may not require extensive diagnosis, because you learned how well each student is doing from the previous lesson.

Bear in mind, however, that some information cannot be absorbed unless necessary prior learning has taken place. Therefore some students will need reteaching of key prerequisite skills. For example, if students are going to conduct a study of the life in a pond, you will want to make sure they have the necessary math skills to summarize their data. Starting the lesson with a quick exercise (not a lecture) that requires students to graphically portray a set of data may provide useful information about who needs a review of this key skill.

Preassessment can also help target those students who already know some of what you are about to teach. For example, before the unit on rocks and minerals, you probably would want to diagnose students' knowledge of this topic. Even if some students have already studied the topic, their retention of the information could vary widely. You could pass around three rocks and have students write about what they observe and know about them. In this way you can tailor the lesson for those who have more or less experience with rocks and minerals. Gathering such information is especially important at the beginning of the year when you do not know each student's background knowledge and capabilities.

2. Objective(s) and Purpose

- Communicates to the students the learning goal(s)
- Motivates students (by explaining the purpose—how the lesson relates to real life)

Telling the students both the objective(s) and the purpose of the lesson provides further focus as well as that valuable commodity, motivation. In direct lessons, you tell students what it is you expect them to be able to do by the end of the lesson (the *objective*), how you will assess them, and what level of performance or culminating authentic activity you expect from them. Students also want to know why it is important to study the topic and how it will be useful to them or others in real life—the *purpose*.

Clearly stated objectives are crucial, not only to help keep your lesson on track but also to motivate students. When you tell the students the objective, you will want to put it in their language, not in the formal way you wrote it when you were planning. So instead of making a statement like "The students will be able to define *point of view*," you would say, "By the end of the week, when I ask you to define *point of view*, I would like you to be able to explain what it means to you and give two examples from books we have read."

Telling the students, "Today we're going to work on point of view" is not an example of conveying the objective because you have not stated any expected behavior. The students don't know how they'll be evaluated, nor do they know the learning they'll be expected to demonstrate as a result of the activities.

Telling the students the purpose further motivates them. It lets them see how useful the new knowledge, skill, or attitude will be. In the lesson example, you would provide the objective and then say, "It's important for us to understand point of view because later we will be writing stories where you will use at least two different points of view and we will be reading those stories to the fourth graders next month."

When explaining to students the objective and purpose of the lesson, it is important to clarify how the lesson relates to the overall objectives and purpose as expressed in the unit rationale. The principle to follow is to relate "this" to "that." Thus when giving the objective and purpose of the lesson in the example, you might emphasize that understanding "why the Revolutionary War was revolutionary" (a key question) requires taking multiple points of view.

CHECK YOUR UNDERSTANDING

Look back at some objectives you have written. Pick one that you believe is suitable for direct instruction. Write down two ideas for set activities that will (a) focus your learners actively and (b) encourage them to transfer their existing knowledge of your topic. Also indicate how you'll find out what they do and don't know already (preassessment). Then indicate how you will tell students the objective and purpose of the lesson.

Share your ideas with a classmate to see if you understand each component similarly.

Lesson objective: _____

_____

Set (focus, transfer, preassessment): _____

_____

Objective told to students: _____

_____

Purpose told to students: _____

_____

3. Information and Modeling (with checks for understanding throughout)

- Explains and demonstrates information
- Uses variety in presentation styles and appeals to various learning styles
- Provides a conceptual structure for information
- Uses verbal labels to point out key elements of examples
- Involves learners actively after each chunk of information

In this phase, you provide the relevant *information* about the topic at hand. Teachers can provide information through a variety of sources: lectures, experts (in person or on the Internet), readings, videos, multimedia presentations, or the Internet, to name a few. As you present information, you *model,* or show it. Periodically, you *check for understanding*—you stop to allow students to summarize or use the material just presented. The information in Chapter 2 on learning and memory provides some guidelines to keep in mind during the presentation of information.

First, you must consider students' individual learning needs. Because of the varied backgrounds and experiences of your students, it is important to appeal to as many learning preferences as possible. This will require, in particular, applying the learning principle of variety (see Chapter 6). You'll want to give students the opportunity to encounter the material in a number of ways—for example, through reading, listening, viewing, and touching.

Modeling goes on while you are presenting information. Remember: Don't just tell it to them; show it to them. Posters, overhead transparencies, multimedia materials, pictures, objects to pass around and explore, demonstrations, chalkboard illustrations—all of these aids help make the verbal information visual and tactile, thus appealing to the learning needs of your students. Think about the difference between a description of a desert environment without visuals and one that is accompanied by a video, or a trip to a website illustrating a trip across desert terrain. Even your best verbal description is likely to be more effective when supported by a model. And, of course, it is essential to model each skill we teach, whether it is using a calculator or putting scissors away safely.

Verbal labeling is the technique of pointing out, in words, an idea or element you want students to notice. Verbal labeling of the essential aspects of a visual aid or demonstration is important when you are explaining how to do a project or a particular procedure. For example, when teachers give directions for an assignment, they should show an excellent example of that assignment and explain why each part is exemplary (Wiggins, 1994, 1996). The verbal labeling is necessary because students may look at the model and not understand which elements are the most important. For instance, a student might look at a poster and assume it's good because of its size, rather than because it conveys the essential information and the colors are vivid. Students need to know why it is a good example. Similarly, as we demonstrate a procedure or skill it is essential to label what we are doing so students recognize important steps.

Next, you must consider the principle of conceptual focus and the fact that the memory searches to structure information into meaningful networks. How can you present information in an organized way? First, divide the information into logical chunks in your mind. Outline it or diagram it so that the concepts, the generalizations, and the links between the elements of information become clear to you. (Remember the concept map you created in Chapter 3.) Then create a poster, an overhead transparency, or other visual aid that makes this organization obvious to students. The concept map in Chapter 3 shows the organization of the information in the Revolutionary War unit.

As you are presenting information, refer to the concept map or diagram often to let students know how the current pieces of information are related to those they've already covered and those to come. Have students actively process each chunk after it has been presented. If there are four main points in your minilecture, stop after each one and have students work with what they have learned. For example, a minilecture on the water cycle would be more effective if supported by a diagram and if the teacher stops at each stage of the cycle to actively involve students with the content. This could be done through asking students to summarize, act out the water's path, or add to their own diagrams at each stage. If you are showing a long video, preview it to determine where to stop so students can actively process the information. In this way, they will solidify their understanding of the material.

CHECK YOUR UNDERSTANDING

Take the objective you used for the set activity you designed earlier and outline the essential content. Plan two or three specific ways you could present the information so your students will remember it. How will you appeal to different learning styles? How can you help students find the conceptual organization of the information? Share your ideas with others.

Objective: _____

_____

Content outline: _____

_____

Ways to make information meaningful (use ideas from Chapters 4 and 5): _____

_____

4. Checking for Understanding (active processing)

- Done periodically during information giving
- Allows students to actively process information (e.g., write, talk, vote)
- Provides information about student understanding of information presented

Although it is listed as a separate phase of the lesson, checking for understanding is interspersed throughout the information and modeling phase as shown in Figure 7.1.

Checking for understanding has two purposes. The first is to enable students to digest the information in small chunks, so that each phase is meaningful to them before the next piece is presented. You probably have had the unpleasant experience of sitting

Checking for Student
Understanding

FIGURE 7.1   Checking for Understanding During Information and Modeling

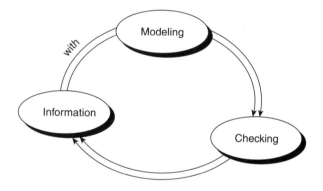

in an hour-long lecture with no opportunity to process, digest, or otherwise interact with the material presented. When you are given large amounts of complex information without any time to actively process it, you retain little of it. While the amounts of information presented to elementary grade students would be much shorter, the active processing is just as essential.

Recall that short-term memory has a limited capacity. If students receive too many pieces of information at once, they overload and begin to forget. Their attention usually wanders and they are no longer learning—or at least not the content we had planned for them to learn. The younger the children, the more quickly the wandering begins. Checking for understanding allows students to actively process information in logical chunks, thus making it more easily remembered.

The word *active* is important here. Recall the principle of active processing from Chapter 6. Passive learning is rarely as meaningful as **active learning**. Discussing the ideas or answering a few true-false questions about the information presented keeps that information in the memory system longer and increases the likelihood of transfer to long-term memory. In reviewing research on effective classroom strategies, Marzano, Pickering, and Pollock (2001) note that making and testing hypotheses is an effective way to help students process information. Although hypothesis testing is often associated with inductive teaching, Marzano, Pickering, and Pollock particularly note the effectiveness of deductive hypothesis testing, in which students generate and test hypotheses based on principles they have been taught. This type of hypothesis testing could fit well into several sections of a direct lesson, including checking for understanding. Students could be asked to imagine, "What would happen if. . . ." and later test their hypotheses. When students explain their hypotheses, the teacher gains important information on students' thinking and students gain practice in logical thinking.

One researcher (Rowe, 1974) suggested the "10-2 rule," which refers to about 2 minutes of active student involvement for approximately every 10 minutes of information presented. According to this rule, if you were teaching a unit on rocks, you might explain the characteristics of sedimentary rocks and show examples (with verbal labeling of essential qualities) for about 10 minutes. You would not go on to explain the second type of rock (igneous rocks) until you had given students a short activity in which they could summarize or apply the information already presented—for instance, classifying examples and nonexamples of sedimentary rocks. Then you would go on to explain and model the characteristics of igneous rocks and again check for understanding. The 10-2 rule may be appropriate for older elementary and middle level students, but for younger students, more frequent checking will be appropriate. Figure 7.1 illustrates the cyclical nature of this phase of a lesson.

A second purpose of checking for understanding is to find out how well students have absorbed the material. This relates to the concept of continuous assessment, which is one of the six principles for designing learning experiences presented in Chapter 6. Without information on students' understanding of the material presented, you would have a difficult time deciding what to do next—go on or reteach. Staying in tune with what students are thinking also keeps you on your toes. You may also think of this process as *formative assessment*—not for grading but for formulating decisions about where to go next with students (Black & Wiliam, 1998).

Often teachers find that their students have misunderstood something they said. Perhaps the teacher just didn't explain it clearly enough or said something that was downright confusing. When teachers check for students' understanding, they can reexplain and model the original information in a new and clearer way. Pausing periodically to assess how students are constructing meaning provides excellent cues to help teachers decide how to proceed.

What activities are useful in checking for understanding? This is where the active participation strategies in Table 7.1 come in. They might include techniques such as having students write a 1-minute summary to be read aloud, giving true-false questions that students vote on, or having students think of questions for others to answer. The least helpful way to check for understanding in most situations is to ask, "Are there any questions?" Many students (especially the shy or less successful ones) do not want to call attention to their lack of understanding. Thus the fact that no one has any questions may reveal little about students' actual grasp of the material.

CHECK YOUR UNDERSTANDING

Try this exercise to check your own understanding of this section. Write T if the statement is true, F if it is false.

_____ 1. An informational lecture is the opening activity of a direct lesson.

_____ 2. The best way to model is to state the information.

_____ 3. Understanding is checked after all the information is presented.

_____ 4. A video is one way to provide information.

_____ 5. It is impossible to check for understanding during a video.

The only true statement is item 4. Why are the others false?

5. Guided Practice

- Allows students to gain mastery through practice
- Provides activities that match the objective(s) (congruence)
- Allows teacher to monitor learning and adjust accordingly

The purpose of **guided practice** is to give students an opportunity to practice with the skills or information until they are confident and have mastered the objective. Recall the importance of repetition and meaningfulness for the transfer of information into long-term memory. The critical aspect here is that the practice is guided by the teacher. Reviewing research on practice, Marzano, Pickering, and Pollock (2001) drew two key generalizations: (a) mastering a skill takes a fair amount of focused practice and (b) during practice, students should adapt and shape what they have learned. The practice sections of direct lesson design are planned to accomplish both aims.

The teacher constantly monitors to check student progress. If students are in a large-group practice activity responding to teacher questions with hand signals, the teacher is there to see how students are doing and to correct any misunderstandings. If the students do a few problems or exercises from a book or worksheet, the teacher circulates among students without spending too much time with any one student. In this way, errors can be caught early before they become ingrained by repeated practice. If many students are making the same kinds of errors, the teacher can adjust the lesson by reteaching the whole group (or a subgroup) in a different manner.

The guided practice activities should follow the concept of congruence by being relevant to the lesson objective. Most practice activities should lead directly to the accomplishment of the objective. For example, if the teacher wants students to be able to interpret the Declaration of Independence and tie it to their lives, and they read multiple reports on the development of the document, the activity and the objective are closely matched. Understanding the origins of the document will be helpful in understanding (and later interpreting) the text. If, however, the teacher asks students to copy the first parts of the Declaration from the book, there is little match between this rote activity and the higher level objective of interpreting and applying such a complex document.

You may ask, What is the difference between a check for understanding exercise and guided practice? Although monitoring student progress is a key aspect in both phases of the lesson, they differ in purpose and in scope. First, consider the purpose. Teachers check for understanding to help students process the information being presented and to find out how they are doing. Teachers provide guided practice to give students a chance, under close supervision, to gain proficiency by working with the new information. The goal of guided practice is mastery of the skill; checking for understanding is merely finding out if students understood what was just presented.

The other difference between the two lesson phases is in the scope of the amount of information. Teachers check for understanding of the most recently presented chunk of information, not all of the information together. They provide guided practice so the student can put all the chunks together in a practice situation. Guided practice thus encompasses all the information presented in the lesson, whereas checking focuses only on the small chunk just presented.

Guided practice may be written or oral; it may include many of the same participation activities referred to in Table 7.1. Throughout the practice time, the teacher

TABLE 7.1 *Suggestions for Increasing Student Participation (To be used during Set, Checking, Guided Practice, or Review)*

Small-Group Activities

1. Discuss with a partner
   Examples:
   • In your own words, explain to your partner how the pistons in a car engine work.
   • Share with your partner the guidelines to keep in mind when writing an expository paragraph.
   • Discuss with your partner the meanings of these 10 terms from our anatomy unit.
2. Discuss in small groups
   Keep the group size to three, four, or five so that each student can participate. Appoint a recorder to summarize the findings of the discussion.
3. Write questions
   Examples:
   • Write one question about what we have just been studying. Try it out on a person near you. If that person can't answer the question, pass it to me. At the end of the period, I'll answer all questions that have been turned in.
   • Write two questions based on the topic "Planning Nutritional Meals." We'll use them tomorrow for a review of the unit.
4. Brainstorm
   Brainstorming can be done as a group or with a partner. Define the topic or problem. For example, the topic may be "questions students think will be covered on an exam."
   Examples:
   • On your scratch paper, jot down as many terms as you can think of that are related to the topic we began studying yesterday. In 5 minutes we'll discuss these terms.
   • Repeat the same process as in the previous example, but share the ideas with a partner.
5. Debate
   Discussion of both sides of a question involves more students when done in small groups. In teaching debate techniques, first explain the structure and guidelines. Then, with the help of a student, demonstrate a debate for the group.

TABLE 7.1 *Continued*

Small-Group Activities

6. *Peer group teaching*
   Using students as tutors can be an effective learning device for both the tutor and tutored.
7. *Role-playing*
   Simulating an event brings new perspectives to any lesson. Role-playing involves more students when done in small groups (rather than by one group in front of class), and it reduces the risk factor.

Whole-Group Activities

8. *Oral reading*
   Oral reading can be done in two ways.
   a. One student can read while the rest of the class follows with markers, their eyes, or their fingers.
   b. The entire class can read aloud together. For special dramatic effects, the boys and girls can alternate reading, etc.
9. *Whisper answer in teacher's ear*
   The teacher can select random students to whisper the answer to him or her.
10. *Provide wait time for covert rehearsal of responses* (Tobin, 1980)
    Waiting at least 3 seconds for an answer is a critical element in effective questioning of an entire class. Ask the students who have arrived at an idea to do something overt, such as put their right hand on the table, fold their arms, etc. Promote even greater participation by telling the class how many have given the signal. For example, say, "Well, already 12 people have signaled that they know the answer." Wait until a sufficient response number is obtained. Then call on one randomly selected student to answer the question.
    Examples:
    • Which were the three Axis countries during World War II? (Pause) I can tell you're thinking. I see five hands, six, eight, lots more. Let's see, I think I'll call on Ted. (He responds) How many agree?
    • I want you to think about whether this blueprint would be practical for a house in an area that has a climate like southern California's. I'll call upon someone in about 1 minute.
11. *Unison response*
    A teacher signal will indicate when the class should respond. For example, the slow raising of the teacher's hand means preparation. The abrupt lowering signals the point for the class response.
    Examples:
    • I'll point to a word and say a definition. If the definition I give is correct, please reply all together, "Yes." If it's incorrect, all say, "No."
    • I'll read some statements about the digestive process. If the statement is true, everyone responds together, "True," etc.
    • We'll check the answers to this worksheet together. I'll say the number of the question, then all of you respond with the answer on your paper. If the response is clear, we won't need to discuss that question. If it's garbled, we'll stop to clarify. (This will work only with short, one-right-answer responses.)
12. *Consecutive response*
    Each student is responsible for recalling the previous student's response.
13. *Polling by raised hands*
    Casting votes or canvassing for information—the data can be recorded on a chart visible to the entire class. Or, when a student responds, teacher can ask those who agree to raise their hands.
14. *Pointing*
    Using an individual pictorial representation (map, diagram, picture), the students can point to the correct answer.
15. *Cross/uncross arms*
    Examples:
    • I'll read a series of statements about different kinds of angles. If you agree with the statement, cross your arms; if you don't agree, don't cross your arms.
    • If you agree with Toby's opinion, cross your arms.

TABLE 7.1 *Continued*

Whole-Group Activities

16. *Flash answers in groups*
    Flash cards made by students can be used in a variety of ways: true-false cards (color-coded for ease of reading), chemical elements, vocabulary review, and color-coded classifying.
    Examples:
    • We've talked about the three branches of our federal government. (Students are divided into groups, and each group has three cards, each one stating a different governmental branch.) I'll read a government duty (such as making laws). As a group, decide which branch of government would be responsible for that duty, and then hold up the correct card.
    • There are three animal classifications listed on the board, and they are color-coded. Each group has three pieces of paper, each a different color. I'll read the name of an animal, and as a group you decide which category that animal belongs to. Then hold up the appropriate piece of paper.

17. *Flashers*
    A short answer can be written either on a laminated notebook with a water-soluble pen or on an individual chalkboard.

18. *Thumb signals (done at chest level in a personal, low-key manner)*
    Examples:
    • I'll read several statements about how to make a collar for a blouse. If the statement is true, put your thumb up. If it is false, put your thumb down. If you're not sure, put your thumb to the side.
    • If you agree with Jim's explanation of a zone defense, put your thumb up, etc.

19. *Finger signals (done at chest level in a personal, low-key manner)*
    Examples:
    • The three kinds of rock formations are listed on the board by number. I'll say a characteristic of a certain rock formation; you put up the appropriate number of fingers for the one that is being described.
    • The five main characters from the novel are listed on the board by number. If the statement I read refers to the first one, put up one finger. If it refers to the second one, put up 2 fingers, etc.
    • I'll play several chords on the piano. If it's a major chord, put up one finger; if it's a minor chord, put up two fingers.

20. *Flash cards*
    Examples:
    • You've made flash cards for your new Spanish vocabulary. Study them alone for 5 minutes. Then we'll do some spot checking.
    • You've made flash cards for this week's vocabulary words. Practice then with a partner for 10 minutes. Then we'll have our quiz.

21. *Cross/uncross arms or legs, look up or down, thumbs up or down, pencils up or down*
    The opposite positions can indicate positive/negative, higher/lower, or any two-part test of opposites.

Adapted from Napa County, CA Essential Elements of Effective Instruction Training Materials.

monitors, assists, and gauges students' success. Having students do entire worksheets or long assignments from books in class is not necessarily the best guided practice because students may be practicing errors or may become stuck for a long time while the teacher is trying to get around to everybody. If worksheets or book assignments are used, students should work on a few of the problems or questions before the teacher brings the whole class together to check their success on those few items. If there is a high degree of success, then students may proceed on their own, with light supervision from the teacher.

6. Assessment

- Gathers information about individual mastery of the objective
- Helps teacher decide how to proceed with each student

It is essential to find out who has and has not met the objective by conducting a brief assessment. This activity may be a quick example or a short project that students do on their own, such as completing two or three math problems or writing a short poem. If students cannot perform the skill adequately at this point, they are likely to experience failure when going on to independent work. The assessment may show, however, that some students would be bored by more practice and need to proceed to independent work or extension. This is one place where teachers may differentiate the instruction to meet the needs of each student by deciding who gets reteaching and who gets to go on to more practice or extension activities.

You may be asking, Isn't guided practice enough to ensure they've met the objective? Remember, students' correct performance on a guided practice activity does not necessarily mean they can perform well on their own. During the practice, they may have received help from the teacher or from their peers. At this point, you will not know which students are capable of succeeding on their own. Therefore you may need a special assessment activity that lets you know *how well each student can perform without your help.*

Sometimes it is possible to gather enough information about achievement during guided practice so that a separate assessment activity is not required. If, however, you skip this phase and find that many students are unsuccessful during independent work, you may conclude that you did not obtain adequate information about who was ready to go on and who wasn't.

Notice how each phase of the direct lesson design includes some form of assessment—during the set (preassessment), during input (checking for understanding), and during guided practice (monitoring). Such continuous assessment gives you valuable information about the students' concerns, misunderstandings, thinking, and prior knowledge. Without this information, instructional decisions are often misguided or irrelevant.

What do you do with those students who are still struggling with the guided practice activities or "fail" the assessment? It is a reality of teaching that not all students learn at the same rate. Thus some students may be ready to go on to independent work while others will need reteaching or more teacher-assisted practice. At this point in the lesson, you use your assessment information to decide who falls into which group.

7. Reteaching (for those still struggling) and/or Independent Practice or Extension (for those who need more practice or challenge)

- Attends to individual needs by reteaching, or
- Provides further practice to develop fluency/automaticity, or
- Extends learning

Through assessment, teachers determine which students have not achieved the learning stated in the objective. *Reteaching* may be necessary because the first round of set, objective/purpose, information/modeling/checking, and guided practice did not work. That is, the student has not yet achieved the objective.

It is important to find out where the problem lies. You can look for evidence of misunderstanding in the student's guided practice and assessment activities, or you may orally check with the student. In any case, when you think you have found the problem, you will want to reteach.

Reteaching may include further direct instruction, or some other approach. It is not, however, just covering the content in the same way a second time. Chances are that the first teaching approach did not work. Therefore try appealing to a different learning style or type of intelligence, or try a different type of guided practice activity. For example, if you presented the information on air using illustrations from a science text, then during reteaching you might use an experiment or demonstration, or have students make up a song about air taking up space.

Often you will find that several students have not succeeded on the lesson and need reteaching. If so, you may wish to pull those pupils aside while the other students are working independently. Or you may assign students to mixed-ability cooperative learning teams, in which the misunderstanding must be cleared up before the group proceeds. Another idea is to use peer teaching (Ernst, 1995; Powell, 1997) to help the student master the objective. Individual help before or after school may also be useful. More ideas for modifying instruction for special student needs may be found in Chapter 9.

You may be thinking, Is it worth taking the time to reteach? Where will I find the time? Experience has shown that it is well worth the effort. Not all students succeed on the first try, and they should have a second chance. Furthermore, research on mastery learning (Bloom, 1984) indicates that, with continuous assessment of student learning and reteaching where needed, students who would normally be near the average of the class can rise to achievement levels typical of the top 10%.

Independent practice is designed to increase students' fluency and ability to perform with ease the activity stated in the objective. For example, although some students may be able to slowly recite the times tables correctly, they may need more practice before they can recall them quickly and without much effort. Independent practice takes place with little or no teacher guidance. It may be performed in or out of class. Homework is one example of independent practice.

In some cases, more work of the type done in guided practice would seem boring and repetitive to students. For example, after students have shown that they can distinguish a noun from a verb in sentences, having them repeat that activity during independent practice would seem senseless. An *extension* of their learning might be for them to look at magazine articles and find nouns and verbs, or to look for nouns in poetry, or even on TV. They are working with the same skills, but in a different setting, with more complex examples, or at a slightly higher level of learning. For example, activities that ask students to identify similarities and differences among key concepts and to portray those differences through a variety of means (graphically, through metaphors, through classifying, etc.) are particularly effective at enhancing student understanding of content (Marzano, Pickering, & Pollock, 2001).

The independent practice and extension activities do not have to be closely guided by the teacher, but students should receive immediate feedback on their work. Since many students have difficulty working independently, they will also need feedback on how well they work on their own. Thus, teacher monitoring (or at least visual scanning) is a good idea, especially if you are reteaching a small group at the same time. Chapter 9 contains more ideas on structuring independent work.

CHECK YOUR UNDERSTANDING

With another student, trade off explaining and giving examples of the following terms: *guided practice, assessment, reteaching, extension,* and *independent practice.* Each of you should write definitions of two or three of the terms, then exchange your work with your partner's. Try not to look at your notes. Be sure to explain the terms in your own words. Check the accuracy of your understanding by looking back over the previous section.

REFLECTING ON THE IDEAS

Like most things in teaching, direct instruction has benefits and challenges. Imagine a classroom that used only direct instruction. What strengths and weaknesses do you envision?

When to Use Direct Lessons

The direct lesson is not recommended for every type of content. For example, you might initiate a teaching sequence for some concepts with an inductive lesson and use direct lessons for follow-up and practice. Direct lessons tend to be less effective with (a) abstract, "fuzzy" concepts, such as *majority, equity, justice, discrimination, freedom, ethics,* and *beauty;* (b) wholistic content that does not lend itself easily to sequencing of skills (such as reading comprehension and the writing process); and (c) content that includes a high degree of judgment or that has a substantial affective flavor—for example, politics, artistic expression, or debates (Cawelti, 1995).

Content that has a high degree of structure lends itself well to direct teaching. Examples of such content are writing an introductory sentence, concepts with clear rules, many math and science operations, problem-solving steps, the rules for debating, classroom rules and procedures, and some foreign language instruction. Some people think direct lessons can be used only with lower level cognitive skills (memorization and comprehension). However, researchers (Beyer, 1997, 1995; Brown, 1978; Rosenshine, 1992) have shown success in using direct teaching to enhance students' higher level cognitive skills (e.g., concept learning, comparison, contrast, and analysis). These researchers argue that too often students are given a higher level task without explicit direct teaching on how to attack that task (Williams & Colomb, 1993). Many students have not learned such skills on their own and need modeling, explanation, and guided practice before they can operate at the higher levels of thinking. For example, students who are taught procedures designed to enhance creative thinking, such as brainstorming, SCAMPER, or Creative Problem Solving, are more likely to be successful in tasks requiring creative thinking (see Starko, 2000). Teaching the skills or procedures themselves might be considered comprehension, but they can then be applied to many more complex activities. Thus direct teaching may be used to support both lower and higher level cognitive objectives as well as psychomotor and some affective objectives.

Examples of Direct Lessons
A Direct Lesson: Latitude and Longitude

Objective (For teacher use)

Given latitudinal and longitudinal readings, students will be able to find a city on a map.

Set

Teacher holds up flat Mercator projection map. "How are this map and a football field alike? How are they different? Everyone jot down a few ideas and be ready to tell me." Teacher walks around and reads what students write, waits a few seconds, and calls on four randomly selected students. (Focus and Diagnosis)

"We studied earlier about the difference between a globe and a flat map. Now we'll learn just a few more details about flat maps." (Transfer)

Objective (Learning outcome told to students in their words)

"By the end of this lesson, you will be able to use these lines on a map to find cities on the map."

Purpose (Why we're learning this; how we/you will use it in the future)

"We'll use this skill later when we role-play the pioneers' trips in our Westward Expansion unit."

Information/Modeling

Teacher explains and labels latitude and longitude lines, the equator, the prime meridian, and the numbering system used for degrees of latitude and longitude. Points to them on large wall map. Uses a memory aid (mnemonic device): "L*at*itude is *at* the equator; *long*itude is a *long* up and down line."

Check for Understanding

Teacher asks students a series of questions based on information that has been presented. Examples: "What are these lines called?" "What is the prime meridian?" (Teacher uses wait time and random selection of students.)

Information/Modeling

With a globe, teacher explains and illustrates how latitude and longitude lines intersect and how to determine north and south latitude, east and west longitude. (Teacher has previously determined by content analysis the order in which these terms and concepts should be presented.)

Check for Understanding

Teacher asks a few oral true-false questions to which all students respond with an overt signal (e.g., thumbs up or down). Depending on responses, teacher decides to reinforce some concepts or go on.

Information/Modeling

Three latitudinal/longitudinal readings are listed on the chalkboard. Teacher illustrates how to use this information to determine which world city is at each of these specific locations. Teacher thinks aloud to illustrate the thinking process and to encourage self-monitoring—metacognition. (Metacognition is discussed in Chapter 8.)

Guided Practice

1. Teacher puts three latitudinal/longitudinal readings on the chalkboard. Teacher gives students 2 minutes to work in groups of three to find the cities on a globe. Then the teacher has a few students of varied achievement levels come to the globe to identify each city and asks the others if they agree.

2. Teacher distributes a copy of a flat Mercator projection map to each student. Teacher has large cards made with a latitudinal/longitudinal reading listed on each card. Holds up one at a time. Students may work in pairs if they wish. They determine the correct city for each card according to the information provided and jot down the name of the city on a piece of scratch paper. After students figure the answer for each card, the teacher points to the correct city on the wall map and names the city. Students who agree raise hands.

3. Extra guided practice is planned, but may not be necessary if students are successful. If not used here, it may be used for reteaching or review. It is a worksheet with five latitude/longitude readings. Students work on them with assistance from teacher or other students.

Assessment (To make sure every student has achieved the objective)

Teacher writes two final latitudinal/longitudinal readings on the chalkboard. The students use their globes to write down the name of the appropriate city.

Teacher does not provide help at this point. Teacher checks each student's answer individually. Students who do not complete this correctly are given reteaching in a small group with a globe while the others do independent practice.

Independent Practice or Extension (This can be done without teacher guidance, perhaps as homework)

Teacher provides a worksheet that lists 10 latitudinal/longitudinal readings. Students use their maps to determine which city is being described and write the name of the city on the worksheet next to its description.

Extension (If more practice seems boring)

Students create fictional maps with cities and latitudinal/longitudinal coordinates. This activity will be followed up with practice and extension the next day. The second step in working with latitude and longitude will be introduced—that is, students determine the latitude and longitude of specific cities.

This lesson will be followed up with reteaching, review, and extension on the next days. All skills, once learned, will be reviewed intermittently. Answers are checked and feedback/reteaching is provided. To consider differentiation for this lesson, you might use a pretest to see if some students already have this skill. If so, those students might skip directly to the extension activity.

A Direct Lesson for Early Grades: Putting Away Supplies

Objective (For teacher use)

At the end of center time, students will be able to return center materials and supplies to the correct location with minimal confusion.

Set

While students are working, teacher has put the rack of scissors in the wrong place. Teacher role-plays being unable to find the scissors she needs. "Oh no, what am I going to do? I need scissors and I can't find them. Someone must have put them in the wrong place. What am I going to do?" She then "spots" the scissors and returns them to their correct location.

Objective (Learning outcome told to students in their words)

"That was really a problem. I thought I wasn't going to be able to cut out the things for this bulletin board because I couldn't find the scissors. Today we are going to learn how to put away some of our most important supplies so everyone can find them when they need them."

Purpose (Why we're learning this; how we/you will use it in the future)

"This is important because when we work together as a class we'll be using many things. All of us want to be able to find the things we need to learn. If supplies are in the right place, we'll always be able to find them."

Information/Modeling

Teacher explains the labeling system for the shelves, showing the pictures and words associated with scissors, crayons, and paste. She demonstrates where each item is to be stored.

Check for Understanding

Teacher asks students a few questions such as, "Where would this paste go?" and "If I found this crayon on the floor, what should I do with it?" She asks students to put the supplies where they belong.

Information/Modeling

Teacher explains and demonstrates procedures for returning unused paper and paper scraps to the art center.

Check for Understanding

Teacher holds up pieces of paper and students signal one finger if it should go in the paper pile, two fingers if it should go in the scrap pile, and thumbs down if it should go in the recycling.

Guided Practice

Teacher places an object to be returned on each table. Students are to decide where the object goes and point to the correct location. At the teacher's signal, the runner for each table returns the object. If students are successful, teacher indicates students are now ready to work on an art project.

Assessment (To make sure every student has achieved the objective)

Assessment will take place after the next activity. Teacher asks students to complete a simple art task. At the end of the activity she signals for cleanup (as previously taught) and observes students, making note of those who appear to have difficulty putting materials back correctly.

Independent Practice or Extension

This skill will be practiced throughout the school year. As new materials are added to the classroom, additional instruction may be required.

Extension/Differentiation

Students with exceptional organizational or language skills may be asked to devise a system for storing new supplies or to create labels for additional classroom items.

If you have students with limited motor abilities or other impairments that would make cleanup difficult, they may be assigned a rotating "pick-up buddy" to assist with the tasks.

SUMMARY

This chapter has provided information on formal and informal direct teaching and two approaches to formal direct teaching. The use of storytelling was described as an important strategy for making information vivid and easy to learn. Direct lesson design was presented as an efficient way to help students learn well-structured content. It may be less effective with loosely structured, abstract, or affective content. Direct teaching incorporates many aspects of effective instruction: congruence among objectives, activities, and evaluation; organization of concepts for long-term learning; rehearsal and practice; appeal to a variety of learning styles; active student involvement; and continuous assessment of the learner. Although you will not use direct teaching every minute of every day, it is a valuable structure for the design of some lessons.

■ *Practice Activity: Using the Elements of a Direct Lesson Design*

Create a direct lesson to meet one of the cognitive objectives you have written. Use the example lesson as a guide. Be sure to write your formal objective at the top of the page. Just for practice, include each element of the lesson design as if it were a recipe. Write out all the activities you would do with students. You do not have to write out every word you would say, except when telling students the objective and purpose. After planning for each activity, have a peer or your instructor give you feedback using the criteria listed on the Peer Feedback Form at the end of the chapter in Figure 7.2.

■ ■ ■

FIGURE 7.2 Peer Feedback Form

```
                                                    Time Started: _____
                                                    Time to End: _____

                    Name of teacher _____

                              PEER FEEDBACK FORM
                          DIRECT LESSON MICROTEACHING

1. SET                                              Look for examples of
        ____Elicited active involvement             principles of learning:
        ____Diagnosed learners                      1. CULTURAL CONTEXT
        ____Referred to previous learning

2. OBJECTIVE(S)                                     2. CONCEPTUAL FOCUS
        ____Told students the behavior
            expected at the end of the lesson       3. PRIOR KNOWLEDGE
            (and how they will be assessed)

3. PURPOSE                                          4. HIGHER LEVEL THINKING
        ____Told students why it's important
            to learn (authentic project/real use)   5. ACTIVE PROCESSING

4. INPUT                                            6. VARIETY
        ____Communicated the structure/
            organization of information
        ____Modeling—showed it

5. CHECKING FOR UNDERSTANDING                       COMMENTS:
        ____Used questioning strategies that got all involved

6. GUIDED PRACTICE
        ____Helped students to use the information
        ____Gave enough practice to lead to success
        ____Practice exercises matched the objective(s)

7. ASSESSMENT
        ____Checked each student's mastery of objective
```

UNIT PREPARATION

Examine the unit time line you prepared for the last chapter. Consider each objective to determine whether you believe it would be most effectively taught through direct or inductive strategies. You may need to read the next chapter before finalizing the decisions. Begin preparing direct lessons for lessons that meet the criteria listed in this chapter. Begin with a lesson that teaches a specific skill, a set of procedures, or well-organized facts. Submit at least one lesson for feedback before proceeding. Depending on your instructor's requirements, you may do a few detailed lesson plans and outlines of additional lessons or you may do detailed lesson plans for the entire unit. Your lessons will probably evolve as you continue to learn about teaching strategies. As you plan, remember to keep in mind all the things you have learned about the students in your class and adapt your planning to meet their needs.

PORTFOLIO ACTIVITY

Use the practice activity at the end of the chapter summary to create a portfolio item. Include your lesson plan and your reflections on the lesson you taught. It will be important to be able to discuss why you made the planning choices you did and what you would do next. It may be helpful to tie to the planning principles in Chapter 6. Think about what your assessment within and after the lesson showed you about what students learned and how that should help you plan the next activities. You should be able to tie your planning directly to student learning.

SEARCH THE WEB

There are many websites in which teachers share their lessons. The quality of those lessons varies widely. Examine some of the lessons on the Companion Website. You will find a variety of lesson plans and many other resources at sites linked to the "Discipline Specific Resources." You may also want to examine "Ask Eric Lesson Plans" at http://ericir.syr.edu/Virtual/Lessons. Notice how many activities are primarily inductive and how many direct. Select a lesson you consider particularly outstanding to share in class. Use the principles you have learned to explain why the lesson is a good one.

REFERENCES

Ausubel, D. (1968). *Educational psychology: A cognitive view.* New York: Holt, Rinehart, & Winston.

Beyer, B. K. (1995). *Critical thinking.* Bloomington, IN: Phi Delta Kappa.

Beyer, B. K. (1997). *Improving student thinking: A comprehensive approach.* Boston: Allyn & Bacon.

Black, P., & Wiliam, D. (1998, October). Inside the black box: Raising standards through classroom assessment. *Phi Delta Kappan, 80,* (2), 139–144.

Bloom, B. (1984, May). The search for group instruction as effective as one-to-one tutoring. *Educational Leadership, 41* (8), 4–17.

Brown, A. L. (1978). Knowing when, where, and how to remember: A problem of metacognition. In R. Glaser (Ed.), *Advances in instructional psychology* (pp. 77–157). Hillsdale, NJ: Erlbaum.

Cawelti, G. (Ed.). (1995). *Handbook of research on improving student achievement.* Alexandria, VA: Association for Supervision and Curriculum Development.

Costa, A., & Liebman, R. (1997). *Supporting the spirit of learning: When process is content.* Thousand Oaks, CA: Corwin Press.

Cruickshank, D. R. (1990). *Research that informs teachers and teacher educators.* Bloomington, IN: Phi Delta Kappan.

Egan, K. (1986). *Teaching as storytelling: An alternative approach to teaching and curriculum in elementary school.* Chicago: University of Chicago Press.

Ernst, M. P. (1995). *The effect of peer teaching on middle school learners' skill performance, cognitive performance and comfort level.* Thesis, University of Wyoming. Accession No. 32651139, ERIC (Internet).

Fritz, J. (1977). *Can't you make them behave, King George?* New York: The Putnam & Grosset Group.

Hunter, M. (1976). *Rx: Improved instruction.* El Segundo, CA: T.I.P. Publications.

Joyce, B., Showers, B., & Weil, M. (1996). *Models of teaching.* Boston: Allyn & Bacon.

Marzano, R. J., Pickering, D. J., & Pollock, J. E. (2001). *Classroom instruction that works: Research-based strategies for increasing student achievement.* Alexandria, VA: Association for Supervision and Curriculum Development.

McGuire, M. (1997). Taking a storypath. *Educational Leadership, 54* (6), 70–72.

Peacock, L. (1998). *Crossing the Delaware: A history in many voices.* New York: Simon & Schuster.

Powell, M. A. (1997). *Peer tutoring and mentoring services for disadvantaged secondary school students.* Sacramento, CA: California Research Bureau, California State Library.

Powell, R. R. (1992). The influence of prior experiences on pedagogical constructs of traditional and nontraditional preservice teachers. *Teaching and Teacher Education, 8* (3), 225–238.

Rosenshine, B. (1987). Explicit teaching. In D. C. Berliner & B. V. Rosenshine (Eds.), *Talks to teachers* (pp. 75–92). New York: Random House.

Rosenshine, B. (1992, April). The use of scaffolds for teaching higher-level cognitive strategies. *Educational Leadership, 49,* 26–33.

Rowe, M. B. (1974). Wait time, review, and instructional variables. *Journal of Research in Science Teaching, 11,* 81–84.

Starko, A. J. (2000). *Creativity in the classroom: Schools of curious delight.* Mahwah, NJ: Lawrence Erlbaum.

Tobin, K. (1980). The effect of an extended teacher wait time on science achievement. *Journal of Research in Science Teaching, 17,* 469–475.

Wang, M., Haertel, E., & Walberg, H. (1993). What helps students learn? *Educational Leadership, 51* (4), 74–79.

Wiggins, G. (1994). Toward better report cards. *Educational Leadership, 52* (2), 28–37.

Wiggins, G. (1996, Spring). Anchoring assessment with exemplars: Why students and teachers need models. *Gifted Child Quarterly, 40* (2), 66–69.

Wiggins, G., & McTighe, J. (1998). *Understanding by design.* Alexandria, VA: Association for Supervision and Curriculum Development.

Williams, J. M., & Colomb, G. G. (1993, October). The case for explicit teaching: Why what you don't know won't help you. *Research in the Teaching of English, 27* (3), 252–264.

CHAPTER 8

Models for Teaching:
Inductive Approaches

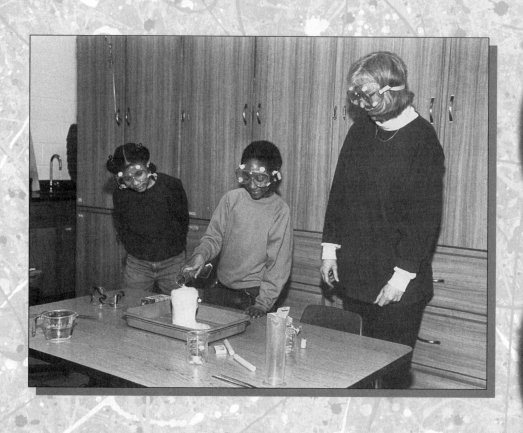

CHAPTER OVERVIEW

In Chapter 7, we described ways to structure teaching using direct instruction—instruction in which the focus of the lesson is on the teacher providing information directly to the students. Many times, however, powerful learning occurs not when a teacher tells students something directly but when they discover something themselves through their own experiences. This chapter will explore strategies for teaching that follow this pattern of experience and discovery. These strategies are characterized as *inductive* teaching.

 ## CHAPTER OBJECTIVES

When you have completed this chapter, you will be able to:

1. describe key components of inductive teaching; and
2. design, teach, and reflect upon inductive experiences including experiences designed to build concepts, inquiry lessons, authentic research, problem-based learning, role play, and simulation.

■ *Opening Activity*

Think of a time, outside of school or other formal class settings, when you learned something that was really interesting. It may have happened during a trip to a local science museum, a walk on the beach, or any other time when exciting learning occurred without the specific guidance of a teacher. Share your experiences with one or two classmates. Discuss what, if anything, your experiences have in common.

■ ■ ■

 ## INDUCTIVE TEACHING: FORMAL AND INFORMAL

In the previous chapter we discussed a variety of ways in which learning can occur directly, through the presentation of information needed. This can occur in informal ways, as it does among family or friends, or in unplanned teachable moments in schools. It also can occur in structured teaching activities, through the use of storytelling or direct lesson design. However, much learning—in and out of school—does not occur through direct teaching. That learning stems from conclusions drawn *inductively*.

When an argument or process of logic is said to be inductive, it proceeds from the specific to the general. That is, individuals draw general conclusions based on particular examples. If you notice that your four red-haired friends also have fair skin and draw the conclusion that red-haired people are fair-skinned, that is inductive reasoning. If you read five fables and conclude that they have characteristics in common, that is also inductive. Detectives (particularly the TV variety) use inductive reasoning when they draw conclusions about what happened at the crime scene from isolated bits of evidence.

Much of the learning that occurs in daily life is inductive. We learn most concepts through experience with examples rather than through direct teaching. Many times, powerful learning happens, not when a teacher tells us something is true, but when we discover something ourselves or share it with others. Perhaps you can remember the first time you noticed the similarities between the pattern of the veins on a leaf and the branches of a tree, and started looking around for other things that branched. Or maybe you remember your curiosity when you noticed how many fairy tales revolved around the number three, or the excitement when your friends experimented to see which method of sand castle construction was most resistant to waves. Perhaps you recall more recent discoveries: suddenly seeing connections between Greek mythology and a contemporary movie, or noticing words in a politician's questionnaire designed to bias the results. Each of these is an important insight, yet none was covered by teachers in a direct learning experience.

Although some content and skills can be appropriately taught through direct teaching, there are many other ways individuals construct meaning. Think of the number of ideas, words, and skills a student has learned before entering school. Few of those ideas were taught directly. Children learn concepts such as *happy, tired, dog,* or *ice cream* through their experiences with the world around them. It is unlikely that many students listened to a lecture or watched a movie to learn the generalization that, as the temperature rises, ice cream gets softer and melts. Yet most students enter kindergarten with that understanding. One of the teacher's roles is to structure school experiences to allow students to discover important ideas.

Individuals construct meaning best when they interact with new information in real contexts and use it in meaningful ways. Like direct teaching, inductive teaching occurs in school in both formal and informal ways. Much informal inductive teaching occurs through the physical environment of the classroom and the routine of the school day. Minute by minute, we are providing students with the experiences that build basic concepts. Much important teaching, particularly in early years, occurs as we structure situations that allow students to have experiences with content and learn to label those experiences appropriately.

It is important to note that informal teaching is not necessarily unplanned. It is true that school days are full of teachable moments, some of which cannot be anticipated. But it is also the case that good teachers plan their classrooms and their days to increase the likelihood of teachable moments. For example, a kindergarten teacher who knows that part of his curriculum is teaching the concepts *over, under, around,* and so forth may choose to have a construction area in the classroom with blocks and an assortment of vehicles. This is not just an area for developing motor skills—although that certainly is a part of its purpose—but a place where it is likely the teacher will be able to talk to students about the fact that they have built a bridge *over* the river or the truck will need to go *around* the pile of blocks. This teacher is not directly teaching the concepts *over* or *around,* but is providing students with experiences that allow them to build the concepts.

Similarly, a classroom with a fish tank, a rabbit, and a collection of plants provides experiences that help students develop richer understanding of the concepts of *living, nonliving, plants,* and *animals.* Classroom weather stations, collections of artifacts borrowed from a children's museum, a collection of books displayed on a table, or a portion of the school yard "adopted" for careful observation throughout the year all provide experiences that form the basis of new concepts. Careful thought about the teaching environments we provide and the cues we give students for interacting with those environments are important parts of planning. Sometimes these environments are structured in centers, as described in Chapter 9.

Field trips are a complex example of structuring the learning environment to provide experiences on which concepts can be based. Restored villages that allow students to simulate life in the past, children's museums with interactive exhibits, or visits to a theater with a backstage tour provide learning beyond the direct instruction that usually takes place there. For example, students touring the wings of a theater probably will hear the guide point out the ropes used for flying scenery, the counterweights, the area for set construction, controls for the many lights, and so on. But while there, students also are experiencing a host of sights and sounds that build new concepts and new connections—about the illusion of scenery, the use of pulleys, and the roles of individuals behind the scene. These connections may prove valuable far beyond the immediate moment. In those settings it is important to provide focus on the key ideas we hope to teach without losing our appreciation of the additional learning that takes place in a rich environment.

Thoughtful use of technology can broaden the classroom environments without leaving the physical classroom. Consider the informal lessons learned by following an expedition across the desert or exchanging data with a class from another state or country. In addition to the core content of the project, students will learn many other concepts and lessons through their exposure to new environments, new people, and new ideas. More specific ideas for technology-infused curriculum can also be found in Chapter 9.

REFLECTING ON THE IDEAS

Observe an elementary classroom. Think about the concepts that are being built through the classroom environment. Try to identify things the teacher says or does that maximize student learning through that environment.

Think about your own classroom. You might want to begin a list of things you would like to include in your classroom to support inductive learning.

FORMAL INDUCTIVE TEACHING

If the students are to develop a clear understanding of the concepts and generalizations we are trying to teach, they will have to experience the ideas and work with them in ways that make sense in their lives. In many cases this type of interaction is best facilitated in lessons or activities that focus on the students' interaction with information. Formal inductive teaching focuses on structuring such interaction so that it happens as a carefully planned aspect of instruction.

In direct lessons a teacher is likely to present an idea or skill and then cite specific examples of how it may be applied, whereas in inductive lessons the students are given the examples and they figure out the concept or generalization that ties the examples together. *It is only an inductive lesson if the students engage in inductive thinking* (Joyce, Showers, & Weil, 1996). It is often tempting, as a teacher, to present the examples and

FIGURE 8.1   The Relationship of Bruner's Structure of Knowledge to Inductive Lessons

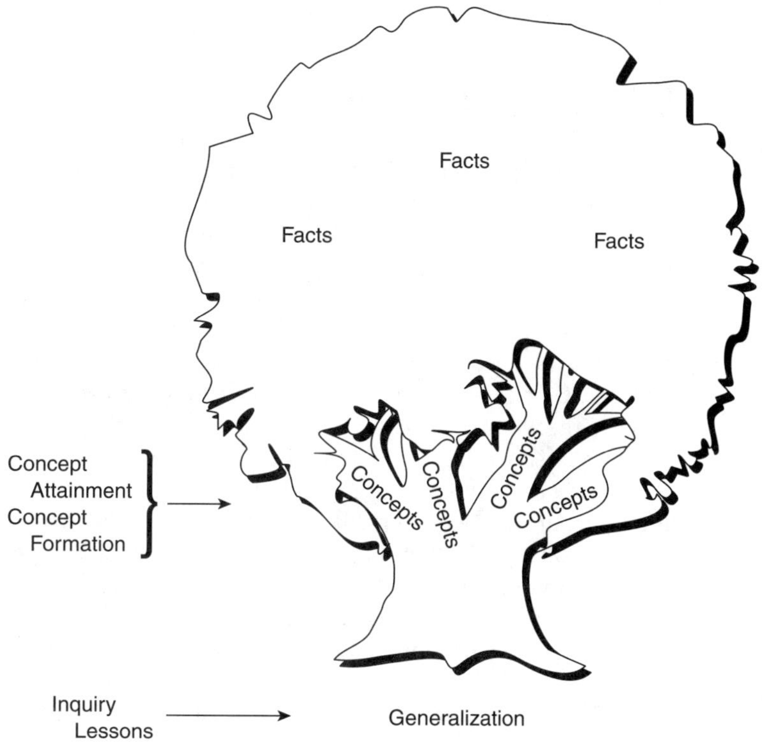

then point out to students the conclusions they should draw. This shortcuts the process. While students often benefit from cues that direct them to new understanding, powerful learning can result from the opportunity to figure things out independently. The resulting "aha" moment is not likely to be forgotten.

Go back for a moment to Bruner's structure of knowledge in Chapter 2. The tree image shown there illustrates how facts, concepts, and generalizations relate to one another. Figure 8.1 shows how several types of inductive lessons relate to that structure-of-knowledge tree. Inquiry lessons tend to result in the discovery of a generalization, principle, or explanation. Concept attainment and concept formation lessons result in deep understandings of concepts and key ideas. There are three basic types of inductive lessons: (a) experiences designed to build concepts, (b) inquiry experiences requiring the interpretation and application of data, and (c) authentic research. Lessons 3 and 6 in the sample unit are examples of inductive lessons.

Experiences Designed to Build Concepts

This section presents two types of concept-based lessons: (a) **concept formation**, where students classify data or information into categories and label the key organizing features as concepts, and (b) **concept attainment,** where students look at examples and nonex-amples of a particular concept, find common characteristics, and then determine the name of the concept.

Concept Formation Lessons

Taba's (1967; see also Joyce, Showers, & Weil, 1996) concept formation lessons have three basic components. First, students are asked to *list,* or enumerate, data regarding a particular question or problem. For example, students might be asked to list all the types of fuel they can think of or all the animals in the nearby woods. Next, students are asked to *group* items with similar characteristics. For example, they may be asked, "Which types of fuel are most alike?" or "Divide the animals into groups that are alike in some way." This process may be assisted through questions such as, "How are solar power and gasoline alike? How are they different?" or "You have said the frog and the robin both lay eggs. Do any other animals on your list lay eggs? Are there any other egg-laying an-imals in the woods?" The final step of a concept formation lesson is to *label* the concepts. In these lessons, the teacher may be hoping to develop the concepts of *renewable* and *nonrenewable resources* or basic classifications of animals. In teaching the concept of *leader* in her American Revolution unit, Gloria could choose a concept formation lesson to help students develop the concepts of *military leaders, political leaders*, and so on.

In planning a concept formation lesson, there are two major considerations. First, it is important to plan a question or problem that will allow students to generate a list of data rich enough to include the concept you wish to develop. Imagine, for example, that you want to plan a concept development lesson around the concepts of *wants* and *needs*. If you start out with the question, "Imagine you had $500. Let's list all the things you might buy," it is possible that all the items listed might be wants. In that case, it would be impossible to develop the desired concepts without asking additional ques-tions. Alternatively, you could pose the question, "Imagine that for one month your par-ents put you in charge of the family's finances. They will give you all the income and you are responsible for all purchases for the month. How will you use the money?" With that introduction, it is more likely that at least some students will mention food, electricity, rent, and so on. In Gloria's leadership lesson, if her first question is, "Who were leaders in the revolution?" it is likely that students will produce a list that will be sufficient to develop the concepts of *military* and *political leaders*. However, if Gloria wants them to understand the leadership roles of other types of individuals, she will need to plan care-fully. She might choose to broaden her question, for example, "What people played im-portant roles in winning the American Revolution?" in hopes of getting a more comprehensive list. Alternatively, she might stick with a more limited concept of leader for this lesson, and later, after subsequent lessons have developed the concept more fully, return to add to the list.

The second key to a successful concept development lesson is recognizing when students need additional questions to assist them in focusing the categories. It is always wise to try to predict in advance what types of categories may be initially formed and how to guide students to the desired concepts. Sometimes very general questions may be helpful. For example, you may ask students to form the smallest number of categories they can in which all items are still alike in some way. Other times you may need to be more specific: "Let's think about the animals' covering. Squirrels have fur. Do any other animals on the list have fur?" Concept formation lessons or activities may stand alone or be part of a sequence leading to further interpretation of data.

Concept Attainment Lessons

A related type of lesson also is designed to help students develop new concepts. Whereas a concept formation lesson requires students to determine criteria and develop categories, concept attainment lessons require them to identify the attributes that differentiate categories already formed by someone else. This is done through the analysis of examples and nonexamples of the concept to be attained (Bruner, Goodnow, & Austin, 1977; Joyce, Showers, & Weil, 1996). The examples and nonexamples are called *exemplars*.

A concept attainment lesson begins with the teacher presenting exemplars and categorizing them as yes (an example of the concept to be developed) or no (a nonexample). By comparing "yes" and "no" exemplars, students begin to form ideas (silently) about the critical attributes of the concept. After a number of exemplars have been presented, students are asked to describe the characteristics or attributes that the yes examples presented thus far have in common. As additional examples are presented, students may be asked to categorize them as yes or no, and determine whether the criteria originally developed continue to hold. After additional examples, criteria may be refined and concept labels developed. After the teacher gives the technical label (if there is one), students are asked to produce examples of their own. Finally, students describe their thinking and how their ideas changed as they moved through the activity.

Imagine, for example, that you wanted your students to be able to use *inductive thinking* to discover the meaning of *natural resources*. Note the lesson develops two objectives/outcomes: the thinking skill and the content understanding. The lesson might proceed as follows:

1. Teacher introduces the activity by presenting the following exemplars, one at a time, and asks the students to find what the positive examples have in common. They should use the negative examples to clarify what the concept is not.

trees (yes)	houses (no)	Mississippi River (yes)
bathtub (no)	sun (yes)	furnace (no)
oil (yes)	tent (no)	granite (yes)
cement (no)	wind (yes)	fans (no)
soil (yes)	natural gas (yes)	gasoline (no)

2. Students form ideas about what all the yes examples have in common and write a definition using critical attributes. For example, one guess might be "things outside," with the critical attribute that all the yes examples are found outdoors. Students do not initially share ideas.

3. Teacher gives additional unlabeled exemplars for the students to label as yes or no. For example, coal (yes) or T-shirt (no). Teacher asks students to share their definitions.

4. Teacher names the concept and restates the definition in terms of the critical attributes. Students are then asked to generate more exemplars. Teacher might listen to students' ideas and then say, "Yes, the critical attributes of the 'yes' examples are that they occur naturally and can be used to meet our wants and needs. Now think of something else that might be called a natural resource." Students are called on to share their examples, which might be *the ocean* or *plants*.

5. Students describe (in writing or discussion) their thoughts on how they formed their definitions and labels, and how they tested them when new exemplars were given. Students might say that they put into one category two exemplars that had a similar quality and then looked at another yes item to see if it fit into that category. Then they would contrast those three examples with the no item. When a new exemplar was given, they again tested it against the yes and no exemplars to see if it fit. (This part refines their thinking skills.)

There are three major steps in developing a concept attainment lesson. First, you must carefully define your concept. Decide on its key attributes. Think about which attributes are critical (essential for this concept) and noncritical (common but not essential). For example, if the concept is *mammal*, critical attributes are that mammals are warm-blooded, are covered with hair or fur, and give birth to live young and nurse them. A noncritical attribute is that many mammals have four legs and live on land. It is important to develop your concept attainment lesson to clarify as many of the critical attributes of the concept as possible.

Next, you need to select your exemplars. Exemplars may be provided in the form of words, phrases, pictures, or even concrete items. You will need to select examples and nonexamples that will highlight critical attributes. It would be extremely difficult to provide examples such that students would identify them as warm-blooded. You could, however, provide examples that would highlight other relevant characteristics. For example, in choosing the examples and nonexamples of the concept *mammals* you might anticipate that students may initially think that the concept is *animals in the zoo* or *animals in the woods*. You could help clarify these misconceptions by including a snake or an ostrich as nonexamples. If you use pictures of these animals including their eggs, you could focus attention on important attributes. Using a whale as an example may be confusing if students don't know whales have hair or give birth to live young. A picture of a nursing whale may be an important clue.

Finally, you will consider the order in which to present the examples and nonexamples. In most cases, broadly differing examples are given first, with finer and finer distinctions presented as the concept is developed. For example, you might decide to present pictures of a bear and a fish early in the lesson and save the whale photo for later fine-tuning of the concept. Concept attainment lessons work best for concrete concepts in which the critical attributes are clear. They are much more difficult to plan for more abstract concepts that are open to interpretation. For example, a concept attainment lesson probably is not the best means by which Gloria might teach the concepts of *liberty* or *freedom* because it would be extremely difficult to agree upon clearly defined examples and nonexamples.

In determining the order of the exemplars, it is important to consider the purpose of the activity. If, as in a concept attainment lesson, the intent is to provide students with information from which they can build a new concept, it is most appropriate to start with clear examples and save those that demand careful analysis for later in the lesson. Occasionally, activities resembling concept attainment lessons are used to review or reintroduce already learned concepts. In this case, teachers sometimes use "trickier" examples first and allow clues to become more and more obvious until students guess the concept. This can be a highly motivating and appropriate introduction to a lesson, but is not a concept attainment lesson because students are attempting to identify a concept they have already internalized. See Figure 8.2 to compare key features of various types of inductive lessons.

FIGURE 8.2   Inductive Approaches

Lesson Type	Use	Key Attributes/Student Activities
Concept formation	Develop concepts	1. List data 2. Categorize data 3. Label concepts
Concept attainment	Develop concepts	1. Examine examples and nonexamples of concept 2. Identify new exemplars as examples or nonexamples 3. Generate rules/criteria for concepts 4. Develop or receive concept labels
Suchman's inquiry	Form generalizations	1. View a puzzling event 2. Ask "yes" and "no" questions to explain the event and/or identify important variables 3. Test hypotheses by asking questions or manipulating variables 4. Draw conclusions
Other inquiry	Form generalizations	1. Examine data set 2. Make hypotheses regarding data 3. Test hypotheses on additional data 4. Draw conclusions
Authentic research	Produce new knowledge	1. Learn about a topic 2. Pose questions that can be investigated through descriptive, historical, or experimental research 3. Choose the appropriate research design and sources of data 4. Gather data 5. Examine data 6. Draw conclusions

REFLECTING ON THE IDEAS

Try the concept attainment activity that follows. Go through steps 1–5 of the preceding lesson with a partner, verbally.

The number on a football jersey (no)

The second-place winner in a race (yes)

The serial number on a radio (no)

The seventh person in a graduating class (yes)

A telephone number (no)

The number-one song on the charts (yes)

What did you get out of this exercise that you would have missed if you had been taught the concept of *ordinal data* using direct teaching?

Inquiry Lessons: Interpreting and Applying Data

Experiences that involve interpreting and applying data are frequently called inquiry lessons. **Inquiry lessons** require students to inquire, examine information, make hypotheses, gather data, and draw conclusions. They get students actively involved in discovering a generalization that explains a puzzling event or set of data. Inquiry lessons are particularly valuable because they involve students in many of the processes of authentic investigation used by adults in a variety of fields. They also capitalize on students' natural curiosity and desire to find solutions to puzzling or problematic situations (Caine & Caine, 1997).

Suchman's Inquiry

One variety of inquiry lesson was developed by Suchman (1962; Joyce, Showers, & Weil, 1996). In this model, the teacher begins the activity by explaining the inquiry process and the ground rules. Students are not given any response from the teacher except "yes" or "no" during the questioning period. The teacher presents a puzzling event—something that conflicts with our typical notions of reality. The students ask questions to get more information and see under what conditions different results would occur. Students, through their questions, begin to isolate relevant variables and to form hunches about causal relationships (hypotheses). Through questions or experiments that test their hypotheses, they formulate an explanation for the puzzling event. Finally, the teacher leads students to analyze their own thinking processes.

A concrete example may help you understand how this model of inquiry works. The objectives here are to develop students' ability to (a) see patterns in the evidence and form a hypothesis to explain why an event occurs, and (b) describe how air pressure, direction, and speed interact to create lift. Note that the first objective relates to a thinking skill, and the second one relates to content understanding.

1. Teacher presents a discrepant event (after clarifying ground rules). Teacher blows softly across the top of an 8 1/2″ by 11″ sheet of paper, and the paper rises. She tells the students to figure out why it rises.
2. Students ask questions to gather more information and to isolate relevant variables. Teacher answers only "yes" or "no." Students ask if temperature is important (no). They ask if the paper is of a special kind (no). They ask if air pressure has anything to do with the paper rising (yes). Questions continue.
3. Students test causal relationships. In this case, they ask if the nature of the air on top causes the paper to rise (yes). They ask if the fast movement of the air is important (yes). Then they test out the rule with other material—for example, thin plastic or paper airplanes.
4. Students form a generalization: If the air on the top moves faster than the air on the bottom of a surface, the object rises. This is because the fast-moving air exerts less air pressure. Later lessons can tie this experience to other important effects of air pressure and/or principles of flight.
5. Teacher leads students in a discussion of their thinking processes. What were the important variables? How did they put the causes and effects together? And so on.

Other Inquiry Lessons

Other inquiry lessons involve students in drawing conclusions, not about a particular puzzling event, but about a set of data. For example, in one lesson students made and investigated hypotheses about the relationship between advertising strategies and product type by examining a collection of advertisements cut from magazines. Students examined the *data set* (magazine ads), made *hypotheses* about *variables* (product and strategy), and tested their *conclusions* (looking at additional print or TV ads). The key attributes of inquiry lessons are examining data, making hypotheses, and drawing conclusions. This cycle may be repeated as many times as it seems productive.

For example, you might want to create an inquiry lesson to help your students develop a generalization regarding the relationship between scarcity and cost. You might divide students into small groups and provide them with a set of data regarding an imaginary product. For example, the data might describe the number of floogles available in various years, and their cost. Students may be challenged to investigate the data and make hypotheses about the cost of floogles. Hypotheses may be tested by examining additional data on floogles in more recent years. If desired, you could ask students to extend their hypotheses to other items. If the cost of floogles rises when floogles become scarce, does that pattern hold for other commodities? Data may be examined for real items that have changed dramatically in availability, for example DVD players. Like other inductive experiences, this lesson would include discussion of the thinking processes students used to reach the conclusions. This inquiry lesson could end with the floogles after one or two class periods or extend to include many areas and weeks of investigation.

Many fascinating inquiry projects can be conducted when classrooms share data from different parts of the country or the world through one of the web-based teacher exchanges. Imagine sharing information on the acidity of rain, the numbers of various types of insects, or weather conditions with students in different geographical locations.

Students can have the opportunities to make and test a variety of hypotheses—while also having the opportunity to learn about another location in a meaningful way.

REFLECTING ON THE IDEAS

Two teachers are discussing a student, John, in the teachers' lounge. John attends class regularly, turns in all his homework, and seems to be succeeding in practice activities, but is failing most of the quizzes. This is a puzzling set of circumstances! With a partner, develop four *hypotheses* that might explain the apparent contradiction. For each hypothesis, give a *strategy* for finding out if it is true.

Present your hypotheses and strategies to another team. Discuss your thinking as you moved through the process. Assume that the correct explanation of John's performance is test anxiety. What did you get out of the exercise that you would have missed if you had been told about John's test anxiety directly?

Authentic Research with Students

Traditional inquiry lessons and most "research" conducted in elementary schools are planned by teachers. Teachers develop the questions, structure the activities, and know in advance the conclusions students should draw. Many valuable activities take this format. However, few researchers in the real world would undertake inquiry projects for which the end result is predetermined. If students are to experience authentic learning, at least some of their inquiries should result in genuine research. Whereas inquiry activities entail drawing conclusions from data selected and controlled by teachers, authentic research analyzes data as it is found in the world around us. Such activities appeal to the way the human brain naturally learns by engaging students with meaningful, complex experiences (Caine & Caine, 1997). Because this type of research entails drawing conclusions from specific bits of data, it can be considered an inductive experience. For more information on conducting research with your students, see Starko (2000) or Starko and Schack (1992).

Defining Authentic Research

What is authentic research? Although there are a variety of activities that might be appropriately labeled *research,* most research efforts share certain basic characteristics. *Random House Webster's Dictionary* (1993) defines research as "diligent and systematic inquiry into a subject in order to discover facts or revise theories" (p. 565). The essence of research is the production or discovery of new information. Researchers address questions and problems for which they do not have ready solutions, and through their efforts add to the body of knowledge. This role as a *producer of information* is key to this type of research—and to authentic learning.

If teachers are to help students function as true researchers, it is necessary to tackle problems for which the teachers do not have ready answers. Teachers and students cannot conduct research to determine the items in the USDA Food Guide Pyramid, but they could investigate food preferences of fourth graders in their school. And although the class cannot research the name of the first U.S. president, they might research the history of their school building. In authentic research, the teacher must give up holding the final solution and take on the role of fellow investigator, never quite sure what the data will bring. Key to this changed role of the teacher is assisting students in posing genuine research questions, questions to which there are no predetermined answers and for which data are available.

A full discussion of research techniques appropriate for elementary students is beyond the scope of this book. It is, however, appropriate to consider basic types of research questions that might be investigated by your students. Consider how each type might be used to enhance the basic curriculum or to encourage students to investigate areas of interest.

Types of Research

Three types of research can be particularly appropriate for students: *descriptive, historical,* and *experimental* (Starko & Schack, 1992). A knowledge of the various types of research is helpful in deciding the kinds of questions that might be asked. If, for example, students are interested in recycling (or recycling is to be studied as part of the regular curriculum), one way to develop possible research questions is to think about how the topic of recycling might be explored through each of the major research types. What kind of descriptive research might be conducted about recycling? How might recycling be studied from a historical perspective? Could the students design an experiment dealing with recycling?

Descriptive Research

Descriptive research is, of course, research that describes. It can be thought of as research that answers the question, How are things now? Its main purpose is to portray a current situation as systematically and accurately as possible. Public opinion surveys, descriptive observations, consumer research, and analyses of current test data are all types of descriptive research. If a school reports average reading test scores for a building or grade, if *Consumer Reports* describes the repair records of various types of CD players, or if *Parade* lists the 10 top-selling snack foods in the country, they are reporting the results of descriptive research. Students who survey the community regarding recycling practices, conduct election polls, plan taste tests to determine the preferred brand of pizza, or observe the types of insects found on school grounds are conducting descriptive research.

Descriptive research is probably the easiest type of research for young students. Such studies can often be conducted in a relatively short period of time. Observation, surveys, and interviews lend themselves to this type of research. Think about how descriptive research could be used to enhance a science or social studies unit. If, for example, you plan a first-grade unit on homes in the community, you might include a simple survey to determine how many students live in houses, apartments, trailers, and so on, or an observational study on building materials on homes near the school. You would not need to directly teach the generalization, "Communities contain many kinds of homes." Students would draw that conclusion from the data. If you plan a unit on nutrition, the class might survey students' favorite snack foods, or interview parents regarding their views on artificial sweeteners for children.

The data collection and analysis necessary in these types of surveys are essential parts of the math curriculum in most elementary schools. Some data collection activities are brief, conducted in a single class period. These might include students creating graphs from stick-on notes or linking plastic cubes to illustrate the number of students who prefer cats or dogs, vanilla or chocolate ice cream. Such activities use inductive thinking to draw conclusions about ice cream or pet preferences, while practicing creating and reading graphs. Others might be more elaborate and span a period of weeks—for example, a study collecting data on the percentage of sugar in students' favorite cereals. In one class a similar study culminated in letters to cereal companies suggesting that sugar content of some favorites be reduced to allow students to add sugar to taste. Think of the number of skills and content areas encompassed in that study: nutrition, percentages, graphing, letter writing and composition, and consumer activism.

Older elementary students can learn to plan survey questions to minimize bias—and to identify bias in political or commercial surveys. This understanding can be essential in making good sense of advertising that claims, "The research says. . . ."

Historical Research

If descriptive research answers the question, How are things now? *historical research* answers the question, How did things used to be? Its purpose is to reconstruct the past as accurately and objectively as possible. You probably do not see historical research reported in popular publications as often as you do descriptive research, but it still surrounds us. A newspaper interview with a former mayor about his or her term, a book on pioneer women based on their diaries, or even a magazine article titled "Fifty Years of Swimsuits" are reporting historical research. Students who interview their parents about the parents' school experiences, investigate the past occupants of stores on Main Street, or learn about the American Revolution by examining diaries, etchings, or the lyrics of popular music of the period are also doing historical research.

Much historical research is interesting and appropriate for elementary-age students. Before discussing it further, however, we'd like to issue one caution: the younger the students, the closer to home we must stay. Young children have a difficult time distinguishing history and fantasy. After all, George Washington and Snow White both lived "long ago and far away." However, even primary students can investigate information about their immediate family or possibly their school. Community history may seem very abstract, but "How is second grade today different from when our parents were in school?" is a very real question about real people. It is a powerful way to examine some of the primary-grade social studies outcomes about change and stability over time. Intermediate age students are, of course, more likely to be able to deal with issues of local, state, or possibly even world history in a professional manner.

One of the key differences between historical research and typical library research is the reliance of historical research on *primary sources*. In a typical research report on clothing of the Civil War period, a student would go to an encyclopedia, reference book, or other *secondary source*; take notes; and summarize the information read. A student doing historical research on the same topic would look for primary sources of information. This might include looking at paintings of the period, reproductions of catalogues, museum displays, or old magazines. The student would look for similarities and variations and draw conclusions from the data.

Many types of resources are valuable in historical research. Some may be available in local libraries or museums, or through interlibrary loan. In many cases, reproductions of paintings, books, magazines, or catalogues are available and are more durable than the originals. Most libraries have archives of older material on microfiche or other media. Increasingly, students may also have access to primary sources through the Internet and other forms of electronic communication. Although locating materials for historical research may seem daunting (especially with the encyclopedia so readily available), historical research provides benefits to students that are unavailable by any other means. Aside from the obvious benefits of library and critical thinking skills, this type of research makes history come alive. Students who have been touched by the words and sounds and images of real people from long ago, who have considered those people's lives and points of view, and have drawn conclusions from those lives, form links with history that are not forged in other ways. This power to touch the reality of history makes historical research a vital tool to consider, especially for intermediate teachers who are charged with teaching state and local history. You may find many local resources in your library, and you may also find it worthwhile to haunt flea markets and used book stores to find sources for your personal collection that tie in with major units in your curriculum.

For example, a teacher who commonly teaches the history of the community may canvass library sales or flea markets for reproductions of early maps, old postcards depicting the community, or histories of local families. Such materials could allow students to investigate questions as diverse as, How have the boundaries of our town changed since 1800? and, What were the most common architectural styles in our community in 1920? How closely does the current restoration resemble the original buildings? A sixth-grade teacher who teaches American history may want to acquire a few old *Life* magazines or recordings of period music (such as "Good-by Mama I'm Off to Yokohama") to add to the unit on World War II. Such additions might result in a class investigation into point of view in news coverage or an individual study comparing music written about World War II with that written about the Vietnam War. Students are able to experience the thrill of touching the world of the past and investigating the way bona fide historians do.

In preparing for the American Revolution unit, Gloria will want to investigate ways to bring students into contact with primary documents from the period. Of course, it is not likely that she will have access to actual artifacts from the period—and if she did, they would not be likely to survive many years of active use by her students. However, there are many sources that reproduce primary sources that can be used by children. Many books about the period include drawings, paintings, and etchings from the time period. Children can analyze them for information about events, clothing, architecture, and so on, just as historians do. The famous Paul Revere etching of the Boston Massacre provides an outstanding opportunity to discuss bias even in primary sources—as well as the use of propaganda during the Revolution (see Hakim, 1999, for an explanation appropriate for elementary-age children). *Cobblestone* magazine regularly includes segments from primary sources. Museum shops can prove rich in sources for real and simulated historical research. One of us returned from a trip to a local museum with a small lamp that could have been used in the Revolutionary period and a reproduction of the first cookbook printed in the United States (Simmons, 1958). Both artifacts could be analyzed in the same ways the originals might have been, enhancing understanding of the lifestyle in the Revolutionary period.

Experimental Research

Perhaps the most typical image that enters your mind when you hear the word *research* is that of the bubbling tubes and strange concoctions of a scientist in the midst of an experiment. Of course, true experimental research is an important type of research design—with or without the test tubes! This type of research is designed to investigate cause-and-effect relationships by exposing experimental groups to some type of treatment. It answers the question, What would happen if. . .?

Experimental research, unlike descriptive or historical research, manipulates variables. That is, the individual conducting the experiment must be able to change at least one aspect of the situation being studied in order to determine the effects of those changes. For example, a researcher investigating the effects of a particular drug must be able to give the drug to some patients and not to others in order to determine its effectiveness. This manipulation of variables is called the *treatment.* All experimental research involves a treatment (though it is usually not a drug!). Researchers do not merely describe a situation, they change it.

Many medical studies, some studies comparing the effectiveness of teaching techniques, and research comparing the effects of various insecticides are examples of true experimental research. Many science fair winners are students who have conducted experimental research. For example, one student compared the growth of beans under normal classroom conditions with that of beans grown on a rotating "Ferris wheel," on which centrifugal force would interfere with the force of gravity. The student provided a treatment—a change in gravitational forces—and studied the results.

Experimental research can sometimes be complex and difficult. However, even very young students can conduct simple experiments with sufficient guidance. One humorous example happened in a first-grade classroom. In the midst of a typical discussion of the needs of plants, Alex raised his hand. "Do you think," he asked thoughtfully, "that if we put milk on the plants instead of water, they would grow better?"

His teacher replied, "I don't know. Why do you think that might happen?"

"Well, milk makes us grow stronger than water. Maybe it would work for plants, too." Alex had made a hypothesis!

"How could we find out?" the teacher asked.

"Well, we could pour milk on our bean plants and see if they grow."

"But how will we know if the milk made any difference? Maybe they would have grown just the same anyway."

(Long pause.) "We could put water on some and milk on some and see which grow more. That would be fair."

Alex had seen the necessity for the other key component of experimental research, the *control group.* To assess the effects of any treatment, it is necessary to have an equivalent group that does not receive the treatment in order to compare results. Alex did pour milk on some bean plants and water on others and carefully observed their growth.

After about 2 weeks, he came to two conclusions:

1. The plants that were given milk grew to just about the same height as those that were given water.
2. Milk, when left in the sun for 2 weeks, is not pleasant to have in the classroom.

The experiment ended when neither the researcher nor his teacher could tolerate the smell another day! Despite its untimely end, Alex's research was a true experiment. A treatment (milk) was applied to an experimental group, which was compared to a randomly selected control group. Students had the opportunity to make hypotheses, gather data, and draw conclusions as would any investigator.

CHECK YOUR UNDERSTANDING

Identify the following as examples of *descriptive* (D), *historical* (H), or *experimental* (E) research.

_____ 1. A report of repair records of new cars in a given model year

_____ 2. Taste tests comparing popular cola drinks with generic brands

_____ 3. Interviews with all living former superintendents of a particular school district

_____ 4. Using different brands of fertilizer in different areas of the garden and comparing results

_____ 5. Examining paintings from the 1860s to learn about clothing of the era

_____ 6. Counting number and type of birds that come to feeders painted different colors

Answers: D, D, H, E, H, E

Problem-Based Learning

Another approach that demands inductive thinking is problem-based learning (Glasgow, 1997). In some ways, problem-based learning stands the traditional learning sequence on its head. In traditional classrooms (or, at least, in those traditional classrooms engaged in projects), students are taught the content and skills associated with a particular body of knowledge. Then they are assigned a project that requires them to use their newly acquired knowledge in complex ways. Such projects are a tried-and-true method of teaching and are the backbone of many classrooms. Suppose, however, that you were to assign the project at the beginning of the unit, before students had the knowledge or skills necessary to succeed. Problem-based learning proceeds in much the same way.

As you might guess from the name, problem-based learning starts with a problem. It has its roots in medical schools where, instead of presenting medical students with lists of symptoms to memorize, some educators began presenting students with hypothetical patients whose complaints must be investigated. In most cases, in or out of medical school, the problem is contrived. It simulates a real-world problem but is selected or created by the teacher. The problem is chosen because it requires students to use content

*Well-Structured Situations
Allow Students to Discover
Important Ideas*

and processes the teacher wants to address. Content and skills are acquired by students and taught by the teacher as students become aware that they are necessary.

As students explore various aspects of the problem, teachers model the types of inquiry they hope students will pursue, for example: What is going on here? What do we know? What do we need to know in order to understand the situation? As students become more proficient at questioning, teachers are able to fade into the background as fellow problem solvers.

For example, one problem-based unit created for middle level students has students facing a large truck overturned in a creek, blocking traffic and spilling liquid (Center for Gifted Education, 1993). As students ask questions about the situation, it becomes clear that the liquid, hydrochloric acid, poses a danger to the ecological systems of the creek. Over the course of several weeks, students investigate the likely course of the acid and experiment with strategies for neutralizing acids and bases. Core content includes the concept of *systems*, acids and bases, and methods of scientific investigation. Older students have investigated simulated outbreaks of Legionnaires' disease, taken on the role of German gallery directors forced by the Nazi government to rid their collections of degenerate art, or acted as marriage counselors in a family relations class (Dooley, 1996; Savoie & Hughes, 1994; Stepien & Gallagher, 1993). Younger students have attempted to create ecosystems that will survive on an earthlike planet, made recommendations for locating fossils in an imaginary landscape, and assisted a farmer in identifying the best crops for particular locations. Some problem-based activities can extend for weeks, some even for an entire school year. Others may last only a few days.

The success of a problem-based unit is determined by two things: (a) the structure of the problem and (b) the skill of the teacher in guiding students. A good problem for a problem-based unit can be described as a well-structured, ill-structured problem. The problem is ill structured in that it is "fuzzy," containing multiple avenues for investigation and no clear answer. It is well structured in that the situation presented to students has been designed carefully to require the content and skills planned by the teacher. If, for example, you wanted to plan a problem-based activity that would include students experimenting with simple machines, you would have to make sure that the situation presented requires simple machines for solution.

The teacher in a problem-based activity can shift between traditional and nontraditional roles. During much of the activity, the teacher is encouraging students to be independent investigators through questioning and modeling. At other times, when students have determined that specific content is necessary, teachers may shift to a more traditional role and provide needed information. For example, in the acid-spill problem described earlier, once students realize they need more information on acids, the teacher provides several lab activities in which students can learn the required information. Problem-based learning can be powerful. It parallels quite closely what people in business and other professions do every day, and students love it.

Some approaches to elementary mathematics can be seen as paralleling the structure of problem-based learning. In these approaches, students are given mathematical problems to solve before they have been taught the mathematical procedures and algorithms necessary to solve them (see, for example, Kamii 1985, 1989). For example, primary students might be asked to figure out the number of soup labels collected by three classrooms or how many pizzas they would need in order to give each student two pieces. Students are encouraged to develop their own strategies for solving these problems—an inductive strategy for developing mathematical procedures. Kamii believes that having students interact with numbers in these meaningful ways develops mathematical concepts more effectively than teaching mathematical procedures directly.

Metacognition and Planning Inductive Experiences

The various inductive activities provide ample opportunities for higher level thinking. Regardless of whether you are having students engage in authentic research, problem-based learning, or any other type of inductive activity, the basic processes of categorization, analysis, hypothesis testing, and drawing conclusions from data remain the same. Each experience also provides opportunities for **metacognition**—thinking about one's own thinking processes. Metacognition can be a valuable asset for students' understanding of content and skills of effective learning (Costa & Liebman, 1997; Tishman, Perkins, & Jay, 1995).

Imagine that while reading a chapter in this book, you turn a page and suddenly realize that you do not understand a word of what you have read. You are thinking about your own understanding; you are engaging in metacognition. As a result of this insight, you decide to reread the page. Many students are unsuccessful at learning tasks because they lack awareness of their own thinking or because their preferred strategy is ineffective. To make matters worse, they often lack the tools to examine their own thinking and to generate a more successful strategy.

One part of metacognition is an awareness of one's own *commitment, attention,* and *attitude* toward a task. A second aspect is the exertion of metacognitive control over the learning process: knowing *what information is important, which strategies to use,* and *how to apply a selected strategy.* For example, when solving a math word problem, a student might need to select the relevant information and decide whether a chart would be helpful in analyzing the data.

FIGURE 8.3   Steps to Inductive Approaches

Lesson Objectives: 1. Thinking/Metacognition
2. Content Understanding, Application, etc.

1. *Exploratory activity:*
   Examine data or view a puzzling event.
2. *Find patterns and/or make hypotheses:*
   Attempt to make sense of the data by creating categories, looking for patterns or making hypotheses.
3. *Test hypotheses:*
   Examine additional data to test hypotheses and see if patterns or categories still make sense.
4. *Form concepts or generalizations:*
   Students draw conclusions from data.
5. *Metacognition:*
   Examine the thought processes used to find patterns and draw conclusions.
6. *Apply understanding in a new situation:*
   Guided or independent practice activities use concepts or generalizations.

Note: Stages 2 and 3 may be repeated as often as necessary.

The third aspect of metacognition occurs when the student *monitors* how well the planned strategies are working and *checks progress* made toward the goal. In the math problem, the student checks to see whether the chart does, in fact, help solve the problem or whether another strategy might be more helpful (Marzano et al., 1988).

What does all this have to do with inductive approaches? Teachers select inductive strategies because they want to develop their students' thinking and problem-solving skills. Notice that the last step of many of the lessons described is metacognition. In any inductive experience, students can share how they approached the task, what strategies they used, and how they monitored their performance during the task. Such discussions are especially useful for students who lack adequate planning and self-monitoring strategies; they benefit from their peers' modeling of metacognition (Caine & Caine, 1997).

Although each type of inductive experience discussed has unique attributes, they usually include five basic stages: (a) *exploring data,* (b) *finding patterns* or *making hypotheses,* (c) *examining additional data to test hypotheses,* (d) *using conclusions to form concepts* or *generalizations,* and (e) *metacognition.* The middle stages, finding and testing patterns or hypotheses, may be repeated as many times as necessary. The five basic steps are frequently followed by some type of application activities. The list in Figure 8.3 may be helpful in planning inductive lessons.

Role-Play

Somewhere between a structured inquiry lesson and the informal experiences that provide the basis for so much concept development, fall role-play and simulation activities.

In these activities we plan situations in which students can interact with important concepts—much as we might plan a classroom environment. However, in these activities we structure the environment so that students can simulate interaction with places, materials, and situations that would be impossible in the actual classroom. Role-play and simulations can provide opportunities both for students to build new understanding and to demonstrate understanding developed in other activities.

Role-plays can be effective tools for enhancing understanding of content and developing social understandings (Joyce, Showers, & Weil, 1996). In role-playing activities, students take on a role—that is, pretend they are a particular person or thing—to solve a problem or act out a situation. Role-playing may be done in small groups simultaneously or by one group in front of the whole class. For example, students might form pairs to act out effective listening with a partner by reflecting back what was heard. Unlike a skit or play, role-plays are not scripted. The words to be spoken are not planned in advance. Students improvise the words and actions they believe to be most appropriate to the problem situation. A role-play is usually a brief activity, completed in one class session.

Role-playing is an excellent way to assist students in developing varied points of view by considering issues from more than one perspective. Such understandings are particularly valuable in social studies and language arts, in which exploring the reasons for individuals' actions is essential. Gloria's American Revolution unit could provide multiple opportunities for students to role-play: George Washington meeting King George, a brother siding with the British and a sister siding with the colonists, or a woman trying to convince a friend to join the boycott of British cloth. They might role-play a new ending to their historical fiction novels or devise role-plays to help them remember key vocabulary.

Role-playing can also be a valuable tool in developing students' social and life skills. It may be used in a planned sequence of dilemmas devised by the teacher as well as for dealing with particular classroom issues. Students may role-play alternate solutions to conflicts, methods for dealing with peer pressure, interview or telephone skills, or appropriate responses to students with disabilities.

There are four main steps in planning a role-play:

1. Select the general problem area to be addressed. In choosing a topic, you will want to consider your students' needs, interests, and backgrounds. In addition to selecting a problem area that is relevant and interesting, it is important that you select a topic on which students have sufficient prior knowledge to take on roles knowledgeably (or provide such background before attempting the role-play). If you are role-playing in content areas, background knowledge can make the difference between an amusing skit and a powerful learning experience.

2. Define the specific situation to be portrayed. A good role-play puts the characters in a specific situation that requires action. For example, if the general topic is dealing with sharing on the playground, you might set up a situation in which one student is bouncing his or her new ball and two others would like to play kickball. The first student doesn't want to lose the ball or take any chances on its being kicked onto the roof. Content-related role-play activities must also be clearly defined. If the topic is westward expansion, a situation might be created in which a parent discusses the move west with

a son or daughter who doesn't want to leave home, friends, and toys behind. Choose the specific characters to be portrayed, the situation, and the action that must be taken. For example, the son or daughter moving west must make a decision about which one possession he or she will bring. It would probably be helpful to provide information to the students about the available possessions.

3. Plan a role for the audience. Students not playing particular roles must have an active part in the role-play experience. For example, they may be listening for particularly effective arguments, deciding which of several solutions they think is best, or deciding what they might do in a particular character's place.

4. Decide how you will introduce the role-play. Some role-play situations might be introduced by a story, others by a discussion of the issue or by small-group sharing.

When actually conducting the role-play experience, follow these steps:

1. Provide the introductory activities (readiness, objective, purpose, directions).
2. Explain clearly and explicitly the situation to be enacted.
3. Select students for each role and assign the observation task to the audience.
4. Provide students with necessary time to prepare for their roles and clarify responsibilities as needed.
5. Give the observers of the role-play a task to perform during the role-play.
6. Conduct the role-play one or more times. If you repeat a scenario, you can give more students the opportunity to participate, as well as obtain varied points of view. You may also have students perform the role-play in small groups all at one time, or in paired groups with one performing for the other.
7. Debrief the experience in a class discussion. For some role-plays you may wish to discuss each version as it occurs; for others you may prefer to withhold discussion until after several versions have been portrayed. In either case, be sure to allow ample time for students to respond to the role-play experiences. Helping students understand why individuals made particular choices, what those individuals were thinking and feeling, and what alternative choices might have been made is at the heart of what can be gained from role-playing activities.

REFLECTING ON THE IDEAS

Suzanne has a box of costume materials in the corner of her kindergarten classroom. Students frequently use the costumes during free time to enhance their dramatic play. One day they may use a white jacket to portray a doctor caring for a doll. Another day the same jacket might be used to costume a cafeteria worker. Both role-play and dramatic play are valuable educational experiences. How are they similar and different? Consider both the activities themselves and the purposes the activities serve.

Simulations: Human and Electronic

In role-play activities, the goal is to allow students to understand people, perspectives, and events by taking on the roles of particular individuals in specific situations. The goal of simulations is similar, but more complex. Whereas role-play activities generally encompass short, tightly defined problem-solving situations, **simulations** are designed to allow all students to experience a simplified version of reality over a more extended period of time. Role-play usually involves a small number of students at a time and is generally completed within a class period. Simulations are likely to involve many students over a period of days, weeks, or even months. For example, a role-play activity regarding local government might involve a student portraying a citizen discussing an issue of concern with a member of the town council. If several pairs of students portrayed the same situation, the activity might take approximately 45 minutes. Younger children's role-plays would be much shorter. In contrast, a simulation on local government would probably involve the entire class. Each student might have a role as a citizen or member of the government. Citizens might organize into special interest groups to lobby officials. Public hearings might be held and testimony given by interested parties. Bills might be introduced, go through committees, and be addressed by the council. Such activities might easily last several weeks.

In good simulations there are a variety of roles that demand differing strengths and interests. Students address complex situations from points of view that vary with the needs and interests of their role. The results of a simulation must not be predetermined. Events should take place as a natural consequence of student actions. For example, one common form of simulation is a courtroom reenactment. These may range from realistic contemporary situations to trials of historical or literary figures (for example, a trial charging Goldilocks with breaking and entering). The guilt or innocence of the character should be assessed by the jury based on evidence presented. If one attorney does a better job arguing and preparing than the other, he or she is likely to win the case. Teachers may provide information on procedures or other necessary input, but they should not direct students' actions. Students should act as they believe their role demands. To do this will quite often require time for students to research their roles so they can be as accurate as possible in their portrayal of the character and situation.

Naturally, the depth and complexity of simulation that is appropriate for a group of students will vary with the age of the students and their familiarity with simulations and role-play. Primary students may set up a simulated postal system that functions for several weeks or a Mexican market that operates only for a day. Intermediate students may set up businesses, a banking system, or a simulated stock market. Some classes (or even whole schools) have created minisocieties, complete with currency, daily expenses, and employment for all students. In such minisocieties, students may spend a portion of each day earning the classroom currency necessary to rent their desks, pay their portion of the lighting bill, and cover other expenses. Some may earn their living as part of the government, others by operating banks, businesses, or publishing companies. Minisocieties may operate for a few weeks or for most of the school year. It is also possible to simulate historical events. Students might take on roles of individuals organizing a party traveling westward or spend a day (or longer) simulating life in medieval times.

Some interesting and challenging simulations are available commercially. For example, a commercial archaeology simulation was used successfully with students as young as sixth grade (Lipetsky, 1982). Teams of students created imaginary societies and appropriate artifacts. The artifacts were exchanged (or actually buried) and other students tried to learn as much as possible about the civilizations from the remaining artifacts. The resulting difficulties brought new appreciation for both the field of archaeology and the tentative nature of research. Bear in mind that not all materials labeled *simulation* actually involve students in important aspects of real life. Materials purporting to be simulations that involve students with dragons or talking space creatures probably have other goals.

A variety of excellent simulations are available on computers. Although computer simulations are less likely to involve an entire class simultaneously, they allow students to experience the results of decisions that would be impossible or dangerous in real life. Computer simulations can allow students to impact their environment, travel to dangerous places, and conduct elaborate experiments that could not be managed in a school. Some computer simulations allow students to interact with participants in other states or countries.

The guidelines for assessing computer simulations are similar to those for other simulation materials. The simulation should present a version of reality that is simplified for students' use, but as complex and authentic as is appropriate for the grade level. Results should be determined by students' participation and should be a natural consequence of students' actions and real-world forces, not primarily of luck or chance. For an in-depth discussion of computer-generated simulations, see Dowling (1997).

If you would like to create a simulation activity for your class, there are four key questions that may prove helpful (Jones, 1985; see also Adkins, 1996 for steps in designing environmental simulations). The questions may be considered in any order you wish, but they all need to be answered before the simulation can begin.

1. *What is the problem?* In this question you will consider the general topic, area, or problem to be addressed. Imagine, for example, that you have decided to develop a simulation around the idea of waste disposal, particularly landfill.

2. *Who are the participants?* Participants in a landfill simulation might include homeowners and businesses that use the landfill, city officials, scientists studying groundwater, the owner of a waste disposal company that transports material to the landfill, and so on.

3. *What do they have to do?* In this question you determine the goal of the simulation. It is usually helpful to set up a situation in which some sort of problem needs to be addressed in a particular format. In the landfill simulation, you might set up a situation in which the local landfill will be too full within the next 18 months. The town council must hold a hearing to get community input, then prepare a long-range plan for waste disposal.

4. *What do they have to do it with?* This concerns the physical materials that will be available for participants. You may consider creating "role cards" for some roles—for example, "You are B.G. Hauler, owner of Waste, Inc. You have a contract with the city to haul waste to the current landfill. It represents 85% of your company's business." You may also consider providing documents such as a regional map showing alternative landfill sites or procedures for conducting hearings. Materials for a simulation may be simple or elaborate, depending on your needs, desires, and creativity. You may want to start with a fairly simple simulation and add complexity (and materials) over several years.

■ *Practice Activity: Designing a Role-Play*

Select a belief, attitude, or value you want to enhance in your students. With a partner, design a role-play activity that may help students grow toward that value.

■ ■ ■

■ *Practice Activity: Designing a Simulation*

Imagine that you want to plan a simulation that would help students understand the functioning of your state government or some other topic suitable to your subject area. Work with a small group to decide:

1. Who might be participants in such a simulation?
2. What situation could form the framework for the simulation? What would the participants try to do?
3. What materials would you need to prepare or gather for the simulation to function effectively?
4. How would you debrief (conduct a discussion) so students gain meaning from the activity?

■ ■ ■

SUMMARY

In inductive approaches, the teacher's role shifts from that taken in direct instruction. In both cases the teachers are responsible for creating experiences that allow students to learn, but they do it in different ways. In direct teaching the teacher is responsible for the explicit presentation of content, through lecture, reading, storytelling, or the use of media. In inductive approaches the teacher does not present key ideas directly, but provides the data from which students can draw conclusions. Selecting data to be presented and structuring the tasks so that students are likely to discover important ideas are key to the success of inductive approaches.

Whenever you want students to get practice in inductive thinking (categorizing, hypothesizing, problem solving, and so on), you would select an inductive approach. When you feel your students need structured experiences with particular concepts in order to construct meaning (when telling is not enough), an inductive approach may be appropriate. If you want to encourage metacognition and higher level thinking, inductive approaches are a good choice. Inductive lessons may take more time than direct lessons, but they have the advantage of meeting at least two objectives at the same time: they teach the content *and* a higher level thinking strategy useful in everyday life. The following practice activities give you many options for planning inductive lessons.

■ *Practice Activity: Concept Formation*

Imagine that you want to teach a concept formation lesson on one of the following concepts: *proper nouns, coniferous trees,* or *nonverbal communication.* Plan a question you might ask that would prompt students to develop a set of examples that could be categorized to form the desired concept.

■ ■ ■

■ *Practice Activity: Concept Exemplars*

Generate a concept appropriate for a grade level and subject you might teach. You may be able to identify an appropriate concept in a unit you are planning. Think of positive and negative exemplars. The exemplars may be words, symbols, phrases, or paragraphs. Describe when you might use this type of approach. How might it be mixed and matched with parts of other types of lessons?

■ ■ ■

■ Practice Activity: Designing a Concept Attainment Lesson

Develop a concept attainment lesson for the concept of *figurative language* or another concept taken from one of your college courses. Try to choose a concept that is not completely familiar to most adults. Teach the lesson to several friends or classmates. Pay particular attention to how the order of your exemplars affects their experience. Reflect on how their learning might have been different if you had taught the same content as a direct lesson.

■ ■ ■

■ Practice Activity: Designing an Inquiry Lesson

Think of a generalization, principle, theory, or rule that is important in a unit you might teach. Consider whether the generalization can best be demonstrated through a puzzling event or a set of data. Plan an inquiry lesson to teach the generalization, and teach it to a small group.

■ ■ ■

■ Practice Activity: Authentic Research

Imagine that you are teaching a third-grade class. Like most third graders, your students are very interested in toys. You have decided to take advantage of this high level of interest to teach research skills. List as many projects as you can in which your students might conduct authentic research that relates in some way to toys. Try to include descriptive, historical, and experimental research.

■ ■ ■

■ Practice Activity: Problem-Based Learning Project

Design a problem-based project for your unit. Carry out the investigation yourself before you have students do it. Share what you designed with classmates. How did you feel doing the research? How might these feelings affect students carrying out similar projects?

■ ■ ■

■ Practice Activity: Microteaching and Observation

Observe a classmate teaching an inductive lesson. Use the microteaching guide that follows to analyze the elements of the lesson.

Microteaching Guide

1. Use exploratory activity
2. Find patterns and/or make hypotheses
3. Test hypotheses
4. Form concepts or generalizations
5. Demonstrate metacognition
6. Apply understanding in a new situation

Note: Stages 2 and 3 may be repeated as often as necessary.
Which of the following learning principles were evident in this lesson?

- Cultural context
- Conceptual focus
- Prior knowledge
- Higher level thinking
- Active processing
- Variety

■ ■ ■

 ## UNIT PREPARATION

Review your unit outline and plan inductive lessons for the appropriate objectives. Submit at least one lesson for feedback to make sure you are using the lesson structure correctly. You may want to use the electronic bluebook for this purpose. Consider these lessons to be in draft form until you read the next two chapters. They are likely to give you ideas for revising your lessons to make them more effective for the range of children in your class.

 ## PORTFOLIO ACTIVITY

Prepare several examples of inductive lessons. Be sure to include a variety of lesson types and to review your lessons with the six principles in mind. Be prepared to explain why each lesson is particularly suited to the content you are teaching.

You may wish to create a diagram of the classroom you would like to prepare. Consider the concepts that could be developed through your classroom plan and label the diagram accordingly.

 ## SEARCH THE WEB

Many of the Companion Website links you visited in Chapter 7 also contain inductive lessons, or sources that could be used to structure inductive lessons. Think, for example, how some of the historical materials under "Discipline-Specific Resources" could be used to create lessons incorporating historical research. You will also find many materials under "Libraries, Museums, and Archives" that can be used to create inductive lessons.

REFERENCES

Adkins, C. (1996, April). Ten steps to better simulations. *Science Scope, 19,* 28–29.

Bruner, J., Goodnow, J., & Austin, G. (1977). *A study of thinking.* New York: Wiley.

Caine, R. N., & Caine, G. C. (1997). *Education on the edge of possibility.* Alexandria, VA: Association for Supervision and Curriculum Development.

Center for Gifted Education. (1993). *Acid, acid everywhere: A unit designed for grades 4–6.* Williamsburg, VA: College of William and Mary, School of Education.

Costa, A., & Liebman, R. (1997). *Supporting the spirit of learning: When process is content.* Thousand Oaks, CA: Corwin Press.

Dooley, C. (1996). Problem-centered learning experiences: Exploring past, present, and future perspectives. *Roeper Review, 19,* 192–195.

Dowling, C. (1997). Simulations: New worlds for learning? *Journal of Educational Multimedia and Hypermedia, 6* (3-4), 321–337.

Glasgow, N. A. (1997). *New curriculum for new times: A guide to student centered problem-based learning.* Thousand Oaks, CA: Corwin Press.

Hakim, J. (1999). *A history of us: From colonies to country. Book 3* (2nd ed.). New York: Oxford University Press.

Huffman, D. (1997, August). Effect of explicit problem solving instruction on high school students' problem-solving performance and conceptual understanding of physics. *Journal of Research in Science Teaching, 34*(6), 551–570.

Jones, K. (1985). *Designing your own simulations.* New York: Methuen.

Joyce, B., Showers, B., & Weil, M. (1996). *Models of teaching.* Boston: Allyn & Bacon.

Kamii, C. (1985). *Young children reinvent arithmetic.* New York: Teachers College Press.

Kamii, C. (1989). *Young children continue to reinvent arithmetic.* New York: Teachers College Press.

Lipetsky, J. (1982). *Dig 2.* Lakeside, CA: Interact Publications.

Marzano, R. J., Brandt, R. S., Hughes, C. S., Jones, B. F., Presseisen, B. Z., Rankin, S. C., & Suhor, C. (1988). *Dimensions of thinking.* Alexandria, VA: Association for Supervision and Curriculum Development.

Marzano, R. J., Pickering, D. J., & Pollack, J. E. (2001). *Classroom instruction that works: Research-based strategies for increasing student achievement.* Alexandria, VA: Association for Supervision and Curriculum Development.

Random House Webster's Dictionary. (1993). New York: Random House.

Savoie, J. M., & Hughes, A. S. (1994). Problem-based learning as classroom solution. *Educational Leadership, 52* (3), 54–57.

Simmons, A. (1958). *The first American cookbook: A facsimile of "American Cookery," 1776.* New York: Dover Publications.

Starko, A. J. (2000). *Creativity in the classroom: Schools of curious delight.* (2nd ed.). Mahwah, NJ: Lawrence Erlbaum.

Starko, A. J., & Schack, G. D. (1992). *Looking for data in all the right places.* Mansfield Center, CT: Creative Learning Press.

Stepien, W., & Gallagher, S. (1993). Problem-based learning: As authentic as it gets. *Educational Leadership, 50* (7), 25–28.

Suchman, J. R. (1962). *The elementary school training program in scientific inquiry.* Report to the U.S. Office of Education. Urbana: University of Illinois.

Taba, H. (1967). *Teachers' handbook for elementary school social studies.* Reading, MA: Addison-Wesley.

Tishman, S., Perkins, D., & Jay, E. (1995). *The thinking classroom.* Needham, MA: Allyn & Bacon.

Wiggins, G., & McTighe, J. (1998). *Understanding by design.* Alexandria, VA: Association for Supervision and Curriculum Development.

CHAPTER 9

Facilitating Structures and Strategies

CHAPTER OVERVIEW

Phil Schlechty, a prominent school reformer, has coined the term **knowledge work** to describe student activity in the classroom. "Knowledge work is nothing more or less than using ideas, concepts, problem-solving skills, analytic skills, and applying facts to achieve some end....What teachers are trying to do is engage students in working on knowledge, rather than having students passively absorb knowledge" (Sparks, 1998, p. 39).

If students' learning and retention require that they interact with, rehearse, and critically examine information, how will you provide the opportunity for this to happen? Think of some strategies or learning structures that will engage students in meaningful ways with the ideas you want them to learn.

You probably thought about some of the most interesting things you did in elementary school; or perhaps you recalled some creative teaching strategies used by teachers you have observed. One of us recalled a covered wagon learning center that resulted in a lifelong curiosity about the settlers of the western United States. Another remembered a school weather station that "broadcast" reports over the intercom each morning. It is the teacher's job to give the students opportunities to work with content in ways that will help them learn. The purpose of this chapter is to introduce several structures and strategies that actively engage students in "knowledge work." These include:

Questioning and discussion
Group learning activities
Academic service-learning
Technology
Centers, contracts, and skills of independent learning

The final section of the chapter discusses how to plan for the use of classroom time.

 ## CHAPTER OBJECTIVES

After you have completed this chapter, you will have the ability to

1. describe effective strategies for questioning and discussion and apply them in lessons;
2. design various types of group learning activities and critique their strengths and weaknesses;
3. design academic service-learning activities related to a unit of study;
4. create activities that use technology to enhance the depth and quality of learning;
5. plan, implement, and assess the effects of various types of centers and contracts;
6. describe key activities to prepare students for independent learning; and
7. make decisions about the use of instructional time.

 ## SECTION 1. QUESTIONING AND DISCUSSION

Section Objective

After you have completed this section, you will be able to describe effective strategies for questioning and discussion and apply them in lessons.

◼ *Opening Activity*

If students' learning and retention require that they interact with, rehearse, and critically examine information, how will you provide the opportunity? List some ways you can think of to get students to participate in a classroom discussion.

_____

_____

_____

_____

_____

◼ ◼ ◼

This section deals with two important teaching techniques: **questioning** and **discussion**. Questioning and discussion can take place in many types of educational experiences. For example, direct lessons may use questions to check for understanding. Inductive lessons use questions to help students form categories or to challenge them to make a hypothesis. Many units are organized around key questions. Discussions can be used to practice, develop, and challenge ideas introduced in any type of lesson, or as an aid in an inductive strategy, guiding students to find generalizations among their thoughts and experiences. Excellent questioning and discussion skills are particularly essential in inductive lessons (Caine & Caine, 1997).

Questioning

You will frequently want to engage your students through effective questioning techniques. Questioning is one of the most powerful tools of any teacher. It can serve many purposes: focusing student attention, helping students to interact with content, encouraging students to express values or opinions, and facilitating classroom management. In summarizing some of the key research regarding questioning and cuing, Marzano, Pickering, and Pollack (2001) made four generalizations.

- Cues and questions should focus on what is important as opposed to what is unusual. Teachers tend to structure questions around what they believe students will find interesting or unusual rather than around key ideas. The irony is, the more students understand about a topic, the more interested they tend to be—so questions that increase understanding will increase interest, but not necessarily vice versa.
- Higher level questions produce deeper learning than lower level questions. Unfortunately, most questions teachers ask tend to be lower level questions.
- Waiting briefly before accepting responses from students has the effect of increasing the depth of student responses. You will read more about this phenomenon in the section about wait time.
- Questions are effective learning tools even when asked before a learning experience. In this case questions serve to focus student attention rather than check their understanding.

FIGURE 9.1   Teacher and Student
Questioning and Discussions

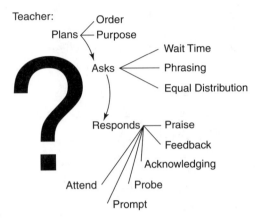

This section provides more detail on strategies that will help you follow these recommendations. It considers techniques for phrasing questions effectively and strategies to promote interaction with all your students: planning questions, pacing and phrasing questions, distributing questions, and responding to student answers. Figure 9.1 illustrates these aspects of questioning.

Planning Teacher Questions

A carefully planned sequence of questions can lend clarity and structure to a lesson, leading students from one main idea to the next. Although it is important to maintain flexibility to respond to students' ideas, needs, interests, and opinions, it is equally important to begin questioning with a clear plan. Questions that are prepared in advance are more likely to focus on lesson objectives and provide for both higher level and lower level thinking than questions produced on the spot.

One of the key considerations in planning questions is *why* you are asking the question(s) in the first place. The type of question you would use to check students' comprehension of previously presented material is likely to be different from questions designed to have students evaluate content or defend opinions. Some of the *purposes* for questions are:

- Checking students' understanding (formative assessment)
- Tying information to students' prior knowledge or experiences
- Having students process information by looking for inferences, implications, and so forth
- Allowing students to practice supporting ideas and opinions with evidence
- Leading students to discover a new concept, principle, or generalization
- Learning about students' interests, ideas, or concerns
- Focusing students' attention on important ideas
- Modeling the importance of questioning

It is also important to consider the *order* in which you will ask questions. There is no one correct way to sequence questions. Sometimes you may wish to begin with an open-ended (divergent) focusing question and narrow the topic down through questions that involve descriptions and comparisons for answers. At other times you may prefer to proceed from lower level to higher level questioning. You should select the sequence of questions that corresponds best to your lesson objectives.

Plan ahead of time the manner in which you will ask the questions so you don't fall into the trap of having the same few students answering every question. Will you use wait time by asking the whole group the question, telling all students to think of an answer, and randomly selecting students to respond? Will you raise a question, then ask students to tell the answer to a partner? Will you pose a question to be discussed in small groups before calling for a response? If you note these ideas in your plans, you will be more likely to provide variety in your questioning techniques. Table 7.1 provided a wealth of questioning strategies that promote maximum student participation.

Pacing and Phrasing Questions

How will you pace and phrase your questions? One of the most important concepts in pacing questions is **wait time**, which refers to the period between the time a teacher asks a question and the time he or she asks another question, questions another student, or answers the question (Atwood & Wilen, 1991). Rowe (1974) discovered that the average wait time for each teacher was less than 1 second. No wonder students sometimes have trouble finding time to think! In studies in which wait time was increased to 3 seconds or longer, numerous changes were observed (Tobin, 1980; Tobin & Campie, 1982):

Length of responses increased.
Number of voluntary responses increased.
Complexity of responses increased.
Student questions increased.
Student confidence increased.
Student failure to respond decreased.

There is no one perfect amount of wait time. In quickly paced recall questions, short amounts of wait time are appropriate. In divergent questioning, or questions requiring higher level thinking or evaluation, longer wait time allows students sufficient time to formulate answers, consider more than one perspective, or reflect on other students' responses. In general, however, you will probably do best pacing your questions more slowly than feels natural at first, allowing "think time" before asking for responses.

At the beginning, you will probably need to carefully structure your wait time. If both you and your students are accustomed to a rapid-fire pace of questioning or calling only on volunteers, it will take practice to change those habits. Some teachers use a formal think time in which a hand signal communicates that no responses will be accepted until everyone has a chance to think. Other teachers simply discuss the idea of wait time with their students and do not call on anyone until an appropriate time has passed. To avoid the distractions of excessive hand waving, some teachers ask students to cross their arms when they are ready to answer. The key is to communicate to students that you will wait until they *all* have an opportunity to think, and that you expect *every* student to think carefully and be prepared to respond.

The *phrasing* of your questions can have an impact on your students' thinking processes. In general it is best not to start a question with a student's name, such as, "Gina, why did Lafayette agree to help the colonists?" All the other students know immediately that they are not being questioned and can ignore both the question and the answer. In this case, more students would have thought about Lafayette's motivation if the question had been phrased, "Everyone think about why Lafayette agreed to help the colonists. (Wait time) Gina? (Wait time)." It is also advisable to avoid the "Who can tell me" habit of asking questions. Such phrasing invites students to call out the answer, thus depriving the others of valuable mental rehearsal of the material.

Distributing Questions Equitably

Even when teachers call for responses after a question, students do not always have an equal chance for classroom interaction. Research has noted numerous inequalities in the opportunities students have to respond to the question. Many teachers call on high-achieving students much more frequently than low-achieving students, males more than females, White students more than students of color, students at the front more than students at the back, or even students on one side of the classroom more than the other.

Any time an unequal pattern of questioning develops, some students have greater opportunity to meaningfully process the material and transfer the information to long-term memory than others. It also sends nonverbal messages to students about which youngsters in the classroom are considered more capable or important. Research in classrooms that have implemented more equitable questioning patterns indicates that they lead to greater interaction by all students, more willingness to respond, and increased questioning by students (Good & Brophy, 1997).

How can you distribute questions and teacher attention equitably to your students? Some teachers like to use props to ensure that all students have an equal chance of being asked a question. Popsicle sticks or index cards with student names on them can be pulled at random. Other teachers keep track of who they call on by making a mark on their seating chart each time they call on or speak to a student. Every day or two they check to see who is getting called on and who needs to be called on more. In this way they can monitor their own distribution of attention and questions. Finally, you can ask a friend or peer to observe a lesson you teach and note the students with whom you interact. Such observations can provide valuable information for improving questioning patterns.

Responding to Student Answers

Once a student has responded to a question, you will need to decide whether to praise, acknowledge, redirect, probe, prompt, correct, or ask a new question. One major factor in making this decision is saving the dignity of the student and knowing how a student will react to different types of public responses by the teacher.

Although *praise* can be important in creating a positive classroom atmosphere and building self-esteem, it must be used carefully (Brophy, 1998). Praise that is vague, routine, or repetitive quickly becomes meaningless. A response of "good" after every student answer is almost like no response at all. Praise that is global ("You are always such a good student") does not help students identify the characteristics of their work that led to their success. It is better to give specific feedback about the performance, not the student ("You made excellent use of figurative language in your description of the forest").

Global, vague praise also has the potential to create or increase emotional problems. Individuals who are led to believe that they are always expected to be good students may become fearful of challenging tasks or open-ended situations. Teachers must also be alert for students who are embarrassed by being praised publicly. For many students, a private comment is more welcome than public praise given during class (Good & Brophy, 1997).

Finally, praise can be seen as a terminal response, frequently ending discussion or thought. If you ask a higher level or divergent question and give elaborate praise to the first answer, other students are less likely to respond, assuming the "right" answer has already been given. Some research has indicated that giving rewards too early may have a detrimental effect on problem solving or higher level thinking (Costa & Liebman, 1997). Other research suggests that the use of **evaluative praise** ("Good work") can be damaging to motivation and creativity in higher level tasks. Students may be left with the impression that something is good or bad simply because the teacher says so (Good & Brophy, 1997).

Informational feedback is less problematic because it tells students which characteristics of their efforts were particularly effective—for example, "You really had a lot of evidence to back up your ideas." Each teacher needs to be sensitive to the effects of praise in the classroom. In many cases, praise is most appropriate for unmotivated or reluctant learners, lower grade students, lower level cognitive tasks, or practice of previously learned material. In other cases, silence or *acknowledgment* of responses ("I understand" or "That's one possibility") may be more appropriate and lead to continued student efforts. You may also wish to accept the response nonverbally (perhaps through a nod) or *redirect* the question to another student: "What do you think, Ben?"

When student responses are unclear or incomplete, it is important to **probe** for further clarification or information. A general probe such as "Please explain further" or "Tell me more about your thinking on that" may be appropriate. In other cases it is best to be more specific. If, for example, a teacher asks the class, "How did Washington's troops feel at Valley Forge?" and a student responds, "Happy," the teacher should probe, "Why were they happy?" If the student replies, "Well, they were cold and hungry, but they knew they were fighting for an important cause and I think that would have made them happy," the teacher would plan a much different response than if the student had said, "They were camping out, and camping is fun."

When probing, be aware of your responses to ethnic, achievement, and gender groups in the classroom. Probing must be equitable; teachers who seek responses from as many students as possible send the message that all students are considered capable and are expected to participate.

If a student answer is inaccurate or incomplete (or if the student gives no answer), you may wish to **prompt**, or cue the student toward a more successful response. It is important to help students understand which parts of an answer were correct and which were incorrect, while providing information that may lead to a completely correct response. The process of prompting students requires care and sensitivity, so that students have every opportunity for success without embarrassment. For example, if Mr. Holmes asks, "What are the characteristics of mammals?" and Cheryl replies, "They live in the water," Mr. Holmes might correct her and then provide a prompt to lead Cheryl to a correct response. A prompt often involves asking another question. "No. Although some mammals live in the water, not all mammals live in the water. Remember yesterday when we talked about the cow being a mammal? What were some of the characteristics of the cow we said were shared by all mammals?" This type of prompting may lead Cheryl to a more complete response.

Good teachers should not only question students but listen effectively to what students say. Teachers can improve their listening through attending behavior and through active and reflective listening. **Attending behavior** refers to a variety of verbal and nonverbal responses that signal to students, "I am listening to you. I believe that the things you have to say are valuable." Nonverbal signals include eye contact, an empathetic facial expression (for example, nodding or smiling), relaxed body posture (signaling "I have time to listen to you"), and comfortable physical proximity (distance). Verbal signals can include silence, which is a chance for the teacher to reflect and the speaker to continue; brief verbal acknowledgments, such as "I see" or "Yes"; or brief summaries of the speaker's statements.

Attending behaviors are often viewed as common courtesy. Unfortunately, without conscious attention, they may be lost in the flurry of classroom activity, in which the critical moment of silence or careful eye contact may seem difficult to maintain. However, with care and practice, you will be able to signal to your students that, no matter how busy you are, you value the things they are saying.

You can also signal students that you are paying attention to them by *active* and *reflective listening*. **Active listening** entails identifying both the intellectual and emotional attitude of the speaker. If Jared says, "This is a dumb book," he is conveying an emotional as well as an intellectual message. You should carefully observe nonverbal cues and consider all you know about Jared to discern what the message might be. Jared might be saying, "I am upset because I don't understand this book" or "I am offended by the stereotypes presented here" or "I read this three years ago and I am bored."

After actively listening to a student, you may reflect, or restate, the message you thought you received. **Reflective listening** may involve paraphrasing the statements ("You don't like the book") or expressing both the statement and the inferred emotion ("You seem upset about reading this book"). Reflective listening is a powerful tool that must be used with care. It is particularly valuable when emotions are high and misunderstandings easy, or in situations in which clear understanding is critical. Try to be sensitive to the amount of reflecting that is sufficient to elicit clarity without becoming monotonous or parrotlike.

Encouraging Students' Questions

The teacher should not be the only person asking questions in the classroom. Students' questions are important in at least two ways. First, it is important that students feel free to ask questions when they do not understand a lesson or assignment. If students sense that such clarifying questions are unacceptable, they are likely to languish in confusion or move forward practicing content incorrectly. Neither experience is likely to lead to effective learning.

Second, students should feel free to ask questions that go beyond the content being taught. The essence of this type of question is not, "I do not understand," but "I wonder." Wondering is an important key to learning and creativity. Productive people wonder all the time—about the things they see, the things they hear, the things that trouble them, and the things that bring them joy. Unfortunately, students seldom experience this type of questioning in school. A typical school question generally has one correct answer, and it can be found in the back of the book. The real world is not like that. Teaching students to question and to wonder is to provide them with a skill for lifelong learning.

There are at least five strategies you may consider to encourage student questions:

1. Teach students the difference between checking for understanding and genuine questions. Help them understand that you will ask them many questions to which you already know the answers. You do this because you need to check to see if they are learning important content. Sometimes they, too, may want to ask clarifying questions to make sure they understand something you are teaching. Make sure students know you will be pleased to respond to such questions. Help students understand the difference between these activities and your real questions—questions that make you curious because you don't have an answer.

2. Model questioning behaviors. Share your puzzlement and curiosity with your students. Sometimes this may be as simple as a casual comment, "Isn't it interesting how the leaves turn such different colors? I wonder why some turn red, some turn yellow, and some just seem to get brown?"

3. Teach students to ask questions. You may want to do a lesson on what constitutes a question, why people ask questions, and why questions are important. Consider lessons focusing on questions one could ask about a given event, experiment, story, or idea. Rosenshine, Meister, and Chapman (1996) found that teaching students the cognitive strategy of generating questions resulted in significant gains in reading comprehension.

4. Respond to student questions with respect. One second-grade student came stomping home from school, disgusted with her teacher's use of the KWL reading strategy. (KWL is a technique in which students are asked what they *know* about a topic, what they *want* to know, and, later, what they have *learned*.) Her complaint was, "I don't know why they bother with the *W* anyway. She asks us what we want to learn and then we just do what the teacher wants to do anyway!" Although it is impossible to investigate every question posed by an enthusiastic group of students, they should have confidence that at least some of their questions will be addressed and others will be met with enthusiasm and suggestions for follow-through. One teacher even created a bulletin board on which to hang interesting questions. Not all the questions were investigated, but they all were acknowledged as valuable.

5. Teach students the investigative skill of the disciplines. That is, teach them how to ask good questions within various subjects. When studying history, teachers should help students understand what kinds of questions historians ask and how they investigate them. In science, teachers should teach students how scientists develop questions and design experiences to test them. (This is a far cry from the follow-the-cookbook procedures

of many science activities.) Language arts teachers can discuss how authors decide what to write and the kinds of issues they try to address. In each case, students are exposed to the mental processes of wondering within the context of a particular discipline.

CHECK YOUR UNDERSTANDING

How might you use reflective listening to respond to the following students' comments?

Jane (looking at the floor): I hate going to lunch.
You: _____

Miguel (smiling broadly): I'm going to be on the citywide quiz bowl team!
You: _____

Conducting Discussions

What is the difference between asking questions and having a discussion? Think about the differences before you read on. Some of the possible points you may have thought of are (a) the relative extent of participation by students and by the teacher, (b) the focus of communication, and (c) the classroom atmosphere. In questioning, the teacher is almost always the focus of attention. Communication travels from teacher to student, back to teacher, and is redirected to another student, forming a pattern like a many-legged spider, with the teacher at the center.

In a discussion, the patterns of communication are much more diverse. The initial stimulus may come from the teacher. Additional comments may travel from student to student, with students adding questions or comments as desired. Figure 9.2 illustrates the difference between questioning and discussion. Whereas questioning is sometimes directed at quizzing students, discussion is an open-ended exchange of ideas designed to share information and possibly to reach consensus, rather than to seek the so-called right answer (Gall & Gall, 1990).

A good classroom discussion is a valuable learning experience, full of opportunities for higher level thinking and ties to student interests and experiences. Like many worthwhile goals, however, it is a challenge that requires planning, patience, and practice. Many students spend years in school without participating in a real discussion. Their inexperience can sometimes turn discussions into questioning sessions in which all at-

FIGURE 9.2   Interaction Patterns in Questioning and Discussion

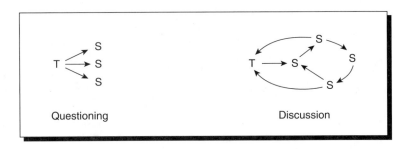

tention is focused on the teacher, and students attempt to discern exactly what the teacher wants. Because they find it difficult to imagine that the teacher wants them to express opinions (to say nothing of asking questions of their own), they expend enormous energy trying to find the right answer.

Key to a successful class discussion is an open-ended topic. There is little point in discussing the year the American Revolution started, or the sequence of events in *Johnny Tremain*. Facts, sequences, or issues on which there is already consensus do not make good discussion topics. Concepts that are fuzzy, issues generating a genuine difference of opinion, or opportunities to tie personal experiences to content provide more chance for successful expression.

If you want students to raise questions during class discussions, you may wish to structure activities to practice such behaviors. Students can be asked to write questions about stories they've read, current issues, historical dilemmas, or almost any other content. Some teachers even explain the levels of Bloom's taxonomy (see Chapter 4) to their students, to enable them to write higher level questions for class discussions. Try to reinforce students' questioning behaviors, letting them know you are glad that they are seeking information, clarification, or opinions.

In many classes it is useful to plan numerous experiences with paired or small-group minidiscussions before attempting to share ideas with an entire class. Students may be asked to describe to a partner their favorite character in a story or to discuss in a group of five the items they would bring with them in a covered wagon. A pair of students might debate the pros and cons of proposed legislation, with a third student noting major arguments. Such activities accustom students to talking to one another without depending on the teacher to direct the conversation. They also provide needed variety, even in classes already adept at whole-group discussion.

During a discussion, the teacher (or other discussion leader) may serve several roles:

1. Provide the initial stimulus for discussion.
2. Provide additional information, clarification, or correction of misinformation as needed.
3. Paraphrase, summarize, or compare student positions to add clarity.
4. Maintain the focus of the discussion. This role demands good judgment and a gentle hand. Although class discussions must not stray far from the topic at hand, occasional diversions can provide significant information about students' needs, wants, and values. In general, discussion leaders should try to keep discussion on the topic of concern.
5. Respond to student comments with acceptance, rather than praise or criticism. Remember that either praise or criticism can be viewed as a terminal response, cutting off further discussion. If one student's response is effusively praised, other students are apt to think that it was the right answer and may hesitate to comment further. Of course, if students' comments are met with personal criticism or harassment, neither they nor others are likely to continue. Students will benefit from instruction on expressing disagreement without fear of being insulted.
6. Draw the discussion to a close through summarizing and/or seeking compromise or consensus.

As you conduct classroom discussions, be aware of the patterns of student interactions. You may want to ask an observer to keep track of student contributions during one class day. You can encourage contributions from all students by using small groups and by teaching skills of discussion and cooperation.

It is not enough to write in your lesson plan, "Conduct class discussion." You will have to do much more detailed planning than that. The reflective teacher makes many key decisions to engage students successfully in question-and-answer and discussion activities. The selection of questions, how they are phrased, the teacher's reactions to student answers, and equity in response opportunities are just a few of the considerations when planning lessons. Discussions must be carefully planned to evoke the engagement, curiosity, and energy of students. The best teachers take care to plan their questions and discussion prompts before the lesson begins. They also think deeply about how to respond to students in ways that maintain students' dignity and interest.

■ *Practice Activity. Planning Teacher Questions*

Reread the section of text dealing with questioning and discussion. Develop two questions that could be used to check students' understanding of the section. Next, plan two questions that would be appropriate for a discussion of some controversial issue raised in the section. Take turns asking your questions in a small group. Don't forget to use wait time.

■ ■ ■

SECTION 2. GROUP LEARNING ACTIVITIES

One of the most natural things children do is socialize. Years ago "socializing" was considered a problem in schools—often cause for disciplinary action. Now we know that a silent classroom is not necessarily a good one. There are many reasons to believe that social interaction is an important part of school learning. Remember from Chapter 2 that social learning theory suggests that students need to interact with adults and with peers in order to develop new concepts. Glasser (1990, 1997) identified "affiliation" as one of the five basic needs of young people. "Collaboration" and "absence of threat" are two of the eight key factors present in a classroom that is compatible with how the brain learns (Caine & Caine, 1997; Kavolik, 1994). In order for students to be able to interact and collaborate productively, we need classroom structures that allow those interactions to take place. Almost any set of recommendations for school and instructional reform includes greater use of small-group, cooperative learning. This strategy fulfills students' need for affiliation while teaching explicitly how to work productively and courteously in a group. In addition, the research base supports the effectiveness of this method for promoting both cognitive and affective learning (Johnson & Johnson, 1999; Slavin, 1995).

Making Student Grouping Decisions

One of the most important decisions a teacher makes in planning learning experiences is how to form instructional groups. The most reasonable question about grouping seems to be not, "Should we group or shouldn't we group?" but, "What grouping arrangements best meet the needs of these students for a particular activity?" Although the effectiveness of rigid, long-term groupings based on ability can be questioned, flexible within- or between-class groupings based on particular academic needs are associated with increased achievement (Slavin, 1994).

If students are to have choice, challenge, and autonomy, they must spend at least part of the school day outside whole-group instruction, either as individuals or in small groups. If they are to learn cooperation, they must spend time in cooperative groupings. No one pattern precludes the others or meets all students' needs. Most students should probably spend part of the school day working in larger, heterogeneous groups. They should also spend some time on individual tasks, projects, and interests; and some time in small groups. The small groups may be heterogeneous or homogeneous, skills-based or interest-based, depending on the needs of the students and the demands of the task. Most experts agree, however, that students should be included in multiple groupings so they do not become labeled or stereotyped as a result of always being in the same group (Cohen et al., 1994; Cohen, 1998).

At times, you may want students to work in groups based on the need for a particular skill. This type of grouping is particularly appropriate for basic skills instruction, or instruction in areas that have been previously introduced but not mastered by all students (i.e., for reteaching). More targeted groupings can provide an appropriate level of challenge for every student. Few things will kill motivation more quickly than repeated practice in a long-mastered skill, or instruction on a task that is impossibly beyond a student's current skill level. Remember, however, that research indicates negative effects when low-ability students are grouped homogeneously for longer periods of time (Lou et al., 1996).

In addition to specific skills needs, some complex tasks are best suited to more homogeneous groups. Particularly challenging problem-solving activities or projects may be appropriate for students with demonstrated abilities in a particular area, but may be unsuitable for a whole-class task. At times, groups of students with more limited skills can benefit from tackling a research task that presents a challenge to them but would be less challenging to others. Managing the task alone can provide chances for problem solving and persistence that might not occur in a more heterogeneous group. Chapter 10 contains more information on differentiated instruction that may assist you in generating ideas for both homogeneous and heterogeneous groups.

At other times, groups may be based on students' expressed interests. Sharan and Sharan's (1992) group investigation model has students generate questions they would like to explore about a particular topic. Then students divide into groups according to the questions they would most like to investigate. For example, Gloria Jackson's class might divide into groups to study various aspects of the lifestyle in 1776. One group may study techniques of farming, another food preparation and storage, still another music or recreation of the period. The groups may be heterogeneous in skill level, but homogeneous in interests. The next section discusses a particular way of teaching with heterogeneous groups that can develop the ability to work harmoniously and productively with others.

Cooperative Group Learning

Cooperative group learning is a specific type of group learning with particular characteristics. A cooperative learning group is a mixed group that "sinks or swims" together because each person is responsible for the others' learning. When discussing cooperative learning (Johnson & Johnson, 1999), it is important to contrast it with individualized learning and competitive learning. In **individualized learning**, students each work on their own to accomplish an objective. Students are not compared with one another; they work to achieve a preset standard. Individual structures are useful when students are well motivated and need little guidance.

Competitive learning is often present in today's schools. In competitive classrooms, student performance is judged against the average performance of all students. Recall the characteristics of norm-referenced evaluation presented in Chapter 5. If some students succeed, others must be less successful because of the limited number of A grades available. Tests in competitive classrooms are graded on the curve, so the idea is to do better than someone else. The effect of too much competition on students may be selfishness, low self-esteem, and poor communication skills.

Cooperative classrooms are characterized by an attitude of interdependence. The students work to help their team members achieve the objectives. Each student is held individually accountable and receives an individual score. Teams with a score greater than the minimum level set by the teacher may receive special recognition or a reward. Students in such classrooms learn to value giving and receiving help. They also learn to work together toward a common goal—a skill that is essential for both effective workplaces and democratic communities.

REFLECTING ON THE IDEAS

Discuss with friends their experiences in school. Do they remember examples of individualized, competitive, or cooperative learning? What was your experience with each type of structure? How did you feel? How did your friends feel? Come to class prepared to discuss your own and your friends' experiences.

The main reason to use cooperative learning, in addition to its obvious social benefits, is that it can assist student learning. The research on cooperative learning is impressive. Students at many levels who received some cooperative activities (approximately 60% of class time, with the balance spent in individual and competitive learning) had higher achievement, better retention, higher level reasoning skills, greater empathy for those who are different, and higher self-esteem than students who had little or no cooperative learning (Johnson & Johnson,1999; Walberg, 1999).

How does cooperative learning work? It is not simply putting students into groups and assigning a task. There are four critical components of cooperative lessons: *face-to-face interaction, positive interdependence, individual accountability,* and *cooperative skills learning.*

Face-to-Face Interaction: Grouping Decisions

As you learned in Chapter 2, many students learn best when involved in purposeful interaction about authentic tasks. Cooperative learning is an excellent way to structure such interaction. Group size is an important factor. As groups become larger, it is harder to get every student actively involved. Groups of two, three, or four seem to be most productive. Students must learn to work closely together; face-to-face interaction is essential to group learning.

Most long-term cooperative groups are mixed in ability or in social makeup. For example, a group of three students may contain one high achiever, one low achiever, and one middle level achiever. Or if social integration is a goal, the groups may be composed of popular and less popular students. Ethnic and home background may be the basis for creating heterogeneous groups. Language proficiency and gender may be taken into account in setting up mixed groups.

When students who don't typically interact with one another are in a face-to-face, interdependent situation, many social barriers are broken down and students learn to value those who are different from themselves. This social integration can be particularly important in upper elementary (or middle school) grades where the preadolescent need to fit into a peer group begins to be a primary motivating force. One teacher forms long-term groups by having students privately list the names of three students they would like to have in their group. In this way students get to have some input into the group structure. The teacher uses this information to mix students who appeared on few lists with those who are particularly outgoing and caring with others. In such groups the isolated student begins to feel included and valued.

For informal, short-term groups you might assign students randomly by "counting off," by the color of their clothes, or by giving playing cards to students as they enter the room. Such random groupings make sense at the beginning of the year when little is known about each student, and for quick on-the-spot activities (e.g., check for understanding with a neighbor).

Positive Interdependence

Positive interdependence always starts with a group goal—a task that can only be accomplished by the group (e.g., a single product signed by all group members to indicate what they contributed and that they understand the whole project). Students need a reason to begin to help each other learn. How is a sense of positive interdependence achieved? Typically, group members are made to feel interdependent by *limiting materials* (e.g., only one copy of a worksheet or one pencil is given to the group); *jigsawing* the material into sections, with the expert on each piece of the puzzle teaching the other group members; *assigning roles* (e.g., a checker, an encourager, and a recorder); and/or offering *group rewards* (e.g., if all members succeed, each member receives a privilege or points). The latter approach (reward interdependence) appears to be one of the most powerful aspects of group learning (Slavin, 1995).

In such interdependent structures, all students must do their part in helping the others learn the material or accomplish the task. If one person does not learn, the whole group has failed to help that student. Thus students learn how to help each other. One of the simplest ways to use reward interdependence is to have a group of three coach each other for a quiz or test. Then, after assigning individual grades, give special recognition, privileges, or rewards to the groups in which every member reached the minimum performance level specified.

TABLE 9.1   *Cooperative Group Role Descriptions*

Reader	Reads the material aloud to group; makes sure all are listening
Writer/recorder	Fills in forms; writes as group dictates
Materials manager	Gathers materials, supplies, information
Timer	Keeps track of time; keeps group on task
Checker	Checks to be sure all agree on group's answer or information selected for a project
	Makes sure each member can explain the answer or information selected and say why
Summarizer	Periodically stops to summarize what has happened so far, or to clarify information gathered
Coach/organizer	Makes sure each member has a chance to participate equally; checks that each member agrees on directions; mediates disagreements
Encourager	Gives praise and encouragement to group members
Presenter	Presents the group's product to class or other audience

The assigning of specific roles to students is another way to introduce interdependence. The students will need to receive very clear directions on their particular role. Many teachers do this by using laminated role description cards. Table 9.1 displays several roles.

Occasionally you may find a student who either wants to dominate the group or refuses to get involved. These students will require coaching and support in the social skills required for group work. They also can be assisted by thoughtful assignment of roles. For example, the role of recorder might suit a shy student or one who needs to learn to listen carefully. The encourager role is appropriate for students who are tentative and need a positive, low-key role, and for those who tend to use put-downs. Being a summarizer is good for those who tend to isolate and for those who need practice in putting thoughts into words. The timekeeper role is good for those who need an important or easy role, or for those who tend to wander (mentally or physically) away from the task. One warning: Students should not always be given the same role; they need to learn to stretch into other areas and responsibilities.

Individual and Group Accountability

Have you ever worked on a group project and felt resentful because one or two people did all the work, but everyone got the same grade? This should not happen in well-structured cooperative groups because every group member is held individually responsible for his or her own learning. It is always crucial for the teacher to continually assess each student's understandings and growing competence. This is especially true in cooperative groups, where one person's understanding can too easily be assumed to represent everyone's level of understanding.

Accountability may be accomplished by giving students a quiz, with grades recorded in the teacher's book as usual. Or the teacher may rotate among the groups with a clipboard, making random spot checks by asking students questions about material they are supposed to have learned. When students are completing a worksheet together, you may ask all the students to sign their name on the sheet, to indicate that all members agree with the answers and that every student can explain why each answer is correct. Another way to encourage **individual accountability** within the group is to assign the role of checker to a student who is responsible for gauging each person's understanding by asking questions, requesting summaries, and quizzing the other group members. A deeper discussion of the role of assessment in cooperative learning may be found in Johnson and Johnson (1999).

REFLECTING ON THE IDEAS

With a partner, explain how cooperative learning differs from more traditional group work. Be sure to include the three essential attributes of cooperative learning discussed so far.

Cooperative Skills Learning

Students don't always walk into the classroom knowing how to help other students or how to work in a group to complete a task. Yet such skills are crucial at home, in the workplace, and in myriad social situations. One of the key skills listed in the Secretary's Commission on Achieving Necessary Skills (SCANS) Report (U.S. Department of Labor, 1993) is teamwork and collaborative problem solving. It is therefore important to teach students how to build and maintain trust, to communicate, to lead, and to manage conflict or controversy. Imagine how successful our relationships would be if we all had such skills!

How are cooperative skills taught? First, a diagnosis (preassessment) is necessary. It is instructive to put students in cooperative groups to complete a simple task—for example, to solve a puzzle and make sure every person can independently explain how to find the solution. Then, walk around with a clipboard, taking notes on which social skills are present or lacking. You may find that many students do not know how to share, that they do not give each other positive feedback and encouragement, or that they interrupt each other. If you find some important social skills lacking, now is the time to teach them—one at a time.

Most experts agree that focusing on only one or two social skills per lesson is enough. It may take several weeks of work on one area before you see improvement. For example, you might spend an entire marking period emphasizing the skills of giving encouraging comments to others, listening without interrupting, and using the other person's name. Figure 9.3 provides a list of common social skills. Remember, students will need long-term practice and reinforcement before a social skill will become automatic, so don't try to do too much too fast.

You may use a variety of strategies to teach social skills: direct explanation, modeling, and practice; discovery or inductive activities; or role-playing. Of course, the work in cooperative groups provides practice of the skills. This is where monitoring, self-assessment, and giving feedback are crucial.

FIGURE 9.3   Common Social Skills and T-Chart

Social Skills	Chart on Encouraging Others	
	Looks like 👁	**Sounds like** 👂
• Staying with the group • Using quiet voices • Taking turns • Not using put-downs • Asking for help • Summarizing aloud • Criticizing ideas, not people • Using first names • Contributing ideas • Praising • Encouraging others • Saying "please" and "thank you" • Paraphrasing	• Smiling • Leaning forward • Eye contact	• "Good job" • "That's a good idea" • "Yes!"

Following are some ideas for teaching cooperative skills:

1. Help students *understand* what the specific social skill is. Telling students to co-operate is too vague and will result in little success. Many young people cannot comprehend an abstract idea like respect until they see and hear it in action. Asking specific questions about the behaviors included in the social skill can make it concrete and easier to understand. For example, you may lead students in a discussion, asking "What does giving encouragement look like?" (e.g., leaning forward, smiling) and "What does it sound like?" (e.g., "Good job!" "That's a good idea"). You may write these behaviors on the board on a T-chart, as shown in Figure 9.3. You may also wish to have students demonstrate what the skill looks like through role-playing.

2. Make sure students know *why a particular skill is useful*. For example, show students how learning to give encouragement will make it easier for them to get along with their siblings or with other people. Let students know how they'll be rewarded (personally and externally) by using the skill.

3. Help students *practice* the skill while they work in groups. You may assign roles ("Today, Joe is the encourager") or you may assign a group observer ("Lola, today you put a checkmark next to each person's name when they encourage another student"). You may even create a special nonacademic activity that promotes application of the skill—for example, having students talk in pairs about a hobby while making a conscious effort to encourage the other student to talk and share. Of course, you will observe the groups and record examples of encouraging behaviors. After more practice, this skill will become more automatic for students.

4. Allocate class time *to discuss students' use of the social skill*. The processing or discussion of the use of the social skill may be done within the small group ("Lola, show your observation results to the group and have members discuss how well they encouraged each other today"). Or you may give specific feedback to individuals or groups by reading aloud the encouraging statements you recorded as you observed the groups.

These feedback and debriefing sessions will take approximately 10 minutes a day at first. Later, you may need to spend only a few minutes per week to discuss how the desired social skills are progressing.

Developing cooperative groups takes time, persistence, and effort. Keep in mind the main cooperative skills you know the students need to focus on. Then, every time you do an activity, remind students to think about the one or two social skills that need polishing. Review the T-chart if necessary. At the end of every activity, make sure the groups assess their progress on cooperative skills. Then, discuss with the groups how they can get better. Keep groups together long enough to learn how to be productive; if they keep switching, there is little opportunity to resolve conflicts and build trust.

The topic of developing trust is important to consider. Think of a group you are in and how long it took you to become comfortable. Trust does not develop overnight, but teachers can help it along. The first weeks are a particularly important time for building a sense of community in the classroom (see Chapter 11). When students don't feel comfortable on a team, they often are less productive. Early on, invest some time in group trust-building activities. It will pay off in the long run!

Other Models of Cooperative Learning

In **Teams-Games-Tournaments (TGT)** (Slavin, 1995), heterogeneous teams of four to five members coach one another as they prepare for team competitions. The teams practice with the content questions for part of each period over a few days. At the tournament on Friday, students from each team are assigned to different three-person tables with other students of similar achievement levels. The questions are usually taken from a current chapter, study guide, or other topic. All tables play at once. The first contestant picks a number card and tries to answer the corresponding question on a handout. Points are earned by successfully answering a question or correcting another's answer. Each person at the table scores points for his or her own team. The points are then totaled to determine each team's score. Rewards and recognition, often in the form of a newsletter announcing the team scores, are provided. Before the next tournament, the teacher may change the composition of the tournament tables to ensure even competition. The students practice in heterogeneous groups, but only compete against those of similar achievement levels, with questions geared to that level.

In **Student Teams—Achievement Divisions (STAD)** (Slavin, 1994), a similar process is used to prepare for the tournament, but teams compete against one another by taking an individual quiz. Quiz scores are converted into team points by computing each member's improvement over the last quiz score and summing them or by awarding points based on the team's improvement over past group averages.

In **Jigsaw** (Aronson, Blaney, Stephan, Sikes, & Snapp, 1978; Clarke, 1994; Draper, 1997), each "home" group member is given a topic or set of materials to teach to the other team members. Students then regroup with others who have the same topic (expert groups) and prepare to teach their group about that topic. This is a good time for the teacher to exert some quality control by providing clarification of key points or misunderstandings with each expert group. Next, students return to their home group to teach their part to the others. A quiz or other form of individual accountability results in a group score and a reward or recognition for the winning team.

Jigsaw is a complex structure but can work well with many elementary school students. For example, imagine a jigsaw review activity with different groups teaching others about parts of speech, or a science activity in which different groups became expert on one living thing in an ecosystem. Only when all the information was shared could students envision the entire habitat.

In summarizing research on cooperative learning strategies, Marzano, Pickering, and Pollack (2001) make the following recommendations.

- Organizing groups based on ability levels should be done sparingly.
- Cooperative groups should be kept small in size, no more than 3–4 students.
- Cooperative learning should be applied consistently and systematically but not overused.

Examples of Cooperative Learning

Example 1: Writing Friendly Letters

The following example illustrates a cooperative learning lesson on letter writing. The teacher has finished several lessons on the correct format for friendly letters and now wants students to apply these ideas. Notice how two objectives are specified (one content objective and one social skill). All four decisions about grouping, interdependence, individual accountability, and cooperative/social skills must be clear in the teacher's mind before the actual lesson plan can be made.

Objectives:

- Students will be able to recognize and correct errors in letters.
- Students will encourage each group member to participate. (social skill)

Decisions (before lesson is taught):

Group size:
3 (mixed according to proficiency in writing)

Cooperative skills:
Encouraging participation. Taught directly at beginning, monitored by teacher during task, and self-assessed and discussed by students at end.

Materials:
3 letters with formatting and grammar errors per group; 1 pencil per group; 1 piece of paper per group

Task:
One person in the group will show his or her letter to the rest of the group. He or she will explain to the group what is incorrect. Then he or she will illustrate how to correct the letter. Group members check accuracy. Roles are then rotated.

Interdependence:

Provided by limited materials, group rewards (points given for correct answers during spot check), and job roles that are rotated after each student's turn:

Writer: Holds letter, explains the error, and corrects it
Checker: Checks writer's correctness
Encourager: Gets all group members involved

Individual accountability:

Spot checks by teacher with recording level of students' performance on a chart and quick individual reteaching.

Lesson Procedure:

Opening:

First, teacher asks students to jot down two things they could say or do to encourage each group member to participate in today's activity. Teacher uses their ideas to fill in T-chart and reminds them she will be rotating among the groups looking for this skill. Teacher explains the other objective (correcting letters) and clarifies the purpose: later they will be using the skills when they write letters to grandparents or other relatives. Reminds students to look at the wall chart illustrating correct letter format.

Constructing meaning and using/applying:

Teacher forms the groups, assigns and explains roles, and gives directions for the task. Teacher explains the group rewards and how students will be held individually responsible for their learning (spot checks). Students perform the task as teacher walks around and takes notes on "encouraging" behavior.

(Individual accountability) Cognitive learning assessment:

Toward the end of the group time, teacher goes to each group and picks two students to justify the corrections made in the group's letters. When the task is completed, students share correct answers with another group, and confusing points are explained by the teacher.

Social skill processing:

Next, groups rate themselves from 1 (low) to 5 (high) on a self-assessment form on their ability to encourage each member and discuss needed improvements in their groups. Finally, the teacher reads examples she heard of students encouraging one another and gives positive feedback.

REFLECTING ON THE IDEAS

In the preceding lesson, heterogeneous groups are used to teach about letter writing. There is no differentiation of activities for students who have differing skill levels. What are the potential difficulties with this structure? What are the benefits?

Example 2: Lesson on "Journey to Jo'burg"

In this lesson, students are reading a novel about the journey of a young Black South African girl and her brother from their small village to a large city in search of their mother. The novel illustrates how the young girl begins to have a different perspective about her life during apartheid. Again, all four elements of cooperative learning are used, but activities are differentiated, and choices are allowed for students needing more or less challenge.

Content standards:

- Explain how a particular public issue became a problem and why people disagree about it.
- Use narratives and graphic data to compare the past of a community with present-day life in those places.

Objectives:

Students will be able to

- describe how oppression and apartheid affected Black South Africans' lives
- distinguish how life for many Black South Africans during apartheid is different than the students' own lives
- use active listening when working in groups (social skill)

Decisions (before lesson begins):

Group size:
5 (racially diverse; 1 strong reader, 2 average readers, and 2 struggling readers)

Positive interdependence:
Roles (connector finds connections between novel and outside world; discussion director creates open-ended questions and directs the discussion; analyzer finds situations, feelings, or locations that are different from the experiences of characters in the book; vocabulary definer finds new, puzzling, or important words, looks them up in a dictionary, and creates a sentence with each one; illustrator draws 2 pictures related to the reading). Limited materials (there is only one copy of each completed role sheet). Jigsaw (each student has one piece of the entire task).

Individual accountability (assessment):
Each student makes a project (e.g., diorama, poem, letter, or journal entry) to show his or her understanding of the key objectives related to the novel. Each project will be assessed using a common rubric that reflects the understandings stated in the lesson objectives.

Cooperative (social) skill:
Active listening (taught at beginning of lesson, monitored with teacher feedback during group work, assessed and discussed by the group at the end).

Materials:

Novel, *Journey to Jo'burg* by Beverley Naidoo; overhead with Word Splash words; individual role sheets with clear instructions.

Task:

Once a week, after students have read a section of the novel, each student will complete his or her own role sheet (different role for each group member). In the group, they share the information they have collected during literature circle time. Afterwards, a class discussion will explore the groups' findings.

Lesson Procedure:

Opening (set, objective, purpose):

Set: Before beginning to read the book, put "Word Splash" on overhead. In assigned groups, students make predictions about the book based on the words given. These are discussed as a large group. Each day the book is discussed, students go back to their predictions to see how well they match the actual story.

Cognitive objectives and purpose: Teacher tells students about the final project. They will each use narratives and graphic data to (a) explain and show how oppression and apartheid affected Black South Africans' lives and (b) compare and contrast life for many Black South Africans during apartheid with the students' own lives. Explains how important it is to recognize that each person has value regardless of his or her race; that each student needs to value the input of fellow classmates no matter how much they differ from each other.

Social skill (teaching, objective, and purpose): The teacher asks students to discuss with their neighbor what it feels like when an adult or friend just does not listen to them. A few randomly selected students share their feelings. Then the teacher explains the importance of listening actively, and models examples. Students practice in pairs by discussing what they did the night before. Teacher explains that they will be using active listening and the teacher will be checking it during their group work, and that at the end of the group work, they will be discussing how well they listened to each other.

Constructing meaning and using/applying:

Teacher explains the task, assigns the roles, and clarifies each role and the importance of each person doing his or her part. (The roles have been modeled and practiced on prior days.)

As the groups are discussing the novel, teacher walks around checking to see that each role sheet is completed, observing students' use of the social skill and answering questions. After 20 minutes, teacher leads a discussion of the themes and examples of how the students' lives here are different from or the same as the main character's life during apartheid.

Assessment of cognitive learning (individual accountability):

At the end of each session, the groups discuss and write down what they felt were the most important parts of the novel and why they thought this. Then teacher leads a group discussion on this topic. (At the end of the entire novel, each student does the individual project described earlier and presents it to his or her group.)

Processing of social skill:

Students individually complete a "Group Reflection" form including the following items:

I listened actively to each of my group members and tried reflecting back to them what they said. (rating from 1—true to 3—false)
I encouraged the views of the person speaking. (rating from 1–3)
Our group had a productive session. (yes or no)
We made sure everyone understood the material. (yes or no)
Everyone felt comfortable about sharing his or her thoughts. (yes or no)
My group could have been better by ....
One thing we did well was.....

Teacher leads a class discussion about what students liked and disliked about the activity and if they changed their mind about something because of something a group member said.

Adaptations/differentiation:

Cultural diversity: Groups are formed so students from different cultures are together.
Struggling students: Readers of different levels are grouped together; struggling readers can begin reading the novel at home or after school with parental or mentor assistance.
Advanced and gifted students: Will have more complex roles and assignment choices (e.g., creating ideas for final projects).
Students with learning disabilities: Will have specific segments broken down with specific direction as teacher monitors the groups (e.g., stand up if you need to while you read).

Cautions, Differentiation, and Cooperative Groups

Much of the literature on cooperative learning stresses the importance of heterogeneous groups. Students in heterogeneous groups can learn to help one another, get along with those who are different from themselves, and understand the value of diversity. Unfortunately, improperly used heterogeneous groups can also cause a host of problems (Cohen et al., 1994; Cohen, 1998). Less able students can rely on more able students to carry out the tasks for them. More able students can become resentful or bored at having to repeatedly explain to team members information that they easily mastered themselves.

Either of these two difficulties could occur in the letter-writing lesson cited earlier, particularly if skill levels are highly diverse. If, for example, one of the group members is unable to read the letters—or one member has been corresponding regularly in letter form for years—picking out errors in a letter may not be an appropriate group task.

This difficulty might have been minimized through differentiation. If, for example, students who were already extremely adept at letter writing were engaged in alternative activities, they may be more appropriately challenged. The groups would still be heterogeneous, but only within the range of students needing practice on that skill. Students who have difficulty reading could work with an assigned buddy—or a particularly sensitive and helpful group member. Alternatively, students could be given varied assignments within the group—perhaps letters of varying difficulty with more or less sophisticated errors. Examples of varied assignments are seen in the roles provided in the second cooperative lesson on the novel. Additional information on differentiating cooperative groups can be found in Chapter 10.

Sometimes the primary goal of heterogeneous groups is social; in this case, content learning is less important. But most group learning should have important content outcomes for all the students involved. If heterogeneous groups are to provide motivation, challenge, and interdependence for all students, cooperative tasks must be carefully planned. In many cases this can be accomplished through the use of more complex tasks like the cooperative lesson example on reading and analyzing the novel.

When using cooperative learning, look carefully at the tasks and make sure that the interdependence assumed in the group goals is real. Sometimes group tasks produce group efforts that are more illusion than substance. Cohen (1986) and Cohen et al. (1994) suggested guidelines for cooperative learning tasks that avoid these pitfalls. The key is that cooperative learning tasks, particularly those for heterogeneous groups, should be tasks for which having group participation is a genuine asset for everyone in the group.

Academic Service-Learning Provides Learning Through Service

This emphasis reflects the way groups function in business and society. Automobile manufacturers do not typically use groups to fill out reports or gather facts. Those tasks are more efficiently done individually. Groups are important on design teams, in think tanks, and in many other problem-solving situations. A good group task is one that benefits from many strengths, abilities, and points of view. Cohen's guidelines may be grouped in the following clusters:

1. *Cooperative learning tasks should have more than one answer and/or more than one path toward a solution.* No student or students should be able to come to the task with the solution in hand. For example, imagine that instead of gathering facts about Sitting Bull as a cooperative learning exercise, the class had the opportunity to learn the basic facts surrounding Sitting Bull and the events at Little Big Horn from a movie or class discussion. Then, cooperative groups might be charged with designing a suitable monument for the battle site of Little Big Horn. There is no simple solution to this task. Each student's opinion could be valuable in helping the group decide on a focus and perspective for their monument. Pointing out the real contributions of group members considered low-status by their peers can be a powerful strategy for combating inequality (Cohen, 1998).

2. *Cooperative learning tasks should be intrinsically motivating and should offer challenge to all students.* Students should work together to create a worthwhile product, not simply to earn team points. Intrinsically motivating tasks, like the monument assignment, involve making choices about interesting topics at a level of challenge suitable for students' knowledge and skills.

3. *Group tasks should allow students to make different kinds of contributions.* They should demand a variety of abilities and skills. Jan may be able to read and analyze reference materials easily. Jose may be able to see issues from more than one point of view. Sally may be able to draw, and Cherilyn to organize materials and keep the group on task. Each contribution is needed and valuable.

4. *Cooperative learning tasks should involve multiple media and multisensory experiences in addition to traditional text.* Complex experiences are good education under any circumstances. In a heterogeneous group, they increase the probability that each student will have the opportunity to take in information and express ideas in the form that best matches his or her learning style.

■ *Practice Activity: Jigsaw Activity*

In your class, count off so that you have teams (home groups) of four members. Spend 5 minutes getting to know each person (remember and use first names). Now join with another group of four and pick a partner from the other group so that you now have four pairs. The first pair will become experts on face-to-face interaction, the second pair will work on positive interdependence, the third pair will become experts in individual accountability, and the fourth pair will take cooperative skills.

With your partner, get ready to explain your piece of the puzzle to the others in your original team. Provide specific examples in your explanation and create a visual aid to help you convey the information. Prepare for your teaching with your partner for 10 minutes.

Now go back to your original team (home group) and have each person explain (and model) his or her piece of content. The others should discuss the ideas and create their own examples. To make things interesting, have the person whose birthday is the earliest in the year be the checker to make sure each person can explain the section before moving on to the next point. You have 20 minutes to make sure all members of your group can explain all four aspects of cooperative learning and give examples. You will be quizzed at the end of this time.

■ ■ ■

■ *Practice Activity: Designing a Cooperative Learning Activity*

With a partner, design a cooperative lesson for content you might teach. Be sure to include the four aspects of cooperative learning in your plan. How will you form groups? How will you create interdependence? How will you assess each individual accountability? Which cooperative skill will you emphasize and how will you teach it? Does your activity lead to genuine interdependence? Share your written plans with other pairs. Use the following form to make decisions and create a lesson.

■ ■ ■

Lesson Plan

Decisions to Make When Planning for Cooperative Learning

Cognitive lesson objective(s):_____

_____

Cooperative (social skill) objective:_____

_____

Group size and selection (trust activity needed?):_____

_____

Positive interdependence (plan more than one type—limited materials, jigsaw, roles, group reward):_____

_____

Roles for group members:_____

_____

Individual accountability (assessment) method for content knowledge:_____

_____

Teaching, modeling, feedback, and group processing or self-assessment of social skill:_____

_____

Materials:

_____

_____

Procedures

Opening (set, objective, purpose):_____

_____

Directions for task: _____

_____

Teaching/reviewing social skills (may be part of opening): _____

_____

Teacher monitoring social skills/helping during the task: _____

_____

Individual accountability (assessment) of cognitive learning: _____

_____

_____

Processing of social skills:_____

—Individual, group, and/or whole class?_____

—Form for self-assessment? _____

_____

Reflections and redesign notes for next time: _____

_____

_____

_____

SECTION 3. ACADEMIC SERVICE-LEARNING

Throughout this text we have emphasized the importance of authentic learning—learning that engages students in meaningful tasks. One structure that is designed to engage students in such activities is **academic service-learning**. As an introduction to academic service-learning, it may be helpful to examine a successful curriculum project that incorporated the use of this methodology. As you read, think about the characteristics of this project that would lead it to be classified as "academic service-learning."

Brice-Heath and Mangiola (1991) initiated a cross-age tutoring program in which culturally and linguistically diverse students who were labeled "at-risk" mentored younger students in reading. In order to develop their mentoring ability, the fifth graders videotaped the mentoring sessions and analyzed their strengths and weaknesses through written observations. Through discussion, fifth-grade students worked together to find ways to increase their repertoire of teaching strategies and increase their effectiveness.

In addition, they developed a mentoring handbook that described key reading strategies for helping young children learn to read. This reading handbook was written for an authentic audience of parents. Throughout this project the fifth graders gradually became confident as readers themselves. Their characterization of themselves as poor readers began to change as they took on the role of "expert." Academic service-learning in this context served to improve the fifth graders' literacy skills, empower them to transform the world for others, and create a more cohesive school community.

All of the critical attributes of an academic service-learning project are present in the mentoring project just described. The following definition of academic service-learning highlights these key attributes:

> Academic service-learning is a teaching methodology that utilizes community service as a means of helping students gain a deeper understanding of specific course objectives, acquire new knowledge, and engage in civic activities. (Jacoby, 1996; Stacey, Rice, Hurst, & Langer, 1997)

Academic service-learning encourages students to provide a *service*. Unlike service projects that are conducted by clubs, church groups, or civic organizations, it is *academic* in that it is structured to teach key content areas, in this case reading. But that is not all. From this definition, we can infer that providing real-world experiences alone will not lead to optimum learning unless teachers provide structured opportunities for student *reflection*. For learning to be meaningful, students must have ample opportunities for metacognition and reflection on their experiences. For example, metacognitive reflection activities in the context of a tutoring program might take the form of journal prompts such as, "What presented the most challenge as you mentored the student?" and "What mentoring strategy seemed most effective and why?" Also valuable are partner dialogue, whole-class discussion, and the creation of regular progress reports that require both description and analysis.

You may have parallel experiences as you engage in field activities as part of your teacher preparation program. If, as we hope, you have the opportunity to use the lesson designs you have learned from this book in a classroom setting (your academic content), those experiences will result in much more powerful learning if you have the opportunity to discuss your experiences and thought processes with an expert professional, record them in a reflection journal, and/or share them with peers. This is academic service-learning at an adult level. You are able to learn and reflect about teaching while serving students and schools.

One of the most important aspects of academic service-learning is a developing sense of community. In a community all of us have opportunities to both serve and be served. Each individual is an important contributor to the whole. Academic service-learning experiences will be most successful when students enter a community ready to share responsibility with and respect those they serve rather than to "fix" things (Kendall, 1990 cited in Jacoby, 1996). The fifth-grade students will be more effective and caring mentors as they respect the challenges faced by the younger students and appreciate the effort that goes into learning to read. They will gain more from the experience as they recognize how much they can learn from the younger children. To ensure reciprocity, teachers can explicitly discuss and model effective cooperative behaviors such as active listening, seeking clarification and elaboration through questioning, and encouraging others.

In order for academic service-learning to be successful, it is important that everyone involved understand the goals of the activities. Teachers should communicate important outcomes to all stakeholders in the project—community members, students, and arents. These outcomes are often quite diverse. They include cognitive, affective, ethical, civic, and career-related outcomes. Think for a moment about the diverse outcomes that could be attained through the mentoring project. Certainly there were cognitive outcomes, as students' reading skills improved. But there were important affective, civic, and ethical outcomes as well. Fifth-grade students developed confidence, learned to respect the struggles inherent in learning, and experienced the ethics of care and service. Perhaps some of them even began thinking about teaching as a career.

Teachers can play important roles in encouraging students to see themselves as participating citizens who can take action to improve their school and community. Academic service-learning projects are most often designed to engage students in problem solving around authentic societal problems. The following activities could be used for academic service-learning.

Creation and implementation of strategies to welcome and support newly arrived immigrant children in the school community

Development of oral histories for individuals living in nursing homes

Instruction of younger students to become critical television viewers

Creation and implementation of solutions to environmental problems in the community such as a neglected park

Development of a peer-tutoring/mentoring program for younger students

Beautification projects in the community or school environment

Projects such as these help students recognize the relevancy of their education and realize their own role in improving the quality of life in their communities. As an instructional methodology, academic service-learning promises to promote young people's activism and academic achievement through service.

REFLECTING ON THE IDEAS

With a colleague, brainstorm ideas for service in your community that could be suitable for elementary-age children. Choose one or two and think about how you could teach important academic outcomes through that service. You might make a chart listing the service-learning opportunity on one side and the standards or outcomes to be taught on the other. Consider including this chart in your portfolio as a demonstration of your understanding of academic service-learning.

SECTION 4. INFUSING TECHNOLOGY IN INSTRUCTION

One of the challenges and adventures of teaching in the 21st century will be finding ways to use emerging technologies to improve teaching. The use of technology has been heralded as the key to educational reform and a necessity for holding the attention and interest of the "net generation" (Dede, 1998; Tapscott, 1999). There also have been cautions about the appropriateness of some types of technology with young children (Healy, 1998; Tell, 2000). Schools have also been given the responsibility to assure that all students have the opportunities necessary to develop the technological skills essen-

FIGURE 9.4   National Education Technology Standards for grades P–2 and 3–5

Prior to completion of Grade 2, students will

1. use input devices (e.g., mouse, keyboard, remote control) and output devices (e.g., monitor, printer) to successfully operate computers, VCRs, audiotapes, and other technologies
2. use a variety of media and technology resources for directed and independent learning activities
3. communicate about technology using developmentally appropriate and accurate terminology
4. use developmentally appropriate multimedia resources (e.g., interactive books, educational software, elementary multimedia encyclopedias) to support learning
5. work cooperatively and collaboratively with peers, family members, and others when using technology in the classroom
6. demonstrate positive social and ethical behaviors when using technology
7. practice responsible use of technology systems and software
8. create developmentally appropriate multimedia products with support from teachers, family members, or student partners
9. use technology resources (e.g., puzzles, logical thinking programs, writing tools, digital cameras, drawing tools) for problem solving, communication, and illustration of thoughts, ideas, and stories
10. gather information and communicate with others using telecommunications, with support from teachers, family members, or student partners

Prior to completion of Grade 5, students will

1. use keyboards and other common input and output devices (including adaptive devices when necessary) efficiently and effectively
2. discuss common uses of technology in daily life and the advantages and disadvantages those uses provide
3. discuss basic issues related to responsible use of technology and information and describe personal consequences of inappropriate use
4. use general-purpose productivity tools and peripherals to support personal productivity, remediate skill deficits, and facilitate learning throughout the curriculum
5. use technology tools (e.g., multimedia authoring, presentation, web tools, digital cameras, scanners) for individual and collaborative writing, communication, and publishing activities to create knowledge products for audiences inside and outside the classroom
6. use telecommunications efficiently to access remote information, communicate with others in support of direct and independent learning, and pursue personal interests
7. use telecommunications and on-line resources(e.g., e-mail, on-line discussions, web environments) to participate in collaborative problem-solving activities for the purpose of developing solutions or products for audiences inside and outside the classroom
8. use technology resources (e.g., calculators, data collection probes, videos, educational software) for problem solving, self-directed learning, and extended learning activities
9. determine which technology is useful and select the appropriate tool(s) and technology resources to address a variety of tasks and problems
10. evaluate the accuracy, relevance, appropriateness, comprehensiveness, and bias of electronic information sources

tial for success in our rapidly changing environment while also attending to their developmental needs. To this end the International Society for Technology in Education (ISTE) has developed National Educational Standards (NETS) for students, outlining the technical literacy skills appropriate for each level. The NETS standards for students P–2 and 3–5 are included in Figure 9.4. The complete standards are available at the ISTE website. As we consider the content standards our students must address, meeting these technological standards poses an additional challenge.

It is certainly true that technology has enormous potential for challenging traditional ways of teaching and learning. Since no teacher can possibly equal the volume of knowledge available electronically, emerging technologies have the potential to shift the roles of teacher and learner alike (Medina, Pigg, Desler, & Gorospe, 2001). It is also true that, like any other strategy or tool, it can be used wisely or unwisely, effectively or ineffectively. Although it is beyond the scope of this text to fully review either the issues surrounding emerging technology or to provide comprehensive guidelines for its use, this section will briefly discuss some ways technology can effectively be infused in our instruction—providing both improved instruction and opportunities for students to address NETS standards.

Key to understanding the effective use of technology in teaching is a basic premise: technology is not a type of lesson nor a teaching approach. Technology provides us with an assortment of tools that can be used in a variety of types of lessons. They will work more or less well depending on the context. For example, various types of presentation software such as PowerPoint can be used to illustrate the "input" portion of a direct lesson for older students or adults. They can provide clear cues to the organization of the content and allow links to interesting graphics, video clips, and so on. However, the logistics of setting up such a presentation and the relative abstraction of the graphics (as opposed to concrete objects in hand) would make this technology much less appropriate for a minilecture on addition or place value in first grade. And using presentation software for a direct lesson based on storytelling is likely to interfere with the eye contact that is an important part of the interaction between storyteller and audience. In the first instance, the use of technology is likely to enhance the older students' attention and interest, as well as focusing attention on the structure of the content. The second example might be helpful to young children, but probably not as helpful as concrete math manipulatives. In the third instance the technology could have a negative impact on the storytelling lesson.

This illustration leads to another perhaps obvious but important premise: It makes sense to use technology when doing so allows us to do something new or to do more effectively something we already do. Using technology simply because it is new is not reflective teaching. Finding ways to enhance our teaching using technology can be an exciting adventure for a reflective teacher.

Technology and Direct Instruction

In direct instruction, technology can be used at several stages of a lesson. In an opening (set), a video clip from a multimedia encyclopedia or other data source (CD, DVD, or web-based) can catch students' attention. The same types of sources, with or without presentation software, can provide illustrations to clarify or enliven a minilecture. A projection system that allows you to create and display a spreadsheet can be helpful for teaching data analysis—particularly when you can create and present an appropriate graph with the click of a button.

In many cases technology can provide appropriate practice or application activities. These may not only be the familiar drill-and-practice software packages, but should include more complex activities that require students to use technology to show what they know. Whereas students only a few years ago were often limited to writing reports, painting murals, and creating an occasional diorama, today's elementary school students—with appropriate instruction and technical support—can create multimedia presentations, videos, and websites. Such projects, if carefully constructed, require complex thinking and problem solving in addition to knowledge of the content being presented.

Technology and Inductive Teaching

One of the most powerful ways to use technology is for inductive teaching: both formal and informal. In particular, the Internet can enlarge the span of the informal inductive teaching we conduct through the creation of our classroom environments. As students develop concepts through interaction with the posters, plants, art, and animals in a classroom, so too they can develop concepts as they follow scientists exploring under the ocean, communicate with classes in other parts of the country, or problem-solve with an electronic mentor. Each of these opportunities may be structured into a formal lesson, but they also provide experiences with other people and places on which concepts and principles will be built for years to come.

Using the Internet and other technologies can vastly expand the opportunities for data collection and analysis in inquiry teaching. For example, students studying weather could conduct a study of weather data and patterns at their school. But the *Kids as Global Scientists* project allowed students to study and compare weather data from across the country. On a smaller scale, many students have graphed the numbers of various colors of M&M candies in a bag for a classic inductive activity on probability. Teaching students to use a spreadsheet to collect and organize the same data adds both a new level of sophistication to the activity and a new, useful skill. This is a good example of using technology to do a similar activity in a better way.

More and Better Tools

Many effective uses of technology allow students to do their work more easily or powerfully. Using word processors to facilitate student writing greatly eases the editing and revising processes. This is of particular assistance to students whose motor control presents challenges while writing. Reading lessons on material taken from the World Wide Web—particularly lessons on critical reading and analysis—can be timely and effective. Computer graphics programs can help students illustrate their ideas.

The research opportunities presented by the Internet—while demanding careful consumerism and media savvy—vastly expand the materials available in the school library. For example, if Gloria Jackson wanted her students to research important people, events, or information on lifestyles from the Revolutionary War period, many relevant sites would be available—from general sites like the *American Revolution Homepage* to subject-specific sites such as *Spy Letters of the American Revolution* or a time line on the history of food, leading to period recipes. In particular, students would have access to primary source materials via the web that are unlikely to be available any other way. For example, students might study three accounts of the Boston Massacre, analyzing the point of view expressed in each one. By bookmarking the sites she finds most appropriate, Gloria could help students make the most efficient use of research time.

In addition, the global communications made available through the Internet provide new and powerful opportunities for real-world problem solving. Through electronic communication, students can gather and analyze data, share concerns across state and national boundaries, and work with others on areas of common concerns. This type of activity, when tied to a teaching unit, provides opportunities for authentic learning beyond those available to any single classroom.

Virtual Architecture

Judi Harris (2002) described a wide variety of activities that can be used to infuse technology into instruction in meaningful and often powerful ways. She uses the term *virtual architecture* to describe structures that define various types of "telecomputing activities." These are divided into two broad categories: those focused primarily on communicating and collaboration with distant colleagues and those focused on research using resources located elsewhere. Numerous examples of such activities can be found at the website associated with the book at http://ccwf.cc.utexas.edu/~jbharris/Virtual-Architecture. Here we will give a brief description of her structures for the first category of activities, "telecollaboration and telepresence" (p. 17). They can help to raise our sights and our expectations of the ways students can use technology.

- *Keypals.* Students pair off with students in another location to communicate electronically, often on topics of mutual interest.
- *Global classrooms.* Two or more classrooms in different locations study a common topic during the same time period. Students might read a common novel or study the same social studies topic. Perhaps Gloria's students might share information and resources with another class studying the Revolution.
- *Electronic appearances.* Students have the opportunity to communicate with a subject matter expert, usually on a one-time basis. For example, they might conference with a NASA scientist or favorite author.
- *Telementoring.* Sometimes subject experts are available for longer term relationships as mentors for individual or class projects.
- *Question-and-answer activities.* A variety of "ask the expert" sites allow students to pose questions to individuals in many areas of expertise.
- *Impersonations.* Impersonation projects are activities in which individuals communicate with each other in character. For example, a project at Monticello allows students to "communicate" with Thomas Jefferson.
- *Information exchanges.* Information exchanges from around the world can provide data for inductive analysis ranging from slang words from around the world to indigenous insect species.
- *Database creation.* Some information exchanges also entail organizing information into databases that can be exchanged and studied. These include information on bird sightings and a collection of children's artwork illustrating animals around the world that start with different letters of the alphabet.
- *Electronic publishing.* Many classes and schools have created websites to share information and student work. Larger scale publishing opportunities include student journals and art galleries created via the web.

- *Telefieldtrips*. Students can visit locations around the world via the web. They can visit specific sites or follow adults researching historical sites or specific environments in a type of virtual expedition. Some expeditions provide students with daily updates and the opportunity to pose questions to the travelers. For example, Conyers and Rauscher (2000–2001) describe the ways students shared in a trip across Antarctica, learning about everything from weather to the effects of temperature on various lubricants.
- *Pooled data analysis*. Like database creation activities, these projects involve students in collecting and analyzing data. In this case both the data collection and the analysis are collaborative activities—including a variation of the M&M probability activity mentioned previously.
- *Information searches*. In these gamelike activities, students are provided with clues and must use reference materials to answer questions. For example, one game asked students to research an interesting landmark and design clues to its identity. Clues were posted weekly in a competition to identify the most landmarks.
- *Peer feedback activities*. These activities encourage students to give helpful suggestions regarding peers' efforts, often as a type of long-distance editing.
- *Parallel problem solving*. Students in multiple locations work to solve a similar problem and then compare experiences and data. One of the most popular of these activities involves creating crates to protect dropping eggs.
- *Sequential creations*. Students join with distant classrooms to compose sections to a poem, song, or other creation.
- *Telepresent problem solving*. Students come together in virtual conferences, often to discuss topics of global importance.
- *Simulations*. Like "in person" simulations, Internet simulations provide students the chance to experience slices of life ranging from western expedition to the Mideast peace negotiations.
- *Social action projects*. The Internet can serve as a vehicle for global humanitarian efforts, many focusing on environmental issues.

Access and the Technology Gap

Although technology-infused curriculum can generate enormous student enthusiasm and develop important knowledge and skills, it is important to consider ways to structure the activities to provide access to all students. There is a gender divide in the ways boys and girls use technology—and the divide continues into adulthood (American Association of University Women, 1998; Weinman & Haag, 1999). In a similar fashion, use of technology varies enormously along cultural lines. As you use the diversity principle to reflect on gender and cultural issues throughout your teaching, special attention should be paid to activities involving technology. For example, considering how groups and responsibilities are divided when using technology can provide important opportunities for boys and girls of all cultures to experience technical competence. Some teachers have found that when computer access in the classroom is limited it is necessary to allocate opportunities for both assigned and free-choice activities. Otherwise students who may be interested but less assertive, or a bit unsure of their technical expertise, may not be willing to compete with highly motivated users for time on the machines.

Many students do not have ready access to computers outside school. It is important to be sure that students who come from technology-rich homes do not have unfair advantages in class assignments over those who must complete their work in school or in the community library. There is a delicate balance to be found between accepting and appreciating students' outside efforts and discouraging those for whom such activities are an unreasonable expectation. As we work to infuse technology in our curriculum, it will be important to help all our students become involved in meaningful ways.

SECTION 5. CENTERS, CONTRACTS, AND SKILLS OF INDEPENDENT LEARNING

One of the factors that allows flexibility in planning large- and small-group lessons—with or without technology—is students' pursuit of independent learning activities. Independent activities can provide opportunities for students to practice skills appropriate for individual needs but not for the whole group. They can also allow students the opportunity to investigate questions of interest or to design creative projects that are unique to their individual concerns, styles, or needs. If students are to have opportunities for individualized practice or investigative activities, all students in the class must be taught the skills of independent working. These skills are not just for the most able, the most creative, or the most motivated. If you are to concentrate your attention on helping a group or individual, at some point each student must be able to work without your direct guidance.

Two of the most common vehicles for implementing independent learning activities are *centers* and *contracts*. Each of these strategies has many possible variations and implementations in diverse subjects and grade levels. This section describes general definitions, uses, and patterns. It is up to you to adapt the general framework provided to the needs, interests, and abilities of your students.

SECTION OBJECTIVES

After you have completed this section, you will be able to

1. describe key activities to prepare students for independent learning;
2. plan, implement, and assess the effects of a learning center, interest-development center, exploratory center, or student learning contract; and
3. describe the use of multiple centers in organizing activities in an elementary classroom.

Centers

In this section we describe three types of centers: learning centers, interest-development centers, and exploratory or independent play areas. Physically, learning centers and interest-development centers look much the same. They entail a designated area of the classroom designed to facilitate independent work on a particular topic or discipline. Centers may be constructed in study carrels, on tabletops, on a pair of desks in the corner, or in virtually any structure that can store materials and provide directions. The differences between learning centers and interest-development centers are in intent. A learning center is designed to introduce or reinforce a specific part of the regular curriculum. An interest-development center is designed to spur curiosity and interest in areas outside the regular curriculum. Related to both learning and interest-development centers are exploratory or independent play areas that may be used in early grades.

Learning Centers

Because a **learning center** is designed to reinforce the core curriculum, all or most students will probably be required to complete work at the learning center. However, the nature of a center makes it easy to provide choice within the requirements and to vary the difficulty of assignments for individual students. Students may be required to complete two activities of their choice, or one "red" (easier) and one "blue" (more challenging) activity. You may also vary center assignments according to students' strengths and needs.

In constructing a center the first decision is topic. Some centers are focused on particular skills—for example, reading maps or solving word problems. Some may be focused on specific materials such as geoboards, math manipulatives, or interactive software. Still others center on areas of content such as birds, weather, or mobiles. Some teachers create multiple centers related to a thematic unit, as described later in this chapter. You may choose to create a center for a topic that needs extra reinforcement, one for which you want to provide differentiated assignments for varied student needs, or one for which the limited quantity of materials makes it impossible for a large group of students to work all at a time. For example, Gloria may decide to devote one corner of the room to a center on historical research related to her unit. The material is important for all students, but the limited number of resources available might make it difficult for an entire class of students to be working with them at once.

Once the topic has been determined, the next step is to gather available materials. If, for example, the topic is birds, you could start by gathering books, magazines, video- and audiotapes, examples of nests, and available materials. You would look for computer software and websites related to your topic. Next, you could brainstorm a list of possible activities that could be pursued independently by individuals or small groups. Typically, activities would focus on, or branch off from, key concepts and generalizations planned for the unit. Activities should include opportunities for data gathering, problem solving, individual research, and creative expression, in addition to more traditional vocabulary practice and fact-gathering exercises. Such an activity allows for higher level thinking and authentic learning that may vary from student to student.

The unit on birds might be planned around four general content clusters: general characteristics of birds' and their life cycle, variation in birds' bodies in diverse environments, effects of development on birds' habitats, and observing bird behavior. The list of possible activities could include a crossword puzzle of relevant vocabulary and directions for building a bird feeder found in the science text. Perhaps the library has a computer program that allows students to observe the effects of environmental changes on the bird population. You might locate a website that gives tips on bird-watching or a site where students can add their observations to a database of bird-watchers. In addition, you might decide students could observe the number and types of birds visiting feeders holding different types of seed, research the effects of DDT on large birds, create a brochure teaching younger children about bird-watching or what to do if they spy a nest of baby birds, or even design a fantasy bird adapted to a new environment. Each of these activities has the potential to be carried out independently and reinforces one of the content emphases for this unit. You would need to decide which activities might be done during class time with supervision, which will be required center activities, and which will be electives. It is also important to decide if and how assignments will be varied to meet students' needs, how the center will be formatted, when it will be used, and how you will monitor activities done at the center.

Interest-Development Centers

In most ways, the construction and use of **interest-development centers** parallel those of learning centers. They, too, start with a topic. However, the topic is generally not part of the regular curriculum. It may be selected because of student interest, as an offshoot of a unit, or as an extension of some local or national event. Next, activities are listed. However, because the intent is not to reinforce content but to spur student interest, the activities are likely to be more wide-ranging and less tied to specific generalizations. For example, if you were to plan an interest-development center on photography, you could include activities on constructing pinhole cameras, taking and developing pictures, studying the lives and art of great photographers, the development of photography, historical research based on photographs, the use of photography in motion research, stop-action photography, the development of moving pictures, and so on. The goal is not to have everyone in the class understand basic processes of photography, but to have as many students as possible find some question, idea, or activity that looks interesting enough to investigate. Interest-development centers reinforce not just content, but the values of choice and independence.

Exploratory or Independent Play Areas

In early grades, particularly in pre-K through first grade, classrooms may be organized using **exploratory** or **free play areas** that parallel other center activities in the same ways that informal direct or indirect teaching parallels formalized lesson plans. These areas are typically designed not to organize specific tasks, but to allow students to interact with materials in ways that provide background or reinforcement for concept development. Planned well, they set the stage for plentiful teachable moments. For example, in a second- or third-grade classroom studying communities, center activities might include opportunities to read and write about workers in the community, sort picture cards into those representing goods and services, tally the number of building materials found on Main Street, or construct birdhouses to lure birds to a local park. In a kindergarten classroom, students might engage in some similar activities. However, their classroom might also include a costume area that encourages students to role-play various community workers, a block area with various vehicles, or a play store in which students can pretend to buy and sell goods.

With careful planning and teacher interaction, exploratory areas help students develop and practice key concepts through play. Teachers observing children interacting with materials in these areas have the opportunity to help students label concepts appropriately. For example, when the teacher says, "Look, Susan is dressed in a white lab coat today. Susan, are you going to be a doctor who helps sick people or a veterinarian who helps sick animals?" the comment serves many purposes. It can help students build the generalization that particular types of clothing are associated with specific occupations, that doctors who help animals have a specific name, and that Susan may want to consider a variety of interesting careers. In other cases, the teacher may want to participate in activities to model important ideas. For example, a teacher might say, "Where is your truck going? Mine is bringing apples to the store so people can buy them." The concepts developed in these interactions provide important background for later more sophisticated studies of interdependence in communities.

Reflective use of exploratory centers demands a careful balance between teacher observation and interaction. Students need plentiful opportunities to explore and interact with materials independently. Too much teacher direction can shortcut chances for concept development—while the teacher loses important opportunities for assessment of students' independent activities. However, as indicated earlier, exploratory areas set the stage for modeling and labeling activities that provide essential scaffolding for student learning.

Using Multiple Centers

The abilities to cooperate with others working toward a mutual goal and to select and pursue individual goals are both important aspects of development that should be supported in classrooms. In support of these goals, some teachers use centers as a key organizational feature in their planning. In most of these classes there are multiple centers operating throughout the school year, often organized around a curriculum theme. Because these classrooms include multiple centers, each center is usually simpler than those described previously, often containing only one or two key activities. These change at regular intervals; usually at least some change every week.

There are many ways to organize multiple centers in a classroom. One traditional way is to organize centers around subject areas: a math center, a language arts center, an art center, a science center, and so on. Some teachers use these centers as independent units supplementing concepts in particular areas. For example, if the class were studying plants, the science center might contain books about plants, materials for planting seeds, and so on. The math center might contain math manipulatives and problem-solving activities, and the language arts center a cozy corner for reading.

Another way to use subject-focused centers is to center all activities around a thematic unit. Imagine, for example, the first-grade theme centered around *Clifford the Big Red Dog* described in Chapter 3. For a period of 1 to 2 weeks, all centers might contain activities that relate to Clifford. The language arts center would be full of Clifford books and writing activities relating to Clifford. Perhaps there would be skills activities such as identifying words that start with *cl* or listing synonyms for "big." The math center could contain measuring activities featuring the size of Clifford's paws or dish, or problems that require calculating total pounds of dog food consumed. The science center might lead children to investigate what dogs need to be healthy or what animals are related to dogs. In this case the centers are related by a topic and used to teach and reinforce a variety of concepts and skills. It is also possible to take the same approach to an abstract theme. For example, the kindergarten unit on patterns might contain activities such as reading and writing patterned books in a language arts center, tasks that require creating of patterns with wooden geometric shapes in the math center, and art activities that could range from potato prints to creating patterns using a computer graphics program.

A third approach to organizing multiple centers is to create centers around multiple intelligences rather than subject areas. Imagine the Clifford unit centered around intelligences.

Linguistic	Read and write about Clifford
Logical-Mathematical	Solve problems about Clifford's size
Visual-Spatial	Build a model house for Clifford, plan a yard that could accommodate Clifford comfortably
Bodily-Kinesthetic	Pantomime a story about Clifford
Musical	Create or choose music that expresses the idea of "big"
Interpersonal	Discuss how Clifford might have felt when he grew so big
Intrapersonal	Write or draw about something that makes you different
Naturalist	Learn about animals who are related to dogs, make a chart of their family tree

As you can see, organizing centers around multiple intelligences often leads to some ideas that are very similar but other ideas that are quite different from those organized around traditional subject areas.

REFLECTING ON THE IDEAS

Imagine you are Gloria Jackson, planning multiple centers to support her American Revolution unit. Decide whether you would prefer to organize your centers around subjects or intelligences. Jot down some ideas for center activities and share them with a colleague.

Teachers who use centers as a major part of the curriculum typically have blocks of time set aside for center use. Some teachers divide students into groups and assign them to rotate among centers in a block of time. Other teachers require that students complete specific activities at each center but allow students to choose the order in which they complete the work. There are, of course, many variations on both approaches. Visiting a variety of classrooms that use centers in different ways can be helpful in envisioning the flexibility available with this structure.

Contracts

Learning contracts provide a structure that allows a student and teacher to agree upon a series of tasks to be completed in a given time frame. Many contracts are designed to allow students to work independently through a body of required content or carry out an individual project during times when part of the class is involved in other activities.

The appropriate complexity and duration of contracts vary enormously with the students' maturity and experience with independent work. Most teachers would immediately agree that the first independent contracts completed by primary students should entail no more than one or two work periods. The same is true for many older students who have never worked outside of whole-group teacher-directed lessons before. Like other aspects of independent learning, facility with contracts must be developed gradually, starting with simple short-term forms and working up to more complex tasks.

Most contracts entail specific assignments drawn from the regular curriculum, and optional activities that may be drawn from the curriculum or planned around student interests. Regular curriculum assignments may be specific pages to be completed or concepts that must be mastered in preparation for some type of evaluation. When dealing with basic skills, many contracts can be tailored to individual students' needs through the use of preassessment. Optional activities might be planned by the teacher or the student. The older the students and the more experienced in independent learning, the more input they should have in planning the optional activities. Open-ended activities based on student interests and those emphasizing individual investigations, problem solving, and expressing creative ideas should be an important part of this section of the contract (see Figure 10.1 in Chapter 10 for samples).

Contract activities may be pursued during any independent work time: while other students are involved in skills instruction, when other assignments have been completed, or at any other time designated by the teacher as appropriate for independent work. It is not necessary to have all students working on individual contracts in any given subject. You may want to begin with a small group of students who have demonstrated independent working skills. As the year progresses, the opportunity to work on independent contracts can be expanded or rotated to other students.

Teaching Skills of Independence

The first key to making the transition to independent work is to realize that you will need to teach students how to work independently. It is not sufficient to tell them to be independent; you must *teach* them how to do it. In most cases you may start this process by planning a series of lessons on working independently. These lessons should be planned and executed with as much care, planning, and practice as any other lesson.

If you teach intermediate grades, do not make the mistake of assuming that because your students have been through several years of school, they have already mastered skills of independent learning and are ready to learn on their own. Many students may have had little or no experience with independent tasks. In fact, students who have experienced many years of totally teacher-directed instruction may have particular difficulty making the transition to a more autonomous learning style. Not only will they not have acquired necessary skills of planning, time management, and organization, but they may have come to see the teacher as their primary source of information and direction. They may have little confidence in their own efforts.

In most cases you may start this process by planning a series of lessons on "independent work time." These lessons should be planned and executed with as much (and possibly more) care, planning, and practice as any other teaching units. Major topics should include:

- Becoming independent
- Uses of independent work time
- Planning your time
- What to do if you are stuck or don't understand a task
- How to signal the teacher for assistance or a conference
- Expectations about noise, conversation, and so forth
- Rules about materials
- Choice activities and what to do when tasks are completed
- Long-term versus short-term planning

There are no set procedures that are better than all others. There is no single best strategy for students to follow if they are stuck or don't understand a task. The key is that there must *be* a strategy. Strategies could include asking tablemates, posting a sign or signal so the teacher knows there is a problem, or going on to alternative activities. Students should know which procedures are to be followed and in what order.

Once procedures are established and taught to students, independent work time—the time students are to work on their own without teacher direction—can be initiated. The goal is to move students from seatwork—during which they may be quiet but all activities are chosen, directed, and monitored by the teacher—to a period of time in which many activities are planned, organized, and implemented by students.

The first time you have independent work time, don't try to introduce any new content. The important lesson is independence. Give the students an assignment (preferably one with enough challenge that some students may practice getting assistance) and two or three choice activities. During the work time, do not try to give other instruction. You may wish to circulate and give feedback on their independent work skills, but do not assist with content except through the procedures established for independent work time. After the independent work time, discuss the results with the class. Identify areas of difficulty and devise strategies to reduce them. Students should be aware of independence as a goal and monitor their progress toward that end.

The next stage in establishing independent work time involves students working independently while you work with individuals or small groups. This is a good opportunity to pull together groups needing work on a particular skill, or to work with individuals needing assessment or help with projects. Be sure that you are seated so that you can easily see the class while working with small groups. Students need to know that you are aware of all activities in the room. Try not to interrupt the group to answer individual questions, but refer students to procedures for independent work time. You may wish to circulate and answer questions between your work with instructional groups.

Remember that independent work skills are complex and will be built over time. Early in the year most whole-class choice activities should be fairly simple, building in complexity as the year progresses. You may wish to progress from activities not directly tied to academic content such as brainteasers or logic puzzles, to activities reinforcing class content, to activities that explore new content such as interest-development centers or independent projects. Gradually increase students' responsibilities from short- to long-term planning and time management. Initially, long-term projects may be broken into subsections with due dates that you determine for your students. Later, scheduling may be planned together as a group, and eventually by individuals.

REFLECTING ON THE IDEAS

Imagine you are planning a lesson on "What is an independent worker?" How would you explain independence to your students? What characteristics or behaviors would you emphasize? Be ready to share your ideas in class.

SECTION 6. PULLING IT ALL TOGETHER

One of the most challenging—and interesting—parts of planning for elementary classes is figuring out how everything fits together. Unlike secondary schools where teachers typically plan for single subjects to be taught in specific blocks of time, many elementary teachers plan for multiple subjects to be taught throughout the entire school day. Making decisions about how to use the available time is an important teaching skill.

Using instructional time wisely requires many levels of planning. At the broadest level, teachers often create a global plan for the school year, either for single subjects or interdisciplinary themes, identifying large blocks of time for particular areas of content. This type of planning can be particularly helpful for beginning teachers who are concerned about attending to required content in a timely way.

For example, a primary teacher might block out the science content by months, using the district curriculum guide, state standards, and knowledge of the local environment. If students are to study seeds and plant growth in the Midwest, that study might logically take place in September when many seedpods are evident on local plants, or during May when gardens can be planted outside. A unit on weather could take place any month.

Doing this type of planning for several subjects can allow you to recognize in advance times that may be challenging for particular subjects. For example, if, as part of your languages arts curriculum, you plan to put on a play during January, it is likely that the large amount of rehearsal time needed may cut into time for other subjects. It would be wise to think about incorporating some interdisciplinary objectives during that time period.

Of course, it is also possible to divide the year into time periods according to interdisciplinary themes—or even to have a single theme for the year divided into subcategories. For example, an intermediate teacher might choose to divide the year into quarters with a main theme for each: exploration, interdependence, power, and heroes. Not all subjects will fit each theme, but the themes can be used to organize much of the curriculum. Science content on energy could fit into the "power" theme along with content on the establishment of balance of power in the Constitution and literature exploring uses of power.

Kavolik (1986) suggests creating a yearlong theme that will integrate one or more subjects across time. This could range from using a single subject theme such as "animals" with monthly themes such as "farm animals," "jungle animals," and so forth to organize science instruction, to using the same theme to organize two subjects (for example, science and language arts), to a single theme that organizes three or more subjects for the school year. This type of planning is complex—particularly as the demands to incorporate specific content standards in particular years become more intense—and will not be mastered your first year. But many teachers find that using a yearlong theme helps them make connections among units and provides a helpful context for students.

Like most beginning teachers, you will probably find that many things take more or less time than you planned. Having a yearlong outline will help you gauge whether you and your students are moving toward your long-range outcomes in a timely manner. Talking to more experienced teachers can be very helpful as you make your first attempts to plan for an academic year.

Similar processes will help you plan subjects over the course of shorter periods. When you do your unit planning, you will plan the number of days you expect to spend on each area of content and outcome. Like all good teachers, you will know that plans will be subject to change according to your students' needs, while still being aware of the need to attend to the realities of limited time and important outcomes.

Finally, it will be important to plan the timing and order of subjects and activities through the school day. There is no single way to do this well, but there are some guidelines that will be helpful. First, it is wise to establish routines that give shape to your school day. Some classes start with morning meetings; others have stories after recess, math moments after lunch, or sharing time at the end of the day. A predictable routine not only makes it easier to plan, but provides security to children with high need for structure. Most teachers have a general routine for the times of day they teach specific subjects, plan for center time, or conduct theme instruction. Although these time allocations should never be rigid, they can be helpful in outlining the day.

As you think about your day, plan for variation in whole-group, small-group, and individual activities; quiet times alternating with more physical activity, and so forth. It is important to have enough variety, support, and challenge that each student—regardless of learning style, prior knowledge, or skill level—has appropriate activities every day. Since students differ in so many ways, this will not be easy. It will require careful planning and differentiation of some activities. Most beginning teachers will plan this level of differentiation for only one or two subjects.

Here are two examples of teachers' planning for a morning centered on language arts. Notice how the teachers have allowed for some whole-class activities and some activities that are differentiated according to students' needs. Each day begins with whole-class activities during "morning meeting" (Kriete, 1999) and then varies with student needs.

Teacher 1

Monday	8:30–9:00	Morning meeting
	9:00–9:20	Preassessment of skills
	9:20-10:00	Whole-group experiences with novel

	10:00–10:30	Journals, individual reading, teacher works with students with particular skill needs—some who need additional assistance, some who need additional challenge
Tuesday	8:30–9:00	Morning meeting
	9:00–9:30	Whole-group experiences with novel
	9:30–10:00	Begin small-group assignments in genre: students read one of three novels based on interest and/or skill level
	10:00–10:30	Skills lesson for students identified through preassessment; other students work on genre assignment, contracts, or individual reading
Wednesday	8:30–9:00	Morning meeting
	9:00-9:40	Trios of students work on genre assignments with those reading the same book, using graphic organizer to identify characteristics of characters
	9:40–10:00	Whole-class discussion comparing novels
	10:00–10:30	Journals, as on Monday

Teacher 2

Monday	8:30–9:00	Morning meeting
	9:00–9:40	Introduce theme for the week
	9:40–10:00	Preassessment of language arts skills
	10:00–10:30	Students rotate to two theme centers
Tuesday	8:30–9:00	Morning meeting
	9:00–9:30	Skills instruction for students identified in preassessment; any students not needing skills instruction at centers with choice activities
	9:30–10:00	Students from skills group work on practice activity; teacher introduces other group to contracts
	10:00–10:30	Students from skills group in centers with choice activities; contract students work on contract assignments
Wednesday	8:30–9:00	Morning meeting
	9:00–9:45	Students rotate through required activities at two more centers
	9:45–10:15	Students who need additional skills work (on the basis of Tuesday's practice activity) with teacher, contract students work on contracts, other students choose either to begin contracts or use choice activities at centers
	10:15–10:30	Students with contracts check in with teacher, others with practice or choice activities

Notice the amount of variety that was planned in a short period of time. Students had the opportunity for whole-group, small-group, and individual activities. Both teachers planned ways to provide extra support and practice to students who needed additional skills instruction and additional challenge for those who did not, without resorting to traditional preset groups. Flexible grouping, that varies according to student need, can provide opportunities for individualization within a classroom community.

SUMMARY

As a beginning teacher, you will need a variety of strategies for planning tasks large and small. From the moment-to-moment planning of questions and responses to broader planning for days or months, each decision affects the ways students learn and the relationships in your classroom. You will need strategies for helping students learn independently and activities to help them learn together. You will need activities that focus on your classroom and activities that open your classroom to the world. Mastery of this complex set of strategies is part of the process of becoming a professional educator. As you progress from field experiences to student teaching to the beginning years of your teaching career, you will find that returning to the information in this chapter will help you incorporate these ideas in increasingly sophisticated ways. Support from other teachers, professional reading, and staff development also will be important as you continue the journey into professionalism.

■ Practice Activity: Observing Questioning

Observe a teacher's questioning patterns. Use a seating chart to keep track of the number of boys and girls who are questioned and the number of higher level and lower level questions asked. Do any students ask questions? Who? What patterns do you find?

■ ■ ■

■ Practice Activity: Interviewing Teachers

Do one or both of the following:

1. Interview a teacher about the processes he or she uses to do long-range planning. If possible, obtain a copy of the long-range plan for one or more subject areas. Compare your findings with a colleague. Think about the processes you think will work best for you.
2. Interview a teacher about the structure he or she uses to organize the school day. Make a template or diagram to describe the day's routines. Compare your findings with colleagues.

■ ■ ■

UNIT PREPARATION

During this time you should be refining your lesson and assessment plans. Using what you have learned in this chapter, consider how you can add variety, challenge, and interest to your plans. Your instructor may have specific strategies or assignments to add to your basic unit. For example, you may want to create an independent learning activity that could be placed in a center to supplement your unit, or compile a list of children's resources that could facilitate independent work.

PORTFOLIO ACTIVITIES

Create a plan for your school day, outlining the routines you believe will be important. Be prepared to discuss your choices and how you believe they will support student learning.

Create and use a learning center. Include one or two photographs of your center in use, along with descriptions of the activities.

SEARCH THE WEB

Continue to search the web for new lesson ideas and materials. One of the richest resources is provided by the federal government of the United States.

FREE (Federal Resources for Educational Excellence) is a source of thousands of materials that can be used by teachers.

> http://www.ed.gov/free

Education World provides lesson plan databases in all subject areas and monthly updates regarding new sites on particular topics.

> http://www.education-world.com

In addition to the Virtual Architecture site mentioned previously, you'll want to review sites on educational technology listed on the Companion Website under "Technology and Teaching."

REFERENCES

Atwood, V. A., & Wilen, W. W. (1991). Wait time and effective social studies instruction: What can research in science education tell us? *Social Education, 55*(3), 179–181.

American Association of University Women (AAUW) Educational Foundation. (1998). *Gender gaps: Where schools still fail our children.* Washington, DC: Author.

Aronson, E., Blaney, N., Stephan, C., Sikes, J., & Snapp, M. (1978). *The jigsaw classroom.* Beverly Hills, CA: Sage.

Brice-Heath, S., & Mangiola, L. (1991). *Children of promise.* Washington, DC: National Education Association.

Bridwell, N. (1997). *Clifford the big red dog.* New York: Scholastic Books.

Brophy, J. (1998). *Motivating students to learn.* Boston: McGraw-Hill.

Caine, R. N., & Caine, G. C. (1997). *Education on the edge of possibility.* Alexandria, VA: Association for Supervision and Curriculum Development.

Clarke, J. (1994). Pieces of the puzzle: The jigsaw method. In S. Sharan (*Ed.*), *Handbook of cooperative learning methods* (pp. 34–50). Westport, CT: Greenwood Press.

Cohen, E. G., Lotan, R. A., Whitcomb, J. A., Balderrama, M. V., Cossey, R., & Swanson, P. E. (1994). Complex instruction: Higher order thinking in heterogeneous classrooms. In S.

Sharan (Ed.), *Handbook of cooperative learning methods* (82–96). Westport, CT: Greenwood Press.

Cohen, E. G. (1986). *Designing group work*. New York: Teachers College Press.

Cohen, E. G. (1998). Making cooperative learning equitable. *Educational Leadership, 56*(1), 18–21.

Costa, A., & Liebman, R. (1997). *Supporting the spirit of learning: When process is content.* Thousand Oaks, CA: Corwin Press.

Conyers, J. G., & Rauscher, W. C. (December 2000–January 2001). An antarctic adventure. *Educational Leadership, 58*(4), 69–72.

Dede, C. (Ed.). (1998). *ASCD Yearbook 1998: Learning with technology*. Alexandria, VA: Association for Supervision and Curriculum Development.

Draper, R. J. (1997, September–October). Jigsaw: Because reading your math book shouldn't be a puzzle. *The Clearing House, 71*, 33–36.

Gall, J., & Gall, M. (1990). Outcomes of the discussion method. In W. Wilen (Ed.), *Teaching and learning through discussion: The theory and practice of the discussion method.* Springfield, IL: Chas. J. Thomas.

Glasser, W. (1990). *The quality school: Managing students without coercion.* New York: Harper Row.

Glasser, W. (1997, April). A new look at school failure and school success. *Phi Delta Kappan, 78*(8), 597–603.

Good, T., & Brophy, J. (1997). *Looking in classrooms* (7th ed.). New York: Longman.

Harris, J. (2002). *Virtual architecture* (2nd ed.). Eugene, OR: International Society for Technology in Education.

Healy, J. M. (1998). *Failure to connect: How computers affect our children's minds—for better or worse.* New York: Simon & Schuster.

Jacoby, B. (Ed.). (1996). *Service-learning in higher education.* San Francisco: Jossey-Bass.

Johnson, D., & Johnson, R. (1994). Learning together. In S. Sharan (Ed.), *Handbook of cooperative learning methods* (51–65). Westport, CT: Greenwood Press.

Johnson, D., & Johnson, R. (1999). *Learning together and alone: Cooperative, competitive and individualistic learning.* Boston: Allyn & Bacon.

Kavolik, S. (1986). *Teachers make the difference.* Village of Oak Creek, AZ: Susan Kavolik and Associates.

Kavolik, S. (1994). Brain-compatible learning. *Video Journal of Education, 3*(6).

Kriete, R. (1999). *The morning meeting book.* Greenfield, MA: Northeast Foundation for Children.

Lou, Y., Abrami, P., Spence, J.C., Paulson, C., Chambers, B., & d'Appollorio, S. (1996). Within-class grouping: A meta-analysis. *Review of Educational Research, 66*(4), 423–458.

Marzano, R. J., Pickering, D. J., Pollock, J. E. (2001). *Classroom instruction that works: Research-based strategies for increasing student achievement.* Alexandria, VA: Association for Supervision and Curriculum Development.

Medina, K., Pigg, M., Desler, G., & Gorospe, G. (2001). Teaching generation.com. *Phi Delta Kappan, 82*(8), 616–619.

Rosenshine, B. V., Meister, C., & Chapman, S. (1996, Summer). Teaching students to generate questions: A review of intervention studies. *Review of Educational Research, 66*, 181–221.

Rowe, M. (1974). Pausing phenomena: Influence on quality of instruction. *Journal of Psycholinguistic Research, 3*, 203–224.

Sparks, D. (1998) The educator, examined: An interview with Phillip Schlechty. *Journal of Staff Development, 19*(3), 38–42.

Sharan, Y., & Sharan, S. (1992). *Expanding cooperative learning through group investigations.* New York: Teachers College Press.

Slavin, R. E. (1995). *Cooperative learning: Theory, research and practice* (2nd ed.). Boston: Allyn & Bacon.

Slavin, R. E. (1994). Student teams—Achievement divisions. In S. Sharan (Ed.), *Handbook of cooperative learning methods* (3–19). Westport, CT: Greenwood Press.

Stacey, K., Rice, D., Hurst, K., & Langer, C. (1997). *Academic service-learning K–12 training manual.* Ypsilanti, MI: Eastern Michigan University.

Tapscott, D. (1999). Educating the net generation. *Educational Leadership,* 56(5), 6–11.

Tell, C. (2000, October). The I-generation—from toddlers to teenagers: A conversation with Jane M. Healy. *Educational Leadership,* 58(2), 8–15.

Tishman, S., Perkins, D., & Jay, E. (1995). *The thinking classroom.* Needham, MA: Allyn & Bacon.

Tobin, K. (1980). The effect of an extended teacher wait time on science achievement. *Journal of Research in Science Teaching,* 17, 469–475.

Tobin, K., & Campie, W. (1982). Relationships between classroom process variables and middle school science achievement. *Journal of Educational Psychology,* 74, 441–454.

United States Department of Labor. Secretary's Commission on Achieving Necessary Skills. (1993). *Teaching the SCANS competencies.* Washington, DC: U.S. Department of Labor.

Walberg, H.J. (1999). Productive teaching. In H.J. Waxman & H.C. Walberg (Eds.), *New directions for teaching practice and research* (pp. 75–104). Berkeley, CA: McCutcheon Publishing Corporation.

Weinman, J., & Haag, P. (1999, February). Gender equity in cyberspace. *Educational leadership,* 56(5), 44–49.

CHAPTER 10

Differentiation and Diversity

CHAPTER OVERVIEW

Throughout this text we have discussed the importance of recognizing individual differences in students and suggested various approaches to instruction. These strategies are helpful in planning lessons that are appropriate for students with a variety of learning styles, interests, and abilities. This chapter takes another look at strategies that will be useful as you work to differentiate the curriculum for a variety of learners. This chapter offers information and techniques to help you make decisions regarding the particular needs of students with educational disabilities, gifted and talented students, culturally diverse and bilingual students, and students in urban schools. The first section of the chapter discusses the principles and characteristics of differentiated instruction. Sections 2–5 focus on the characteristics and needs of students discussed, describe teaching strategies appropriate for such students, and explain how these strategies may sometimes be useful for all students.

■ *Opening Activity*

Hannah Lewis, a first-year teacher, sits at her desk at the end of a long October day. So far, she has found her third-grade class to be extremely hectic but rewarding. Hannah has enjoyed the diversity in her large urban school. Her carefully prepared management system has proved valuable in creating a classroom atmosphere that is warm but businesslike. Although much of the material has been review, Hannah is pleased that most of her students are completing their assignments successfully. Best of all, Hannah feels as if she is beginning to really know her students—their likes and dislikes, strengths, weaknesses, and interests. Today, however, that knowledge is starting to cause her some concern.

The students are all so different. It is easiest to worry about John. Although he is the oldest child in his class, John has the most difficulty learning basic skills. His reading is slow and laborious and he has not mastered basic writing skills. So far he has not caused any trouble, but last year's teacher said he used to argue with her and would not participate in class.

Maria, on the other hand, has caused some problems already. Her ready wit sends the class into fits of laughter, often at the teacher's expense. She is a leader on the playground, devising games and fantasies for others to play or act out. Her work is erratic. Although her creative writing is outstanding, her math and spelling are average at best, and she frequently hands in late or incomplete assignments. Hannah often wonders if Maria is really listening to her.

Rosa is another story. Raised in a Spanish-speaking home, Rosa spent her first 2 years in school in a bilingual program. She speaks English fairly well, but her grammar is weak and her reading is not much better than John's. Rosa never volunteers in class, and Hannah is seldom sure whether she understands the lesson.

Joe is the star of the class. Whenever a lesson is lagging or a point seems unclear, Hannah can count on Joe to come up with the correct answer. His assignments are always complete and accurate. If a topic is mentioned in class, Joe frequently finds a newspaper article or book from home that can serve as an additional resource. Hannah has heard other teachers reminiscing about how much they enjoyed Joe in previous years. Hannah enjoys him, too, but she continues to have nagging doubts about the work he is doing in class. Is Joe really learning anything?

As she thinks about John, Maria, Rosa, and Joe and her carefully prepared unit on mythic heroes and heroines, Hannah wonders how she can ever teach the subject in a way that will reach all her students.

Think for a moment about John, Maria, Rosa, and Joe. What characteristics of these students may have an impact on their learning in Hannah's class?

John: _____

_____

Maria: _____

_____

Rosa: _____

_____

Joe: _____

_____

■ ■ ■

Hannah is facing a common dilemma. Although teachers learn important principles of planning and instruction, those principles are always put into practice on a particular day, in a particular lesson, and with a particular group of students. The artistry in teaching consists of knowing how to take into account the context of the lesson—that is, which principles and strategies are most important to emphasize in each set of circumstances.

This chapter will help you differentiate your planning and instruction for individual variation, with special emphasis on the students almost every teacher encounters: learners with special needs. The following sections will guide you in planning for students like John, Maria, Rosa, and Joe. As you read, remember that none of the special needs addressed are mutually exclusive. A student may be gifted and bilingual; a slower learner may come from a cultural background that affects school performance. There are, of course, many other combinations. It is important to consider each student first as an individual. Only then is it helpful to think about some of the special needs often found in particular groups of young people.

 ## SECTION 1. DIFFERENTIATED INSTRUCTION

As we discussed in Chapter 6, differentiated instruction is instruction that is designed to flex to meet the varying needs of students within a class. If you intend for all children to learn, you must plan instruction that can accommodate many types of learners with widely varied backgrounds. You will need to plan some activities for the whole class, some for small groups, and some for individual students. Now that you know more about different types of lessons and instructional strategies, you can better reflect on how differentiation can (and must) occur. This section elaborates on principles and characteristics of differentiated instruction. The following sections discuss a variety of types of special needs that will require even more differentiation than you might initially plan.

Tomlinson (1999) outlines principles that guide differentiated classrooms. Think about how many of these principles already guide your planning.

1. The teacher focuses on the essentials. Teachers in differentiated classrooms focus instruction around core concepts, principles, and skills of a discipline. (See Tomlinson, 2000, for a discussion of standards-based instruction and differentiation.)

2. The teacher attends to student differences. Teachers in differentiated classrooms are aware of individual differences and of their responsibility to all the students in their classrooms.

3. Assessment and instruction are inseparable. In these classrooms assessment is ongoing and diagnostic. Instructional decisions are based on assessment, not on what is found on the next page of a teacher's guide.

4. The teacher modifies content, process, and products. This principle provides some cues as to basic ways instruction can be differentiated in response to assessment. The teacher may modify the *content* that is learned, the *processes* by which it is learned, or the *products* through which students demonstrate their learning. Modifying content may mean skipping practice of already mastered skills or additional practice activities on content other students may have learned in previous years. It also can mean variation by interest or prior knowledge. Modifying process may mean that some students work with the teacher in a small group while others work independently on similar material. It could mean that some students receive a homework assignment to read about key terms before they are introduced in class, or others are given resource materials too complex for most of the class to analyze. Modifying products could entail choices among different products or variations on a product assigned to different students. For example, if all students are writing historical fiction, some students may be challenged to write a new ending for an already familiar story, some to recount a major event in story form, and still others to write in first person—a task requiring greater abstraction and flexible thinking. All three are higher level tasks but they provide varying levels of difficulty.

Differentiated classrooms do not make these modifications all day long, only when they make sense. Tomlinson (1999) recommends:

> Modify a curricular element only when (1) you see a student need and (2) you are convinced that modification increases the likelihood that the learner will understand important ideas and use important skills more thoroughly as a result. (p. 11)

5. All students participate in respectful work. A differentiated classroom does not mean a room in which some students learn important content or engage in challenging higher level thinking and others do not. All children work toward essential goals. But teachers in these classrooms understand that we do not show respect for student differences by ignoring them. Respectful teaching entails respecting the readiness level of each student, expecting each student to grow, offering escalating challenges as students develop understanding, and providing all students with equally interesting, important, and engaging work. The writing example given earlier represents an effort to provide all students with interesting creative work while still allowing differing levels of challenge.

6. The teacher and students collaborate in learning. The teacher in a differentiated classroom is the leader, but students are important participants in the community. Students

help the teacher identify appropriate goals, monitor progress, analyze successes and failures, and learn from experience. As they do this, they become active participants in their own learning.

7. The teacher balances group and individual norms. Differentiated instruction requires attention to group goals (often outlined as state standards and benchmarks) and individual goals. If a student enters a grade without having mastered key parts of earlier curriculum, the teacher will need to balance targeted activities designed to teach earlier skills with supported instruction in grade-level content as appropriate. Both sets of goals are essential. In a parallel fashion, students who enter a grade well above the expected skill level will need both group and individual goals in order to learn.

8. The teacher and students work together flexibly. As described in earlier chapters, good teaching entails great variety in strategy, group structure, amount of choice, and so on. Differentiated instruction requires a large and varied repertoire of teaching strategies and the flexibility to use them in diverse combinations as they meet students' needs.

Many of the strategies we have discussed can be used to facilitate differentiation. Centers can be a natural setting for activities at varied levels. A similar structure called **stations** sets out areas of the classroom in which students can work on varied tasks simultaneously. Tomlinson (1999) describes a fourth-grade math class with five stations. In the teaching station, students have direct instruction from the teacher. In the proof place, students use manipulatives or drawings to solve problems and defend their solutions to a partner. In the practice place, students practice the type of computation on which they need work. In the shop, they work on application problems helping out a shopkeeper named Mr. Fuddle who always seems to have a mathematical dilemma. In the project place, students work on long-term projects that require the use of mathematics—for example, redesigning the classroom or planning and conducting surveys. On some days the whole class may work together, but on most days students are assigned to a station through a names-on-pegboard system. Not all students spend the same amount of time at each station, but all students go to all stations in the course of 1 to 2 weeks.

Contracts also can facilitate differentiation. They can be used for individual assignments or as a class activity with two or three possible contracts—each with challenging options appropriate to a particular level. Figure 10.1 shows the beginning of two possible contracts that might be used in a unit on insects. Another similar structure, agendas, provides students with an individualized list of tasks to be completed in a specified amount of time. Generally, students determine the order in which they work on the tasks—often while the teacher circulates, coaching and monitoring. Agendas can work well in conjunction with centers. Figure 10.2 is an example of a personal agenda.

Tiered activities is a key strategy when teachers want to ensure that students all work on key skills or essential ideas but still address varied learning needs. For example, a student who struggles with reading or abstract thinking still needs to be able to understand the dilemmas of a character in a particular story. A student who reads several years above grade level still needs to learn from the character's choices. If both students are given identical assignments, at least one is likely to be frustrated and experience limited learning. A tiered activity could be used to provide multiple avenues to the same key learning, but with varied levels of difficulty. Students could discuss the plot and the influences on the character in a whole-class discussion or in heterogeneous groups with guide questions. Some

FIGURE 10.1 Sample Contract Segments

Contract 1

Insect Study

Name _____

1. Draw a diagram of an insect, illustrating all the major body parts.
2. Choose one insect and create a flip book illustrating its life cycle. Attach a written description of the life cycle to the flip book. Explain how this insect's life cycle is like or unlike that of other insects.
3. Using your science notebook, observe at least five insects in your environment. Sketch or describe each insect. Note when and where you observed it, what the insect was doing, and what you observed about the insect's environment.

Contract 2

Name _____

Science Choose an insect that interests you. Draw a diagram of your insect, labeling all important body parts.	Science Investigate your insect's environment. Write a description of the environment and how your insect is suited for the environment(s) in which it lives.	Science/Technology Use a search engine to locate three sites that describe your insect. Using the rating form, rate the sites for information, ease of use, and potential bias.
Music Create a work of music inspired by your insect. You may use the collection of percussion instruments or other instruments of choice.	Language Arts Write your autobiography if you were your chosen insect. Create at least three illustrations for your story.	Math Calculate how much space would be needed to hold 10,000 of your insect. If you want, calculate the space for 1 million insects

---

students (including the first student) might be assigned to create a collage illustrating the influences they felt were most important in the character's choices. Others might be assigned to write a dialogue in which one character explains the choice to another. Still other students (perhaps including the more advanced student) could be assigned to write about an original character who responded to similar influences in a different way.

Another approach to varied reading levels is a reading workshop program (Towle, 2000), one of several approaches to reading designed to address individual needs in a heterogeneous class without resorting to traditional static groups. In a reading workshop, skills lessons are targeted at either the whole class or small groups, depending on need. The bulk of reading time is spent on self-selected reading and responding. The details of the program are too complex to describe here, but it is important to note that a good language arts

FIGURE 10.2 Personal Agenda

Personal Agenda for _____

Starting Date _____

Completion Goal _____

Teacher and Student Initials	Task	Special Instructions
	Complete first-person descriptions of Boston Massacre.	Be sure that at least one of your descriptions is from someone not involved in the combat.
	Read your historical novel.	Keep track of new vocabulary in your reading log. Make notes of areas in which you identify historical consistency or inaccuracies.
	Complete problem-solving activities 26–30.	Try to find at least three ways to solve problem 28.
	Write a rough draft of your plan for your demonstration project using simple machines. After the draft has been reviewed, complete the plan according to the directions.	Do not begin your final draft or your project until the rough draft has been reviewed. Remember that the final report must be word processed.

program will have multiple opportunities for individual choices in reading and writing. Any approach that allows for differential assignments can facilitate differentiation.

One of the key skills for teachers who want to differentiate instruction is learning to differentiate within heterogeneous cooperative groups. This type of differentiation can link the advantages of working with many types of students to the strengths of assignments targeted to specific needs. Schniedewind and Davidson (2000) describe several strategies for differentiating within cooperative learning. One strategy entails varying the complexity of tasks within heterogeneous groups. For example, in a jigsaw activity students can each become expert on key pieces of information, but they need not work from resources of equal length or complexity. Cooperative groups also can enhance individualized work. For example, students can help partners study individualized spelling lists or help each other stick to time lines on long-term projects.

Carefully planned peer tutoring activities can benefit many students. Keep in mind, however, that pairing students from the two extremes of your class—those who learn most easily and quickly with those who have the most learning difficulties—may not be the best strategy. Students learn best from a model they perceive is similar to themselves. If the perceived differences are too great, modeling may be less effective. And in any peer tutoring structure it is important to make sure that tutoring represents only a limited portion of the school day—particularly if the tutor is already highly skilled in the content being taught. For the majority of their day, tutors, too, should be learning content that is new to them. In their article, Schniedewind and Davidson (2000) respond to an important question about differentiated instruction.

> Do students feel awkward or resentful about such differentiated assignments? We have found that students know one another's capabilities quite well although they don't necessarily talk about them. One teacher explained to her students that differentiated assignments help her fulfill her job of challenging each student . We've found that students feel more comfortable when teachers acknowledge and engage them in discussion about the tension-producing subject of academic difference. Afterward, students can focus on learning with less anxiety. (p. 25)

We have found that a matter-of-fact acknowledgment of differences among students—in the context of a classroom in which it is clear all are valued—does, in fact, merely recognize what students already know. Different students are good at different things. Recognizing and appreciating those differences, rather than acting as if difference is something to hide, can be the basis of an accepting community and provide chances to genuinely celebrate differing accomplishments.

Whatever the strategy, the key to successful planning for elementary classes is to remember that classes never learn anything. Only individual children learn, one at a time. Whatever lessons and units you plan must be adapted in ways that meet individual students' needs. You might want to look again at the sample schedules for morning activities in Chapter 9. Think about how the movement from large- to small-group activities can ensure that all students have the opportunity to learn. As you look at those plans and think about the challenge of meeting so many students' needs, you probably are feeling a little overwhelmed. Sometimes good teaching can feel like an overwhelming task to even the most experienced professionals. Few teachers with typical-sized classes can differentiate for every student or for every lesson. It is important to begin to prioritize your lessons to determine when differentiation is most important.

First, you'll want to consider the content. Content that focuses on basic skills or that is primarily a review from previous years is most likely to be strengthened through differentiation for able learners. Content that requires numerous prerequisite skills or complex abstract thinking may pose enough of a challenge that some students will need extra levels of support. Next, consider the students themselves, particularly those with the most extreme individual needs. If you have students whose current levels of achievement are a year or more above or below grade level, working with those students' most clear-cut needs can provide a place to start. Finally, in planning for a day or a week, consider each student's experience over that period of time. A reasonable rule of thumb is that all students—even those whose needs are significantly different from the norm—should spend at least part of every day engaging in activities that specifically target their needs. The following sections discuss the students for whom differentiation will be most crucial, those with particularly diverse needs.

SECTION 2. TEACHING STUDENTS WITH EDUCATIONAL DISABILITIES

Section 2 Objectives

After you have completed this section, you should be able to

1. describe characteristics of students with educational disabilities;
2. describe special instructional needs of students with educational disabilities;
3. design instructional strategies that are appropriate for such students;
4. plan lessons in your curriculum area that are adapted to meet the needs of students with disabilities; and
5. explain how activities that are appropriate for students with educational disabilities may be used in lessons for an entire class.

For much of the history of American education, students with physical, emotional, and mental disabilities were taught in special educational environments by instructors trained to teach such children. In the case of a severe disability, the student was taught in a location other than a regular school. If the disability was modest, the student's classroom was typically in a public school, usually in an area set apart from the school's traffic patterns. In either case, young people with disabilities were isolated from the regular public education system and thus from teachers and students in regular classes. However, the second half of the 20th century has seen dramatic changes in the education of such students. Almost every public school classroom now includes one or more students with educational disabilities. Many districts still employ specialists trained in various disabilities, but all teachers must become familiar with the major types of disabilities and strategies for accommodating young people with disabilities in the regular classroom.

What Are Educational Disabilities?

A **disability** is a condition that results in a reduced competency to perform some task or behavior, whether the condition is physical, emotional, or intellectual. Disabilities that impede regular educational activities are called *educational disabilities*. Everyone suffers from some degree of disability, in the sense that we all have traits that keep us from performing some tasks at optimum levels. Many people have poor eyesight or poor color discrimination, are awkward at sports, or are shy with strangers. However, these disabilities are mild enough that we can easily reduce their effects or correct them. It may be useful to think of disabilities as existing within a continuum of competency. For example, consider a continuum of visual acuity, from individuals with excellent eyesight (perhaps those who can read the numbers on the jerseys from the top row of a football stadium!) to those who have no sense of sight. Somewhere in the lower 25% of that continuum we would begin to classify persons as disabled. Reduced competency can be categorized as *mild, moderate, severe,* or *profound*. The major classifications of disabilities include students with the following impairments:

1. **Mental impairments**. Such students function less well than the norm at all levels of learning. In the activity at the beginning of this chapter, John may have mild mental impairment. Many students with mild mental impairments need extra assistance with

both traditional school curriculum and basic social and communication skills. In its moderate and severe form, intellectual impairment is accompanied by difficulty in adapting to regular classroom expectations and routines and difficulty in getting along with the teacher and other students. Children with such impairments will need instruction giving special support in daily living skills.

2. **Physical or other health impairments**. Such students have disabilities that reduce their capability to perform psychomotor tasks involving small- and large-muscle movement, such as manipulating writing instruments and books, or moving around the classroom. Often the impairment results in reduction in the student's stamina, alertness, and vitality. However, many students with physical impairments have no mental impairment. Common causes of physical impairment are birth defects, disease, and accidents.

3. **Sensory impairments**. Such students have reduced visual or auditory competency. Some teachers have performed a great service for students and their parents by identifying a mild sensory impairment that could be compensated for by glasses or hearing enhancements. In more severe cases, the young person has limited or no vision or hearing, and adapted teaching must be used to reduce the effects of the disability on learning. Many forms of adaptive technology can assist students with sensory impairments in learning and communicating what they have learned.

4. **Speech impairments**. Such students have reduced competency in speech communications. A common source of speech impairment is a severe hearing loss that reduces the student's ability to reproduce speech patterns.

5. **Emotional impairments**. Such students display repeated inappropriate behavior to the extent that it affects their academic growth, social maturity, and relationships with adults and peers. It is important to distinguish a person who acts out from time to time from the person with emotional impairments whose inappropriate behaviors are frequent and distinctive. Some individuals with emotional impairments are identified because they are verbally or physically aggressive, and prone to repeated outbursts that upset classroom routines. However, students with emotional impairments may also be fearful, passive, or withdrawn.

6. **Learning disabilities**. Such students demonstrate a reduced competency to perform some behaviors, while performing as well as or better than peers on other tasks. Unfortunately, because of the limited nature of the disability and an individual's efforts to compensate for areas of weakness, learning disabilities may not be identified until many years of schooling have passed. Conversely, some young people are wrongly identified as learning disabled when the true cause of disability may be a physical, mental, or emotional impairment. In fact, of all the disability areas, learning disabilities are the most controversial. Because of the imprecise nature of diagnosis, there are major disagreements about the nature of a learning disability and the criteria to be used to classify a student as learning disabled. More than 40 definitions for *learning disabilities* have been proposed, but none has been universally accepted (Heward, 2000). Varying types of learning disabilities may impair a student's ability to read, attend to stimuli, understand figurative language, or accurately assess spatial relationships.

Some kinds of impairments are much more commonly occurring than others. Ninety-one percent of the children and youth receiving special education services are reported in four disability categories: learning disabilities (51.1%), speech and language impairments (20.1%), mental impairments (11.4%), and emotional disturbances

(8.6%). The vast majority of these individuals (85%) have mild disabilities. Children with disabilities in special education represent approximately 10% of the entire school-age population (Heward, 2000). These statistics make it clear that virtually every teacher will encounter students with disabilities in general education classes.

All of the listed impairments may occur in a range from mild, to moderate, to severe, to profound. At some level of disability a person loses the capacity to function in society without external assistance. The degree to which individuals are assisted determines the degree of handicap they experience. A **handicap** is the disadvantage one suffers from the effects of a disability. The extent to which an individual is handicapped is a result of both the severity of the disability and the degree of assistance offered by society. For example, a person with physical disabilities who uses a wheelchair will be handicapped by facilities that are inaccessible, but not in areas designed to accommodate wheelchair access. A student with a learning disability who is unable to read a science test is handicapped if required to take a written exam. Although it is impossible to prevent all handicaps caused by disabilities, teachers have a responsibility to minimize the handicapping effects of disabilities in their classrooms. In the case of a reading disability, the teacher could allow the student to take the science test orally. The student would still have a learning disability, but would not be handicapped in taking the science exam.

Educational Disabilities in School

Understanding the relationship between a disability and a handicap is helpful in interpreting the motivation for the events of the late 1960s and 1970s that culminated in the passage of the Individuals with Disabilities Education Act (IDEA). Originally known as the Education for All Handicapped Children Act (EHA) or Public Law 94-142, this legislation has been amended four times. The 1990 amendments renamed the law, often referred to by its acronym, IDEA.

The purpose of IDEA is to

. . . assure that all children with disabilities have available to them. . . . a free appropriate public education which emphasizes special education and related services designed to meet their unique need, to assure that the rights of children with disabilities and their parents or guardians are protected, to assist states and localities to provide for the education of all children with disabilities, and to assess and assure the effectiveness of efforts to educate children with disabilities. (IDEA, 20 U. S. C., 1400 [c])

The law has six major principles.

1. Schools must educate all children. Regardless of the nature or the severity of the disability, no child with disabilities can be excluded from public education.
2. Schools must used nonbiased and multifactored methods of assessing disabilities. Tests must be administered in the child's native language, and placement cannot be made on the basis of a single score. This principle is intended to protect students from inaccurate assessments affected by cultural bias or single observations.
3. Education for students with disabilities must be provided at public expense, including an **individualized educational program (IEP)** designed to meet the child's unique needs.

4. Students must be educated in the least restrictive environment (LRE) appropriate to their needs. Students with disabilities cannot be segregated into special classes or schools unless the nature of their disabilities is such that they cannot receive appropriate education in a general education setting with supports. To ensure that students have access to the least restrictive environment possible, schools must provide a continuum of services.

5. Schools must provide due process to protect the rights of students with disabilities and their parents. Parental consent must be obtained for evaluations and placement decisions. When the school and the parents disagree, specific requirements for due process must be adhered to.

6. Parents (and where appropriate, students) should have the opportunity to collaborate with schools in the design and implementation of specialized services (Heward, 2000).

In a 1987 review of the impact of the Education for All Handicapped Children Act, Singer and Butler concluded that the EHA had been a singular success. They stated that 20 years earlier, most Americans

> would have flatly denied the feasibility of instituting in every school system in the country, a program of individualized education, however imperfect, for 11 percent of the nation's children. Yet, this was done within a few years of EHA's implementation. Regular education teachers, special education teachers, school administrators and others at the local level have demonstrated a remarkable degree of dedication to the law's goals and an equally remarkable willingness to subsidize the program with their own efforts. (p. 151)

In fairness, it must be noted that this success was not accomplished without significant problems. Then and now, the sheer size of the change and the number of disability areas created administrative, logistical, clerical, and instructional burdens for the schools. Each disability area has its unique characteristics and challenges. Many students with physical and sensory impairments need special equipment, materials, and support personnel. Some students who are classified as disabled qualify for government support because they are also economically disadvantaged; others do not. Some disabilities are hard to identify, particularly in students with multiple disabilities or students for whom English is not the primary language. Despite such difficulties, however, IDEA has successfully mandated enormous changes in the education of students with disabilities.

To provide all students with the least restrictive environment possible, a continuum of services has evolved.

1. *Full-time regular classroom.* In this option, students with disabilities spend the entire school day in a regular classroom. Placing students with disabilities in regular classrooms has been called mainstreaming or, more recently, inclusion. The teacher in a classroom with one or more students with disabilities may receive support and consultative services from a special education specialist. In some cases, the specialist may also provide supplementary services or instruction to students within the regular classroom. In other cases the student may be accompanied by a part- or full-time assistant appropriate to his or her disability.

2. *Regular classroom for a majority of the school program.* In this case, the student has the outside support of a resource teacher trained in special education and other professional personnel who specialize in the particular disability involved. The student is with his regular student peers for most of the day but may spend several hours each week in a resource setting.

3. *Self-contained classroom for a majority of the school program.* In this option, the student is taught in a special education classroom and mainstreamed into the regular classroom for varying amounts of time and for appropriate content activities. Such students may join a regular classroom for a limited amount of time each morning or afternoon, or for special subjects such as music or physical education.

4. *Self-contained classroom for the instructional program but within the regular school building.* Placement in the regular building permits the student with disabilities to participate in individually prescribed experiences and extracurricular activities.

5. *Separate school.* When special schools are located on the same campus as other school buildings, the proximity can permit students with disabilities to participate in appropriate parts of the extracurricular program. Students with severe disabilities may need more protective services than can be provided by public schools and require full-time residential programs.

It is likely that you will have one or more students with disabilities in your classroom for all or part of the school day. Each student will require an IEP. An IEP must include the following, for each student:

(A) a statement of the child's present levels of educational performance,
(B) a statement of annual goals, including short-term instructional objectives,
(C) a statement of the specific educational services to be provided and the extent to which the child will be able to participate in regular educational programs,
(D) the projected date for initiation and anticipated duration of such services, and
(E) appropriate objective criteria and evaluation procedures and schedules for determining, on at least an annual basis, whether instructional objectives are being met.
(Public Law 94-142, 1975, Sec. 4, a, 19)

In addition to describing the nature of the IEP, the law stipulated that the plan must be cooperatively developed by the student's teacher and the student's parent(s) or guardian, and approved by the designated school administrator or special education supervisor. Although the federal law does not do so, some states require that IEPs be prepared not just for students with disabilities but for students identified as gifted as well. If a student in your classroom requires an IEP, a specialist should work with you to plan the individualized program and to clarify your role in carrying out the plan.

Note that the IEP has a similar structure to a unit plan or lesson design. Each is a system beginning with goals that are analyzed and phrased as clearly stated objectives. Activities are designed to help students meet the objectives, and evaluation procedures are used to determine if the objectives have been met. If additional instruction is needed, it is provided. Throughout instruction, there is consideration for students' learning styles, prior knowledge, and experience.

The major differences between an IEP and a unit plan or lesson design are that the IEP is a learning prescription for an individual student and that parents are more directly involved in its preparation and execution. You may also recognize that the IEP rests on criterion-referenced evaluation rather than norm-referenced evaluation principles—that is, evaluation is based on a student's achieving a predetermined performance standard rather than on a comparison with the performance of other students. Because of the attractive characteristics of the IEP process, its individual perspective on achievement, the way in which it involves parents, and its systematic structure, some educators have proposed that all students be taught through individualized educational plans.

REFLECTING ON THE IDEAS

Assume that an influential group of citizens recommended that all students be taught through the IEP process. What would be the advantages and disadvantages of that recommendation? Is it a worthy goal? Is it workable and practical? Briefly explain your views, and discuss the recommendation with others.

Inclusion

The passage of IDEA has meant that many students with disabilities spend all or part of the day in regular classrooms. This practice is often referred to as inclusion. There is no clear consensus on the definition of inclusion (Kauffman & Hallahan, 1994–1995). Some individuals use the term only to refer to full-time placement of students with disabilities in general education classrooms. Others would include more limited time in regular classrooms within the definition. Some advocates for individuals with disabilities believe that the best way to ensure equitable treatment for students with disabilities is to place all students in regular classrooms all the time. This practice is known as **full inclusion**. Inclusion involves the integration of students with severe disabilities into regular classrooms. Generally the educational programs for students with severe impairments center on the development of functional life skills—eating, communication, and hygiene. Although such students often spend the majority of their time in special education, they are sometimes able to join regular classrooms for appropriate activities (Raynes, Snell, & Sailor, 1992; Rogers, 1993). In an inclusion classroom the test is whether the severely disabled student benefits from participation in the regular classroom work and not whether the student is able to maintain a work performance level similar to that of other students (Goodlad & Lovitt, 1993).

Where inclusion is common practice, the student does not follow assistance personnel and services; rather, the personnel and services follow the child. These personnel may include resource teachers who work with students individually or in small groups, paraprofessionals who assist with physical care and other needs, translators for students with physical impairments, readers for those with visual impairments, and many others. In an inclusion program, a cooperative relationship and a shared sense of responsibility develop between the student's regular classroom teacher and these special education personnel. If inclusion is to be successful, all members of the educational community must work together to meet the needs of students with disabilities.

A school that successfully implements inclusive education has been characterized as a place where the following occur on a regular daily basis.

1. *Heterogeneous grouping.* Students are organized in classrooms in which the proportion of students with disabilities approximates the natural proportion in the population. In an elementary classroom this might include one student with severe disabilities, several with mild disabilities, and many students without identified disabilities.
2. *A sense of belonging to a group.* The students with disabilities are considered part of the group rather than special guests. They are welcomed into a classroom community.
3. *Shared activities with individualized outcomes.* Students may share learning activities without necessarily sharing the same goals within the activity. This could include differentiated objectives within a curriculum or social objectives for some students being pursued at the same time as content goals.
4. *Use of environments frequented by persons without disabilities.* Educational experiences take place in environments in which most individuals do not have disabilities, such as general education classrooms.
5. *A balanced educational experience.* Inclusive education seeks a balance between academic and social goals. Neither is given absolute priority (Giangreco, Cloninger, Dennis, & Edelman, 1994).

An inclusive school would not be characterized by a particular set of practices as much as by the commitment of its staff to continually develop its capacity to accommodate the full range of individual differences among its learners. Simply placing students with disabilities in general education does not constitute inclusion and will not guarantee that children with disabilities will learn and behave appropriately or that they will be accepted by other students. It is important that teachers, often with the help of special education specialists, educate nondisabled students about their classmates. Properly implemented, inclusive classrooms have demonstrated successes from preschool to high school, and from mild to severe impairments (Esposito & Reed, 1986; Guralnick, 1981; Hanline & Murray, 1984; Johnson, Rynders, Johnson, Schmidt, & Haider, 1979).

Despite these successes, full inclusion has its critics (see, for example, the variety of positions in the January 1995 issue of *Educational Leadership*). The levels of support provided, type and severity of disabilities, and number of inclusion students in a particular classroom all contribute to the success or failure of the effort. Snell and Janney (2000) describe some of the lessons they learned in creating successful inclusion experiences. Teachers who were successful in implementing inclusion modified their typical role to share responsibility for the focus (included) students with a special education professional. Typically, classroom teachers maintained primary responsibility for the class and the focus child when he or she was being treated like classmates. Special education professionals took the lead when the focus child was being treated differently. Classroom teachers modified classroom routines and arrangements to accommodate physical needs of focus students and modified instructional activities in order to allow focus students to participate. This might entail modifying activities to allow academic participation (for example, a reduced or differentiated list of spelling words) or simply social participation (for example, holding a book while other children are reading). Special education teachers taught individualized objectives separately but within the classroom. Relationships with other students were most successful when teachers treated focus students as much like other students as possible, encouraging age-appropriate behavior and backing off most social interactions with other children.

Farlow (1996) described strategies for successful inclusion at the secondary level. They include supports for inclusion students and curriculum adaptations to maximize student success. Farlow's suggestions are easily adapted for elementary students and are summarized as follows.

Supports for Students

1. Allow peers to facilitate learning. Reading buddies, playground pals, and other types of assistants can help students function in general education settings.
2. Structure class activities to make peer support available. If cooperative learning and peer tutoring are part of the classroom routine, inclusion becomes part of a natural climate of helpfulness. It is important, however, to be sensitive to the amount of time nondisabled students spend as peer tutors—particularly if the material being studied is something they mastered long ago. Peer tutoring can be a powerful learning experience, but it is also important to make sure all students spend most of the school day learning material that is appropriate to their own level.
3. Prime students to be successful. Being introduced to ideas or materials before they are presented to the class can add to students' success. Communication with parents, reading guides, and early assignments can help students gain important prior knowledge before a new topic is introduced to the class as a whole.
4. Give students valued roles. Students with disabilities often have strengths that can allow them to play important roles in school organizations, teams, and classrooms. To the degree they successfully manage roles that are valued in the school community, students become an accepted asset of the group. In one of our classes a first-grade student with a disability was exceptionally compassionate and helpful when students were hurt during playground activities. Her role as "class nurse"—dispenser of hugs, occasional Band-Aids, and assistance in finding an appropriate adult—was valued by her peers.
5. Use existing expertise. Learn from teachers who are successful with inclusion students. One graduate student did a research project in which she interviewed teachers in her district who were particularly successful with inclusion students. Her conversations with those teachers enriched her own teaching practice—as well as providing an interesting graduate project!

Adaptations of Curriculum

1. Use independent prompts. If students need cues to classroom routines or other skills, written or audiotaped directions can provide assistance without disrupting others. For example, direction cards taped to a desktop can remind students of classroom routines or steps in an assignment.
2. Vary the amount of work required. Some students with disabilities work much more slowly than other students. In such cases, a reduced assignment can provide needed practice without placing an unreasonable burden on the student. Some students are much more successful if an assignment is literally cut into smaller sections—for example, strips of additional facts one at a time rather than a whole page.

3. Adjust delivery of information. A variety of means of presenting information—pictures, media, storytelling, oral reading—can assist students for whom reading is a challenge.

4. Allow students to express information in varied ways. Students who may not be able to express content in writing may be able to explain it, draw it, or choose from among several possibilities.

5. Present alternative activities. At times a class activity may be inappropriate for a particular student. Providing an alternative activity is a reasonable solution. In a classroom in which many students frequently do differing kinds of assignments, such flexibility will seem natural.

Strategies for Teaching Students with Disabilities

Some general recommendations can be made for teachers regardless of the nature of the students' disabilities. You will recognize that several of the ideas are also recommended for optimum learning for all children.

- Learn as much as you can about the needs of students in your class. Consult with the special education professional in your building or district to gain additional insights into students' learning styles and strengths as well as strategies to accommodate the disability. For example, a student with a mild mental impairment is more likely to be successful if presented with small chunks of information and given considerable reinforcement. A student with a mild hearing impairment will benefit from sitting near the speaker, with an unobstructed view for lip reading. A student with a more severe impairment may need a translator. You can also use your knowledge of students' interests and strengths to plan individual or class activities particularly suited to their needs.

- Avoid calling special attention to the student's disability. Although a matter-of-fact acceptance of a disability is appropriate (you certainly cannot ignore the fact that Paul cannot see the board or Susan cannot read), it is important to relate to students as individuals, not as members of a group. It is no more appropriate to make generalizations about people with disabilities than it would be to base broad generalizations on race or gender.

- Do not make assumptions based on the disability. Do not assume that the person with a disability is unhappy. Do not assume that individuals with disabilities are disabled in all areas, or are less mature than those without disabilities. It is inappropriate to treat a mentally impaired 10-year-old whose intellectual level is that of a 5-year-old in the way you would treat a typical 5-year-old, or to treat a preadolescent who is blind or has a physical disability like a small child (Biklen & Bogdan, 1977).

- Establish a classroom environment in which it is a common practice for students of different backgrounds and capabilities to learn from each other. Use cooperative learning activities to integrate students of different backgrounds and abilities so they can teach each other. Use a clear management system. Do not accept inappropriate behavior from a student with a disability that you would not accept from others. You may choose a less serious consequence, but do not communicate the message to the rest of the class that John or Maria can get away with unacceptable behavior. Such inconsistencies may lead to misbehavior or resentment by other students.

- Be enthusiastic and give positive reinforcement in response to the performance of students with disabilities. However, as for all students, praise that is repetitious, insincere, or overly broad is not helpful and can be damaging.

- Be sure to have a systematic framework to organize your classroom activities. Some students with emotional, intellectual, or learning impairments need a carefully established structure in order to work most effectively. Clearly defined objectives, with activities and evaluation procedures that logically follow from these objectives, communicate a sense of security and predictability to all students.

- Consider using a criterion-referenced evaluation approach in judging the performance of a student with a disability. Students with disabilities are more apt to be successful if your goal is to move each child to greater competence rather than to rate that child in comparison with others.

- You may wish to consider using the IEP format for all your students. Begin with a small portion of your requirements and assess how it works. You could meet with each student to develop a plan for an individual project. Help each student develop a project goal and transform it into objectives, activities, and a product that can be evaluated to determine if the objectives have been met.

- Finally, become an advocate for the student with a disability. Lobby for alternative learning materials—for example, interesting literature and social studies books that parallel the text for regular students but at a different reading level. Lobby for facilities and materials that can reduce the handicaps of students with visual or hearing impairments. See education for students with disabilities as their right as members of society rather than as a privilege granted to them.

There are also numerous strategies that are particularly appropriate to specific disabilities. It is impossible in this brief space to provide a comprehensive description of teaching methods for students with disabilities. However, a brief list of additional strategies that may prove useful for students with varied types of disabilities is given in the following paragraphs. Although strategies are suggested for a particular type of disability, many strategies are appropriate for multiple student needs. Working as a team with a special education professional, you will be able to plan for strategies most suited to the students in your class.

Students with mental impairments often find it easier to learn skills and procedures in small incremental steps. They will need more detailed and elaborate directions than other students. Carefully analyzing the task at hand can allow you to provide appropriate directions and prompts. For example, a young student with a mild mental impairment may initially need a set of reminder pictures to remember the correct order in which to put on outdoor winter clothing (mittens after all zippers are complete, for example). In a similar fashion, it may be necessary to provide a detailed checklist for a student learning to write a complete sentence or add fractions.

Students with mental impairments benefit by active involvement in lessons, with the opportunity for frequent responses. Response cards or other signaling devices can be helpful. Other types of active involvement can include choral reading, computer-aided instruction, and activities that call for physical responses such as clapping or moving in specific ways. Similarly, students with mental impairments benefit from frequent feedback. Feedback is most effective when it is immediate, positive, frequent, and differential ("You did five more than yesterday") (Heward, 2000). This type of feedback is not difficult in a small group but can be challenging when working with a whole class. When students are participating in large-group activities it can be helpful to create "secret signals" to let the student know you notice and appreciate his or her appropriate responses and behavior without having to allow the student to respond to every question. For example, walking by and briefly touching the student's desk, or giving a subtle thumbs-up signal or other agreed upon gesture can provide needed reinforcement. As the student matures, time without reinforcement can increase.

Students with learning disabilities benefit from explicit explanations of what is expected. Being clear about objectives and providing support materials and examples can be helpful. For example, students with learning disabilities may find graphic organizers and diagrams particularly helpful. Many students benefit from templates to guide their note taking or help them follow a minilecture. Mnemonic devices can help some students recall content more readily. Many students with learning disabilities benefit from very explicit teaching of study, organizational, and problem-solving strategies. For example, students may need clear step-by-step directions about how to record homework assignments, address a word problem, or structure a story.

Many other types of support strategies can be effective, depending on the nature of the disability. Some students with learning disabilities benefit from guides to help them follow along a line of text or transparent overlays that cut the glare on their papers. Special education specialists should be able to assist you with specific strategies targeted to a student's disability. Some students will need adjusted deadlines or adjusted assignments to accommodate a slower pace of work. If a disruption in routine is expected, for example a school assembly, many students with learning disabilities will benefit from advanced preparation and rehearsal of the new activity. Sudden changes in structure can be distressing.

Similarly, students with emotional impairments benefit from predictable routines and preparation for anticipated changes. For many such students, learning self-management skills is as important as content learning. Opportunities for self-monitoring—for example, a checklist on which the student assesses the period's success in keeping class rules—can help students begin to learn self-management. Students with emotional impairments also need many opportunities to see positive models of peer interactions. Morning meetings, class councils, cooperative learning activities, and peer mediation programs can all be helpful sources of peer modeling. Perhaps most important, students with emotional impairments need teachers who can accept the child without accepting inappropriate behavior and who can develop empathetic relationships. This is not easy; it demands patience, maturity, and self-control. But with the assistance of an empathetic teacher and a skilled specialist many students with emotional impairments can learn the skills and behaviors necessary to succeed in school and in life.

Learning Together

The integration of students with disabilities into regular school classrooms has been a consistent element of local, state, and federal education policy since the 1970s. There are a number of advantages to the practice: the opportunity for cooperative learning; the lessening of isolation experienced by special students; the democratic values that are strengthened; the reduction in stereotypes, prejudice, misconceptions, and outright superstition concerning individuals with disabilities; and the promise it holds for the continuation of such values into the adult world.

Drawbacks of inclusive education can include the increased costs of enhanced support needed for educating students with disabilities in multiple environments, instructional demands on the regular classroom teacher, and the additional paperwork burden on districts. Most educators believe that integrating a student with disabilities into a regular classroom requires additional effort and commitment on their part. Nevertheless, these same educators are working toward an adaptive education system in which all young people can achieve their maximum potential.

SECTION 3. TEACHING GIFTED AND TALENTED STUDENTS

Section 3 Objectives

After you have completed this section, you should be able to

1. describe characteristics of gifted and talented students;
2. describe special instructional needs of such students;
3. list instructional strategies that are appropriate for gifted and talented students;
4. plan lessons in your curriculum area that are adapted for gifted and talented students; and
5. explain how activities that are appropriate for gifted and talented students may be used in lessons for an entire class.

What Is a "Gifted" Student?

There is no consensus on what constitutes a "gifted" student. Traditionally, giftedness has been identified by a high score on an IQ test, a measurement closely associated with school success. A student who scored in the top 1%, 2%, or 5% of the population (depending on the district) was likely to be highly adept at school learning and was considered to be gifted. One of the problems with equating giftedness with high IQ is that IQ is not a particularly good predictor of adult giftedness. If all students are given an IQ test, it will not necessarily identify the next Einstein or Madame Curie or Phillis Wheatley. Moreover, the information that is being learned from studies in human intelligence makes the limitations of IQ tests increasingly clear.

As you learned in Chapter 2, contemporary theories of intelligence are multifaceted. Whether you consider Sternberg's (1985) triarchic theory, Gardner's multiple intelligences (Gardner, 1983; see also Checkley, 1997), or other emerging theories, it is clear that no single number can represent the complexity of any individual's intellectual ability. Individuals may demonstrate outstanding capabilities in many dimensions. For example, according to Gardner's theory, a student with exceptional linguistic intelligence will probably have different abilities and needs than one who is exceptional in logical-mathematical, spatial, or interpersonal intelligences. Whatever model of intelligence is considered, there is no doubt that students' prior knowledge, cultural background, and previous school experiences have a significant impact on test scores. Although IQ scores may reasonably predict the ease with which students may succeed in traditional schooling, they cannot assess an individual's total intellectual or academic potential—or identify giftedness (see Colangelo & Davis, 1997, for a more complete discussion of conceptions of giftedness).

In 1993 the U.S. Department of Education proposed a definition that limited the use of the word **gifted** to adults and focused on developing talent in children. It defined young people with outstanding talent as those who

> show the potential for performing at remarkably high levels of accomplishment when compared with others of their age, experience, or environment . . . in intellectual, creative, and/or artistic areas . . . leadership capacity . . . or specific academic fields. (p. 26)

The definition further notes that such young people "require services or activities not ordinarily provided by the schools" and that outstanding talents are present in "all cultural groups, across all economic strata, and in all areas of human endeavor" (p. 26). This definition marks an important shift from an emphasis on giftedness as a trait (either you have it or you don't) to a characteristic that is developed over time and affected by experience. The definition's emphasis on talented students' needs for specialized services has provided support for programs for the gifted and talented.

Another definition was proposed by Renzulli (1978). His definition might best be understood through the following exercise. Take a moment and think of five people, living or dead, you would consider to be gifted. What do the people you named have in common? It is likely that you thought of individuals who developed an important idea, were responsible for a major invention, made a scientific discovery, or created a work of art, literature, or music. One way to describe these individuals is to call them **creative producers**—producers of information and art rather than simply consumers. (Does this bring to mind the discussion of authentic learning?) Now think about the ways in which we have traditionally labeled students as gifted. Is the rationale the same? In most cases, students have been labeled as gifted because they are skillful consumers of information. They take the input teachers give them and "return" it on tests, without necessarily doing very much to change or improve it.

Renzulli believes that we have attached the gifted label to two different types of ability, so he devised two new categories. **Schoolhouse giftedness** is the ability to consume, analyze, and reproduce information, whereas **creative productivity** is the ability to generate new information. Both schoolhouse giftedness and creative productivity are important. Einstein certainly could not have devised the theory of relativity if he had not consumed his physics! However, schools have traditionally paid much more attention to the consumption than to the production of information. Renzulli's **three-ring conception of giftedness** (see Figure 10.3) was designed specifically to reflect research on creative producers, in the hopes that, if we identified the ways in which giftedness "works" in adults, we might be able to identify or encourage it in young people.

There are important ties between Renzulli's concept of creative productivity and authentic learning. Schoolhouse giftedness—emphasizing the reproduction and analysis of information—must be only part of what students achieve in schools. It may be useful to consider the definition of giftedness that Renzulli believes can help explain high-level creative productivity in adults.

FIGURE 10.3 The Three-Ring Conception of Giftedness (*The Schoolwide Enrichment Model* by Renzulli & Reis. Creative Learning Press, 1985.)

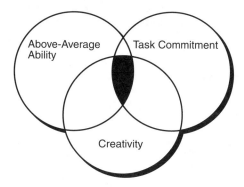

The three-ring conception of giftedness consists of three interlocking circles: above-average ability, creativity, and task commitment. Adult creative producers are of above-average intelligence, but not necessarily from the top 1%, or even the top 5%, of the population. They also work creatively, and with great commitment to the tasks they choose. Of course, their ability, task commitment, and creativity must be in the same area. If an individual has above-average ability in math, creativity in cooking, and task commitment to an improved golf swing, it is not likely that gifted behavior will result. One of the functions of schools can be to help students identify areas of ability and interest, and work to develop creativity and task commitment in those areas. It is unrealistic to expect even the brightest students to come to school with their abilities, creativity, and commitment already fully developed; that is part of the teacher's responsibility.

CHECK YOUR UNDERSTANDING

List three different ways in which giftedness may be defined. Think of someone you know who might be considered gifted according to each definition.

1. _____

2. _____

3. _____

WHAT ARE GIFTED STUDENTS LIKE?

There is no simple answer to the question, What are gifted students like? Some children may be very good at one or more school subjects. Other children may be creative, always ready with a new idea. Some will have a wide variety of interests; others will pursue one specialized area. Special interests or abilities do not always show up in obvious ways, or even in ways that make the teacher's job easier. Maria, at the beginning of the chapter, showed creativity in her writing and extracurricular activities, but also in the humor directed against her teacher. Picasso was frequently reprimanded in school because he refused to do anything but paint. He was demonstrating creativity and task commitment, but not in the ways his teachers may have expected.

CHECK YOUR UNDERSTANDING

The following list gives characteristics often associated with gifted students.

Large knowledge base
Good memory
Unusually varied and/or intense interests
Highly developed verbal skills
Ability to process information rapidly and accurately
Flexibility in thinking, with ability to see many points of view
Persistence
Awareness of relationships among diverse ideas
Ability to generate original ideas
Enjoyment of abstract ideas
Intense opinions or emotions
Sensitivity to feelings of self or others
Concern for global issues: war, hunger, and so forth
Sense of humor

Choose three characteristics and describe how they might be manifested in schools in positive or negative ways. For example, a student with a fine sense of humor may add zest to the class or disrupt lessons with inappropriate comments.

1. _____

2. _____

3. _____

Under what circumstances do you think the negative behaviors would be most likely to take place? Although there are many possible causes for negative behavior, bright students who are not intellectually challenged by classwork sometimes find alternative forms of challenge through disruptive activities.

Characteristics of giftedness may also be hidden. It is easy to see evidence of intelligence in a successful student like Joe, but what about Rosa? Teachers should look for signs of special interests or abilities in students whose other needs may prevent the teachers from noticing the students' giftedness. Sometimes cultural differences may obscure teachers' understanding of students' abilities. If they anticipate that bright students will ask many questions, they may be less open to noticing the abilities of a Native American whose tribal customs promote silent watching and listening as signs of respect. Various types of disabilities may also lead teachers to miss signs of advanced ability. It may be more difficult to recognize advanced reasoning in children whose hearing impairment has delayed the development of language or whose learning disabilities affect their reading. Some students may—consciously or unconsciously—hide their gifts, either because they fear social isolation or because their experience has taught them that good work is rewarded with more work. If most math students are assigned 20 problems and above-average math students are assigned 30, many bright students "beat the system" by performing like average students.

The assumption that gifted students will make it on their own is a fallacy, especially if "making it" means living up to their potential. Like all learners, bright students need instruction appropriate to their individual capabilities. Some districts provide special programs for bright students. Students identified as gifted and talented spend part or all of the day in classes designed to provide challenging experiences. Sometimes these classes focus on specific sections of content and are designed for students with strengths in particular areas. For example, an advanced creative writing class may be offered for especially able or interested writers. Other schools offer advanced independent study options or seminars that allow students to investigate a variety of interests or strengths. In still other cases, resource people assist teachers in planning for gifted students in their classrooms. In some areas the appropriateness of specialized instruction for gifted students has been called into question, with questions raised regarding elitism and the distribution of resources (see, for example, Sapon-Shevin, 1994). However, even in districts with special programs, most gifted students spend the majority of their time in regular classrooms, under the direction of a classroom teacher.

But What Do I Do with Gifted Students?

Giftedness is a complex concept and identification is not simple. Therefore the question remains: What can teachers do with bright students in their classrooms, regardless of whether they have been officially labeled as *gifted?* One course of action is to consider two basic questions. First, which parts of the regular curriculum has the student already mastered (or could the student master quickly with little assistance)? Second, what alternative activities will allow the student to learn and be challenged at an appropriate level?

There is a basic assumption underlying these questions that may seem simple, but is profoundly important. It is the obligation of every teacher to make sure that each student in the classroom has the opportunity to learn. The teacher's first obligation is not to the body of content designated kindergarten or fourth grade—or even the state standards—it is to the students. Meeting that assumption with students who have special needs is a challenge. In the case of particularly able learners, it means finding things for students to learn even if they arrive in September already knowing large amounts of the designated curriculum. If, for example, a fifth-grade student enters the classroom having worked her way through an algebra book during the summer, she is not likely to improve in mathematics if the only experiences provided are the same as those provided most fifth graders. Students who spend sixth grade reading *Mein Kampf* or *Macbeth* need challenges beyond the typical language arts program.

Students who enter 1 or 2 years "ahead" have less extreme needs, but the principle is still the same. Teachers faced with such students may not breathe a sigh of relief and assume they need not worry about students who can already meet the grade-level goals. It is the teachers' responsibility to set new goals for the students to reach. The importance of examining curriculum goals for prior mastery is not limited to the top few students in a grade or a class. In one study, fourth-grade students were tested on the content of their math text before they had used it for the school year. Sixty percent of the students in one suburban group could score over 80%! Similar results were obtained with students in fourth- and tenth-grade science and tenth-grade social studies (Education Products Information Exchange, 1979). Assessing students' regular curriculum is important for all students, and it is particularly vital for able learners, who often enter a grade having already mastered a substantial portion of the content to be taught.

Regular Curriculum

One strategy for dealing with the regular curriculum is called **curriculum compacting** (Reis, Burns, & Renzulli, 1992; Renzulli & Smith, 1979). In its simplest form, compacting involves diagnosing which of the skills in a particular unit of study some of your students have already mastered. In one study, elementary teachers found that this ranged from 24% to 70% of the regular curriculum (Reis & Purcell, 1998). Throughout this text we have emphasized the importance of assessing students' prior knowledge before beginning instruction. In curriculum compacting, this assessment is particularly focused on identifying areas of the curriculum that may be unnecessary or repetitious for some students. For example, before beginning a math chapter, you might give a pretest covering the main skills in the unit. Some teachers use unit tests for this purpose; others use excerpts from workbooks or worksheets or devise their own tests. If you discover that any of your students have already mastered these skills, it would not be appropriate for them to spend a lot of time practicing or reviewing the same material. In 1888, J. M. Greenwood wrote, "When once a child has learned that four and two are six, a thousand repetitions will give him no new information and it is a waste of time to keep him employed in that manner" (p. 13). Instead of repeating previously learned content, students could test out of some material and be provided with alternative activities. In the unit on the Revolution, Gloria may discover that two or three students have already mastered the map skills she plans to incorporate in the unit. If so, she can allow those students to pursue other activities during the time she plans to focus on map work.

In other cases, especially when the instruction deals with concepts rather than skills, gifted students may not have mastered the material yet but can do so more quickly than other students. For these students you might consider contracts (see Chapter 9) or other forms of independent study. Recall from Chapter 9 that a **contract** generally identifies activities that must be completed to help a student master the regular content, as well as related enrichment activities. The contract also specifies how new knowledge and skills will be evaluated.

However, the use of independent contracts or other independent work does not release you from your responsibility as a teacher. Although many bright students can master material with much less direct instruction than average students, you must still identify areas in which instruction is needed. Sometimes such instruction may be provided on an individual basis, perhaps while other students work on a practice activity, or a student may receive instruction with a large or small group of students needing to learn the same skill. Periodic individual conferences can be helpful in assessing students' progress, as well as in identifying areas of difficulty and planning further activities. Sample contracts can be found in Figure 10.1.

Alternative Activities

If students' curriculum has been compacted, they will complete the regular assignments in less time than average students. It is necessary to decide how best to use the additional time. One basic decision is between acceleration and enrichment. **Acceleration** is the pursuit of the regular curriculum at a faster pace (for example, going on to the fourth-grade math book while in third grade). Acceleration can encompass advancement in a single subject (such as going on to the next math book), grade skipping, or early entrance to college. Since acceleration affects students' studies years after it occurs, many districts have guidelines for its use. It is important to find out your district's policies regarding acceleration.

Enrichment, the incorporation of activities outside the regular curriculum, can be divided into three general categories. One type of enrichment can be developed by *adapting assignments* or techniques in the regular curriculum to provide additional challenge. Many gifted students thrive on inquiry, induction, role-playing, simulation, and other activities that encourage higher level thinking while teaching content. The higher levels of Bloom's taxonomy can be helpful in generating ideas for assignments. Of course, teachers must take into account not only the students' abilities, but their prior knowledge of the content to be taught. For example, in the unit on the Revolution, Gloria Jackson may consider substituting additional higher level assignments for those designed to teach basic facts for students with a great deal of prior knowledge or exceptional independent learning skills. Rather than constructing a time line of basic events, such students may be challenged to investigate events occurring at the same time in diverse cultural groups (for example, learning about American Indian activities during the same time period) or to compare events in the American Revolution to the revolution in France.

Alternative Activities Can Be Used to Meet the Learning Needs of Students Who Have Mastered the Regular Curriculum

A second category of enrichment is *interdisciplinary teaching*. Of course, interdisciplinary teaching can be an appropriate organizational strategy for all students. However, it is particularly suited to students whose excellent abstract reasoning abilities allow them to make ties among ideas in various disciplines. Interdisciplinary planning for gifted students is usually organized around abstract themes, such as patterns or revolution. For example, students studying the American Revolution might also examine the idea of revolution in other disciplines. How might scientists like Barbara McClintock be considered revolutionaries? What would constitute a revolution in art? In sports? How are revolutions in other disciplines similar to or different from the American Revolution?

The third type of enrichment often recommended for bright students is *independent investigations* that culminate in some type of product. The types of projects pursued should encompass the same categories as the "real problems" described in Chapter 2: investigation of research questions, involvement in activism, or communication of some aesthetic. The skills of independent learning discussed in Chapter 9 can be particularly valuable as individuals or small groups investigate topics of interest. Many times, parent volunteers or other community mentors can give valuable assistance to students interested in particular topics.

These activities may or may not parallel the general curriculum. Renzulli (1993) describes Elaine, a third-grade student reading on the adult level with a special interest in women of scientific accomplishment. In order to meet her needs, her third-grade teacher first addressed the regular curriculum by allowing Elaine to substitute books in her interest area for the third-grade reader. Twice a month, Elaine met with a mentor who was a journalist specializing in women's issues. (Elaine's teacher was fortunate to have a building enrichment specialist who arranged this match.) During language arts time, when most students were practicing skills Elaine had previously mastered, she developed a questionnaire and interview questions to be used with local women scientists and university science faculty. Although this activity used language arts skills, it did not closely parallel other children's reading activities. It is also possible to work with students in individual projects more closely related to core content. Gloria might encourage students to undertake projects having to do with the Revolution—for example "translating" a period cookbook into modern recipes and trying them out or searching the Internet to compare drafts of the Declaration of Independence.

Even with such help, allowing and encouraging individual investigations can be challenging. Within classes where differentiated instruction is the norm, it is much easier. But even small beginnings can be important. For exceptionally able students, finding the opportunity to be challenged in an area of strength and interest part of the time is better than no opportunity at all.

The Enrichment Triad

Renzulli (1977) referred to independent investigations as "Type III enrichment"—individuals or small groups pursuing real problems. Two other types of enrichment can help lead students to Type III projects. The three types of enrichment form the **Enrichment Triad Model** (see Figure 10.4).

The first, Type I enrichment, consists of general exploratory activities designed to help students identify their interests and to encourage them to investigate these inter-

FIGURE 10.4 The Enrichment Triad

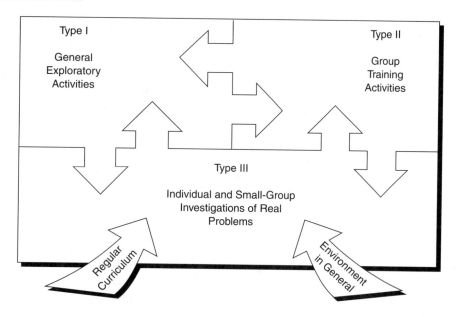

ests further. It includes activities, materials, and resources (e.g., guest speakers, displays, movies, books, and interest-development centers) that extend education beyond the regular curriculum. Any time you set up an interesting display, show a movie expanding the curriculum, or have a guest speaker in your classroom, you are providing a Type I activity. The broader the range of topics presented during the year, the better. The key to providing a meaningful Type I activity is the debriefing questions that follow it. Because a Type I activity is intended to help students identify their interests, the questions should not simply assess whether students have understood the material but should raise additional questions, pose problems, and find out which students are interested in pursuing the topic. For example, after an environmentalist has discussed acid rain, you could ask students whether they think there is acid rain in their area, what questions they still have about acid rain and how they could find answers, or if they would like to learn how to test for acid rain. The most important objectives of Type I enrichment are to (a) expose students to as many varied topics as possible and (b) encourage them to identify areas of interest and learn more about them.

Type II enrichment is composed of group training activities that can provide students with the tools they need to become independent investigators. Skills of independent learning can be taught as described in Chapter 9. Other activities might include the development of advanced skills in research (like using Internet seach engines, databases, or microfiche), data gathering, problem solving, or interviewing. The gifted-education specialist in your district can provide ideas, techniques, and materials. If your district does not have such a specialist, you may wish to consult the professional literature or your state Department of Education for suggestions.

Planning both Type I and Type II enrichment for many students can help you identify students with the interest and motivation to pursue an individual Type III project. Some leaders in the field of education of the gifted and talented are recommending that many students be provided with the skills and opportunities necessary to develop diverse abilities (Feldhusen, 1992; Renzulli, 1993). They envision a shift from concern about identifying students who can be labeled as gifted to a focus on developing talents in all students. This text's emphasis on authentic learning and real-world problem solving reflects a similar view. However, it is clear that students with exceptional abilities will still need additional challenge and support in pursuing enrichment opportunities that may not be suited to the needs of all students.

You may, at times, wish to provide students with a choice of assignments and encourage able students to select challenging tasks. Of course, not all bright students have the same interests and strengths. If you expect students to put forth efforts that are beyond those expected of other children, the tasks must not only challenge them but interest them. You should also make sure that gifted students do not spend too much time working in isolation. If students are able to bypass or condense significant amounts of the regular curriculum, it may be helpful to identify a group of intellectual peers with whom they can work for part of the school day. Sometimes advanced classes or independent study seminars provide this opportunity. Students also may form a cluster group in a heterogeneous class, a group of same-grade students from different classes who come together for instruction or independent work, or a group of mixed-grade students working on a particular project. Such arrangements may demand creative scheduling, but they can be invaluable in helping students meet important intellectual and social needs.

REFLECTING ON THE IDEAS

Choose a unit topic you might teach. Briefly list three enrichment activities that might be suitable for a student who has already mastered much of the unit content.

1. _____

2. _____

3. _____

Did your activities require higher level thinking, interdisciplinary ties, and/or independent investigation and problem solving?

Affective Needs of Bright Students

Like all young people, highly able students have affective as well as cognitive needs. They need to have friends, feel part of the group, and enjoy social interaction. Although characteristics may vary with degree of exceptionality (Shaywitz et al., 2001), most exceptionally bright students are well liked and socially adept. There are, however, some characteristics of bright students that can impact their emotional needs.

One of the factors that most affects bright students (particularly in primary grades and below) is the differences in their levels of physical, intellectual, and emotional maturity. Since most highly able students function at physical and emotional levels close to their chronological age, they may develop intellectually in ways that are difficult affectively. Adults may expect them to behave in a manner suiting their intellect rather than their age. (In fact, many bright students are told to act their age when they are doing just that!) They may wish to discuss topics in which classmates have little interest. They may also develop concerns that are difficult emotionally. Younger students can become enmeshed in issues of violence, poverty, death, and so forth, without the emotional maturity to handle them. For example, one primary-school girl sent her life savings to earthquake victims and then wept every night during the news when she had nothing more to give. Her age-mates had difficulty understanding why she was so upset about people she didn't know.

These differences in developmental levels mean gifted students need to have many types of peers. It is important that they have interaction with others working on the same instructional level. A third-grade girl who does math at the sixth-grade level may need sixth-grade peers in math class, a fifth-grade friend with whom to discuss stamp collecting (or earthquakes), and third-grade friends on the soccer team.

Teachers of bright young people must be wary of the dangers of perfectionism. Some children go through years of school without ever encountering challenging work. They come to expect that everything they do in school will be easy and that they should be able to complete their tasks without struggle. Sometimes students develop an image of themselves that demands that everything they do be done perfectly—anything less is seen as failure. This type of perfectionism can be disabling and potentially dangerous to healthy emotional development. If students' needs are correctly diagnosed and challenging work is provided beginning in early grades, some perfectionism can be avoided. If you encounter students who have difficulty taking risks or attempting challenging tasks for fear of making an error, it will be important to start with small challenges and increase gradually, while modeling your own willingness to try, fail, and try again.

Serving Many Students

Strategies recommended for gifted students are important for other students as well. Many students will benefit from preassessment and curriculum compacting, especially at the beginning of the year. Interdisciplinary teaching, Type I exploratory activities, instruction in Type II skills, and involvement in real-world problem solving can be appropriate for a wide range of students. One of the most important trends in the field of education of the gifted and talented is the adoption of many of the strategies used with gifted students into general education (Feldhusen, 1996; Renzulli, 1993). In fact, the Accelerated Schools Model uses strategies typically employed with gifted students (including accelerated math) to accelerate and enrich the whole-school curriculum for urban, at-risk students (Brandt, 1992; Goldberg, 2001; Hopfenber, Levin, & Chase, 1993). This trend brings many benefits for a wide range of students. Renzulli and Reis (1997) described a Schoolwide Enrichment Model in which enrichment activities are used to structure a range of activities for all students.

However, there is one potential danger. If many of the strategies recommended for bright students are used for all students, some teachers may be led to believe that gifted students' needs are automatically being met within the regular curriculum and teachers need have no further concerns about them. This is not true. In a 1993 report, *National Excellence: A Case for Developing America's Talent,* the U.S. Department of Education called the lack of achievement in our most able learners a "quiet crisis" in education.

> In a broad range of intellectual and artistic endeavor, America's most talented students often fail to reach their full potential. . . .Despite sporadic attention over the years to the needs of bright students, most of them continue to spend time in school working well below their capabilities. The belief espoused in school reform that children from all economic and cultural backgrounds must reach their full potential has not been extended to America's most talented students. They are underchallenged and therefore underachieve. (p.5)

There is an enormous range of students who may be considered gifted. Students who are functioning slightly above grade level may need only slight adaptations in curriculum. However, there are also students in virtually every school who are functioning (or capable of functioning) substantially beyond grade-level expectations. Sometimes such students are easy to spot, such as the first grader who enters school reading near-adult books. Other students may appear to be only slightly advanced, either because they have learned to hide their abilities in order to avoid sticking out or because no one has asked them to attempt anything more difficult. A few years ago, the authors became aware of a sixth-grade student who was particularly able in math. Neither the student nor his parents felt he was being challenged by the math curriculum. The teacher had planned a flexible program that allowed students to progress through the sixth-grade curriculum at different paces, so she felt the student's needs were being met. Finally, the parents had the student take part in a "Talent Search" program in which 12-year-old students take the SAT test along with high school juniors. The student scored over 700 on the math portion of the SAT, well ahead of most high school students. Only then did the teacher realize that small adaptations of curriculum would not be sufficient to meet this particular student's needs.

The challenge, then, is to help *all* children learn. Much of what is good for bright students can be used with most students in the classroom. However, educators must still be open to recognizing special needs and advanced abilities that demand more challenge than even the best general curriculum can offer. Providing needed adaptations can help all students find school to be a place of learning, challenge, and opportunity.

SECTION 4. TEACHING CULTURALLY DIVERSE AND BILINGUAL STUDENTS

Section 4 Objectives

After you have completed this section, you should be able to

1. list instructional strategies that are appropriate for culturally diverse students, with special attention to individuals of color and bilingual students;
2. plan lessons in your curriculum area that are adapted to meet the needs of each group; and
3. explain how activities that are appropriate for culturally diverse and bilingual students may be used in lessons for all students.

Home and family backgrounds are important in determining the experiences, attitudes, interests, and beliefs that pupils bring to school. Students come to school with a diversity of languages, cultures, and experiences that affect their school performance. Just as you should know as much as possible about your students' learning styles and prior academic experiences, you have to take into account language and cultural diversity and consider how this variety may affect students' interactions.

Teaching for Equity

In Chapter 2, the definition and characteristics of *culture* were introduced and discussed. The differences between the Anglo–Western European macro culture and the several micro cultures that coexist with it in the United States were identified.

Because of their skin color, early immigrants from Europe often were willing and able to assimilate into American culture without having to give up their unique cultural attributes. They could identify with the Anglo–Western European culture and adopted the concept of the "American melting pot." However, some people, because of their skin color, were forced to assimilate and prevented from practicing their own culture, beliefs, traditions, and language. Historically, because of enforced segregation, many have been underserved by our schools. Despite the abolition of most formerly legal forms of discrimination, the continued shadow of racism remains (Quality Education for Minorities, 1990).

In recent years, cultural pluralism—where ethnic groups retained their cultural heritage, traditions, and values while still adopting aspects of the Anglo-Western culture—emerged as an alternative to the melting pot. Unfortunately, this concept of cultural pluralism has not been completely accepted in our society. Judgments about students' abilities, potential, or even interests are sometimes made through the cultural lens of the Anglo-Western culture. Remember John, at the beginning of the chapter? John had trouble learning basic skills, had been in frequent fights, and would not participate in class. When majority children have such difficulties, the school is most likely to contend that there is a problem with the instruction, or a mismatch between the curriculum and the child's level of development (Hale-Benson, 1986). If John is a student of color, however, he is 2.3 times more likely to be labeled as educable mentally impaired than a White child ("Status of Black Children," 1989). Although there certainly are educable mentally impaired students of all races, and such children need special educational support, it is crucial that the evaluation of students' abilities be based on their performance on appropriate tasks, not on racial or cultural stereotypes.

Three main conditions support cultural pluralism in the schools (Banks, 1994):

1. Positive teacher expectations
2. A learning environment that encourages positive intergroup contact
3. A pluralistic (multicultural) curriculum

Other helpful approaches for diverse groups of students are to raise self-esteem and use culturally relevant teaching.

Positive Teacher Expectations

Students tend to perform at the level expected of them by the teacher. Research has indicated that in classes where teachers held higher expectations for *all* students, higher general student performance resulted.

Too many African American, Native American, or Latino students are considered slow and difficult to teach. These expectations of inferiority are often passed on to the students, who, by their behavior, turn the expectations into self-fulfilling prophecies. In other words, students tend to behave as teachers expect them to behave. If a teacher labels a student as a low achiever, less is expected and demanded from that student. If the teacher perceives a student to be a high achiever, more is expected and demanded from that student. This view of a student's expected performance is communicated to the student by verbal and nonverbal behaviors. Good (1981) cited many ways in which teachers behave toward students they perceive as low achievers. The teachers he studied

- provided general, often insincere praise,
- provided them with less feedback,
- demanded less effort from them,
- interrupted them more often,
- seated them farther away from the teacher,
- paid less attention to them,
- called on them less often,
- waited less time for them to respond to questions,
- criticized them more often, and
- smiled at them less.

Students who are perceived as high achievers, on the other hand,

- were given more opportunities for responses,
- were asked higher level questions,
- received more praise and detailed feedback,
- were given prompts or probes if they seemed to be having difficulty,
- were allowed more time to respond to questions, and
- were provided supportive communications (i.e., active listening, physical closeness, courtesy, acceptance of feeling, compliments).

Positive Learning Environment

Four basic conditions are necessary if social contact between groups is to lessen prejudice and lead to friendly attitudes and behaviors (Bennett, 1986):

1. Contact should be sufficiently intimate to produce reciprocal knowledge and understanding between groups.
2. Members of various groups must share equal status.
3. The contact situation should lead people to do things together. It should require intergroup cooperation to achieve a common goal.
4. There should be institutional support—an authority and/or social climate that encourages intergroup contact.

One research study found that successful teachers in culturally diverse situations were flexible, creative, well organized, enthusiastic, warm, firm, and consistent risk takers. They had high expectations, a high energy level, and a commitment to the teaching of all children. They had a repertoire of many teaching strategies, and they were able to find a compatible mode that would engage students in learning (Shade, 1990). Teachers who have studied learning style differences, particularly cross-cultural differences, will have an advantage in developing such a repertoire (see, for example, Shade, 1997).

Teaching students from culturally diverse backgrounds also requires a restructuring of teaching attitudes, approaches, and strategies. It requires becoming a facilitator and director of the learning process, rather than an information giver. The classroom should become more group-oriented and cooperative. Students should become more involved in their learning, and the telling of facts must be replaced with demonstrations and modeling (Hollins, 1994). Although all young people, regardless of their color, benefit from the general teaching strategies outlined in this text, some teaching and learning activities are particularly important in culturally diverse classrooms.

Effective teachers in culturally diverse situations

1. have a clear sense of their own ethnic and cultural identities,
2. look at cultural differences among students as cultural assets (Boykin, 1994),
3. communicate high expectations for the success of all students and a belief that all students can succeed,
4. are personally committed to achieving equity for all students and believe they are capable of making a difference in their students' learning,
5. develop a bond with their students and cease seeing their students as "the other,"
6. provide an academically challenging curriculum that includes attention to the development of higher level cognitive skills,
7. add meaning to instruction in an interactive and collaborative environment,
8. include contributions and perspectives of the various ethnocultural groups that compose our society, by using a multicultural curriculum,
9. use an affective curriculum (Harmon, in press),
10. encourage community members and parents or family members to become involved in students' education and give them a significant voice in making important school decisions related to school programs (i.e., resources and staffing), and
11. use culturally congruent teaching methods (Cole, 1995).

Multicultural Curriculum

As described in Chapter 2, the American culture is a macroculture composed of many microcultures making it a multicultural and pluralistic society. According to Banks (1999), ". . . education within a pluralistic society should affirm and help students understand their home and community cultures" (p. 4). A multicultural curriculum is designed to promote and value the diversity of all cultures in our country, while helping students to see the commonalties among all groups. In a positive multicultural environment

- teachers expect all students to achieve, regardless of race, sex, class, or ethnicity,
- the learning environment encourages positive contact between all students,
- instructional materials are reviewed for bias,
- the curriculum includes the historical experiences of all cultures,
- efforts are made to develop an understanding of, and appreciation and respect for, all cultures,
- goals and strategies reflect cultural learning styles of all students,

- time is spent dispelling misconceptions, stereotypes, and prejudices, and
- bulletin boards and classroom exhibits display people of many backgrounds.

Students in a multicultural classroom learn to appreciate the capabilities of others as well as their own strengths. Multicultural education involves providing the best education for students that preserves their own cultural heritage, prepares them for meaningful relationships with other people, and enables them to lead productive lives in the present society without sacrificing their own cultural perspective (Hollins, 1994).

Goals for multicultural education should provide for

1. the development of historical perspectives and cultural consciousness,
2. the development of intercultural competence,
3. the reduction of racism and ethnic prejudice and discrimination, and
4. the development of social action skills (Bennett, 1986).

Historical perspectives involve knowledge of the world views, heritage, and contributions of diverse cultures, including one's own culture. In a music class a teacher might include music from many different cultures, rather than just focusing on classical music from Europe. Intercultural competence is the ability to interpret intentional communication (language, signs, gestures), some unconscious cues (body language), and customs in diverse cultures. Simulation activities could be used in social studies classes to experience how a lack of communication and knowledge of other cultures affects interactions with each other.

One way to reduce prejudice and discrimination is to teach students strategies for detecting bias in the media. Such activities can help students clarify their own values, and help them clear up misconceptions and erroneous beliefs about the superiority of some races. Social action skills include self-expression, decision making, making choices, setting goals, and problem resolution. Students' feelings of personal and political effectiveness can be developed through these activities, community activism, or classroom projects.

Activities That Enhance Self-Esteem

Because culturally diverse students and students from lower socioeconomic levels often feel less valued, it is important to find ways to increase their self-esteem. The following activities build students' self-esteem through positive relationships among teachers and students.

- Check your perception of students. Ask yourself if you really expect the students to achieve. A study from the University of Chicago found that the major factor in student performance was not parent demography or per-pupil expenditure, but teacher expectations (Kunjufu, 1984). Don't use a student's home environment or social status as an excuse for poor achievement.
- Encourage students to take a more challenging educational path. This will convey the message that you have confidence in their abilities. Provide role models with others from the same cultural background. Inform students about opportunities in many fields. Involve community organizations and local businesses and industries. Recruit school graduates to assist in this area.

- Watch the language you use. Grant (Hale-Benson, 1986, p. 179) found that social scientists used harsher terms when describing African Americans and more neutral terms when describing Whites. For instance, African Americans were seen as belonging to the "drug culture," whereas Whites had a "chemical dependency problem." African Americans had "illegitimate children"; Whites chose "single motherhood." Teachers can also be guilty of discrimination in vocabulary.
- Learn about the culture of your students. Understanding their traditions will help you see how students view and interpret their world.
- Let students know that effort is valued. Attribution theory indicates that students' beliefs about the reasons for success and failure can greatly influence their perception of the task and their achievement of a successful outcome. When students believe that they are successful because they have put effort into a task, they experience a greater feeling of pride and are more likely to work hard on tasks in the future than if they feel their success was caused by luck.
- Strive to maintain a positive classroom climate. Clear explanations, positive reinforcement, and activities that encourage interaction among students can all contribute to classroom tone.
- "Catch 'em being good." Find opportunities to tell students how much they are valued by you and how bright and promising you know they are (Collins, 1992).
- Provide opportunities for students to discuss their concerns regarding prejudice, discrimination, and other kinds of social injustices. Bibliotherapy, or the use of carefully selected literature containing characters and challenges similar to those of the students, is a highly effective technique.
- Look to the community and the family for role models and mentors for students. Although posters of famous and exceptional individuals contribute to students' appreciation of diversity, real-life role models who are accessible to students have the greatest impact.

Culturally Relevant Teaching and Other Instructional Strategies

Culturally relevant teaching refers to methods of teaching that empower students to grow intellectually, socially, and emotionally by using cultural referents in teaching knowledge and skills (Harmon, in press; Pang, 2001). Instructional strategies are procedures or steps that teachers use to facilitate students' attainment of stated objectives. There is no right or wrong strategy, for all students learn differently. When a strategy matches a student's preferred learning style, student success is more likely. The following strategies can help to make the classroom more stimulating and students more flexible learners.

- Take cultural characteristics into consideration when beginning instruction and selecting instructional strategies. Students in some cultures prefer oral/aural communication, and are field dependent, expressive, flexible, and humanistic. Preassessment of your students early in the year will give you insights into these variations in learning preferences.
- Check students' prior knowledge. Some students miss the point of a lesson because they don't have the background knowledge that could put the text and ideas presented in meaningful context.

- Relate content to students' lives. Knowing about students' interests and backgrounds can help you provide valuable links. Using examples, similes, metaphors, and stories from students' cultures can provide bridges for understanding.
- Provide kinesthetic activities (writing, physical games, role-playing); visual images (photographs, charts); auditory experiences (records, music); and interactive (group discussion) and haptic strategies (drawing, painting, sculpturing) (Shade, 1990).
- Provide field trips and other background-enriching activities. If students have not had the experiences necessary for learning a particular subject, you can plan appropriate activities to provide the requisite background knowledge.
- Engage students in meaningful real-world tasks. When students see that learning has a purpose (e.g., solving a real problem or doing an authentic project), they are more likely to stay engaged.
- Use cooperative learning strategies. Many students who do not achieve individually do well with group activities (see Chapter 9).
- Be flexible in grouping students. Heterogeneous grouping can be effective. Research shows that interracial work teams among students are one of the most powerful ways to improve performance (Bennett, 1986). If you do group students homogeneously for some activities, don't always put the same students together.
- Teach students test-taking skills. Practice test-taking environments. Familiarize students with the routines of tests, use practice drills, teach study skills for use in test taking, reduce stress through relaxation skills, and discuss time management.
- Assess students through multiple measures. Allow students to be evaluated through personal interviews, oral tests, and practical assignments.

Bias must be removed from materials used in teaching. Materials that are biased ignore the existence and often demean the personal characteristics of some students. They can distort conditions and largely ignore the student's perspective. If biased or racist language passes unchallenged, students are harmed by the demeaning depiction of the group (Southern Poverty Law Center, 2001).

Pang (2001) focuses on culturally relevant teaching that is structured by an ethic of caring. Her work is powerful regardless of school setting, but is particularly important in diverse urban settings. She suggests five approaches for restructuring curriculum to incorporate both cultural diversity and a focus on caring relationships.

1. Include themes or threads in your curriculum that focus on language, culture, power, and compassion.
2. Use a comparative orientation of study presenting diverse perspectives on the issue , theme, event, or concept.
3. Employ an issues-centered orientation.
4. Restructure existing units by using a culture/caring/justice filter.
5. Teach by example. (p. 204)

As Pang observes, the fifth approach is one of the most powerful. When teachers treat students with respect, fairness, and open-mindedness, students are likely to respond in kind. If teachers demonstrate interest in diverse ideas and cultures, it is much more likely students will do so as well.

REFLECTING ON THE IDEAS

Observe a teacher interacting with students in a variety of circumstances: in class, on the playground, in the cafeteria, and so on. Observe the interactions that you believe convey high or low expectations for students. Observe actions you believe demonstrate an ethic of caring.

Teaching Bilingual Students

Some culturally diverse students whose family traditions and customs are quite different from those associated with the majority culture may also be impacted by limited proficiency in English—the language spoken by the macro culture and therefore the medium of communication in the nation's public schools. Bilingual students will benefit from good teaching and planning, as well as from many of the activities suggested for culturally diverse students. In addition, the following ideas may be helpful:

- Review students' files extensively. Make sure you are clear on the history of the students' educational experiences. A student who was successful in fractions in her native country needs different strategies in math from one who was unable to learn fractions because of language difficulties, even if neither can express knowledge of fractions in English.
- Make and maintain contact with parents. Realize that some parents may be reluctant to contact the schools because of their limited English proficiency. Others may view American schools as a threat to their native culture or to their authority as parents. Convey both your respect for the student's native culture and your academic goals.
- Learn as much as you can about the cultures of the students in your class. Make contact with parents, local cultural associations, bilingual education specialists, academic specialists in various cultures, and others with knowledge of the countries. Be especially attuned to patterns of communication, taboos, and structures of authority.
- Consider a buddy system or cross-grade tutoring. A buddy within the class might be assigned to help a bilingual student communicate and learn the logistics of school. An older, successful bilingual student can provide tutoring and can serve as a powerful role model.
- Be cautious about cooperative learning in the beginning, particularly structures in which groups compete with one another. Cooperative learning assumes an ability to communicate and function within an educational system that may not be reasonable for a non-English-speaking student. Avoid putting students in situations they are unable to handle; the results are likely to be a sense of personal inadequacy and a feeling of having let their groups down.
- Present as much material visually as possible. Movies, pictures, filmstrips, and demonstrations can assist students with language development.
- Whenever possible, share information and positive role models from diverse cultures, with emphasis on those cultures represented in your room. Parent presentations, studies of the contributions of varied groups, and the selection of music, celebrations, and games from non-Western lands all send a message that all cultures are important.
- Be patient. Adapting to a new language and culture is a long and difficult task, even for a young person. Time, energy, and genuine affection will be necessary for students to integrate that task into the already complex demands of school.

REFLECTING ON THE IDEAS

Imagine that the principal comes to your room and informs you that in 1 week a Polish student will be joining your class. The student speaks limited English and will receive 1 hour per day of specialized language instruction. How will you prepare for the student's arrival? What strategies might you use once the student has arrived? Write down your ideas; then discuss them with one or more colleagues.

SECTION 5. TEACHING IN URBAN SCHOOLS AND OTHER SETTINGS

Section 5 Objectives

After you have completed this section, you should be able to

1. discuss the major factors influencing the success of some teachers in urban schools;
2. compare and contrast the influencing factors for successful urban teachers with those for successful rural and suburban teachers;
3. compare and contrast the views of successful urban, rural, and suburban teachers concerning such important factors as learner needs and characteristics, society/home community/culture, and the availability of funding and resources;
4. relate the PREMIER model of successful urban teaching with instructional principles presented elsewhere in the text; and
5. describe the potential benefits of parental involvement and integrated services schools on student achievement.

Although schools cannot accomplish everything, Edmonds (1979) argued, "We can, whenever and wherever we choose, successfully teach all children whose schooling is of interest to us. We already know more than we need to do that" (p.24). If this belief is to be proven true, it will have to be demonstrated in urban schools. It is in such schools that the racial, cultural, and social contradictions between the teachers and students often create barriers that significantly endanger learning.

Consider that the teaching force in the United States is predominantly White; almost 90% of those currently teaching trace their family histories back to Europe (Pasch, Krakow, Johnson, Slocum, & Stapleton, 1990). Most were fortunate enough to be nurtured as children in emotionally and financially secure families. They were successful students and graduated from small-town or suburban schools and then achieved a college degree. Their background and experiences were overwhelmingly influenced by the dominant Anglo-European culture.

Teachers employed in the foreseeable future can expect to be employed in urban schools. They are likely to be teaching children of color, from African American and Latino cultures, but also children from families who recently emigrated from one of the many Asian or Middle Eastern countries (Hodgkinson, 1988). It is a good bet that the urban school districts in which these teachers work will be large and bureaucratic. The school districts will be underfunded, and thus the buildings will be old and possibly deteriorating. There will be little money available for necessary supplies and equipment.

Too many students in each urban classroom will come from families facing unemployment, financial problems, and health emergencies. Too often, families will be headed by a single parent who must face these problems with inadequate support. Differences in resources between urban and suburban districts, particularly given the needs of many urban populations, can cause striking levels of inequality (Kozol, 1992).

Given the importance of the need, it is vital to identify those factors that allow some teachers and students to succeed, even in potentially difficult environments. In a recent study looking at high-achieving culturally diverse inner-city students and their teachers, students were able to identify what they believed were characteristics of effective teachers (Harmon, in press). Exemplary teachers

were culturally competent,
viewed cultural differences as cultural assets—not deficits,
held high expectations for all students,
used a multicultural curriculum incorporating higher level thinking skills and creative
    problem solving,
used an affective curriculum including conflict management skills,
used culturally relevant teaching methods,
used differentiation,
used role models and mentors,
provided a disciplined environment through an authoritative and democratic
    management style, and
involved the family and the community.

Note that one of the key concepts in the preceding list is cultural competence. Culturally competent teachers possess self-awareness and self-understanding, cultural awareness and understanding, and social responsiveness and responsibility. They use appropriate techniques for teaching all students. The process of becoming culturally competent begins with the opportunity to learn about one's own cultural heritage and the influence of that culture on teaching. Cultural awareness and understanding involves learning how cultural differences and conflicts influence teaching and learning. Teachers who work to develop racial harmony in their classroom by demanding respect of individual differences are demonstrating social responsiveness and responsibility. Armed with this knowledge and understanding, culturally competent teachers are able to use instruction methods that enable all of their students to learn.

REFLECTING ON THE IDEAS

Consider your own cultural heritage. Think about the values that are most important to you, the standards you set for exemplary behavior and achievement, and the ideas you consider most interesting. How will those ideas and values affect your interactions with students whose cultural norms are different from yours?

One of the authors has been active in a consortium of three urban teacher education projects engaged in a 2-year research project to identify the factors that influence successful urban teachers (Pasch et al., 1992). After analyzing data from 90 urban teachers in three large cities, the researchers developed a model for teaching success in urban schools represented by the mnemonic PREMIER. These elements and others are supported by Haberman's (1995) research on "star" teachers of children in poverty. Note, too, the similarity to the Harmon study described earlier. Successful urban teachers

1. are *Purposeful*. They set high, yet achievable expectations, identify the purpose(s) for learning in each new unit and lesson, establish and communicate clearly stated objectives, and teach the relationships between previous learning and upcoming learning tasks.

2. are *Respectful of Diversity*. This principle encompasses the importance teachers attach to knowing the characteristics of the student, the environment in which the student lives, and its probable effects on the student. Finally, teachers add to their success when they accept and care for young people from different backgrounds and lifestyles than their own.

3. employ *Experience-Based Methods and Activities*. The importance of a curriculum that has relevance to the life of the urban student—that not only identifies the contributions of culturally diverse people to American and world civilization and culture but challenges students to interpret, analyze, compare, and evaluate these contributions—captures the essence of experience-based learning. This principle also subsumes the benefits derived from role-playing, simulations, and activities that permit young people to observe, touch, and manipulate objects in contrast to activities that rely exclusively on verbal symbols.

4. *Manage the Urban Classroom Effectively*. The focus of this principle is on physical, emotional, and relational environments and their impact on student behavior. Chapters 11 and 12 discuss the research- and experience-based principles and practices that enable any teacher to be successful as a classroom manager.

5. *Individualize Instruction*. Each student is an individual and has the right to be treated as such. Alternating direct lesson designs with those based on active, discussion-based activities helps meet the needs of a variety of students. Inductive lessons that require students to investigate and discover concepts and principles should also be used.

6. are *Excellent Communicators*. This principle suggests that purposeful teaching is not complete until ideas, relationships, and expectations are communicated, before, during, and after instruction. Teachers in the study often referred to the importance of responding appropriately to students' answers, questions, and comments.

7. are *Reflective in Thought*. This principle develops the importance of self-evaluation and metacognition while teaching, with special attention to reflection after instruction. Successful teachers also communicate to students what they are teaching, share alternative ways to structure a lesson or activity, and thus assist students to become more aware of their own thought patterns (see also Cole, 1995).

REFLECTING ON THE IDEAS

Leaving the principle "Manage the Urban Classroom Effectively" aside, consider how the other PREMIER principles relate to concepts taught in other chapters. What ideas you have learned thus far do you think will be most important in teaching in an urban environment?

Parental Involvement

In the 1990s, there was growing attention to the importance of home/school cooperative efforts to improve educational outcomes. Research studies over a 30-year period have demonstrated the positive results on school performance from school/home partnerships (Henderson & Berla, 1995). After examining over 85 studies, Henderson and Berla conclude that when parents are involved with a school, their children perform better in that school. In wealthy communities where family income and educational achievement is high, parents have traditionally been active in school activities. As the pace of life increases and parents work to juggle careers and families, maintaining those levels of involvement is difficult. In urban and rural communities extra effort is needed to bring parents and school administrators and teachers closer together.

The evidence has been of such persuasive weight as to encourage the National PTA to develop and disseminate the booklet National Standards for Parent/Family Involvement Programs (National PTA, 1997). Parent involvement has been identified as one of the eight National Education goals:

> Every school will promote partnerships that will increase parental involvement and participation in promoting the social, emotional and academic growth of children. (National PTA, 1997, p.4)

The PTA describes six types of home/school involvement based on the framework established by Joyce Epstein (Epstein, 1995; Sullivan, 1997). The standards include (a) frequent and predictable two-way communication between home and school, (b) enhancing parenting skills and capabilities, (c) assisting and enhancing student learning, (d) encouraging parents to engage in volunteering activities in the school, (e) participating in school decision making and advocacy, and (f) enabling parents and schools to create additional partnerships for collaborating with the community. Of course, these standards are applicable in urban and nonurban communities.

■ *Practice Activity: Home and Family Involvement*

Working with colleagues in class, divide into six groups, one focusing on each of the types of home/school involvement. Brainstorm things you will be able to do as a beginning teacher to support each type of involvement.

■ ■ ■

Integrated Services Schools

In his last book, *Basic Schools: A Community for Learning*, Boyer (1995) argued for an integrated approach to schooling, one that serves the "whole child." In addition to a solid academic program and a partnership between home and school, an integrated services school provides "basic health and counseling services for students, referrals for families, and a new calendar and clock, with after-school and summer enrichment programs for learning and creative play" (Boyer, 1995, p. 153). The move toward more integration of school and community services can take a variety of forms. In some areas, schools establish more formal links with health and social service agencies than in traditional schools. There, educational personnel have systematic communication with a variety of agencies, allowing for quick and convenient referrals and consultation. In other schools, sometimes called **full-service schools**, the school itself becomes the hub for services. Health, government, and social service agencies establish a presence within the school itself (Dryfoos, 1994; William-Boyd, 1996). In these cases, teachers do not have to refer a student or parent to a health clinic, counselor, or social service agency somewhere in the city; they can simply help them walk to another part of the building. In urban settings (or in impoverished rural settings) in which many students have complex sets of needs, such supports can be particularly valuable.

In *Basic Schools*, Boyer gives credit to James P. Comer, a Yale University child psychologist, for his early and continuing efforts to create schools that provide a range of professional services to children (Boyer, 1995, p.168). Recall from Chapter 1 that Comer emphasizes student development along six developmental pathways and supportive relationships among adults and children. Today, there are hundreds of **Comer schools** across the nation, predominantly in low-income school districts. These schools utilize the Comer School Development Program to integrate pupil services with parental collaboration to foster child development as a necessary foundation for educational progress and academic achievement (Finn-Stevenson & Stern, 1997; Goldberg, 1997; Haynes, 1996; Squires & Kranyik, 1995–1996). When a Comer School Development Program is fully functioning, every child in the school is supported by a significant adult presence at home, at school, and in the community at large. As we consider the directions schools must take during the 21st century, it seems likely that they will form the focus of services not traditionally considered part of the schools' mission. Think about the impact on your effectiveness—and on your students' lives—if basic health, safety, and economic concerns could be addressed efficiently and effectively in a single environment.

SUMMARY

The extraordinary range of student strengths, needs, interests, experiences, values, difficulties, learning styles, and a host of other variables makes it impossible for a one-size-fits-all approach to be very successful in any classroom. On the other hand, the realities of classroom life dictate that you will have few opportunities to plan individually for each one of your students. This poses a dilemma that has puzzled teachers for generations: How do I balance the seemingly limitless variety of students' needs with the basic limits of time, space, and human energy?

Fortunately, you have a host of options between inflexible planning and infinite variety. If teachers assume the right way to teach is when all students do the same things in the same way, any variation in that pattern is likely to seem an unreasonable expectation. On the other hand, if teachers assume that having students engage in a variety of activities is the normal process of teaching, fewer adaptations will need to be made, because the regular classroom routines will already accommodate a variety of students' needs. The more differentiation and variety you plan as part of your normal course of teaching, the fewer worries you will have about adapting to the needs of individual students. Just like a stretchable piece of clothing fits more sizes, the more flexible the curriculum, the less it will need to be adapted.

■ *Practice Activity: Adapting Mythic Heroes and Heroines*

Think back to the four students described at the beginning of this chapter and to Hannah's planned unit on mythic heroes and heroines. What advice might you give Hannah for activities or strategies that would enhance the unit for her students? List at least two suggestions for each student. Compare your list with a friend's. Discuss the characteristics that helped you diagnose each student's instructional needs.

■ ■ ■

PORTFOLIO ACTIVITY

Your plan for differentiating your teaching unit can make a good portfolio activity. Learning to differentiate instruction for various groups of students simultaneously is enormously challenging. Be prepared to talk to interviewers about how you hope to accomplish this. You will not become expert at differentiation during your first year, but you can begin the important habit of thinking of students as individuals first.

SEARCH THE WEB

The Companion Website section on "Special Education" has links related to both disabilities and gifted education. Also, review the "Parents and Community" section for links on parent involvement and community-school partnerships.

UNIT PREPARATION

As you have planned your teaching unit, you should have kept in mind the needs, interests, and circumstances of the students for whom you are planning. Now that you have some basic plans in place, it is important to examine those plans to find places you will need to differentiate instruction. Here are some questions to get you started. Note the kinds of adaptations or alternative plans that will be necessary to meet all your students' needs.

1. What skills are you assuming when planning class activities? These might be skills associated with the content you are teaching or general skills such as reading, adding, or using a scissors. What supports will you plan for students who lack prerequisite skills?
2. Are there students in your class who may not have had experiences common to other students or who are likely to have trouble learning through the types of lessons you are planning because of a disability? How will you adapt your instruction?
3. Are there students in your class who learn exceptionally rapidly or who have a great deal of background knowledge about your topic? How will you make sure they learn information that is new to them?
4. Are there parts of this unit that should be omitted for some students? Are there places where multiple options might allow for differing styles, backgrounds, or levels of challenge?

REFERENCES

Banks, J. A. (1999). *An introduction to multicultural education* (2nd ed.). Boston: Allyn & Bacon.

Banks, J. A. (1994). *Multiethnic education: Theory and practice.* (3rd ed.). Boston: Allyn & Bacon.

Bennett, C. I. (1986). *Comprehensive multicultural education: Theory and practice.* Newton, MA: Allyn & Bacon.

Biklen, D., & Bogdan, R. (1977). Handicappism in America. In B. Blatt, D. Biklen, & R. Bogdan (Eds.), *An alternative textbook in special education* (pp. 205–215). New York: Love Publishing.

Boyer, E. (1995). *Basic schools: A community for learning.* Princeton, NJ: Carnegie Foundation for the Advancement of Teaching.

Boykin, A. W. (1994). Harvesting talent and culture: African American children and educational reform. In R. Rossi (Ed.), *Schools and students at risk.* New York: Teachers College Press.

Brandt, R. (1992). On building learning communities: A conversation with Hank Levin. *Educational Leadership, 50* (1), 19–23.

Checkley, K. (1997). The first seven . . . and the eighth. A conversation with Howard Gardner. *Educational Leadership, 55* (1), 8–13.

Colangelo, N., & Davis, G. A. (1997). *Handbook of gifted education* (2nd ed.). Boston: Allyn & Bacon.

Cole, R. W. (Ed.). (1995). *Educating everybody's children: Diverse teaching strategies for diverse children.* Alexandria, VA: Association for Supervision and Curriculum Development.

Collins, M. (1992). *Ordinary children, extraordinary teachers.* Charlottesville, VA: Hampton Publishing Co.

Corcoran, T. B., Walker, L. J., & White, J. L. (1988). *An imperiled generation: Saving urban schools.* Princeton, NJ: The Carnegie Foundation for the Advancement of Teaching.

Dryfoos, J. (1994). *Full-service schools.* San Francisco: Jossey-Bass.

Edmonds, R. (1979). Effective schools for the urban poor. *Educational Leadership, 37,* 15–24.

Education Products Information Exchange (EPIE). (1979). *Grant progress report NIE-G-790083.* Mimeographed. Stony Brook, NY: Author.

Epstein, J. (1995). School family, community partnerships: Caring for the children we share. *Phi Delta Kappan, 77* (9), 701–712.

Esposito, B. G., & Reed, T. M. (1986). The effects of contact with handicapped persons on young children's attitudes. *Exceptional Children, 54,* 224–229.

Farlow, L. (1996). A quartet of success stories: How to make inclusion work. *Educational Leadership, 53* (5), 51–55.

Feldhusen, J. F. (1992, August). *Talent identification and development in education (TIDE).* Paper presented at the Second Asian Conference on Giftedness, Taipei, Republic of China.

Feldhusen, J. F. (1996). How to identify and develop special talents. *Educational Leadership, 53* (5), 66–69.

Finn-Stevenson, M., & Stern, B. (1997). Integrating early-childhood and family-support services with a school improvement process: The Comer-Zigler initiative. *Elementary School Journal, 98* (1), 51–66.

Gardner, H. (1983). *Frames of mind.* New York: Basic Books.

Giangreco, M. F., Cloninger, C. J., Dennis, R. E., & Edelman, S. W. (1994). Problem-solving methods to facilitate inclusive education. In J. S. Thousand, R. A. Villa, & A. I. Nevin (Eds.), *Creativity and collaborative learning: A practical guide to empowering students and teachers.* Baltimore: Brookes.

Goldberg, M. (1997). Maintaining a focus on child development. An interview with Dr. James P. Comer. *Phi Delta Kappan, 78*(7), 557–559.

Goldberg, M. (2001). An interview with Henry Levin: A concern with disadvantaged students. *Phi Delta Kappan, 82* (8), 632–634.

Good, T. L. (1981). Teacher expectations and student perceptions: A decade of research. *Educational Leadership, 38,* 415–422.

Goodlad, J., & Lovitt, T. (Eds.). (1993). *Integrating general and special education.* New York: Macmillan.

Greenwood, J. M. (1888). *Principles of education practically applied.* New York: D. Appleton.

Guralnick, M. J. (1981). The social behavior of preschool children at different developmental levels: Effects of group composition. *Journal of Experimental Child Psychology, 31,* 115–130.

Haberman, M. (1995). *Star teachers of children in poverty.* W. Lafayette, IN: Kappa Delta Pi.

Hale-Benson, J. (1986). *Black children: Their roots, culture, and learning styles.* Baltimore: Johns Hopkins University Press.

Hanline, M. F., & Murray, C. (1984). Integrating severely handicapped children into regular public schools. *Phi Delta Kappan, 66,* 273–276.

Harmon, D. (in press). They won't teach me: The voices of African American inner city students. *Roeper Review.*

Haynes, N. (1996). Creating safe and caring school communities: Comer School Development program schools. *Journal of Negro Education, 65* (3), 308–314.

Henderson, A. T., & Berla, N. (1995). *A new generation of evidence: the family is critical to student achievement.* Washington, DC: Center for Law and Education.

Heward, W. L. (2000). *Exceptional children: An introduction to special education.* Upper Saddle River, NJ: Prentice Hall.

Hodgkinson, H. (1988). An interview with Harold Hodgkinson: Using demographic data for long-range planning. *Phi Delta Kappan, 70* (2), 166–170.

Hollins, E. (Ed.). (1994). *Teaching diverse populations: Formulating a knowledge base.* Albany, NY: State University of New York Press.

Hopfenber, W. S., Levin, H. M., & Chase, C. (1993). *The accelerated school resource guide.* San Francisco: Jossey-Bass.

Individuals with Disabilities Education Act of 1997. U.S. Public Law 105–17. 105th Cong., 4 June 1997.

Johnson, R., Rynders, J. R., Johnson, D. W., Schmidt, B., & Haider, S. (1979). Interaction between handicapped and nonhandicapped teenagers as a function of situational goal structuring: Implications for mainstreaming. *American Educational Research Journal, 16,* 161–167.

Kauffman, J. M., & Hallahan, D. K. (1994–1995). *The illusion of full inclusion: A comprehensive critique of a current special education bandwagon.* Austin, TX: PRO-ED.

Kozol, J. (1992). *Savage inequalities.* New York: Harper.

Kunjufu, J. (1984). *Developing positive self-images and discipline in Black children.* Chicago: African-American Images.

Marland, S. P. (1972). *Education of the gifted and talented: Report to the Congress of the United States by the United States commissioner of education and background papers.* Submitted to the United States Office of Education. Washington, DC: Government Printing Office.

National Education Association. (1978). *Education for all handicapped children.* Washington, DC: Author.

National PTA. (1997). *National standards for parent/family involvement programs.* Chicago: Author.

Pang, V. O. (2001). *Multicultural education: A caring-centered, reflective approach.* New York: McGraw-Hill.

Pasch, M., Krakow, M. C., Johnson, C., Slocum, H., & Stapleton, E. (1990). The disappearing minority educator: No illusion, a practical solution. *Urban Education, 25,* 207–218.

Pasch, S., Pasch, M., Johnson, R., Ilmers, S., Snyder, J., Stapleton, E., Hamilton, A., & Mooradian, P. (1992). Reflection of urban education: A tale of three cities. In *Diversity, the 1992 research yearbook* (pp. 9–30). Reston, VA: Association of Teacher Educators.

Public Law 94-142. (1975). Sec. 4.

Quality Education for Minorities Project. (1990). *Education that works: An action plan for the education of minorities.* Cambridge, MA: Massachusetts Institute of Technology.

Raynes, M., Snell, M., & Sailor, W. (1992). A fresh look at categorical programs for children with special needs. *Phi Delta Kappan, 73* (4), 327.

Reis, S. M., Burns, D. E., & Renzulli, J. S. (1992). Curriculum compacting: *The complete guide for modifying curriculum for high ability students.* Mansfield Center, CT: Creative Learning Press.

Reis, S. M., & Purcell, J. H. (1998). An analysis of content elimination and strategies used by elementary classroom teachers in the curriculum compacting process. *Journal for the Education of the Gifted, 16* (2), 147–170.

Renzulli, J. S. (1977). *The enrichment triad.* Mansfield Center, CT: Creative Learning Press.

Renzulli, J. S. (1978). What makes giftedness? Reexamining a definition. *Phi Delta Kappan, 60,* 180–184.

Renzulli, J. S. (1993). *Schools are places for talent development: Applying "gifted education" know-how to total school improvement.* Storrs, CT: National Research Center for Gifted and Talented.

Renzulli, J. S., & Reis, S. M. (1997). *The schoolwide enrichment model* (2nd ed.). Mansfield Center, CT: Creative Learning Press.

Renzulli, J. S., & Smith, L. H. (1979). *A guidebook for developing individualized educational programs for gifted and talented students.* Mansfield Center, CT: Creative Learning Press.

Rogers, J. (1993). *The inclusion revolution. Research bulletin no. 11.* Bloomington, IN: Phi Delta Kappa Center for Evaluation, Development and Research.

Sapon-Shevin, M. (1994). *Playing favorites: Gifted education and the disruption of community.* Albany, NY: State University of New York Press.

Schniedewind, N., & Davidson, E. (2000). Differentiating cooperative learning. *Educational Leadership, 58* (1), 24–29.

Schumaker, J.B., & Deshler, D. D. (1995). Secondary classes can be inclusive, too. *Educational Leadership, 52* (4), 50–51.

Shade, B. J. (1990). *Engaging the battle for African American minds.* Washington, DC: National Alliance of Black School Educators.

Shade, B. J. (Ed.). (1997). *Culture, style, and the educative process: Making schools work for racially diverse students* (2nd ed.). Springfield, IL: Charles C. Thomas.

Shaywitz, S. E., Holahan, J. M., Freudenheim, D. A., Fletcher, J. M., Makeuch, R. W., & Shaywitz, B. A. (2001). Heterogeneity within the gifted: Higher IQ boys exhibit behaviors resembling boys with learning disabilities. *Gifted Child Quarterly, 45* (1), 16–23.

Singer, J. D., & Butler, J. A. (1987). The Education for All Handicapped Children Act: Schools as agents of social reform. *Harvard Educational Review, 57* (2), 125–152.

Snell, M. E., & Janney, R. E. (2000). Some things we've learned about inclusion. In W. L. Heward, *Exceptional children: An introduction to special education* (pp. 236–237). Upper Saddle River, NJ: Prentice Hall.

Southern Poverty Law Center (2001). *Responding to hate in school.* [On-line]Available: www.splcenter.org/teachingtolerance/tt-index.html:

Squires, D., & Kranyik, R. (1995–1996). The Comer program: Changing school culture. *Educational Leadership 53* (4), 29–32.

Status of Black children. (1989). [Special issue]. *Black Child Advocate, 15* (4).

Sternberg, R. (1985). *Beyond IQ: A triarchic theory of human intelligence.* New York: Cambridge University Press.

Strother, D. B. (1985). Adapting instruction to individual needs: An eclectic approach. *Phi Delta Kappan, 67,* 308–311.

Sullivan, P. (1997). The PTA's national standards. *Educational Leadership., 55* (8), 43–44.

Tomlinson, C. A. (1995). *How to differentiate instruction in mixed-ability classrooms.* Alexandria, VA: Association for Supervision and Curriculum Development.

Tomlinson, C. A. (2000). Reconcilable differences: Standards-based teaching and differentiation. *Educational Leadership, 58* (1), 6–11.

Tomlinson, C. A. (1999). *The differentiated classroom: Responding to the needs of all learners.* Alexandria, VA: Association for Supervision and Curriculum Development.

Towle, W. (2000). The art of reading workshop. *Educational Leadership, 58* (1), 38–41.

U.S. Department of Education. (1993). *National excellence: A case for developing America's talent.* Washington, DC: Author.

Wang, M. C., Reynolds, M. C., & Walberg, H. J. (1986). Rethinking special education. *Educational Leadership, 44,* 27–28, 31.

Wang, M. C., Reynolds, M. C., & Walberg, H. J. (1988). Integrating the children of the second system. *Phi Delta Kappan, 20,* 248–251.

Wang, M. C., & Walberg, H. J. (1985). *Adapting instruction for individual differences.* Berkeley, CA: McCutchan.

William-Boyd, P. (1996). *A case study of a full-service school: A transformational dialectic of empowerment, collaboration and communitarianism.* Unpublished doctoral dissertation, Lawrence, KS: University of Kansas.

TOPIC 3

Creating a Positive Learning Environment

Classroom Management:
Traditions, Programs,
and Goals

CHAPTER OVERVIEW

An understanding of effective classroom management is basic to professional practice and should be a significant part of a teacher's decision making. Knowledge of what constitutes sound classroom management can provide answers to a new teacher's numerous questions: Why is there so much concern among teachers about classroom management? How does a teacher establish an environment that enhances learning? What are the forces that affect a teacher's responses to student behaviors? What management programs or strategies have proven to be most workable?

This chapter describes and analyzes the beliefs, guidelines, and practices of two approaches to classroom management: behavior management and humanistic/developmental. In addition, it offers insights and practical suggestions gleaned from researchers who observed successful classroom managers in action and considers how a variety of management strategies can be considered part of a developmental continuum. Reflective teachers will have to make decisions by selecting the approaches that best fit their philosophy, meet student needs, and complement school expectations.

Chapter 12 will describe one approach, the Rational Approach to Practical School Discipline, that blends features of the management approaches described in this chapter. Here, again, the teacher decision maker will have to select appropriate strategies that meet the individual problem, set the tone for positive interactions, and structure the environment to match the teacher's style.

■ *Opening Activity*

You are a new member of the Landstown School staff. During a prep period in mid-September, you overhear Ken Cowan discussing a discipline problem with three teachers. Examine the responses made by Sandy and Marilyn to the problem Ken is having with Kevann, one of his students.

> *Ken:* Kevann disrupts my class every five minutes. It's so frustrating. He is such a sweet respectful young man, but I have to tell him to stop talking, visiting, or wandering aimlessly in my class. I plead with him to stop. He stops for a few minutes and then he is back disrupting again. I'm at my wit's end. I need to observe a bit more, maybe talk to last year's teacher.
>
> *Sandy:* Ken, have you taught students your classroom rules and consequences for misbehavior? I spend the first two weeks of class creating an environment in which the students learn that they will receive rewards for positive behavior and punishment for negative behavior.
>
> *Marilyn:* My approach is very different. I want students to develop self-discipline, to take responsibility for their own behavior, and to realize that when they misbehave, they disappoint me and diminish what we can do together that day. I use group meetings and individual conferences to gain insights about my students' needs, resources, and feelings. I find that these practices make it possible for the students to participate actively in managing the classroom.

Using the information provided, describe the approach to classroom discipline management reflected by each teacher.

Sandy: _____

_____

Marilyn: _____

_____

■ ■ ■

Sandy & Marilyn represent differing traditions of classroom management. Like other aspects of your teaching, your approach to management will be shaped by many factors. Approaches to management often are defined by the schools of thought that shaped the psychological principles undergirding the programs. The behaviorist tradition in psychology holds that human behavior is shaped through experiences with reward and punishment. This perspective frames the beliefs and strategies used in the behavior management approaches to management characterized by Sandy in the example. Humanist psychology holds that healthy human development is a natural process of growth that will unfold in positive directions unless blocked. Humanist approaches are more likely to lead to management strategies like those described by Marilyn. The degree to which you implement strategies based on these traditions is likely to be based on your own beliefs and values, school requirements, and your students' experiences and developmental levels.

In nearly every yearly opinion survey between 1973 and 2000, the national Gallup Poll reported that parents, students, and teachers regarded discipline among the most serious problems facing the public schools (Gallup & Elam, 1997; Rose & Gallup, 2000). The public has remained consistent in its perception that (a) students in the public schools of the United States lack discipline and (b) improved discipline is the answer to many of the schools. Unfortunately, as the case study about Kevann reveals, there are serious differences of opinion about what methods and practices are most effective in addressing discipline and management problems in schools.

As a teacher, you will make decisions each day on methods and practices to maintain order in your classroom. The achievement of a disciplined and well-managed classroom is not as simple as most packaged, widely marketed discipline programs would suggest. On the other hand, it is not as awesome a challenge as many veteran teachers would have you believe. Reality lies somewhere between the two extremes.

The decisions you make in setting up your room and interacting with students are critical. With increasing numbers of young people coming to school from families in which both parents are working, from households headed by a single parent, or from troubled homes and communities, you must be able to enhance a student's personal and social development if you wish to be successful in teaching academic content.

CHAPTER OBJECTIVES

After you have completed the activities in this chapter, you will be able to

1. classify examples of the behavior management and humanistic/developmental traditions of classroom management;

2. describe the components necessary for developing a classroom learning community;
3. explain contemporary research principles related to
   a. establishing classroom rules and routines,
   b. behaviors of effective classroom managers,
   c. preventing classroom disruption, and
   d. saving instructional time;
4. develop classroom rules and routines that are consistent with sound principles of classroom management; and
5. develop and refine your own philosophy of classroom management.

SECTION 1. TWO TRADITIONS OF CLASSROOM MANAGEMENT
Tradition 1: Behavior Management

The behavior management tradition is based on the behaviorist learning theory of B. F. Skinner. Skinner believed that future human behavior is determined by the consequences that followed past behavior. Behavior learning theory was derived from scientific experimentation, including numerous types of animal studies. It was Skinner who developed language that could communicate the nature of behavior theory to people within the field of education (but outside the field of psychology), and thus became its primary spokesperson. According to behavior learning theory, students are more likely to repeat behaviors that have led to positive consequences, and less likely to repeat behaviors that have led to negative consequences. Consequently, the teacher's responsibility is to ensure that positive actions yield positive results.

Many behavior management programs, although based on behavioral theory, incorporate practices derived from other psychological theories. For example, a behavior management program may include a component that dignifies the importance of student feelings and values, a practice derived from humanistic psychology.

What are the common elements of behavior management programs? Among the best known are *contingency management, contracting, the use of praise, noncontingent reinforcement, and rules/reward–ignore/punish.* As you read about each element, consider how it is a logical outgrowth of behaviorist theory.

Contingency Management

Contingency management, sometimes referred to as an *incentive system,* is a widely practiced element in behavior management. Contingency management requires that the teacher control (or manage) reward and punishment in the classroom based on specified criteria. Rewards are *contingent* upon behavior. A student who is ready for the next activity may be praised; students who complete their math in a specified amount of time may earn 5 minutes extra recess.

Contingency management often involves the use of tangible rewards to reinforce appropriate behavior. The basic theme of contingency management is that the worth of a reward you receive in school should be based on the worth of your actions. Often tokens of different values are given and then exchanged for such rewards as books, magazines, free time, or preferred classroom activities. Instead of tokens, play money may be used to redeem desired products from a student store. In some cases, individual adults and the business community contribute products and services to support the token exchange.

Contracting

Contracting is a formalized contingency management process usually implemented through agreement with an individual student. The work to be accomplished by the student, the period in which the contract will remain in force, and the reward (reinforcement) to be given to the student after successful completion of the contract are all specified in writing. The teacher and the student sign the contract; in some cases the student's parents do so as well. The legal overtones of the process are intended to convey a sense of importance and responsibility to the student. Teachers can use discussions of the contract to help students begin to assess and monitor their own behavior. Similar although less formalized arrangements can be made through charts where, for example, a student agrees that he or she will receive a "star" for each morning's assignments completed without disruption, and that a specific reward will follow a whole week of stars.

The Use of Praise

"Catch 'em being good," or the use of praise as reinforcement, can be seen as a specific form of contingency management. It is an immediate reward that reinforces a desirable behavior. For example, after a teacher gives an assignment, he may say, "Take out your social studies book and do so without talking to your neighbor. Thank you, Maxine, for being so prompt in getting out your book. You, too, Tanya and Ivan." These students are recognized because they responded promptly and appropriately. The teacher's recognition both reinforces the desired behavior as exhibited by Maxine, Tanya, and Ivan, and signals the others that desired behavior will be recognized.

Many educators suggest that this method is most effective at the elementary school level. Certainly, it occurs most frequently at that level. However, it has been applied at every grade level, even at the college level. As students get older, they may prefer privately given praise over public praise.

Noncontingent Reinforcement

Noncontingent reinforcement takes place without reference to any particular behavior on the part of the student. At first, this practice would seem contrary to a behaviorist approach. There is no systematic structure or process, only the teacher's use of a smile, the granting of privileges or special activities, or the giving of tokens to deserving students. Students are given positive reinforcement (reward) without a specific contingency behavior (although not when they are actively misbehaving). When positive noncontingent reinforcement is implemented, students generally behave better even in settings other than the ones in which they received reinforcement. For example, giving a big smile in the hallway could result in improved student attitude and behavior during independent math seatwork. The smile had no specific reference to student behavior. It was not based on merit. It was just a human thing to do.

Rules/Reward–Ignore/Punish (RRIP)

Some behavior management programs communicate the theme that if students obey the rules, they receive a reward; if they ignore the rules, they receive a punishment. Referred to as rules/reward–ignore/punish (RRIP), this approach uses freedom from unpleasant consequences as a form of control. In the RRIP system, logical consequences for misbehavior are given the same status as are rewards for good behavior. In the RRIP system, rules are established to set the limits of behavior. In many cases, students participate in the development of the rules. The teacher then acts as the enforcer of the rules. Students who are compliant get rewarded, and those who are not get punished. Both rewards and punishments are administered with little elapsed time after the behavior that prompted them.

There is a difference in philosophy between two groups of RRIP advocates. One group maintains that certain disruptions, such as soft talking, unobtrusive movements, whispered profanity, and the like should be ignored. This strategy is based on (a) the belief that the attention given to misbehavior can, for some students, be rewarding and (b) the recognition that minor disturbances do not disrupt the flow of classroom activity. The second group cautions that at some point the teacher will have to confront the behaviors that are ignored, because they will increase either in frequency or in intensity. This group charges that ignoring some misbehavior sets up a continuing negative pattern that will be more difficult for the teacher to break the longer it remains in force.

CHECK YOUR UNDERSTANDING

Examine the following case study.

Sam, a fifth grader, has been absent from school three times within the last month. Each time he returns, Sam seems distracted in class and he picks on another student before the day ends. Mr. Griffiths is frustrated by Sam's behavior. He decides to design a behavior management contract for Sam. After analyzing Sam's behavior pattern, he focuses the contract on Sam's habit of picking on his classmates. He discusses the proposed program with Sam and they agree on the following contract:

Contract

On Monday, Sam will sign an agreement that he will avoid using any negative words or actions with his classmates on Monday and Tuesday. At the conclusion of the school day on Tuesday, if Mr. Griffiths has observed no negative incidents, Sam will be given time (5 to 10 minutes) after the work is done to choose from a variety of learning activities of his preference.

1. Review and critique the contract agreement between Mr. Griffiths and Sam.
2. Develop your own contract to deal with Sam's behavior. Share it in a group of three to five persons and come to group consensus about what the contract should contain.

You may have been concerned in your critique that Mr. Griffiths chose to focus on Sam's habit of picking on classmates rather than on his distractedness. Focusing on one behavior per contract, and one contract at a time, makes monitoring easier for the teacher and enhances the student's likelihood of success. Mr. Griffiths chose to emphasize safety and the reduction in interpersonal conflict as his first priority—thus the contract to eliminate Sam's picking on other children. When Sam has mastered that behavior, the teacher may then contract to address his attention in class.

Assertive Discipline: An Example of a Behavior Management Program

Assertive discipline, a program developed by Lee Canter (1976, 1989), is based on the rules/reward–ignore/punish approach. Canter and Canter recommend that teachers create a discipline plan for their classroom with the participation of the parents and the school principal. This system includes the following:

1. A list of rules and a series of lessons to teach the students the difference between acceptable and unacceptable school and classroom behaviors. The result of the rules and lessons should be a clear understanding of which behaviors will result in punishment and which behaviors will reap rewards.
2. A short list of discipline consequences, organized from least serious to most serious, to be administered to students if and when they misbehave. For example, the least serious consequence could be the writing of the misbehaving child's name on the blackboard. The most serious consequence could involve a conference among the teacher, the principal, and the child's parents.
3. A list of rewards to be given to students for acceptable behaviors and especially for those behaviors that contribute to classroom learning success. For example, students could exchange tokens for material rewards, or they could receive verbal praise, written notes of appreciation, or independent reading time.
4. Procedures that ensure timely and frequent communication with all parents about the classroom rules and consequences of misbehavior. Contacts with parents of particular students whose pattern of behavior warrants it are also made.

The important thing to remember is that students must be *taught* how to behave, as described later in this chapter. Also, the consequences should be *logical*—that is, logically related to the misbehavior (Albert, 1996; Dreikurs, Grunwald, & Pepper, 1982). Writing "I will not talk to my neighbor in class" 100 times has no logical relationship to the impact of students talking in class—lost learning time. A more logical consequence would be for the student to lose some social time, for example, working on homework during free time. The following is an example of an assertive discipline system:

Rules

1. Listen while others are talking.
2. Walk quietly in the classroom and halls.
3. Bring materials every day.
4. Respect others' property and bodies.

Consequences

Discipline	Rewards
1st infraction = warning (name on board)	*Points accumulated until 50 = class party*
2nd infraction = check by name (miss 1 minute of recess)	*Positive note to parents* *Free games*
3rd infraction = second check (miss half recess)	*Special movie* *Computer time*

4th infraction = third check
(call home)

5th infraction = fourth check
(see principal)

Lunch with teacher
Free time

Letter to Parents

Dear _____,

I will be (student's name)'s teacher this year. I look forward to working with your child in my class. To maintain a positive classroom, we have established the attached rules and consequences. If your child must remain after school, you will be given one day's notice.

I appreciate your support in upholding this system. Please feel free to call or visit me to discuss anything of concern to you.

Sincerely,

Criticisms of the Behavior Management Approach

In recent years, much criticism has been made of the behaviorist approaches to classroom discipline. Alfie Kohn (1996) has raised serious concerns about the coercive nature of behavior management strategies. He claims that students become merely compliant and do not learn about the crucial aspects of human cooperation. Other research calls into question the result of external rewards on students' creativity, critical thinking, and motivation (see, for example, Amabile, 1996; Collins & Amabile, 1999; Amabile, DeJong, & Lepper, 1976; Deci, 1971; Lepper & Greene, 1975, 1978). According to this body of research, when rewards are given for activities that could be intrinsically rewarding, motivation for those activities can actually decrease. Some teachers wonder, "If students' behavior is 'managed,' at what point do students learn to control themselves without external rewards or consequences?"

Similarly, Glickman (1998) maintains that the emphasis on obeying rules precludes the development of a democratic atmosphere in the classroom. Thus valuable opportunities to develop character and care are lost. In 1996 even Lee Canter (the developer of Assertive Discipline) stressed the importance of establishing rapport with students before moving on to discussions of rules, and of involving students in the development of the rules and consequences. His critics (for example, Kohn, 1996) would argue that the teacher-centered focus of assertive discipline would make it an ineffective means for developing a classroom community, even with established rapport.

Tradition 2: Humanistic/Developmental

Although the humanistic tradition has a long history, its application in classrooms became popular in the 1960s and 1970s. Guidelines and practices can be traced to the work of clinical psychologists, school counselors, and mental health professionals studying emotional development. The goal of this approach is to establish a classroom atmosphere in which students' healthy emotional growth and development are supported as part of a natural process. Humanists hope to create and maintain a classroom environment that emphasizes clear, effective communication; shared responsibility; conflict resolution; and the development of student self-control and need fulfillment. Indeed, in this approach the teacher may act as a guide in the classroom rather than as a figure of authority.

The remainder of this section describes two programs that emerged from the humanistic tradition. The first program, *cooperation through communication* (Ginott, 1972), emphasizes the importance of communication in the classroom. The second humanistic program, *reality therapy* (Glasser, 1969), stresses the role of individual conferences and group meetings in establishing a positive environment for learning. These two programs are discussed in detail along with Glasser's (1994) work on quality schools. As you read, think about how each approach exemplifies a humanistic approach.

Haim Ginott: Cooperation Through Communication

Ginott suggests that good behavior is inextricably tied to a good self-concept. The latter is, to a significant extent, built on the messages that adults generally, and parents and teachers specifically, convey to students. It is logical, then, that his model for enhancing students' development—and, in turn, improving their behavior—is based on improving communication. In advancing his teacher-student communication model, he focuses on reducing chaos through *congruent communication*, which he describes as a way of sending messages that are honest and in harmony with the needs of the students and of others (Ginott, 1972). In pursuit of this harmony, Ginott proposes that teachers must (a) express sane messages, (b) deal with feelings, (c) eliminate stereotypes and labels, (d) use praise carefully, (e) build cooperation, and (f) communicate anger. These six principles are the essential building blocks of Ginott's conception of a humanizing, and yet orderly, environment.

Express Sane Messages

According to Ginott, the best teachers send sane messages, in which feelings are appropriate to the situation and the individuals. He observes that adults are too often predisposed to preach, condemn, force, accuse, threaten, and humiliate, resulting in the dehumanization of young people.

One of the essential principles designed to break this pattern is to separate the student's behavior from the teacher's conception of the student. The student should hear very clearly that "your behavior is unacceptable and will not be tolerated, but there will always be a guaranteed safe place for you in my heart." For example, Leesha, a fourth-grade student, was walking about the room without permission and not writing the assigned essay. The teacher said to her, "You have 10 minutes to finish the essay. Let me see how much you have done." This is a sane message because the emphasis is on the child's off-task behavior. A different (less sane) message from the teacher is communicated when she says to Leesha, "Why do you keep walking about? You are always inconsiderate of the others in the room."

Deal with Feelings

Confronting feelings about self and others is one of the most challenging tasks we face. Ginott counsels teachers that they must help students to sort out their feelings. He suggests that teachers play the role of sounding boards to reflect feelings and ideas expressed by students. For example, students may exaggerate the facts about some situation to impress and to gain attention. Suppose Lauri says to the teacher, "I got all the math problems wrong. I know I am dumb." The teacher may try to prove she is not dumb.

These attempts to argue the logic or dispute the facts may be laudable, but according to Ginott a better decision would be to address Lauri's feelings of inadequacy by saying, "That has really made you upset. Well, we all feel that way sometimes. Let's see where you made the mistakes. Understanding that should help you feel better." This demonstrates that the teacher has confidence in Lauri's ability to assess the situation and accepts the student's right to feel bad about her performance in math.

Eliminate Stereotypes and Labels

According to Ginott, teachers have often used irresponsible labels to describe students. Labeling creates stereotypes for others to apply to the student in future years. It fosters a negative self-image in the student. Labeling, Ginott suggests, is especially dangerous when the teacher, from a position of authority, hardens an attitude into a conclusion about a student's academic and social future. One student had a teacher who called her "Pell-mell Pam," to remind her that she was frivolous and often acted without careful thought. Pam struggles with the memories of that label today, some 30 years later.

When students are negatively labeled, their imagination, aspirations, and possibilities for personal growth are disabled to the degree that they accept the label. Any conclusion about a student's social or academic standing may become a self-fulfilling prophecy that stifles the student's potential. To avoid negative labeling, it is best to communicate to the class that you identify with your students' expectations and possibilities for the future. Identify their goals and aspirations and use that knowledge to prompt behaviors that will motivate students to work toward their goals. For example, if a student expresses an interest in an educational career, a teacher might say, "So you want to be a teacher. If I can help in any way, let me know." This does not mean that you confirm the student's choice. It only means that you are ready and willing to communicate with the student about the goal.

Use Praise Carefully

Ginott cautions teachers to avoid giving judgmental praise. Statements such as "Leesha, you are a good student" or "Maria, you are the best student in the class" may make students dependent on others for self-validation or may alienate students. Praise should be focused on a particular performance: "Leesha, I particularly enjoyed the way you used your own experience to show how we can welcome new students in the class," or "Maria, this is the fourth math test in a row that you have gotten 100 percent. That's the kind of work that makes me confident that you are going to achieve your goal to become a math teacher."

A second caution about the use of praise is the tendency we all have to associate correctness with goodness. A student's ability to do schoolwork correctly is no guarantee that he or she is a "good" person. If the teacher—consciously or unconsciously—connects the two traits, some students may seek to exercise more liberties than are reasonably allowed. Conversely, students whose work does not measure up will arrive at the conclusion that they are "not good."

Third, Ginott suggests that teachers avoid praising minimally acceptable behavior, such as sitting down or working quietly. Instead, the teacher should praise the results of that behavior, as in "I appreciate your working so quietly and hard. We really accomplished a lot today." Praise should be expressed when students behave appropriately in an unusual circumstance: "I'm so glad that you solved the problem of who would clean up our lab equipment."

A fourth caution is to refrain from overusing praise, especially when it is not warranted by student behavior. It is tempting to believe that if praise rewards and reinforces behavior, then more and more praise will lead to even better behavior. Unfortunately, students will detect that they are being manipulated and will come to resent it. When they perceive that the praise is insincere, it will lose its positive reinforcement value.

The four cautions are not meant to imply that praise is not worthy and effective. Rather, teachers are encouraged to use praise carefully to avoid the potential pitfalls. You may wish to refer to Chapter 9 for more guidelines on the use of praise.

Build Cooperation

Ginott encourages teachers to build an atmosphere of cooperation in the classroom. He suggests that this is most effectively done when students feel a sense of independence and a sense of responsibility for the environment. Conversely, when students are dependent on external authority, their will to strive for self-control is diminished.

He recommends several ways to enhance cooperation through the development of student independence. First, give students alternative ways to solve classroom problems. For example, in the event that room cleanup after art projects has been unacceptable, the teacher can offer the students a choice of selecting a cleanup committee that quits 10 minutes early and cleans up for everyone or of having the entire class end art activities 5 minutes earlier and begin to clean up.

Second, Ginott reinforces the notion that it is more productive to invite cooperation than to legislate it. He encourages teachers to give students opportunities to make decisions about ways to increase cooperation in the classroom. For example, he suggests that when students are off task, the teacher should reemphasize positive expectations, as in, "Remember, it's now 10:00 and the period ends at 10:20. You should be working on your projects." Such a message reminds the students that they have a personal responsibility for what they do during the next 20 minutes.

Communicate Anger

Lawyers, doctors, construction workers, police officers—in fact, all human beings—get angry in both their personal and their work lives. Teachers are no different. In contrast to those other working people, however, teachers are in physical proximity to those they serve (students) for 5 to 6 hours a day, day after day. It is therefore not uncommon for a teacher's irritation and anger to be fueled by fatigue, student rudeness, classroom emergencies, or disputes with students, parents, or other teachers and administrators. Because the teacher is expected to be warm, gentle, and sympathetic, the public may be surprised when a teacher reveals anger. Yet, Ginott points out, showing anger in front of a class is one of the few times the teacher has the students' full attention.

He advises the use of the *I-message* when showing anger. An I-message contains both a description of the behavior that prompted the anger and an expression of how the behavior makes the teacher feel—angry, frustrated, disappointed. The following are examples of effective I-messages:

- "The put-downs you used during group work made me feel sad because it shows that we have not learned our lessons about cooperation."
- "Tony, when you use those words in class, I feel very unhappy."
- "Sarah, when you interrupt me while I am giving instruction, it upsets me and I become angry."

Ginott contrasts an *I-message* with an accusatory *you-message*, which is much less effective. In a *you-message* the focus is on the student rather than the behavior. For instance, "Stop that fighting. You are making me angry" or "Tony, you must stop saying those nasty words in my class" or "Sarah, you are being rude when you interrupt me!"

REFLECTING ON THE IDEAS

Assume that you are an advocate of Ginott's principles of classroom management. Analyze the following case study:

Mrs. Weaver explained to her third-grade class that she had to speak to a parent outside the classroom. "I will be just outside the door for five minutes," she informed them. "When I return, everyone working on their assignments and behaving will receive five minutes extra recess. Remember you have an assignment that should take you ten minutes or more. Stay on task." She returned in 4 minutes to find most of the class out of their seats, some running, others engaged in a scuffle. She realized that if someone had been hurt, she would have been liable for damages. She clenched her right fist and thumped it into the palm of her hand. Her eyes narrowed in anger. She stood ramrod-straight as the students scurried back to their seats. In a hissing voice forced through clenched teeth, she slowly and deliberately spoke to them:

"I am not going to let myself get mad. I am not going to blame your behavior on your parents and your upbringing. I am not going to let the behavior of some of you ruin the day for me and for the few good students who remained in their seats and continued to do their work. Instead, I am going to calmly ask that you all take your seats and we will continue with class. I trusted you and you responded by being disrespectful of my directions."

How well did this teacher follow Ginott's principles of cooperation through communication? What would you have said if you had been the teacher? Discuss your responses with a classmate.

If you and your classmates decided that Mrs. Weaver was angry but did not express that anger well, you were correct. If you concluded that she really was labeling students by mentioning their upbringing, you are also on target. Finally, her reference to the few "good" students violated Ginott's principle that correctness (behavior) should be separated from goodness (a person's worth).

If Ginott had observed the scene, he might have suggested that Mrs. Weaver express appreciation for those students who settled down quickly when she entered the room. She would have then told the class that she was angry and disappointed about their behavior while she was gone and explained that her feelings were caused by the fact that many of the students had not honored her trust. She should conclude by expressing a willingness to give them a second opportunity soon to show that they can exercise positive classroom responsibility.

William Glasser: Reality Therapy and Quality Schools

William Glasser, a noted psychiatrist, developed his educational program after years of working with troubled youngsters. The basic premise of **reality therapy** (1969) is that a student's past is over and cannot be altered. Regardless of that past, whether happy or sad, students make a choice when they select a behavior, whether that behavior is good or bad. The emphasis is on continued development.

Glasser rejects the idea that the environment from which the student comes determines whether the student will behave well or badly. He is impatient with teachers who find sociological and economic causes to explain or excuse the inappropriate behavior of students. Even though he may concede that these factors influence behavior, he maintains that teachers should not accept them as justifications for inappropriate behavior.

Glasser places the responsibility for deciding to misbehave squarely on the shoulders of the student. He believes that since humans are rational beings, they should make choices that are conducive to their present and future well-being. The fact that students become disruptive indicates that they are not making good choices. The teacher's responsibility is to assist students to make better choices.

In reality therapy, teachers must help students see the value of desired behaviors in the classroom. Teachers can also provide opportunities for students to explore alternative approaches to problem solving. To perform these responsibilities, Glasser recommends two activities: *class meetings* and *individual conferences*. His more recent work (1985, 1994, 1997, 2000) extends these ideas into creating a quality school environment where students are most likely to get their basic needs met. This includes both sound management strategies and instruction that supports success for all students. He believes that successful teaching is built on strong relationships.

Class Meetings

Class meetings, according to Glasser, must be held on a frequent and regular basis. Glasser encourages, as part of the routine curriculum, three types of classroom meetings. In the *social conduct and problem management meeting,* issues related to school and classroom conduct are discussed and ways to improve them are analyzed and evaluated. In the *student progress meeting,* the focus is on students' educational progress and ways to enhance it. The *open-ended discussion* allows the students to make decisions about issues that are important to them.

In class meetings the emphasis is on the identification of one or more problems affecting the class and on finding solutions to them. The teacher's role is to facilitate the discussion while permitting the students to set the direction and the momentum. Glasser recommends that the seating arrangement for meetings be a circle and that the discussion be limited to 30 to 45 minutes. Before closing, the teacher or a designated student should summarize the findings and recommendations.

Individual Conferences

Despite the success of class meetings, individual conferences with students about their behavior and school performance may be necessary. It can be difficult to find time for an individual conference in the regular flow of a school day. It is best that the student conference be held privately, without other students looking on, perhaps before class or after class, during lunch, or before or after school. The time spent one-on-one usually yields positive results in rapport and clarity. Glasser emphasizes that the teacher must demonstrate caring to the student during an individual conference. Caring reinforces self-worth, and self-worth produces a belief that the student can be successful.

Glasser recommends that an individual conference consist of the following eight steps:

Step 1. Individual conferences should stress students' responsibility for their own behavior.

> *Teacher:* Newton, why are we meeting?
> *Student:* I dunno.
> *Teacher:* Newton, why are we meeting?
> *Student:* Because you want to talk to me.
> *Teacher:* Why are we meeting for me to talk to you?
> *Student:* I guess because I would not stay seated.
> *Teacher:* Right!

Step 2. Have students identify the rule that has been broken and explain why the rule is important to individual and class success.

> *Teacher:* Which rule did you break by moving around in class without permission?
> *Student:* No off-task movement.
> *Teacher:* And why do we have the rule?
> *Student:* Because we would lose too much class time if everyone was moving around the room and disturbing others.

Step 3. Regardless of students' background or status, accept no justification that will excuse inappropriate behavior.

> *Teacher:* OK, Newton. You know and I know there is no excuse for that behavior in this room.
> *Student:* I know.

Step 4. Students must acknowledge explicitly or implicitly that their action was inappropriate.

> *Teacher:* So why did you move without permission?
> *Student:* I can't sit for so long without moving.
> *Teacher:* Then we must work out a plan that keeps you on task.

Step 5. Suggest two or three acceptable alternatives for students to select from if the urge to break a classroom rule should become irresistible.

> *Teacher:* Of the three alternatives I suggested, which one do you think is best for you?

Student: Number two.

Teacher: OK, Newton, when you get the urge again, that is what I expect you to do. Do you need me to remind you when you come to class the first few times?

Student: It will help.

Teacher: Then I will.

Step 6. Logical, reasonable consequences must be communicated and affirmed. The teacher should firmly and consistently administer the consequences if students choose an unacceptable alternative.

Teacher: As you know, if you choose not to do what you promised by informing me that you need to move, you will be isolated from the class for fifteen minutes. Neither of us wants that, right?

Student: Right.

Step 7. The effective teacher is persistent, never giving up. This may mean repeating the process again with some students, being consistent and patient, and communicating a positive expectation that they can learn to behave.

Teacher: We will talk again at the end of the week to see how well you have done.

Student: Thank you.

Teacher: If you want to talk with me about it before the end of the week, just let me know.

Student: OK.

Step 8. The teacher should evaluate at the end of the trial period. Never give up on your students. You are their hope for a positive future.

CHECK YOUR UNDERSTANDING

Now that you have examined the eight steps as advocated by Glasser, summarize each in a word or two. Try to do this exercise without reviewing the steps.

Step 1. _____

_____

Step 2. _____

_____

Step 3. _____

_____

Step 4. _____

_____

Step 5. _____

_____

Step 6. _____

_____

Step 7. _____

_____

Step 8. _____

_____

Glasser's Quality Schools and Control Theory

Glasser (1992, 1994) has extended his examination of classroom behavior to emphasize the individual control that students have over their own actions. He refers to this as *control theory* (more recently, **choice theory**, 1997). In these writings he decries the "boss management" approach to governing students and believes that such coercive measures have alienated students and lowered motivation to learn. Glasser's *Quality Schools* books (1992, 1994) describe how schools and classrooms can use a "lead management" approach that will result in true motivation.

Glasser states that students must actually have some real control over their destiny through participating in decisions about the classroom and school. In this way they learn about their own power and the responsibility that comes with such freedom. Teachers must understand that students come to their classes with five basic needs:

1. Survival
2. Love
3. Power
4. Fun
5. Freedom

All actions taken by students are aimed at fulfilling these five needs. If the teacher can remember that the student's behavior is merely an attempt to satisfy one of these needs, then the approach taken will be more sensitive and responsive. As one middle school teacher said, "It is important to remember that when a kid is giving you trouble, it is not really your problem. It is the student's problem and it's simply your job to help the kids resolve their problems. By keeping yourself on the kid's side as you think through a classroom problem you can avoid about 90% of the pitfalls that most teachers fall into in terms of discipline" (L. Ayers, personal communication, August 1998).

The satisfaction of these needs is one of the most important factors for a reflective teacher to consider when making classroom decisions. It will affect the strategies you use (direct, cooperative, or inductive learning), how you set up your rules and procedures (amount of choice and student participation), and how you interact with students.

As a lead manager, you can search for and find ways to meet many of the students' needs while still engaging them in valued learning.

■ *Practice Activity: Examining Tony's Pattern of Misbehavior*

In the first year of your first teaching job at Landstown School, you are drawn into a lunch-hour conversation between two veteran teachers who are exchanging impressions about Tony.

> *Mr. Griffiths:* Tony is helpless. He sits and stares. He does nothing. He is just plain lazy. I told him on Tuesday that if he did not change, I was going to get him out of my class.
>
> *Mr. Henry:* He is not the only one. Most of the kids around here learn nothing at home that is helpful in school. They are insolent and lazy. I asked one of them if he was planning to spend his whole life sitting around watching television. He said, "I don't care."

Both teachers turn in your direction, and Mr. Henry says, "Ms. Hoilette, you don't look very happy with my hypothesis. What would you recommend we do about Tony?" Write a response to Mr. Henry's question. Include at least four principles/practices found within either the **behavior management** or the **humanistic classroom management** traditions. Also, try to help the teachers develop more appropriate conclusions about the students' home situations.

_____

_____

_____

If you began your response by showing respect for the feelings of the two teachers, you have understood what Ginott means about dealing with feelings. Dealing with feelings is necessary with colleagues as well as with students. You may have suggested that your understanding of learning theory leads you to believe that having students interact with the content will enhance learning. Group work might produce more learning success, and would be particularly appropriate in cultures that emphasize cooperation—for example, many Native American and Latino populations. If you counseled that good people can occasionally behave unacceptably, you will have encouraged the teachers to send sane messages instead of messages of condemnation. These three principles—deal with feelings, eliminate stereotypes and labels, and send sane messages—should be communicated to the two veteran teachers. You may then wish to suggest that they analyze Tony's unacceptable behavior and evaluate his level of ability to accomplish the tasks assigned to him by using a contract.

■ ■ ■

SECTION 2. BUILDING THE CLASSROOM COMMUNITY

In deciding among the many possible management strategies, it can be helpful to stop for a moment and consider your goal. Remember in Chapter 3 we suggested that it is necessary to identify instructional goals if we are to meet them. Similarly, if we are to meet our goals in classroom management, we must first determine what they are. Few teachers today aim for the atmosphere that may have characterized some schools 100 years ago—complete silence broken only by the scratching of writing implements. Stop for a moment now and think about the type of atmosphere you would like to have in your ideal classroom.

If you are like many teachers, you envisioned a classroom full of happily engaged students working together on tasks and contributing without conflict. You envisioned students in a learning community. Helping students come together to form a learning community is one of the most important goals of elementary grades. If, as children, our students learn to work together and value one another, those habits and beliefs can be important influences in their life into adulthood. The key questions are, What makes a group a community? and Which type of management system will best get us there?

Sapon-Shevin (1999) described five characteristics of a community.

1. *Security*. In a community it is safe to be yourself, take risks, ask for support, and occasionally fail. In a safe classroom, students are free to share concerns without fear of mockery. They are free to share successes, trusting they will be met with enthusiasm and support. In one first-grade class a boy had struggled with virtually all literacy activities. One day while working individually with his teacher, something "clicked" and the links among letters, sounds, and words suddenly made sense and allowed him to decode new words. He leaped to his feet and raced across the room yelling to his best friend, "Jimmy, Jimmy, you aren't going to believe it. I'm reading; I'm reading!" Jimmy, who had been reading for months, hugged his friend as they jumped up and down. In that community, success was shared. A safe environment is also one in which racist or otherwise demeaning comments are not accepted and evidence of prejudice is addressed, not ignored (Southern Poverty Law Center, 2001).

2. *Open communication*. In a community, questions are accepted and differences are embraced. A student who uses a walker or speaks a different language is treated matter-of-factly. "Jason uses a walker because his legs aren't strong enough for him to walk without it." "Kim is just learning English because he just arrived from Taiwan." "We'll need to listen carefully to Danny because it is hard for him to pronounce some words. Perhaps he can spell them for us."

3. *Mutual liking*. Students in a community genuinely enjoy each other's company. Multiple opportunities to share positive experiences and express appreciation support the development of many friendships.

4. *Shared goals and objectives*. In a community people work together toward common goals. This can be as simple as completing the cleanup in time to listen to an extra chapter from a favorite story or as complex as joint planning of a class trip.

5. *Connectedness and trust*. Feeling connected entails sharing good and bad, excitement, sadness, and fear. It means explaining how hard it is to return to class after the death of a loved one, trusting that the absence has been noticed.

According to Sapon-Shevin (1999, p. 17), "Community is important not just as a place where we feel connected and supported, but as a solid base from which we move out into the world. Being a member of a community can help us to understand that together we are better, together we are stronger."

FIGURE 11.1   Building a Classroom Community

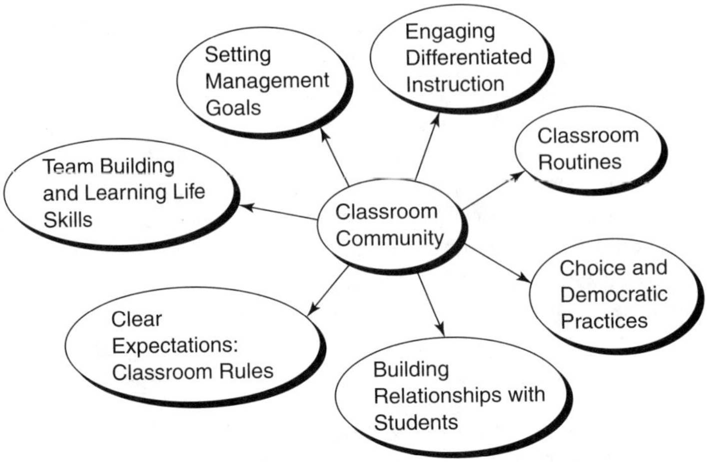

We have identified seven factors that will contribute to your classroom community. These are displayed in Figure 11.1.

Setting Management Goals

Building a classroom community is a complex process that will affect, and be affected by, virtually everything you do in your classroom. First, you must have clear management goals and an understanding of your own management philosophy. We believe that having students work together as a community is an important goal. The goal of community is probably more congruent with humanistic than behavior management approaches, but it is the community that is the goal, not a specific approach. In fact, one way to view the process of community building is helping students grow along a developmental pathway from external control to self-management.

Think about a toddler walking near the street. A responsible adult will want to make sure that the toddler does not walk into the path of cars. Most toddlers are not ready for a complicated explanation of the dangers of motor vehicles. If the child walks near the street, he or she is likely to be swept up by an agitated adult saying "No! Do not run in the street!" in a loud voice. This negative response is consistent with a behavior management approach. However, as children grow older, we know it will not always be possible to watch their every movement. Nor do we want them always stuck on one side of the street fearing the traffic. So as time goes on, children are taught how to look both ways and make good judgments about crossing. At first these habits may be undertaken out of fear or obedience but we hope that eventually young people will realize that careful maneuvering in public places makes life safer and more pleasant for everyone.

Similarly, our goal in classroom management is to help children become more self-directed. As students move from early to middle childhood they should become more adept at self-monitoring and making good judgments about their own behavior. Where students fall on that pathway will be dependent on their past experiences at home, in the community, and in school. Even young children can be capable of making responsible choices in order to have an effective community. Just as we must adjust our teaching to address students' prior knowledge, so our management choices must reflect students' needs at a given moment. Students' culture and prior experience will shape their concepts of what constitutes authority, how directions are given, and what behaviors do—and do not—elicit respect. Understanding differing expectations can help us help our students respond appropriately to varied management styles.

For example, in many urban environments the cultural expectation of authority is that it is direct, sets high standards, and conveys seriousness of purpose. Delpit (1995) quotes a young Black man describing a former teacher.

> We had fun in her class, but she was mean. I can remember she used to say, "Tell me what's in the story, Wayne." She pushed, she used to get on me and push me to know. She made us learn....There was this tall guy and he tried to take her on, but she was in charge of that class and she didn't let anyone run her. I still have this book we used in her class. (p. 37)

Delpit clarifies that this young man was proud of the teacher's "meanness." Her straightforward no-nonsense leadership style commanded his respect. Someone else viewing the same behavior might have characterized it as negative or authoritarian. But for that young man at that moment, it was appropriate. Similarly, Delpit describes the indirect style of giving directions—"Isn't it time to put that away now?" or "Would you like to take out your math books?"—as characteristic of upper middle-class parenting styles. Students who are accustomed to such directives—which sound like questions but are, in reality, commands—are much more likely to obey them. Students from working-class families are much more likely to respond to a clear directive, "Please take out your math books now."

Recognizing the differences in culture and experience with which our students arrive makes the developmental pathway more complicated, and understanding our ultimate goal even more crucial. We want our students to be successful in our classes, in succeeding classes, and in life. Some students' only experiences have been with direct external control. Others have had experiences that are less directive but still controlling. Still others have had experiences that support them in learning self-monitoring and self-management. It is essential to move students toward self-management by building on their current understanding. Students who understand only direct commands can be explicitly taught about indirect language. Students who are accustomed to external control can be taught self-regulation—but it will take time. Even in circumstances in which we determine that external rewards are important—for example, a reward system for a special-needs child who has trouble attending for more than a few moments—the goal is to "wean" children from external control and move toward self-monitoring and self-control. Having a management philosophy and goals helps us understand that "control" is not the end product of effective classroom management. Good classroom management has two goals: the creation of an effective learning environment and teaching the self-management skills of successful adults.

Engaging Differentiated Instruction

The next factor in establishing an effective classroom community is engaging differentiated instruction. Initially it might seem inappropriate to discuss instruction in a chapter about classroom management. But, in fact, one of the most effective management

*Students Can Learn Responsibility
Through Classroom Routines*

tools of all is good teaching. If students are actively engaged in interesting activities, they are much less likely to be engaged in disruptions. If the instruction is differentiated so that students are working on tasks that (reminiscent of Goldilock's porridge) are not too hard, not too easy, but "just right," they are less likely to encounter the frustration that can so often lead to misbehavior. It is certainly true that even the best teachers will encounter management challenges. But they can be minimized by making sure that children spend the maximum amount of time each day busy with interesting appropriate activities.

All of the information in the previous chapters will be important as you consider the impact of instruction on the development of your classroom community. In particular, it will be essential to attend to Chapter 10's discussion of differentiated instruction. Differentiation is a vital part of a classroom community, not just because it makes it possible for many students to be appropriately challenged simultaneously, but because of the messages it conveys about individual differences. Good differentiated instruction, by its very nature, conveys respect for differences. It says that different students have different needs and that is OK. Everyone has interesting and important work to do. This attitude is fundamental to a classroom in which diverse students work together cooperatively.

Classroom Routines

Next, it is important to consider classroom organization and the use of routines. Classroom **routines** are the many small things that can go so smoothly we rarely notice them, or they can be a constant source of confusion and irritation. For example, teachers are constantly passing out and collecting papers. If students know exactly how it is done and have done it many times before, the task can be accomplished with virtually no discussion, disruption, or attention. If each time papers are distributed everyone has to stop and consider how the papers will go and who will manage the effort, large amounts of time can be wasted in confusion.

Routines should be accomplished automatically, with little lost time. For example, a starter procedure for entering class may be: "When you enter class, hang up your coat, put your lunch in your cubby, check the board for bell work, and begin your work."

When this procedure repeatedly functions without the teacher's verbal intervention, a routine has been established. In contrast to the small number of classroom rules described later in this chapter, a teacher may have a large number of routines, including how to form classroom groups, pass out material, begin class, use the bathroom, and so on. Some routines will be established by the teacher and should be taught immediately. For example, bathroom procedures should be taught within the first few minutes of the first day, particularly in early grades. Other routines and procedures can be developed cooperatively with students.

Like differentiated instruction, classroom routines have two purposes in any management system. The first and most obvious purpose is to facilitate the logistics of day-to-day life in a classroom. But routines, too, send implicit messages. Think about the message conveyed by the morning routines in the following two second-grade classes.

In Mrs. Jones's class, students arrive by bus, with some buses arriving 10–15 minutes before others. When students arrive they are to hang their coats on hooks in the hall and line up outside Mrs. Jones's door until the bell rings. When the bell rings they are to enter the classroom and go to their seats, sitting quietly while Mrs. Jones takes attendance. The group that is quietest is the first chosen to come to the rug to receive directions for the day.

Next door in Mr. Shannahan's class, the buses arrive at the same time but the routines are different. When students arrive they hang up their coats and enter the classroom. They find their name on the attendance chart and move it to the correct location. Next they check the board for morning challenge activities or tasks. Depending on the activity, students work independently or with a partner. Assigned students feed the fish and check to see if class pencils need sharpening. One student reports to Mr. Shannahan to see if he needs assistance, while a second student begins her assignment as today's designated assistant for a classmate with a disability who has difficulty moving around the classroom. She sits near the student conversing about last night's activities. When the bell rings, students move to the rug for morning meeting.

REFLECTING ON THE IDEAS

Think about the implicit messages being conveyed by the routines in the two classes. Share your thoughts with a classmate. Compare the routines described with those you have seen in your pre–student teaching experiences. How do the messages compare?

Choice and Democratic Practices

The next component of your classroom practice that will contribute to the development of a community is the incorporation of choice and democratic practices. Democratic practices do not mean abdication of your responsibility as the teacher. They do not mean your classroom is a democracy—it is not. You are an adult responsible for the education and well-being of children. Their choices will not always be appropriate or wise, and thus they cannot be given complete control. However, if you are teaching in the United States, most of these children will grow to be adults who will need to operate within a democratic system. They will need to understand core democratic principles and be able to operate thoughtfully within that system. Democratic classroom practices are designed to prepare them for that role.

In a classroom based on democratic practices, students have opportunities to make reasoned choices, share in decision making, and engage in problem solving. In those experiences they practice the skills they will need to be involved citizens in adulthood. Experiences with choice can range from helping to plan the games for a class party to deciding which of several topics to investigate in a social studies unit. Reasoned choice is more than just providing options. It entails helping students think through the possible options, consider the reasons for making a particular choice, and later evaluate the selection. For example, a class making decisions about games for a class party might list criteria to be used in selecting games: Can everyone play at once? Will it make a mess? Do we have the equipment we need? Is it fun? Some teachers teach Creative Problem Solving (CPS) as a strategy for decision making and planning (Isaksen, Dorval, & Treffinger, 2000; Treffinger, 1995; Treffinger, Isaksen, & Dorval, 2000).

One area in which shared problem solving can be particularly effective is conflict management. There are many programs designed to teach children how to deal with peer conflicts productively (see, for example, Levin, 1994; Porro, 1996; Prutzman, Burger, Bodenhamer, & Stern, 1988). A typical strategy is described by Denton and Kriete (2000). Students are taught four steps.

1. Calming down
2. Explanation of the problem
3. Discussion and resolution
4. Some kind of acknowledgment of closure (handshake, etc.)

Students are taught to use I-statements to deliver emotion-laden messages using the formula "When you _____, I feel _____, because _____, so what I would like is _____" (p. 1). Students may hold conflict resolution meetings (at first with the teacher present) to solve problems. For example (after calming down) John might ask for a meeting and present the I-statement "When you don't let me join the kickball game I feel bad because I don't have anyone to play with, so what I would like is to be on a team." Next David says what he heard John say. "You want to play kickball with us." "Yes." David may also have an I-statement. "When you play with us I feel mad because you don't pay attention and you lose points for our team. So what I would like is for you to pay attention if you are going to be on my team." The meeting would continue until resolution is achieved—perhaps with David agreeing to have John yell "Heads up" if David doesn't see the ball coming.

Building Relationships with Students

In the first chapter of this book we talked about the necessity of building relationships with students in order to teach effectively. Using the model of the bridge, we said that even if the bridge links the students and the content, it will do no good unless the student trusts the teacher enough to come along across the bridge. Similarly, the most carefully thought-out management system will be ineffective without positive personal relationships with students. Glasser (2000) put it succinctly, "Successful teaching is based on strong relationships" (p. 1). Many of the practices described for developing classroom community will help foster positive relationships—treating students with respect, giving them choices, and planning instruction that acknowledges their individuality. But it is also necessary to take the time to make sure each student realizes that you value him or her as an individual. A few moments to talk about the student's dog, or ballet recital, or worries about the best route home are an important investment of time. It is challenging to get to know each student individually, but it is worth it. One of the most powerful tools in building relationships with students is to get to know families. Frequent communication home—particularly about positive things—can provide important opportunities for sharing. Some teachers make special effort to call home whenever a student does something particularly well. Others set up a system in which they contact one family per night, just to touch base and see how things are going. A brief phone conversation can help build relationships with both the student and important family members.

Clear Expectations: Classroom Rules

A **classroom rule** is a statement that informs students which behaviors are acceptable and which are unacceptable in the classroom. Rules are few in number (usually three to seven, for easy recall) and are designed to clarify expectations in the classroom. One group of authors describes rules as intended to instill "habits of goodness" (Horsch, Chen, & Nelson, 1999, p. 224) that promote and sustain community. Just as we feel safer approaching an intersection with a signal or stop sign because it is easier to predict the behavior of oncoming traffic, so rules in a classroom can make it a more predictable and pleasant place. Rules can be used to stimulate conversation and problem solving as well as to enforce behavior. In many classrooms, students work together with the teacher to establish class rules. Of course, the teacher has the ultimate responsibility for rules that will keep students safe and allow learning to take place. But planning rules together can help students feel that they are responsible participants in the community and can encourage cooperation. The following guidelines are useful for establishing classroom rules.

- Effective rules clearly communicate and are linked to logical consequences.
- They should be made with student input and discussion.
- Rules should be phrased with positive expectations.
- Rules need to be clarified, practiced, and enforced to result in the kind of learning environment you are striving to achieve.
- Rules and consequences, like other important school information, should be communicated to parents.

Although virtually every writer in the area of classroom management agrees that rules should be clear, authors differ in how they define "clear." Some writers suggest that all rules result in observable behaviors—much like behavioral objectives. This results in rules such as "remain seated during lessons." However, we believe that teaching students to interpret rules that are written a bit more broadly can be an effective life skill. The following are examples of effective rules for elementary-age children.

1. Be polite and helpful.
2. Focus on today's tasks.
3. Protect all property.
4. Use your words to solve problems.

Of course, students will need assistance in defining what polite and helpful look like, how to solve problems with words, and what it means to be focused on tasks. Conversations regarding the meaning of rules are appropriate for morning meetings. Of course, if students have had a hand in developing the rules, the phrasing is more likely to communicate to them.

REFLECTING ON THE IDEAS

Write five rules for your classroom. Make them understandable, reasonable, and enforceable. Share them with classmates and invite suggestions for improvement.

Team Building and Learning Life Skills

The final component necessary for building a classroom community is team building and learning life skills. In these processes, teachers plan activities specifically designed to promote a cooperative, inclusive classroom atmosphere and teach values, attitudes, and skills that promote community and real-world success. These might include initiative, perseverance, organization, patience, curiosity, and caring (Kovalik, 2000). Sapon-Shevin (1999) describes strategies that help students know each other well, set mutual goals, be honest with one another, and work together. These include the use of literature, songs, and class activities. For example, the picture book *Oliver Button Is a Sissy* (dePaola, 1990) can be used to spur a class discussion on the ways people react when someone's interests don't fit stereotypical ideas. Choosing a class name can build group identity. Singing an introduction song in which each child adds a verse or even "Three Kind Mice" (Sapon-Shevin, 1999, p. 210) can build the idea of a class team. Activities designed to help students practice effective listening or helping strategies also build classroom community. **Morning meetings** can be particularly important in building a sense of common purpose and identity. Morning meetings can be used for daily activities such as reviewing the day's **agenda**, sharing information, playing games, or solving group problems. They can be an important part of a predictable routine.

One model that brings these components together in an effort to establish classroom communities is the Responsive Classroom Model (Horsch, Chen, & Nelson, 1999; Wood, 1999). The model is built around seven beliefs.

1. The social curriculum is as important as the academic curriculum.
2. How children learn is as important as what children learn. Children need both student-directed and teacher-directed experience, and opportunities for choice and discovery.
3. The greatest cognitive growth occurs through social interaction.
4. There is a set of social skills that children need in order to be successful academically and socially. These form the acronym CARES: cooperation, assertion, responsibility, empathy, and self-control.
5. Knowing the children we teach is as important as knowing the content we teach.

6. Knowing the parents of the children we teach is as important as knowing the children.
7. Teachers and administrators must model the social and academic skills they wish to teach their students (Wood, 1999).

Many of the elements of the Responsive Classroom Model probably sound familiar to you, since they echo basic principles of the text: active learning, understanding students, and the importance of relationships in teaching. Basic elements used in implementing the model include morning meeting, rules and logical consequences, classroom organization designed to maximize students' independence, academic choice, assessment and reporting to parents, and guided discovery, in which classroom materials and methods are deliberately introduced to children. Guided discovery focuses on openended questions that allow students to think about the ways to use materials and implement procedures that will work best for everyone. If you are interested in more details on this model you may want to review the website listed at the end of this chapter.

SECTION 3. USEFUL INSIGHTS FROM RESEARCH

Whatever management philosophy or system you espouse, it can be helpful to examine research regarding strategies judged to be effective in establishing and maintaining well-managed classrooms. The following are strategies that have emerged from research regarding management practices.

Research on Classroom Routines

Some teachers are more effective classroom managers than others, in part because of their development and use of positive and effective classroom routines. The following recommendations for establishing classroom routines have been gathered from a number of research reports. They are presented in two groups—a general list and a list specific to the beginning of the school year. As you read them, think about how each contributes to some of the classrooms you have observed.

General Guidelines

1. Greet students on entry to your classroom—meet them at the door, give a pat on the shoulder, shake hands, and/or smile. Use your educational philosophy to guide you in developing a greeting style and be consistent and regular in using it.
2. Begin your class promptly with a mental exercise. This exercise may be a review of a homework assignment, a response to something on the chalkboard, or a discussion by pairs of students of some issue. During this time, you may take attendance, deal with an individual student, and monitor the students. Be prepared to actively engage students' minds each day as soon as they enter your classroom.
3. Take time to communicate your objective and purpose for each lesson. Attentive, focused students are less likely to be disruptive. Active involvement of students during lessons also helps to maintain students' attention.

4. Behavior during lessons should be based on established routines. Among these are signals for responding to teacher questions, appropriate behavior while someone is speaking, rules for movement in the room, guidelines for working in pairs or small groups, and so on. The more complex the behaviors, the more time you will need to teach and establish routines. For example, working at multiple centers or in differing cooperative groups are complex behaviors. In most classes you will need to build toward those activities over time, introducing one skill at a time.

5. Give directions *once*. Begin preparing students in the first week to listen carefully. They will learn to listen after 2 or 3 days of practice.

6. Expected student behavior at independent work stations or centers should be clarified. Issues related to availability and scheduling, use of resources, and potential problems should be considered.

7. Students should know which legitimate activities they may pursue when their work has been completed. For example, free reading or writing in a journal may be long-term assignments.

8. Establish a routine for ending class. Students should understand the routines for closing, cleanup, storage of supplies and equipment, and dismissal.

9. Interruption routines should be developed. Students should be taught what to do if they or the teacher is interrupted. Most students are willing to help develop a list of appropriate activities or behaviors. Let them discuss ideas for staying on task during interruptions. Crossword puzzles, brain teasers, and word searches may be developed for such purposes.

10. Fire, hurricane, and tornado warnings are not the only emergencies. If there are other emergencies (such as possession of weapons, fights, someone in danger), what are students expected to do? Plan these routines and teach students to behave appropriately. Schools should work with law enforcement agencies to establish routines for major safety emergencies. Be sure to learn these procedures and review them regularly. It is important to be mindful of the different needs in different types of emergencies. For example, in a fire emergency the goal is to evacuate the building as quickly as possible. However, if an intruder enters the building with a gun, many law enforcement agencies would prefer that classes remain in locked rooms until the entire situation can be secured. Exiting prematurely could add danger. Consult with your building and district officials to determine what is recommended for your school.

During the *first week of classes* the knowledge students gain from your orientation activities may be more important than the academic content you teach. The first impression students have of you will determine, to a great extent, the way they respond to you throughout the year. Remember the importance of establishing a set for each lesson. The classroom management set you create during the first week of class is even more critical to your success as a teacher than your instructional set each day. To make this management set a supportive one, extend your orientation activities across a full week or two.

Guidelines for Beginning the School Year

Several decisions will have to be made prior to starting the school year. General planning ahead for management, setting a tone, being aware of your first impressions, and establishing order are some of the areas about which you will make decisions. One popular source of ideas for beginning the school year is *The First Days of School* by Wong and Wong (1998). Wong and Wong's emphasis is on clear and orderly classroom procedures. Their recommendations include the following.

I. Planning
    A. Establish clear management objectives about what you want to happen the first day and thereafter. Pay particular attention to the first 15 minutes of class. Anticipate possible external interruptions and determine, ahead of time, responses that will leave in your students' minds the impression that their teacher is businesslike and nice.

II. Setting the tone
    A. Make sure that your meeting and greeting of students leaves them with a warm and expectant feeling.
    B. Introduce humor into your orientation activities and remarks.
    C. Be authentic. Do not play Dr. Jekyll and Mr. Hyde with the sensitivities of students. Introduce them on the first day of class to the teacher you plan to be for the entire year. Contrary to common wisdom, there is no need to refrain from smiling until December. Be firm and friendly from the beginning (Johns, MacNaughton, & Karabinus, 1989, p. 6).
    D. Expose students to a repertoire of reinforcers the first week. Joke, smile, touch, praise, encourage, compliment, use names, incorporate student ideas, and make positive references to the school and the community.

III. Impressions of students
    A. While you try to make a positive impression on students, be equally conscious that you do not develop a negative impression of any students during this first week. Remember that some students will attempt to impress you, others will be fearful, and still others will have had some external experience that will negatively affect their behavior.
    B. Develop an awareness of individual students during this first week. Attempt to match them with their level of need. Be especially conscious of the need to establish a climate that meets their physical and psychological safety and security needs.

IV. Establishing an orderly environment
    A. Make sure that on the first day you discuss room arrangements and classroom routines. If there are start-up activities each day, describe and demonstrate them. It is very beneficial to have students practice all procedures and to provide feedback throughout the first weeks of school.
    B. Introduce the rules during the first 3 days of class. Students should participate in the creation of the rules in your room. Be certain they understand the purpose of these rules, and allow discussions and clarification where necessary. It is your responsibility to enforce rules and to see to it that the rules are focused on learning tasks. Teach the rules each day during the first week at both the knowledge and the higher cognitive levels of learning.
    C. Establish a sense of order by keeping your class together in a large group for the first few days. Allow students to develop a sense of community and to

know that you are securely in charge before you break into small-group activities. When you do, teach and discuss the rules and routines for small-group work. Give plenty of feedback—both positive and negative, as necessary.

D. Implement initial activities that require a high level of student participation. Such activities should be simple, interesting, and pleasant, and should guarantee that all students will achieve a high degree of success.

E. Prepare smooth transitions from one activity to the next. This is a time when a classroom routine can be especially helpful. Teaching a classroom procedure by explaining, demonstrating, and rehearsing it greatly reduces transition time. For example, you may teach students how to get quiet when you raise your hand and say "Give me five." You would practice this and time students each day until the response is quick and automatic.

F. Plan activities to soak up "dead time" at the beginning and end of class and during transition periods. These activities, often referred to as sponges, add instructional time and reduce the opportunities for disruption. They should be easy, pleasurable, and related to valued learning. Brain teasers, writing in journals, board work, and puzzles are some commonly used sponge activities.

All these guidelines should be acted on during the first weeks of school. Begin in the first hours and continue through the following weeks. Reinforce your rules, routines, and expectations throughout the remainder of the year.

Another useful source for beginning the school year is Denton and Kriete's (2000) *The First Six Weeks of School*. Although the book is designed particularly for classrooms using the Responsive Classroom approach (Wood, 1999), its assumptions are appropriate for many teachers striving to develop a classroom community. Its day-by-day schedules and differing suggestions for various grade levels can be helpful to beginning teachers and those changing grade level. The book provides week-by-week guidance with four broad aims:

1. Create a climate and tone of warmth and safety.
2. Teach the schedule and routines of the school day and your expectations for behavior in each of them.
3. Introduce students to the physical environment and materials of the classroom and the school, and teach students how to use and care for them.
4. Establish expectations about ways you and your students will learn together in the year ahead. (Denton & Kriete, 2000, pp. 3–4)

Preventing Classroom Disruptions

In the late 1960s and early 1970s, Jacob Kounin (1970) received a grant from the National Institute of Mental Health to undertake several studies in order to improve teachers' skills in preventing discipline problems. Based on his study of elementary, high school, and college classrooms, he introduced new concepts and terms into the discipline literature. Among the most useful are *overlapping, group alerting, with-it-ness,* and *smoothness and momentum*.

Overlapping

Overlapping is the teacher's ability to attend to more than one event or activity at the same time. Assume the teacher is working with an individual or a small group and a disruption occurs elsewhere in the classroom. The teacher who is able to handle both events without becoming sidetracked is effectively overlapping. For example, an earth science teacher is discussing mountain formations with one group and becomes aware of loud chattering and off-task behaviors among the group working on rock formations. The teacher poses a question to the group with whom she is working and leaves them to find an answer while she gets the rock formation group back on task. Two minutes later she returns to the mountain group to process the question she had posed before leaving them.

REFLECTING ON THE IDEAS

Observe a skilled classroom teacher. Note the number of times the teacher attends to multiple needs simultaneously. Begin now to practice attending to multiple areas of the classroom simultaneously. It can be helpful to observe a classroom in pairs. Afterwards, discuss what you saw. Consider whether there were areas of the classroom of which you were less aware.

Group Alerting

Group alerting is the technique of keeping students' attention when they have yet to be called on to respond. A helpful group-alerting strategy is to use wait time—to ask the question, pause, remind all students to prepare a response, and only then identify the selected student respondent. Thus you ensure that all students will consider the question since they may be called upon to respond. By first naming the student to whom a question will be asked or having a predictable pattern of questioning (alphabetical, or by row and seat), students are allowed to mentally check out of class discussions. Another strategy is to have the first student called upon select another student to help or give an answer to the same question.

With-it-ness

With-it-ness is the extent to which the teacher demonstrates an awareness of student behavior in all situations and in all sectors of the classroom. Students believe that teachers who possess with-it-ness have eyes in the back of their heads. With-it-ness can be measured by the number of times the teacher identifies disruptive behavior as compared with the actual number of occurrences.

Smoothness and Momentum

Smoothness and momentum measures how easily the teacher moves from one lesson to the next without interrupting the instructional flow and student attention. *Overdwelling* is one threat to smoothness and momentum and occurs when the teacher badgers or nags the students about an issue, especially one that is irrelevant to the lesson at hand. The teacher must maintain movement, activity, and attention toward a specific goal. Goal-directedness is essential to smoothness and momentum.

Saving Instructional Time: Time on Task

Jones (1979) developed a program to help teachers reduce the loss of instructional time resulting from student off-task behavior. He arrived at a set of conclusions about disruptive student behavior from observations in hundreds of classrooms (Cangelosi, 1988). According to Jones, some 50% of the available instructional time in the classroom was lost because of disruptive behavior.

Classroom control is strongly influenced by the students' perception of how close the teacher is at any given time. Jones advocated the use of eye contact, facial expressions, gestures, and a take-control appearance that communicates the message that the schoolroom is a place for work. These *low-control* or *low-profile methods* have been identified by other researchers as highly effective in preventing disruption with a minimum of attention and loss of instructional time. For example, the teacher's physical proximity is an effective technique in classroom management. Thus it is recommended that teachers move frequently around and through the classroom.

Jones also examined the way time was allocated in helping students. He reported that teachers believed that they were spending an average of 1 to 2 minutes with each student who needed help when, in actuality, they spent an average of 4 minutes with each student. Consequently, Jones counseled teachers to be more conscious of the way they distributed time to individuals and the group and to be more equitable in that distribution.

One technique for achieving Jones's goal is called *praise, prompt, and leave* (Jones, 1979). First the teacher approaches the student needing help and *praises* what the student has done independently: "Oh, good! You've got the first problem correct." Then the teacher *prompts* the student to make another try by giving a hint or a suggestion: "Number 2 is just like the one on page 16. Try it and I'll be back to check in a minute." The *leave* step is obvious; the teacher leaves, and the student must make another independent attempt. The student has not been reinforced for helplessness by 4 minutes of undivided teacher attention but has been reinforced for independent work and will receive a second praise, prompt, and leave when the teacher returns in a few minutes.

 ## SUMMARY

Since the 1970s, classroom discipline has been identified as one of the most serious problems facing the public schools. Classroom management can be a formidable challenge for teachers during their beginning years in the profession. The first section of this chapter focused on traditions from which discipline philosophies emerge: behavior management and humanistic. Programs that fit within these traditions were presented. The second section of the chapter discussed the range of strategies as they might fit on a developmental continuum and considered aspects necessary for developing classroom community. In the third section of the chapter, insights about classroom management were drawn from the work of contemporary researchers.

If this array of approaches to classroom management seems confusing right now, please heed the words of a wise teacher, Lynn Ayers (personal communication, August, 1998). Just as, in the first chapter, we identified relationships among teachers and students as the heart of the instructional process, so too those relationships are key to effective classroom management.

My motivation has always been very clear to my students: I want to help them learn. If the kids know I am motivated by a concern for them, they will help me teach a camel to swim, if necessary. The key (with controlling behavior) is that the kids have to know the teacher really cares about them and is implementing a behavior system, no matter how dumb or how well-researched it might be, in order to provide a classroom atmosphere that will be in the best interest of the kids themselves. As long as the kids know that, I think any system can work.

Chapter 12 will present and analyze a rational approach to classroom management that emerges out of a variety of philosophies and represents a successful classroom management system.

UNIT PREPARATION

By now you should have completed the first draft of your unit plan and be ready for revisions. Try to read through your lessons as if you'd never seen them before. Imagine that all the content is new to you. Think about the questions you'd ask, where ideas might be confusing, and where you could make connections. One of the important skills for planning is the ability to view the world from another perspective—that of a student who does not already know the material you are teaching. Consider whether the ideas build logically one to another. Think about whether you have provided students with ample opportunities to work with key concepts. Pay particular attention to your culminating activity/assessment. Be sure that your directions and criteria are clear and that you have provided students with the experiences they will need to succeed. Be sure you have used a variety of lesson types to appeal to varied learning styles. You may want to have a colleague review your materials and give you feedback. One hint: The keyboarding and formatting necessary to put your unit into final form will take longer than you think. Be sure to allow yourself plenty of time before the due date for final preparations.

PORTFOLIO ACTIVITY

It is your turn to create your own discipline philosophy, one that best reflects your personality and beliefs. Consider the traditions from which classroom management philosophies emerge, your own experiences as a student, and your goals as a teacher. Be conscious of the extent to which these traditions influence your philosophy about student behavior.

Write your philosophy carefully, understanding that you will one day be called upon to explain it to parents and administrators. Be concise and clear. Attempt to keep the philosophy to a paragraph or two. You may wish to discuss your philosophy with a peer or a group. This philosophy statement should be included in your professional portfolio.

SEARCH THE WEB

Examine the resources available in the "Discipline/Classroom Management" section of the Companion Website. You may also want to read more about specific approaches to classroom management.

Read more about the Responsive Classroom approach at www.responsiveclassroom.org

Read about Susan Kovalik's Lifeskills in the "ITI Overview" found at www.kovalik.com

REFERENCES

Albert, L. (1996). *Cooperative discipline.* Circle Pines, MN: American Guidance.

Amabile, T. M. (1996). *Creativity in context: Update to the social psychology of creativity.* Boulder, CO: Westview.

Amabile, T. M., DeJong, W., & Lepper, M. (1976). Effects of externally imposed deadlines on subsequent intrinsic motivation. *Journal of Personality and Social Psychology, 34,* 92–98.

Cangelosi, J. S. (1988). *Classroom management strategies.* New York: Longman.

Canter, L. (1989). Assertive discipline: More than names on the board and marbles in a jar. *Phi Delta Kappan, 71* (2), 37–40.

Canter, L. (1996, March/April). Discipline alternative: First the rapport—Then the rules. *Learning, 24*(5), 12–14.

Canter, L., & Canter, M. (1976). *Assertive discipline: A take-charge approach to today's education.* Seal Beach, CA: Canter & Associates.

Collins, M. A., & Amabile, T. M. (1999). Motivation and creativity. In R. J. Sternberg (Ed.), *Handbook of creativity* (pp. 297–312). New York: Cambridge University Press.

dePaola, T. (1990). *Oliver Button is a sissy.* New York: Scholastic Books.

Deci, E. (1971). Effects of externally mediated rewards on intrinsic motivation. *Journal of Personality and Social Psychology, 28,* 105–115.

Delpit, L. (1995). *Other people's children.* New York: The New Press.

Denton, P., & Kriete, R. (2000). *A conflict resolution protocol for elementary classrooms.* Northeast Foundation for Children. Available: www.responsiveclassroom.org

Dreikurs, R., Grunwald, B., & Pepper, F. (1982). *Maintaining sanity in the classroom.* New York: Harper & Row.

Elam, S. M., Rose, L. C., & Gallup, A. G. (1991). The 23rd annual Gallup Poll of the public's attitudes toward the public schools. *Phi Delta Kappan, 73* (1), 41–56.

Emmer, E. T., Evertson, C. M., Clements, B. S., & Worsham, M. E. (1997). *Classroom management for secondary teachers.* Boston, MA: Allyn & Bacon.

Evertson, C. M., & Emmer, E. T. (1982). Effective management at the beginning of the school year in junior high classes. *Journal of Educational Psychology, 74* (4), 485–498.

Evertson, C. M., Emmer, E. T., Clements, B. S., & Worsham, M. E. (1997). *Classroom management for elementary teachers.* Boston, MA: Allyn & Bacon.

Gardner, T. G. (1991). *Rational approaches to practical school discipline.* Canton, MI: Six Gards, Inc.

Gallup, A. M., & Elam, S. M. (1997). The 4th annual Gallup Poll of the teachers' attitudes toward the public schools. *Phi Delta Kappan, 79* (3), 212–221.

Ginott, H. G. (1972). *Teacher and child: A book for parents and teachers.* New York: Macmillan.

Glasser, W. (1969). *Schools without failure.* New York: Harper & Row.

Glasser, W. (1985). *Control theory in the classroom.* New York: Perennial Library.

Glasser, W. (1992). *Quality schools.* New York: Harper Collins.

Glasser, W. (1994). *Quality school teachers.* New York: Harper Collins.

Glasser, W. (1997, April). A new look at school failure and school success. *Phi Delta Kappan, 78* (8), 597–602.

Glasser, W. (2000). *Every student can succeed.* San Diego, CA: Black Forest Press.

Glickman, C. (1998). *Revolutionizing America's schools.* San Francisco: Jossey-Bass.

Horsch, P., Chen, J., & Nelson, D. (1999). Rules and rituals: Tools for creating a respectful, caring, learning community. *Phi Delta Kappan, 8* (3), 223–227.

Isaksen, S. G., Dorval, K. B., & Treffinger, D. J. (2000). *Creative approaches to problem solving* (2nd ed.). Dubuque, IA: Kendall/Hunt.

Johns, F. A., MacNaughton, R., & Karabinus, N. G. (1989). *School discipline guidebook.* Boston: Allyn & Bacon.

Jones, F. (1979). The gentle art of classroom discipline. *National Elementary Principal, 58,* 26–32.

Kovalik, S. (2000). *ITI overview* [On-line]. Available: http://www.kovalik.com/whatisoverview.shtml

Kohn, A. (1996). *Beyond discipline: From compliance to cooperation.* Alexandria, VA: Association for Supervision and Curriculum Development.

Kounin, J. (1970). *Discipline and group management in the classroom.* New York: Holt, Rinehart, & Winston.

Lepper, M., & Greene, D. (1978). *The hidden costs of reward.* Hillsdale, NJ: Lawrance Erlbaum Associates.

Lepper, M., & Greene, D. (1975). Turning play into work: Effects of adult surveillance and extrinsic rewards on children's intrinsic motivation. *Journal of Personality and Social Psychology, 31,* 479–486.

Levin, D. E. (1994). *Teaching young children in violent times: Building a peaceable classroom.* Cambridge, MA: Educators for Social Responsibility.

Porro, B. (1996). *Talk it out: Conflict resolution in the elementary classroom.* Alexandria, VA: Association for Supervision and Curriculum Development.

Prutzman, P., Burger, M. L., Bodenhamer, G., & Stern, L. (1988). *The friendly classroom for a small planet: Children's creative response to conflict program.* Wayne, NJ: Avery Publishing.

Rose, R. C., & Gallup, A. M. (2000). The 32nd annual Phi Delta Kappa/Gallup Poll of the public's attitudes toward the public schools. *Phi Delta Kappan, 82* (1), 41–57.

Sapon-Shevin, M. (1999). *Because we can change the world.* Boston: Allyn & Bacon.

Southern Poverty Law Center. (2001). *Responding to hate in school* [On-line]. Available: www.splcenter.org/teachingtolerance/tt-index.html

Stallings, J. A. (1980). Allocated academic learning time revisited, or beyond time on task. *Educational Researcher, 9,* 11–16.

Treffinger, D. J. (1995). Creative problem solving: Overview and educational implications. *Educational Psychology Review, 7,* 301–312.

Treffinger, D. J., Isaksen, S. G., & Dorval, K. B. (2000).*Creative problem solving: An introduction* (3rd ed.). Waco, TX: Prufrock Press.

Wong, H., & Wong, R. (1998). *The first days of school.* Sunnyvale, CA: Harry K. Wong Publications.

Wood, C. (1999). *Time to teach, time to learn: Changing the pace of school.* Greenfield, MA: Northeast Foundation for Children.

12

A Rational Approach to Classroom Management

CHAPTER OVERVIEW

Chapter 11 examined two traditions from which classroom management philosophies emerge—behavior management, and humanistic/developmental. We considered the ways the two approaches may be viewed as stages on a continuum from external control to self-management. In an activity in the chapter, you wrote a classroom discipline philosophy that reflects your personality, beliefs, and values. This philosophy will be a powerful influence when you make teaching decisions. It is likely that your emerging philosophy is a blend of elements taken from more than one tradition. One example of a classroom management strategy with roots in multiple traditions is called the rational approach to classroom discipline.

This chapter describes the **Rational Approach to Practical School Discipline (RAPSD)**, which was developed by one of the authors (Gardner, 1989). Section 1 focuses on what the teacher can do to prevent disruption. Section 2 emphasizes responses to disruptive students. Finally, Section 3 provides a menu of techniques that can be used by the successful rational manager.

■ *Opening Activity*

Based on your knowledge from reading Chapter 11, evaluate Mrs. Henry's responses in the following incident:

Leesha is a student in Mrs. Henry's fifth-grade room. In mid-November, Mrs. Henry was 10 minutes into a lesson on reading graphs when Leesha began playing with Tanya's hair. Mrs. Henry said, "Leesha! Pay attention to the explanation being given, dear." Leesha turned her face to the teacher but continued to play with Tanya's hair. Mrs. Henry continued, "I'm waiting." At this point, Leesha let go of Tanya's hair and began playing with Gerald's jacket. Mrs. Henry resumed her explanation. While looking at the teacher in what seemed like a very attentive manner, Leesha continued to play with Gerald's jacket. After about 6 minutes she initiated a tug of war with Cori over a pencil. Mrs. Henry then told Leesha to "watch it."

How would a behaviorist evaluate Mrs. Henry's handling of Leesha's behavior?

_____

How would a humanist evaluate Mrs. Henry's responses?

_____

What philosophy would you use in handling this behavior? Why would you take that approach?

■ ■ ■

 ## CHAPTER OBJECTIVES

After you have completed this chapter, you will be able to

1. describe the rational approach to classroom management;
2. analyze examples of student and teacher behaviors using Rudolf Dreikurs's misbehavior classification system;

3. discuss and defend student behavior management decisions based on a rational integration of philosophy, attitudes, behavior types, and classroom management techniques;
4. demonstrate confidence in analyzing and determining responses to classroom discipline situations by providing a rational base for your choices;
5. select proactive elements and techniques that are consistent with your classroom philosophy and teaching style;
6. select management elements and techniques that deal effectively with pattern disruption and disrupters; and
7. respond to classroom disruptions with greater confidence.

Rational Philosophy of Classroom Discipline: An Overview

The rational philosophy is eclectic in that management decisions are guided by sound behavioral and humanistic psychology. The rational manager takes from the behavior management tradition an emphasis on consequences following positive or negative behavior. The rational manager also believes that the teacher's needs must be met, but not at the expense of the student. External reinforcers are used to emphasize that the student has a choice to behave well and avoid punishment or to behave inappropriately and be punished.

Similarly, the rational philosophy includes some elements from the humanistic tradition. Constructive expression of students' wants and desires is supported, responsibility is highlighted, anxiety is reduced, and shared authority and a warm environment are advocated. Although in this system teachers are responsible for selecting and enforcing rules and consequences, they are encouraged to involve students in the management of the classroom.

In the rational philosophy the emphasis is on the classroom as a society in which teacher and students learn to work together to develop a more cooperative and just community (Hoover & Kindsvatter, 1997). The laws that govern how teachers manage must be considered and taken seriously. Teachers must make informed decisions about student behavior. Responsibility to the community is of great importance in the rationalist approach to management. The rational classroom manager educates students to be accountable for the standards of behavior in the classroom. This attitude, when held by both teacher and students, works effectively to create a disciplined environment.

Because of the sense of mutual respect built on a belief that all students have equal rights and responsibilities, the rational philosophy can be more responsive to students' cultural, ethnic, and social backgrounds (Hernandez, 1995). At the same time, the teacher must be true to the essential management structure that ensures each student a safe, orderly, and cordial classroom environment.

Rational Approach to Practical School Discipline: Its Structure

The RAPSD program was developed by Trevor Gardner (1989) at Eastern Michigan University. It exemplifies the rational philosophical approach because it is an eclectic blend of behavior management and humanistic ideas. The RAPSD program has two essential elements.

1. It is proactive in that
   a. both the teacher's and students' needs are considered before classroom rules and consequences are established,
   b. the physical organization of the classroom is planned to maximize learning and minimize disruption, and
   c. understandable, reasonable, enforceable rules, classroom routines, and desirable social behaviors are taught through a discipline curriculum.
2. It includes a system for responding to classroom misbehavior. This system
   a. uses Dreikurs's classification system of misbehavior to evaluate the causes of misbehavior,
   b. establishes an information system to record student misbehavior,
   c. uses quality circles to confront disruptive behaviors and disruptive students,
   d. gives students some decision-making power in the class,
   e. implements the positive moments strategy with pattern-disruptive students, and
   f. develops a set of procedures in preparation for classroom emergencies.

SECTION 1. PROACTIVE STRATEGIES TO PREVENT CLASSROOM DISRUPTIONS

The rational manager believes that the management of classroom discipline is divided into two equally important stages. Unfortunately, many teachers spend too much of their creative thinking on the second phase—being reactive to disruptive student behavior. What will I do if Joanna speaks out in class without permission? How will I respond if Paula threatens my authority in front of the entire class? Should I send Mike to the principal's office if he misbehaves again tomorrow? All of these questions are important. However, teachers would gain greater benefits if they were more proactive—understanding teacher and student needs, organizing the classroom to promote learning and prevent disruption, and establishing a discipline curriculum to teach classroom rules, routines, and consequences before disruption occurs.

Teacher and Student Needs

Keith knocked his pencil on the back of the chair in front of him. It was the fourth time Mrs. Ronberg had to tell him to stop in the last 35 minutes. When he was not hitting the pencil, he was pulling someone's hair, throwing spitballs, flying airplanes, or talking without stopping until she reprimanded him for his behavior. Even when he stopped after she spoke to him, he was back at it within 5 minutes. "How does one deal with those irritating behaviors?" Mrs. Ronberg asks.

Keith's behaviors express a need. As a teacher, you should spend a significant part of your planning time assessing and predicting student needs as a way to prevent disruptive behaviors and maintain effective management. If you view student misbehavior as the result of a misplaced attempt to fulfill a need, you are more likely to be effective in channeling or changing the behavior. There are many theories of need and its relation to human motivation. Perhaps the best known is the hierarchical arrangement of needs as developed by Abraham H. Maslow (1954). Maslow conceived of five levels of need, with the lowest need at the bottom:

Level 5. Self-Fulfillment Needs—Attainment of your full potential, being all that you can be

Level 4. Self-Esteem Needs—Reputation, recognition as a valuable and important person, being your own person

Level 3. Love/Belonging Needs—Acceptance by others, friendship, love

Level 2. Safety/Security Needs—Protection from physical and psychological threats and attacks

Level 1. Physical Needs—The most basic and obvious needs: oxygen, water, food, sleep, sex

It requires little imagination to create a scenario in which a student's misbehavior could be the result of unfulfilled needs at level 1 (hunger), level 3 (peer pressure), level 4 (drive to achieve academic recognition), and so on. Note the close correlation with the needs highlighted by Glasser in Chapter 11: survival, love, power, fun, and freedom.

The teacher's needs are also important to consider in classroom management. The emphasis on the teacher's needs by Canter and Canter (1976) was a significant addition to the literature on classroom management (see Chapter 11). When asked by the Canters what teachers want from students, teachers responded with need statements, such as "I don't want hassles from the boys who are trouble makers" (level 2) and "I want them to be good citizens and have positive attitudes" (level 4).

Consideration of the teacher's needs must be balanced by a concern for the needs of students. Failure to balance these two legitimate needs may result in teacher behaviors that encourage rather than prevent disruptive student behaviors. Gartrell (1987) emphasized this very point in his critical review of Canter's assertive discipline program. Gartrell believes that students are controlled but do not learn self-control if the teacher follows the principles espoused by Canter. The student's sense of responsibility may be neglected in an effort to satisfy the teacher's need to control student actions.

Glasser's (1994, 2000) approach appears to strike the appropriate balance. Although teachers are not responsible for fulfilling every need of their students, a major part of their job is creating learning experiences that do fulfill some important student needs while producing the desired learning. In such environments, students have some decision-making power, so they begin to learn self-control and self-regulation.

Classroom Arrangement

We have already discussed the way the classroom environment provides important opportunities for informal learning of academic content through the content and arrangement of materials. Classroom arrangement can either facilitate or hamper various types of class activities. For example, desks in immovable rows make cooperative learning more difficult. The physical arrangement of the classroom also has a significant impact on the way teachers manage and the way students behave. Student desks, the teacher's desk, computers and multimedia equipment, bookshelves, cabinets, learning centers, and other materials and tools must be arranged to maximize instructional results and effective management.

From a management perspective, the primary guidelines for good room arrangements are visibility, proximity, accessibility, and safety (Emmer, Evertson, Clements, & Worsham, 1997; Evertson, Emmer, Clements, & Worsham, 1997). Although there is no one right way to arrange classroom furniture, equipment, and materials, these guidelines provide a foundation on which an effective design can be constructed:

1. Students should be easily visible from all areas of the room. (visibility)
2. The teacher must be able, without difficulty, to move close to students during instruction. (proximity)
3. Frequently used instructional materials and supplies should be kept within easy access. (accessibility)
4. Students should be able to see and hear instructional presentations, demonstrations, and displays. (accessibility/visibility)
5. High traffic areas—for example, around pencil sharpeners—should be free from congestion. (accessibility)
6. Arrangement of furniture, centers, and equipment should be designed to facilitate safety in case of emergency situations—fire, accidents, fights, and so on. (safety)

The traditional seating arrangement of five rows of six seats, shown as A in Figure 12.1, has at least two disadvantages. First, it affords too little opportunity for eye contact (visibility). An observation of more than 500 teachers documented that in the traditional pattern most of the teacher's attention is directed to the students inside the boxed area. Students outside the boxed area tend to be ignored and are likely to become disruptive. Teachers may compensate for this fact by circulating often among students during instruction. However, during whole-class direct teaching (especially when teaching at board, overhead, or computer) it is difficult, if not impossible, to be mobile. A second disadvantage is that it is difficult to get close to students (proximity) when you have to pick your way through rows of desks and chairs. Of course, the arrangement has instructional disadvantages as well, as it provides little flexibility for varied instructional spaces.

Because of the disadvantages of the traditional pattern, you will wish to consider alternatives. Some teachers of older students recommend a semicircular or horseshoe pattern, such as B in Figure 12.1. They find that they can maintain eye contact and move

FIGURE 12.1   Alternative Student Seating Patterns

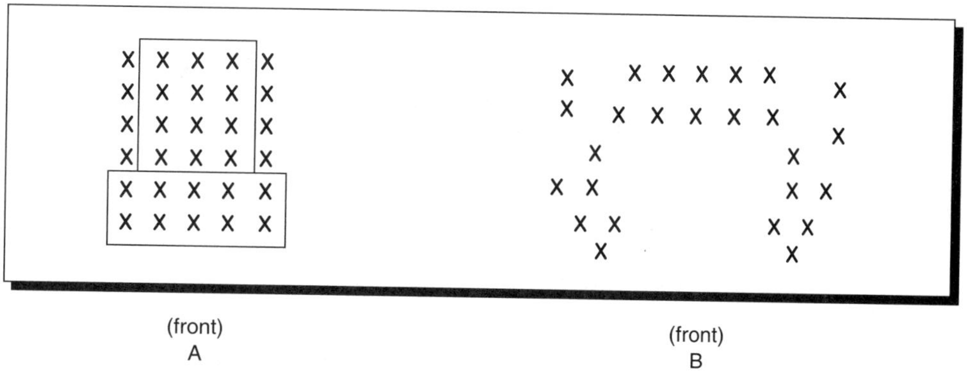

quickly and easily among students. Other teachers recommend a three-sided rectangle (one end open for teacher access) or groups of four or five students at desks or table clusters. In planning seating arrangements, you will also need to consider areas for class meetings, centers, and storage, as well as "passageways" for students to move from one area to another. In a room with multiple instructional areas you may find it helpful to watch the ways children use your room and adjust the arrangement to suit the flow of student traffic. Whatever classroom arrangement you select should be checked for visibility, proximity, accessibility, and safety.

CHECK YOUR UNDERSTANDING

Keith is a busy third grader. He is constantly moving in your class and always ready to start a conversation or examine the activities of other students. Although his behavior is not seriously disruptive, it is annoying. He is especially active when he believes that you cannot see him. How can you use your room arrangement to help solve this problem?

The location of the students' desks is not the only concern in planning a room arrangement. The teacher's desk should be strategically placed to facilitate your management style and philosophy. If you plan to offer any instruction while seated at your desk, it should be placed so that (a) a student can gain easy access and (b) you have visible control over the entire class. If you plan to be up and about most of the time, you'll want to place your desk in an area where you will spend much of your time and be close to routinely used materials. As you contemplate a room arrangement for support furniture, equipment, and materials, ask yourself where you will place the following:

1. Learning resources—charts, maps, books, models, artifacts, and so forth
2. Bookcases
3. Overhead projector
4. Other audiovisual equipment
5. Teacher supplies
6. Classroom materials (paper, textbooks, etc.)
7. Computer(s)

As you plan the location of your instructional tools and materials, you will want to make sure that each decision is consistent with the guidelines of visibility, proximity, accessibility, and safety. After that, you may consider the aesthetics of the placement.

Remember that the room arrangement is likely to affect student responses. Some teachers suggest that cluttered rooms may lead students to value disorder and to submit messy work.

Teaching a Discipline Curriculum

Several studies have shown that a teacher's failure to adequately explain, teach, and enforce management rules and routines often leads to nonproductive student behaviors such as confusion, incomplete assignments, disruption, frustration, and lower academic achievement (Emmer, Evertson, Clements, & Worsham, 1997; Evertson, Emmer, Clements, & Worsham, 1997). Processes for developing classroom rules and routines, together with illustrative examples, were presented in Chapter 11.

The most important rules and routines should enhance a young person's skills as a participant in small and large social groups. Johnson and Johnson (1995) argued that the development of social skills leads directly to the building of personal relationships (see also Kelly, 1982). They asserted that the fostering of such skills is critical for students, since they are learning how to get along with others. The degree to which students accept themselves is a significant predictor of the likely strength of their relationships with others. As Matson and Ollendick (1988) stated: "A person's ability to get along with others and to engage in prosocial behaviors determines popularity among peers and with teachers, parents and other significant adults" (p. 1).

A curriculum for teaching acceptable social behavior should consist of two units: (a) the teaching of classroom rules of conduct and routines, with an appreciation of the reasons for rules, limits, and consequences, and (b) the development of social skills that lead to supportive social relationships among the students and thus to a more productive classroom atmosphere.

Teaching Classroom Rules of Conduct

In teaching rules in a classroom following the RAPSD philosophy, you should follow seven basic steps:

1. Have three to five rules that cover the essential behavior management needs of your class. (The students may participate in developing the rules, but it is your responsibility as the teacher to decide what the rules are.)
2. Present and explain the rules and consequences to your students on the first day of school.
3. Be sure that your students understand these rules and consequences so that they can explain them in their own words by the second day.
4. By the third day, provide simulated situations that allow your students to practice appropriate behaviors. Give ample positive and corrective feedback.
   Note: You will follow steps 2–4 to teach classroom routines such as passing and collecting materials, classroom start-up activities, and end-of-class routines.
5. Continue this practice and feedback until the behaviors and routines are well established. This may take 1 to 3 weeks.
6. Post the rules in a very visible place.
7. Periodically review and practice the rules to reemphasize their importance and value in the environment.

For example, if you want to teach your students to sit quietly during independent work, begin by explaining and modeling the desired behavior. Then check students' understanding of the rule by giving examples of and asking students to label appropriate behavior (sitting, feet on floor, eyes on the work) and inappropriate behavior (standing, crowding around the teacher's desk, talking to a neighbor). Or, you could use the same processes to teach children to ask two friends for help with directions before approaching the teacher. Have your students practice during an independent activity while you carefully monitor and give positive or corrective feedback, perhaps applying rewards or negative consequences later in the week. Before each independent activity, ask the students to state appropriate and inappropriate behaviors. Continue to monitor behavior and give feedback and consequences. By the end of a week or two, your students will have learned how to behave during independent work, and less monitoring will be necessary.

Teaching Social Skills

While one unit of the discipline curriculum focuses on social rules, the second unit emphasizes social skills that help students enhance and strengthen their self-concepts and thus their standing in social groups (Lee, Pulvino, & Perrone, 1998). For example, students should be taught how to avoid being the perennial victim of the class aggressor. To illustrate, consider the following incident:

> *Sarah:* John, you are big, fat, and ugly. (the aggressor)
> *John:* I'm not. (potential victim)
> *Sarah:* Yes you are! You're as big as a truck.
> *John:* I'm going to tell the teacher. You are calling me names.
> *Sarah:* (gets a parting shot) You are a crybaby too.

John runs to the teacher and reports Sarah's behavior. Too often the teacher will respond by moving immediately to discipline Sarah.

> *Teacher:* Sarah, how many times must I tell you…

A scenario like this is played out in some classrooms every day. In a rational classroom, however, the pattern is broken, not just by making it clear that bullying will not be accepted, but also by coaching students to be assertive, poised, and confident in responding to bullies and their verbal taunts. For example, John can learn two simple sentences to use in response to Sarah on subsequent occasions:

> *Sarah:* John, you are big, fat, and ugly. (the aggressor)
> *John:* When you say that, it hurts. (the potential victim)

After that response, most aggressors feel embarrassed and slink away. However, a few will be so hurtful that they may go on to say:

> *Sarah:* That was the whole idea. You are big, fat, and ugly.
> *John:* Then you succeeded in hurting me.
> *Sarah:* What?
> *John:* I am hurt. You are successful.

Most aggressors will apologize and never repeat the performance. Strategies that help students deal with difficult social situations not only facilitate individual development but also promote a more positive classroom environment.

The teacher's responsibility is to help students learn assertive responses that build confidence and the willpower to confront a bully. Your knowledge about individual students will guide you in shaping the counsel you give to the student who is being victimized. In all cases you inform the victim that a helping adult will not always be ready and available; self-help is the best solution. The goal is for every student to feel responsible for the social environment in the classroom. One technique for achieving cooperation is to teach students how to discourage their peers from undesirable behaviors through conflict management. Other social skills might include being supportive, sharing feelings, listening actively, and participating constructively in a group.

Students do not usually learn these skills on their own. Many will need explicit training through a social skills curriculum. This curriculum may be designed specifically for young students with social behavior deficits or for all students. The skills should be taught at the beginning of the year and reinforced periodically throughout the year. Role-playing, simulations, cooperative learning, classroom meetings, direct lessons, and inductive lessons are all appropriate for teaching these crucial social skills.

■ *Practice Activity: Designing Your Own Classroom*

As a new teacher in your school you have been assigned a fourth-grade class with 23 students in a room 25 by 30 feet. Design two room arrangements and organize the furniture and space as you would in the week preceding your first day of school. One design should reflect a room with the basics—desks, chairs, bulletin boards, and so on. The second design should include everything you ever wanted in your classroom. Compare and contrast your designs with others in your class.

■ ■ ■

■ *Practice Activity: Teaching a Social Rule or Skill*

Select a rule or social skill appropriate for a class you might teach. Design a lesson to introduce and model the desired behavior. Make sure that students understand and practice it. Indicate how and when you will follow up to continue teaching the rule or skill.

_____

_____

_____

_____

■ ■ ■

■ *Practice Activity: Evaluating Classroom Arrangements*

Visit two teachers' classrooms and evaluate the layout of the rooms on the basis of the four guidelines of successful room arrangement. If it is useful and the teachers are willing, discuss your conclusions with them. Write a brief report to share with your class for discussion. *Caution:* Be prepared to learn from the teachers. If their rooms are not consistent with the guidelines, there may be extenuating circumstances.

■ ■ ■

SECTION 2. RESPONDING TO DISRUPTION AND THE PATTERN-DISRUPTIVE STUDENT

Dreikurs's Classification System of Misbehavior

In spite of your best efforts to prevent disruptive behavior by developing effective classroom rules, routines, and lessons, students will misbehave. Students who misbehave repeatedly and often are sometimes referred to as **pattern disrupters**. Before deciding how to respond to a pattern of disruption, you need to analyze why all students misbehave. One of the best known theories of student misbehavior is that of Rudolf Dreikurs (Dreikurs, Grunwald, & Pepper, 1982). Dreikurs characterized student's misbehavior according to the goal being sought: attention seeking, power seeking, revenge seeking, or sympathy seeking. The student may or may not be conscious of the reason for the misbehavior. However, it is clear that the goals reflect mistaken efforts to fulfill Maslow's level 3 (love/belonging) needs or level 4 (self-esteem) needs. An excellent resource for more information on Dreikurs's system is *Cooperative Discipline* (Albert, 1996).

Attention Seeking

As social beings, students share a need to belong and to be accepted by others. Students who lack social skills or who have developed patterns of antisocial behavior still seek to be accepted by their peers. Such students may rise frequently to sharpen a pencil, poke other students, or engage in a myriad of distracting activities. They may ask repeated questions or may blurt out answers during oral exercises—both legitimate answers and silly ones. Recognition from the class and the teacher reinforces the belief that the attention seeker is an acknowledged member of the group, albeit one who is recognized for the wrong reasons.

A student engaging in these behaviors legitimately needs attention. However, the teacher should decide the time and the circumstances for giving that attention. Gather enough information to determine the frequency of the inappropriate behavior. When you judge that it occurs often enough to be considered a pattern disruption, decide how and when you will give attention. For example, students who like to talk may be given the opportunity to present information to the class, read a story, or take part in a lesson demonstration. Allowing students to gain attention within the structure of class activities can lessen the need to be disruptive.

Power Seeking

Power seeking is a more desperate attempt on the part of the student to be recognized as an important member of the group. The student can see the teacher's authority as a barrier to the goal of achieving power in the classroom. When Joan calls the teacher a name in front of the class, she hopes that her friends will admire her for her courage. Joan wants other students to conclude that she is free to do whatever she wishes in the classroom.

To confront a student seeking power, you must decide that you are the legitimate authority in the classroom. Since you are the only professional, there is no need to enter a contest that pits you against a student. It is impossible to "win" a power struggle with a child. Simply engaging in the conflict implies that your authority is in question and that your goal is to prevail. Neither of these is supportive of a classroom atmosphere focused on learning and community.

Prepare a series of alternatives to an open war of words. Consider ways to use humor to reduce the level of conflict, invite dialogue, give the student an escape route, or postpone immediate action. In any power confrontation, keep cool. When a student attempts to argue after a reprimand by saying, "I wasn't doing anything. You're always picking on me," don't argue the point. Merely repeat your request ("Please get to work") each time the student attempts to argue. This repetition of your expectation, sometimes referred to as the broken record technique, does not allow the student to pull you into a power struggle. Some authorities suggest taking deep breaths and saying to yourself, "I'm in charge here" before saying anything to a power seeker. Your calmness and dignity let the class know that the problem is being handled with care and respect. Most students do not relish a fight with a teacher. When given an opportunity to avoid one, they will gladly take it.

Unlike other disrupters, most students seeking power seem to be able to do the classwork. You can use this advantage to find ways to give them legitimate status and prominence. The classroom offers many status-enhancing opportunities—for instance, to be discussion leaders, run errands, interview important adults, direct role-playing activities, pass out classroom papers and materials, monitor other students during field trips, and so forth. Students who are granted such opportunities will usually work to preserve the teacher's authority. Although power seekers are typically better than average academically, sometimes less able students exhibit power-seeking characteristics. They, too, can benefit from most of the same leadership opportunities.

Revenge Seeking

A struggle for power with the teacher may result in the student's losing face in the eyes of peers. Or struggles for recognition or other events outside the classroom can result in anger toward adults or authorities in general. In response, the student may turn to ridicule, taunts, and physical attacks in an attempt to hurt and humiliate the teacher. For example, a student may taunt you with the charge that "You can't even spell right" or ask, "Who sold you that ugly tie?" Respond with humor ("Gee, you're right, my dad has bad taste!") and a willingness to work on the problem. Students seeking revenge expect you to get flustered and defensive. Shock them by not indulging this expectation!

Treat this type of student behavior thoughtfully. Instead of giving vent to your first reaction, demonstrate instead that you understand and care: "John, that comment is not like you. Is there anything I can do to help?" Such a response is more likely to prevent further attacks—and to help you understand and help the student. It is better to step outside the traditional role of teacher and let the revenge-seeking student see you as a humane person. The more belligerent the student, the greater the understanding that is required from you. Find out what things interest the student and initiate a conversation. Take every opportunity to build a relationship with the student. Positive attention reduces the urge for revenge.

Sympathy Seeking

Barbara spends most of her class time daydreaming. It makes no difference whether the activity is direct instruction or group work. Ivan's most common statements are "I can't do it," "It's too hard," "I don't understand," or "Will you show me how?" Kezia is satisfied with a D in spelling. She boasts, "My daddy is a worse speller, but we have a house, two cars, and a boat."

Sympathy-seeking students will indulge in one or all of the behaviors illustrated in these examples. They have given up hope that the teacher or their parents will help them. They have given up on themselves, too. They know that you, the teacher, cannot force them to do anything. Yet they depend on you. When students whine or complain, there is a tendency to leave them alone. However, you must recognize their behavior as a display of passive resistance, defiance, and personal defeat. Students engaged in sympathy-seeking behavior should be told in clear and precise terms what is expected of them. They must experience success at the initial levels of performance. Nothing is more powerful in changing their lowered self-concepts than success in reaching expectations.

In Chapter 11 you were introduced to a strategy called praise, prompt, and leave (Jones, 1979). The first step is to praise something the student has done independently: "Good, Mary. You've gotten the problem copied." Asking "What's the trouble?" only reinforces the student's sense of inadequacy. The next step is to prompt the student's attempt to solve the problem by giving a hint or providing direction: "OK, now look on page 68. It helps you with this part." Finally, the teacher leaves, saying, "Try that on your own, and I'll be back to check in 5 minutes." Praising, prompting, and leaving, the teacher does not rescue Mary and thus does not reinforce her helplessness. Rather, Mary is praised for her efforts made and nudged to try to solve it on her own—a lesson in self-sufficiency.

Table 12.1 displays Dreikurs's four classes of misbehavior, the beliefs that support each misbehavior, an example of a student behavior associated with each type, a typical teacher response, and a constructive action guide. To analyze misbehaviors, you must (a) describe the pattern of student misbehavior, (b) classify the behavior into one of the four types, (c) examine your own feelings, and (d) select your response.

CHECK YOUR UNDERSTANDING

Reread the set activity in Chapter 11, in which three teachers—Sandy, Marilyn, and Ken—discussed the misbehavior pattern exhibited by Kevann. Based on your knowledge of Dreikurs's classification system of misbehaviors, answer the following questions:

1. What was the pattern of misbehaviors exhibited by Kevann?

2. Into which type of misbehavior does the pattern best fit?

3. How did the teacher's pattern of responses support your conclusion?

4. Suggest some constructive actions that Ken might have implemented.

TABLE 12.1 *Four Classes of Misbehavior*

Student Behavior Pattern	Student Belief	Teacher Responses	Behavior Type	Constructive Action Guide
Student stops the behavior on teacher command. But soon starts same behavior or another behavior of the same type. Teacher must observe pattern.	Feels that acting out will draw attention of peers or teacher. "I belong only when people are noticing me."	Teacher feels annoyed and frustrated. Wants to coax, guide, and react to student's behavior.	Attention seeking	1. Resist temptation to coax, guide, or overtly react. 2. Code behaviors to ascertain basic pattern. 3. Formalize process to give attention on your own terms. 4. Reinforce possible behaviors. 5. Give noncontingent reinforcement.
Student continues the behavior that the teacher says should stop. May increase intensity of behavior. Seems to ignore teacher although is well aware of command intent.	"I am important and a part of a group only when I control, or when I am proving how strong I can be by standing up to authority."	Teacher feels angry, challenged, provoked, and needs to show who is in charge. Thinks, "I'll show who is boss in this class."	Power seeking	1. Withdraw from the conflict interaction. 2. Provide students with some control. 3. Teach students how to work for and use power constructively. 4. Use students in meaningful ways in the lesson.
Student seeks to hurt teacher or other students physically or verbally. Calls unkind names, tries to ridicule, shows malice, and so on.	"I am worthwhile only when I let others feel fearful of me. I do not expect anyone to like me, so I will not be kind to anyone."	Teacher feels hurt and defensive. Desires to retaliate for self or on behalf of others.	Revenge seeking	1. Do not visibly show hurt. 2. Demonstrate that you care. 3. Be warm and trusting.
Student does not attempt to do work. Always asks for help. Often complains of lack of understanding, although teacher knows student can do the work.	"People will accept me only when they are convinced that I am helpless and unable to do things on any own. My position in the group is enhanced when somebody gets a chance to help me."	Teacher feels despair, discouragement, and helplessness. Will say, "I do not know what else to do with (student)".	Sympathy seeking (display of inadequacy)	1. Make sure the assignment is at the correct level of difficulty for the student. 2. Do not pity, sympathize with, or criticize. 3. Encourage all positive efforts. 4. Do not be mean but be firm about your expectations.

If you concluded that Kevann was seeking attention, you are correct. Why attention seeking? First, look at his misbehavior pattern. He initiates a behavior, stops when the teacher commands him to do so, but repeats the behavior or a similar behavior minutes later. Next, what is the teacher's response pattern? Ken feels annoyed and says, "I am at the end of my wits," "so disturbing," "so frustrating." Kevann's behavior has annoyed him beyond composure. The behaviors of both the student and the teacher suggest that the child is seeking attention. Kevann appears to believe that he belongs to the class only when he draws everyone's attention to himself. He is not conscious of the annoyance of his peers at his repeated disruptions. He thinks that no one will remember he is there unless he takes some unusual steps to remind them.

As you decide on constructive actions to change his behavior, you should be certain, first, to document and analyze the pattern of attention-seeking behavior the child exhibits. Second, the actions you select should not include coaxing, which only reinforces attention seeking. Third, your selected action should ensure that Kevann receives some legitimate attention. For example, as indicated in Table 12.1, you may use noncontingent reinforcement. As you will recall from Chapter 11, noncontingent reinforcement is physical or nonverbal attention or other reward given even though the student has not done anything in particular to earn it. It may be a pat on the back, a smile, or a piece of candy. Equally important is positive reinforcement—an action taken immediately after the student has behaved appropriately. Catch the attention seeker being good whenever possible. In this case, you would give Kevann legitimate attention when he is not deliberately seeking it. (Positive reinforcement and "catch 'em being good" are discussed in Chapter 11.)

You should not assume that your days in the classroom will be taken up analyzing student misbehavior patterns. For the most part, you will worry only about the few students who exhibit frequent and recurring nonproductive behaviors. Distinguishing between incidental disruption and patterns of disruption is important before you select instructional and behavior change strategies. After several class meetings it is usually possible to predict who these students are. Although there is no magic formula or precise recipe for managing discipline effectively, the approaches presented here can make a significant difference when consistently applied.

Establishing an Information System

An accurate information system is a key component of a rational discipline system, after you have determined which student behavior is pattern disruptive. The purpose of such a system is to record the nature and incidence of disruptive behavior so that an appropriate response can be made. The system permits the teacher to plot patterns of disruption on a behavior log; the information includes student's name, description of behavior, place, date and time, and teacher responses. Table 12.2 shows an example of a teacher's behavior log.

With the availability of menu-driven computer spreadsheets, the record keeping, analysis, and retrieval of information can be greatly facilitated if stored electronically. The information in the behavior log helps the teacher detect patterns of student behavior. The identification of these patterns is essential for the teacher to (a) respond appropriately to a pattern-disruptive student and (b) communicate the pattern to the student, parents, and administrators. In any case, the RAPSD teacher acts in a consistent manner

TABLE 12.2 *A Teacher's Behavior Log*

Student's Name	Student's Behavior	Location	Date and Time	Teacher Response
John Rumfelton	1. Moves out of seat and wanders around room while seatwork is in progress	In math class	5/4 9:30 a.m.	Warns John that if the unacceptable behavior continues, he will be consequenced
	2. Calls two students names of which they disapprove	Math period in class	5/10 9:10 a.m.	Points to logical consequences in rules-teaching week and administers consequences—miss 10 minutes of recess
	3. Gets up four times within 30 minutes to sharpen his pencil	In class right after math class	5/20 10:15 a.m.	Administers logical consequences—stay in seat during choice time
	4. Calls Sarah a "rag doll who has no brains"	In class during math	5/30 9:35 a.m.	Administers logical consequences—miss 10 minutes of recess
	5. Calls the principal a "bag of wind with no direction"	On the playground during recess	5/30 10:30 a.m.	Administers logical consequences—miss 10 minutes of recess

Note: This sample of a teacher's log was developed by teachers in an elementary school.

in administering consequences because decisions are based on informed judgment. The teacher makes decisions based on observable patterns of student behaviors.

When a student has demonstrated a pattern of disruption, the RAPSD teacher may decide to place the student in a **positive moments** program for a defined period of time. In this strategy, the teacher blends ideas and practices from the humanistic and the behavior management traditions. Together with an emphasis on individual student differences and an understanding of the social context, the combination of approaches produces the rational tradition of classroom discipline.

Use of Positive Moments

The time the teacher devotes to students, individually or in small groups, is related to their motivation for academic excellence and constructive social behaviors. A positive moments strategy is built on an appreciation of the importance of teacher time spent with two groups—*pattern disrupters* and *cooperatives*. The former term refers to students who indulge in social behaviors that are inappropriate in the school environment. The latter refers to students whose behaviors are desirable and thus promoted in schools.

The positive moments approach is translated into a set of techniques that classroom teachers use to encourage acceptable behaviors. As you review the techniques, consider how the teacher-student interaction affects both the pattern disrupters and the cooperatives. As a result of the interaction, will the pattern disrupter feel that the teacher "knows me, listens to me, helps me, and protects me"?

The techniques are organized into logical groupings—those relating to equity, feedback, rule enforcement, and courtesy and caring. As you read about these techniques, you may wish to develop measuring skills and tools to evaluate yourself on each of them.

Equity

Apportioning Fair Time. The equitable apportionment of positive time to all students is known as *fair time*. Comments of agreement or encouragement and expressions of praise and appreciation are examples of positive time. Critical comments, commands to desist in disrupting the class, requests for justification, or discussion of tasks that do not result in productive learning are examples of negative time. Repeated classroom observations have documented that teachers spend more positive time with cooperatives and more negative time with pattern disrupters. Even when more total time is spent with the disrupters, the major portion of the time is negative.

To alter this relationship, teachers should spend at least 15 seconds of positive time each hour with the disruptive student. Use those 15 seconds to comment on something good about the student. Things you might mention include behavior change, attendance improvement, pleasant smile, family, favorite sport, favorite subject, and favorite pastime. Fifteen seconds can work miracles in changing student attitudes toward knowledge and constructive social behavior. In about 3 weeks, the teacher is likely to observe an increase in fair time, as more positive time is added to the equation and there is less need for negative time with the student.

Teacher Proximity. The results of many studies indicate that, in a typical classroom, there are differential attention patterns. In each case, the students nearest the teacher receive more attention than do students in the rear of the classroom or the farthest from the teacher. Students who work at tables get more positive attention if they are in the group of cooperatives. Teachers should consciously spend more time in the proximity of disruptive students. Thus you will want to review your class seating chart to see where pattern disrupters are seated and adjust seating patterns to focus more positive time on these students.

Distributing Classroom Questions. As you learned in Chapter 4, Bloom developed a taxonomy of cognitive behavior that included six categories, from knowledge through evaluation. The taxonomy may be used to classify classroom questions into two categories: (a) questions that ask only for the recall of information (knowledge and comprehension) and (b) questions that ask students to use the information (application through evaluation).

Just as some teachers distribute questions inequitably among cultural groups (see Chapter 9), questions put to pattern disrupters show systematic bias that denies them the opportunity to use higher level thinking. Teachers have many reasons why they ask the kinds of questions they do of different students, but when students become aware that discrimination exists, they will resent it. To prevent this inequity, teachers should:

- Ask for opinions from all students
- Ask questions that require students to identify relationships among concepts and generalizations and to organize information
- Use inquiry lessons that have no right answers, to help all students think through puzzling phenomena
- Create a system that uses wait time after questioning and ensures a random order of student selection to eliminate systematic bias and increase classroom attention

The teacher's goal is to distribute low-level and high-level, and convergent and divergent questions equally between pattern disrupters and cooperatives, as well as between boys and girls, between high achievers and low achievers, and among students from all cultural groups. The reasoning is that all students will then have less time to be disruptive.

Rephrasing and Cuing. When a teacher rephrases a question to make it more understandable to a student or cues a student to assist in the search for an appropriate response, the results are usually positive. Teachers have reported that rephrasing and cuing are made available to a greater degree to cooperatives than to pattern disrupters. Teachers typically do less probing for the correct answer when questioning pattern disrupters. Whether teachers fear embarrassing their students or believe that they may have failed to teach the material thoroughly, the result is that those who need help the most get help the least.

Feedback

Giving Feedback. Feedback can be positive or negative, constructive or destructive. Positive feedback may not always be constructive. In the example "Right, Keith, you are always correct," the positive feedback creates an unrealistic pressure on Keith and puts him above other students, who by implication are not always correct. Conversely, negative feedback may not always be destructive, as in "Lara, it is better for all of us if you wait your turn." In this example, the negative feedback is a signal of disapproval; however, the feedback contains constructive advice.

Each student, including the pattern disrupter, should expect and get as much positive validation and correction as other students. In an ideal classroom environment, the teacher promptly affirms and corrects the behavior of each and every student.

Sensitivity to the Ripple Effect. A response to one student is a response to all students. Kounin (1970), in observations of K–12 and college classrooms, discovered that teacher responses to a single student were perceived by all students as if the teacher were talking to them. When the response was negative, it had a more extended and deeper ripple effect than a positive response. Pattern-disruptive students are particularly sensitive to the way teachers speak to others. They consistently compare the teacher's response to others with the way the teacher speaks to them, and they feel resentment when they see themselves as victims of the differences in the two treatments.

Giving Praise. The teacher must find a reason to praise each student, each day. When praise is given judiciously, one clearly recognizable praise statement for each student each day is sufficient. The total amounts to about 7 1/2 minutes out of each day for a class of 30 (15 seconds of praise for each student). Brophy (1981) has shown that not enough praise is given to the pattern disrupter who responds with a right or helpful answer. Teachers should be sure that every student receives positive recognition. Bear in mind that students get too much unwarranted praise and too little genuine recognition when they deserve it (Sadker & Sadker, 1985). Consider delaying your praise until you can give it genuinely. Other ideas for effective praise come from Brophy (1981, 1998):

- Praise should express appreciation for achievement, effort, and determination.
- Praise should specify the particulars of the accomplishment.
- Praise should highlight students' effort and ability (not luck).
- Praise should use prior work or performance as the context for describing the present accomplishment.
- Praise must excite. Use variety and spontaneity. Give it energy!
- Praise must be specific to the event, not general to the person.
- Private praise may be as effective as—and for some students, more effective than—public praise.

CHECK YOUR UNDERSTANDING

Describe some examples of positive moments equity and feedback techniques that you have seen used in any classroom.

_____

_____

_____

_____

Rule Enforcement

Being Consistent. The teacher's consistent behavior in enforcing the classroom rules conveys a message of fairness. Regardless of whether the disruption is a minor or major one, the teacher must respond to it in a consistent manner:

- Similar disruptions call for similar consequences.
- Teachers must use care to enforce all rules for every student.
- Establishing too many rules will reduce consistency.

Observing. A teacher must be observant. Recall the concept of with-it-ness, created by Kounin (1970) and discussed in Chapter 11. Pattern disrupters who perceive that the teacher is observing them at all times are likely to engage in appropriate behavior. Teachers must remain alert to classroom behaviors, rhythms, and relationships. A behavior that the teacher may find irritating but that does not affect the learning environment should not be made into an overt issue. Instead, teaching energy is best concentrated on pattern disruptions and clearly unacceptable behaviors in an effort to change them.

Teachers should

- continually scan the room visually, even when working with an individual student,
- observe and respond to patterns of behavior, both negative and positive, and
- demonstrate that they also observe and appreciate effort and appropriate actions.

Employing Desists Appropriately. A desist is a verbal or nonverbal command that identifies the behavior that is causing the disruption and commands the disrupter to stop. Since there are no ideal classrooms, desists will be needed. What is crucial is that they be accurately and equitably used. They should signal or verbally indicate what behavior is required at the moment without calling too much attention to the individual student and without stopping the flow of instruction. If there is no response, then the next step in the discipline agreement or code of conduct should be taken.

Courtesy and Caring

Modeling Courtesy. Visitors from other countries, and many U.S. citizens as well, have accused our nation of lacking civility. Considering the public treatment of the aged, the weak, and the poor, it is not surprising that our schools mirror the lack of hospitality and civility. Teachers should look for ways that respect can be enhanced in such relationships as parent-child, teacher-student, and student-student. Teachers must model that respect, especially when conversing with a disruptive student:

- Teachers should use courteous words, particularly when dealing with a disruption.
- Nonverbal expression (posture and facial expressions) should show sincerity and an absence of anger.
- Verbal and nonverbal expressions should be complementary. On occasion, because of cultural differences, some nonverbal behaviors may be confusing to some students. However, if there is congruence with the spoken words, the true intent will come through.

Exploring Personal Interests. Students have to be convinced that you are interested in them as individuals. Whatever process you use to help pattern disrupters talk about their lives outside the classroom will be invaluable in promoting their cooperation in school. Students feel respected and worthwhile when teachers listen to them and respond to what they say. The personal nature of sharing gives students a sense of importance and belonging, and it permits you to respond as a human being rather than in your role as teacher:

- Find out what you can about students' hobbies and relate them in class at appropriate times.
- Ask students to share their experiences.
- Give writing assignments that require the integration of personal experiences, and show interest in the revelations from pattern disrupters.

Listening. Students who listen learn. Teachers who listen also learn. The art of listening may be one of the teacher's most important assets. Listening is essential for justice, for appropriate response, for gaining time, and for thinking in the classroom. As students talk, the teacher should be sensitive both to what they are saying and to what their words indicate about their feelings and needs.

For example, if Joseph is yelling and speaking abusively to another student, it can be best to let him finish. Extract the essentials from what he said. Respond to those essentials in a constructive manner. If your response is disapproval, take time to make him aware that your disapproval is of his behavior and not of him as a person. It is important that you not only listen to what is said, but also demonstrate an understanding that the student is hurting. Remember the following:

- Listen for feelings and needs as well as for facts.
- Recognize all on-task contributions.
- If you must interrupt a student who is speaking, acknowledge the interruption.

Touching. Babies in a crib move toward a corner, a doll, a blanket—any object with which they can feel contact. The desire to be physically close to another human being is instinctive in children and in adults. As a teacher, look for the appropriate opportunity to touch a student.

Touch can be a useful management technique in the classroom. A light, friendly touch can dissuade a student from engaging in disruptive behavior. The teacher must, however, be careful when touching a student to make it a brief encounter, to ensure that the student will not see the gesture as a threat. Touching a student's hand or tapping the student on the shoulder or upper arm may be sufficient to gain attention. In case of a violent incident, the firm touch should have immediate and commanding effect.

Some school districts expressly forbid the touching of students. The teacher should know district policies on such matters and adhere to them. For some students, touching may help focus their attention; for others, it may be a bewildering or frightening experience. Therefore it is essential that both the nature of the situation and the student's likely response guide the teacher's decision.

Be aware that the pattern disrupter is less likely to be touched by adults, in school and at home. You should not touch a student in the midst of an argument or if the student is angry at you. If the student's anger or disruption is directed at someone or something else, approach from the front and try to accompany the touch with eye contact or words that inform the student that it is the teacher who is touching.

Following are two examples of how touch may be effectively used as a classroom management technique:

1. Ms. Sand has assigned an exercise, but David is reading a comic book. She calmly approaches his desk, touches his hand, and then, while facing him, places her hands on his desk and points to the exercise that has been set. She looks him in the eyes for the count of 3 and leaves.
2. Cindi and Mike are talking excitedly as Mr. Francis gives a dictation. As he continues to dictate, he moves to the desk closest to Mike's and grasps his shoulder gently but firmly. As Mike looks at Mr. Francis, the teacher makes eye contact with Cindi and points to their books. He leaves as quietly as he came. His touching was timed to coincide with the end of a sentence. They will begin to write on the next sentence.

Remember:

- Teachers should touch, but use it with care.
- A touch may be a pat on the shoulder or a gentle nudge.

Accepting Feelings. Dealing with feelings is one of the most mysterious areas of human behavior. Goodlad's research reported in *A Place Called School* suggests that many classroom tasks are accomplished in a bland environment "with little emotion, from interpersonal warmth to hostility" (1983, p. 230). To help overcome the sense of emotional sterility, teachers should be alert to ways of generating feelings in students. Teachers who are able to do this mobilize positive feelings among students and possess the skill to control negative feelings. Experience has shown that students, especially pattern disrupters, learn more in classrooms in which teachers are apt to accept, encourage, and validate student feelings.

Implementing Positive Moments: A Summary

The following list summarizes the key suggestions involved in the implementation of a positive moments approach in your classroom.

Preparation

1. Select two students with disruptive behavior patterns.
2. Establish a baseline frequency (how many times the misbehavior occurred) for 2 weeks before implementing your positive moments approach with the two students.

Implementation

1. Every classroom hour, include 15 seconds of positive time with each student.
2. Touch each student three times each week.
3. Administer consequences when one of the students breaks a rule.
4. Praise each student at least once a week.
5. Give feedback about inappropriate behavior. Clearly articulate that the behavior is unacceptable and explain why it is unacceptable. Reinforce acceptable behavior.
6. Stand close to the students in a friendly way at least twice each week.
7. Use quality circle meetings to explore alternatives to disruptive behavior (see the discussion that follows).
8. Place the two students in a visible location at all times.
9. Plan and implement a strategy that will encourage the students to tell you something about themselves.
10. At the end of each week inform the two students that you have been pleased with their improved behavior. Mention three or four specific good things they have done.
11. Call or write to the parents of the two students and tell them something good about each student.
12. Give each student a responsible task each day for the first week and one each week thereafter.

If First Approach Fails

1. If you do not observe a 30% reduction in disruption in 3 weeks, move to the establishment of a contract with the student and shake hands on it.
2. Ask the student, "What rules have you been breaking?" "What have you been doing that breaks these rules?"

3. Ask, "What are your plans for stopping what you have been doing?" (Work toward a goal. Help the student be realistic.)

4. Ask, "How do you plan to reach the goal?" (Work to develop a plan.)

5. Ask, "How long will it take before I see a change?" (Work toward a specific and realistic time period; the shorter the time interval, the better.)

6. Ask, "How can I help you achieve the goal?" (You may even suggest a way to help.)

7. At the end of the agreed upon period, assess, praise, and/or guide to another contract; reduce or lengthen the time period as necessary. (The goal is to get 1 week of nondisruptive behaviors. Be realistic, as this may not happen until the third or fourth week.)

Organizing and Conducting Quality Circle Meetings

A common activity in RAPSD classrooms is the use of meetings called **quality circles**. Based on Glasser's classroom meetings (see Chapter 11), quality circles are used to reinforce personal and group responsibilities, to process the causes of and the alternatives to misbehavior, to recommend changes in past behavior, and to discuss community issues that affect school life. In a quality circle the group helps the disruptive student to acknowledge the behavior and to plan ways of reducing the severity and incidence of the behavior.

Public disclosure is excluded during a quality circle. That is, the student whose behavior is being discussed is not publicly identified with the disruption. Rather, the students discuss what they would do if faced with the situation that led to the disruptive behavior. The disruptive child listens to the discussion of the problem, without being referred to in person, and privately or publicly decides what changes will be made. In this approach, the problem, not the person, is the focus.

The seating arrangement should be a closed circle, with the teacher seated as a group member. Although misbehavior should always be discussed in the third person, the issues and concerns can be discussed either in the first person or the third person, depending on individual choice. No names should be used except when giving positive reinforcement. The teacher's role is to be a facilitator. Students should be allowed freedom to initiate issues that they believe are affecting class behavior and performance. In closing a quality circle session, everyone is encouraged to summarize what occurred, but no one is required to speak.

When a case of disruptive behavior is being discussed, the teacher will usually close by asking, "What should be done if circumstances create a similar situation that causes another disruption?" This strategy embedded in a quality circle is called *decision therapy*. The focus of decision therapy is to have pattern disrupters make decisions about what they will do in the future. The rationale is that each time a pattern disrupter hears or states a positive, constructive action, it reinforces the chances that the appropriate behavior will be selected on future occasions.

Responding to Emergencies

The RAPSD model also recommends that the teacher develop a set of predetermined procedures in the event of a classroom emergency. For example, what will you do if two students begin a fight in the classroom or in the hallway? If a student brings in a toy gun or knife, what action will you take? What if it isn't a toy? If a student uses expletives or physical or racial slurs to describe you or another student, what will be your response? What will the administration do in any of these emergency cases? Since emergencies are handled in different ways in different schools, you must know your school's emergency procedures. You also should consider four factors when developing an emergency procedure:

1. Personal behavior
   - Be firm and consistent.
   - Remember that developing a disciplined life is not a dramatic event; it's putting a series of correct social habits together progressively.
   - Focus your actions on improving your relationship with the disruptive student(s).
2. Incentives
   - Use an incentive system as a first step to prevent emergencies, but incentives should be soon phased out. Students should be taught to find value in a disciplined environment rather than to behave to secure token rewards.
3. Standards
   - Teach students the socially acceptable behavior in your classroom.
   - Be sure that students know what behaviors are unacceptable in your classroom, including bullying.
   - Don't permit students to avoid responsibility for and the consequences of their actions.
4. Analysis
   - Emphasize low- rather than high-control management.
   - Keep Dreikurs's four types of misbehavior in mind as you analyze what the disruptive student did to create the emergency.

What specifically should you do if a fight breaks out in your classroom or nearby on school property? Even when you are at your best, a fight places you in a tense, irrational, and potentially dangerous situation. Expect to make mistakes in judging who started the fight and what proportion of the responsibility each combatant should be assigned. Be cautious in judging. Avoid, if you can, the role of fight arbitrator. There are two things you can do when encountering a student fight.

First, decide whether it is an individual or a group fight. In individual fights there are only two combatants. Other students may be encouraging the fight, but each of the two combatants represents a social, racial, ethnic, or other subgroup in the class merely by chance. When you investigate, the noncombatants are willing to assign blame to each of the combatants. In the case of an individual fight, stop the fight and then send the two fighters to different corners of the room or to different locations in the school. In some cases, you may need to have the other students leave the room for their own safety. Your school will have procedures for handling fights. Most recommend that a teacher not try to break up a fight alone. Getting help is usually a good idea.

When you have a conference with the two involved in the fight, try to reconstruct the incident as accurately as possible. You may have each combatant write out what happened. Bring the students together and inform them that there is only one story you wish to hear and that is the correct sequence of events. Let them tell their version to each other without interruptions. After the facts have surfaced, expose and explore feelings (Lee et al., 1998).

In most cases, the students will agree on what occurred, thus avoiding the necessity for you to be the judge. Try to avoid identifying a "winner" and a "loser." Even if there is an admission of guilt, let the guilty party leave feeling a winner because you recognized the honest and cooperative behavior.

A group fight can be inferred if (a) three or more students are involved, (b) social, racial, religious, ethnic, or other identifying group epithets are heard, (c) there have been rumors about conflicts between groups, (d) there has been a previous history of group divisiveness, and (e) the atmosphere becomes a tomb of silence as soon as you attempt to investigate what caused the fight. In the case of a group fight, first make sure students not involved in the fight are safe and any who need medical attention are attended to. Then, divide the class into the respective groups and let each group list all the things the other group has done to cause harm. Let each group review the other's lists and correct inaccurate perceptions. Facilitate an open dialogue to restore a community atmosphere and positive attitudes. Have students discuss what should happen if the situation becomes ripe for a repeat fight.

Second, and most important, students should be taught that a fight is the responsibility of both parties. The only excuse for fighting is self defense. A student who is attacked or otherwise bullied should feel safe in reporting the incident to the teacher and expecting that something appropriate will be done about it without the need for fighting.

■ Practice Activity: Analyzing Misbehavior Patterns

To assess your understanding and analysis of the characteristics of Dreikurs's misbehavior classification system, read the following cases and

1. determine the category of misbehavior present in each case,
2. write a response consistent with the recommendations for effective actions on a separate sheet to be shared with colleagues,
3. critique your responses with a peer or with a group, and
4. be aware of the need to recommend practical actions.

Case 1

Ms. Gardner feels that Maxine is the most passive and whining child she has ever had in class. Maxine's mottoes are, "I can't do it," "I don't know how," and "Please show me." The school year is 5 weeks old when Ms. Gardner walks into the staff room with her hands in the air and in a voice expressing exasperation announces, "I give up." After a moment she addresses a fellow teacher, "Molly, you had Maxine in class last year. How did she do?" Molly replies, "I suspect the same as she does for you. We did not seem to do well together. I wish you good luck."

Assume that Maxine is in your class. Analyze her behavior and plan a course of action.

Case 2

While Ms. Pettigrew is at the back of the classroom preparing supplies for a science activity, Brian climbs up on his desk. As he jumps from one desk to the other, she says to him, "Brian, you are not supposed to be on the desk." The rest of the conversation goes like this:

Brian: I know.
Ms. Pettigrew: Well come down, now.

Brian: I don't want to.
Ms. Pettigrew: But you know it's against the rules for you to damage the desk's surface.
Brian: I'm just showing them something.
Ms. Pettigrew: Get down, I said.
Brian: I'll get down pretty soon.
Ms. Pettigrew: Listen, young man. . .

The dialogue continues for 2 to 3 minutes while the rest of the class looks on.

If you classified the misbehaviors in Case 1 as sympathy seeking, you were correct. The student's helplessness and the teacher's surrendering behaviors are evidence of a sympathy-seeking child.

Case 2 illustrates a power-seeking incident because the student continues his inappropriate behavior as he argues with the teacher.

■ ■ ■

■ *Practice Activity: Planning for an Emergency*

Create a plan of action to use if you find three students fighting in the hall. Use the ideas presented in this section.

■ ■ ■

SECTION 3. ADDITIONAL MANAGEMENT TECHNIQUES

The techniques that follow are used by effective managers to maintain order in the classroom. The rational management approach recommends and makes use of all of them. Consider which ones are most consistent with your discipline philosophy and give you the most confidence as a classroom manager.

Nonverbal Classroom Management Techniques

The teacher continuously communicates in every classroom through verbal and nonverbal messages. These messages—conscious or unconscious, purposeful or inadvertent—prevent, help, control, or encourage discipline problems. The following represents a sample of the nonverbal management techniques organized within each of the major sources of nonverbal messages.

Teacher Attire

There are significant data from the business world, from observers of fashions, and from the social science literature to substantiate the effect of dress on people's behavior. Thus it is not surprising that the way teachers dress affects the responses of their students and helps set the tone for classroom control. As a teacher, your dress communicates your attitude toward order, neatness, and appropriateness of behavior for different settings. It conveys a message about your feelings toward societal standards. The community in which you teach has determined acceptable dress standards for teachers. Do not be enslaved by these standards but do respect them. Your attire should be professionally appropriate for each occasion: gym, science class, picnic, and so on. If your choice of dress is of the stiff-collar-and-tie fashion, the hidden message may be one of an exacting and uptight individual—a headmaster or headmistress with little room for understanding. Sloppy clothes, on the other hand, may indicate sloppy attitudes toward students, academics, or order in general. Dress as the professional person you are. Be conscious of the image you want to project. Of course, a professional image in a first-grade classroom can be very different than one in a bank or office building. A sweater with a teddy bear motif or alphabet socks may not be appropriate for many business meetings, but they could convey positive and appropriate messages to children. Modesty, professionalism, and appropriateness should be goals of the rational manager.

Eye Contact

Eye contact may be the most potent nonverbal management technique available to the teacher. Teachers who develop the skill of doing periodic sweeping surveys of their room usually control marginal problems by that means alone. An eye survey may be slow and deliberate with no specific student as a target, or it may be swift and certain in order to jog memories that the teacher is still there and in charge.

Eye contact with an individual says something different from what eye contact with a group says. The situation and severity of the behavioral problem will dictate the method of eye contact that you use. Look at the individual or visually roam around the group so it is obvious who the target is. Expressions of approval and disapproval may be communicated in brief flashes of eye contact. A look must always be purposeful, certain, and timed—not so quick that the student loses the impact, and not so slow that the student believes you are deliberately trying to cause embarrassment. Practice using your eyes as a discipline technique; they will serve you well.

Facial Expressions

Intentional or unintentional facial expressions make a difference in the way students respond to the teacher's management. Teachers should use facial expressions appropriately in an effort to prevent discipline problems or to maintain an air befitting the classroom situation. Facial expressions can indicate concern or anger, in order to give students the opportunity to change their behavior before the teacher must resort to verbal cues (spoken anger, for instance). Anger may be demonstrated by slanting the brows inward and downward, close to the eyes, with the lips firm. The knitted brow can express concern rather than anger. The forever stern look (taut cheek, downturned corners of the mouth) can mean there is no room for tolerance. Be careful not to use mocking smirks. Students are quick to pick these up, unless they are intended in good humor and the students clearly understand that. Smiles can be a powerful means for showing approval and can be much more personal than verbal cues, particularly in some cultures. It can be both a help and a time-saver to use nonverbal rather than verbal cues and to make requests with a smile.

Movement in the Classroom

A teacher must be at ease in the physical setting of the classroom. Teachers should move in a manner that is purposeful, deliberate, and self-confident (Zirpoli & Melloy, 1997). Too often, teachers' movements are unrehearsed, haphazard, or thoughtless. Such move-

Good Communication Is Essential for Effective Classroom Management

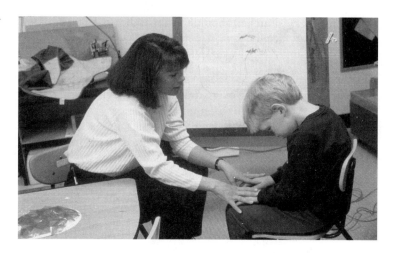

ments can have disruptive effects on the classroom environment. For example, when the teacher gets involved with students or materials right after giving directions, many students will continue to visit.

Control of movement as a form of nonverbal communication is an important aspect of the disciplinary encounter. Fast attack-like motions in response to minor offenses can result in much more severe behavior if a student becomes defensive. A teacher has to make a quick appraisal of the problem and decide on its potential to erupt into something more serious. This decision will dictate the urgency with which the teacher moves and the subtlety or the obtrusiveness of the movements.

Most classroom situations are not emergencies. Thus, you should not overreact to the particular circumstances or students. Finally, don't turn away from the class for a long period of time, as this may indicate lack of communication and invite talking or other behavior that is irrelevant to the lesson.

Using Your Hands

The appropriate use of your hands is a highly effective management technique. Hand messages can be as precise as verbal messages. Hands can point out a particular student, draw attention, signal silence, and so on. For example, after Mr. Roshaw established eye contact with the three girls in the back row, his hand pointed at Cindy and his index finger signaled a "no" to cue her to stop stuffing paper down Todd's shirt. The gesture communicated to Cindy the teacher's disapproval of a potentially disruptive behavior without interrupting the class. Cindy quickly stopped, to avoid drawing negative attention to herself. Finally, do not be tempted to use your hands to maintain control in a threatening fashion, as you may elicit a physical reaction.

The Power of Posture

The teacher's posture affects classroom management as much as—sometimes more than—the posture of students. Standing tall (straight posture) during the execution of a discipline procedure may suggest command or superiority. On the other hand, slouched shoulders may indicate defeat and hopelessness and lead to challenge by some students, or to fear by those who feel that the teacher is not in control.

The examples that follow illustrate some effects that posture may have on management success:

Leaning over students to supervise their work or social behavior is more threatening than stooping.

Moderately slow, deliberate steps, with upright frame and a businesslike facial expression indicate that the teacher is in command.

If your authority is challenged by a student exhibiting a defiant posture, do not back down. Move close enough, after you have given a reasonable direction, so that you are about two long steps away. Look directly at the student. Repeat your command slowly and maintain a comfortable stance. Wait. Maintain eye contact. If and when the student breaks eye contact, acknowledge the response and return to the lesson.

REFLECTING ON THE IDEAS

Assess yourself on each of the six nonverbal techniques. Which one(s) do you need to improve?

	OK	Needs Work	Not Sure
Attire			
Eye contact			
Facial expression			
Movement			
Using your hands			
Posture			

Verbal Cues in Management Techniques

As nonverbal techniques may be called the silent treatment, verbal cues may be thought of as the audible treatment. Verbal cues may consist of complete sentences, phrases, exclamations, grunts, laughter, and so forth. The sensitivity of the teacher toward the student and toward the situation will dictate what verbal response is selected. Verbal cues stand as good a chance of being misinterpreted as nonverbal cues. Quite unconsciously, a teacher may use a word that is loaded—culturally, sexually, or racially. Care in the choice of verbal cues is especially crucial at the beginning of the term, because the students and the teacher do not know each other.

When properly used, verbal expressions can open doors of communication. What a teacher says, how it is said, when it is said, and to whom it is said are all significant elements in a verbal management technique.

Voice Is the Crucial Element

The teacher's ability to manipulate the voice is an essential skill in controlling a classroom. Through tone and volume, voice communicates meaning during an interaction, particularly in a stressful, disciplinary situation. The tone and volume of the voice can create, increase, or lessen stress.

Teachers must enunciate clearly. When commands are given, they should be brief and specific. "John, please be quiet." Sharp, short phrases may be sufficient for reprimands or for attracting students' attention. You may calmly say to students who are talking: "Trevor, Marge." The voice should reflect calm and assurance. Pause long enough for them to regain composure, and proceed with the lesson. Speak distinctly, in a pleasant, friendly voice. Students will listen more attentively and be more likely to ask questions spontaneously if the sound effects are pleasant and harmonious. Tape-recording a few lessons and listening to the tapes can reveal poor speech habits, such as lack of tone variation or too many "uhs."

The teacher who yells is likely to find that students will yell back. If the teacher yells, "John! Be quiet!" the student is likely to shout back, "I'm not talking!" or "OK!" or "I'm not making any noise!" or "What for?" In such a situation, no matter what is said, the result may be anger, a threat, defensiveness, or a contest for power. The teacher's tone often sets the atmosphere for the student's response.

Feelings such as disapproval, annoyance, and anger should be carefully expressed with appropriate voice tone and volume. Know your students. Some are very sensitive, whereas nothing seems to bother others. Some students are just beginning to experiment with the expression of their own feelings. Others have had disapproval expressed to them in a destructive manner all their lives. Teachers must learn to recognize these feelings in students' voices and modulate their own voices accordingly.

Content and Control

The content of verbal communication can become the essence of a teacher's management technique. The message should not be focused on personal approval but on task accomplishment. Instead of saying, "I don't like it when you keep tapping on the desk," the teacher might say, "We will never learn how to do equations if the noise continues" or "It is more difficult for us to understand equations with the continuous tapping." A statement like the first example can be used, but it depends on the relationship of teacher and students for its effect. The latter two examples are task-oriented, and students respond more appropriately to such messages.

Verbal commands such as "Hey, stop that!" have minimal effect in controlling a situation. To maximize the effect of a command, the teacher should be sure that it helps the student involved and the other students who are aware of the situation. Give a clear message: "Mike, stop playing with that car, and start writing your essay." When teachers increase the clarity of verbal desist messages, students are less likely to become disruptive.

Coercive threats are bad management techniques. For example, some teachers often say things such as, "If you do that again, I'll deal with you" or "If you don't stop, you will see what happens." The use of threats will not lessen the chance that the disruption will be repeated. In fact, it may encourage such behavior. The credible use of a threat should be more appropriately called a *warning*. For example, you might say: "John, this is the third time you have shouted without reason in this class. When you choose to do that again, you will miss your free time." Leave it right there. Do not wait for a response. Continue the academic task at hand.

The teacher's message should be delivered with firmness. You are more likely to achieve control if you use a businesslike tone of voice, walk closer to the disrupter, or continue to look at him or her as you go on with the lesson. These actions, when judiciously undertaken, convey to the students the professional quality of your teaching. "I wish you people would pay attention" is what the teacher who expects to lose control would say. Your message should have power. "You have to learn how to identify the sources on these websites so you are not fooled by someone with a particular bias, so let's stick to it." Such a statement demonstrates power accompanied by respect and expectations. Power is in the implication that the teacher has information to give. Respect and high expectations enhance power by establishing a relationship between effort and the achievement of a worthwhile goal.

Responding to Student Blockers

"I Didn't Do It." This is a response common to most students. Many teachers unwisely try to use logic to prove to students that they did do what they were accused of doing. That is precisely what the students want the teacher to do. Teachers should resist the temptation to justify a reasonable action each time one is taken. For example, if you are sure that James behaved inappropriately but he denies it, go ahead and administer the logical consequence you normally use. Do not provide an opportunity for the student to lie. Close the dialogue after the first denial with "James, I know you did it. I saw you do it, and you know that such behavior is unacceptable."

"I Didn't Know." In the rational classroom management program, it is unlikely that a student will say, "I didn't know." The teacher would have spent the first weeks of school teaching which behaviors are acceptable and which are not. Therefore students will have had opportunities to explore both the behavior examples given in class and unfamiliar examples that may emerge later. However, as much as a teacher prepares, a few students generally end up saying, "I didn't know." Your response is to affirm the rule that was broken, in the context in which it was taught. Be calm and professional in the process. You may respond by saying, "Let me remind you of when and how we covered this incident." Administer the consequence that had been agreed upon earlier. In most cases, the student is prepared to accept it. "Now that you know, I'm sure we will never have to deal with this again from you." Return to your academic instruction.

"I Wasn't the Only One." Another comment students will make is, "I wasn't the only one doing it. Why are you picking on me?" The teacher should firmly but quietly reply, "Vonda, I'm sorry. You are the only one I saw, so right now I can only deal with you." The logical consequence should be administered. Be very careful that you are not being unfair to the student. Some students develop a reputation for being disruptive, and it becomes easy for others (students and teacher) to see them as the disrupter in any situation. Be sure that social and cultural stereotypes are not predisposing you to "pick on" certain students unconsciously. For example, if you believe that students from a particular minority group are usually more disruptive than other students, you may, without being aware of doing so, pick on such students disproportionately. However, if you have examined your motive, your judgment, and your decision, and you are confident that you are being fair and equitable, go ahead and do what you have to do without fear.

"You're a Racist." Students may say, "You're the man," "You are for the man," "You've forgotten your roots," "You yell at us but not at them," and a host of other statements that may be summed up as: "You're a racist" or "You're selling out." Statements like these are used by both the dominant and the minority student cultures in an effort to make the teacher feel guilty. Teachers of all races often find themselves defending their actions to prove that they are not what they are made out to be (Hernandez, 1995). Some teachers unwisely try to explain how much they have worked for or supported desegregation efforts. You must remember three points in responding to such accusations:

1. The students know you, and if you are racist, there is nothing you can say at this point that will disprove that belief. If you are not, they know that and are merely trying to anger you.
2. The students' main objective is for you to feel guilty and begin to defend yourself.
3. When you begin to put up a defense, you are responding to students' manipulation.

Instead of offering an explanation, say, "You know that what you did was unacceptable. The consequences are. . ." Repeat the statement as many times as you deem necessary as you administer the consequence. Sometimes it is hard to leave it at that; however, it is the most constructive decision you can make at that point. There are some considerations you may want to contemplate as you make decisions that may be affected by the culture of the student.

Cultural Continuity and Discontinuity

As teachers consider students' behavior, it can be useful for them to reflect on the student's culture of origin before making a decision (Hernandez, 1995). This reflection may be by race, but it should not be assumed that a student's race is enough to predict his or her culture. All students enter the school with a culture that is different from the school culture.

For many White students the cultural difference is minimal. They enter a system that looks and behaves like a business, much like life is at home. This **cultural continuity** quickly provides for them an environment that is less forbidding than it would be for a minority child. Most teachers are White, even in school districts where the population is overwhelmingly minority. The formality and language is reflective of the White population more than it is of any other group. Therefore White students have far less cultural dissonance than do other students.

Where the difference is minimal for most White students it is great for many other students. This difference between the culture of the school and the home is what Ogbu (1992) called **cultural discontinuity**. It is the process through which education as a cultural transmission agent impinges on the normal culture of the student's home and imposes an institutional culture on the child.

Some students accept this imposition as a normal part of education, and others rebel against it. Effective teachers will consider this fact in any analysis of student behavior and design ways to reduce the potential problems inherent in cultural discontinuity.

Planning the first week of school is particularly important because that is when the student begins to feel a sense of identity or isolation. During the first week the student must be made to feel that as much is expected of him or her as of all other students in the class. This expectation must be directed to academics as well as social behavior.

Equally true, you must pay attention to the idiosyncratic behaviors that are common in groups. Make a note of such behaviors without typing them as "good" or "bad." If students do not look you in the eye, you should avoid the temptation of thinking that they are lying or shy. Students who make statements such as "Yes, I would prefer not to have you call my parents," are not necessarily attempting to confuse you. They may be responding as those in their cultures have been trained to respond, or expressing concern for their parents' language skills. You will need to understand the cultures of your students in order to make effective decisions.

Some cultures are more animated than others, but it would be disastrous to decide that someone is very passionate because he or she is from a particular ethnic group. You must get to know your students and respect them for their differences without tolerating unacceptable behaviors. Acceptable behavior does not mean that they behave as you do. Rather it may best be measured in the context of how it prevents or aids learning. The teaching process is a complex web of decisions. Experience progressively reduces the complexity for reflective teachers.

Despite the cultural discontinuity that each student experiences in the school setting, you can reduce the negative impact in the way you manage your room. Validate the importance of each member of your class. Find an opportunity to reinforce the value of each culture, either in lectures, discussions, or as model examples. Effective managers are careful to create a family-type atmosphere in their class where students have an opportunity to question without fear and to disagree freely but appropriately.

REFLECTING ON THE IDEAS

In Section 3, nine additional techniques were presented that have been used by rational managers to assist them in responding to disruptive students. Which three or four techniques were the most meaningful to you? Why? Be prepared to share your list with classmates.

 SUMMARY

Maintaining an environment conducive to learning is a primary responsibility of the classroom teacher. The rational leader-manager formulates policies to communicate reasonable expectations, disciplinary practices, and consequences—both positive and negative—that create a constructive environment in the classroom. Integrating essential elements from the behavior management and humanistic philosophies into the Rational Approach to Practical School Discipline (RAPSD) results in a proactive position that will earn the respect of students, parents, and administrators. Adopting this approach is the first constructive step of the rational manager.

The second step taken by the rational manager is to build a predictable, comfortable, and secure learning environment in the classroom. Creating that environment requires that you teach collective responsibility for managing the classroom, for helping peers stay on task, for sharing, for safety, and for respect, within the first weeks of school. Furthermore, your prudent integration of rules, routine procedures, and management techniques will promote positive individual and group behaviors. Your efforts to be consistent, to respect the civil rights of students, and to prevent rather than punish will be well received.

However, in spite of your best efforts as an effective discipline manager, conflicts and other disruptive behaviors will occur in your classroom. Your knowledge of the causes of misbehavior, combined with your use of quality circles and positive moments strategies, will enable you to be as rational in response to discipline situations as you are in creating a proactive classroom environment in which many discipline situations fail to develop.

Your understanding of the cultural discontinuity that students experience in the classroom and school community will aid the quality of the decisions you make in responding to student needs and managing social behaviors.

Your decisions about management will create or destroy a safe and productive climate in your classroom. You must make those decisions with your best heart and the best skills you have. Be aware that you will make some mistakes in the process of establishing your management style. Do not despair in such cases, but take Glasser's advice given in Chapter 11, "Never give up."

■ *Practice Activity: Revising Your Classroom Discipline Philosophy*

Examine the discipline philosophy you wrote at the conclusion of Chapter 11. What characteristics of the rational approach to classroom management might you use in revising your philosophy? Think specifically of the proactive elements—teacher and student needs, physical organization of the classroom, use of a discipline curriculum—and the elements in a system to respond to discipline situations (Dreikurs's classification system of misbehavior, an information system, quality circles, positive moments, and procedures for responding to classroom emergencies).

■ ■ ■

UNIT PREPARATION

By this time you should be fine-tuning your unit. Be sure that you have a complete reference list and a list of necessary materials. See that any handouts or required visual aids have been completed so that the unit is clear to the reader. Check to make sure that after any revisions you still have continuity from your goals and objectives, to your lesson plans, to your assessment. Use the six principles from Chapter 6 to examine your unit. Trade units with a classmate and give one another helpful suggestions. Proofread your unit carefully for grammar, spelling, and technical errors. Parents, administrators, and the public expect teachers to have exceptional communication skills. It is essential that you be able to express yourself clearly in grammatically correct Standard English.

If you have the opportunity to teach your unit, it is important to analyze your students' learning. Compare the knowledge your students demonstrated in the preassessment with the knowledge demonstrated at the end of the unit. This will take careful analysis if you have used complex assessment since some of the knowledge demonstrated will be embedded within larger activities. Compare the achievement of subgroups within your classroom. Do you see equivalent gains for boys and girls? Students of different cultures? How do the gains of high-achieving and low-achieving students differ? After your analysis, consider how the information you gained would affect your next teaching decisions.

PORTFOLIO ACTIVITY

If necessary, adapt your management philosophy from Chapter 11. You also may want to create or revise a map of your ideal classroom to take into account management, as well as instructional goals. Talk to experienced teachers, observe a variety of classrooms, and examine a number of texts on management strategies. Practice with friends and colleagues until you can easily discuss the types of management strategies you will use and your rationale for discussing them.

If you had the opportunity to teach your unit, your analysis of student work can make a powerful portfolio activity. Be prepared to discuss how your teaching affected your students' learning and how you can use that information to inform your teaching.

SEARCH THE WEB

In the last chapter you should have visited "Discipline/Classroom Management" on the Companion Website at www.prenhall.com/starko. You will find that many other general sites targeted at teachers also have sections on management—for example, Education World (www.education-world.com) and the American Federation of Teachers site (www.aft.org). Using any search engine, see what other links you can find.

REFERENCES

Albert, L. (1996). *Cooperative discipline*. Circle Pines, MN: American Guidance Service.

Brophy, J. E. (1981). Teacher praise: A functional analysis. *Review of Educational Research, 51*, 5–12.

Brophy, J. E. (1998). *Motivating students to learn*. Boston: McGraw-Hill.

Canter, L., & Canter, M. (1976). *Assertive discipline: A take-charge approach to today's education*. Seal Beach, CA: Canter & Associates.

Dreikurs, R., Grunwald, B., & Pepper, F. (1982). *Maintaining sanity in the classroom*. New York: Harper & Row.

Emmer, E. T., & Everston, C. M. (1994). *Classroom management for secondary teachers*. Needham Heights, MA: Allyn & Bacon.

Emmer, E. T., Evertson, C. M., Clements, B. S., & Worsham, M. E. (1997). *Classroom management for secondary teachers*. Boston, MA: Allyn & Bacon.

Evertson, C. M., & Emmer, E. T. (1993). *Classroom management for elementary teachers*. Needham Heights, MA: Allyn & Bacon.

Evertson, C. M., Emmer, E. T., Clements, B. S., & Worsham, M. E. (1997). *Classroom management for elementary teachers.* Boston, MA: Allyn & Bacon.

Gardner, T. (1989). *Rational approach to school-wide discipline.* Manual. Ann Arbor, MI: Pedagogic Press.

Gartrell, D. (1987, January). Assertive discipline: Unhealthy for children and other living things. *Young Children Journal, 42* (2), 10–11.

Glasser, W. G. (1994). *The quality school teacher.* New York: Harper Collins.

Glasser, W. (2000). *Every student can succeed.* San Diego, CA: Black Forest Press.

Goleman, D. (1995). *Emotional intelligence.* New York: Bantam Books.

Goodlad, J. I. (1983). *A place called school.* New York: McGraw-Hill.

Hernandez, H. (1995).*Teaching in multicultural classrooms.* Columbus, OH: Merrill Publishing.

Hoover, R. L., & Kindsvatter, R. (1997). *Democratic discipline: Foundation and practice.* Columbus, OH: Merrill Publishing.

Johnson, D. W., & Johnson, R. J. (1995). *Teaching students to be peacemakers* (3rd ed.). Edina, MN: Interaction Book Company.

Jones, F. (1979). The gentle art of classroom discipline. *National Elementary Principal, 58,* 26–32.

Kelly, J. A. (1982). *Social skills training: A practical guide for interventions.* New York: Springer.

Kounin, J. (1970). *Discipline and group management in the classroom.* New York: Holt, Rinehart and Winston.

Lee, J. L., Pulvino, C. J., & Perrone, P. A. (1998). *A guide for managing conflicts in schools.* Columbus, OH: Merrill Publishing.

Maslow, A. H. (1954). *Motivation and personality.* New York: Harper & Row.

Matson, J. L., & Ollendick, T. H. (1988). *Enhancing children's social skills.* Elmsford, NY: Pergamon Press.

Ogbu, J. U. (1992, November). Understanding cultural diversity and learning. *Educational Researcher, 21* (8) 5–15.

Roff, M., Sell, B., & Golden, M. (1972). *Social adjustment and personality development in children.* Minneapolis: University of Minnesota Press.

Sadker, D., & Sadker, M. (1985). Is the O.K. classroom O.K.? *Phi Delta Kappan, 66* (5), 358–361.

Ullman, C. A. (1975). Teachers, peers and tests as predictors of adjustment. *Journal of Educational Psychology, 48,* 257–267.

Watson, C. R. (1997). *Middle school case studies: Challenges, perceptions and practices.* Columbus, OH: Merrill Publishing.

Zirpoli, T. J., & Melloy, K. J. (1997). *Behavior management: Application for teachers and parents.* Columbus, OH: Merrill Publishing.

CHAPTER 13

Looking Back and Looking Ahead

CHAPTER OVERVIEW

This text has discussed a variety of decisions you will make as a reflective teacher. You will select and analyze instructional goals and objectives and develop activities based on your knowledge of student needs and child development, the subject matter, pedagogy and learning principles, the political and social context, and your educational philosophy.

The text also described direct, inductive, and social lessons; independent activities; how to design lessons for diverse student needs; various approaches to classroom management; and suggestions for creating a successful classroom discipline system.

If you have been studying carefully, you now should have the knowledge you need to begin planning lessons for elementary school. You know about reflective teaching and the complex variables that must affect your decision making if you are to be successful. It all probably feels a little overwhelming. Indeed, our students frequently remark, "I never knew we had to think about so much," or "I don't know how I'm going to manage it all." The students who raise such concerns are wise. They recognize the complexity of the tasks ahead of them, much like new physicians anticipating their careers must worry about the many diagnoses to come. We have remarked more than once that the students we are concerned about are the ones who are so overconfident that they *aren't* worried. They clearly do not understand the challenges ahead. This chapter will do two things. First, it will briefly review the kinds of decisions you will make as a reflective teacher and how you'll continue to make those decisions in the future. Second, and perhaps more important, it will consider why it is worth the time and trouble to be this kind of teacher.

 ## CHAPTER OBJECTIVES

At the end of this chapter, you will be able to:

1. describe the major themes of decision-making presented in this book; and
2. describe the decision the authors believe to be the most important.

 ## SECTION 1. TEACHER AS DECISION MAKER
Decision-Making Model

This book was written to give you workable techniques and principles to enable you to make intelligent teaching decisions that will help your students succeed. This means doing more than following each page of the prescribed textbook for your class, as many consumer teachers do. You will want to act as a designer of units and lessons, drawing on a variety of resources and activities (including your textbooks) that lead students to achieve your main objectives.

The decision-making model presented earlier in this book is illustrated again in Figure 13.1. In the center are listed the factors to consider when you make any teaching decision and when you interpret the effects of your decisions. Three phases of teachers' reflective thinking are shown as a continuous process of decision making: (a) decisions before teaching, (b) decisions during teaching, and (c) decisions after teaching. Now

FIGURE 13.1   Framework for Organizing Curriculum and Instruction

Topic I. Planning for Instruction: Setting the Stage

- Establishing classroom relationships(Chapter 1)
- Understanding the learner and learning (Chapter 2)
- Developing authentic learning activities (Chapters 2 & 5)
- Choosing worthwhile educational goals and outcomes (Chapter 3)
- Analyzing content goals for instruction (Chapter 3)
- Writing instructional objectives and preassessing students (Chapter 4)
- Designing assessment and evaluation procedures (Chapter 5)

Topic II. Implementation: Getting Out There and Teaching

- Designing and teaching the lessons and assessments (Chapters 6–10)
- Direct teaching (Chapter 7)
- Inductive approaches (Chapter 8)
- Teaching for diversity (Chapter 10)

Topic III. Classroom Management: Establishing a Positive Environment

- Developing classroom community (Chapter 11)
- Organizing the classroom for learning (Chapters 11 & 12)
- Dealing with misbehavior (Chapters 11 & 12)

that you have learned more about the teaching process, consider the model once again. You might notice in the process how the change in your prior knowledge alters the level of detail with which you are able to review the model.

Before Teaching: Decisions for Action

When you are planning a lesson or a sequence of lessons, you should take the factors listed in Figure 13.2 into consideration by asking:

What's important for my students in this lesson or unit?
What are the key concepts, generalizations, and facts to be understood?
What is the appropriate depth and scope of this material for students?
What student objective(s) am I hoping to achieve?
What differences among my students should affect the content, process, or products of this lesson?
Which activities will help the students meet my objectives?
How will I assess student learning?
How will I organize the materials and the students for productive learning?
What community resources can I connect to this content?
What conditions can I anticipate that may influence the outcomes of the lesson?

When you can answer these questions, you will feel confident that you have thought through the important decisions. Then you can prepare to put these decisions and plans

FIGURE 13.2   Five Factors Influencing Teaching Decisions

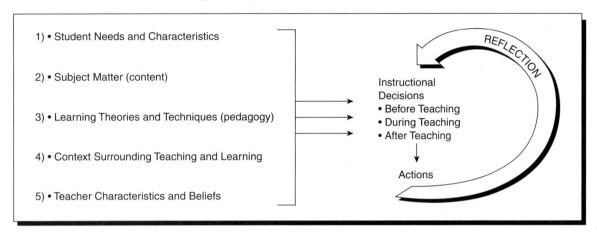

into action. Just before teaching the lesson (perhaps that morning), you might look over the plans one more time and ask yourself the following preteaching reflection questions:

What about the students today do I need to consider and adapt to? Has anything happened today that could change the effectiveness of my planned lesson?
How will I know when students have achieved the objective(s) (assessment)?
What specifically am I looking for?
Is there any particular aspect of teaching that I am working to improve today?
Is there some way I can gather evidence on how well I'm doing in that area (have a friend or student observe, make a tape recording, make notes on my behavior, and so on)?
Are there any problems I'm anticipating, and have I planned strategies to avoid them?
Have I considered the five factors influencing teaching decisions in my plans?

During Teaching: Action, Modifications, and Observation

During the act of teaching, you will be making many decisions each minute. The process can be overwhelming, especially if you have not spent enough time analyzing your plans. The payoff for careful and thorough planning is realized during the actual teaching. When you have done considerable thinking about the activities, students, conditions, your own needs, and potential problems before the lesson, you will not be surprised when plans have to be modified on the spot. In many cases, you will have visualized the potential problems and will have backup plans ready and waiting. Without preplanning, teachers can be frozen into confused inaction (or stunned into inappropriate overreaction) when things do not go as planned.

During your interaction with students, you will usually make minor changes and adjustments to your plans. These will be based on the information you gather as you teach and observe how students are responding. The ability to think on your feet and adjust a lesson to allow maximum student engagement and learning is key to effective teaching.

Sometimes a lesson just does not go well. In such cases, it is important to observe your students carefully; you may even discuss the lesson with one or more students. You will find that the information you obtain from observation and discussion will be useful as you analyze the lesson. Although you may not have enough time to think the problem through in the heat of the moment, you will have time later. You will want to analyze what went wrong and why. Without this knowledge, how will you be able to prevent the same thing from happening again? Your observations and discussions are also crucial when things are going well. Later you'll want to think about why your lesson went particularly well so that you can build on those elements in future lessons.

After Teaching: Reflection and Predictions

After teaching, it is advisable to take time during lunch break, after school, or before school the next day to reflect on the lesson. You might use the following questions as a guide as you look at students' work generated during the lesson:

How did the lesson go? What happened as I hoped it would? What didn't?
What do I know about the students, teaching, and learning that might help me explain why the lesson turned out the way it did?
How well did the students do in accomplishing my stated outcome(s) or objective(s)?
How did they respond to the lesson?
What evidence did I see that led me to this conclusion?
What things did I change in the lesson? Why?
How did I do in the area of teaching I chose to work on? What does the information I gathered show?
Were there any conditions that played a role in the outcome of the lesson (e.g., student needs, physical factors, school context)?
If I could change anything in the lesson, what would it be?
What alternative activities or approaches might be more successful?
What has worked well in similar situations? Why?
Which alternatives will I try next time?
Are there any puzzling questions that remain in my mind that I find myself mulling over during the day? How could I find answers to those questions?

As a result of these reflections, you will plan your next actions. You may also wish to discuss your insights and questions with another teacher, a mentor, or a supervisor.

Of course, no teacher is able to carefully consider each of these many questions regarding every lesson of the day. Still, each question is important. Do not let the fact that you cannot answer every question every time prevent you from asking any questions at all. In most cases, you will find it most effective to choose a focus for your reflection. For many beginning teachers, that will mean selecting one or two lessons each day for careful reflection and analysis. At other times you may decide to focus on a particular subject area or a particular student (or group of students) for careful thought and consideration each day. As you become more comfortable and confident in your teaching, you will be able to expand the range of your reflection to include a wider variety of issues and questions.

REFLECTING ON THE IDEAS

Imagine that earlier today you taught a lesson on the correct use of punctuation at the end of sentences. You told the students they were going to work on writing complete sentences. You showed them a few examples on the board. You had students form sentences at the front of the room by holding word cards and placing the correct "punctuation person" at the end. Finally, you gave them a worksheet that required them to put periods and question marks at the end of the sentences. Students were generally successful on the practice sheet. However, later in the morning when students wrote in their journals, you saw little use of ending punctuation.

You are now at your desk after school, reflecting on your actions and the students' responses. Write several questions you would ask yourself that might help you figure out what to do next. Compare your list with another student's list and come up with suggestions for your next lesson. Be sure you can explain why your plans would help students succeed.

_____

_____

_____

Ways to Improve Your Decision Making

As a teacher, you will want to find ways to examine your own decision making and the effects of your actions on students. Keeping a journal of your teaching experiences may be a helpful way to improve your teaching. Or you may prefer to discuss your experiences with a trusted colleague. If you do ask another teacher to discuss your teaching with you, pick someone who is competent, positive, and willing to be helpful, and who will keep information about individual students confidential.

Peer coaching can be of immense help when you are trying to learn more about teaching. Peer coaching in its simplest form occurs when you visit another teacher's classroom, or that teacher visits yours. You may ask the colleague to look for something specific (for example, whether you are giving all students attention and response opportunities). Or you may just want the teacher to help you examine your entire lesson from a different perspective. If you feel hesitant about having a friend observe you, you may wish to begin peer coaching by observing another teacher, especially one who is strong in an area you need to learn more about. Later, you can ask a trusted colleague to observe you. Perhaps you will find a more experienced teacher to serve as a coach. Such relationships can be extremely helpful for your professional growth (Freiberg, Zbikowski, & Ganser, 1997).

Making an audiotape or videotape of your lesson, or of a particular group of students is another way to gather information on your teaching. The observation forms and reflection in Chapters 7 and 8 can be useful for analyzing what you see and hear on the tape.

Many teachers have found student questionnaires to be a valuable source of insights. Teachers ask students' impressions of certain activities and classroom events. Student names are not required. It provides fascinating reading!

Finally, you may wish to conduct your own student study where you select two or three target students who represent fairly typical teaching challenges. Once a week or so, you take examples of these students' work (or behavior) and analyze (preferably with another teacher) why the students are performing the way they are. Then you brainstorm ways to improve each student's performance, select some strategies, and try them out during the next week or so. Then you collect more work samples, analyze them, decide what might help the student, and try it out. You repeat the cycle until you believe you have found a way to help each of your target students. In this way you can build your case knowledge of strategies that work with different kinds of student challenges.

■ *Practice Activity: Planning for Decision Making*

Write three specific actions you will take during student teaching or during your first year of teaching that will help you grow in your decision making. Think of these as New Year's resolutions.

■ ■ ■

Your role as a professional decision maker will continue throughout your career. If you are to learn and grow as an educator, it is important that you gain information that will contribute to your effectiveness in the classroom. Because knowledge about teaching and learning is increasing rapidly, teachers must make an effort to stay current on trends in educational research. Review the research carefully and look for ways to put the new principles and ideas to use in your classroom. The information in this textbook is just a beginning.

You can gain a significant amount of knowledge and insight throughout your teaching career. Subscribe to professional publications, join educational organizations, and continue to study through graduate and in-service education. As you do so, view the information you learn critically. See how new ideas fit in with tried- and-true principles. Don't be afraid to experiment, to retain ideas you find effective and appropriate, and to reject others. Very few educational trends need be swallowed in their entirety. Your professional judgment will allow you to choose what is best for your students and what fits your personal philosophy and values.

You have the opportunity to begin the process of continuous learning now as you observe teachers in your pre–student teaching or student teaching experiences. Try to enter each situation reflectively. The examples you see in those classrooms will have an enormous impact on the way you teach a class of your own. Watching experienced teachers can give you a chance to learn the practical ins and outs of teaching. It can help you understand how the instructional techniques and principles in this book can be applied with a variety of students in a variety of situations. On the other hand, no teacher is perfect, and no two individuals' educational philosophies and values are identical. Don't be afraid to question, to consider alternatives, or even to say to yourself, "This is something I'll do differently in my own class." You may find, in the end, that your view changes and you decide to adopt a technique you had earlier rejected. Or you may decide that just because something works for one teacher does not mean it is the best way for you.

You will find many opportunities for professional growth through workshops offered during student teaching and your first years of teaching. Take advantage of these opportunities for learning new ideas and gaining new perspectives. It is in such settings that you can sit back and reflect on your own practice. You will receive support for change and experimentation, and you will have the comfort of hearing that other teachers struggle with the same issues that puzzle you! As each year of teaching goes by, you will feel more confident, more comfortable with what you are doing, and clearer about your goals and accomplishments.

As you enter your third or fourth year of teaching, you may find that you have the inclination to face a larger challenge—pursuing an advanced certificate from the National Board for Professional Teaching Standards (NBPTS). Preparing for National Board certification entails honing—and demonstrating—your reflective decision-making skills. The process involves the preparation of a portfolio that documents your best teaching and collaborative efforts and your analysis of what made those efforts effective. You would also go through a series of assessment tasks at a centralized location. Should you attain this certificate, you will find the process has greatly enhanced your own sense of professionalism and respect.

SECTION 2. THE MOST IMPORTANT DECISION

Finally, we must consider the most important decision you will make as a teacher. Teaching is a complex, demanding process. It requires energy, commitment, and resilience. It is impossible to sustain those things over the course of a career without one key decision: Effective teachers choose to believe that teaching makes a difference. Educator Larry Cuban once said, "To teach is to be full of hope" (cited in Anello, Gandolfi, Scott, & Unser, 1998). The hope Cuban speaks about does not happen automatically. It is sustained day by day as teachers choose to believe that their efforts matter. There is evidence to suggest they do (Berliner, 2000; Darling-Hammond, 2000). So, as you approach the beginning of a career that is focused on the future, we'd like to consider a few of the ways teaching makes a difference, to you and to others.

Teaching will make a difference for you. Good teaching will never be boring. As you have learned, a reflective teacher is surrounded by information, challenges, and puzzles about which to reflect. It is true that some teachers have chosen to teach the same content, the same way, year after year. That certainly could get boring. But teachers who are attuned to the individual differences among children, to new ideas about pedagogy, and to interesting ideas from the world around them will find each day brings fresh challenges.

Good teaching brings chances to learn interesting things. Teaching not only gives you the opportunity to learn more about the content you teach, it provides the chance to see the content with new eyes. Looking at the world through the eyes of children, and doing your best to help them see the excitement that can be found there, makes the world come alive. Teaching helps you remember that seeing a butterfly or eating something that has come across the ocean—or even adding two fractions—can be a strange and wonderful thing. It can inspire you to continue to learn, whether it be about Internet adventures that can link your classroom to far corners of the earth or local history that can make your neighborhood come to life. Each new bit of information can be doubly interesting as you consider how it will affect the children who share your days.

Teaching also brings you the chance to learn how human beings learn and grow, how children change their perceptions of the world, and how relationships are built.

*Effective Teachers Choose to Believe
That Teaching Makes a Difference*

Good teachers build relationships with children, with colleagues, and with parents. They learn to listen carefully, to hear alternative perspectives, and to communicate clearly. Teachers have the chance to know and value people they would not know outside their professional world.

But, more important, *teaching makes a difference to the children and to the future*. We teach because we believe our efforts matter. As teachers we share the lessons of our cultures and the universal lessons of humankind. Gardner (1999) believes the best curriculum helps young people understand the things we find to be good, true, and ethical. In elementary school we have exceptional opportunities to share these lessons as many elementary teachers work across and among content areas.

In the sciences we help children see how exciting the natural world can be, balancing new understanding with a sense of wonder. In social studies we help them see the equal wonder of human beings. We teach the ways human beings make decisions based on many factors. As we understand these factors—a moment in history, the forces of geography or economy, the values of a culture—humans' actions make sense. Being able to "try on" these differing points of view helps us understand others, past and present.

Literature and the arts uncover human lives and emotions and begin to explore what is beautiful, what is ethical, and what is true. Math is important not just for calculation but for building appreciation of all that is ordered and seeing patterns in myriad aspects of life. Understanding the workings of the world, and the people and other living things that populate it, can be a source of interest and delight for students and teachers, now and for years into the future. It also prepares students to be contributors to that knowledge, with hope that they can solve the many dilemmas that have puzzled society for decades.

In schools we also teach important values. Although the idea of teaching values can be controversial, the fact of the matter is that every teacher and every classroom teach values. We teach values through our choice of content, our teaching strategies, and our interactions with students. Beane (1998) cited a quotation by John Dewey carved in Dewey's memorial at the University of Vermont.

> We who now live are parts of a humanity that extends into the remote past, a humanity that has interacted with nature. The things in civilization we most prize are not of ourselves. They exist by grace of the doings and sufferings of the continuous human community in which we are a link. Ours is the responsibility of conserving, transmitting, rectifying and expanding the heritage of values we have received that those who come after us may receive it more solid and secure, more widely accessible and more generously shared than we have received it.

As teachers we play a vital role in helping children understand the world they live in; heritage they share; and the values, attitudes, and actions we consider important.

In the United States, one of our most important roles is to prepare students to function in our democratic society. This is more than learning American history or the structures of government, although those are important. Preparing students to work in a democracy means helping them to consider carefully, to make decisions, to work together, to think about others, and to believe their efforts make a difference. The experiences they have in classroom communities form the patterns by which they understand larger communities and the decisions they make about their roles there. If our curriculum brings diverse groups of young people together to live and work together on a daily basis, it teaches many lessons about democratic living: People matter. Kindness matters. Prejudice is wrong. Problem solving works. Hard work pays off. Differences are often interesting and good. We can disagree and still work together. We can make a difference in the world. It takes a whole class to make a community.

Finally, Palmer (1998–1999) said, "Whoever our students may be, whatever subject we teach, ultimately we teach who we are" (p. 10). Through our lives in school we model intelligent, caring adulthood. We demonstrate curiosity; hard work; solving problems without fists; and how to be fair, speak respectfully, value diversity, and plan for the future. Children see themselves through our eyes. If we believe they can learn, they will believe it, too. If we value their abilities, their talents, and their families, they can come to believe those things are important to the world at large. For many students—from all cultures and economic level—school can be an island of stability in a world full of changes and stresses. If, through all those things, they continue to receive our message of hope—our decision to believe we can make a difference—we will have done our best to prepare the next generation of citizens and parents.

In the end, what's it like to be a teacher? Teaching, and the children it brings into your world, will change who you are and how you live your life in ways from the silly to the profound. For many people it means closets full of egg cartons, spare feathers, rock samples, and scraps of plastic—just because you never know when you might need some. For others it means being the only adult on the block to wear pumpkin earrings or shoelaces in school colors, or never being able to pass a bookstore or sale at an office supply house without looking for something for "your" kids.

Teaching will make you laugh. Whether you are surrounded by the silliness of 5-year-olds, the budding puns of middle childhood, or the more sophisticated humor of older children, there will be days when humor abounds. It will bring you moments of joy—watching a child perform an unexpected kindness; witnessing the first moment a student reads, gives a speech, or hits a home run; and watching students find new courage in difficult situations. There will be days when all your planning pays off and children who couldn't understand before now understand, and you know you've made a difference. Those days you'll think, "Yes, I am a teacher!"

Teaching also will bring harder days. There will be days when you drag yourself out of a sickbed because it is easier than planning for a substitute, and the minutes will each seem to last an eternity. Because you are human, there will be days when your patience runs thin. There will be lessons that fail, fire drills that interrupt you, and paperwork that will drive you crazy. There will be days when teaching breaks your heart. There will be children facing situations you cannot change and days those situations will bring you to tears. There will be times when your best efforts to help children fail. And still you choose to keep trying.

Teaching means being in close touch with the everyday dramas of young lives, remembering what it is like to have a best friend—or not have one, to discover the excitement between the covers of a book, or to bang the desk in frustration because your pencil won't create the drawing your mind envisions. It is about being there to celebrate a successful recital or a new tooth or a perfect math paper. It is also about being sad together when pets die—or people die, about being stable when families change, and about being a predictable source of learning and care. It is a tall order. Teaching is about careful planning, but it is also about unplanned moments and unscripted lessons. The people we are when we are with our students teach them what it means to be an adult, to be a professional, to be a caring human being.

This book was written to help you become the best teacher possible: an empowered reflective educator capable of making thoughtful and appropriate instructional decisions. There is no single path or easy prescription for this goal. The information, tools, and guidelines provided here will help you begin. But the art and science of teaching demands not just the best of learning, intellect, and decision making; it also requires insight, sensitivity, persistence, humor, patience, stamina, and joy in the process of learning. Although the goal may seem daunting, there is no profession with greater potential to communicate, to make change, or to touch individual lives. John Steinbeck wrote of a high school teacher who changed more than his understanding of content—she changed the way he viewed the world.

> She left her signature upon us, the literature of the teacher who writes on minds. I have had many teachers who told me soon-forgotten facts but only three who created in me a new thing, a new attitude and a new hunger, I suppose that to a large extent I am the unsigned manuscript of that high school teacher. What deathless power lies in the hands of such a person. (Copyright © 1955 by John Steinbeck. Reprinted by permission of McIntosh & Otis, Inc.)

As you help shape the world for your young students, we hope you use that power wisely and well.

UNIT PREPARATION

If all has gone according to plan, this should be the time to celebrate a task well done. Consider having a unit exhibition to share your accomplishments with classmates.

Planning units is a skill you will practice and hone throughout your teaching career. Once you have developed the skills of unit planning, most of your units probably won't be written out in detail as you did for this class. Instead, you will develop the habits of mind that will allow you to plan effective congruent units with a more abbreviated set of notes. However, when you are on school or district curriculum committees you are likely to need more formalized plans. This unit may be the beginning of your collection of prepared curriculum units. Consider ways to bind and preserve the unit for storage and future use. Although posting original material always runs the risk of unauthorized use, you may want to post part or all of the unit on your personal website to be reviewed by potential employers. Whatever format you choose, we hope you preserve your efforts, adapt them, and use them for years to come.

 ## PORTFOLIO ACTIVITY

Review your portfolio to see if it portrays not just what you know, but who you are as a teacher. You may want to consider a set of core belief statements, a graphic representation of your beliefs about teaching, or some other portfolio entry that will help readers to understand you as a teacher.

Consider having a professional friend read your portfolio and give you feedback. Be sure to choose someone who is a good enough friend to be honest in the critique!

 ## SEARCH THE WEB

There are many professional organizations that can support you in your ongoing efforts to be the best reflective teacher you can be. One of the most comprehensive lists available is found at the website of the American Association of Colleges of Teacher Education. Go to www.aacte.org and follow the link under "Other Resources." You can read more about the National Board for Professional Teaching Standards at www.nbpts.org. You will also want to review "Professional Development" on the Companion Website to find information on portfolio development, national certification, and other professional standards organizations.

 ## REFERENCES

Anello, M., Gandolfi, C., Scott, S. M., & Unser, V. (1998). *To teach is to touch lives forever.* White Plains, NY: Peter Pauper Press.

Beane, J. A. (1998). Reclaiming a democratic purpose for education. *Educational Leadership, 56*(2), 8–11.

Berliner, D. C. (2000). A personal response to those who bash teacher education. *Journal of Teacher Education, 51*(5), 358–371.

Darling-Hammond, L. (2000). How teacher education matters. *Journal of Teacher Education, 51*(3), 166–173.

Freiberg, M., Zbikowski, J., & Ganser, T. (1997, Spring). Promoting mid-career growth through mentoring. *Journal of Staff Development, 18,* 52–54.

Gardner, H. (1999). *The disciplined mind: What all students should understand.* New York: Simon & Schuster.

Palmer, P. J. (1998–1999). Evoking the spirit in public education. *Educational Leadership, 56*(4), 6–11.

Steinbeck, J. (1955, November). Like captured fireflies. *California Teachers Association Journal, 51* (8), 7.

APPENDIX

Example Unit
The Revolutionary War: What's So Revolutionary?

The following example includes the same components you will use in the unit you will design in your methods class. Read it carefully and be ready to ask questions in class about the structure of this unit. Note that the Rationale, Objectives, and Evaluation are interdisciplinary, while only the social studies portions of the concept map and a few sample lessons are provided. Many more lessons would need to be planned and the assessments fully developed before this unit would be ready to be taught.

 ## UNIT RATIONALE AND KEY QUESTIONS

Rationale (for Teachers)

This interdisciplinary unit is designed to help students understand how the Revolutionary War brought forth a set of truly revolutionary concepts in government, while building on ideas and events of the past. It focuses on understanding diverse points of view and on the contributions of varied types of leaders.

Key Questions (for Students)

Have you ever wondered why the Revolutionary War is called "revolutionary" or how a group of untrained soldiers managed to win a war against one of the greatest military powers on earth? Has anyone ever wondered whether George Washington had spies? Or what his family was doing while he was busy fighting? Are you curious about what George Washington ate or what kinds of music he may have listened to? In this unit you'll have the chance to answer those questions. We'll learn *why the Revolutionary War really was revolutionary* and *what kinds of people were needed to win the war.* Some of you may even learn what George or Martha Washington ate!

 ## SOCIAL STUDIES CONCEPT MAP WITH GENERALIZATION(S)

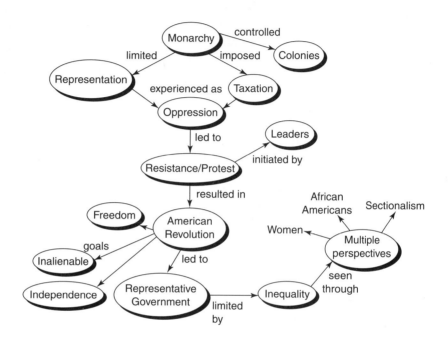

 ## SOCIAL STUDIES CONTENT OUTLINE (FACTS)

Content Outline: Revolutionary War Unit

Key Concepts to Be Taught/Retaught

Democracy, Monarchy, Colonies, Taxation, Equality, Freedom, Inalienable Rights, Independence, Leader, Liberty, Oppression, Multiple Perspectives, Representation, Democracy, Republic, Protest/Resistance, Revolution

---

I. Taxation Without Representation. British Rule: Roots of the Revolution
   A. The Monarchy and Parliament
   B. John Locke and the Rights of Englishmen
   C. Restricting Representation in the American Colonies
   D. Restricting Trade in the American Colonies (Mercantilism)
   E. The French and Indian War (1756–1763)

1. Colonial powers fight for territory in the New World
2. The Native American perspective
3. Quebec, Treaty of Paris, and the end of French control

II. Actions and Reactions: The Revolutionary War
   A. War Debt and the Cost of British Protection: Taxation in the Colonies
   B. Parliamentary Actions and Colonists' Reactions

Crown and Parliament Actions	**American Colonists' Reactions**
Stamp Act (1765)	Stamp Act Congress (1765)
Boston Massacre (1770)	Founding of Sons of Liberty (1772)
Tea Act (1773)	Boston Tea Party (1773)
Intolerable Acts (1774)	Continental Congress (1774)
(Boston Port Act, Quartering Act)	Paul Revere's Ride (1775)
Battles of Lexington and	Minutemen Gather at Lexington
Concord (1775)	and Concord (1775)

   C. Multiple Perspectives
      1. Patriots and loyalists
      2. Free and slave
      3. Rich and poor
      4. Merchants and farmers
      5. Men and women
      6. Northerners and Southerners
   D. Patriot Leaders
      1. John Adams
      2. Samuel Adams
      3. Benjamin Franklin
      4. John Hancock
      5. Patrick Henry
      6. Thomas Jefferson
      7. Thomas Paine
      8. George Washington
   E. Leaders (English)
      1. Monarchy (Crown)
         a. King George III
      2. Parliament (House of Commons, House of Lords)
         a. Edmund Burke
         b. George Grenville
         c. Lord North
         d. William Pitt
   F. The Declaration of Independence (1776)
      1. Committee of the Continental Congress
      2. Thomas Jefferson the primary author
      3. Model document for others to emulate
      4. Issues of freedom, independence, equality, rights, slavery, revolution

G. The Revolutionary War (1776–1783)
   1. American military leaders
   2. British military leaders
   3. Battles and events
   4. Problems of finance and supply
   5. America gains European allies
   6. The home front
   7. Surrender at Yorktown and Treaty of Peace
III. The Aftermath: Struggles for a New Nation
   A. The Articles of Confederation
      1. Nature
      2. Weaknesses
   B. Calls for a New Pattern of Government
      1. Federalist papers
      2. Constitutional Convention (1787)

 ## INTERDISCIPLINARY UNIT OUTCOMES
Social Studies Outcomes

Students will

1. analyze and explain the political, economic, and territorial causes of the American Revolution
2. show a deep understanding of basic concepts such as revolution, liberty, democracy, equality, and so on.
3. place the major events in the Revolutionary War period (1763–1787) in accurate chronological order using a time line
4. explain how the French and Indian War led to the imposition of taxes in the colonies
5. give examples of different forms of governmental authority as they are enacted through a monarchy and a democracy and the use of power without authority
6. create analogies between the different forms of government and rules and structures in their own classroom community and explore them through the creation of differing forms of classroom government
7. describe the different forms of resistance the colonists employed and compare them with forms of social protest used today
8. value the importance of political participation as an instrument of societal improvement
9. define the term *revolution* and explain why the concepts of independence, equality, and democracy as used in 1776 were revolutionary for the period
10. interpret the development and summarize the main points of the Declaration of Independence

11. pose a research question pertaining to a major event, cultural group, or person of the American Revolutionary period, gather information, construct an answer to the question posed, and report the results of their investigation
12. explain how the American Revolution affected various persons including patriots, loyalists, rich, poor, women, Native Americans, and African Americans
13. evaluate one or more major events of the Revolutionary War from two contrasting points of view and use these multiple perspectives to create a story, play, newspaper, or three-dimensional model
14. strive to value and appreciate the perspectives of others
15. compare and contrast multiple perspectives among students regarding everyday classroom issues and life events
16. develop a class definition of a leader and evaluate why an individual from the Revolutionary War should or should not have been considered a leader
17. evaluate the major dilemmas facing the Continental Congress and determine if the compromise regarding slavery was justified; predict what might have occurred had the congress reached a different decision
18. value the importance of ethics when making decisions
19. pose a question regarding the music and art of the Revolutionary period, gather information, construct an answer to the question posed, and present the results in a musical performance

Language Arts Outcomes

Students will

1. express their responses to oral, visual, and electronic texts, and compare their responses to those of others
2. describe and discuss the shared human experience depicted in a work of historical fiction
3. identify the persuasive forms of communication used by the individual authors and speakers of the American Revolutionary period and analyze how their words influenced audience expectations
4. analyze the Declaration of Independence in terms of content, structure, and style
5. use the writing process to construct a simple narrative depicting specific events of the Revolutionary War
6. participate in a literature discussion circle regarding a biography of one important leader or common person of the Revolutionary period

PREASSESSMENT

Informal

Students will freewrite for 5 minutes, everything that comes to mind about the Revolutionary War. Then they will work in groups to create a "mind map" organizing their ideas. Groups will share their maps with the class. The teacher will ask students what things they wonder about the Revolution and list those on chart paper. Those students with extensive knowledge will be distributed through the cooperative groups used for this unit. They will also be offered opportunities for leadership, peer teaching, and special projects. Students' prior knowledge (accurate or inaccurate) will be used to develop key questions and to revise objectives and the culminating project.

Formal Pretest

Students may be given a short pretest to see which facts and concepts they already understand.

SAMPLE SOCIAL STUDIES LESSON PLANS WITH MODIFICATIONS FOR SPECIAL NEEDS STUDENTS

Sample Lesson 1: What Was King George Thinking?

Objectives

Students will be able to

1. explain how the French and Indian War was tied to the imposition of taxes in the colonies
2. describe the rationale for additional taxes from the point of view of King George III
3. define *point of view*.

Opening

Teacher introduces the lesson by reminding students of the many lessons they have had in February about George Washington and how he and others fought with England during the Revolutionary War. Asks students what George Washington and the patriots wanted. Asks students what they think King George, the King of England, wanted.

Teacher tells students they need to listen carefully to find out two things: (a) What did King George want from the colonies? and (b) What kind of a person was King George?

Teacher tells students that when we study history it is important to figure out what the people of the time were thinking if we want to understand why they acted a certain way. If we understand more about what King George was thinking, it might help us understand more about why there was a Revolutionary War.

Building Understanding

Teacher either tells or reads the story of King George from the book *Can't You Make Them Behave, King George?* (Fritz, 1977). Students may be asked who they think King George wants to behave. Throughout the story, teacher asks questions such as the following to check basic understanding of the story. Care is taken to use wait time to allow all students to prepare a response.

Why do you think George prepared so carefully for his wedding?
What do King George's rules for his house tell you about King George?
Why did King George need money?

Why did King George think he should close Boston Harbor?
If you were King George, what would you have done?
What do you think King George would have liked to say to George Washington?

After the story, discuss the two main questions: (a) What did King George want from the colonies? and (b) What kind of a person was King George?

Teacher explains that when people look at a situation in very different ways, they are said to have different points of view, or multiple perspectives. George Washington and King George had very different points of view about how England should get the money it needed.

Applying Understanding

Divide students into pairs. In each pair, the student seated closest to the door should express the point of view of King George. The other student should be George Washington. Together they should create a six-line dialogue about why King George should or should not have imposed new taxes. Save these for Sample Lesson 2.

Students look in the newspaper to find an issue on which there are different points of view.

Modifications

Students who have trouble with writing should be paired with a stronger student for the dialogue assignment. Depending on interest, advanced students may be asked to look for examples of differing points of view in documents from the Revolutionary War period rather than in the newspaper, or to use the newspaper articles to create a bulletin board display on points of view.

Sample Lesson 2: What Were the Colonists Thinking?

Objectives

Students will be able to

1. describe major events and influences in the early Revolutionary War period
2. describe multiple perspectives regarding these events

Opening

Yesterday you learned one author's ideas about the reasons King George thought the way he did. Today you'll learn more about why the colonists were so upset with King George they were willing to start a war with one of the most powerful countries on earth.

Building/Applying Understanding

Students should be divided into groups of approximately four students. Each group is given information on a key idea or event that helped shape colonial thinking. These could include:

Traditional rights of the English
New taxes without representation
Samuel Adams and the Sons of Liberty
Thomas Paine and *Common Sense*
The Boston Massacre
John Adams and revolutionary ideas

Each group should decide which ideas in their information are most important and create a visual representation to explain them. Groups have 20 minutes to work and 5 minutes to explain their visual aid. Three groups will present their work the following day. Teacher uses a simple scoring rubric to assess students' presentations for factual accuracy, focus on key issues, accuracy of points of view portrayed, and use of visuals. This information will be used both to assess various groups' understanding and to make decisions about information that may require clarification or reteaching. After all the presentations are completed, students should review and revise the dialogues created in the previous lesson. They may choose to continue to reflect the points of view of King George and George Washington or they may choose to alter their dialogue to reflect King George and another colonial leader. Visuals should be displayed around the room and elaborated over time as desired.

At the end of the class period, teacher reminds students that one of the topics being discussed is "Revolutionary Ideas." There have been a lot of wars in history, but only a few of them have been called revolutionary. Sometimes other ideas are called revolutionary as well. For tomorrow, students are to ask two different adults for an example of something they consider revolutionary.

Modifications

Struggling students should be working in heterogeneous groups. If necessary, a reader should be assigned to make sure all students have access to the content. In other cases it may be sufficient to place students in a group in which the required reading is more limited. Exceptionally able or knowledgeable students may be placed in a group with challenging reading material or given an alternative source (perhaps from the time period) to share with their group.

Sample Lesson 3: What Makes Something Revolutionary?
Objectives

Students will be able to

1. define *revolutionary*
2. defend an event in history, in their community, in the arts, or in current events as revolutionary

Opening

Last night you collected ideas from adults about things they considered to be revolutionary. Today we are going to use those ideas, along with some new ideas I'll share with you to decide what makes something revolutionary. Later we'll decide whether or not we think the Revolutionary War actually was revolutionary.

Exploratory Activity/Find Patterns/Make Hypotheses

Have students share their ideas about things that are revolutionary and list them on the board. Discuss what the ideas have in common and identify any patterns. Make a tentative list of characteristics of things that are considered revolutionary.

Test/Modify Hypotheses

Teacher provides cards with additional information on historical events that might be considered revolutionary. The information should emphasize key attributes of revolutions (rapid, dramatic, substantial change, often involving overthrow of established powers) and include examples from multiple cultures and venues. They could include examples as varied as the Mexican Revolution, the establishment of the Dance Theater of Harlem, and the entrance of Elizabeth Blackwell into medical school. As a class (or, if desired, in cooperative groups), use the examples to refine the definition of *revolutionary*.

Metacognition

Have students explain the thought processes used in creating and modifying their definitions.

Practice

Using the class definition, students will write a paragraph defending an event in the community, the arts, or current events as revolutionary. Teacher will assess paragraphs for understanding of the revolutionary aspects of the event (social studies), consistency with the established definition (social studies), and the use of supporting facts to make a persuasive argument (language arts).

Modifications

The teacher may wish to assign the event to be defended to each student. This would allow the assignment of more conceptually complex events (for example, the Industrial Revolution) to students who need additional challenge.

Sample Lesson 4: Revolutionary Ideas
Objectives

Students will be able to

1. explain how the concepts of independence, equality, and democracy were used in 1776 and how they are used today
2. describe how these ideas were revolutionary in 1776
3. evaluate whether the compromise regarding the exclusion of antislavery language from the Declaration of Independence was justified and predict the consequences if it had been included

Opening

Teacher has written on the board in large letters: *independence, equality, democracy*.

Teacher asks students to look at the three words on the board. Using a sheet of paper divided into three columns, students should freewrite for one minute about each word, listing all the ideas and associations they can.

Building Understanding

Teacher explains that these revolutionary ideas were important to the colonists. The members of the Second Continental Congress decided to tell King George what they had decided about them.

Teacher tells story of the signing of the Declaration of Independence, including the role of Thomas Jefferson, key ideas in the declaration, and factors surrounding the decision to leave antislavery language out of the declaration. As much as possible, include information on the people and personalities that bring the story to life. Teacher leads a discussion around the following questions. What did these revolutionary words mean to John Adams? What do they mean today? How have our ideas changed? What might have happened if today's ideas had been used in 1776?

Practice

Students will write a letter to the editor of a newspaper either supporting or criticizing the decision to leave antislavery language out of the Declaration of Independence. The letter should include their prediction of what might have happened if the language had been included. Students may choose to write a letter to a colonial newspaper (using only information available at the time) or a modern newspaper, using information available today.

Modifications

Peer editing can be used to assist all students, but particularly struggling students, to refine their letters. Some students may need specific small-group review on the structure of a letter to the editor.

Sample Lesson 5: Revolutionary Time Line

Objectives

Students will be able to

1. create a time line of major events in the Revolutionary War
2. create cartoons depicting major events from a specific point of view

Opening

Teacher explains that they've learned a lot about the different points of view during the Revolutionary War period. Today they will watch a video that portrays events of that time. They will be using a note-taking guide to help them look for the answers to three questions. This information will help them prepare for their cartoon time line project today and to answer another interesting question later in the week.

Building Understanding

Students watch video portraying major events of the Revolution. Using a note-taking guide they record answers to the following questions.

What are some important events leading up to the Revolution?
What does the video tell you about ordinary life during the 1770s? For example, what
do you notice about the clothing, food, transportation, or housing during that time?
Who were some of the important leaders during the Revolution?

After the video, teacher and students list the important events portrayed in the video on one side of the board. They list facts about clothing and so forth on the other side.

Applying Understanding

The information gleaned from the video will be combined with other information from previous lessons to decide on a list of key events to be portrayed in a Revolutionary War time line. The time line should have three parts. In the middle is a time line with each event in its proper place, including a sentence describing each event. On top of each event is an editorial cartoon about the event as it might have been portrayed in a colonial newspaper from a colonial point of view. At the bottom is a cartoon portraying the same event in an English paper. Cartoons should portray the event from the correct point of view and depict time-appropriate clothing, furniture, and so on.

Students can be assigned individual roles or placed in teams to create all three sections of the time line for a given event. If students have not recently created editorial cartoons, it will be necessary to review several examples.

Modifications

Since this is an involved activity, student roles can be assigned as appropriate to their needs and skills. The activity provides an opportunity for complex expression for students who may be more adept at drawing than writing. Particularly interested or able students may add additional information to the time line, if desired.

Sample Lesson 6: All Kinds of Leaders
Objectives

Students will be able to

1. describe the characteristics of a leader
2. defend an individual as either a leader or not a leader, using the class definition
3. use the World Wide Web as an information source
4. evaluate web sources for point of view

Opening

Who are some of the leaders of the Revolutionary War? Today we are going to think about other people who were important to the Revolutionary War and decide if we think they were leaders.

Building Understanding

Teacher asks, "What did the people you have listed do to make them leaders? Do all leaders do those things?"

Teacher asks students to complete a web search on individuals who had various roles during the Revolution: spies, soldiers from various countries, women, children, and others. Teacher reminds students that individuals creating websites, like those who create editorial cartoons or write books, often have particular points of view regarding their topic. In each case the students must discover what the person(s) did and decide whether or not they believe the person(s) exemplified leadership. They should also decide if it is likely the creators of the website had a particular point of view they were trying to portray. These ideas could be recorded in a three-column note-taking sheet.

Applying Understanding

After all students have had the opportunity to complete the search, the class discusses the results and uses them to create a class definition of *leadership*. Each student selects (or is assigned) an individual from a list provided by the teacher. Students should research the contribution of the individual they have selected and create a poster describing why the person should or should not be considered a leader. Posters should be evaluated using a rubric jointly created by students and teacher. If desired, another class may be invited to view the posters and talk to students about their work at a poster session.

Unit Assessment

There will be multiple sources of information used to assess the unit. In many cases, activities completed as part of specific lessons will be used for assessment. For example, the time line and leadership activities will provide important information regarding students' understanding of the concepts of *point of view* and *leadership*. These may be compiled in a portfolio along with other activities designed specifically for assessment. A completed unit would include the rubrics necessary to assess these assignments. If language arts activities were included as part of the unit, of course, they would be added to the following list. The portfolio could include:

- Dialogue created to portray two points of view regarding taxation
- A paragraph defending a particular event as revolutionary
- A letter to the editor regarding the decision to exclude antislavery language from the Declaration of Independence

- Results of a web search
- A poster regarding a Revolutionary War leader
- A culminating product that portrays one or more major events of the Revolutionary War from multiple points of view; this could be a story, play, newspaper, or other product

Many teachers will also choose to give a unit test. This is important, not just to test students' recall of unit information not included in the products listed (for example, the major events on the time line or contributions of specific individuals) but to allow students the opportunity to gain practice in test-taking situations.

Materials

Materials necessary for the unit would be listed in this section. These would include the video, web search information, source materials for students and teacher, and necessary worksheets or note-taking guides.

References

Both student and teacher references, including multimedia materials, should be listed here.

Glossary

Academic service-learning Community service that helps students gain a deeper understanding of specific learning objectives.

Acceleration Pursuing the regular curriculum at a faster pace—for example, working on above-grade-level curriculum, grade skipping, early entrance to school, etc.

Active learning Learning activities that require students to be mentally and/or physically involved as opposed to passively listening.

Active listening A response to a student that summarizes both the emotional attitude and the intellectual content of what the student said.

Advanced organizer An activity at the beginning of a lesson designed to preview the structure of the content to be addressed.

Affective domain Domain that involves emotional behavior—that is, feelings, attitudes, preferences, and values.

Agenda An individualized list of tasks to be completed in a specified amount of time, generally shorter than a contract.

Anticipatory set A type of opening used in direct instruction to focus student attention on relevant content and activate prior knowledge.

Assertive Discipline A management system designed by Lee Canter, based on a behavior management approach.

Assessment The process of measuring the quantity and/or quality of a behavior or the indicator of that behavior.

Attending behavior Verbal and nonverbal responses from a teacher that indicate the student's response is worthy of attention—for example, nodding, smiling, or summarizing the response.

Authentic assessment A performance assessment where the focus of attention is on significant tasks such as student products, exhibits, or performances rather than on right or wrong answers on objective tests.

Authentic learning, authentic tasks Learning that serves a real-world function, using information for a purpose other than simply presenting it to a teacher. Typically entails solving a problem, answering a question, or creating something new and then presenting the results to an interested audience.

Authentic research Inductive lessons in which students collect and analyze data to draw new conclusions. Unlike traditional inquiry lessons, the data is not presented by the teacher, nor are the preferred results identified in advance.

Behavior management A tradition of management based on behaviorist theory, focusing on rewarding desired behaviors and punishing undesired behaviors.

Benchmarks Generally, more specific outcomes than standards. For example, content standards for elementary grades may have grade-level benchmark outcomes.

Bloom's taxonomy of educational objectives The most widely used process for ordering cognitive learning tasks.

Bloom's taxonomy: Analysis A task that consists of unfamiliar data and/or examples but requires a more complex thought process than is elicited from an application task. Analysis requires the taking apart of a complex stimulus.

Bloom's taxonomy: Application A level at which students are required to exhibit complex thought as well as the retrieval of information. A typical task at the application level is to provide unfamiliar math or science data, a historical incident, a quotation, a painting, or a musical selection and ask the student if it is an example of a concept that has been previously learned.

Bloom's taxonomy: Comprehension The level at which students understand material and can express it in their own words or in a similar form.

Bloom's taxonomy: Evaluation   A task in which students must defend their judgmental decisions using a combination of logical argument supported by evidence in fact and the application of predetermined criteria.

Bloom's taxonomy: Knowledge   Tasks that oblige the student to recall, recognize, or reproduce what has been previously learned.

Bloom's taxonomy: Synthesis   The level at which students create an original product, exhibit, or performance that involves the selection, organization, and implementation of a number of concepts and generalizations and requires substantial thought.

Brain-based education   Educational practices based on inferences from neural psychology.

Checking for understanding   Part of continuous assessment that takes place during teaching, checking students' understanding of individual parts of a lesson.

Choice theory (control theory)   A theory by Glasser emphasizing individual choice and accountability for actions.

Comer school   A school based on James Comer's model of school development, focused on coordinating school, parent, and community efforts to facilitate student development.

Compensatory instruction   Circumventing areas of weakness or lack of experience in order to carry on planned instruction.

Competitive learning   A type of learning in which students compete with others in the class to gain a limited number of high grades or rewards.

Concept attainment lessons   Inductive lessons in which students examine examples and nonexamples of a concept, find common charateristics, and define the concept.

Concept formation lessons, concept development lessons   Inductive lessons in which students classify data or information into categories to generate concepts.

Concept mapping   A thought process that culminates in a visual display of relevant knowledge and relationships.

Concepts   Categories or classes of things that share a set of critical characteristics.

Congruence   A match among goals or outcomes, lesson objectives, lesson activities, and assessment.

Constructivism/Constructivist teaching   Education based on the premise that students construct their own understanding through experience.

Content analysis   A process to break down content to be taught into its components parts (i.e., generalizations, concepts, and facts) and to display the relationships among them.

Context   The conditions that surround classroom life: social, cultural, political, and physical.

Contingency management   A system in which teachers reward and punish students based on desired behaviors, often using concrete tokens or incentives.

Continuous assessment   The idea that assessment must take place before, during, and after teaching as an inherent part of the instructional process.

Contract (learning)   An agreement between the student and teacher that directs the tasks to be completed in a given time frame.

Contract learning, as assessment   A strategy in which the standards for receiving a given grade are described to all students. Each student contracts with the teacher to perform certain tasks at a given quality level in order to receive the agreed upon grade.

Contracts   Written agreements outlining activities agreed upon by student, teacher, and sometimes parents.

Controlled assessment   An assessment procedure in which the learners are always aware they are being assessed.

Cooperative group learning   A group where students are responsible for both their own and others' learning.

Cooperative skills learning   A method for students to learn how to interact in ways that promote learning, consensus, and conflict resolution.

Creative producers/Creative productivity   As used by Renzulli, individuals' ability to create—rather than consume—information or art.

Criterion-referenced assessment   A type of *assessment* that considers each student as an individual. The individual's performance is assessed against predetermined performance standards.

Critical pedagogy   Teaching practices that promote more democratic, equitable social relations, even if that means challenging the existing order.

Critical ethical/moral reflection   Reflecting (from multiple perspectives) on the long-term impact of teaching on students' learning and their role in society (e.g., Will this child respect and be kind to others?).

Cultural discontinuity Occurs when the culture of the school differs from the student's home culture.

Cultural pluralism A model in which cultural groups maintain their own identity while adopting some aspects of a joint culture, sometimes contrasted with the "melting pot" model in which cultural identities are merged.

Culturally relevant teaching Teaching that empowers students intellectually, socially, and emotionally by using cultural referents in teaching knowledge and skills.

Culture The learned, shared, and transmitted social activities of a group.

Curriculum The subject matter to be taught, sometimes organized by scope (content) and sequence (order). The term *curriculum* is also sometimes used to include the plans for teaching and the context of learning.

Curriculum benchmarks Narrowly defined outcomes that are expressed in terms of what students are to know or do to demonstrate they have achieved what is expected of them.

Curriculum compacting A strategy for differentiation that involves preassessing students' prior knowledge and eliminating previously mastered material.

Curriculum rationale A section of a unit that describes the content to the student and justifies its importance.

Curriculum standards Global, long-range outcomes or goals for all students.

Developmental pathways, Comer model A model developed by Comer for providing a caring environment that nurtures the development of children in six ways: physical, cognitive, psychological, language, social, and ethical.

Developmentally appropriate practice Educational planning that takes into account the developmental needs of children at different ages.

Differentiated instruction Instruction that is modified to meet differing needs of multiple students simultaneously, usually by providing varied assignments and/or instruction.

Differentiation Varying instruction, assignments, and assessments to fit the level of challenge necessary for each child.

Direct lesson A lesson in which the teacher directly tells students the objective and presents information, usually in a deductive manner, moving from general principles to specific examples.

Disability A condition that results in a reduced competency to perform some task or behavior.

Discussion An open-ended exchange of ideas designed to share information and explore ideas, rather than to seek the "right" answer.

Divergent question An open-ended question that invites multiple perspectives and may be answered with a variety of correct answers.

Dramatic play Unstructured activities in which students often use costumes or props to enact imaginary situations.

Educational assessment A systematic process that leads to a judgment about the ability or achievement exhibited by a person or persons, or the success of an instructional program.

Educational goal A *goal* that provides general direction to the teacher in making crucial decisions about instruction. Similar to a standard.

Electronic appearances A learning activity in which students communicate electronically with a subject matter expert.

Emotional impairments Disability characterized by repeated and inappropriate behavior displayed to the extent that it affects students' academic growth, social maturity, and relationships.

Emotional intelligence Self-awareness, independence, optimism, accountability, empathy, and the ability to manage one's feelings.

Enabling objective A short-term objective leading to a broader outcome.

Enrichment Incorporation of activities outside the regular curriculum to provide additional challenge and/or interest.

Enrichment Triad A model including three types of enrichment: exploratory activities, group training activities, and individual or small-group projects.

Essentialism An educational philosophy that argues that the purpose of schooling is to impart essential knowledge, skills, and attitudes to enable young people to function as fully developed human beings.

Evaluative (global) praise Praise that indicates whether the student response or work is good or bad, but does not specify the aspects that are worthy of praise.

Exhibition   A culminating experience that requires the application of knowledge within specific conditions, usually involving some type of presentation to an audience outside the class.

Exploratory (free play) areas   An area where students develop and practice key concepts through exploration and play.

Facts   Specific statements about particulars—people, things, places, time, or events.

Formative assessment   A type of assessment that provides information for improvement while the person or program has the opportunity to improve.

Full-service schools   Schools that are the hub for a variety of educational and other services including health, social, and governmental agencies all at a single site.

Gender bias   Conscious or unconscious differential treatment of males and females.

Generalization   A statement that expresses a generally true relationship between two or more concepts.

Giftedness   Ability and/or performance beyond the norm in some area. There is no consensus as to the definition of *giftedness* as it pertains to either students or adults.

Global classrooms   Classrooms in different locations that study a common topic during the same time period.

Graphic organizers   Visual depictions illustrating the structure of the content to be taught or task to be addressed. Can be used to introduce a lesson or to structure student responses, often to readings.

Group alerting   The technique of keeping students' attention in a group when they have not yet been called on to respond.

Group investigation   A group-learning strategy where students investigate a particular question of their choice in shared-interest groups.

Guided practice   A type of practice at the end of direct instruction in which the teacher monitors learning and adjusts accordingly.

Handicap   The disadvantage that results from the effects of a disability. These may vary depending on the situation and supports available.

Heterogeneous groups   Grouping students according to differences—for example, mixing males and females in a group or mixing reading performance levels in a group.

Higher level thinking   Using information in some way (analysis, synthesis, evaluation, problem solving, etc.) rather than simple recall.

Homogeneous groups   Grouping students according to similarities—for example, all male groups, all minority groups, all lower-reading-performance groups.

Humanistic approach to classroom management   An approach to classroom management focused on healthy emotional growth as a natural process.

Individuals with Disabilities Education Act (*IDEA*)   The major federal legislation mandating educational services to students with disabilities.

Individualized Educational Program (IEP)   An educational plan required for students with disabilities, outlining goals, strategies, and so on.

Inclusion   A strategy that places students with severe disabilities in general education settings, with appropriate supports. *Full inclusion* programs place all students in general education, eliminating all full-time special education placements.

Independent practice   A type of practice in which students work without teacher monitoring.

Individual accountability   A learning situation in which each student is held accountable for achieving the essential objectives of the lesson.

Individualized learning   A learning activity in which students work on their own to accomplish an objective or preset standard.

Inductive lesson   A lesson in which the teacher provides data or experiences from which students draw conclusions to uncover concepts or generalizations.

Informal instruction   Instruction that occurs as part of the daily interactions in the home, classroom, or community rather than through prepared lessons.

Informational feedback   Feedback that is specific about the aspects of student work that are correct or need to be corrected.

Inquiry lesson   Inductive lessons in which students interpret and apply data to draw conclusions, often to determine generalizations.

Instructional objective   A specific statement of what the student will know or be able to do after the unit or lesson ends. Thus, it is similar to a benchmark. Instructional objectives include **A**udience, **B**ehavior, **C**onditions, and **D**egree elements.

Interdisciplinary instruction Instruction planned to use multiple disciplines and help students understand their interrelationships.

Interdisciplinary thematic instruction Instruction planned around a theme that is meaningful across disciplines.

Interest-development center A center where a child can engage in activities that stimulate interest in areas outside the regular curriculum.

Intrinsic motivation Motivation that comes from within the student, rather than from outside forces.

Jigsaw A cooperative group strategy that requires each member to become an expert on one part of the whole lesson and teach it to the other students.

Key questions Questions that focus a unit of instruction by providing provocative or interesting areas for exploration.

Knowledge work Student activity that involves using ideas, concepts, problem-solving skills, and applying facts to achieve some end.

KWL A strategy for collecting information on what students Know, Want to know, and Learn about a topic.

Learning center A center where a child can engage in activities that introduce or reinforce a specific part of the regular curriculum.

Learning disabilities A reduced competency to perform some behaviors while performing as well or better than peers on other tasks. These disabilities may be evident only in particular subject areas.

Learning process analysis A process that breaks down tasks into higher and lower learning levels to determine what students are to do with the content that is presented to them.

Learning style Variations in individual ways of learning across all domains, including differences in taking in and processing information.

Least Restrictive Environment (LRE) A term from the Individuals with Disabilities Act. *The least restrictive environment* clause requires that students with disabilities be placed in the educational environment appropriate to their needs that is closest to a general education setting.

Less is more The principle that students will learn more if instruction focuses on fewer ideas in greater depth.

Lesson design All the activities necessary to teach a specific objective, may span one or more than one day.

Lesson plan Describes activities for a single day, usually for one subject.

Limited materials interdependence In cooperative groups, each student must share with others the essential materials (e.g., only one sheet of directions, or one pencil).

Mainstreaming A practice in which students with disabilities spend part or all of the school day in a general education setting. The term *mainstreaming* originated with reference to students with mild to moderate disabilities.

Mastery learning An individualized approach for use in a structured instructional program. It is based on the belief that all students can be successful in achieving all objectives if additional learning time is allowed for those who may need it.

Mental impairments Students function less well than the norm in all areas of learning.

Metacognition Awareness of one's own thinking.

Modeling More than simply demonstrating, *modeling* also requires careful explanation of the processes being demonstrated.

Morning meetings Whole-class activity used to begin the day, usually containing a greeting, sharing, group activity, and news/announcements.

Multicultural curriculum Curriculum designed to promote and value diverse cultures while helping students to see the commonalities among groups.

Multidisciplinary instruction Using multiple disciplines to study a topic.

Multiple intelligences A model developed by Gardner establishing profiles of intelligences across at least eight domains.

National Board for Professional Teaching Standards (NBPTS) An organization offering advanced national teacher certification in a variety of areas.

Natural assessment A type of *assessment* that requires no artificially constructed testing environment. The learners are not aware that they are being assessed.

Noncontingent reinforcement Reinforcement that is given without reference to any specific behavior.

Norm-referenced assessment A type of *assessment* that considers each student in relationship to every other student in the group. That is, the evaluator examines all the scores and determines where each individual's score fits within the distribution.

Open-ended question   A question with many potential correct responses.

Outcome   A goal for instruction describing what students should be able to understand or do, often describes broad rather than specific behaviors, sometimes used synonymously with *goals*.

Overlapping   Teacher's ability to attend to more than one event or activity simultaneously.

Pattern disrupters   According to Dreikurs, students who misbehave repeatedly. Pattern disrupters are divided into attention-seeking, sympathy-seeking, power-seeking, and revenge-seeking behaviors.

Pedagogical content knowledge   Knowledge about teaching and learning that is specific to a particular discipline or body of content.

Pedagogy   Knowledge about teaching and learning, including knowledge of human development, learning theory, multicultural education, teaching methods, assessment, and classroom management.

Peer tutoring   Activities in which students assist classmates or younger students with assigned activities.

Perfectionism   Individuals' pursuit of excellence to the degree that it becomes debilitating. Nothing short of perfection can be accepted.

Performance assessments   Assessment tasks that demonstrate understanding by asking students to use information in a real or realistic context.

Personal progressives   The wing of the Progressive Movement that views the curriculum as a flexible menu of options that responds to the felt needs and interests of each individual child.

Physical or other health impairments   Disabilities that reduce students' capability to perform psychomotor tasks and/or affect stamina, vitality, and so on.

Portfolio   A collection or display of student work collected for assessment purposes.

Positive interdependence   A cooperative learning situation in which students are responsible for the success of each group member; they "sink or swim together."

Positive moments   A management strategy in which teachers include 15 seconds of positive time with a pattern-disruptive student every hour, and incorporate positive touch and informational feedback into interactions with disruptive students.

Preassessment   The process of diagnosing student performance prior to instruction.

Prior knowledge   All the knowledge and experiences students bring to instruction, including general cultural understandings, relevant information, and misconceptions.

Probe   A request for more information from a student following an incomplete or unclear response.

Problem-based learning   Learning structured around a complex problem. Students learn content and processes as necessary to solve the problem, rather than being given the problem after the skills are learned.

Professional development   Growth and learning activities that enhance the professional practice of the teacher.

Progressivism   An educational philosophy that emphasizes thinking, the child, and democratic values and processes rather than predetermined subject matter.

Prompt   A hint or suggestion to help a student respond correctly following an incomplete or incorrect response.

Psychomotor domain   The *domain* that consists of learning that is sensory in nature, ranging from involuntary, reflexive movements to complex chains of skillful and purposeful behavior.

Quality circle   A group meeting in which students anonymously discuss problem behaviors and alternatives for problem solving.

Questioning   A technique in which the teacher or students pose questions; the teacher is the focus of attention. Often contrasted with discussion used to review and practice information.

Rational Approach to Practical School Discipline (RAPSD)   An eclectic approach to school management developed by Gardner.

Rationale   An introduction to a unit explaining the content and purposes of the unit.

Reality therapy   An approach designed by Glasser based on the premise that a student's past is over and he or she must now make choices about future behavior. It emphasizes the use of individual conferences and group meetings to establish a positive environment for learning.

Reconstructionism   An educational philosophy that is characterized by a belief that schools should prepare the future adults of society to work for and to demand societal change.

Reflection   Thinking about, interpreting, and analyzing one's own experiences with the goal of improving one's practice or learning. In teaching, *reflection* is the ability to make rational educational choices and take responsibility for those decisions. *Reflective teaching* is reflection in action, carrying through the decisions made.

Reflective decision maker   An active designer of curriculum, instruction, and assessments who makes rational educational choices and takes responsibility for those choices by reflecting on their effects.

Reflective listening   A brief summary of a student's response to indicate that it was heard and understood.

Reliability   The property of an assessment that is concerned with consistency or stability from one performance to the next so that one can be confident that the performance is a representative measure.

Remedial approach, remediation   Teaching prerequisite skills before going on to new instruction.

Responsive Classroom Model   A model of classroom organization designed to promote both academic and social learning.

Reward interdependence   A cooperative learning situation in which students strive to help each member succeed, so that each member will receive a reward.

Role-play   An activity in which students take on a role to solve a problem or act out a situation.

Routines, classroom   Procedures for carrying on everyday classroom functions: distributing papers, walking through the halls, and so on.

Rubric   A scoring guide that reveals to the student how the authentic performance or product will be assessed.

Rules, classroom   A statement that informs students which behaviors are acceptable and unacceptable in the classroom.

Scaffolded instruction   Strategies used to bridge gaps between students' prior experiences and content to be taught, often involving teacher modeling desired strategies and gradually shifting responsibility to students.

Schema (singular, schemata)   Cognitive structures that link knowledge together in individualized patterns to establish concepts and relationships.

Schoolhouse giftedness   A term introduced by Renzulli, reflecting individuals' ability to take in and process information, as in traditional schools.

Sensory impairments   Reduced visual or auditory acuity.

Simulation   An activity in which students experience a simplified version of reality, either through complex extended role-play or through electronic "virtual" experiences.

Social Progressives   The wing of the Progressive movement that views school curriculum as providing preparation for successful adult life in a democratic society.

Specific praise   Praise that describes the specific aspects of the student's performance that are worthy of praise.

Speech impairments   Reduced competency in speech, often caused by a hearing loss.

Standardized tests   Tests that are administered and scored in exactly the same way for all students, frequently mass-produced national tests.

Standards   Outcomes to be attained by students at particular levels, usually broad. At this time most states have adopted specific content standards.

Stations   Areas in the classroom where students can engage in differing activities simultaneously. Generally contain a narrower focus of activities than a center, often a single activity.

Student needs and characteristics   Students' culture, developmental level, background knowledge, mood, learning styles, interests, and needs.

Student teams—Achievement divisions   A model of cooperative learning in which members prepare each other for a quiz (which may be different for various achievement levels). Teams with highest gains win.

Subject matter   The content to be taught, usually specified by national, state, and district curriculum standards.

Summative assessment   Used to make educational decisions about persons or programs after instruction terminates.

Target paper   An example of an assignment used to portray for students the various criteria for an exemplary performance.

T-chart   A list of what a particular social skill looks like and sounds like, often used in cooperative group lessons.

Teacher characteristics and beliefs Teacher philosophy, confidence, enthusiasm, cultural background, intelligence, commitment, values, beliefs, prior experiences, and attitudes.

Teacher consumer A teacher who uses textbooks, units, and lessons designed by others without critically examining their quality or appropriateness for his/her students.

Teacher designer A teacher who adapts and/or creates curriculum while considering a number of variables.

Teams-Games-Tournaments A model of cooperative learning in which members prepare each other for team competitions. In the tournament, students are grouped with others of similar achievement levels from different teams.

Technical reflection Reflecting on the short-term impact of teaching and learning strategies (e.g., Did I use this technique correctly?).

Technology gap The gap between those with access to computers or other technology and those without access.

Telefieldtrips Visiting locations around the world through electronic communications.

Telementoring Mentoring through electronic means.

Telepresent problem solving Discussing problematic situations electronically.

Thematic instruction Instruction planned around a theme that is meaningful across disciplines.

Three-ring conception of giftedness A model of creative/productive giftedness comprising above-average ability, creativity, and task commitment.

Tiered activities Activities in which all students work on the similar activities and content but at different levels of difficulty.

Transmitted knowledge Knowledge gained from courses, discussions with teachers, observations, textbooks, and research.

Triarchic theory A theory of intelligence developed by Sternberg including the ability to process information, response to novelty, and ability to respond to the environment.

Understanding Mastery of content to the extent that one can use it in a new situation.

Understanding performances Activities that require students to demonstrate understanding by using information in new situations, typically planned for assessment purposes.

Unit A coordinated series of lessons that leads to a broad goal.

Validity The property of an assessment that makes it an accurate gauge of what it purports to measure.

Verbal labeling Pointing out in words an idea or element you want students to notice, giving notice that something is important.

Wait time Waiting long enough after a question to allow students to prepare an answer; this results in more equitable student involvement and deeper thinking.

With-it-ness The extent to which the teacher demonstrates an awareness of student behaviors in all situations and areas of the classroom.

Zone of proximal development Level of instruction at which information is beyond the child's current understanding but close enough to be reachable with scaffolding by a teacher.

Index